This book is dedicated to the memory of Gerald Cole and to Phil Kelly's family – especially Rebecca, Toby, Jacob, Ben and my father, Paul F. Kelly

CONTENTS

PART TWO: MANAGEMENT IN PRACTICE

PART THREE: FUNCTIONAL MANAGEMENT – MARKETING, PRODUCTION (OPS), HRM, FINANCIAL AND IS/IT

PART FOUR: GLOBAL MANAGEMENT

MANAGEMENT THEORY AND PRACTICE

EIGHTH EDITION

GERALD A. COLE
PHIL KELLY

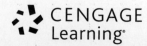

CENGAGE
Learning

Australia • Brazil • Mexico • Singapore • United Kingdom • United States

**Management Theory and Practice,
8th Edition**

Gerald A. Cole and Phil Kelly

Publisher: Andrew Ashwin

Development Editor: Abigail Jones

Content Project Manager: Melissa Beavis

Manufacturing Buyer: Elaine Field

Marketing Manager: Vicky Fielding

Typesetter: Cenveo Publisher Services

Cover design: Adam Renvoize

For product information and technology assistance,
contact **emea.info@cengage.com**.

For permission to use material from this text or product,
and for permission queries,
email **emea.permissions@cengage.com.**

British Library Cataloguing-in-Publication Data
A catalogue record for this book is available from the British Library.

ISBN: 978-1-4080-9527-0

Cengage Learning EMEA
Cheriton House, North Way, Andover, Hampshire, SP10 5BE, United Kingdom

Cengage Learning products are represented in Canada by Nelson Education Ltd.

For your lifelong learning solutions, visit **www.cengage.co.uk**

Purchase your next print book, e-book or e-chapter at **www.cengagebrain.com**

Printed in China by RR Donnelley
Print Number 01 Print Year 2015

PREFACE

The aim of this 8th edition of *Management Theory and Practice* is to provide a contemporary, comprehensive and accessible introduction to the principal ideas and developments in management. A holistic text, it covers a wide range of management topics and is really three books in one. Key management theories are outlined within, as expected of a textbook. It also, through inclusion of management skill sheets, aims to develop readers' business and management (transferable) skills. Finally, through chapter questions and a rich case study, building across all sections of the book, it provides real world business problems, enabling readers to practise applying their skills and knowledge within a safe environment. The book also seeks to signpost a wide range of specialist management books and articles and helps readers navigate their way through the vast topic of management. Targeted at undergraduates either studying a management degree or business module on a variety of other degrees, the book is also intended as a foundation text for higher degrees and management courses.

Management theory has developed into a wide-ranging and assorted subject. Interestingly, new theories tend to enhance or complement but not negate older theories. Thus, every management student should be encouraged to study the past 100 years of management theory! Taylor's early twentieth-century work on scientific management, for example, is still very much alive today in contemporary organizations. What is different now is the emphasis placed on particular aspects of management theory and how theories become blended within the organization's specific context. In order to introduce a broad range of topics we have structured this book into many short chapters, with numbered paragraphs for easy reference. The chapters are grouped by topic and topics form one of four book parts. Part 1 seeks to identify what is meant by the term management and focuses more on management theory. Starting with the classical theories of management (scientific and bureaucratic) we trace the development of management theory throughout the twentieth century. Human relations and social psychological theories, leadership, group and systems theories are explored. This leads to a review of contemporary approaches to management and a discussion about how companies add value throughout the supply chain. Part 2 focuses on management practice, adopting the POMC (Planning, Organizing, Motivating and Controlling) framework. The context of management is explored and tools and techniques to analyze the environment presented. We then discuss strategy, before considering how companies organize themselves to attain goals and perform effectively and efficiently. In Part 3 we consider the work of the major business functions of Marketing, Operations, HR, Finance and IT. Finally, in Part 4 we take a closer look at the impact of globalization and consider how we might lead and manage when operating internationally. The structure enables the reader to dip in and out of the many aspects of management.

Whilst retaining many aspects of the 7th edition, shortlisted for a literary award – 'Management Book of the Year', which made the book an international bestseller, we have updated and created new chapters, making extensive revisions. We have also developed skills and case study sheets to enrich the pedagogical features, making the book more engaging and supportive of either traditional or problem-based and blended learning. Whilst the chapter structure is similar, we have added new chapters such as Managing the Supply Chain, Strategic Aspects of Management, Organizing for Innovation, Managing Risk, Managing the Procurement Function, Managing the Logistics Function, International HRM (IHRM), Managing

Information Resources, Leading Globally and Managing Globally. Every chapter has defined learning outcomes and key concepts, and identifies glossary terms, an introduction, text and conclusion. There are chapter figures, end-of-chapter questions, suggested web links and reading for most chapters. Each section has skills sheets providing detailed guidance on how to apply specific management models, tools and techniques. Furthermore there are supplementary resources such as an extensive multiple choice test bank, case study sheets, and PowerPoint slides, teaching and learning guidance notes. The overall structure of the book is influenced by various management subject frameworks to ensure the core management topics are covered.

We hope you will find the book useful and that it provides some insight into management. The changes discussed should enhance the book's appeal, making it more useful to contemporary readers and management practitioners. Feedback on the content, style and pedagogical features is welcome – please email Dr Phil Kelly, p.kelly1@ljmu.ac.uk with your comments.

ABOUT THE AUTHORS

The late **Gerald Cole** wrote the first and earlier editions of this popular book. His pioneering work in a wide variety of organizations, both large and small, in the public and private sectors provided a rich management experience from which to draw. This was complemented with Board Level experience – he held four Non-Executive Directorships. Gerald drew from this knowledge and experience in higher education and was an external examiner in various management courses at Middlesex University. The breadth of his knowledge and experience was translated into other books which included works on Personnel and Human Resource Management, Strategic Management, and Organizational Behaviour; the popularity of his books is evidenced by the number of subsequent editions published. For example, he wrote five editions of *Personnel and Human Resource Management*. His books have been on the reading lists of several management institutes and are used by many university courses.

Dr Phil Kelly has a Doctorate in Business Administration from Manchester Business School (MBS) and has worked for over 20 companies in almost as many countries. He has worked at all management levels in SMEs and large MNEs and operated as a Line Manager, Senior Manager, Company Director, Board Member and Consultant. After 15 years practising management around the world he became a Senior Lecturer at Liverpool Business School (LBS). An experienced, award-winning, tutor, he has an MA (distinction) in Teaching and Learning in Higher Education and is a Senior Fellow of the Higher Education Academy. Phil has written several management books including *International Business and Management*, and *The Business Environment*. Presently, Phil teaches on a variety of postgraduate degree programmes such as the MBA, along with HR and BIS undergraduate programmes at LBS and is supervising five PhD students. In addition he is a principal examiner for a leading professional institute. He is regularly consulted on a wide range of contemporary business issues.

ACKNOWLEDGEMENTS

I would like to thank Gerald Cole for his inspiring work on the earlier editions that laid the platform for the 7th and 8th editions. The Publisher thanks the Cole estate for its cooperation and support in helping to keep Gerald's work alive and of benefit to students. I would like to take this opportunity to thank all of those individuals whose insight, time and hard work have contributed to this book – especially my wife, Rebecca. Special thanks go to Abbie Jones, the Development Editor at Cengage Learning, for her patience, support and management of the project. Exceptional thanks go to all of those in the formal review process; their feedback and suggestions for improvement helped shape the book. Numerous individuals contributed towards the thinking behind the book, through conversations, conferences, seminars and writings. Huge benefit has resulted from the views and experiences of business educators and practitioners from the UK and around the world. Personal appreciation goes to many individuals including staff from Liverpool Business School (LBS) based within the Faculty of Business and Law – especially Bob McClelland and Roger Pegum. May I also thank the LJMU business students and staff for trialling aspects of the text. Grateful thanks also to a variety of companies and publishers for permission to reproduce copyright material. Acknowledgements are listed at the end of the text. Likewise, thank you to the various organizations providing case study and vignette materials.

The Publisher would like to thank the following academics who supplied feedback on the original proposal and during the writing process:

Desmond Gargan, National College of Ireland

Peter Stokes, University of Chester

The Publisher also thanks various copyright holders for granting permission to reproduce material throughout the text. Every effort has been made to trace all copyright holders, but if anything has been inadvertently overlooked, the Publisher will be pleased to make the necessary arrangements at the first opportunity (please contact the Publisher directly).

Dr Phil Kelly

Digital Support Resources

All of our Higher Education textbooks are accompanied by a range of digital support resources. Each title's resources are carefully tailored to the specific needs of the particular book's readers. Examples of the kind of resources provided include:

- A password protected area for instructors with, for example, a testbank, PowerPoint slides, and an instructor's manual
- An open-access area for students including, for example, useful weblinks and glossary terms

Lecturers: to discover the dedicated lecturer digital support resources accompanying this textbook please register here for access: **http://login.cengage.com**.

Students: to discover the dedicated student digital support resources accompanying this textbook, please search for MANAGEMENT: THEORY AND PRACTICE on: **www.cengagebrain.co.uk**

Digital Support Resources

All of our Higher Education textbooks are accompanied by a range of digital support resources. Each title's resources are carefully tailored to the specific needs of the particular textbook's readers. Examples of the kind of resources provided include:

- A password-protected area for instructors with, for example, a testbank, PowerPoint slides, and an instructor's manual.

- An open-access area for students including, for example, useful weblinks and glossary terms.

Lecturers: to discover the dedicated digital support resources accompanying this textbook, please register here for access: http://login.cengage.com.

Students: to discover the dedicated student digital support resources accompanying this textbook, please search for MANAGEMENT: THEORY AND PRACTICE on: www.cengagebrain.co.uk.

PART I
MANAGEMENT THEORY

Every practising business manager who seeks to improve their skills, abilities and their performance, and the performance of their organizations, should be concerned with the knowledge and application of management theories from across the past century. Yet there exists this persistent view that management theory and practice are polar opposites or that older management theories are no longer relevant. Management is one of those bodies of theory and practice whose concern might be described as 'rational intervention in human affairs'. This book will make sense of management theory from the present and the relevant past to help guide future managerial action. We start with management theory in the first part of the book and include practice in subsequent parts.

The opening chapter provides an overview of developments in management theory asking what 'management' means. The theoretical framework for Part 1 (Chapters 2–11) is based on the idea that management activities can best be analyzed in terms of essential groups of activities, namely planning, organizing, motivating and controlling (decision-making being inherent in all) and including leadership. Whilst this approach omits some aspects of management, it nevertheless simplifies the study of the theoretical basis of the subject. There are five sections to the first book part, each broadly represents a particular management era but all remain of relevance today.

CLASSICAL THEORIES OF MANAGEMENT

This section contains two chapters which describe and comment on the main ideas of the leading classical theorists. Chapter 2 focuses on the search for principles of management and draws upon the work of Henri Fayol and then considers scientific management (Taylorism) and the scientific management school. This leads into Chapter 3 where Max Weber's idea of bureaucracy is described.

HUMAN RELATIONS AND SOCIAL PSYCHOLOGICAL THEORIES

Whereas the exponents of classical theory were principally concerned with the structure and mechanics of organizations, the human relations and social psychological theorists focused on the human factor at work. These were invariably academics – social scientists – interested in people's behaviour in the workplace. They were particularly interested in human motivation, group relationships and leadership. Chapter 4 introduces the concept of 'motivation', and describes the famous Hawthorne Studies conducted in the USA almost 70 years ago. A brief outline of the ideas of Mary Parker Follett follow, then the chapter continues with an explanation of the ideas of several early contributors to motivation theory in the 1950s and 1960s, notably Maslow, McGregor, Herzberg, Likert, Argyris and McClelland.

Chapter 5 summarizes the work of later theorists, including Vroom's so-called 'expectancy theory', and the contributions of Locke, Kelley and Skinner.

THEORIES OF LEADERSHIP AND GROUP BEHAVIOUR

This section of the book examines some leading concepts in the related fields of leadership and group behaviour. Chapter 6 describes different ways of looking at leadership, discusses the tensions between concern for the task and concern for people, and summarizes a number of important theories of leadership. Chapter 7 looks at crucial aspects of the workplace, behaviour of people in groups and examines some features of the working of groups, including the effect of competition and the task of team-building.

SYSTEMS AND CONTINGENCY APPROACHES TO MANAGEMENT THEORY

The dominance of first the Classical School and second the Human Relations/Social Psychological Schools was overtaken by a more comprehensive approach to the study of management in organizations. This more recent approach views the organization as a system of interrelated sets of activities which enable inputs to be converted into outputs (a transformational process). The approach enables theorists to study key elements of organization in terms of their interaction with one another and with their external environment. Whereas, in the past, the explanations were in terms of structures or people, now it is possible to identify theories which seek to explain or predict organizational behaviour in a multidimensional way by studying people, structure, technology and environment at one and the same time. The most recent formulations of systems theories tend to be labelled contingency theories because they emphasize the need to take specific circumstances, or contingencies, into account when devising appropriate organizational and management systems. Chapter 8 introduces the concept of 'systems' as applied to organizations, and describes some of the major developments in the growth of systems theory, whilst Chapter 9 summarizes developments in contingency theories.

MODERN APPROACHES TO MANAGEMENT THEORY

Part 1 ends with two short chapters, outlining a number of key issues facing modern organizations, and identifies a selection of the theorists helping practising managers address these issues. The first chapter of this section considers the transformational process in more detail and the concept of value creation through the value chain. This is then discussed in the context of a broader value system – the supply chain. All the issues to which we refer are dealt with in various chapters throughout the remainder of the book.

CASE STUDY

To enable holistic and deeper thinking whilst enabling management theory to be put into practice – we will adopt a single case running through the book as a collection of case study sheets with activities. The case is outlined here and further case study sheets can be found online.

A BRIEF HISTORY OF SKATEBOARDING

Dreamed up by skaters who wanted to 'surf the streets', skateboarding was invented in the 1950s in California. Initially, boards were home-produced, as there were no manufacturers of boards until the early 1960s. Skateboarding gained credibility in the 1990s, as ESPN hosted the first ever 'X' games (televised across the world). Skateboarding is an action sport which involves riding and performing tricks using a skateboard. Skateboarding can also be considered a recreational activity or a method of transportation. A skateboard is a small piece of wood in the shape of a surfboard with four wheels attached to it. A lone person rides the skateboard,

controlling the movement with their feet. While some use skateboards as transportation over short distances, most are used to perform stunts.

SKATEBOARD HARDWARE

The basic elements of the skateboard include the board or deck, the wheels, and the trucks, which connect the wheels to the board, and allow the board to turn. Each skateboard wheel is mounted on its axle via two bearings. Mounting hardware, used to attach the trucks to the board, is a set of eight bolts, usually an Allen or Phillips head, and corresponding locknuts. Risers are used to increase the space between the truck and the deck. This allows the truck to twist further without causing wheel bite (when the wheel touches the deck and stops spinning). In addition, grip tape (a sheet of paper or fabric with adhesive on one side and a surface similar to fine sand paper on the other) may be applied to the top surface of a board to allow the rider's feet to grip the surface and help the skater stay on the board while undertaking tricks. Skateboards have been customized in many ways using colour, different materials, sizes, shapes and graphics.

FIGURE 1 Skateboard hardware

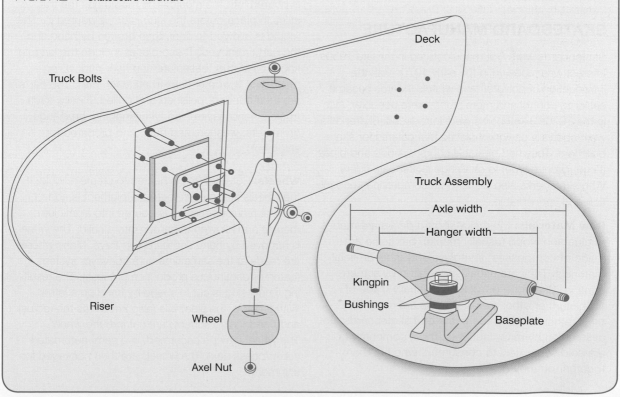

SKATEBOARD INDUSTRY

Some writers claim that skateboarding is one of the fastest growing sports not only in America but worldwide. Participants in the sport have been growing exponentially, already surpassing the popularity of several more traditional sports. One of the reasons skateboarding has become so popular (over 15 million enthusiasts in the USA) is that it has such a universal and open appeal. Skateboarding has been a significant business since the late 1970s. Since then skating, and the board sports industry, has been commercially driven. The skateboarding industry has evolved into a multi-billion dollar business. It is thought that the hard goods (boards, wheels and trucks) account for a much smaller amount of sales than the softer goods such as clothing, hats and shoes. Consequently, not all consumers are skaters. The skate industry posted US retail sales of approximately $7 billion in 2008 (around $6.2 billion in 2010) according to the Surf Industry Manufacturers Association (SIMA). The industry is typically made up of manufacturers who create the parts and assemblers who put them together to form a wide variety of products. Downstream, skateboards are typically purchased from specialist shops and the Internet.

SKATEBOARD MANUFACTURE

Skateboards were first manufactured in the late 1950s. Interest was renewed in the early 1970s with the introduction of polyurethane wheels (boards became easier to control and more stunts were possible). Also in the 1970s, skateparks were introduced. Skateparks were specially designed places that catered for skateboarders. They had obstacle courses, pools and pipes (large, circular type) to challenge skateboard riders. With skateparks also came more competition, recognition and sponsorship.

Raw Materials: Most skateboard decks are made of glue and wood (usually maple), but some are made of composites, fibreglass and other artificial materials. They are usually decorated by screen-printing. Skateboard trucks are usually made of aluminium or other metal. Wheels are made of polyurethane. While some low-end skateboards are assembled by manufacturers, most components are sold separately to consumers who put them together on their own.

THE MANUFACTURING PROCESS

Deck: A piece of maple wood undergoes a treatment that allows it to be peeled into veneers (thin sheets of wood) that are then delivered to the deck factory. Each veneer is then put into a glue machine which evenly coats each veneer with wood glue. Each skateboard is made of several layers of veneer. Stacks are put into a mould inside a hydraulic press. The mould creates the nose, concave, and tail of each skateboard. The resulting laminate sits in the press for anywhere from a few minutes to a few hours. The longer the time, the more naturally the wood and glue set. After the laminates are removed from the press, eight holes for the truck mount are drilled. A worker – called the shaper – takes the newly drilled board and, with a previously made template, hand-shapes each deck with a band saw. The deck is hand sanded and coated with a paint or sealant. After the deck is dry, a decorative design may be added by screen-printing. The decks are then dried and readied for shipment.

Trucks: First a master truck pattern is hand tooled and used to construct a mould for making the actual truck. Aluminium is heated to over 700°C in a furnace, reducing it to a liquid. This liquid aluminium is poured into the mould. The mould has the truck's axles in place before the aluminium is poured in. The mould is allowed to cool, then broken by hand and the parts removed. These pieces include the kingpin knob, pivot cup, baseplate and riser pad. Using machines, a worker heat-treats each part. The parts are then grinded, polished and drilled. Finally, each truck is hand-assembled with kingpins, brushings, grommets, washers and nuts, and prepared for shipment.

Wheels: Polyurethane is heated to create a liquid. If the wheels are to be coloured, a pigment is added and the resulting mixture is poured into aluminium moulds and allowed to harden into a solid. The wheel is removed by hand and cured on trays. Many wheels are made at the same time on a conveyor system (batch or continuous production process). The resulting wheel slug is cut to shape by hand on a lathe. With a blade, the sidewalls (also known as the radius) and tread (riding surface) are cut into the wheel. The wheel may be decorated, in a semi-automated sub-process next. The wheels are then packaged for shipment.

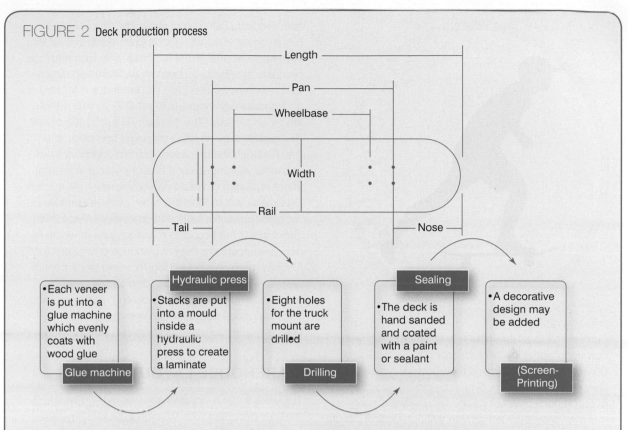

FIGURE 2 Deck production process

Length

Pan

Wheelbase

Width

Rail

Tail

Nose

Glue machine
• Each veneer is put into a glue machine which evenly coats with wood glue

Hydraulic press
• Stacks are put into a mould inside a hydraulic press to create a laminate

Drilling
• Eight holes for the truck mount are drilled

Sealing
• The deck is hand sanded and coated with a paint or sealant

(Screen-Printing)
• A decorative design may be added

Assembling the Skateboard: After purchasing/ manufacturing the three separate components, the consumer or manufacturer must put them together. Once assembled, grip tape is needed to provide traction on the board. Grip tape comes in a large rectangular sheet, bigger than the actual deck. It is smoothed over by hand to get rid of any air bubbles. Using a file, the edge of the board under the grip tape is defined. With a blade or scissors, the extra parts of the grip tape are removed. With an awl or another sharp, pointed object, the eight truck holes are exposed through the grip tape, and the mounting bolts are placed. The truck is then installed over the bolts and tightened with the locknuts. One set of bearings and a spacer are placed on each of the four truck axles. The wheel is then attached, flush with the bearings and spacer. The other set of bearings is put in the wheel. The wheels are secured with washers and a lugnut. The skateboard is now ready to be ridden.

Quality Control: When the components are purchased separately, the consumer must follow all instructions for their own safety. All screws must be tightly secured so that they will continue to hold the trucks in place while stunts are performed. Manufacturers continually check the finished boards to see that they are secure and meet safety requirements.

STARTING YOUR OWN SKATEBOARD SHOP

There are many specialized skateboard shops worldwide – thousands just in the USA. There are also numerous board, truck and wheel products created by manufacturers. Diversified shops may also sell longboards and scooters. (A longboard is a longer variant of a skateboard, commonly used for cruising, downhill racing, slalom racing, sliding and/ or transport.) Ideally, the shop should be in a good location. An ideal site would be near a skatepark or an area where skaters visit often. Shops cater for different needs from new to professional skaters. New skaters may find skateboards in the lower price range more attractive until they gain additional experience. Experienced skaters may value higher-quality skateboards that are more expensive. Experienced skaters are more likely to purchase parts and assemble boards by themselves whilst the novice will seek out a ready assembled board. Additional products can include T-shirts, hats, bags, footwear and first aid kits.

Sources: **http://www.madehow.com/Volume-6/ Skateboard.html**

ScaterBoys is an example of a small manufacturing company within the skateboarding industry. Scater-Boys offer skateboards as their primary product. They also provide skateboarding accessories and clothing. The company was established as a reseller but has more recently pursued growth through vertical integration and has taken to manufacturing/assembling its own products using procured parts. The company has a variety of trading goods (purchased in their final form from UK and global suppliers who then resell the products directly to consumers (indirect) and directly to consumers (worldwide). The company is located in an industrial warehouse built in 1990. In year 1 there are 21 employees. The company is run by the owner (MD) assisted by an office manager and clerk, and five managers/team leaders (plant/production, sales, accounts, warehouse and procurement/purchasing). There is a team of five employees responsible for making skateboard products; a team of three employees are responsible for sales and customer service; two clerks assist the accounts manager (one of whom is part time); there are three warehouse employees (one focuses more on inbound logistics and stock control and the withdrawal of stock/parts for the production team) the other two focus on picking, packaging and shipping goods outbound. Cleaning services and company accounts are contracted out.

WAREHOUSE LAYOUT

The warehouse is approximately 30m by 50m and the total occupied floor space is 2000m². Bays are approximately 2.5m by 5m.

FIGURE 3 Warehouse layout

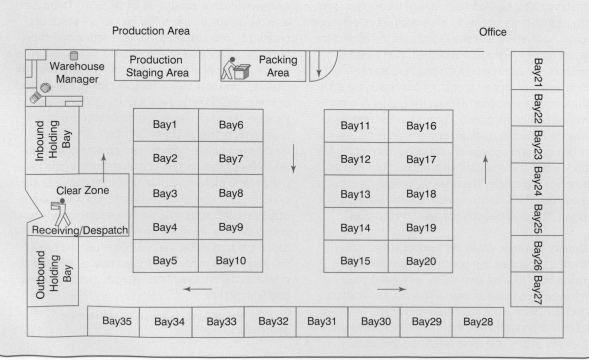

BUSINESS PROCESSES

The core business processes include fulfilment, procurement and production.

Fulfilment: A customer order is received by email, fax, telephone or post by the sales team who enter details into the ScaterBoys system to create an internal sales order. The warehouse pick, pack and ship the goods (using an external courier). If the customer is a business then an invoice is generated with 28 day terms. Consumers pay at the time of placing an order (typically by credit card). Accounts process the payment of invoices (receivables) as they arrive.

Procurement: When inventory is running low or a customer orders goods not in stock, procurement place orders with suppliers. Goods are then received inbound at the warehouse where staff store the goods and update systems accordingly. Accounts will receive the invoice from suppliers and will then pay the supplier.

Production: The production manager plans operations based on either a supply (make-to-stock) or customer-led approach, though they tend to make-to-order. Upon the issuance of a planned order, the warehouse withdraws the parts needed by the production team to make the skateboards. The boards are assembled and then placed into the inventory.

Information Systems: Until recently the company had utilized several stand-alone computers. A SAGE application was used to manage orders and accounts, a custom built access database managed the inventory. Spreadsheet packages were used to manage suppliers and products. This was, however, far from satisfactory with employees having to go from computer to computer to swap files and printout forms to instigate work etc. In some cases data had to be printed from one system and re-entered into another.

As a result of a number of problems, growth and a desire to be more efficient, the company recently procured a new integrated and networked system to manage all operational and primary aspects of the company. This new system eliminated the problem of having to re-enter data and have multiple versions on different computers. Everyone now had access to the same information but actions are restricted by a user set of privileges.

Revenues: In the first year that you encounter the company they record annual revenues of £3 million. Revenues grow in the second year.

 Further resources available at the ScaterBoys website managed by Dr Phil Kelly.

USING THE SCATERBOYS CASE STUDY

The case study (downloaded from the companion website) enables detailed, integrative problem-solving and the practice of management. When used by student groups it can develop teamwork, critical thinking and transferable skills (interpersonal, communication, problem-solving and presentation skills) and enables students to translate management and business theory into practice. Furthermore, it presents an opportunity to engage in day-to-day operations, management tactics and strategy. Completion of tasks and activities allows students to gain appreciation of business processes, structure, integrated roles/functions and responsibilities. Completing the case activities provides a rich experience and opportunity for reflection. It also enables alternative learning styles, supporting problem-based learning (PBL) and action learning – (learning by doing). Overall, this will engage and motivate students, encourage independent and collaborative learning, participation and involvement, whilst developing higher order cognitive skills.

A case study sheet has been created for each book section (see Table 1). Whilst each case study sheet can form a stand-alone activity there is also an opportunity to integrate them into a more comprehensive management project. When used in this way we suggest posing the following overarching management challenge: 'The MD has asked your team to analyze the current business and make recommendations for efficiency improvements that could take immediate or short-term effect. You should also identify ways to make the company more effective'. Students could present their recommendations in report or presentation form, or both. They could deliver feasibility studies, budgets, management reports or business memos for example. Finally, they could be encouraged to reflect on the group work aspects of the case. A comprehensive assessment of learning might include (1) a multiple-choice question test of specific chapters, (2) a business report, (3) a presentation to the MD and

FIGURE 4 Roles

| Sales | Warehouse | Purchasing | Production | Accounts |

(4) an individual or group reflection. Alternatively, the various case and resource sheets and data could be used in a business simulation.

Whilst case sheet activities can be attempted individually, we recommend creating student groups (role playing the ScaterBoys management team) that remain together throughout a teaching course/semester. This facilitates the development of transferable group work skills and builds critical thinking opportunities into the case activities as each group member can hear a range of alternative viewpoints as they solve, collectively, the business problems posed. Ideally the groups will comprise five members and each will role play a specific ScaterBoys function, e.g. Sales, Warehouse, Production, Accounts and Procurement. For advice on group formation we recommend the following publications: (1) Kelly, P. (2009), 'Group Work and Multicultural Management Education Programmes', *Journal of Teaching in International Business*, 20(1), 80–102 and (2) Kelly, P. (2008), 'Achieving desirable group-work outcomes through the group allocation process', *Team Performance Management*, 14(1/2), 22–38. Kelly advocates a mixed pair approach to group formation.

RESOURCES:

- Each case sheet can be downloaded by the reader or tutor as a pdf (and distributed to the class)

- **Activity Answers**: Each case sheet activity has a suggested answer. The answer book can be downloaded by tutors from the companion website

- **Skills Sheets (SS)**: For each case sheet there is a corresponding skills sheet which should be used by the reader, in conjunction with the management theory presented in the chapters, to answer the case questions and complete activities

- **ScaterBoys website**: Further resources (including role briefings/guides) can be downloaded from the ScaterBoys website: **www.scaterboys.com**

TABLE 1 Case study parts

	Title	Book Content	Overview
1	Bureaucracy and Efficiency	Ch. 1–3 SS 1	How might ScaterBoys make efficiency gains through the adoption of bureaucratic ideas?
2	Motivation	Ch. 4–5 SS 2	Design an employee satisfaction survey; discuss how to motivate employees.
3	Groups, Teams and Leaders	Ch. 6–7 SS 3	Evaluate the MD as a leader; review the CRM team.
4	Organization and Structure	Ch. 8–9 SS 4	Create a diagram showing ScaterBoys as an open system; build a business case for flexibility; evaluate differentiation, integration, centralization and formalization; discuss structure – classify it as mechanistic or organic.
5	SCM and Process Modelling	Ch. 10–11 SS 5	Create process maps for ScaterBoys; write a brief description of the supply chain and critically discuss how value is created at ScaterBoys.

6	Analyzing the Environment	Ch. 12–15 SS 6	Create a SWOT supported with a PESTEL analysis, analysis of competition and the internal environment; and evaluate organizational culture.
7	Strategy	Ch. 16–19 SS 7	Create vision and mission statements; list core values and goals; list strategic initiatives and create a policy document.
8	Organizing	Ch. 20–26 SS 8	Draw an organization chart; create job descriptions; prepare a PowerPoint briefing explaining how managers might better engage the workforce; propose efficiency improvements within the warehouse operation.
9	Control	Ch. 27–29 SS 9	Prepare a short report that (a) identifies targets for control and (b) discusses control mechanisms; write a business memo discussing coordination; discuss quality and evaluate the usefulness of the IRM risk standard.
10	Marketing	Ch. 30–34 SS 10	Conduct a marketing audit; identify and describe the important market segments; critically evaluate the RFM method; assess and discuss the customer purchasing criteria; manipulate the marketing mix and create a marketing plan.
11	Operations Management	Ch. 35–38 SS 11	Undertake an ABC analysis; create a new reverse logistics process; calculate the EOQ; review the use of barcode and RFID technology; discuss stockouts; discuss lean operations; create a short memo exploring possible coordinates for warehouse relocation or a second warehouse and conduct a high-level review of the application of technology in ScaterBoys.
12	HRM	Ch. 39–43 SS 12	Write a draft promotion, absence or health and safety policy; design a new performance appraisal form; write a grievance or performance appraisal procedure; create a briefing memo to explain cultural difference.
13	Financial Management	Ch. 44–45 SS 13	Calculate the NPV, IRR and ROI for investment opportunities; write a memo reviewing how prices could be set; write a procedure for creation of a master budget.
14	Information Resource Management	Ch. 46–47 SS 14	Create a feasibility study for the acquisition of an entry level ERP solution and create a covering memo to the MD outlining the acquisition process.

Section One
Introduction

CHAPTER 1
MANAGEMENT – AN INTRODUCTION

Key Concept

- Management

Learning Outcomes   Having read this chapter, you should be able to:

- explain, through the use of the LANDSCAPE acronym, what is meant by the term 'management'
- define management
- discuss the eclectic and sometimes non-linear nature of management theory
- argue why it is important to study management theory over the past 100 years
- recognize why simply studying management theory is unlikely to make you an effective manager.

1.1 INTRODUCTION – WHAT IS MANAGEMENT?

1.   How does the newly promoted or developing manager know what they are expected to do when asked to manage? It is hard for new managers to know what to aim for when developing, or to judge whether a manager is effective or not, if we do not have a shared view of the concept. Yet there is no easily cited all-encompassing definition of what a manager is and what it means to manage. In this chapter we will seek to outline an explanation of what management is, developed further in remaining parts of the book. In answering such a question we will explore what a manager is and what it means to manage. Many textbooks, journal and practitioner articles have provided useful insights that help us understand aspects of management. However, those new to management may soon get confused as discussions include reference to theories of management, skills, roles, the environment, activities, functions, processes, levels and more! Consequently, we have developed an acronym and framework to structure thoughts on this issue. We believe that this collection of thoughts, insights, perspectives and explicit knowledge describe the LANDSCAPE (features) of MANAGEMENT.

2.   **LANDSCAPE** not only suggests a broad backdrop but is also a useful acronym for a range of features used to define management:

MANAGEMENT	
L	evels of management
A	ctivities of management
N	ovel aspects of management
D	ealings (roles, doings, duties, deeds) of management
S	cience of management (eclectic set of management theories)
C	raft of management (skills and competencies required to practice)
A	rt of management (the creative, innovative and visionary activities)
P	redispositions of managers (how we see management challenges)
E	nvironment for management (context)

We discuss each of these elements of management in more detail next before identifying a succinct definition of management within the context of the organization.

1.2 LEVELS (AND TYPES) OF MANAGEMENT

3.   An important determinant of the meaning of management is the level of managerial work undertaken. Organizations are often conceived in terms of a hierarchy. There are those at the top and bottom of an organization. The nature of managerial work, authority and organizational influence (power) is determined by managerial level. Thus, management means different things at different levels. Despite this, Chan and Renée (2014) suggest companies distribute leadership across all management levels. The key to a successful organization is having empowered leaders at every level, because outstanding organizational performance often comes down to the motivation and actions of middle and frontline leaders, who are in closer contact with the market.

4.   Managers at the bottom are more operational, concerned with facilitating employee performance in their day-to-day work. Often referred to as first line or first level managers, their responsibilities may be of a functional/specialist nature (i.e. different types of manager) and are typically responsible for a primary activity associated with the production of goods and services. The planning and decision-making activities of such managers typically have a time orientation measured in days or weeks. This level may include departmental heads in larger organizations.

5.   Middle managers are more senior, typically having responsibility for a business unit or major department. They may be 3rd or 4th line managers, i.e. they may have first or second line managers reporting to them. Their decisions tend to be more tactical/strategic and they may have responsibilities which include developing sources of competitive advantage. Middle managers tend to be less concerned with individual performance (other than for their direct reports) and more with coordinating the efforts of groups of people as well as allocating resources and putting senior management plans into action.

6.   Finally there are the senior managers of the organization (aka top managers) who head up significant parts of the organization, determine strategy and collectively represent the management team. They will have middle managers reporting to them and may have titles such as senior manager, director, vice president or similar. The most senior manager in this group is known as the Chief Executive Officer (CEO) or Managing Director (MD). These managers and the management team are responsible for the whole organization, for attaining goals and overall performance. Their focus is more on the external environment and meeting its needs and challenges. Decisions taken by this group of managers have a significant impact upon the organization and the effect may be witnessed over several years. Managerial levels will be revisited in Section 9 when the concepts of organizing and structure are considered in detail.

1.3 ACTIVITIES OF MANAGEMENT – THE PROCESS OF MANAGEMENT

7.   We may also gain an insight in what it means to be a manager by considering the major work activities they do. A structured set of activities designed to produce a specified output is termed a process. The process of management is concerned with the transformation processes of organizations; how inputs are converted to outputs through work. As Drucker (1955) first described it, almost 60 years ago, management is concerned with the 'systematic organization of economic resources' and its task is to make these resources productive. Management may therefore be viewed as a part of the transformation process.

8.   Management is not an activity that exists in its own right. It is rather a description of a variety of activities carried out by those members of organizations whose role is that of a 'manager', i.e. someone who either has formal responsibility for the work of one or more persons in the organization or who is accountable for specialist advisory duties in support of key management activities. These activities have generally been grouped in terms of planning, organizing, motivating (also associated with leadership by some scholars) and controlling. These groupings describe activities which indicate broadly what managers do in practice.

9.   The groupings of management activities can be summarized as follows:

PLANNING: deciding the organizational objectives or goals and how to meet them

ORGANIZING: determining and coordinating activities and allocating resources and responsibilities for the achievement of plans

MOTIVATING: meeting the social and psychological needs of employees in the fulfilment of organizational goals, and

CONTROLLING: managing the implementation of plans, monitoring and evaluating activities, and providing corrective mechanisms.

These traditional groupings – the POMC approach – are the ones chosen to represent the framework for this book. It is appreciated that they do not tell the whole story about what constitutes management, but they are a convenient way of describing many of the key aspects of managerial work in practice. Inherent in each activity is decision-making (Chapter 16).

The approach, shown in Figure 1.1, focuses on actions of managers:

FIGURE 1.1   **POMC approach to management**

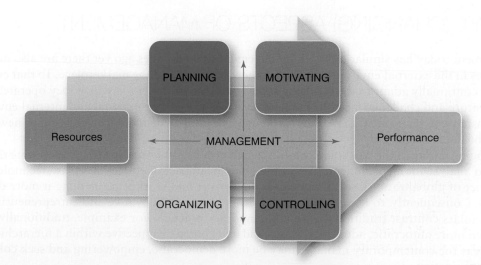

PLANNING

10. Planning is a management activity which involves decisions about ends (organizational aims/objectives), means (plans), conduct (policies) and results. It is an activity taking place against the background of the organization's environment (discussed later). Planning can be long term, as in strategic and corporate planning, medium term, as in the setting of annual departmental budgets or even short term (immediate future) such as organizing the staff rota for the coming weeks. In summary, planning is the formalization of what is intended to happen at some time in the future; it concerns actions taken prior to an event, typically formulating goals and objectives and then arranging for resources to be provided in order to achieve a desired outcome. Section 8 describes the major aspects of planning.

ORGANIZING

11. Plans have to be translated into action – determining activities and allocating responsibilities (and resources) for their achievement; activities must be coordinated through an appropriate structure and other mechanisms. Communications are an important means to allocate and coordinate work activities. Aspects of organizing are dealt with in greater detail in Section 9.

MOTIVATING

12. Motivating is about activating the driving force within individuals by which they attempt to achieve some organizational goal. We consider some of the most significant theories of motivation in Chapters 4 and 5. The motivating activities of managers, however, are essentially practical in their intent for, in setting plans and executing them, managers have to gain the commitment of their employees.

CONTROLLING

13. Controlling ensures or assures plans are properly executed; assuring the organization functions as planned; activities are concerned essentially with measuring progress and correcting deviations. The basic functions of control are to establish targets and standards of performance, to measure actual performance against targets/standards and to take corrective actions where appropriate. Control activities act as the feedback mechanism for all managerial activities. Their use is, therefore, crucial to the success of management. Key aspects of control are discussed in Section 10.

1.4 NOVEL (CHANGING) ASPECTS OF MANAGEMENT

14. Management today has similarities with management some decades ago yet there are also many differences as forces in the external environment change the workplace and the marketplace. To that end, organizations must continually adapt to the changing forces of the environment in which they operate. Change is a common feature and challenge faced by management. Changes in the external and internal environments present a constant stream of new challenges for managers. Change demands the creation of new ideas and solutions to business needs.

15. The changing nature of the workplace was discussed by Kelly and Ashwin (2013). Adopting the PESTLE framework to analyze the environment, the authors note the impact of employment law, technology, migration (a product of globalization), social norms on the market and workplace; making it more diverse and multicultural. Consequently, to manage also means to be creative, innovative and entrepreneurial.

16. Many scholars contrast traditional with contemporary practice. For example, traditionally managers may have been more autocratic, adopting a command and control perspective within a hierarchical organization. Whereas the contemporary manager may be more democratic, empowering and seek collaboration in a flatter organization.

1.5 DEALINGS OF MANAGEMENT

17. The POMC approach and our understanding of management may be enhanced when we take account of the variety of roles that managers can be called upon to play. Mintzberg's analysis of managerial characters identified ten key roles, which clearly encompass more than just planning, organizing, motivating and controlling. Mintzberg (1973) describes these roles as 'organized sets of behaviours identified with a position', and gathers them into three main groupings, as follows:

Interpersonal roles	Informational roles	Decisional roles
Figurehead	Monitor	Entrepreneur
Leader	Disseminator	Disturbance handler
Liaison	Spokesman	Resource allocator
		Negotiator

18. The important issue for understanding what management means is that managers fulfilling different roles will be called upon to do different things. The leader may set goals (visionary) and win the support of employees; the liaison role requires relationship management skills; the disseminator requires good communication skills whilst the resource allocator may need good analytical skills. In some cases the role will benefit from knowledge of relevant theories, whilst in other cases the role may develop through practice. We consider theory next but will consider practice from a management craft perspective later.

1.6 SCIENCE OF MANAGEMENT (THEORY)

19. Continuing with the LANDSCAPE acronym we now move onto 'S'. The Science (theories) of management is about explicit management knowledge generated from the documented experiences of practising managers and the use of empirical data to derive principles, frameworks and tools for managers to use – typically to analyze the organization and its environment. Theories help us to understand causes and relationships. However, theory is generally speculation. This book is about theory and practice and we may draw a distinction between the two – the former is more about a proposed explanation – in some cases theory can be thought of as a model of reality – whilst the latter is more about action, translating an idea into action – engaging in an activity.

20. There are many different non-mutually exclusive management theories (eclectic) which will be outlined next and discussed further in the remainder of Part 1 of this book. Management theories, or approaches to

FIGURE 1.2 Management theory – the building blocks

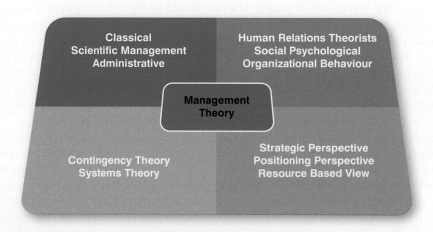

management, tend to be clustered and several major categories are recognized (see Figure 1.2). Collectively, each contributes to our overall understanding of management.

21. The earliest contributors to our (classical) understanding of management theory included practising managers as well as social scientists. More recent theorists have tended to be academics or management consultants. The early theorists can be divided into two main groups – the practising managers, such as Taylor and Fayol, and the social scientists, such as Mayo and McGregor. The **classical approach to management** was primarily concerned with the structure and activities of formal or official organization. Issues such as the division of work, the establishment of a hierarchy of authority, and the span of control (the number of people who should be under the direct control of a manager) were seen to be of the utmost importance in the achievement of an effective organization. The work of these contributors to classical theories of management is described in the next section (Chapters 2 and 3).

22. The practising managers tended to reflect upon, and theorize about, their personal experiences of management with the object of producing a set of rational principles (laws) of management which could be applied universally in order to achieve organizational efficiency (detailed in the next chapter). The resultant 'theories' of management were concerned primarily with the structuring of work and organizations, rather than with human motivation or organizational culture, for example. The label generally ascribed to these theorists is 'Classical', or, in some cases, 'Scientific Managers'. Their approaches were generally prescriptive, i.e. they set out what managers ought to do in order to fulfil their leadership function within their organization.

23. While Fayol and Taylor were grappling with the problems of management, a German sociologist, Max Weber (1864–1924), was developing a theory of authority structures in which he identified a form of organization to which he gave the name '**bureaucracy**'. The distinguishing features of a bureaucracy were a definition of roles within a hierarchy, where job-holders were appointed on merit, were subject to rules and were expected to behave impartially. Weber's ideas and their impact upon modern organization theory are discussed in more detail in Chapter 3.

24. The social scientists, by contrast, were academics, whose starting point was research into human behaviour in the workplace. At first most of their studies were also linked to concerns about efficiency, including the effects of physical working conditions on employees. Subsequent theorists were more interested in the human factor at work, and thus concentrated their attention on issues such as employee motivation, interpersonal communication and leadership style. Their focus was as much on individual satisfaction as on the efficient use of resources. Typical labels that have been assigned to these early social scientists include 'Human Relations Theorists' and 'Social Psychological School'. They were concerned primarily with social relationships and individual behaviour at work. The fundamental idea behind the human relations approach to management is that people's needs are the decisive factor in achieving organizational effectiveness. The work of these theorists and the results of their research are covered in Chapters 4–5.

25. By the late 1960s another group of theorists began to challenge the dominance of human relations and psychology. These were theorists that viewed organizations as complex systems of people, tasks and technology. Their work was grounded in the idea of organizations as social systems, and produced a more comprehensive view of the behaviour of people at work, based on the interaction of a number of variables, such as structure, tasks, technology and the environment. Later theorists of this school were given the label 'Contingency Theorists', since their ideas were based on what was appropriate in given circumstances, i.e. where the effect on people of one variable was contingent on its relationship with one or more others.

26. This group recognized that human or social factors alone were not the most important consideration in achieving organizational effectiveness. They recognized that organizations were part of a larger environment within which they interacted and in particular were affected by technical and economic factors just as much as social factors. This approach is described in greater detail in Chapters 8–9.

27. Arising out of the **open systems** approach is an essentially pragmatic 'theory' which argues that there is no one (management) theory at present which can guarantee the effectiveness of an organization. Management has to select a mix of theories which seem to meet the needs of the organization and its internal and external pressures at a particular period in its life. This has been termed a contingency approach to management.

28. Towards the end of the twentieth century, business management came to consist of branches, such as: human resource, operations or production, strategic, marketing, financial and information technology

management. Theorists of management, such as Mintzberg, Porter, Peters and Moss Kanter, adopted a strategic perspective. The emphasis in management theorizing in the latter part of the twentieth century was on organizational effectiveness, with its focus on strategic issues. This emphasis implies more than just efficiency, which is concerned with 'doing things right'. Effectiveness is primarily a question of 'doing the right things' even more than performing them efficiently. Thus, the concerns of such theorists have been topics such as developing strategic mission and implanting organizational values/culture (i.e. doing the right things) as well as managing change, promoting quality management, achieving organizational excellence, facilitating personal empowerment and optimizing stakeholder relationships. Some of the leading ideas in these areas of interest are described in Section 6.

29. Strategic management theories looked for means to attain competitive (and sustainable) advantages by focusing on the organizations' external environment – competitive positioning perspective. Later, scholars turned to the internal environment, developing a perspective on strategy that emphasizes the importance of capabilities (sometimes known as core competencies) in determining sustainable competitive advantage. This perspective was labelled the resource based view (RBV).

30. In the twenty-first century, scholars and practitioners find it increasingly difficult to subdivide management into functional categories. As an alternative, people think in terms of the various core business processes such as fulfilment or production. This has been labelled as a horizontal perspective of management (as opposed to the vertical, hierarchical and silo aspects of traditional/functional management).

1.7 CRAFT OF MANAGEMENT

31. Having outlined major areas of management theory (management as science) we now recognize the controversy as to whether management is a science at all. Some scholars have argued whether management is an art or craft. Exponents of management as craft argue that managing can be learned only by working under a skilled practitioner in a non-academic setting and by observing and copying what he or she does. In this way the manager will learn from their own experience.

32. Management as a craft is a perspective that emphasizes managerial skills and competencies. There have been many attempts to categorize managerial skills and competencies. For simplicity we suggest adopting a framework using the CHART acronym. Managers need Conceptual skills to see the holistic nature of the organization; Human skills to work with others; Analytical skills to aid understanding of business problems; Relationship skills to communicate with a wide range of stakeholders and Technical skills in order to accomplish tasks in efficient ways. Since skills emphasize a person's ability to actually do something well they are more concerned with practice than theory. Thus you can CHART your way through the management LANDSCAPE!

33. Many scholars support management as science, craft and art, i.e. some aspects of management can be codified and written down; made explicit for others to read and follow. Other aspects of management (skills and competencies) are more tacit and not easily codified or written down. Such skills have to be observed and practised. Under this perspective, management is a practice where art, craft and science meet.

1.8 ART OF MANAGEMENT

34. Mintzberg suggests that management work is more an art than a science and is reliant on intuitive processes and a feel for what is right. In pursuit of competitive advantage, companies and their managers are always on the lookout for new ideas; this is about creativity and innovation. Creativity involves the application of imaginative thought which may lead to new ways of seeing things and result in innovative solutions to a problem or the initiation of change (Kelly and Ashwin, 2013). For other scholars it is simply the ability to produce novel and useful ideas. Since creativity can lead to new products and services, novel applications and cost savings it is an important aspect of management. Protagonists of management as art or craft will cite numerous examples of the successful managers who have never studied the theories of management!

1.9 PREDISPOSITIONS OF MANAGERS

35. Other scholars have attempted to understand management from the perspective of the individual manager as a decision-maker who has differing values which impact upon the choices he/she may make – regardless of theory or rational thinking. Child (1997) introduces a perspective labelled 'strategic choice' – the process whereby power-holders within organizations decide upon courses of strategic action.

36. Strategic choice followed the 'determinism' theories, the 'contingency' views, giving attention to organizational decision-makers. The decisions of managers are coloured by their values, attitudes and beliefs; the sources of which include culture (e.g. professional, corporate or national membership), experience and training. Predispositions impact evaluations, cognitions and mental process and therefore choices and actions.

37. Thus what it means to be a manager and to manage will also be dependent upon the individual manager concerned – how they perceive the world and believe they should operate within it. None of us sees the events in our lives in a totally objective way. Our views of reality are determined by our own personal attitudes, values, beliefs and expectations. We then filter everything through this lens that makes up our individual 'world view' and assign meaning to the people, things and events in our lives based on our personal interpretation. We make sense of a situation and then respond through our actions; our perceptions (the meanings we attach to incoming information) shape our actions.

1.10 ENVIRONMENT FOR MANAGEMENT

38. Earlier we noted the important role of the environment in the meaning of management when we outlined contingency theory, i.e. the way we manage depends upon the challenges faced in the environment. The external business environment is typically analyzed or considered using the PESTLE framework or categorization schemes that seek to analyze the degree of predictability or uncertainty within it. The framework categorizes environmental influences into six main types: political, economic, social, technological, legal and environmental. Factors (forces) within each category influence what the organization does and how the organization works (is managed). The environment is therefore the context for management, presenting challenges, opportunities and threats. It therefore defines the problems managers will face. It defines laws governing work and trade and is made up of consumers with needs to be satisfied by the business.

39. The degree of uncertainty in the environment may constrain the planning process. If there is significant change and the environment is dynamic, forecasting – as one aspect of management – becomes less beneficial and other management methods or perspectives must be adopted. Similarly, rigid structures (organizing) may be too slow to respond to new challenges and more agile methods selected to enable flexibility and speed of response.

40. Kelly and Ashwin (2013) argue that businesses have to operate both in an internal environment and an external one. These two environments are not mutually exclusive and issues that affect the internal environment not only affect decision-making on issues that the business takes internally but also these decisions will feedback to effects on the external environment.

41. The context of management will be explored in more detail within Section 7 of this book. In summary, we have now explored the meaning of management through the LANDSCAPE framework. An understanding of management levels, activities, novel aspects and change, duties and roles, science and theory, management craft and art, the predispositions of managers and the environment should help illuminate what it means to be a manager and to manage. Having explored the landscape of management we are now in a position to consider succinct definitions of management.

1.11 THE MEANING OF MANAGEMENT – CAN WE DEFINE IT?

42. Taking everything we have discussed thus far and turning it into a succinct definition of management is a non-trivial task! Indeed it is worth noting there is no generally accepted definition of 'management',

although the classic definition is still held to be that of Henri Fayol. His general statement about management, in many ways, still remains valid after almost a century and has only been adapted by more recent writers, as shown below:

'To manage is to forecast and plan, to organize, to command, to coordinate and to control.'

Fayol (1916)[1]

'Management is a social process … the process consists of … planning, control, coordination and motivation.'

Brech (1957)

'Managing is an operational process initially best dissected by analyzing the managerial functions … The five essential managerial functions (are): planning, organizing, staffing, directing and leading and controlling.'

Koontz and O'Donnell (1984)

'Five areas of management constitute the essence of proactive performance in our chaotic world: (1) an obsession with responsiveness to customers; (2) constant innovation in all areas of the firm; (3) partnership – the wholesale participation of and gain sharing with all people connected with the organization; (4) leadership that loves change (instead of fighting it) and instils and shares an inspiring vision; and (5) control by means of simple support systems aimed at measuring the "right stuff" for today's environment.'

Peters (1988)

The definitions proposed by Brech (1957), and Koontz and O'Donnell (1984) represent changes of emphasis rather than principle.

43. It has to be recognized that the above definitions are extremely broad. Basically, what they are saying is that 'management' is a process enabling organizations to set and achieve their objectives by planning, organizing and controlling their resources, including gaining the commitment of their employees (motivation).

44. The search for a comprehensive definition of 'management' that is not over-generalized still proceeds. In the meantime, this book deals with management as a collection of activities involving planning, organizing, motivating and controlling. This approach is helpful in enabling the work of management to be analyzed.

45. Whatever view is preferred concerning the definition of management, it is clear that it can only be discussed within the context of an organization. Brech (1965) once described organizations as 'the framework of the management process'. It must be recognized, however, that this 'framework' can be described in several different ways. The first distinction is between the use of the word 'organization' to describe the process of organizing, and its use to describe the social entity formed by a group of people.

46. As yet there is no widely accepted definition of an organization. Nevertheless, as the following quotations suggest, there are some commonly accepted features of organizations such as purpose, people and structure.

'Organizations are intricate human strategies designed to achieve certain objectives.'

Argyris (1960)

'Since organizations are systems of behaviour designed to enable humans and their machines to accomplish goals, organizational form must be a joint function of human characteristics and the nature of the task environment.'

Simon (1976)

---

[1] Fayol's work became more generally known with the 1949 publication of General and industrial administration, the English translation of the 1916 article 'Administration industrielle et générale'.

'Organizations are systems of inter-dependent human beings.'

Pugh (1990)

'Organizations are set up to achieve purposes that individuals cannot achieve on their own. Organizations then provide a means of working with others to achieve goals ... likely to be determined by whoever is in the best position to influence them.... A key characteristic of organizations is their complexity.'

Stewart (1994)

47. An organization then is a group of people with a common purpose who work together to achieve shared goals. The collection of work groups that has been consciously designed by management to maximize efficiency and achieve organizational goals is referred to as the formal organization. However, scholars also recognize the informal organization, the network of relationships between members of an organization which form of their own accord, on the basis of common interests and friendship.

48. In the preceding paragraphs we have explored many of the facets of management and noted that this includes leadership, planning, organizing, motivating and controlling. We have outlined aspects of management theory which can prescribe what the manager and leader should be and should do. Yet the reality is often messy and less consistent with the theory. According to Gallup (based on a recent survey), only 30 per cent of employees actively apply their talent and energy to move their organizations forward. Fifty per cent are just putting their time in, while the remaining 20 per cent act out their discontent in counterproductive ways. A main cause of employee disengagement is poor leadership, Gallup says. Chan and Renée (2014) recently investigated what managers actually do. They discuss 'as-is' leadership – the activities that employees see leaders (and managers) actually engaging in. One study of middle managers revealed that employees viewed them as rule enforcers who 'played it safe'. They spent more time on activities like requesting frequent progress reports, enforcing rules and seeking justifications for action by more junior staff and less time creating a safe learning environment, explaining the strategy clearly, empowering front line managers or coaching people. Thus, management theory is not always put into practice! Organizations may have managers who do not know how to lead and manage, lack the skill to do so or choose not to. According to Chan and Renée (2014) most executives recognize that one of their biggest challenges is closing the vast gulf between the potential and the realized talent and energy of the people they lead. Managers don't intend to be poor leaders. The problem is that they lack a clear understanding of just what changes it would take to bring out the best in everyone and achieve high impact.

CONCLUSION

49. We have devoted this chapter to an exploration of the meaning of management: to be a manager and to manage. The task of management is carried out in the context of an organization. Over the past century or so there have been numerous coherent theories developed to explain what management is and how to practise it. Early ideas about management were put forward at a time when organizations were thought of as machines requiring efficient systems to enable them to function effectively. The emphasis, therefore, was on the efficient use of resources, especially human resources, in the service of a mechanistic model of organizations. Later theorists modified this approach by taking account of social and environmental as well as technical factors in the workplace. Their emphasis was as much on employee satisfaction as on organizational effectiveness. Modern approaches to the analysis of organizational effectiveness do not necessarily rule out the ideas put forward by earlier theorists, but emphasize that they must be evaluated in the context of an organization's overriding need for flexibility in responding to change in its external and internal environment, in order to meet the competing demands of all its various stakeholders – customers, suppliers, employees and shareholders, etc.

50. In this chapter we explained what is meant by 'management' and 'organization'. There is no generally accepted definition of 'management' but we consider it to be coordinated activities (forecasting, planning, deciding, organizing, commanding) to direct and control an organization. It may also embrace leadership, depending how it is defined, a matter discussed in Chapter 6.

QUESTIONS

1   In your own words explain what management theory is. In your answer you should identify major contributors to a theory of management and discuss the origin of their contribution. You should contrast different ideas about management that have evolved over time.

2   Discuss management's preoccupation with effectiveness and efficiency. Evaluate the importance of effectiveness and efficiency to the scientific managers (bureaucrats), systems/contingency theorists and contemporary managers – which of the concepts features greatest in their theories?

3   Reread the ScaterBoys case notes and then discuss what management is likely to mean in this SME. In your discussions you should make reference to the management LANDSCAPE.

4   Contrast a SME like ScaterBoys with a large company that you are aware of. What differences might you expect to find when contrasting views of what management means according to managers of each company?

USEFUL WEBSITES

The Institute of Management: **www.managers.org.uk**
Management Guru: **www.mgmtguru.com/mgt301/301_Lecture1Page2.htm**
Brief history of early management thinking
HRM Guide: **www.hrmguide.co.uk/history/classical_organization_theory_modified.htm** Classical organization theory – Henri Fayol

Institute of Business Consulting: **www.ibconsulting.org.uk/**
The Institute of Business Consulting is the professional body for all consultants and business advisers.
Chartered Management Institute: **www.managers.org.uk/listing_with_description_1.aspx?id=10:255&id=10:63&id=10** Certificate in Management Consulting
Department of Business Innovation & Skills: **www.bis.gov.uk**

REFERENCES

Argyris, C. (1960) *Understanding Organizational Behaviour*, Tavistock.
Brech, E.F.L. (1957) *Organisation, The Framework of Management*, Longmans.
Brech, E.F.L. (1965) *Organization – the Framework of Management*, 2nd edn, Longman.
Chan, K.W. and Renée, M. (2014), 'Blue Ocean Leadership', *Harvard Business Review*, May, 92(5): 60–72.
Child, J. (1997), 'Strategic choice in the analysis of action, structure, organizations and environment: Retrospect and prospect', *Organization Studies*, Berlin 18(1): 43–76.
Drucker, P. (1955) *The Practice of Management*, Heinemann.
Fayol, H. (1949) *General and Industrial Management*, Pitman.

Kelly, P. and Ashwin, A. (2013) *The Business Environment*, UK: Cengage Learning.
Koontz, H. and O'Donnell, C. (1984) *Management*, 8th edn, McGraw-Hill.
Mintzberg, H. (1973) *The Nature of Managerial Work*, Harper & Row.
Peters, T. (1988) *Thriving on Chaos – Handbook for a Management Revolution*, Macmillan.
Pugh, D.S. (1990) *Organisational Theory: Selected Readings*, 3rd edn, Penguin.
Simon, H.A. (1976) *Administrative Behaviour*, 3rd edn, Collier Macmillan.
Stewart, R. (1994) *Managing Today and Tomorrow*, Macmillan.

Section Two
Classical Theories of Management

CHAPTER 2
THE SEARCH FOR PRINCIPLES OF MANAGEMENT

Key Concepts

- Management, principles of
- Scientific management
- Span of control
- Specialization

Learning Outcomes   Having read this chapter, you should be able to:

- identify the general principles of management defined by classical theorists
- evaluate the principles of scientific management
- evaluate Urwick's principles of management.

1.   In the previous chapter we outlined what is meant by the term management, using the LANDSCAPE acronym to organize thoughts on the matter. We noted management theory to be management as science and acknowledged numerous theories spanning the past 100 years. Bridgman and Cummings (2014) believe there is evidence of an increasing aversion towards history within management education. Today's management textbooks typically have little space devoted to management's history. They suggest students want to learn about how to manage in the present and the future – not about how it was done in the past. However, they note that some books are written that engage with management's defining ideas and critically evaluate their continued relevance. In this chapter we focus on earlier theories whilst mindful from the outset that many of the ideas and aspects of early theories continue to have use today. We also noted that theory has a number of meanings – one being the creation of laws or principles that enable explanation of a phenomenon. Understanding management principles will develop your understanding of what management means – what you may do when you are managing within your organization.

2.   The search for universally applicable principles of management began in the industrial heartlands of Europe and America in the last years of the nineteenth century. This chapter firstly describes the most important ideas on management proposed by the Frenchman, Henri Fayol, at the beginning of

the twentieth century. Particular attention is paid to his definition of management, and to his general principles of management, which may then be compared with similar principles proposed by other classical writers. The chapter continues with an account of Taylor's ideas concerning 'scientific management' in the workplace, together with brief references to other individuals sharing his viewpoint. The chapter ends with summaries of the ideas of two latter-day scientific managers, Urwick and Brech, who developed many of Fayol and Taylor's ideas in the period following the Second World War.

2.1 HENRI FAYOL

3. Henri Fayol (1841–1925), the celebrated French industrialist and theorist, began his working life as a young mining engineer at the age of 19. He spent his entire working life with the same company, rising to Managing Director at the age of 47, and only retiring after his 77th birthday! Under his leadership the company grew and prospered despite its near-bankrupt state when he took over. His entrepreneurial successes won him considerable fame and popularity, and when, in 1916, he published his major work on management ('Administration Industrielle et Generale'), he ensured himself a place in the annals of industrial history. The publication brought to light the distillation of a lifetime's experience of managerial work.

2.2 FAYOL'S DEFINITION OF MANAGEMENT

4. Fayol prefaced his famous definition of management by stating what he considered to be the key activities of any industrial undertaking. He outlined six such key activities, as follows:

1)	Financial	e.g. securing capital.
2)	Accounting	e.g. providing financial information.
3)	Security	e.g. safeguarding property.
4)	Technical	e.g. production.
5)	Commercial	e.g. buying and selling.
6)	Managerial	e.g. planning and organizing.

5. Explaining the final activity he stated that to manage is to 'forecast and plan, to organize, to command, to coordinate and to control'. He considered forecasting and planning to involve looking to the future and drawing up a plan of action. Organizing was seen in structural terms, and commanding was described as 'maintaining activity among the personnel'. Coordinating was regarded as essentially a unifying activity. Controlling meant ensuring that things happened in accordance with established policies and practice. It is important to note that Fayol did not see managerial activities as exclusively belonging to the management. Such activities are part and parcel of the total activities of an undertaking. Having said this, it is important to point out that Fayol's general principles of management take a perspective which looks at organizations from the top downwards. Nevertheless, they do have the merit of taking a comprehensive view of the role of management in organizations. Thus, Fayol's analysis has more far-reaching implications than Taylor's ideas on scientific management, which were centred on the shop floor.

2.3 FAYOL'S PRINCIPLES OF MANAGEMENT

6. In his book Fayol lists 14 so-called 'principles of management'. These are the precepts which he applied most frequently during his working life. He emphasized these principles not as absolutes but capable of adaptation, according to need. He did not claim his list was exhaustive, but only that it served him well in the past. The 14 'principles' listed below in Figure 2.1 are given in the order set out by Fayol, but the comments are a summary of his thinking on each point.

7.   Fayol's General Principles have been adopted by later followers of the classical school, such as Urwick and Brech. Present-day theorists, however, would not find much of substance in these precepts. From our present-day viewpoint, the following general comments may be made:

A   The references to division of work, scalar chain, unity of command and centralization, for example, are descriptive of the kind of formal organization that has come to be known as bureaucracy. Fayol, in true classical fashion, was emphasizing the structural nature of organizations.

B   Issues such as individual versus general interests, remuneration and equity were considered from a paternalistic management point of view. Today, questions concerning fairness, or the bona fide conflict of interests between groups, must be worked out jointly between management and organized labour, often with third party involvement by the State.

C   Although emphasizing the hierarchical aspects of the business enterprise, Fayol was well aware of the need to avoid an excessively mechanistic approach towards employees. Thus, references to initiative and esprit de corps indicated his sensitivity to people's needs as individuals and as groups. Such issues are of major interest to theorists today, the key difference being that whereas Fayol saw these issues in the context of a **rational model of organization** structure, the modern organizational development specialist sees them in terms of adapting structures and changing people's behaviour to achieve the best fit between the organization and its customers.

D   Fayol was the first to achieve a genuine theory of management based on a number of principles which could be passed on to others. Many of these principles have been absorbed into modern organizations. Their effect on organizational effectiveness has been subject to increasing criticism over the last 20 years. This is mainly because such principles were not designed to cope with modern conditions of rapid change, flatter structures and increased employee participation in the decision-making processes of the organization.

FIGURE 2.1 Fayol's principles of management

1. Division of work	Reduces the span of attention or effort for any one person or group. Develops practice and familiarity.
2. Authority	The right to give orders. Should not be considered without reference to responsibility.
3. Discipline	Outward marks of respect in accordance with formal or informal agreements between firm and its employees.
4. Unity of command	One man one superior!
5. Unity of direction	One head and one plan for a group of activities with the same objective.
6. Subordination of individual interests to general interest	The interest of one individual or one group should not prevail over the general good. This is a difficult area of the management.
7. Remuneration	Pay should be fair to both the employee and the firm.
8. Centralization	Is always present to a greater or lesser extent, depending on the size of company and quality of its managers.
9. Scalar chain	The line of authority from top to bottom of the organization.
10. Order	A place for everything and everything in its place; the right man in the right place.
11. Equity	A combination of kindliness and justice towards employees.
12. Stability of tenure of personnel	Employees need to be given time to settle into their jobs, even though this may be a lengthy period in the case of managers.
13. Initiative	Within the limits of authority and discipline, all levels of staff should be encouraged to show initiative.
14. Esprit de corps	Harmony is a great strength to an organization; teamwork should be encouraged.

2.4 TAYLOR AND SCIENTIFIC MANAGEMENT

Vignette

Despite origins in the early twentieth century, scientific management principles can be found in many contemporary organizations. Consider McDonald's for example. The company was formed during the first half of the twentieth century, at a time when scientific management dominated management thinking. Adopting the process that revolutionized the auto industry, McDonald's used an assembly line to prepare food and improve the *efficiency* of the restaurant. They called it the Speedee System. One of the founders regarded consistency and maintaining control of his restaurants as the key to business success. As the number of restaurants grew, he needed a way to instil his motto of 'quality, service, cleanliness and value' into the franchisees who would be running them. In 1961 he established 'Hamburger University' to help determine scientifically the best ways to make burgers and train staff. Today's McDonald's restaurants still incorporate classic production line procedures in the kitchen. Each employee is typically in charge of a certain task so that orders are filled quickly. The success of the company and its management approach may be reflected in the fact that McDonald's is the world's largest restaurant chain with more than 34 000 restaurants worldwide and employing 1.8 million people (one in every eight American workers has been employed by McDonald's) to serve more than 68 million people per day, (about 1 per cent of the world's population) 75 burgers every second.

8. The following paragraphs summarize the key ideas of the pioneers of 'scientific management' – Taylor, Gilbreth and Gantt – and comment on the main consequences of their work.

9. Frederick Winslow Taylor (1856–1915), like Fayol, was one of the early practical manager-theorists. Born in Boston, Massachusetts, in 1856, he spent the greater part of his life working on the problems of achieving greater efficiency on the shop floor (the concept of efficiency was also considered in Chapter 1). The solutions he proposed were based directly on his own experience at work, initially as a shop-floor worker himself and later as a manager. His career began as an apprentice in engineering. Having served his time he moved to the Midvale Steel Company, where, in the course of 11 years, he rose from labourer to shop superintendent. It was during this time that Taylor's ideas of 'scientific management' were born. In 1889 he left Midvale to work for the Bethlehem Steel Company, where he consolidated his ideas and conducted some of his most famous experiments in improving labour productivity. Taylor was keen to share his ideas with others, which he achieved through his writings, most notably 'The Principles of Scientific Management' published in 1911. After his death, his major works were combined and published as 'Scientific Management' in 1947. He did not meet Henri Fayol and it is possible that he did not know of Fayol's analysis of management.

2.5 THE SETTING FOR SCIENTIFIC MANAGEMENT

10. The last 20 years of the nineteenth century were a time for facing up to the often ugly realities of factory life. From the employers' point of view, efficiency of working methods was the dominant issue. The gathering pace of the industrial revolution in the Western world had given rise to new factories, new plant and machinery; labour was plentiful. The problem was how to organize all these elements into efficient and profitable operations.

11. It was against this background that Taylor developed his ideas. He was passionately interested in the efficiency of working methods. At an early stage he realized that the key to such problems lay in the systematic analysis of work. Experience, both as a worker and as a manager, had convinced him that few, if any, workers place more than the minimal effort into their daily work. He described this tendency as 'soldiering', which he subdivided into 'natural' soldiering, i.e. humans' natural tendency to take things easy,

and 'systematic' soldiering, i.e. the deliberate and organized restriction of the work rate by employees (the calculated efforts by workers to produce far less than they are capable of). According to Taylor, reasons for soldiering appeared to arise from three issues:

- fear of unemployment

- fluctuations in earnings from piece-rate systems

- rule-of-thumb[1] methods permitted by management.

Taylor's answer to these issues was to practise 'scientific management'.

2.6 THE PRINCIPLES OF SCIENTIFIC MANAGEMENT

12. Taylor recognized the measures he proposed would appear as more than just a new method – they would be revolutionary! He stated at the outset that 'scientific management' would require a complete mental revolution on the part of both management and workers.
13. In its application to management, the scientific approach required the following steps:

- develop a science for each operation to replace opinion and rule-of-thumb

- determine accurately from the science the correct time and method for each job

- set up a suitable organization to take all **responsibility** from the workers except that of actual job performance

- select and train the workers

- accept that management itself be governed by the science developed for each operation and surrender arbitrary power over workers, i.e. cooperate with them.

14. Taylor saw that if changes were to take place at the shop-floor level, then facts would have to be substituted for opinion and guesswork. This would be done by studying the jobs of a sample of especially skilled workers, noting each operation and timing it with a stopwatch. All unnecessary movements could then be eliminated in order to produce the best method of doing a job. This best method would become the standard to be used for all like jobs. This analytical approach has come to be known as Work Study, the series of techniques now utilized all over the world (see Chapter 39).
15. In Taylor's time the usual practice at the work organization level was for the management to leave working methods to the initiative of the workers – what Taylor called rule-of-thumb. His suggestion that managers should take over that role was certainly new. Not only that, it was controversial, for he was deliberately reducing the scope of an individual's job. Contemporaries said it turned people into automatons. Taylor argued that the average worker preferred to be given a definite task with clear-cut standards. The outcome for future generations was the separation of planning and controlling from the doing, or the fragmentation of work. **McGregor's Theory X** assumptions about people (see Chapter 4) are essentially a description of the managerial style produced by Taylor's ideas. In the 1990s, ideas such as job enrichment and work design have been translated into practice precisely to combat the fragmentation effects of years of **Taylorism**. Another comment of Taylorism is that the gradual deskilling of work has been accompanied by a rise in educational standards, thus tending to further increase worker-frustration.
16. Taylor felt that everyone should benefit from scientific management – workers as well as managers. He disagreed with the way most piece-rate systems were operated in his day, as the practice was for management to reduce the rates if workers' earnings went up beyond an acceptable level. Taylor's view was that, having measured scientifically the workers' jobs and set rates accordingly, then efficient workers should

---

[1] A general guideline, rather than a strict rule; an approximate measure or means of reckoning based on experience or common knowledge.

be rewarded for their productivity, without limit. The difficulty for most managers was that they lacked Taylor's expertise in measuring times and had to resort to arbitrary reduction in rates where measurements had been loose.

17. So far as the workers were concerned, scientific management required them to:

- stop worrying about the division of the fruits of production between wages and profits

- share in the prosperity of the firm by working in the correct way and receiving wage increases of between 30 per cent and 100 per cent according to the nature of the work

- give up their ideas of soldiering and cooperate with management in developing the science

- accept that management would be responsible, in accordance with the scientific approach, for determining what was to be done and how

- agree to be trained in new methods, where applicable.

18. One of Taylor's basic theses was that adoption of the scientific approach would lead to increased prosperity for all. It was, therefore, much more important to contribute to a bigger cake than to argue about the division of the existing cake. Needless to say this kind of approach did not receive much favour with the trade unions at the time. Taylor saw them as a decidedly restrictive influence on issues such as productivity. In his view, wages could now be scientifically determined, and should not be affected by arbitrary factors such as union power or management whim. His own experience had shown the considerable increase in earnings achieved by workers adopting their part of the scientific approach.

19. In terms of work-organization, the workers were very much under the control of their management in Taylor's system. Taylor felt that this would be acceptable to them because management's actions would be based on the scientific study of the work and not on any arbitrary basis. It would also be acceptable, argued Taylor, because of the increased earnings available under the new system. He claimed that there were rarely any arguments arising between management and workers due to introduction of the scientific approach. Modern experience has unfortunately shown Taylor's view to be considerably over-optimistic in this respect. The degree of trust and mutual cooperation, which Taylor felt to be such an important factor in the success of scientific management, has never been there when it mattered. As a result, although workers' attitudes towards Work Study have often been favourable, the ultimate success of work-studied incentive schemes has always been rather limited owing to workers' feelings that the management was attempting to 'pin them down', and to management's feelings that the workers had succeeded in 'pulling the wool over their eyes' concerning the timing of key jobs.

20. In support of his Principles, Taylor demonstrated the benefits of increased productivity and earnings which he had achieved at the Bethlehem Steel Works. He described to his critics an experiment with two shovellers – 'first-class shovellers', in his words – whose efforts were timed and studied. Each man had his own personal shovel, which he used regardless of the type of ore or coal being shifted. At first the average shovel load was about 38 pounds and with this load each man handled about 25 tons of material a day.

21. The shovel was then made smaller for each man, and the daily tonnage went up to 30. Eventually it was found that with smaller shovels, averaging about 21 pounds per load, the daily output rose even higher. As a result of this experiment, several different sizes of shovel were supplied to the workforce to enable each man to lift 21 pounds per load whether he was working with heavy ores or light coals. Labourers who showed themselves capable of achieving the standards set by the two 'first-class' shovellers were able to increase their wages by 60 per cent. Those who were not able to reach the standard were given special training in the 'science of shovelling'. After a 3-year period, Taylor and his colleagues reviewed the extent of their success at the Bethlehem Works. The results were impressive: the work of 400–600 men was being done by 140; handling costs per ton had been reduced by half, and as Taylor was quick to point out, that included the costs of the extra clerical work involved in studying jobs; and the labourer received an average of 60 per cent more than colleagues in neighbouring firms.

2.7 SCIENTIFIC MANAGEMENT AFTER TAYLOR

22. Three important followers of scientific management were Frank and Lilian Gilbreth and Henry Gantt. All made significant contributions to the study of work.

23. The husband-and-wife team of Frank and Lilian Gilbreth, who were somewhat younger than the pioneering Taylor, were keenly interested in the idea of scientific management. In his now famous Testimony to the House of Representatives Committee in 1912, Taylor describes how he was first approached by Frank Gilbreth who asked if the principles of scientific management could be applied to bricklaying. Some 3 years later Gilbreth was able to inform Taylor that as a direct result of analyzing, and subsequently redesigning the working methods of typical bricklayers, he was able to reduce the number of movements in laying bricks from 18 per brick to five per brick. The study of task movements, or '**motion study**' as it was known, was a development of Taylor's ideas and represented the Gilbreths' major contribution to basic management techniques.

24. A particular feature of the Gilbreths' work was its detailed content. 'Measurement' was their byword, and the Science of Management, as they termed it, consisted of applying measurement to management, and of abiding by the results. They were convinced it was possible to find the 'one best way' of operating and undoubtedly they went a long way towards the ideal. As employers, the Gilbreths practised what they preached. They laid down systematic rules and procedures for the efficient operation of work and insisted upon adherence to these rules and procedures. In return, their employees were paid well above competitors' rates, and, into the bargain were freed from unnecessary effort and fatigue. With this approach, the separation of the planning from the doing was complete. Employees had no discretion whatsoever once the scientific process had determined how the job should be done. Although these ideas were challenged at the time, they could not be ignored by the new industrial age and its obsession with ideas of efficiency. Whilst few people were prepared to follow the Gilbreths' methods closely, the basic techniques were implemented and today (as Method Study) they represent one of the key measures used by management to organize and control working methods in a wide range of industries. The Gilbreths also left a legacy in the form of symbols to map business activities. **Flow chart** symbols were introduced by them to represent work steps pictorially, thus aiding analysis and communication.

2.8 HENRY GANTT

25. Gantt was Taylor's contemporary colleague at the Bethlehem Steel Company. Whilst accepting many of Taylor's ideas on scientific management, Gantt felt Taylor's ideas did not afford the individual worker enough consideration. Although Taylor himself could not have been accused of making employees work unduly hard, in any way, his methods were used by less conscientious employers to squeeze as much production as possible out of their workforce. This was particularly true in respect of piece-rate systems. Gantt introduced a payment system whereby performance below what was called for on the individual's instruction card still qualified the person for the day-rate, but performance of all the work allocated on the card qualified the individual for a bonus. Gantt discovered that as soon as any one worker found that he could achieve the task, the rest quickly followed. Better use was made of the foremen, because they were sought after by individuals who needed further instruction or help with faulty machines. As a result, supervision improved, breakdowns were minimized and delays avoided by all concerned. Eventually individual workers learned to cope with routine problems on their own. Gantt's bonus system also allowed workers to challenge the time allocated for a particular task. This was permitted because Gantt, unlike the Gilbreths, did not believe there was a 'one best way', but only a way 'which seems to be best at the moment'. Gantt's approach to scientific management left some discretion and initiative to workers, unlike those of his colleague, Taylor, and of his fellow theorists, the Gilbreths.

26. Although it was his ideas on the rewards for labour that made Gantt a notable figure in his day, he is best remembered nowadays for his charts. The **Gantt chart** was originally set up to indicate graphically the extent to which tasks had been achieved. It was divided horizontally into hours, days or weeks with the task marked out in a straight line across the appropriate numbers of hours or days, etc. The amount of the task achieved was shown by another straight line parallel to the original. It was easy from such a chart to assess actual from planned performance. There are many variations of the Gantt chart in use by project managers today, and a simple example is given below in Figure 2.2.

FIGURE 2.2 Gantt chart

Period	Week 1	Week 2	Week 3	Week 4
Planned Output	1000 units	1000 units	1000 units	1000 units
Actual Output	**850 units**	**900 units**	**1000 units**	**1100 units**
Weekly Actual	▬▬▬		▬▬▬	▬
Cumulative	▬▬▬▬▬▬▬▬▬▬▬▬▬▬▬▬▬▬			

2.9 COMMENTS ON THE SCIENTIFIC MANAGEMENT SCHOOL

27. Scientific management is evaluated in the table that follows:

BENEFITS	DRAWBACKS
• its rational approach to the organization of work enabled tasks and processes to be measured with a considerable degree of accuracy	• it reduced the worker's role to that of rigid adherence to methods and procedures over which he had no discretion
• measurement of tasks and processes provided useful information on which to base improvements in working methods, plant design, etc.	• it led to fragmentation of work due to emphasis on the analysis and organization of individual tasks or operations
• by improving working methods it brought enormous increases in productivity	• it generated a 'carrot-and-stick' approach to the motivation of employees by enabling pay to be geared tightly to output
• it enabled employees to be paid by results and take advantage of incentive payments	
• it stimulated management into adopting a more positive role in leadership at the shop-floor level	• it placed the planning and control of workplace activities exclusively in the hands of the management
• it contributed to major improvements in physical working conditions for employees	• it ruled out any realistic bargaining about wage rates since every job was measured, timed and rated 'scientifically'.
• it provided the foundations on which modern work study and other quantitative techniques could be soundly based.	

Whilst it is true that business and public organizations worldwide have benefited from, and are continuing to utilize, techniques which have their origins in the Scientific Management movement, it is also a fact there has also been a reaction against the basic philosophy of the creed. Tasks and processes are re-integrated, individuals demand participation in the key decision-making processes, and management prerogatives are under challenge everywhere by individuals and organized groups alike. On balance, the most important outcome of scientific management was that it stimulated ideas and techniques for improving the systematic analysis of tasks at the workplace. It also undoubtedly provided a firm launch pad for a wide variety of productivity improvements in a great range of industries and public services.

28. The major disadvantage of scientific management was that it subordinated the employee to the work system, and so divorced the 'doing' aspects of work from the planning and controlling aspects. This led to:

- the creation of boring, repetitive jobs

- the introduction of systems for tight control over work, and

- the alienation of shop-floor employees from their management.

2.10 URWICK

29. Lyndall Urwick was an enthusiastic and prolific writer on the subject of administration and management whose experience covered industry, the Armed Forces and Business Consultancy. He was strongly influenced by the ideas of Henri Fayol, in particular. Urwick was convinced the only way that modern man could control his social organizations was by applying principles, or universal rules, to them. In one of his best-known writings – 'The Elements of Administration' – published in 1947 he set out numerous principles which, in his view, could be applied to organizations to enable them to achieve their objectives effectively. Like other classical writers, Urwick developed his 'principles' on the basis of his own interpretation of the common elements and processes which he identified in the structure and operation of organizations. On this basis, the principles represented a 'code of good practice', which, if adhered to, should lead to success in administration, or management as we would call it today.

30. In 1952, Urwick produced a consolidated list of ten principles, as follows:

The Principle of

OBJECTIVE – the overall purpose or objective is the raison d'être of every organization.

SPECIALIZATION – one group, one function!

COORDINATION – the process of organizing is primarily to ensure coordination.

AUTHORITY – every group should have a supreme authority with a clear line of authority to other members of the group.

RESPONSIBILITY – the superior is absolutely responsible for the acts of his subordinates.

DEFINITION – jobs, with their duties and relationships, should be clearly defined.

CORRESPONDENCE – authority should be commensurate with responsibility.

SPAN OF CONTROL – no one should be responsible for more than five or six direct subordinates whose work is interlocked.

BALANCE – the various units of the organization should be kept in balance.

CONTINUITY – the structure should provide for the continuation of activities.

31. As a statement of classical organization theory, Urwick's list would be difficult to better, concentrating, as it does, mainly on structural issues. Compared with Fayol's Principles of Management, Urwick's list is less concerned with issues such as pay and morale, for example. Its emphasis is very much upon ensuring the organizational mechanisms are right.

32. There is no doubting the rational appeal of Urwick's 'principles', especially in relation to the internal environment of the organization. Organizations, however, do not operate in a vacuum. They must interact with their external environment as discussed in the previous chapter (they are open systems). Where modern studies have found weaknesses in Urwick's 'principles' is precisely on this point. The 'principles' tend to assume that it is possible to exert control over the issues mentioned, but many current trends, particularly in Western society run counter to several of the 'principles'. For example, attitudes towards greater sharing of authority at work are likely to clash with the Principle of Authority and the Principle of Correspondence. Similarly, attitudes towards the reintegration or enrichment of jobs will conflict with the Principle of Specialization, the Principle of Definition and the Span of Control.

33. Organizations are not self-contained. They must respond to the pressures of an external environment – social, technological, political, legal and economic. Urwick's 'principles', therefore, are not easily introduced into modern organizations. They can and are adopted with modification in several cases, but will always be suspect because they fall into the category of 'what ought to be' rather than 'what actually is' in terms of the realities of organizations today.

34. Urwick's ideas in general achieved considerable popularity with business organizations on both sides of the Atlantic because of their common sense appeal to managers. In more recent times, however, Urwick's emphasis on purpose and structure has not been able to provide answers to problems arising from social attitudes, external market pressures and rapidly changing technology. His ideas are now a little archaic. They prescribe only a part of what is needed for organizational health today.

2.11 BRECH

35. Brech wrote widely on management and organizational issues. Whilst sharing Urwick's concern with the development of principles or general laws of management, Brech was also concerned with the development of people within the organization. His approach was basically a classical one, but tempered to some extent by the prevailing human relations theories of the 1950s and 1960s. He saw management as a process, a social process, for planning and regulating the operations of the enterprise towards some agreed objective, and carried out within the framework of an organizational structure. Key issues for Brech in the formation of the structure were:

- defining the responsibilities of the management, supervisory and specialist staff
- determining how these responsibilities were to be delegated
- coordinating execution of responsibilities
- maintaining high morale.

36. Brech's own list of the principles of organization overlapped considerably with those of Fayol and Urwick. It was less dogmatic in approach than the others, but was nevertheless concerned with the division of responsibilities, lines of communication, unity of command and the allocation of authority, to give just a few examples. Fundamentally, in his view, the principles existed to maintain a balance between the delegation of managerial responsibility throughout the organization and the need to ensure unity of action as well.

37. Writing in the 1970s, Brech regretted there was still no general agreement about a fundamental body of principles of management. Until such principles are developed, he argued, it will be impossible for management to gain recognition as a science, or indeed as a profession. He believed that such principles, or basic laws of management, could be deduced from an analysis of the nature of the management process and this is what he himself attempted in the footsteps of Fayol, Urwick and others. However, he conceded that the development of principles would probably be acceptable only on the basis of first-hand research into management practices – a view which would undoubtedly have pleased researchers such as Henry Mintzberg (1973), Rosemary Stewart (1994) and others who believe that it is primarily through research into managerial behaviour that a body of relevant knowledge or fundamental truths may emerge.

2.12 SCIENTIFIC MANAGEMENT TODAY

38. A century has now passed since Taylor's (1911) 'The Principles of Scientific Management'. Taylor presented a systematic, 'one-best way' approach to management organized around scientific principles: developing a science of work; the separation of conception from execution; the scientific selection, training and development of workers; and the provision of incentives to develop cooperation with workers. Evans and Holmes (2013) in their recent book, 'Re-Tayloring Management', set out to assess the extent to which these principles are evident in today's organizations (Bridgman and Cummings 2014). They ask if management is still driven by Taylor's obsession for efficiency and control. Evans and Holmes argue contemporary workers are just as constrained by Taylor's principles of scientific management as the industrial workers that Taylor studied in the early twentieth century (2013:1). On the question of Taylor's continued influence, the authors conclude that ideas such as total quality management, business process re-engineering and lean

production (discussed later in this book) are descendants of Taylorism. The obsession with control through monitoring and performance measurement remains.

CONCLUSION

39. Many scholars consider scientific management as the origin of 'management'. This chapter considered early thoughts and important ideas on management – coordinated activities (forecasting, planning, deciding, organizing, commanding) to direct and control an organization – and the search for universally applicable principles of management; 14 elements of what was involved in a managerial role, as developed by Fayol. Several of these principles are considered later in the book. For example, authority is considered in Chapter 3. Next, we considered Taylor's ideas concerning 'scientific management', considered later in Chapter 22. This is a school of classical management theory, dating from the early twentieth century. It is based on the application of work study techniques to the design and organization of work in order to maximize output – increase productivity (to find the 'one best way' of performing each task); it is a form of job design theory and practice which stresses separation of task conception from task execution and motivation based on economic rewards (see also Taylorism). We introduced McGregor's Theory X, and Theory Y is considered later in Chapter 4. We also introduced the terms mechanistic system and specialization, considered later in Chapter 9. Finally, the chapter closed summarizing ideas of two latter-day scientific managers, Urwick and Brech, who developed many of the concepts of Fayol and Taylor in the period following the Second World War. Like others of his time, Taylor clearly believed in the universalist one best way of managing. It is no surprise to find that many see Taylor as the 'founding father' of management.

QUESTIONS

1 Identify the general principles of management defined by classical theorists.

2 Develop your own principles or general laws of management and explain why they could be universally applicable.

3 Critically compare and contrast your principles with those proposed by others, particularly with management scholars who are regarded as classical writers.

4 Investigate McDonald's further and discuss how scientific management has influenced the organization. Evaluate how scientific management is used, commenting on benefits and drawbacks. List five other organizations which could be used to demonstrate ideas from scientific management and briefly explain why they are good examples.

USEFUL WEBSITES

Accel-Team: **www.accel-team.com/scientific/scientific_02. html**

Reviews scientific management.

REFERENCES

Bridgman, T. and Cummings, S. (2014) Book review: 'Re-tayloring management: Scientific management a century on', *Management Learning*, 45(2): 242–245.

Evans, C. and Holmes, L. (2013) *Re-Tayloring Management – Scientific Management a Century On*, Gower.

Mintzberg, H. (1973) *The Nature of Managerial Work*, Harper & Row.

Stewart, R. (1994) *Managing Today and Tomorrow*, Macmillan.

Taylor, F. (1911) *The Principles of Scientific Management*, Harper & Brothers.

CHAPTER 3
BUREAUCRACY

Key Concepts

- Authority
- Bureaucracy
- Power

Learning Outcomes   Having read this chapter, you should be able to:

- list the main features of bureaucracy
- describe and discuss the bureaucratic form of organization
- list and describe three types of legitimate authority
- distinguish power from the concept of authority
- evaluate bureaucracy, commenting on side-effects and dysfunctions.

1.   In Chapter 1 we made reference to **bureaucracy**. Bureaucracy is a term with several meanings and this has led to genuine misconceptions about what it truly means. The most common meanings are as follows:

- Bureaucracy is an organizational form with certain dominant characteristics, such as a hierarchy of authority and a system of rules.

- Bureaucracy is 'red tape', i.e. an excess of paperwork and rules leading to gross inefficiency. This is the negative sense of the word.

- Bureaucracy is 'officialdom', i.e. all the apparatus of central and local government. This is a similar meaning to red tape.

2.   In this chapter the term 'bureaucracy' is interpreted as an organizational form. The object of the chapter is to describe and discuss this important and all-pervading form of organization, with particular reference to the fundamental work of Max Weber.

3.1 MAX WEBER

3.   Max Weber (1864–1920) spanned the same period of history as those early pioneers of management thought, Fayol and Taylor, to whom we have already referred. Unlike them, however, Weber was an academic – a sociologist – and not a practising manager. His interest in organizations was from the point of view of their authority structures. Weber wanted to find out why people in organizations obeyed those in

authority over them. It was in his publications that the term 'bureaucracy' was used to describe a rational form of organization which today exists to a greater or lesser extent in practically every business and public enterprise.

4.   In his analysis of organizations, Weber identified three basic types of legitimate authority: traditional, charismatic and **rational-legal authority**. Before describing these, it will be helpful to understand what he meant by the expression 'legitimate authority'. First, the concept of authority has to be distinguished from that of power. **Power** is the means by which one person may influence another to behave in a certain way. Authority, on the other hand, implies acceptance of rule by those over whom it is to be exercised. It implies that power may only be exercised within limits agreeable to subordinates. It is this latter situation to which Weber refers when he talks about legitimate authority.

5.   The three types of legitimate authority described by him can be summarized as follows:

- **traditional authority** – where acceptance of those in authority arises from tradition and custom (e.g. as in monarchies, tribal hierarchies, etc.)

- charismatic authority – where acceptance arises from loyalty to, and confidence in, the personal qualities of the ruler

- rational-legal authority – where acceptance arises out of the office or position of the person in authority, as bounded by the rules and procedures of the organization.

It is this latter-mentioned form of authority which exists in most organizations today and this is the form to which Weber ascribed the term 'bureaucracy'.

3.2 BUREAUCRACY

6.   The main features of a bureaucracy, according to Weber, are as follows:

- a continuous organization of functions bound by rules

- specified spheres of competence, i.e. the specialization of work, the degree of authority allocated and the rules governing the exercise of authority

- a hierarchical arrangement of offices (jobs), i.e. where one level of jobs is subject to control by the next higher level

- appointment to offices are made on grounds of technical competence

- the separation of officials from the ownership of the organization

- official positions exist in their own right, and job holders have no rights to a particular position

- rules, decisions and actions are formulated and recorded in writing.

7.   The above features of bureaucratic organization enable the authority of officials to be subject to published rules and practices. Thus authority is legitimate, not arbitrary. It is this point more than any other which caused Weber to comment that bureaucratic organization was capable of attaining the highest degree of efficiency and was, in that sense, the most rational known means of carrying out 'imperative control over human beings'.

8.   Weber felt that bureaucracy was indispensable for the needs of the large-scale organization, and there is no doubt that this form of organization has been adopted in one way or another by practically every worldwide enterprise of any size. The two most significant factors in the growth of bureaucratic forms of organization are undoubtedly size and complexity. Once an organization begins to grow, the amount of specialization increases, which usually leads to an increase in job levels. New jobs are created and old jobs redefined. Recruitment from outside becomes more important. Relationships, authority boundaries and discipline have to be regulated. Questions of control and coordination became all-important.

9.   Thus a small, relatively informal, family concern can suddenly grow into quite a different organization requiring new skills and new attitudes from its proprietors. Although size almost inevitably implies

complexity, there are also issues of complexity for smaller organizations. These can arise out of the require-ments of sophisticated modern technology, for example. In such an environment, specialized and up-to-date skills are required, the span of control has to be small, questions of quality control are vital and lastly, but by no means unimportantly, a keen eye must be kept on the competition. Add to all these points the rules and regulations of governments and supranational bodies, such as the European Union (EU) and the World Trade Organization (WTO), and the result is a highly complex environment, which can only be controlled in a systematic form of organization. Indeed, one of the challenges to modern management is to maintain a 'lean' organization in such circumstances.

3.3 BUREAUCRACY AFTER WEBER

10. Weber's contribution to our understanding of formal organization structures has been a major one. No subsequent discussion or debate on this topic has been possible without reference to his basic analysis of bureaucratic organization. Nevertheless, without disputing the basic proposition that bureaucracy is the most efficient means of organizing for the achievement of formal goals, several researchers since Weber have established important weaknesses in the bureaucratic model.

11. These researchers have identified a number of awkward side-effects or 'dysfunctions' of bureaucracy. These can be summarized as follows: Rules originally designed to serve organizational efficiency have a tendency to become all-important in their own right. Relationships between office holders or roles are based on the rights and duties of each role, i.e. they are depersonalized, and this leads to rigid behaviour (predictability). Decision-making tends to be categorized, i.e. choices are previously programmed and this discourages the search for further alternatives, another form of rigidity. The effects of rigid behaviour are often very damaging for client or customer relations and also for management–worker relationships; customers are unable to obtain tailor-made services, but have to accept standardization; employees must work within a framework of rules and controls which has largely been imposed upon them. Standardiza-tion and routine procedures make change and adaptation difficult when circumstances change. The exercise of 'control based on knowledge', as advocated by Weber, has led to the growth of experts, whose opinions and attitudes may often clash with those of the generalist managers and supervisors.

12. One particularly well-known follow-up to Weber's theories was conducted by an American sociologist, Alvin Gouldner. He studied the effects of introducing a bureaucratic system into an organization which had been very informal and indulgent in its management style. The head office of a small gypsum (plaster of Paris) company had appointed a new manager to improve plant efficiency. His new approach led to replacement of informal methods of working by formalized procedures such as work study and production control. These changes were resented by the workforce and the eventual outcome was a reduction rather than an increase in the efficiency of operations. In studying this situation, Gouldner identified three differ-ent patterns of bureaucracy operating within the one organization. These were as follows:

MOCK BUREAUCRACY. This expression was applied by Gouldner to situations where the rules and procedures were imposed by an outside body (e.g. Head Office) and where they were either ignored, or were merely paid lip service by the employees concerned. In this situation a separate set of 'rules' (i.e. their own) was developed by these employees.

REPRESENTATIVE BUREAUCRACY. In this case the rules were followed in practice because both management and employees agreed on their value.

PUNISHMENT-CENTRED BUREAUCRACY. This description was applied to situations where either the manage-ment or the employees imposed their rules on the other. Disregard of the rules was seen as grounds for imposing sanctions. Each side considered its rules as legitimate, but there was no common position.

13. Weber's thinking on bureaucracy was dominated by his view of the rationality of the concept. Gouldner, by contrast, helped to indicate that opinions and feelings are also a key ingredient in the success of a bureaucratic form of organization. Whereas Weber emphasized the structural aspects of organization, Gouldner emphasized behaviour. He saw that rules not only generated anticipated

responses, e.g. obedient behaviour, but also unanticipated responses, e.g. minimum acceptable behaviour. Therefore, in any one organization, there will be a tendency to respond to the rules in any one of the three ways described above, the response being dependent upon how and why the rules were introduced.

14. Handy (1999) describes bureaucracies as 'role cultures' based on logic and rationality. In the role culture, power comes from position power, i.e. the authority of the office, as determined by rules and procedures. Such a culture offers security and predictability to its members, but can be frustrating for those who are ambitious and results-oriented. Handy sees bureaucracy as a Greek temple, based on the firm pillars of its speciality departments and ideally constructed for stability. Its very stability is a drawback in times of change. The Greek temple is not designed for adaptability.

15. However one chooses to describe a bureaucracy, there is little doubt that it is by far the most frequent form of organization in society. The question which needs to be asked is not so much 'is this organization a bureaucracy?' but rather, 'to what extent is this organization a bureaucracy?' The evidence seems to suggest that there is something of the Greek temple in every organization!

3.4 EFFICIENCY AND EFFECTIVENESS

16. Thus far, in this book, we have referred to two fundamental and generic objectives of organizations (and management) – first, to be effective (do the right thing) and second, to be efficient (do things right). In this chapter we have highlighted the crucial role of bureaucracy in organizational efficiency. When environments are relatively stable or placid, organizations need not concern themselves as much with their effectiveness (the right thing today will be the right thing in 5 or 10 years' time). Consequently, bureaucracy remained in favour throughout much of the twentieth century.

17. However, significant changes in business environments as a result of deregulation (increased competition), globalization and technological change (travel, Internet and mobile telecoms in particular), towards the end of the century, increased environmental turbulence, necessitating continuous change within organizations. This presents a more perpetual 'effectiveness' challenge – organizations must ask constantly whether they are doing the right thing. Such a challenge calls for creativity, risk taking, entrepreneurial activity and the management of uncertainty; it requires dynamic, flexible, learning and adaptable organizations.

18. Consequently, throughout the latter part of the twentieth century, many business scholars and practitioners argued that aspects of bureaucracy stifled the attitudes and behaviours required from employees. As a result, excessive formalization (red tape) was often removed, generalists were favoured over specialists and decision-making was decentralized to improve responsiveness in many, or at least in parts of organizations. Less work was standardized and controlled and a more results-oriented or self-regulatory control framework favoured. Hamel (2014) asks how we overcome formal hierarchy and how can individuals learn to lead without authority? According to Hamel, managing is largely about controlling and coordinating but today's challenges include finding ways to reduce 'top-heavy management structures' whilst maintaining efficiency. Focusing on coordination and control, Hamel believes that in most organizations managers hold everything together; they connect activities, teams, programmes and business units. For such organizations the assumption seems to be that coordination requires a hierarchy of coordinators. Hamel points out the problem that hierarchy adds costs and reduces responsiveness. He believes we need ways of integrating complex activities with little management overhead. On the subject of control he believes that managers are often the enforcers (refer back to Chapter 1) and that it is their job to ensure that procedures are followed, budgets are met and 'slackers are punished'. However, the supervisory infrastructure again is costly and disempowering. 'We need organizations where control comes less from rules and sanctions, and more from norms and peers. We need to radically reduce the management costs associated with both coordination and control'. Thus coordination and control (discussed in this chapter as key features of bureaucracy) are said to be critical to organizational health (Hamel, 2014). However, organizations must think carefully about how they accomplish them. Interestingly, Hamel discusses other factors such as motivation (to be discussed in the next chapter), noting the need to 'unleash' contribution.

CONCLUSION

19. It is important to recognize that organizations do not simply decide to be bureaucratic or not – all large organizations are bureaucratic to some degree. The question is – how much? Bureaucracy describes a form of business administration based on formal rational rules and procedures designed to govern work practices and organizational activities through a hierarchical system of authority (see discussions on standardization, centralization, formalization and specialization). Bureaucracy emphasizes efficiency. In the next chapter we will consider employee motivation (also a factor of productivity – efficiency – and effectiveness). In doing so, we will consider bureaucracy and its impact upon motivation. We will also revisit a number of related concepts such as power and authority (such concepts also feature in later chapters).

QUESTIONS

1   Compare and contrast Fayol's principles of management and Weber's description of bureaucracy.

2   Discuss the main advantages and disadvantages of the ideal type of bureaucracy, as described by Weber.

3   Critically evaluate the contribution of the classical/traditional school of management theorists to our understanding of organization.

4   List the main features of bureaucracy.

5   Evaluate bureaucracy, commenting on side-effects and dysfunctions.

REFERENCES

Hamel, G. (2014) 'Beyond Bureaucracy', *Leadership Excellence*, 31(1): 10–11.

Handy, C.B. (1999) *Understanding Organizations*, 4th edn, Penguin.

SKILL SHEET 1 **Efficiency and Bureaucracy**

This skills sheet consists of two parts: part 1 considers how to evaluate efficiency and part 2 how to measure bureaucracy. The sheet should be used in conjunction with Chapters 2 and 3 and case sheet 1.

Evaluating Efficiency in Organizations

Organizational efficiency is a vast subject both theoretically and practically. In this skills sheet we seek to outline and introduce the topic. **Efficiency** (performing work right) in general describes the extent to which time, effort or cost is well used for the intended task or purpose. Efficiency is measurable, quantitatively determined by the ratio of output to input. In business it is typically about the accomplishment of a job (work) with a minimum expenditure of time, effort and other transformational resources. Productive efficiency occurs when the company is utilizing all of its resources efficiently. **Productivity** is a related measure of output from a production process, per unit of input. For example, labour productivity is typically measured as a ratio of output per labour-hour – an input. Efficiency is frequently associated with cost and cost reduction. This is highly important since companies may compete on cost. Reduced costs can enable price reductions and increased margins (profit). Aside from financial performance, efficiency is also associated with waste and therefore sustainability and 'green' goals. Typically associated with efficiency is benchmarking and KPIs. **Benchmarking** is the process of measuring and comparing data with competitors and Best-in-Class (BIC) companies to identify opportunity for improvement and to achieve a higher level of performance. **Key Performance Indicators** (KPIs) describe parameters that are used to measure previously defined business goals and may reflect the **critical success factors** of the company, department, or project (see skills sheet 12). Efficiency measurements may be based upon time taken to perform certain tasks; frequency of tasks per hour or full-time equivalent[1] (FTE). Efficiency measures may also consider utilization of space or equipment etc. Productivity is simply a measure of the number of *work units* processed in a given amount of time, either by an employee or by department. Work units can be orders, calls, shipments, etc. as appropriate for each function or process activity. Examples are the number of orders per hour, calls per hour; the average sales in currency per FTE. The exact metric varies within companies and between functional areas, based upon what is deemed critical to the particular business and function. In summary there are many types of input and output to measure and these may be within processes, procedures, departments, systems, facilities, etc. Examples are presented next.

Efficiency within Business Process: Workflow and Procedures

FULFILMENT (Sales, Invoicing, Warehouse, Collections) **Sales**: evaluating the efficiency of the sales team: Orders (by Telephone, Mail) processed per hour/FTE and time taken to raise invoices.

Warehouse Performance: A key goal is to minimize the number of times a product is handled, and the number of steps (process and on-foot!) an employee has to take to move the product through the facility to be shipped. Flow charts (see skills sheet 5) may be used to help identify problems. They can be used to show the tasks (work steps) in sequence and the duration of each step. Analysis may suggest unnecessary steps, new methods or technological enablers. Some organizations measure the labour (FTE or hours) to perform necessary operations of receiving, moving, storing, retrieving, order picking and shipping. This may be determined by employee effort and/or distance/time travelled to bays in the warehouse. The next area to examine is the fulfilment facility itself, specifically, the layout and whether there is enough space and whether this space is being utilized efficiently and cost-effectively. Evaluate (1) the storage capacity of the facility. Is the whole 'cube'-square footage and height being used efficiently? Or is there something that can be done to optimize stacking height with racking or layout changes? (2) layout: work paths should be designed to minimize travel time and merchandise movement. Departments and teams should be situated logically in relation to one another to minimize travel between them.

[1] A unit that indicates the workload of an employed person. (An FTE of 1.0 means that the person is equivalent to a full-time worker.)

Inventory levels: One way for companies to be efficient and competitive is by keeping inventory levels down – not tying up too much money in stock (see sheet 11). Inventory turnover measures how quickly the company is moving merchandise through the warehouse to customers.

Inventory Days = 365 Days / (Average Cost of Goods Sold[2]/Average Inventory)

Around 40 inventory days (the number of days to cycle through the inventory – also known as the 'days-to-sell' figure) may suggest an efficient company. Broadly speaking, the smaller number of days, the more efficient a company – inventory is held for less time and less money is tied up in inventory. If the number of days is high, that could suggest that sales are poor and inventories are piling up in warehouses.

Cash Flow, Collections and Accounts Performance: A company that provides customer credit, or that allows payments over time, needs to manage collections. The accounts receivable cycle starts with a sale (credit sales) which in turn creates a receivable (monies due the company), and then, ultimately converts into cash. The length of time that it takes a company to complete this cycle, from sale to accounts receivable to cash, is the collection period. The shorter the collection period, the less time cash (capital) is tied up in the business process, and thus the better for a company's cash flow. A shorter collection period indicates an efficient company. Accounts receivable is the money that is currently owed to a company by its customers. Analyzing the speed at which a company collects what it is owed can be indicative of a company's financial efficiency. If a company's collection period is growing longer this may indicate inefficiency. Determine how many days, on average, the company takes to collect its accounts receivable:

Receivables Days = 365 Days / (Revenues/ Average Receivables)

Dividing revenue by average receivables gives a receivables turnover ratio. This shows how many times the company turned over its receivables in the annual period. Similarly, calculate the Days in Accounts Receivable (A/R) – (1) determine the number of days in a period (2) determine the average daily revenue, and then (3) divide that number into the accounts

[2] Cost of goods sold (COGS), or 'cost of sales' can be found in the company Consolidated Statements of Income or master budget data.

receivable. For example, consider a specific quarter (90 days) and determine the revenue over that period (e.g. €90 000) this represents average daily revenue of 1000 per day. Then determine the Accounts receivable on the books at the end of that period (e.g. €60 000). Divide the A/R (60 000) by the Avg. daily revenue (1000) = 60 days in accounts receivable. What this calculation indicates is that on average it will take 60 days to collect what it is owed. Companies also measure the cost to perform specific tasks (cost-per-transaction metric) such as creating an invoice or PO.

Cost-per-transaction = total costs (associated with a task – labour etc.) / number of transactions e.g. orders generated that year

Alternatively, the number of invoices or POs etc. processed per FTE may be analyzed.

PRODUCTION

Productivity can be measured in several ways: e.g. Output per worker or hour of labour; Output per hour/ day/week; Output per machine; and Unit costs (total costs divided by total output).

Efficiency within Systems

Does a system provide the functionality and flexibility needed? Does it support efforts to maximize space and labour efficiency? Does the system provide reports that are adequate to monitor performance? Is the system compatible with the use of bar codes or RFID technology? Any system should provide the necessary functional components to permit easy and accurate entry of orders; and easy and timely access to customer, order and inventory information.

WHAT NEXT: FROM MEASUREMENT TO ACTION… Once information has been gathered and analyzed it should reveal what the company does well and what needs to be improved (areas of inefficiency). This should then be translated into an action plan. Rarely will it be possible to change everything immediately; when prioritizing areas for action consider the Pareto's 80/20 Law. Where can the biggest improvements from the smallest number of changes be achieved? Think about the TQM philosophy of continual improvements over time (see Chapter 28).

Bureaucracy: Is this a bureaucratic company?

In Chapter 3, paragraph 7 we noted Weber commented that bureaucratic organization was capable of attaining the highest degree of efficiency. Scholars over time have attempted to measure the degree of bureaucracy within companies in order to determine the impact upon performance. They have also developed tools to help individuals appraise their preference to work in such organizations. This has been done in order to reduce employee stress and improve satisfaction by facilitating a better fit between employee and workplace. Example questions used to indicate and measure bureaucracy follow:

	Strongly Agree	Agree	Undecided	Disagree	Strongly Disagree
Samples of questions are provided as a framework to focus your analysis of organization and individual preference. Score each item (strongly agree = 5 through to strongly disagree = 1) – a higher score indicates a more bureaucratic company; maximum score = 35					
A superior should expect subordinates to carry out orders without question					
A person should not volunteer opinions to his superior outside of his own area of specialization					
Formality, based on rank or position, should be maintained by members of an organization					
People are better off when the organization provides a complete set of rules to be followed					
Length of service in an organization should be given almost as much recognition as level of performance					
Everything (rules, procedures, job descriptions, etc.) is written down					
Personnel are hired and promoted based on competence and experience					

It is important to remember that companies can be more or less bureaucratic in many different ways – some aspects of bureaucracy may be of benefit whilst others may be to the detriment of the company. In some cases the pursuit of efficiency may be to the detriment of effectiveness and vice versa; they may – to some extent – be mutually exclusive (this is about the pursuit of cost and differentiation advantages).

Am I suited to work in a bureaucratic company?

Bureaucratic orientation refers to the tendency of some employees to prefer authority and norms, strict adherence to procedures and rules, and impersonal and formal work relationships. Example questions used to indicate and measure a preference for bureaucracy follow.

I like a predictable organization				
Every employee should have a detailed job description/specification				
Work roles should be specialized				
Promotion should be based on demonstrated technical competence				
I like rules, policies and procedures – they provide necessary guidance				
Authority should be clearly related to position in each department				
Senior managers should set objectives and communicate them downwards				

A higher score indicates a preference for a more bureaucratic company.

Section Three
Human Relations and Social Psychological Theories

CHAPTER 4
MOTIVATION – 'WHAT' MOTIVATES PEOPLE

Key Concepts

- Content theories of motivation
- Hierarchy of needs
- Motivation

Learning Outcomes Having read this chapter, you should be able to:

- explain what is meant by the term motivation (in the workplace)
- compare the work of several prominent social scientists on motivation at work.

Vignette

MOTIVATION AT WORKPLACES

IT TAKES TWO TO TANGO

The *Daily Star*, of Bangladesh, recently reported on the challenge of motivation in the workplace. Accepting that 'getting people to give their best at work … is one of the most enduring and slippery challenges faced by managers', they recognize determining what motivates human beings is 'a centuries-old puzzle'. Influential thinkers about human behaviour – like Aristotle, Adam Smith, Sigmund Freud and Abraham Maslow – have tried to understand its nuances and create theories about why people act in particular ways. According to the *Daily Star*, a McKinsey survey has shown that employee motivation has slumped throughout the world, with morale lower in almost half of all companies. The *Star* concludes that it is more important than ever for managers to find ways to retain and motivate high performing employees. However, as the article title, 'It Takes Two To Tango' suggests, there is also an onus on employees to think about ways 'to keep themselves motivated and improve their morale'. Motivation is an important issue for all organizations around the world, yet the theories on which motivational practices are designed are Western – 'American to be more precise'. Consequently the *Star* argues for local – home-grown – models to be developed which take into consideration the local cultural context and customs and tradition of the people.

1.   This is the first chapter devoted to Human Relations and Social Psychological Theories. Whereas the exponents of classical theory were principally concerned with the structure and mechanics of organizations, the human relations and social psychological theorists focused on the human factor at work – the behaviour of people in the workplace. They were particularly interested in human motivation, group relationships and leadership. Managers can make use of a number of motivational theories to help encourage employees to work harder. Chapter 4 introduces the concept of 'motivation', and motivational theory. The chapter opens with an explanation of the basic concept of motivation, and follows this with a summary of different models of motivation proposed by Schein (1988). Next we provide an account of the celebrated **Hawthorne studies**, conducted in the USA some 70 years ago. The chapter continues with an outline of the work of a number of American social scientists, namely Follett, Maslow, McGregor, Herzberg, Likert, Argyris and McClelland.

4.1 THE CONCEPT OF MOTIVATION

2.   Human motivation studies aim, in essence, to discover what it is that triggers and sustains human behaviour (in the workplace). **Motivation** is a driving force that encourages individuals to behave in particular ways as they seek to achieve a goal. Not all theorists focus on the **process theories of motivation**. In fact, most of the early theorists were interested in the drives and/or needs of people at work, i.e. the **content aspects theories of motivation**.

3.   A very basic and simplified model of motivation is shown in Figure 4.1. This suggests that a stimulus, such as hunger (physical) or the desire for company (social) gives rise to a response. This response takes the form of some kind of behaviour, which leads to an outcome which is either satisfactory or unsatisfactory. Where the behaviour is appropriate, satisfaction is achieved. Where it is not, the stimulus remains in the form of frustration, and the process begins again.

4.   Understanding human motivation is a complex matter. Sometimes a person's motives may be clear to themselves, but quite puzzling to others. In other situations both the individual and those affected by their behaviour understand what is driving them. In some situations, especially where stress is involved, the individual concerned may be totally unaware of their motives, whereas others may see them quite clearly. It is important for those in managerial and supervisory positions to be aware of these issues, and to take account of their own prejudices in this area of their work. This is because our efforts to understand others are coloured by our attitudes towards them and the assumptions we make about their behaviour. If we assume that a particular group of workers is hardworking and reliable, we tend to treat them with respect and trust; if, however, we see them as lazy and unreliable, we are likely to treat them as requiring close control and supervision.

5.   Schein, a professor at the MIT Sloan School of Management, has made a noteworthy mark on the field of organizational development and social psychology. He propounded a classification of managers'

FIGURE 4.1 **A basic model of motivation**

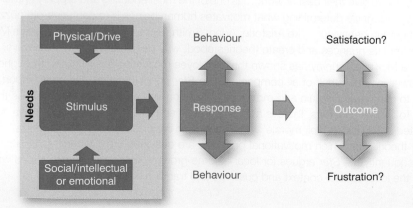

assumptions about people based on a review of earlier approaches to motivation. His classification follows a broadly chronological pattern as follows:

- **Rational-economic** model. This view of human motivation has its roots in the economic theories of Adam Smith in the 1770s. It suggests that the pursuit of self-interest and the maximization of gain are the prime motivators. According to Schein, this view places human beings into two main categories: (1) the untrustworthy, money motivated, calculative masses, and (2) the trustworthy, more broadly motivated moral elite whose task it is to organize and control the masses. Such an approach is evident in the work of Taylor and the Gilbreths (see Chapter 2), and the entrepreneurs of mass production techniques.

- Social model. In the 'social model', Schein drew heavily on the conclusions of the Hawthorne researchers. This view sees people as predominantly motivated by social needs – the need for personal relationships. The implication for managers is that emphasis on attending to people's needs over the needs of the task leads to greater productivity as well as higher morale. Such a view, according to Schein, needs to be treated with some reservations.

- Self-actualizing model. This concept is based on Maslow's theory of human needs (see below), which, whilst allowing for the influence of other needs, stresses as the prime motivator individual need for self-fulfilment. The implication for managers is that people need challenge, responsibility and autonomy in their work if they are to work effectively. There is some research evidence to support such a view, especially amongst professional and highly skilled employees.

- Complex model. Schein proposes this model of motivation as more comprehensive than the earlier models. It presupposes that understanding people's motivation is a complex business in which several interrelated factors are at work. Managers in this situation need to be sensitive to a range of possible responses to employee motivation dependent upon the differing work and team environments. Schein himself prefers to see motivation as a form of 'psychological contract' between the organization and its employees, based on their respective expectations of each other's contribution. Ultimately, the relationship between an individual and his or her organization is both interactive and interdependent.

6.   Schein's classification helps us to relate the major approaches to management theory with the concept of motivation, the basis of which is that human motives are directed towards desired ends, and that behaviour is selected consciously or sometimes instinctively, towards the achievement of those ends. Differing opinions have emerged as to what constitutes these ends and how they are best met in the work situation. Several of the most well-known theories are outlined in the following paragraphs, commencing with the findings arising from the research carried out by Mayo, Roethlisberger and Dickson in the Hawthorne Studies.

4.2 THE HAWTHORNE STUDIES

7.   Professor Elton Mayo is associated with the social research carried out at the Hawthorne plant of the Western Electric Company in Chicago, USA, between 1927 and 1932, and named the Hawthorne Studies. In these studies, the emphasis was on the worker rather than on work. Unlike Taylor and the scientific managers, the researchers at Hawthorne were primarily concerned with studying people, especially in terms of their social relationships at work. Their conclusions were that people are social animals – at work as well as outside it – and that membership of a group is important to individuals. Group membership leads to establishment of informal groups within the official, formal groupings as laid down in the organizational structure.

8.   These conclusions gave rise to the idea of social man (now the social model) and to the importance of human relations. Elton Mayo has been described as the founder of the human relations movement, whose advocates stressed the need for managerial strategies to ensure that concern for people at work was given highest priority. This movement, if it can be described as such, spanned the period from the mid-1920s to the mid-1950s, after which there was a gradual trend away from the social model, and its close relation – the self-actualizing model, towards the complex model, where people operate in highly variable organizational environments.

4.3 ELTON MAYO

9.   Elton Mayo (1880–1949) was an Australian by birth, a psychologist by training, and, according to some, a natural PR man by inclination! At the time of the Hawthorne studies he was Professor of industrial research at the Harvard Graduate School of Business Administration. He was already involved in a study of issues related to fatigue, accidents and labour turnover at work when he was approached for advice by executives of the Western Electric Company. The company, which prided itself on its welfare facilities, had begun a number of studies into the effects of lighting on production and morale. It had discovered, to its surprise, that the groups of workers who were the subject of study improved their productivity whether their lighting was improved or not. Clearly some factor other than the impact of physical improvements was at work. The company management decided to seek external assistance.

10. Their decision was to bring considerable fame to Mayo, in particular. His popularization of the results of the Hawthorne Studies made an enormous impact at the time. The social model was seen as a rebuttal of the ideas of scientific management, with its emphasis on the task and the control of work. Subsequent decades have also been greatly influenced by the findings at Hawthorne, with Mayo gaining most of the credit.

11. The studies were carried out over several years in a number of different stages, as follows: Stage one (1924–1927). This was conducted by the company's own staff under the direction of Messrs Pennock and Dickson. As mentioned above, this stage was concerned with the effects of lighting on output. Eventually two groups of comparable performance were isolated from the rest and located in separate parts of the plant. One group, the control group, had a consistent level of lighting; the other group, the experimental group, had its lighting varied. To the surprise of the researchers, the output of both groups increased. Even when the lighting for the experimental group was reduced to a very low level, they still produced more! At this point Pennock sought the help of Mayo and his Harvard colleagues.

12. Stage two (1927–1929). This stage became known as the Relay Assembly Test Room. The objective was to make a closer and more detailed study of the effects of differing physical conditions on productivity. At this stage, it is important to note, there was no deliberate intention to analyze social relationships or employee attitudes. Six women workers in the relay assembly section were segregated from the rest and placed in a room of their own. Over the course of the experiments the effects of numerous changes in working conditions were observed. Rest pauses were introduced and varied; lunch times were varied in timing and in length. Most of the changes were discussed with the women before being implemented. Productivity increased whether the conditions were made better or worse. Later studies included altering the working week. Once again output increased regardless of the changes. By the end of stage two the researchers realized they had not just been studying the relationship between physical working conditions, fatigue, monotony and output, but had been entering into a study of employee attitudes and values. The women's reaction to the changes – increased output regardless of whether conditions improved or worsened – has come to be known as 'the Hawthorne Effect'. That is to say, the women were responding not so much to the changes as to the fact that they were the centre of attention – a special group.

13. Stage three (1928–1930). Before the relay assembly test had come to an end, the company had decided to implement an interview programme designed to ascertain employee attitudes towards working conditions, their supervision and their jobs. The interviews were conducted by selected supervisors, initially on a half-hour, structured basis. Eventually the interview pattern became relatively unstructured and lasted for 90 minutes. Despite this, the numbers interviewed reached over 20 000 before the programme was suspended. The wealth of material gained was used to improve several aspects of working conditions and supervision. It also became clear from the responses that relationships with people were an important factor in the attitudes of employees.

14. Stage four (1932). This was known as the bank wiring observation room. In this study 14 men on bank wiring were removed to a separate observation room, where, apart from a few differences, their principal working conditions were the same as those in the main wiring area. The aim was to observe a group working under more or less normal conditions over a period of 6 months or so. The group soon developed its own rules and behaviour – it restricted production in accordance with its own norms; it short-circuited the company wage incentive scheme and protected its own sectional interests against those of the company.

The supervisors concerned were powerless to prevent this situation. The group had developed its own unofficial organization, run in such a way that it was able to protect itself from outside influences whilst controlling its internal life too.

15. Final stage (1936). This stage was commenced some 4 years after stage four because of the economic difficulties of the depression. This final stage was based on lessons learned from the earlier studies. Its focus was firmly on employee relations and took the form of personnel counselling. The counsellors encouraged employees to discuss their problems at work and the results led to improvements in personal adjustments, employee–supervisor relations and employee–management relations.

16. The official account of the Hawthorne studies was written not by Mayo but by a Harvard colleague (Roethlisberger) and one of the company's own researchers (Dickson). Their detailed descriptions of the research did not appear until 1939, sometime after Mayo had already highlighted the studies in his popularized account published 6 years earlier.

17. There have been many criticisms of the way the Hawthorne Studies have been interpreted more recently, see for example, Levitt and List (2011) and Hassard (2012). Mayo's references to them were included in writings, which propounded his theories about man and industrial society. As a result, his use of the studies was biased towards his own interpretation of what was happening. For the official evidence one must look to Roethlisberger and Dickson. Modern researchers point out that their Hawthorne colleagues overlooked important factors in assessing their results. They also adopted some unreliable methods for testing the evidence in the first place. However, everyone is agreed the Hawthorne Studies represented the first major attempt to undertake genuine social research. Important lessons were learned, and, perhaps even more importantly, many questions were raised by these studies.

18. The main conclusions to be drawn from the Hawthorne research are:

- Individual workers cannot be treated in isolation, but must be seen as members of a group.

- The need to belong to a group and have status within it is more important than monetary incentives or good physical working conditions.

- Informal (or unofficial) groups at work exercise a strong influence over the behaviour of workers.

- Supervisors and managers need to be aware of these social needs and cater for them if workers are to collaborate with the official organization rather than work against it.

19. The Hawthorne experiment began as a study into physical conditions and productivity. It ended as a series of studies into social factors: membership of groups, relationships with supervision, etc. Its most significant findings showed that social relations at work were every bit as important as monetary incentives and good physical working conditions. Demonstrated also was the powerful influence of groups in determining behaviour at work. By modern standards of social research, the Hawthorne studies were relatively unsophisticated in their approach. Nevertheless, they represented a major step forward for the social sciences in their study of work organizations. Also, by their model of 'social man', they did much to further the humanization of work. Group work will be discussed further in Chapter 7.

4.4 MARY PARKER FOLLETT

20. The ideas of Mary Parker Follett, an American social worker, management consultant and pioneer in the fields of organizational theory and organizational behaviour, were so far ahead of her time that most of them were ignored. The fact that she was a woman, trying to speak out in a man's world, was undoubtedly another factor. In her principal piece on the workplace, published after her death, 'Dynamic Administration' (1941), she moved forward the work of the Hawthorne researchers by concluding that human problems were not just important, but were central to the success of organizations. In particular, she argued the case for giving greater not less responsibility to people at work. Follett was aware of the importance of teamwork, and the role of the leader, which she saw in holistic and shared terms. The leader's role was to envision the future and to empower others to achieve that future. She herself did not use the modern

expression empowerment, but that is clearly what she meant. Her idea of leadership meant gaining the collaboration and respect of others and reconciling conflicts. Such a leadership approach depended upon the interaction of leader and followers.

21. Follett suggested there were three ways of dealing with conflict: by domination, by compromise or by integration. Today we would refer to her integration as a 'win–win' solution. Domination implies a 'win–lose' outcome, and compromise a 'lose–lose' situation, in which neither side is content. She was strongly against the notion that conflict was a matter of 'either-or', as this meant that alternative solutions were restricted from the outset. Today, Follett's ideas are acknowledged, as writers and historians look back across the twentieth century, free from prejudices.

22. The emphasis on people as the most crucial factor in determining organizational effectiveness was researched further by scholars of the social psychological school of motivation. They recognized that people have considerably more than just physical and social needs. The dominant concept here is that of self-actualizing man, and the influential contributors here are the American social scientists Maslow, McGregor, Herzberg, Likert, Argyris and McClelland.

4.5 MASLOW'S HIERARCHY OF NEEDS

23. Abraham Maslow's hierarchy of needs is one of the most popular models in leadership writing. Developed in 1948, the hierarchy of needs is pervasive across many disciplines, including business, management, marketing, education and psychology. Maslow argues that staff can be motivated through means other than pay. His studies into human motivation led Maslow to propose a theory of needs, which explain why people work, based on a hierarchical model, with basic needs at the bottom and higher needs at the top, as in Figure 4.2. This theory made a considerable influence on developments in management theory during the 1950s/1960s due partly to the simplicity of the model and partly to the identification of higher-level needs.

24. The starting point of Maslow's hierarchy theory, first published in 1954, is that most people are motivated by the desire to satisfy specific groups of needs. These needs are as follows:

- physiological needs – needs for food, sleep, etc.

- safety needs – needs for a stable environment, relatively free from threats

- love needs – needs related to affectionate relations with others and status within a group

- esteem needs – needs for self-respect, self-esteem and the esteem of others

- self-actualization needs – the need for self-fulfilment.

25. The second and most central point of Maslow's theory is that people tend to satisfy their needs systematically, starting with the basic physiological needs and then progressing up the hierarchy. Until a particular group of needs is satisfied, a person's behaviour will be dominated by them. Thus, a hungry person is not going to be motivated by consideration of safety or affection, for example, until after his hunger has been satisfied. Maslow later modified this argument by stating that there was an exception to the rule in respect of self-actualization needs. For this group of needs it seems that satisfaction of a need gives rise to further needs for realizing one's potential.

26. Maslow's theory provided a useful early framework for discussions about the variety of needs people may experience at work, and the ways in which their motivation could be met by managers. One criticism of the theory is that systematic movement up the hierarchy does not seem to be a consistent form of behaviour for many people. Alderfer (1972), for example, argued that individual needs were better explained as being on a continuum, rather than in a hierarchy. He considered that people were more likely to move up and down the continuum in satisfying needs at different levels. He concluded that there were really only three major sets of needs – existence needs (i.e. the basics of life), relatedness needs (i.e. social and interpersonal needs) and growth needs (i.e. personal development needs). Drucker (1974) commented that Maslow had not recognized that when a want was satisfied, its capacity to motivate was changed. An initially satisfied want that was not sustained could, on the contrary, become counter-productive and act as a disincentive.

FIGURE 4.2 **Hierarchy of needs**

4.6 McGREGOR – THEORY X AND THEORY Y

27. Like Schein's classification of managers' assumptions about people, McGregor's Theory X and Theory Y are sets of assumptions about behaviour. In proposing his ideas, McGregor pointed to the theoretical assumptions of management that underlie its behaviour. He saw two noticeably different sets of assumptions made by managers about their employees. The first set of assumptions regards employees as being inherently lazy, requiring coercion and control, avoiding responsibility and only seeking security. This attitude is what McGregor termed Theory X. This is the theory of scientific management, with its emphasis on controls and **extrinsic** rewards. Schein's rational-economic model (see para. 5 above) is very similar to that of Theory X.

28. McGregor's second set of assumptions sees people in a more favourable light. In this case employees are seen as liking work, which is as natural as rest or play; they do not have to be controlled and coerced, so long as they are committed to organizational objectives. Under proper conditions they will not only accept but also seek more rather than less responsibility, i.e. people are able to exercise imagination and ingenuity at work. These are the assumptions of Theory Y. They are closely related to Maslow's higher-level needs and to Schein's self-actualizing model.

29. Theory X and Theory Y have made their greatest impact in the managerial rather than in the academic world. The two labels have become part of the folklore of 'management style', which will be examined in the chapter on leadership (Chapter 6). They do help to identify extreme forms of management style, but there is a danger that they may be seen only as polar extremes, representing an either/or style. In real-life a blend of the two theories is more likely to provide the best prescription for effective management.

4.7 HERZBERG'S MOTIVATION-HYGIENE THEORY

30. Herzberg's studies of the mid-twentieth century concentrated on satisfaction at work. In the initial research some 200 engineers and accountants were asked to recall when they had experienced satisfactory and unsatisfactory feelings about their jobs. Following the interviews, Herzberg's team came to the conclusion that certain factors tended to lead to job satisfaction, whereas others led frequently to dissatisfaction (see Figure 4.3). The factors giving rise to satisfaction were called motivators. Those giving rise to dissatisfaction

were called **hygiene factors**. These studies were later extended to include various people in manual and clerical groups, where the results were claimed to be quite similar.

FIGURE 4.3 Factors affecting job attitudes

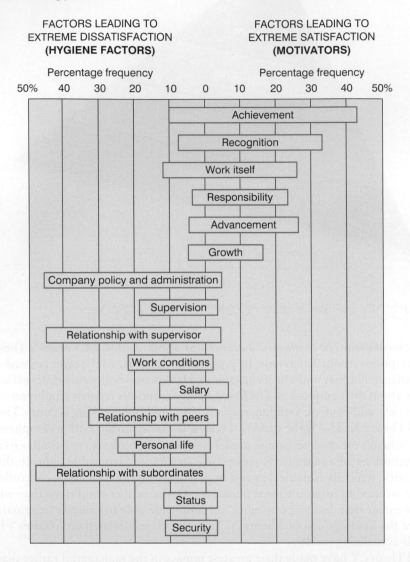

Note: The *length* of each 'box' denotes the frequency with which the factor occurred in the situation described by the respondents. The overlap of the boxes across the centre line indicates: (a) that motivators have their *negative* aspects, e.g. lack of achievement can lead to dissatisfaction and (b) that hygiene factors have their *positive* aspects, e.g. salary can be a source of satisfaction.

31. The most important motivators, or satisfiers, to emerge were the following:

- achievement
- recognition
- work itself
- responsibility
- advancement.

Herzberg pointed out that these motivators were intimately related to the content of work, i.e. with its intrinsic challenge, interest and the individual responses generated by them.

32. The most important hygiene factors, or dissatisfiers, were as follows:

- company policy and administration
- supervision – the technical aspects
- salary
- interpersonal relations – supervision
- working conditions.

Herzberg noted that these dissatisfiers were more related to the context or environment of work than to its content. When in line with employee requirements, such factors could smooth the path of working life, but in a taken-for-granted way. When these factors were out of line with employee's expectations, they could be a source of difficulty and complaint, and definitely provided grounds for dissatisfaction at work. This lack of a positive aspect to these factors led Herzberg to call them 'hygiene' factors, because whilst they contributed to the prevention of poor psychological health, they did not make a positive contribution to employee sense of well-being, at least not in any lasting way.

33. The key distinction between the motivators and hygiene factors is that whereas the presence of motivators can bring about positive satisfaction, the presence of hygiene factors can only serve to prevent dissatisfaction. To put it another way, if motivators are absent from the job, the employee is likely to experience real dissatisfaction. However, even if the hygiene factors are provided for, they will not in themselves bring about substantial job satisfaction. Hygiene, in other words, does not promote good health positively, but only acts to prevent ill-health.

34. If we apply Herzberg's theory to the ideas and assumptions of earlier theorists, it is possible to see that Taylor and colleagues were thinking very much in terms of hygiene factors (pay, incentives, adequate supervision and working conditions). Mayo, too, was placing his emphasis on a hygiene factor, namely interpersonal relations. It is only when we consider the ideas of the neo-human relations school that motivators appear as a key element in job satisfaction and worker productivity.

35. Herzberg's motivation-hygiene theory was well received by practising managers and consultants for its simple and vivid distinction between factors inducing positive satisfaction and those causing dissatisfaction. It led to considerable work on so-called job enrichment, i.e. the design of jobs to ensure they contained a greater number of motivators (to be discussed in Section 9). The approach here is to counter the effects of years of Taylorism, in which work was broken down into its simplest components, and over which there was no responsibility for planning and control. Herzberg's ideas were less well received by fellow social scientists, mainly on grounds of doubt about (a) their applicability to non-professional groups and (b) his use of the concept of 'job satisfaction', which they argued was not the same thing as 'motivation'.

4.8 LIKERT

36. Likert's contribution to the concept of motivation, and its applicability to the world of work, came mainly from his work as Director of the Institute of Social Research at the University of Michigan, USA. The 'Michigan studies' were described by Likert, in 1961, who theorized about high-producing and low-producing managers. The former, according to his research, were those who achieved not only the highest productivity, but also the lowest costs and the highest levels of employee motivation. The latter, by comparison, produced higher costs and lower employee motivation.

37. Research indicated that the high-producing managers tended to build their success on interlocking and tightly knit groups of employees, whose cooperation had been obtained by thorough attention to a range of motivational forces. These included not only economic and security motives, but also ego and creativity motives (self-actualization, in Maslow's terminology). Another key feature noted by the Michigan researchers was that, although the high-producers utilized the tools of classical management – work study, budgeting, etc. – they did so in a way that recognized the aspirations of employees, by encouraging participative approaches.

38. A dominant theme in Likert's discussion of these 'new patterns of management' is the importance of supportive relationships. Management can achieve high performance when employees see their membership of a work group to be 'supportive', that is to say when they experience a sense of personal worth and importance from belonging to this work group. High-producing managers and supervisors tended to foster just such relationships with, and within, their groups.

39. The idea of supportive relationships is built into Likert's view of the ideal organization structure. Supportive relationships lead to effective work groups which can interact with other effective groups in an overlapping form of organization. In this form of structure certain key roles perform a 'linking pin' function. A head of a section, for example, is a member not only of their own group but also of their managers' group. Their manager or supervisor, in turn, is a member of a further group higher up the organizational hierarchy, and so on. Such an organization still has the basic shape of a classical organizational pyramid, but operates in practice on the basis of interlocking teams as opposed to separate specialisms. This form is shown diagrammatically in Figure 4.4.

FIGURE 4.4 **Overlapping group form of organization**

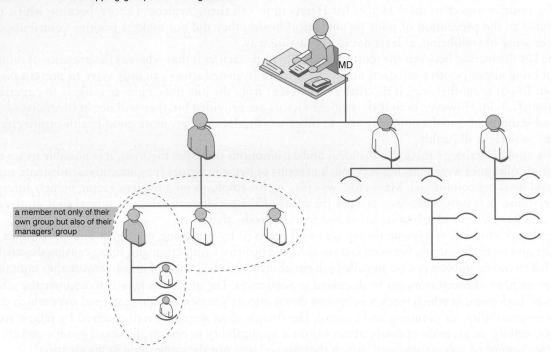

a member not only of their own group but also of their managers' group

40. In reviewing his work on motivation, leadership and organizational structures, Likert distinguished between four separate systems, or styles of management. These are founded on a number of differing assumptions about human behaviour and are useful when compared with Schein's classifications and McGregor's theory X – theory Y. The four systems are as follows:

–   Exploitative-authoritative where power and direction come from the top downwards, where threats and punishment are employed, where communication is poor and teamwork non-existent. Productivity is mediocre.

–   Benevolent-authoritative is similar to the above but allows some upward opportunities for consultation and some delegation. Rewards may be available as well as threats. Productivity is fair to good but at the cost of considerable absenteeism and turnover.

–   Consultative where goals are set or orders issued after discussion with subordinates, where communication is both upwards and downwards and where teamwork is encouraged, at least partially.

    There is some involvement of employees, as a motivator. Productivity is good with only moderate absenteeism etc.

– Participative-group is the ideal system. Under this system, the keynote is participation, leading to commitment to organizational goals in a fully cooperative way. Communication is good both upwards, downwards and laterally. Motivation is obtained by a variety of means. Productivity is excellent and absenteeism and turnover are low.

41. The exploitative-authoritative system corresponds closely to Schein's rational economic model and McGregor's theory X. The benevolent-authoritative system can be considered as a similar, but softer, approach. The consultative system is fairly close to the idea of the social model. Finally, the participative-group system is more like Schein's self-actualizing model and very close to the idea of theory Y. The exploitative-authoritative system, at one extreme, is highly task oriented, whilst the participative-group system is highly people oriented at the other.

4.9 ARGYRIS

42. Professor Argyris was one of Likert's contemporaries. His initial interests, whilst at Yale University, were in the relationship between people's needs and the needs of the organization. He suggested the reason for so much employee apathy was not so much because of laziness, but rather because people were being treated like children. This led to what he called the immaturity-maturity theory, which suggests that the human personality develops from immaturity to maturity in a continuum, in which a number of key changes take place. The characteristics of the immature personality can be described as passive, dependent, erratic and shallow interests, unvaried behaviour, having a short-term perspective, generally subordinate and a lack of self-awareness. Contrastingly, the mature personality has the opposite characteristics and can be described as active, independent with deeper interests, having varied behaviour and a long-term perspective, generally in equal or superior positions and more self-awareness and control.

43. Against the above model of maturity, Argyris sets the features of the typical classical organization: task specialization, chain of command, unity of direction and span of control. The impact of this type of organization on individuals is that employees are expected to be passive, dependent and subordinate, i.e. they are expected to behave immaturely! For individuals who are relatively mature, this environment is a major source of frustration at work. This frustration leads to individuals seeking informal ways of minimizing difficulties such as creating informal organizations that work against the formal hierarchy.

44. The lessons for motivation are important. For the more we can understand human needs, the more it will be possible to integrate them with the needs of organizations. If the goals of the organization and the goals of individuals can be brought together, the resulting behaviour will be cooperative rather than defensive or downright antagonistic (a matter discussed by Ouchi, 1980). Argyris's ideas, therefore, favour a self-actualization model of man with some of the attributes of complex man too.

4.10 ACHIEVEMENT MOTIVATION

45. Whilst many social psychologists have studied common factors in human motivation, others have focused on differences between individuals. One such researcher, whose work is well known, is McClelland of Harvard University. He and his team drew attention to three sets of needs in particular, as follows:

- the **need for achievement (n-Ach)**
- the **need for power (n-Pow)**
- the need for affiliation, or belonging (n-Aff).

McClelland isolated n-Ach as a key human motive, and one that is influenced strongly by personality and by environment.

46. Persons with a high need for achievement tend to have the following characteristics:

- their need for achievement is consistent

- they seek tasks in which they can exercise personal responsibility

- they prefer tasks which provide a challenge without being too difficult and which they see as within their mastery

- they want feedback on their results

- they are less concerned about their social or affiliation needs.

47. The major disadvantage of persons with high n-Ach is that, by definition, they are task-oriented and less concerned with relationships. These characteristics are not always suitable for those whose responsibility is to get work done through people, i.e. managers and supervisors. This may not be a problem for an entrepreneurial figure in a small organization, but what of the high achiever working in a typical industrial or commercial bureaucracy? In the latter case high n-Ach can be frustrated by the constraints imposed by delegating responsibility. Nevertheless, McClelland's ideas were important as a contribution to our understanding of motivation at work, and how the concept of n-Ach might be applied in practice.

CONCLUSION

48. This (and the next) chapter is mainly concerned with the basic management and leadership problem of how we motivate or persuade others to do what we want them to do. Since it is part of a manager's job to get work done through others, managers need to understand why people behave as they do (that is, what motivates them) so they can influence others to work towards the goals of the organization. The chapter began with an explanation of the basic concept of motivation, and was followed by a summary of different models of motivation; we provided an account of the Hawthorne Studies and continued with an outline of the work of a number of American social scientists, namely Follett, Maslow, McGregor, Herzberg, Likert, Argyris and McClelland.

QUESTIONS

1   What are the similarities between Schein's description of the Rational-Economic Model, McGregor's Theory X and Likert's System 1 (Exploitive-Authoritative)?

2   What is the 'Hawthorne Effect'? What are the implications of this for those undertaking research into human behaviour in the workplace? In your answer you should argue why the Hawthorne Studies were considered to be so important in their time.

3   What are the essential differences between motivators and hygiene factors in Herzberg's theory of motivation.

4   How can an understanding of the need for achievement be of use to managers in industry and commerce?

5   Discuss the significance of the Hawthorne experience at Western Electric.

USEFUL WEBSITES

The Institute of Management: **http://www.managers.org.uk**
 Harvard Business School library: **www.library.hbs.edu/hc/hawthorne/intro.html**

Harvard Business School library information about the Hawthorne studies and human relations movement
Frederick Herzberg: **www.businessballs.com/herzberg.htm**
 Frederick Herzberg motivational theory

REFERENCES

Alderfer, C. (1972) *Existence, Relatedness and Growth*, Collier Macmillan.

Drucker, P. (1974) *Management: Tasks, Responsibilities, Practices*, Heinemann.

Hassard, J S. (2012), 'Rethinking the Hawthorne Studies: The Western Electric research in its social, political and historical context', *Human Relations* 65(11): 1431–1461.

Levitt, S D. and List, J A. (2011), 'Was There Really a Hawthorne Effect at the Hawthorne Plant? An Analysis of the Original Illumination Experiments', *American Economic Journal: Applied Economics* 3(1): 224–238.

Ouchi, W.G. (1980) 'Markets, Bureaucracies, and Clans', *Administrative Science Quarterly* 25(1): 129–141.

Schein, E. (1988) *Organizational Psychology*, 3rd edn, Prentice-Hall.

CHAPTER 5
MOTIVATION – 'HOW' MOTIVATION OCCURS

Key Concepts

- Attribution theory
- Equity theory
- Expectancy theory
- Goal theory
- Reinforcement
- Theory Z

Learning Outcomes   Having read this chapter, you should be able to:

- explain the process theory of motivation
- recall the expectancy theory of motivation
- recall the equity theory of motivation
- recall the goal theory of motivation
- discuss Theory Z and its application to Western organizations
- discuss how attribution theory may help managers to motivate their employees.

1.   Work motivation has been of interest at least since the 1930s, stimulated in large part by the famous Hawthorne studies (previous chapter), which focused mainly on the effects of supervision, incentives and working conditions, (Locke and Latham, 2004). The motivation theories discussed in the previous chapter have been labelled 'content theories' of motivation, because they focus on the needs, drivers or triggers of human behaviour in the workplace. This chapter examines some of the ideas proposed by those whose focus is mainly on the process of motivation rather than its content. Not surprisingly, these theories tend to be called 'process theories' of motivation. Process theories of motivation focus upon what people are thinking when they decide whether or not to place effort into a particular activity. One of the best known of the process theories is Expectancy Theory, which we outline first. This is followed by a brief consideration of other later theories of motivation, including Equity, Goal, Attribution and **Reinforcement** Theory, and an analysis of Japanese motivational practices given the name of '**Theory Z**'.

5.1 EXPECTANCY THEORY

2.   The development of this theory of motivation is based on the work of the American, Victor Vroom, during the 1960s. A key point of his theory is that an individual's behaviour is formed not on objective reality but on his or her subjective **perception** of that reality. The core of the theory (see Figure 5.1) relates to how a person perceives the relationships between three things – effort, performance and rewards. Vroom focused especially on the factors involved in stimulating an individual to place effort into something, since this is the basis of motivation. He concluded there were three such factors, each based on the individual's personal perception of the situation. These were:

EXPECTANCY, i.e. the extent of the individual's perception, or belief, that a particular act will produce a particular outcome.

INSTRUMENTALITY, i.e. the extent to which the individual perceives that effective performance will lead to desired rewards.

VALENCE, i.e. the strength of the belief that attractive rewards are potentially available.

This approach to the concept of human motivation, with its emphasis on the psychological mechanisms which trigger effort, differs markedly from that of the content theorists whose work was described in the previous chapter. The basic model developed by Vroom, indicating the components of effort that can lead to relevant performance and appropriate rewards, can be summarized in Figure 5.1.

3.   It is important to note that Vroom distinguishes 'valence' from 'value'. He does so by defining the former in terms of the anticipated satisfaction the individual hopes to obtain from the outcome or reward, and by defining 'value' in terms of the actual satisfaction obtained by the individual. According to Vroom the three factors – Expectancy, Instrumentality and Valence – combine together to create a driving force (Force), which motivates an individual to instil effort, achieve a level of performance and obtain rewards at the end. Vroom suggested that Force was a multiple of Expectancy and Valence (encompassing Instrumentality) in the formula: Force = Expectancy × Valence (or $F = E \times V$).

4.   Effort alone, however, may not necessarily lead to effective performance. Other factors are involved, such as the individual's own characteristics (personality, knowledge and skills) and the way in which they perceive their role. For example, the prospect of promotion could be seen by a newly appointed employee as an attractive prospect (valence), but their expectancy of gaining promotion could be low, if they perceive that promotion is attained primarily on length of service. In such a situation, performance does not lead to rewards, so effort in that direction is not seen as worthwhile. In any case, effort does not necessarily lead to effective performance, if the individual has insufficient knowledge and skills, or if their perception of their role does not equate with that of their superior, for example.

5.   Other factors which are not shown may also affect performance, e.g. constraints of the job, organization style, etc. Effort, therefore, does not always result in effective performance. It is also true that effective performance may not always lead to the rewards anticipated by the individual. Nevertheless, on both counts, it is not the reality which spurs on the individual but the prospect of effective performance and/or desirable rewards. It is the individual's perception of the situation that is the vital part of this theory.

6.   Rewards may be classified in two categories – (1) intrinsic and (2) extrinsic. Intrinsic rewards are those gained from fulfilling higher-level personal needs, such as self-esteem and personal growth. The individual can exercise a degree of personal control over these. Extrinsic rewards, by comparison, are those provided by the organization and thus outside the control of the individual, such as pay, promotion and working conditions. Several research studies have suggested the rewards associated with intrinsic factors are more likely to be perceived as producing job satisfaction. The extrinsic rewards are less likely to match individual expectations.

FIGURE 5.1 Expectancy theory

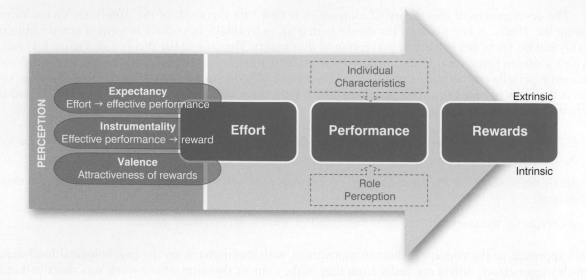

7.   Thus, **Expectancy Theory** is a process theory which argues that individual motivation depends upon the valence of outcomes, the expectancy that effort will lead to good performance and the instrumentality of performance in producing valued outcomes. The main features of Expectancy Theory are, it:

- takes a comprehensive view of the motivational process

- indicates that individuals will only act when they have a reasonable expectancy that their behaviour will lead to the desired outcomes

- stresses the importance of individual perceptions of reality in the motivational process

- implies that job satisfaction follows effective job performance rather than the other way round, and

- has led to developments in work redesign, where emphasis has been laid on intrinsic job factors, such as variety, autonomy, task identity and feedback.

5.2 EQUITY THEORY

8.   Have you or a colleague ever been demotivated upon discovering that a similar employee has received better benefits than you (for the same or less work)? A theory of motivation which focuses on people's feelings of how fairly they have been treated in comparison with the treatment received by others is termed Equity Theory. The basis of this theory, in a work context, is that people make comparisons between themselves and others in terms of what they invest in their work (inputs) and what outcomes they receive from it. As in the case of Expectancy Theory, this theory is also founded on people's perceptions, in this case of the inputs and outcomes involved. Thus, their sense of equity (i.e. fairness) is applied to their subjective view of conditions and not necessarily to the objective situation. The theory states that when people perceive an unequal situation, they experience 'equity tension', which they attempt to reduce by appropriate behaviour. This behaviour may be to act positively to improve their performance and/or to seek improved rewards, or may be to act negatively by, for example, working more slowly (cf. Taylor-type soldiering) on the grounds of being under-rated or under-paid or may even result in an exit from the organization.

9.   Equity Theory suggests that people are not only interested in rewards as such, which is the central point of expectancy theory, but they are also interested in the comparative nature of rewards. Thus, part of the

attractiveness (valence) of rewards in a work context is the extent to which they are seen as comparable with those available to the peer group. Such thinking, however, is best applied to extrinsic rewards, such as pay, promotion, pension arrangements, company car and similar benefits, since they (a) depend on others for their provision, and (b) have an objective truth about them. **Equity Theory** cannot apply in the same way to intrinsic rewards, such as intrinsic job interest, personal achievement and exercise of responsibility, which by their very nature are personal to the individual, entirely subjective and therefore less capable of comparison in any credible sense. Nevertheless, so far as extrinsic rewards are concerned, managers would be well advised to reflect on the ideas of Equity Theory, especially in recognizing that subjective perceptions are extremely powerful factors in motivation.

5.3 GOAL THEORY

10. **Goal Theory**, a theory of motivation, is based on the premise that people's goals or intentions play an important part in determining behaviour. Goal-setting theory has arguably become one of the dominant motivational theories in organizational behaviour (Fried and Slowik, 2004). Goals guide people's responses and actions and direct work behaviour and performance, leading to certain consequences or feedback. The thinking behind Goal Theory is that motivation is driven primarily by the goals or objectives that individuals set for themselves. Unlike Expectancy Theory, where a satisfactory outcome is the prime motivator, Goal Theory suggests that it is the goal itself that provides the driving force. Locke (1967) first proposed the idea that working towards goals was in itself a motivator. His research indicated that performance improved when individuals set themselves specific rather than vague goals. When these specific goals were demanding, performance was even better.

11. Goal theorists also argue that an individual's motivation is enhanced when feedback on performance is available. Other important factors include goal commitment (i.e. the extent to which the individual is committed to pursuing the goal even when things get rough), and self-efficacy (i.e. the perception that one has the ability to achieve the goal). Goal commitment is likely to be enhanced when goals are made public and when they are set by the individual rather than imposed externally. Clearly, the concept of goal 'ownership' is important here. Self-efficacy is a belief that a person is capable of achieving their goals, which were set as realistic, though challenging.

5.4 ATTRIBUTION THEORY

12. Managers frequently have to make judgements about employees and employees will frequently judge themselves and colleagues. They will often make attempts to determine the causes of behavioural outcomes (work performance). For example, expectancy and goal theory will often require a manager to reward an employee. The reward will normally only be given if the manager judges that desirable work outcomes arose as a consequence of employee behaviour (motivation and work). In this chapter we have also discussed equity theory whereby employees make comparisons between themselves and others; in doing so, they will be judging themselves and others and attributing causes to behaviour. Attribution is the process by which we ascribe causes to events as well as to our own and others' behaviour. It is part of the overall perceptual process. **Attribution Theory** is used to explain aspects of discrimination within the organization and may also be used to explain aspects of motivation. When explaining or describing behaviour and its relationship with performance, people tend to consider internal and external forces. The internal forces relate to personal attributes such as ability, skill, amount of effort, etc., whereas external forces may include environmental factors, organizational rules and policies, resources, etc. Attribution is an important process because the subsequent responses depend upon how individuals interpret the original causes. When judging subordinate performance, if the manager perceives the cause of outcome (e.g. work output) to be internal and based on employee behaviour (ability, skill, effort and motivation) then a reward is likely to be given. However, should the manager believe that external factors caused the outcome then rewards may be withheld. A number of theories have been proposed to explain whether managers are more or less likely to attribute cause to employee ability or the situation (external force). **Self-serving bias** describes a

situation whereby individuals attribute success to their own abilities and failure to the situation. However, when we judge others we tend to assume that failure is due to lack of ability rather than caused by the situation (Actor–observer effect). Specific conditions may determine when people judge behaviour to be intentional. The presence of a relevant goal, intention, possession of relevant skills, etc. are likely to influence a judgement that considers internal forces to be at work in causing the outcome.

13. Employees who do not meet targets or objectives may blame external factors/forces and as a result may reduce the level of future effort. In situations where the manager fails to give a reward, judging outcomes to have been caused by external forces, and employees perceive their good performance to be due to their ability and effort, then the lack of recognition and reward may well have a demotivating effect. Attribution Theory is as much an issue of perception between individuals as a theory of motivation. Nevertheless, by providing another way of looking at people's behaviour, it can add to our understanding of the motivational process.

5.5 REINFORCEMENT THEORY

14. Whereas Attribution Theory has strong links with ideas about human perception, Reinforcement Theory, as applied to motivation, has major connections with learning theory, and especially the work of the late American behaviourist, Burrhus Skinner. The Reinforcement Theory of motivation suggests that a given behaviour is a function of the consequences of earlier behaviour. Thus, it is argued, all behaviour is determined, to some extent, by the rewards or punishments obtained from previous behaviour, which has the effect of reinforcing current actions. In this sense all behaviour is caused by external sources, since we can have little control over the consequences of our actions. So, if an individual's efforts to contribute new ideas to a team are consistently met with an indulgent but apathetic approach by the management (i.e. Negative reinforcement), then the individual is likely to be discouraged from making further suggestions, and may even seek to change his or her job. Where, by comparison, the individual is encouraged to share new ideas and help to develop them (i.e. Positive reinforcement), then the person is likely to generate even more ideas.

15. Strict Reinforcement Theory would argue that an individual's own understandings, emotions, needs and expectations do not enter into motivation, which is purely about the consequences of behaviour. However, modifications of the theory (e.g. Social Learning Theory) do allow for the effect of individuals' perceptions of the rewards/punishments obtained by others as a contributor to motivation. Thus, an employee is not just affected by the consequences of his own actions at work, but is able to infer 'appropriate' behaviour from what he sees as the consequences for others of their behaviour. Reinforcement Theory is not concerned with what motivates behaviour, or how, and is not strictly a theory of motivation. It is more concerned with control of behaviour (i.e. Power over others).

16. Supporters of Reinforcement Theory offer some important guidelines to those intending to use it as a motivating tool in the workplace. Typical suggestions include the following:

- positively reinforce desired behaviour
- ignore undesirable behaviour, so far as possible
- avoid using punishment as principal means of achieving desired performance
- provide reinforcement as soon as possible after the response
- apply positive reinforcement regularly
- assess positive and negative factors in the individual's environment
- specify desired behaviour/performance in quantifiable terms.

17. The underlying assumption behind this approach is that people are there to be controlled, and that management's task is to provide the 'right' conditions to encourage high performance. This is not quite such a negative view of people as is suggested by McGregor's Theory X (see previous chapter), but Reinforcement Theory is not too far removed from that concept of human motivation.

5.6 THEORY Z – THE JAPANESE APPROACH

18. The reference in the previous paragraph to McGregor's Theory X is timely, for it leads us into the last 'theory' in this chapter – 'Theory Z'. This describes an approach to employee motivation based on Japanese management practices. The phrase was coined by an American exponent of Japanese approaches to management, William Ouchi, who used it to describe attempts to adapt Japanese practice to Western firms. Theory Z is the management style that combines various aspects of scientific management and behaviouralism; the characteristics include long-term employment, development of company-specific skills, participative and collective decision-making and a broad concern for the welfare of workers.

19. In the last quarter of the twentieth century, considerable attention was given to the success of Japanese manufacturing industries. One of the key factors in their success, according to Ouchi, has been their approach to their management of resources, especially people. Among the key features of Japanese industrial organizations, notes Ouchi, are the following personnel-related factors:

- There is a high degree of mutual trust and loyalty between management and employees.

- Career paths are non-specialized with life long job rotation as a central feature of career development.

- Decision-making is shared at all levels.

- Performance appraisal is long-term (i.e. the first appraisal takes place 10 years after joining the company).

- There is a strong sense of collective responsibility for the success of the organization, and cooperative effort rather than individual achievement is encouraged.

20. Although Ouchi recognizes that many of the features of Japanese management cannot be translated into Western industrial society, he believes that certain features can be applied in a Western context. Despite the participative management style implied by the above theory, it is important to note the Japanese have taken up many of the ideas of Taylor (see Chapter 2), but, in contrast to Western industrialized nations, they have emphasized the importance of the human resource element in achieving production efficiency using Taylor's methods. The acceptance of Taylorist approaches to manufacturing has enabled the Japanese to capture an enviable place in world markets for their manufactured goods. It is not that the Japanese are particularly innovative, but they have found the secret of achieving a standard of production control which ensures a consistently excellent product. This standard has been achieved because of thorough attention to human resource issues as well as to questions of technology, quality and cost control. Backed by financial policies aimed at long-term growth rather than short-term profits and a worldwide view of product marketing, Japanese manufacturing companies have set a high standard for their competitors to follow. Critics of Japanese manufacturing companies have pointed to the slow processes of decision-making, the lack of risk taking, the reliance on a myriad of small firms and part-time employees, the docile nature of the trade unions and the imprisoning effect of lifetime employment in one company. It is precisely because of such criticisms that Japanese management practices must be adapted if they are to be employed successfully elsewhere. For Ouchi, Theory Z focused on increasing employee loyalty to the company by providing a job for life, with a strong focus on the well-being of the employee, both on and off the job. According to Ouchi, Theory Z management tends to promote stable employment, high productivity, and high employee morale and satisfaction.

5.7 THE FUTURE OF WORK MOTIVATION THEORY

21. From discussion so far we note that the concept of motivation refers to internal factors that drive action and to external factors that can act as inducements to action. The three aspects of action that motivation can affect are direction (choice), intensity (effort) and duration (persistence). Motivation can affect not only the acquisition of people's skills and abilities but also how and to what extent they utilize their skills and abilities (Locke and Latham, 2004). According to Steers, Mowday and Shapiro (2004) the topic of

employee motivation plays a central role in the field of management – both practically and theoretically. Managers see motivation as an integral part of the performance equation at all levels. Indeed, the topic of motivation permeates many of the subfields that compose the study of management, including leadership, teams, performance management, decision-making and organizational change. They note that many of the ideas emerging from the 1960s and 1970s have subsequently been extended and further developed; indeed there has been new work focusing on goal-setting theory, job design, reward systems, punishment, innovation and creativity, and cross-cultural influences on work behaviour. However, they also note that by the 1990s, intellectual interest in work motivation theory – at least as measured by journal publications – seemed to decline.

22. In 2004 the 'Academy of Management Review' Special Topic Forum focused on the future of work motivation theory. This forum was used to discuss new research directions to help understand what motivates workers to work. This acted as a platform for further work on motivation. For example, Michaelson (2005) believes we need to enhance our understanding of *why* workers should be motivated to work; the author notes the connection between worker motivation and productivity within individual and group performance. Michaelson discusses the meaningful work literature, the so-called objective conditions that institutions have a moral obligation to provide, include free choice to enter, honest communication, fair and respectful treatment, intellectual challenge, considerable independence to determine work methods, democratic participation in decision-making, moral development, due process and justice, non-paternalism and fair compensation. He concludes, 'Surely, meaningful work is an important work motivator. It is also obvious that productivity is an important motivation for work motivation theory.'

CONCLUSION

23. In this and the previous chapter we considered the problem of how we motivate or persuade others (employees etc.) to do what we require of them. Motivation theories are important to managers and others seeking to be effective leaders. Whilst there is no all-encompassing explanation, the aforementioned theories (alongside those outlined in the previous chapter) are helpful in understanding motivation.

QUESTIONS

1   Motivation of subordinates is an important aspect of a manager's job. Outline methods that may motivate a person to work and perform well in the workplace.

2   In what respects is Expectancy Theory novel in its approach to motivation at work?

3   What is 'Theory Z', and to what extent can its underlying assumptions be transferred to non-Japanese manufacturing companies?

4   Compare and contrast process and content theories of motivation. In your answer you should (a) explain what is meant by a process theory of motivation and then what constitutes a content theory of motivation and (b) list and describe three examples of each.

5   Critically evaluate process theories of motivation and their application in the management of workplace behaviour – which do you consider to be the most important and why?

USEFUL WEBSITES

Institute for employment studies: **www.employment-studies. co.uk/consult/index.php?id=mwb&tab=work**

Motivation and well-being

REFERENCES

Fried, Y. and Slowik, L,H. (2004) 'Enriching goal-setting theory with time: An integrated approach', *Academy of Management Review*, 29(3): 404–422.

Locke, E. (1967) 'Toward a theory of task motivation and incentives', *Organizational Behaviour and Human Performance*, 3(2): 157–189.

Locke, E.A. and Latham, G.P. (2004) 'What should we do about motivation theory? Six recommendations for the twenty-first century', *Academy of Management Review*, 29(3): 388–403.

Michaelson, C. (2005) 'Meaningful Motivation for Work Motivation Theory', *Academy of Management Review*, 30(2): 235–238.

Steers, R.M., Mowday, R.T. and Shapiro, D.L. (2004) 'The future of work motivation theory', *Academy of Management Review*, 29(3): 379–387.

SKILL SHEET 2   MOTIVATION: 'What' and 'How'

Previously we focused on efficiency; continuing the theme of productivity, this skills sheet considers human resources as inputs and how to motivate employees to produce more. Use the sheet in conjunction with Chapters 4 and 5 and case sheet 2.

There are two parts: (1) DIAGNOSIS (measuring motivation) and (2) INTERVENTIONS (how to motivate others in the workplace):

1. DIAGNOSIS: measuring and assessing motivation

Motivation etc. may be 'observed' routinely or measured quantitatively through a deliberate and structured approach (questionnaire/survey). We can diagnose and measure (a) attitudes within the workforce (b) how managers are likely to attempt to motivate (manager motivational preferences) or (c) motivational techniques preferred by employees

(A) SATISFACTION, COMMITMENT AND ENGAGEMENT SURVEYS

As a start point managers need some indication of the level of motivation and satisfaction within the workforce. When managing a team they will want to judge individual levels of motivation and continuously monitor them. Designing an employee motivation and satisfaction questionnaire and survey requires research skills. Careful thought should be given to what needs measuring and why. Several related work attitudes may be of interest. Interest started with the concept of job satisfaction and its influence on productivity and performance.

	Strongly Agree	Agree	Undecided	Disagree	Strongly Disagree
Questionnaires[1] may seek to measure overall or satisfaction within a distinct area of work. There are a number of questions that can be asked of the workforce, such as:					
Most days I am enthusiastic about my work					
I feel fairly satisfied with my present job					
Each day at work seems like it will never end					
I find real enjoyment in my work					
I consider my job to be rather unpleasant					

The concept of *commitment* (to a goal, organization or occupation) is often measured to indicate the attachment an individual feels. Commitment is about acceptance and belief in the organization's values; willingness to exert effort to help the organization meet its goals and the desire to remain with the organization. Clearly the effort aspect is of interest to those seeking to motivate others. *Organizational identification* is a similar and measurable concept that deals more with the emotional aspect of organizational membership – the feeling of pride and esteem from association with an organization.

Finally, a relatively new construct, *employee engagement*, has emerged to reflect a positive work-related state of mind characterized by high levels of energy, enthusiasm and identification with one's work. Whilst there are overlaps amongst these concepts, each is regarded as a distinct construct.

Aside from quantitatively measuring motivation, managers will, daily, consider qualitative indicators of motivational levels. One way to do this is to compare the performance of team members. Whilst employee productivity is not necessarily the same as employee motivation, it can provide a good estimate of the

[1] These are simple/crude self-diagnostic instruments for discussion purposes.

amount of effort an employee is investing in the business. Other useful indicators may include absenteeism, late submission of work, evading responsibility, arriving late/leaving early, taking long breaks and general symptoms of apathy.

(B) WHAT IS YOUR MANAGEMENT/MOTIVATIONAL STYLE?

THEORY X/Y

Instructions: rate the degree to which **you** agree or disagree with the following statements

Scoring (add up the score for the boxes you ticked. Column 1 = 1 point, Column 2 = 2 points … Column 5 = 5 points

	Strongly Agree	Agree	Undecided	Disagree	Strongly Disagree
Most people will try to do as little work as possible					
Most employees must be closely supervised in order to get them to perform to expectations					
For most, work is not as natural as play or recreation					
Most employees actually prefer to be told exactly what to do rather than having to figure it out for themselves					
Most workers care little about the organization's goals					
Most employees would prefer increased job security to increased responsibility					
Employees generally contribute little when asked to participate in making decisions or solving problems					
Most people will not use their own initiative or do things that they have not been specifically assigned to do					
Most employees will not exercise self-control and self-motivation – managers must do this for them					
It is basic human nature – people just naturally dislike work					
Theory X beliefs <21 [mixed Theory Y and Theory X beliefs] **>30 Theory Y beliefs**					

Theory X (authoritarian style – carrot and stick approach): feel the sole purpose of the employee's interest in the job is money – therefore likely to believe employees will show little ambition without an appealing incentive program (rewards of varying kinds are likely to be adopted). Managers rely more heavily on punishment, fear and coercion as motivational techniques; tend to micro-manage and very closely supervise employees. **Theory Y** (participative style – supportive climate): management assumes employees may be ambitious and self-motivated; believe that the satisfaction of doing a good job is a strong motivation – motivate through autonomy, empowerment, collaboration, listening to and valuing etc. The challenge for management with Theory Y workers is to create a working environment (or culture) where workers can show and develop their creativity.

(C) MOTIVATION AND PERSONALITY: LOCUS OF CONTROL

Aside from using any of the motivational theories discussed in Chapters 4 and 5 to understand employee needs we may also consider employee personality when determining what techniques to employ. Locus of control (LOC) in social psychology refers to the extent to which individuals believe they can control the events that affect them. At one end of the continuum are high internals who believe that opportunity to control their own behaviour rests within themselves. At the other end of the continuum there are high externals who believe that external forces determine their behaviour. Appraise your LOC

	A/B
Instructions For each pair of statements, select the one statement that best describes how **YOU** feel, (Select a or b) – the item you believe to be truer than the other – this is about your personal belief, there are no right or wrong answers. Answer all.	
(a) Many of the unhappy things in people's lives are partly due to bad luck (b) People's misfortunes result from the mistakes they make	
(a) Without the right breaks one cannot be an effective leader (b) Capable people failing to become leaders have not exploited opportunities	
(a) I have often found that what is going to happen will happen (b) Trusting to fate has never turned out as well for me as making a decision to take a definite course of action	
(a) Exam questions tend to be unrelated to course work thus studying is pointless (b) For the well prepared student there is rarely if ever an unfair test	
(a) Getting a good job depends mainly on being in the right place at the right time (b) Becoming a success is a matter of hard work, luck has nothing to do with it	
(a) It is unwise to plan far ahead as many things are a matter of good or bad luck (b) When I make plans I am almost certain that I can make them work	
(a) Most people don't realize the extent to which their lives are controlled by accidental happenings (b) There really is no such thing as luck	
(a) In the long run bad things that happen to us are balanced by the good things (b) Most misfortunes are the result of lack of ability, ignorance, laziness or all three	
(a) Sometimes I can't understand how teachers arrive at the grades they give (b) There is a direct connection between how hard I study and the grades I get	
(a) Many times I feel that I have little influence over the things that happen to me (b) It's impossible for me to believe chance/luck plays an important role in my life	
Add up all of the As (1 point) and Bs (2 points) – then subtract 10 points. A high score (>6) indicates an external locus while a low score (<5) an internal locus of control.	

If a person generally believes that they are in control of their destiny, they are more likely to exhibit great effort to achieve high performance. Those with an internal locus of control tend to be self-motivated and need less external approval and reward; they are more likely to make their own decisions (seeking out autonomy etc.). Those with a higher external locus of control respond more readily to external praise; they may feel unable to influence organizational decision-making regardless of their actual feelings about the issue being discussed; such people are more likely to look to others for what is appropriate.

2. How to motivate others in the work-place

Diagnosis may help identify a need to modify employee behaviour through motivational techniques and interventions. When intervening, it is important to understand the preferences of ourselves as managers and the employees for which we may be responsible. Others may not be motivated by the same factors as us and so methods need to be carefully selected with the individual in mind. Motivational methods include:

LOWER ORDER NEEDS e.g. **PAYMENT METHODS**
Managers may motivate using a variety of payment methods:

~ Time rate: pay for the number of hours worked
~ Overtime: pay extra for working beyond normal hours
~ Piece rate: pay for the number of items produced
~ Commission: staff paid for the number of items sold
~ Performance related pay: pay a bonus for meeting targets
~ Profit sharing: pay a part of any profits made by the business
~ Salary: pay monthly no matter how many hours are worked
~ Fringe benefits: payments in kind, e.g. a company car

CHANGING BEHAVIOUR: **Contingent rewards** are concerned with specific desirable behaviours. A manager may identify a set of desirable behaviours to develop. The behaviours will be monitored and then rewarded if observed. For example, a manager may want to motivate attendance and reward reduced absenteeism.

HIGHER ORDER NEEDS: **NON-PAY METHODS**

Managers can motivate using factors other than pay through:

~ Job rotation: rotate worker through diverse tasks – reduce boredom
~ Job enlargement: extend the range of job duties/ responsibilities
~ Job enrichment: provide more interesting and challenging tasks
~ Empowerment: share information and power with employees
~ Autonomous teams: create empowered groups
~ Goal setting: SMART goals, 'owned' by the employee

JOB CHARACTERISTICS MODEL (JCM): Managers can motivate employees who are focused on higher order needs by making work interesting. The JCM, designed by Hackman and Oldham attempts to use job design (see Section 9) to improve employee motivation. They show that any job can be described in terms of five key job characteristics:

1. **Skill Variety** – number of skills required to perform the job.
2. **Task Identity** – how meaningful the job is in relation to others.
3. **Task Significance** – perceived importance of the job.
4. **Autonomy** – degree of freedom/discretion in doing the job.
5. **Task Feedback** – extent of clear, specific, detailed, actionable information about the effectiveness of his or her job performance.

The core dimensions listed above can be combined into a single predictive index, called the Motivating Potential Score (MPS), calculated, as follows:

$$MPS = \frac{\text{Skill Variety} + \text{Task Identity} + \text{Task Significance}}{2} \times \text{Autonomy} \times \text{Feedback}$$

Jobs that are high in motivating potential must be high on at least one of the three factors that lead to experienced meaningfulness, and also must be high on both Autonomy and Feedback. If a job has a high MPS, the job characteristics model predicts that motivation, performance and job satisfaction will be positively affected and the likelihood of negative outcomes, such as absenteeism and turnover, will be reduced.

EMPLOYEE ENGAGEMENT

Employers want employees who are motivated and committed, who identify with their organization – engaged employees – because they deliver improved business performance. To create an engaging workplace:

~ Allocate responsibilities for engagement
~ Communicate a clear vision, mission and goals
~ Don't micro-manage. Give employees a degree of discretion
~ Managers should be visible leading by example
~ Create opportunities to work on challenging projects
~ Encourage participation (involvement), sharing ideas and concerns
~ Encourage and reward initiative and new ideas
~ Involve People in the planning
~ Allow employees autonomy and empower
~ Provide CSR opportunities
~ Make employees feel appreciated
~ Measure employee performance
~ Demonstrate personal interest and care about employees
~ Communicate and celebrate successes
~ Personally thank staff (feedback timely and specific)

Section Four
Theories of
Leadership and
Group Behaviour

CHAPTER 6
LEADERSHIP – THEORY AND PRACTICE

Key Concepts

- Appointed leader
- Charismatic leadership
- Contingency theory of leadership
- Functional leader
- Leadership
- Power
- Principle-centred leadership
- Situational leadership
- Traits approach to leadership

Learning Outcomes Having read this chapter, you should be able to:

- review the main theories of leadership
- discuss alternative styles of leadership
- compare various types of leader
- contrast the leader and manager roles.

1.   In this chapter we continue with the question of what is meant by the term management? In Section 2 we focused on efficiency, whereas we now focus on effectiveness. Every manager and business leader must consider, as a matter of routine, the attainment of organizational goals and superior performance. This presents issues of effectiveness (strategy/goals) and efficiency (the use of resources). Whereas the internal environment may dominate when the focus is on efficiency, the external environment comes to the fore when considering effectiveness. This chapter explores the concepts of leadership (and management) and will focus on leaders' use of power to influence and persuade followers (employees in most cases) to act in ways which help the organization attain its goals. Chapter 6 describes a number of different ways of looking at the concept of leadership, discusses the tensions between concern for the task (Chapters 2/3) and concern for people (Chapters 4/5), and summarizes a number of important theories of leadership. Leadership is a concept which has fascinated humankind for centuries, but only in recent years has theory of leadership emerged. A review of the main theories of leadership is followed by a discussion of the alternative styles of leadership available in practice, to a person in a management or supervisory position.

6.1 WHAT IS LEADERSHIP?

Vignette

What type of leaders are the people listed below – how do they differ?

Heir to the throne, Prince Charles

Virgin Group founder, Richard Branson

US President, Barak Obama

Governor of the Bank of England, Mark Carney

German Chancellor, Angela Merkel

Head of the British Armed Forces, General Sir Nick Houghton

2.   Before defining 'leadership', it would be appropriate to reflect briefly on the various types of leader identified, and to consider some of the practical difficulties arising from the different types of leader. The most important types of leader are as follows:

CHARISMATIC – gains influence mainly from strength of personality, e.g. Mandela, Obama, Branson, and others. The difficulty with **charismatic leadership** is that few people possess the exceptional qualities required to transform all around them into willing followers! Another issue is that personal qualities or traits of leadership cannot be acquired by training; they can only be modified by it.

TRADITIONAL – position is assured by birth, e.g. kings, queens and tribal chieftains. This is another category to which few people can aspire. Except in the small family business, there are few opportunities for traditional leadership at work.

SITUATIONAL – this is an approach to leadership which argues there is no one correct way to lead for all situations and leaders need to adjust their style according to the situation they are in.

APPOINTED – influence arises directly out of position, e.g. most managers and supervisors. This is the bureaucratic type of leadership, where legitimate power arises from the nature and scope of the position within the hierarchy. The problem here is that, although the powers of the position may be defined, the job holder may be unable to implement this power because of weak personality, lack of adequate training, or other factors.

FUNCTIONAL – when leadership varies with the task, rather than the person. In other words, functional leaders adapt their behaviour to meet the competing needs of the situation. This particular leadership type will be examined more closely later in the chapter.

PRINCIPLE-CENTRED – whose approach to leadership is influenced by moral and ethical principles, involving considerations of equity, justice, integrity, honesty, fairness and trust.

3.   Leadership, then, is something more than just an aspect of personality, tradition, opportunism or appointment. It is intimately connected with actual behaviour and attitudes towards oneself and others. The way in which the leadership is carried out is influenced strongly by cultural factors (see Chapter 14), and this is an important consideration for senior management given the extent of globalization in many industries. For present purposes, we can define 'leadership' as the process of influencing others to understand and agree about what needs to be done and how to do it, and the process of facilitating individual and collective efforts to accomplish shared objectives. Leadership is a dynamic process and there is no 'one best way' of leading – leadership is essentially about striking the right balance between the needs of people, task and goals in a given situation.

FIGURE 6.1 **The key leadership variables**

4. The main variables in the leadership process can be illustrated as shown in Figure 6.1.

The critical variable in the above is the leadership role. Using his or her skills and knowledge, drawing on personal qualities and adhering to principles of integrity and trust, a leader has to make the best of the other three variables. Perhaps all three might be favourable at a particular time, but the likelihood is that one or other of task, group members and situation will be problematic, and thus the leader will be challenged. The task facing the leader and the group may be complex, and there will always be the need to consider individual goals or targets within the overall objective. The group members themselves may not always have the best blend of knowledge and skills, and they may need motivating to achieve the overall objective (see previous chapters). There will always be issues of group morale to be considered, as well as the needs of individuals. Finally, the situation or environment (both internal and external) are important. The interactions within the group (see next chapter) and with the leader are major factors affecting outcomes. Cultural traditions may need to be considered where the group is not homogeneous. There will always be external pressures of one kind or another that might not be favourable to group progress, and there may be problems with insufficient resources to support the group in its efforts. Finally, we should not forget the emotional sides of leadership. As suggested by McGovern (2014), your job as a leader is 'to tap into the power of that higher purpose – and you can't do it by retreating to the analytical. If you want to lead, have the courage to do it from the heart'. At this point we might ask what, if any, is the difference between leadership and management?

6.2 LEADERSHIP AND MANAGEMENT

5. In the preceding chapters we have explored theories of management and asked what is meant by the term management. We drew on the work of Fayol and others to help us define what is meant by managing (planning, organizing, motivating and controlling). We have also outlined ideas of power and authority (as separate concepts); we noted an emphasis on efficiency (scientific management) and discussed types of authority through Weber's idea of bureaucracy (Chapter 3). This chapter builds upon previous chapters, with a discussion regarding what is meant by the terms leader and manager, continuing with the theme of what leaders and managers are required to do. Leadership has been defined in terms of traits (**traits approach**), behaviours, influence, interaction patterns, role relationships and occupation of organizational positions. Most definitions of leadership infer a process whereby one person influences another. In the case of organizational leadership, people are influenced to do what is beneficial for the organization. Gary Yukl, a leading American researcher with interest in leadership, power and influence and motivation, defines leadership as the process of influencing others to understand and agree about what needs to be done and how to do it, and the process of facilitating individual and collective efforts to accomplish shared objectives. Typically associated with the concept of influence is motivation, discussed in the previous two

23. Bales' ideas have been adapted by a number of British researchers, notably Rackham and Morgan (1977), who have used their version as the basis for improving skills in interpersonal relationships and for interaction process analysis. Their list utilizes the following categories of possible behaviour in groups:

- proposing (concepts, suggestions, actions)

- building (developing another's proposal)

- supporting (another person or their concepts)

- disagreeing

- defending/attacking

- blocking/difficulty stating (with no alternative offered)

- open behaviour (risking ridicule and loss of status)

- testing understanding

- summarizing

- seeking information

- giving information

- shutting out behaviour (e.g. interrupting, talking over)

- bringing in behaviour (involving another member).

Experience in the use of such categories can enable observers of group behaviour to give constructive and relevant feedback to group members, instead of rather generalized or anecdotal descriptions of what has appeared to have taken place.

24. Categories of behaviour are a key element in distinguishing roles in groups. Feedback to groups can help members see what kind of role they played in the proceedings. Role is not quite the same as position (or job). The latter is concerned with the duties and rights attached to a particular job title. The former is concerned with how the job is performed, and is affected by the expectations of superiors, of organizational policies, of colleagues and subordinates as well as the expectations of the job holder himself or herself. This web of relationships has been called the role-set.

25. In any group activity a number of roles are likely to be performed – for example, the roles of 'leader', 'peacemaker', 'ideas person', 'humourist' and 'devil's advocate' to name but a few. In informal groups roles may emerge in line with individual personality and know-how. In formal groups many roles are already defined, such as Chairman, Secretary, Visiting Expert and others. Sometimes members of a group experience a conflict of roles. For example, a union representative may feel a conflict between his or her need to fulfil a spokesman role for constituents, and the need to act responsibly as an employee of the company.

26. The items discussed here are essentially about actual behaviour in a group. This behaviour is part of a dynamic or constantly changing process within the group, which can be influenced by individuals in response to issues that have occurred during task undertaking. Thus, even where the immediate constraints impose tight restrictions on behaviour, the group can still be effective if individuals are motivated to work together to achieve their objectives.

7.5 COMPETITION AND CONFLICT BETWEEN GROUPS

27. So far we have been discussing behaviour within groups. Another important aspect of group behaviour is inter group relations and the impact of the group on the individual. Since every organization is made up of a number of different groups (e.g. IT, Marketing, Operations) of employees, the question of collaboration between groups is vital for obtaining an overall balance in the social system. As Lawrence and Lorsch were at pains to point out, integration is as crucial to organizational success as differentiation. Breaking an organization down into smaller units (workgroups), in order to cope adequately with the diversity of

tasks faced, creates opportunities to develop task interests and special know-how, but, at the same time, it also fragments the organization, creating rivalries and competing interests which can be damaging to the organization's mission. An understanding of both the good and bad consequences of intergroup competition can therefore be of considerable help to an organization's management.

28. The first systematic study of intergroup competition was made many years ago by Sherif and colleagues in the USA. They organized a boys' camp in such a way that two deliberately created groups were formed for the experiment. Various devices were used to encourage the development of separate identities between the two groups. As the camp progressed, a number of interesting changes took place both within and between the groups. WITHIN GROUPS – Collections of individuals, with no special ties with each other, grew into closely knit groups; the group climate changed from being play-oriented to work-oriented, and leadership tended to become more autocratic; each group became more highly structured and placed a much greater emphasis on loyalty and conformity. BETWEEN GROUPS – Each group began to see the other group as 'the enemy', hostility between groups increased whilst communication between them decreased; stereotyped opinions of the other side began to emerge, especially negative stereotypes.

29. Conflict between groups and their members and employee behaviour can be explained, to some extent, by Social Identity Theory (SIT). Belonging to groups (both socially and at work) affects the way we think about and see ourselves (whom we are) and the way others think about and see us. Such thinking impacts upon behaviour, the way we behave and the way others behave in relation to ourselves and the groups to which we may belong. The way we view ourselves is determined in part by the groups to which we belong (social identity). Thus, social identity defines the person and appropriate behaviours for that person. This typically happens through social comparison – individuals not only compare themselves with other individuals with whom they interact, but they also compare their own group with similar, but distinct, out-groups. We all see ourselves as members of various social groupings, which are distinguishable and hence different from other social groupings. According to SIT, people tend to classify themselves and others into various social categories, such as organizational membership, religious affiliation, gender and age cohort. As these examples suggest, people may be classified in various categories, and different individuals may utilize different categorization schemas. Categories are defined by typical characteristics abstracted from the members.

30. The consequence is that by identifying with certain groupings but not others, we come to see the world in terms of 'us and them'. Whilst group membership may have its benefits (self-esteem, privilege) it can also be a source of conflict and may, through generalizations and stereotypes, determine inappropriate behavioural responses. The group can impact upon (1) perceptions of individual members (2) individual performance (3) individual behaviour and (4) individual attitudes.

31. In social identity theory, a social identity is a person's knowledge that he or she belongs to a social category or group. A social group is a set of individuals who hold a common social identification or view themselves as members of the same social category. Through a social comparison process, persons who are similar to themselves are categorized with the self and are labelled the in-group; persons who differ from them are categorized as the out-group. The consequence of the social comparison process is people come to see themselves as members of one group/category (the in-group) in comparison with another (the out-group), and the consequences of this categorization include conflict and prejudice.

32. SIT suggests that much inter group conflict stems from the very fact that groups exist. More specifically, in SIT it is argued that (a) given the relational and comparative nature of social identifications, social identities are maintained primarily by inter group comparisons and (b) given the desire to enhance self-esteem; groups seek positive differences between themselves and reference groups. This suggests groups have a vested interest in perceiving or even provoking greater differentiation than exists and disapproving of the reference (out-) group on this basis. Difference can determine the ability of people to work effectively and efficiently together in pursuit of common goals.

33. Inter group competition, as was noted above, has its advantages and disadvantages. The prime advantages are that a group develops a high level of cohesiveness and a high regard for its task functions. The main disadvantages are that groups develop competing or conflicting goals and that inter group communication and cooperation breaks down. Since the Sherif study, several researchers have followed up with studies of conflict resolution between groups. The general conclusions are that to reduce the negative side-effects of inter group competition, an organization would need to: encourage and reward groups on the basis of their contribution to the organization as a whole, or at least, to large parts of it, rather than on individual group

results; stimulate high interaction and communication between groups, and provide rewards for inter-group collaboration; encourage movement of staff across group boundaries for the purposes of increasing mutual understanding of problems; and avoid putting neighbouring groups into a situation where they are competing on a win–lose basis for resources or status, for example.

34. Not all conflict is harmful. On the contrary, disagreement is an essential element in working through problems and overcoming difficulties. The conflict of ideas when put to the service of organization or group goals is in fact the sign of a healthy organization. What is to be avoided is the point-scoring conflict that develops between groups who see their relative success and status vis-a-vis their neighbours as being more important than the pursuit of the common good.

7.6 TEAMS, TEAM-BUILDING AND VIRTUAL TEAMS

35. A team implies a small, cohesive group that works effectively as a single unit through being focused on a common task. What, then, are the characteristics of effective teamwork? Research suggests they are as follows:

- clear objectives and agreed goals

- openness and confrontation

- support and trust

- cooperation and conflict

- sound procedures

- appropriate leadership

- regular review

- individual development

- sound intergroup relations.

36. Long-term research into management team skills has been carried out by Dr Meredith Belbin and colleagues. The result, after studying numerous teams at Henley Management College, showed that team behaviour fell into one or more of eight fairly distinct **team roles**, as follows:

- Chairman – An individual who can control and coordinate the other team members, who recognizes their talents but is not threatened by them, and who is concerned with what is feasible rather than what is exciting or imaginative.

- Shaper – This is another leader role, but one in which the role holder acts much more directly to shape the decisions and thinking of the team.

- Innovator – This type of person provides the creative thinking in a team, even if a concern for good ideas overshadows his ability to be sensitive to other people's needs.

- Monitor/Evaluator – The strength of this role lies in the holder's ability to analyze issues and suggestions objectively.

- Company Worker – Whilst the first four roles provide the major inspiration and leadership, this role provides for implementation of ideas by the role holders' ability to translate general ideas and plans into practice.

- Team Worker – This role meets the needs of the team for cohesiveness and collaboration, for role holders tend to be perceptive of people's needs and adept at supporting individuals.

- Resource Investigator – A person in this role looks for resources and ideas outside the team with the aim of supporting the team's efforts.

- Completer – This is an individual whose energies are directed primarily to the completion of the task, and who harnesses anxiety and concern towards getting the job done on time and to a high standard.

37. Individuals are likely to be predisposed (an individual's behavioural tendency in a team environment) to behaving in one or two predominant roles, even though they may show tendencies towards others. The dominant role is closely linked to particular reasoning abilities and personality characteristics, but is also affected by the priorities and processes of a manager's job. An effective team is one that is likely to have a range of roles present in its make-up. Belbin concluded that the ideal team would be composed of one Chairman (or one Shaper), one Innovator, one Monitor Evaluator and one or more Company Workers, Team Workers, Resource Investigators or Completers. Since ideal conditions are rarely present, managers have to build their teams from the people they have and encourage a greater degree of role flexibility. However, a manager can benefit from understanding the distinctions between the roles and making an assessment of the role strengths of his own staff. Knowing what to expect as well as what not to expect from colleagues enables the manager to avoid potential tensions or even group breakdown.

38. There are many types of group within the organization such as the functional, cross-functional, self-managed, task force, virtual and executive team. They vary in size and degrees and interdependence and consequently their need for communication, coordination, control and leadership. Each can vary in relation to degrees of autonomy, authority, diversity of membership, stability of membership and the duration of existence.

39. Globalization, increased competition and improvements in communication technologies have driven many organizations to rely upon virtual teams – a team that uses mainly electronic interaction in order to achieve objectives without the need to function as a team in the traditional sense of the term.

40. A further team type is now more common as a result of globalization – the multicultural team. As organizations globalize their operations the frequency with which employees will interact with people from different countries will increase. Further, domestic populations are becoming more diverse, suggesting that domestic organizations will also need to learn how to manage more heterogeneous workgroups than they have managed previously. Kelly (2009) warns us that diversity appears to be a double-edged sword, increasing the opportunity for creativity as well as the likelihood that group members will be dissatisfied and fail to identify with the group. A group that is diverse could be expected to have members who may have had significantly different experiences and, therefore, significantly different perspectives on key issues or problems. However, such differences can create serious coordination and communication difficulties for groups. He advises that we allocate more time to allow diverse groups to become cohesive.

CONCLUSION

41. In this chapter we recognized the important role of groups in helping organizations attain their goals but argued that not all groups are effective; they need to work at developing cooperative structures. Stages of development, group structures and dynamics were considered alongside tools to classify certain types of group behaviour and the roles group members may adopt. Aside from considering within-group issues we also considered the challenges associated with inter group working. We closed with a discussion about teams, recognizing there to be many types of team. More recently, as a result of social and technological forces, organizations have given increased attention and made greater use of virtual and multicultural teams.

QUESTIONS

1 How are group norms established, and why are they sometimes in conflict with the norms of the organization as a whole?

2 What are the implications of Belbin's research for team development or team building?

3 List the factors influencing effective teamwork. Take four of the factors and write a short paragraph on each.

4 Define what is meant by the term 'a group' and with reference to at least one stage model, describe how groups develop.

5 Compare and contrast effective and ineffective groups – what makes a group effective?

USEFUL WEBSITES

Belbin Associates: **www.belbin.com** Brief outline of Belbin Team Role Theory

Management Library: **managementhelp.org/grp_skll/teams/ teams.htm** Team Building

REFERENCES

Kelly, P.P. (2008) 'Achieving desirable group-work outcomes through the group allocation process', *Team Performance Management*, 14(1/2): 22–38.

Kelly, P.P. (2009) *International Business and Management*, Cengage Learning EMEA.

McGregor, D.M. (1960) *The Human Side of Enterprise*, McGraw-Hill, New York.

Rackham, N. and Morgan,T. (1977) *Behaviour Analysis in Training*, McGraw Hill.

Tuckman, B.W. (1965) 'Developmental Sequence in Small Groups', *Psychological Bulletin*, 63(6): 384–399.

Tuckman, B.W. and Jensen, A. (1977) 'Stages of Small-Group Development Revisited', *Group and Organization Studies*, 2(4): 419–427.

SKILL SHEET 3   **Working in Groups**

Use the sheet in conjunction with Chapters 6 and 7 and case sheet 3.

1. FORMING A GROUP

Group allocation (initial formation stage) refers to the process of selecting group or team members and assigning them to a specific group. Members can be allocated to groups (1) randomly (unbiased but may not create a good structure) (2) by self-selection (subjective, people choose who they like – not necessarily someone they can work with productively – less likely to result in a diverse team but may have high levels of social cohesion) (3) manager selection (more objective but less likely to start socially cohesive) and (4) or a hybrid approach (mix pairs: members pair up with the person they want to work with; manager adds pairs).

2. GROUP STRUCTURE

ATTITUDES: How well do you work with others – do you need to work on your interpersonal skills – is your attitude to teamwork likely to be a barrier?

Quick crude test to get you thinking – (Score: 1 point for column 1, 2 points for column 2 and so on. Add up the points. There may be a need for you to develop your skills if the score is < 15)	Usually	Quite Often	Sometimes	Seldom	Almost Never
I find it quite difficult to connect and interact with other people I have not met before					
I tend to get into arguments if people don't see my point of view					
I feel uncomfortable in social or group work situations					
I tend to focus more on what a person is saying than their non-verbal signals					
I find it almost impossible not to interrupt if something someone says triggers a really good idea					

ROLES: Complete the Belbin Self-Perception Inventory:
http://www.belbin.com/rte.asp?id=400

The personal skill inventory identifies eight team roles and your preference(s). Use this to evaluate groups and their structure.

3. GETTING STARTED

At the first meeting discuss members' knowledge, skills and abilities relevant to the project. Create goals and objectives.

GOALS AND SMART OBJECTIVES: Shared goals can unify and motivate. Goals should be outcome-oriented and developed by the team to ensure buy-in and ownership. Objectives are the steps (sub-goals) to achieve the goal(s). Objectives should be SMART: Specific (significant, stretching but simply worded – Who is involved?), Measurable (motivational and manageable), Attainable (appropriate, agreed, assignable and actionable), Relevant (goals that matter) and Time-bound (specify by when it will be achieved). Objectives should be allocated and monitored.

CONTRACT (FORMALIZING STRUCTURAL ARRANGEMENTS): whereas few work groups will have a written contract, the student group may benefit from the formulation of one. The contract provides an opportunity for a group to specify contact information, preferred methods of communication, action plans, meeting schedules, goals, and consequences of actions (or inactions) of group members. Action Plans: Present your group's 'plan of attack' for completing the project/assignment. In essence, address how you will split the workload.

MEETINGS: Effective meetings achieve the meeting's objective, take up a minimum amount of time and leave members feeling satisfied. Consider what you want to achieve. Do you want a decision, to generate ideas, are you getting status reports or communicating something or are you making plans? Create an agenda considering the following factors: Priorities – what must be covered? What needs to be accomplished at the meeting? Who needs to attend the meeting? In what order should topics be covered? Where and when will the meeting take place?

4. GROUP DEVELOPMENT

	Almost Never – 1	Seldom – 2	Occasionally – 3	Frequently – 4	Almost Always 5
STAGES: This questionnaire is to help you assess at what stage your team normally operates. It is based on the 'Tuckman' model of Forming, Storming, Norming and Performing. Instructions: Next to each question, indicate how often your team displays each behaviour by ticking the appropriate column. You should complete the questionnaire independently – then discuss.					
1 We have agreed procedures to ensure that things run smoothly					
2 We are quick to get on with the task in hand and do not spend too much time planning					
3 Our team feels that we are all in it together and share responsibility for success or failure					
4 We have comprehensive procedures for agreeing our objectives and planning the way we will perform tasks					
5 Team members are afraid or do not like to ask others for help					
6 We take our team's goals and objectives literally, and assume a shared understanding					
7 The leader tries to keep order and contributes to the task at hand					
8 We do not have fixed procedures; we make them up as we go					
9 We generate lots of ideas, but we do not use many because we fail to consider them, rejecting without fully understanding them					
10 Team members do not fully trust other members and closely monitor those working on a specific task					
11 The team leader ensures that we follow the procedures, do not argue, do not interrupt, and keep to the point					
12 We enjoy working together; we have a fun and productive time					
13 We have accepted each other as members of the team					
14 The team leader is democratic and collaborative					
15 We are trying to define our goal and tasks that need to be done					
16 Many of the team members have their own ideas about the process and personal agendas are widespread					
17 We accept each other's strengths and weaknesses fully					
18 We assign specific roles to team members (team leader, facilitator, timekeeper, note taker, etc.)					
19 We try to achieve harmony by avoiding conflict					
20 The tasks are very different from what we imagined and seem very difficult to achieve					
21 There are many abstract discussions of the concepts and issues, which make some members impatient with these discussions					
22 We are able to work through group problems					
23 We argue a lot even though we agree on the real issues					
24 We are often tempted to go above the original project scope					
25 We express criticism of others constructively					
26 There is a close attachment to the team					
27 It seems as if little is being accomplished with the project's goals					
28 The goals we have established seem unrealistic					
29 Although we are not fully sure of the project's goals and issues, we are excited and proud to be on the team					
30 We often share personal problems with each other					

| 31 There is a lot of resisting of the tasks we need to do | | | | | | |
| 32 We get a lot of work done | | | | | | |

SCORING: Next to each survey item number below, transfer the score that you give that item on the above questionnaire. For example, if you scored item (1) with a 3 (Occasionally), then enter a 3 next to item one below. When you have entered all the scores for each question, total each of the four columns.

Item	Score	Item	Score	Item	Score	Item	Score
1		2		4		3	
5		7		6		8	
10		9		11		12	
15		16		13		14	
18		20		19		17	
21		23		24		22	
27		28		25		26	
29		31		30		32	
Total							
Stage	Forming	Storming		Norming		Performing	

The highest of the four scores indicates the stage of your team. If your highest score is ≥ 32, it is a strong indicator of the stage of your team. If your lowest score is <16, it is a strong indicator that your team is not in this stage. If two of the scores are almost the same, you are probably going through a transition phase, except: If you score highly in both the Forming and Storming phases then you are in the Storming Phase; If you score highly in both the Norming and Performing Phases then you are in the Performing Stage; If there is only a small difference between three or four scores, then this indicates that you have no clear perception of the way your team operates; performance is highly variable, or that you are in the storming phase.

OBSERVING GROUP BEHAVIOUR: Periodically, the group should stop its task work and discuss the way in which the group is functioning. Members can improve the way the group works by reflecting on how they work together. Nominate one group member to be a Participant observer – A person who is skilled enough to both participate in group work and observe the group process at the same time. The Participant observer should observe the group and place a tick in the relevant member's column each time a particular behaviour is observed (see table). List group members and nominate as A, B, C, etc.

Less participation					
Seeking information					
Giving information					
Disagreeing/criticizing					
Supportive					
Summarizing					
Clarifying					
Talking over others					
Taking on roles, e.g. time-keeper					
Other behaviours					

At the end of the meeting the observer delivers a summary of observations as group feedback. The group should discuss the feedback and consider any action.

	A	B	C	D	E
Taking initiative					
Drawing in others					
Main participator					

5. PERFORMING: Group problem-solving tools

Conventional group problem-solving can often be undermined by unhelpful group behaviour. Consider using the following tools: BRAINSTORMING: Brainstorming is used to harness group effort and create ideas. Brainstorming steps:

1. When everyone is gathered, appoint one person to record the ideas that derive from the session.
2. Clearly define the problem you wish to solve, and lay out any criteria that you must meet.
3. Give people plenty of quiet time at the start of the session to write down their own ideas. Then, ask them to share their ideas, whilst giving everyone a fair opportunity to contribute. Do not evaluate ideas yet. With Round-robin Brainstorming, people contribute ideas in turn – gets people to contribute without being influenced by others.
4. Once everyone has shared their ideas, start a group discussion to develop ideas, and use them to create new ideas. Building on the ideas of others is one of the most valuable aspects of group brainstorming.
5. Group similar ideas into themes; rank and select ideas.

6. TEAM BUILDING

Guidelines for effective teamworking:

~ Establish clear group goals and gain commitment; ensure that all members understand and accept the objectives
~ Distribute leadership and power and encourage broad participation
~ Select members with appropriate skills, knowledge, and, if possible, a mix of preferred team roles and types
~ Pay attention to both task and process
~ Accept that feelings may run high during early storming, and when working in a mixed group
~ Value all contributions
~ Review both task progress and group process at regular intervals
~ Explore the reasons for disagreements and conflict – encourage constructive feedback and critical thinking; ensure members face conflict rather than avoid it

7. MANAGING CONFLICT (procedural steps)

1) Issue Identification: what are the issues underlying the conflict? Parties should share their perceptions and feelings of the issue and their own position. Attempt to identify the causes of the conflict. Arrive at a mutual understanding of the issues before moving on to the next step.
2) Envision what the future would be like if the conflict were resolved.
3) Generate a wide variety of possible solutions. Do not evaluate ideas at this stage. Use brainstorming or a similar technique to generate ideas.
4) Evaluate and select the preferred option for implementation.

8. MANAGING LOAFERS AND DIFFICULT MEMBERS

SOCIAL LOAFING SCALE The inclination for individuals to apply less effort when working as part of a group, i.e. to let others do the work 15–20 = Loafer; > 20 a significant loafer	Almost Never – 1	Seldom – 2	Occasionally – 3	Frequently – 4	Almost Always 5
Defers to others responsibilities he/she should assume					
Puts less effort in when others are around to do the work					
Doesn't do a fair share of the work					
Absent from or significantly late to group meetings					
Uses less effort compared with when he/she works alone					

If any group member scores a '4' in any column then the group should discuss how to deal with them; consider:

~ Using constructive confrontation – discuss group goals and the loafing behaviour
~ Using an independent facilitator/observer
~ Giving them a chance to explain and correct their behaviour
~ If they do not change then consider expelling them from the group

Section Five
Systems and Contingency Approaches to Management Theory

CHAPTER 8
ORGANIZATIONS AS SYSTEMS

Key Concepts

- Socio-technical system
- System
- Systems approach
- Systems thinking

Learning Outcomes   Having read this chapter, you should be able to:

- review the role of systems theory in understanding organizations
- list the main characteristics of open systems
- explain what is meant by the term cybernetic system
- identify the key variables considered in the systems approach to organizations
- list four types of environment
- discuss the five sub-systems at work in organizations.

Vignette

SAMSUNG MISSES FORECAST AS SMARTPHONE WORRIES DEEPEN

In 2013 Samsung's performance fell below expectations as growth in sales of its best seller Galaxy phone began to fall and new rivals emerged to 'eat away' at its market share. The Galaxy propelled the South Korean firm into the top rank of smartphone makers in 2012, overtaking Apple Inc. Samsung, like other significant world players, face the challenge of shrinking margins, in an industry where companies 'live and die by their ability to stay ahead of the innovation curve'. The company is expected to launch wearable devices to complement its smartphone business. One approach to uncertainty in the wider environment, adopted by Samsung and many large companies, is to diversify. 'Samsung's got diversified businesses. When one business lags, it's got others outperforming and propping up the overall profit,' said a Fund Manager. The company has been spending heavily on marketing and R&D (research and development), and recently invested greatly in distribution channels, including opening brand shops.

1.   The dominance firstly of the Classical School, followed secondly by the Human Relations/Social Psychological Schools, has been overtaken by a more comprehensive approach to the study of management in organizations. This more recent approach views the organization as a system of interrelated sets of activities which enable **inputs** to be transformed into **outputs**. This view attempts to bring together the Classical and Human Relations approach.

2.   A **systems approach** is a management approach whereby attention is focused on the total work of the organization and the interrelationships of structure and behaviour and the range of variables within the organization. The organization is viewed within its total environment and the importance of multiple channels in interaction emphasized.

3.   This approach, which is described in more detail below, enables theorists to study key elements of organization in terms of their interaction with one another and, importantly, with their external environment. Whereas, in the past, the explanations were in terms of structures OR people, now it is possible to identify theories which seek to explain or predict organizational behaviour in a multi-dimensional way, by studying people, structure, technology and environment at one and the same time. Review the opening vignette. Samsung is an organization which can be described in terms of its people structure, technology and environment. It is evident that the success of the organization is dependent upon its ability to meet the needs of the consumers within the volatile environment in which it operates.

8.1 SYSTEMS THEORY

4.   Defined at its simplest, a system is a collection of interrelated parts which form some whole – like the human body. Systems may be 'closed' or 'open'. Closed systems are those which, for all practical purposes, are completely self-supporting and thus do not interact with their environment. An example would be an astronaut's life-support pack. Open systems are those which do interact with their environment, upon which they rely for obtaining essential inputs and for the discharge of their system outputs. Social systems (e.g. organizations) are always open systems. A basic model of an open system is shown diagrammatically in Figure 8.1.

FIGURE 8.1 Basic model of an open system

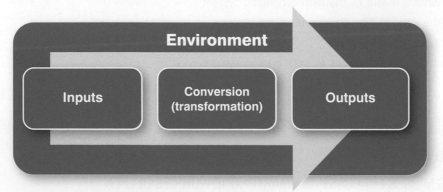

5.   Samsung is a system – a collection of interrelated parts which form the whole organization. Parts identified in the case include marketing, R&D and the distribution channel. We may also add manufacturing, warehousing, sales, accounts, etc. as other parts. Operating in their environment they must source raw materials for manufacture (inputs) and create outputs – products like the smartphone for which consumers are willing to pay.

6.   The three major characteristics of open systems are as follows:

- they receive inputs or energy from their environment

- they convert these inputs into outputs

- they discharge their outputs into their environment.

In relation to an organization (like Samsung), the inputs include people, materials, information and finance. These inputs are organized and activated to convert human skills and raw materials into products, services and other outputs which are discharged into the environment, as shown in Figure 8.2. Note that some scholars discuss inputs solely in terms of the raw materials required for the product/service whilst others include the inputs used to make the product or service (see transformational resources – people, processes, knowledge, technology, etc.).

FIGURE 8.2 The organization as an open system

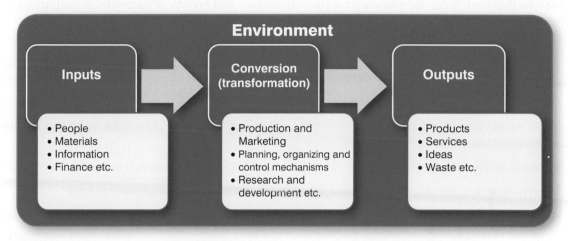

7.   A key feature of open systems is their interdependence on the environment, which may be relatively stable or relatively uncertain (like the smartphone industry) at a particular point in time. This feature is of considerable importance to business enterprises which need to adapt to the changing fortunes of the market-place if they are to flourish. A classification of environments is provided later in the chapter.

8.   Most systems can be divided into **sub-systems**. For example, the human body – a total system – encloses a number of major sub-systems, such as the central nervous system and the cardiovascular system, to name but two. Organizations have their sub-systems as well, e.g. production, marketing and accounting sub-systems. The boundaries between sub-systems are called interfaces. These are the sensitive internal boundaries contained within the total system, and they will again be referred to shortly. In the meantime it is important to consider a few points about system boundaries. Organizational boundaries are defined as much by corporate strategy as by actual fact. The boundaries of an organization are not visible, since the boundaries of a social system are based upon relationships. Thus, whilst certain factual elements such as physical location do have some impact upon an organization's boundaries, it is the results of management decisions, i.e. choices, that really determine where the organization ends and the environment begins. Similarly, whilst the physical presence of machinery, for example, may determine in part some of the internal boundaries of the organization, it is ultimately a matter of corporate or departmental strategy which decides where the production system begins and where it ends.

9.   In any organization, some employees work consistently at the external boundary. These are the people who have to deal with the inputs and the outputs to the system, e.g. those responsible for raising capital, purchasing from suppliers, identifying customer requirements, for example, and those responsible for sales, distribution, etc. Other employees work consistently on internal boundaries, i.e. at the interfaces between the various sub-systems of the organization. These people may be responsible for the provision of services to others in the organization, e.g. management accountants, HR professionals, facilities managers, etc. They may be responsible for integrating activities, e.g. managers and supervisors. In fact, it is becoming increasingly recognized that 'boundary management' is of vital importance to the effectiveness of those in managerial and supervisory roles. Boundary management in this context means establishing and maintaining effective relationships with colleagues working in neighbouring sub-systems (in strategic aspects of management, Michael Porter refers to these as 'linkages' – see Chapter 10).

10. Whilst organizations are open social systems, taken as a whole, their sub-systems may be either open or closed. Production sub-systems and accounting sub-systems tend to be closed systems, i.e. they are relatively self-contained and are affected in ways which are usually predictable. Marketing and R&D activities tend, on the other hand, to work best in open systems, i.e. where they can be aware of, and adapt to, key influences in the external environment. In the main, closed systems are required for stability and consistency, whereas open systems are required for unstable and uncertain conditions. Closed systems are designed for efficiency (Section 2), open systems for survival. The early Classical theorists were expounding a closed systems approach. Developments in Human Relations, by contrast, were biased towards open systems. The modern consensus appears to be that both types are necessary for the maintenance and growth of successful organizations.

11. The common characteristics of open systems are as follows:

- inputs

- throughput or conversion (transformation), e.g. the processing of materials and organizing of work activities

- output, e.g. of products or services

- cyclic nature, e.g. the returns from marketing the output enable further inputs to be made to complete the cycle of production

- feedback enables the system to correct deviations; organizations tend to develop their own 'thermostats'

- differentiation, e.g. the tendency to greater specialization of functions and multiplicity of roles

- equifinality – open systems do not have to achieve their goals in one particular way. Similar ends can be achieved by different paths and from a different starting point.

12. Giving consideration to the aforementioned characteristics of open systems, the input–conversion–output model, shown in Figure 8.2, now must be expanded to take in the key factors of feedback. The result of including feedback from output to input is to produce a so-called 'closed loop' system. A closed loop system is basically a self-regulating system, such as a thermostat in a heating system or, to take a business example, a budgetary control system in a departmental operating plan. In each case, information fed back to the input side of the system enables corrective changes to keep the system on course, i.e. in a steady state. The revised model of the organization as an open system can now be drawn as in Figure 8.3.

FIGURE 8.3 **The basic cycle of the organizational system**

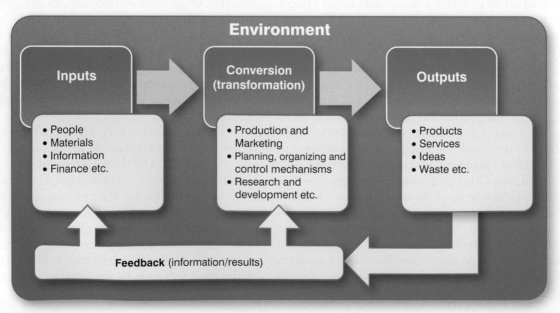

13. The revised model shows the consequences of the outputs as information and results. The information can take many forms, e.g. sales volumes, new orders, market share, customer complaints, etc. and can be applied, as appropriate, to control the inputs and conversion processes. The results are the revenues and profits fed back into the organization to provide further inputs and so ensure the survival and growth of the system.

14. An adaptive system such as the one described above is sometimes referred to as a 'cybernetic' system; the term 'cybernetics' in this context means the study of control and communication. Cybernetics was made prominent by Norbert Wiener in the late 1940s, but is still very much a developing science. The essence of a cybernetic system is self-regulation on the basis of feedback information to disclose a shortfall in performance against standards and to indicate corrective action.

15. The late Stafford Beer was a British theorist, consultant and professor at the Manchester Business School. He is best known for his work in the fields of management cybernetics. In the late 1950s Beer published his first book about cybernetics and management, building on the ideas of Norbert Wiener, especially for a systems approach to the management of organizations. Beer was arguably the first to apply cybernetics to management, defining cybernetics as the science of effective organization (see the viable system model).

16. Katz and Kahn set out to describe their view of social systems and their related sub-systems. Advocating an open system approach, they identified five sub-systems at work within organizations:

1) **Production/Technical:** Concerned with the accomplishment of the basic tasks of the organization (production of goods, provision of services, etc).

2) **Supportive:** Procure the inputs and dispose of the outputs of the production sub-system. They also maintain the relationship between the organization as a whole and the external environment.

3) **Maintenance:** concerned with the relative stability or predictability of the organization. They provide for the roles, the rules and the rewards applicable to those who work in the organization.

4) **Adaptive:** The first three systems above serve the organization as it is. The adaptive sub-systems, by comparison, are concerned with what the organization might become. They deal with issues of change in the environment, e.g. in marketing, and research and development.

5) **Managerial:** These comprise the controlling and coordinating activities of the total system. They deal with the coordination of sub-structures, the resolution of conflict, and the coordination of external requirements with the organization's resources. An important managerial sub-system is the authority structure which describes the way the managerial system is organized for the purposes of decision-making. Remember the five sub-systems (Managerial, Maintenance, Adaptive, Production and Supportive) with the M-MAPS acronym.

8.2 DEVELOPMENTS IN SYSTEMS THEORY

17. The Human Relations theorists set out to humanize the workplace and this they did but at the expense of studying the organization as a whole. They did not address themselves sufficiently to the many major problems that can arise in practically every organization, for example the problem of dealing with the tensions between the requirements for structure and the needs of people. Questions of conflict were dealt with in terms of avoidance whereby attention was diverted towards motivation and leadership. A further difficulty with the Human Relations approach was its emphasis on the practical application of ideas rather than on the conceptual development of organizational theory. This is not to deny the usefulness, to practising managers in particular, of the propositions of human relations, but it suggests the need to look elsewhere for a fuller explanation of behaviour in organizations.

18. This is where we turn to theorists who see organizations as complex social systems, responsive to a number of interdependent and important variables. The key variables of greatest interest to those adopting a systems approach to organizations are as follows:

- people – as individuals and in groups
- organizational structures

- environment – the external conditions affecting the organization
- technology – in terms of the technical requirements of work.

These variables are best remembered by the acronym POET. Whereas earlier theorists studied individual variables in isolation, the systems theorists study the relationship between two or more variables. Initially, the Tavistock researchers, for example, looked at the relationships between people and technology and between structure and environment. Later studies conducted by Pugh and colleagues have developed a more comprehensive and multi-dimensional approach, utilizing all the above variables. The principal developments in systems theories of organizational design are discussed in the following paragraphs.

8.3 THE TAVISTOCK GROUP

19. The London-based Tavistock Institute of Human Relations has been engaged in various forms of social research for over 60 years. Despite its title, the Institute has developed a reputation for its contribution to systems theory. In particular, Trist and Bamforth introduced the concept of 'socio-technical' systems and Rice and Emery promoted several important ideas relating to open-systems theory and types of environment.

20. The Trist and Bamforth studies took place in the 1940s and focused upon changes in the method of extracting coal from British pits. The researchers were interested in the effects of mechanization on the social and work organization at the coal face. Before mechanization, the coal had been extracted by small, closely knit teams working as autonomous groups. They worked at their own pace, often isolated in the dark from other groups. Bonds established within groups became important outside work as well as during the shift. Conflicts between competing groups were frequent and sometimes violent, but were always contained. This was the system which operated before the coal-cutters and mechanical conveyors were introduced. It was called the shortwall method.

21. The mechanized coal face was completely different. It consisted of a long wall which required not small groups, but groups of between 40 and 50 men, plus their supervisors. These men could be dispersed over 200 yards, and they worked in a three-shift system. The new system (longwall method), was essentially a mass-production system based on a high degree of job specialization. Under the former shortwall method, each team had provided all the skills required, but in the longwall arrangement the basic operations were separated between the shifts. So, for example, if the first shift cut the coal from the face, the second shift shovelled it into the conveyor, and the third shift advanced the coal face along the seam. Even within each shift, there was a high degree of task specialization.

22. The social consequences of the new method, arising from the breakdown of the previously closely integrated social structure were increased haggling over pay, inter-shift competition for the best jobs, the seeking of scapegoats in other shifts and a noticeable increase in absenteeism. The results of the radical change in working methods, and the miners' adverse response to them, led Trist and Bamforth to the conclusion that effective work was a function of the interdependence of technology (equipment, physical layout and task requirements) and social needs (especially relationships within groups). It was not sufficient to regard the working environment as either a technical system or a social system. It was a combination of the two: a socio-technical system.

23. Eventually a so-called 'composite longwall method' was developed which enabled the needs of the social system to be met, whilst at the same time utilizing the benefits of the new mechanized equipment (the technical system). Tasks and working arrangements were altered so that the basic operations could be carried out by any one shift, and tasks within each group were allocated by the members. Payment was changed to incorporate a group bonus. The outcome of the composite methods was increased productivity, reduced absenteeism and a lower accident rate.

24. Alongside the coal-mining studies mentioned above, the reputation of the Tavistock group was also assured by Rice's studies into the calico mills at Ahmedabad, India. In his book Rice (1958) elaborated upon key aspects of systems theory as applied to organizations, two of which are selected for inclusion here: his concept of systems, and views on work design.

25. Rice saw any industrial system (e.g. a firm) as an open system, importing various items from its environment, converting them into goods, services and waste materials and then exporting them into the environment. Within the total system of the firm he suggested there were two main systems in existence: an operating system and a managing system. The operating system dealt with the import, conversion and export of the product or service, whilst the managing system dealt with the control, decision-making and communication aspects of the total system. Each system could have one or more sub-systems, which was why it was necessary to develop the managing system, in order to coordinate the interaction of all the systems and sub-systems.

26. Rice's view of systems can be compared usefully with those of Handy who identified not only the operating system but also the adaptive, maintenance and information systems in activating the various parts of the total organization. It is these last three which align most closely with the managing system formulated by Rice. On balance, the more modern analysis is the clearer of the two in helping to establish the prime focal points of the managing system.

27. The studies at Ahmedabad produced, amongst other things, some interesting conclusions about the design of work. These can be summarized as follows: (a) effective performance of a primary task is an important source of satisfaction at all levels of work (b) the capacity for voluntary cooperation is more extensive than is often expected (c) there is great benefit in allowing individuals to complete a whole task (d) work groups of eight seem to have the best chance of success for achieving group tasks (e) there is a clear relationship between work effectiveness and social relations and (f) where group autonomy has been established, unnecessary interference by supervisors will be counter-productive.

28. The above findings have been incorporated into current ideas on the design and redesign of work, to try and meet social and psychological needs of employees as well as the requirements of changing technology. They also share much common ground with Herzberg's ideas of motivation and job enrichment.

8.4 OPEN SYSTEMS AND THE ENVIRONMENT

29. The final example of the work of the Tavistock Group relates to another key factor in systems theory – the nature of the environment. Emery and Trist (1965) were the first to produce a classification of environments. They described four types of environment from: (1) Placid, randomized (unchanging and predictable) environment, through (2) Placid, and (3) Disturbed, through to (4) Turbulent. This describes a dynamic and rapidly changing environment in which organizations must adapt frequently in order to survive.

30. Emery and Trist were particularly interested in the turbulent category of the environment. This is an area where existing formal or bureaucratized structures are ill-suited to deal with their environment. According to the writers, more and more environments are experiencing turbulence without the corresponding organizational flexibility.

31. Burns and Stalker theorized that companies facing a changing environment may need to adopt an organic organizational structure in order to adapt rapidly to changes. Such companies have a de-centralized decision-making arrangement to enable speedy adaptation to changes in the marketplace. On the other hand, companies operating in a stable environment would benefit from continuing with a mechanistic structure, where policies remain constant for a long period of time, decision-making is centralized around a few people and tasks remain essentially the same.

32. Finally, we should note that viewing organizations as systems has limits and the systems approach and way of thinking is not without criticism. As has already been noted, organizations are more than simple physical systems and include people and the complex interactions between these people. Individuals have free-will and behaviour is not always predictable. Social systems are much more complicated than single human systems. The adoption of systems models can lead to mechanistic and overly rationalistic theories. That said, the systems approach and systems thinking has formed the backbone of organizational analysis.

CONCLUSION

33. In this chapter we have described the evolution of management and organizational theory. The classical approach may be criticized for viewing organizations without regard for their people. Similarly the

human relations approach, emphasizing people without organizations is also subject to criticism. Neither the classical nor human relations approach considered organizations in turbulent environments whereas the systems approach takes a holistic perspective, encouraging managers to view organizations both as a whole and as part of a larger environment (open system). The approach considers the interdependency of organizational parts, changes in one part – technical or social – will affect other parts, a concept we build upon in the next chapter.

QUESTIONS

1   What are the major differences between the approach of the systems theorists and those of (a) the Classical theorists and (b) the Human Relations theorists?

2   Review the role of systems theory in understanding organizations.

USEFUL WEBSITES

UK Systems Society (UKSS): **www.ukss.org.uk**
The Society is committed to the development and promotion of 'systems' philosophy, theory, models, concepts and methodologies for improving decision-making and problem-solving for the benefit of organizations.
Tavistock Institute: **www.tavinstitute.org**

The TIHR is dedicated to the study of human relations for the purpose of bettering working life and conditions for all humans within their organizations, communities and broader societies and to the influence of environment in all its aspects on the formation or development of human character or capacity.

REFERENCES

Emery, F.E. and Trist, E.L. (1965) 'The Causal Texture of Organizational Environments', *Human Relations*, 18(1): 21–32.
Rice, A.K. (1953) 'Productivity and social organization in an Indian weaving shed: an examination of the socio-technical systems of an experimental automatic loomshed', *Human Relations*, 6: 297–329.

Rice, A.K. (1958) *Productivity and social organization*, London: Tavistock Publications.

CHAPTER 9
CONTINGENCY APPROACHES TO MANAGEMENT

Key Concepts

- Contingency approach
- Differentiation
- Integration
- Mechanistic system
- Organic system
- Situational approach

Learning Outcomes Having read this chapter, you should be able to:

- discuss what is meant by the contingency approach to management
- contrast mechanistic and organic systems
- distinguish six primary variables of structure
- explain the congruence model of organizational behaviour based on the system paradigm
- evaluate the contribution of systems theory to theories of management and organization.

Vignette

HOW WELL DO YOU HANDLE CHANGE?

Change is commonplace in the manufacturing (operations) function which must strive constantly to meet customer demands, fulfil regulatory requirements, seek ways to improve performance or adapt to new technology. The operations function therefore faces the challenge of managing change effectively. To examine the challenges facing manufacturers today an independent research firm conducted a survey of more than

250 manufacturers to understand how they approach change within the factory. Survey responses revealed that manufacturers make minor changes every month or two, moderate changes a few times a year, and major changes once or twice a year. The chief drivers for change focused on improving product quality and production efficiency/cost (internal focus). Following these challenges are strategic, market-driven issues related to new products and changes in market demand, i.e. an external environment focus.

1.   Whereas earlier management scholars argued for universal management principles (one size fits all), scholars of the latter half of the twentieth century found evidence to suggest management and organizations need to fit with the unique situation and context of the firm. The work of latter scholars was categorized under contingency theories which were, themselves, born out of systems theories. Contingency theories suggested previous theories such as Weber's bureaucracy and Taylor's scientific management had failed because they neglected to mention that management style and organizational structure were influenced by various aspects of the environment. There could not be 'one best way' for leadership, management or organization.

2.   The most recent formulations of systems theories tend to be deemed contingency theories because they emphasize the need to take specific circumstances or contingencies into account when devising appropriate organizational and management systems.

3.   There is no clear distinction between the systems approach and the **contingency approach** to the management of organizations. The latter has developed out of the findings of the former. A systems approach highlights the complexity of the interdependent components (parts) of organizations within equally complex environments. A contingency approach builds on the diagnostic qualities of the systems approach in order to determine the most appropriate organizational design and management style for a given set of circumstances. Essentially the contingency approach suggests that issues of design and style depend upon choosing the best combination, in the light of prevailing (or forecast) conditions, of the following variables: (a) the external environment (b) technological factors (c) human skills and motivation and (d) structural variables.

4.   Reconsider the opening case. Change is a process allowing organizations to align themselves continually with external forces. If the context and environment change (the given set of circumstances) then so too must the organization since the two are interdependent.

5.   Unlike the Classical and Human Relations approaches to the management of organizations, the contingency approach does not seek to produce universal prescriptions or principles of behaviour. It deals in relativities, not absolutes. It is essentially a **situational approach** to management. The contingency approach does not turn its face against earlier approaches, but adapts them as part of a 'mix' which could be applied to an organization in a particular set of circumstances.

6.   The label 'contingency approach' was suggested by Lawrence and Lorsch (1967). Their important contribution to this approach will be summarized shortly. Burns and Stalker introduced the concept of mechanistic and organic types of structure and discussed them in relation to the environment; Joan Woodward is noted for her key studies into the effects of technology on structure and performance; finally, the so-called Aston group (Pugh, Hickson *et al.*) have undertaken interesting studies into several of the technology-structure variables within organizations. The following paragraphs look at several important research studies which have dealt with two or more elements of this 'organizational mix'.

9.1 BURNS AND STALKER

7.   A pioneering and renowned study of the environment–structure relationship was conducted in England and Scotland during the 1950s by Burns and Stalker. Twenty firms in the electronics industry were studied regarding how they adapted to changing market and technical conditions, having been organized initially to handle relatively stable conditions.

8. Researchers were particularly interested in how management systems might change in response to the demands of a rapidly changing external environment. As a result of their studies they devised two distinctive 'ideal types' of management system: **mechanistic systems** and **organic systems**. Key features of both systems are summarized below.

9. Mechanistic systems are appropriate for conditions of stability. Their outstanding features are as follows: a specialized differentiation of tasks; a precise definition of rights, obligations and technical methods of each functional role; a hierarchical structure of control, authority and communication; a tendency for vertical interaction between members of the concern; a tendency for operations and working behaviour to be dominated by superiors; and an insistence upon loyalty to the organization and obedience to superiors.

10. By contrast, organic systems are appropriate for conditions of change. Their outstanding features can be summarized as follows: individual tasks relevant to the total situation of the concern are adjusted and redefined through interaction with others; a network structure of control, authority and communication, where knowledge of technical or commercial aspects of tasks may be located anywhere in the network; a lateral rather than vertical direction of communication through the organization; communications consist of information and advice rather than instructions and decisions; and commitment to the organization's tasks is seen to be more important than loyalty and obedience.

11. Burns and Stalker did not see the two systems as complete opposites, but as polar positions between which intermediate forms could exist. They also acknowledged firms could move from one system to the other as external conditions changed, and that some concerns could operate with both systems at once. Burns and Stalker stressed they did not favour one or other system. What was important was to achieve the most appropriate system for a given set of circumstances – a perfect expression of the contingency approach!

9.2 JOAN WOODWARD

16. The Woodward studies, conducted by a small research team from the South East Essex College of Technology during the period 1953–1958, were initially aimed at assessing the extent to which classical management principles were being translated into practice by manufacturing firms in the area, and with what success. Information on various aspects of formal organization was collected from 100 firms. In terms of structure, for example, the number of levels of management varied between two and 12, and spans of control (the number of persons directly supervised by one person) ranged from ten to 90 for first-line supervisors.

17. The team concluded there was little in common amongst the most successful firms studied, and there was certainly no indication that classical management principles were any more likely to lead to success than other forms of organization. At the time this was considered to be rather disconcerting, given the popularity of classical ideas.

18. Drawing no positive conclusions from the first part of their studies, Woodward's team turned their attention to the technological data collected. The question they posed was as follows: is there any relationship between organizational characteristics and technology? In attempting to answer this question, the team made a lasting contribution to the theory of organizations by establishing the key role of technology as a major variable affecting organizational structures.

19. Their first step was to find some suitable form of classification to distinguish between the different categories of technology employed by the firms concerned. Three main categories were eventually selected as follows: (1) Unit and Small Batch Production. This included custom-made products, the production of prototypes, large fabrications undertaken in stages and the production of small batches (2) Large Batch and Mass Production. This encompassed the production of large batches, including assembly-line production, and mass production and (3) Process Production. This included the intermittent production of chemicals in a multipurpose plant, as well as the continuous flow production of liquids, gases and crystalline substances.

20. When the firms in the study were allocated to their appropriate categories and then compared by their organization and operations, some discernible patterns emerged. For example, process industries tended to

utilize more delegation and decentralization than large-batch and mass production industries. This was just one aspect of the link between technology and organizational structure. Others included the following:

- The more complex the process, the greater the chain of command, i.e. there were more levels of management in the process industries than in the other two categories.

- The span of control of chief executives increased with technical complexity, i.e. the number of people directly responsible to the chief executive was lowest in unit/small-batch production firms and highest in process production.

- By contrast with the point above, the span of middle management decreased with technical complexity, i.e. fewer people reported to middle managers in process production than in large-batch/mass production firms, who in turn had fewer people than in unit/small-batch production.

21. As well as the differences mentioned above, there were also some interesting similarities. For example the average number of workers controlled by first-line supervisors was similar for both unit/small-batch and process production – and these were noticeably fewer in number than for mass production situations. Another similarity between unit/small-batch and process production was that they both employed proportionately more skilled workers than mass production categories. Woodward's team also found that firms at the extremes of the technical range tended to adopt organic systems of management, whereas firms in the middle of the range, notably the large-batch/mass production firms, tended to adopt mechanistic systems.

22. Having established some definite links between organizational characteristics and technology, Woodward's team turned its attention to the relationship, if any, between these two factors and the degree of business success (profitability, growth, cost reductions achieved, etc.). They found the successful firms in each category were those whose organizational characteristics tended to cluster around the median figures for their particular category. So, for example, a process production firm would be better served by a taller, narrower structure backed up by an organic system of management rather than by a flatter, broader structure, operated mechanistically. On the other hand, a mass-production firm would appear to benefit from a flatter, broader structure, operated in a mechanistic way. Firms in either category which did not display the appropriate characteristics would tend to produce less than average results.

23. Woodward concluded that the predominance given to the classical theorists, especially in respect of the application of their ideas in practice (span of control, unity of command, definition of duties, etc.), only made sense when viewed in terms of large-batch/mass production processes. Classical ideas did not seem appropriate for other categories of production. Her research strongly suggested that not only was the system of production a key variable in determining structure, but that also there was a particular form of organization most suited to each system.

9.3 LAWRENCE AND LORSCH

24. A few years later, Lawrence and Lorsch developed an open systems theory of how organizations and organizational subunits adapt to best meet the demands of their immediate environment. Initially Lawrence and his colleague studied the internal functioning of six plastics firms operating in a diverse and dynamic environment.

25. The major emphasis of their study was on the states of differentiation and integration within organizations.

26. Differentiation was defined as more than mere division of labour or specialization. It also referred to the differences in attitude and behaviour of the managers concerned. More recently it has been defined as the degree to which the tasks and the work of individuals, groups and units are divided up within an organization. To some extent, differentiation fragments the organization.

Integration was defined as the quality of the state of collaboration existing amongst departments – the process of achieving unity of effort amongst the various sub-systems in the accomplishment of the organization's task. Thus integration is about the extent to which units in an organization are linked together and their respective degree of independence. Organizations must balance differentiation and integration to be successful. They must determine how much differentiation is required and then how much integration.

27. In approaching their studies, Lawrence and Lorsch adopted the view that there was probably no one best way to organize. They aimed to provide a systematic understanding of what states of differentiation and integration were related to effective performance under different environmental conditions. In essence they argued about **Environmental determinism** – a perspective which claims that internal organizational responses are wholly or mainly shaped, influenced or determined by external environmental factors.

28. Lawrence and Lorsch's main conclusions were as follows:

- The more dynamic and diverse the environment, the higher the degree of both differentiation and integration required for successful organization.

- Less changeable environments require a lesser degree of differentiation, but still require a high degree of integration.

- The more differentiated an organization, the more difficult it is to resolve conflict.

- High-performing organizations tend to develop better ways of resolving conflict than their less effective competitors. Improved ways of conflict resolution lead to states of differentiation and integration that are appropriate for the environment.

- Where the environment is uncertain, the integrating functions tend to be carried out by middle and low-level managers; where the environment is stable, integration tends to be achieved at the senior end of the management hierarchy.

9.4 THE ASTON GROUP

29. The Aston group – Pugh, Hickson and others (now dispersed, but originally at the University of Aston, Birmingham), began a major study into various aspects of structure, technology and environment in the late 1960s. Pugh and his colleagues concluded that the impact of technology on organizational structure must be related to company size. In small organizations they deemed technology to be critical to structure, but in large organizations other variables tended to confine the impact of technology to basic operating levels.

30. The importance of the Aston group was that they adopted a multi-dimensional approach to organizational and contextual variables, i.e. they developed the idea of an 'organizational mix' which could be applied to an organization at a particular point in time in order to achieve successful results. This contingency approach has provided the basis for further research into what represents the ideal structure for an organization in the light of a particular grouping of circumstances.

31. The Aston study distinguished six primary variables of structure and considered them against a number of contextual variables. The structural variables were as follows: (1) Specialization (of functions and roles) (2) **Standardization** (of procedures and methods) (3) Standardization of employment practices (4) **Formalization** (extent of written rules, procedures, etc.) (5) **Centralization** (concentration of authority) and (6) **Configuration** (shape of organization). These variables were considered in a number of different contexts, including the following: Origin and history; Ownership (owner-managers, shareholders, parent company, etc.); Size of organization; Charter (i.e. Number and range of goods/services); Technological features (in several dimensions); Interdependence (balance of dependence between the organization and customers, suppliers, trade unions, etc.).

32. Amongst the conclusions reached by the Aston team was the relevance of size to the structural variables. As an organization grows beyond the stage at which it can be controlled by personal interaction, it must be structured more explicitly. Larger size tends to lead to (a) more specialization (b) more standardization (c) more formalization but (d) less centralization. Overall, the researchers concluded it was possible to predict, fairly closely, the structural profile of an organization on the basis of information obtained about the contextual variables.

9.5 MODELS BASED ON THE SYSTEM PARADIGM

33. Whilst the systems perspective is valuable, systems theory by itself may be too abstract a concept to be a usable tool for managers. Consequently, a number of organizational theorists have attempted to develop more pragmatic theories or models based on the system paradigm. There are a number of models now in use.
34. The organizational system model proposed, in 1965, by Harold Leavitt of the Carnegie Institute of Technology, is made up of four major components (see Figure 9.1):

task (the organization's purpose)

people (those who carry out the task)

technology (tools and computers etc.), and

structure.

35. Leavitt argues the components are interdependent with one another and a change in any one of the components will result in change amongst the other three. This model is grounded in systems thinking but is not based on open system theory, i.e. forces in the external environment are not modelled.
36. A decade later, Nadler and Tushman developed their congruence model for diagnosing organizational behaviour, see Figure 9.2. Recognizing the organization is influenced by its environment, their model embraced both systems and open system theory. Nadler and Tushman (1989) divided their model into inputs, process and outputs. Their (transformation or internal) process contained similar components to the model proposed by Leavitt. Inputs came from the environment, including organizational history and current strategy, which help define how people in the organization behave. Nadler and Tushman also argued a need for the transformational process components to be congruent or 'fit' with each other. Nadler and Tushman (1989) did however recognize that such congruence may present advantages and disadvantages. In the short term a system with high congruence is an effective and performing system, however, such

FIGURE 9.1 **Organizational system model**

FIGURE 9.2 Congruence model of organizational behaviour

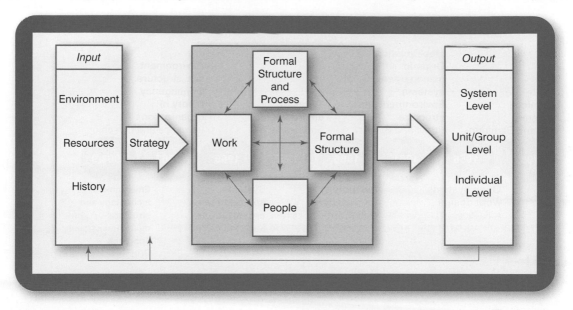

a system may be resistant to change. Their model suggests there is no one best way to organize. Rather, the most effective way of organizing is determined by the nature of the strategy as well as the work, the individuals who are members of the organization, and the informal processes and structures (including culture) which have emerged over time.

37. Like the other theories presented within this part of the book, contingency theory is not without criticism. In the Introduction we noted that contingency theorists suggested that earlier theories such as Weber's bureaucracy and Taylor's scientific management had failed because they neglected the view that management style and organizational structure were influenced by various aspects of the environment. Towards the end of the twentieth century, Child (1997) made an important contribution to management theory noting that we should not simply consider the environment and rational determinants of structure (contingency theory) without consideration of the managers themselves: the people who made choices about how to manage.

38. Child discusses the integrative potential of **strategic choice** theory within organization studies and examines its contribution to an evolutionary perspective on the subject. Strategic choice followed the 'determinism' theories and the 'contingency' views, giving attention to organizational decision-makers. 'Strategic choice' is a process whereby power-holders within organizations decide upon courses of strategic action (in this case, structure). The decisions of such managers are coloured by their values, attitudes and beliefs; the sources of which include culture, experience, education and training. Values, attitudes and beliefs (and personality) impact upon evaluations, cognitions, mental process and actions. Despite the criticism (it is an oversimplification), some scholars continue to defend and apply contingency theory, particularly in change management theory and practice. The contribution of the theory remains important.

CONCLUSION

39. If we now review management theory over the past 100 years (previous chapters) we can appreciate how management thinking evolved. We can witness an eclectic set of theories, with some developed from others and some able to coexist mutually. We started with the rational and general classical theories which neglected motivation and were then supplemented with the human relations theories. As the twentieth century evolved, so too did markets and the extent of change and uncertainty. Contingency theories were proposed to take account of various aspects of the environment – now seen as an independent variable. Figure 9.3 summarizes the principal systems and contingency approaches to organization and management theory. The contingency approach emphasizes the need for flexibility. The approach argues there

FIGURE 9.3 The principal systems and contingency approaches to organization and management theory

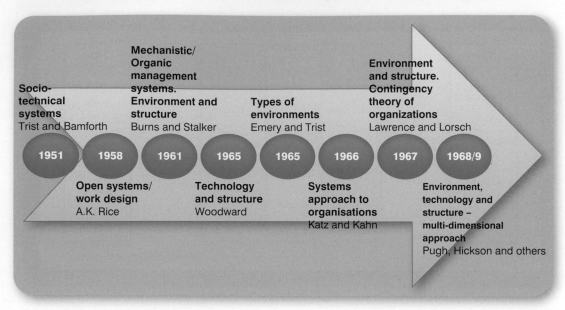

cannot be 'one best way' for leadership, management or organization. Whilst the classical theorists argued for universal principles of administration, the simple idea behind Contingency theory is that organization structure should be dependent upon the organizational context, i.e. it should be regarded as a contingent variable. However, this did not mean that the classical theories were now defunct. With input from systems theory, management was now seen as a mixture of theories, determined by the environment. The general model implicit in contingency theory is shown in Figure 9.4. Finally, our understanding of management was enhanced with the idea of strategic choice theory. Power-holders within organizations decide upon courses of strategic action (in this case, structure). The decisions of such managers are coloured by their predispositions.

FIGURE 9.4 General model of contingency theory

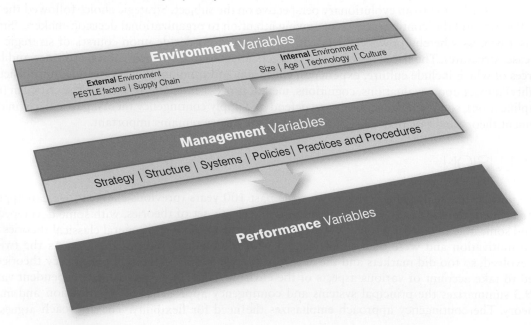

QUESTIONS

1 In what ways is the concept of 'integration' important for organizations?

2 How would you summarize the principal contributions to organization and management theory of: Joan Woodward's Essex studies and the Burns and Stalker studies?

3 In what ways could the Aston group's study be said to have furthered understanding about the analysis of organizations?

4 In approaching their studies, Lawrence and Lorsch took the view that there was probably no one best way to organize. Discuss this viewpoint with reference to the contingency approach and the views of other theorists.

5 Discuss what is meant by the contingency approach to management and to organizational design/structure.

6 Whilst the systems perspective is valuable, systems theory by itself may be too abstract a concept to be a usable tool for managers. Identify and explain the congruence model (proposed by Nadler and Tushman) based on the systems paradigm.

REFERENCES

Child, J. (1997) 'Strategic choice in the analysis of action, structure, organizations and environment: Retrospect and prospect', *Organization Studies – Berlin*, 18(1): 43–76.

Lawrence, P.R. and Lorsch, J.W. (1967) 'Differentiation and Integration in Complex Organizations', *Administrative Science Quarterly*, 12(1): 1–47.

Nadler, D.A. and Tushman, M. (1989) 'Organizational Frame Bending: Principles for Managing Reorientation', *Academy of Management Executive*, 3(3): 194–204.

SKILL SHEET 4 **Organizational Mix (Structure)**

Use this sheet in conjunction with Chapters 8 and 9 and case sheet 4.

1. ASSESSING THE ENVIRONMENT

The measurement of environmental uncertainty is a significant challenge. Organizations attempt to understand their environments in two key ways. First, they seek to measure the degree of uncertainty and turbulence (predictability) at a holistic and general level of analysis and second, they analyze the specific factors of the external environment (political, economic, social etc.) – the factors that influence aspects of the organizational mix. PESTLE analysis is considered in Section 7 and so we will focus on the degree of uncertainty and the dependent variable of flexibility in this skills sheet. Environmental uncertainty is not a simple concept and we may be concerned with matters such as predicting how an environmental change may impact upon the organization; we may also want to predict what may happen as a result of the organization changing something. Furthermore, the interest in the environment may be considered in terms of what the organization may be able to control. Of course some factors will be more important than others. It is therefore a complex task to measure environmental uncertainty and aspects of the environment may be used to inform structural decisions or to influence leadership and management style. We may be interested in turbulence, complexity, predictability or heterogeneity. No questionnaire is perfect for environmental analysis and there are usually concerns over such instruments (scales, questions, fact or perception). Despite this, we have created a simple measurement tool to help in the understanding of the environment(s) for a given firm.

Choose a company to analyze and consider the country within which it is operating. Then complete the PERCEIVED UNCERTAINTY IN THE BUSINESS ENVIRONMENT questionnaire below. Indicate the extent to which you believe the various items can be predicted in the country/industry under analysis. You must tick a box (1–5) for each item listed. Tick box 1 if the item is easy to predict; 2 = moderately hard; 3 = somewhat hard; tick box 4 for an item that

is difficult to predict and if the item is unpredictable (in your view) tick box 5.

Scoring: add and compute the mean score (1–5) for each of the four sections. Sum the mean scores. You should have a value between 4 and 20. The higher the score, the harder it is to predict the environment and it is therefore more uncertain, possibly dynamic/turbulent. Scores are of relative use when comparing countries, industries or periods in time.

Perceptions of environmental uncertainty are expected to manifest in strategy, structure and the decisions made by senior managers. Generally, companies operating in more dynamic, turbulent or less predictable environments will need to be more adaptable (flexible) when coping with external change. In the sections following the questionnaire we consider aspects of the organization mix (structural variables) and the arguments to be more or less flexible, differentiated, centralized, formal or mechanistic.

	1	2	3	4	5
1 GOVERNMENT POLICY AND THE ECONOMY					
1.1 Tax policies					
1.2 Monetary policy					
1.3 Interest rates					
1.4 Exchange rates					
1.5 Inflation rate					
2 ORGANIZATION INPUTS AND RESOURCES					
2.1 Availability of trained labour					
2.2 Labour and Union disagreements					
2.3 Quality of inputs, raw materials and components					
2.4 Availability of inputs, raw materials and components					
2.5 Prices of raw materials					
3 MARKET AND COMPETITION					
3.1 Customer preferences					
3.2 Demand					
3.3 Changes in competitor prices					

3.4 Changes in competitor strategies						
3.5 Entry of new firms						
4 STAKEHOLDER BEHAVIOUR						
4.1 Investors						
4.2 Regulators						
4.3 Suppliers						
4.4 Customers						
4.5 Pressure groups						

2. FLEXIBILITY VERSUS INFLEXIBILITY

As was noted, firms operating in more unpredictable environments seek out flexible ways of working so that they can cope with changes. Flexibility is a complex construct with many meanings. It is the degree to which an operation's process can change what it does, how it is doing it, or when it is doing it. It may be viewed as a performance dimension that considers how quickly operations and supply chains can respond to the unique needs of customers; the ability of the organization to change what it does quickly. In terms of products or services this can relate to introducing new designs, changing the mix, changing the overall volume and changing the delivery timing. The concept covers a combination of *practices* which enable organizations to react quickly and cheaply to environmental changes. If the company is operating in a fast changing environment with little predictability then it must be able to adapt to the changes quickly. It must be flexible.

PRACTICES – what can organizations do to be more flexible?

~ Use early warning indicators, KPIs with self-regulation – the adaptive system
~ Delayer to enhance responsiveness and the speed of decision-making ('Flexible firm'); use empowerment and autonomy (span of control, management levels)
~ Flexible budgets
~ Flexible manufacturing technology/systems (see also just-in-time (JIT)) – Manufacturing technologies designed to improve job scheduling, reduce set-up time and improve quality control
~ Goods and service design flexibility – the ability to develop a wide range of customized goods or services to meet different or changing customer needs; see also Mix flexibility – the operation's ability to produce a wide range of products and services

~ Volume flexibility – operation's ability to change level of output or activity to produce different quantities or volumes of products and services over time
~ Workforce flexibility in terms of pay (see 'Flexible pay' and Flexible benefits), contractual rights, hours and conditions, and working practices ('Functional flexibility', Abolishing demarcation rules and skill barriers so that workers can take on a variety of jobs) – see also 'core' and 'peripheral' workforces and outsourcing
~ Flexible working arrangements – Flexibility on patterns of work organization and the workforce, including part-time work, annual hours contracts and flexitime; start/finish times of a worker may be varied without exceeding daily/weekly hours of a normal working day/week over a specified period
~ Numerical flexibility – matching employee numbers to fluctuating production levels or service requirements
~ Flexible specialization – allocation of time and labour according to consumer demand. Staff receive extra training and resources to widen specialist skills
~ Requiring jobseekers to show a willingness to move location, change occupation and accept radically different terms of employment

Building the Business Case for Flexibility:
Flexibility in some cases may help reduce or eliminate costs, speed up decision making and therefore make the organization more responsive and better able to provide an improved service to customers. Flexibility has, in the past, been positioned as simply a benefit to employees. However, there is widespread evidence that employers also gain tremendous benefit from providing flexibility over when and how work gets done. Not only are there cost benefits (such as reduced absenteeism and overtime costs in production environments) but also talent management (attracting the best employees), greater job satisfaction and higher levels of engagement. On the downside there are disadvantages. Aside from compromises to efficiency (reduced specialization, increased set-up costs, reduced economies of scale), some will argue that because buildings have to be left open longer, extra lighting and heating costs can result; employees find it difficult to work from home; requires investment in new technologies in order to communicate with employees who decide to perform their duties from home; lack of supervision; if

the business requires team meetings or collaborative work sessions, flexitime may result in key employees being absent. Trying to find a time when everyone needed to attend a meeting is available can be difficult with rotating or constantly changing schedules. How flexible is your organization?

3. DIFFERENTIATION AND INTEGRATION

Organizational design considers the manner in which management achieves the right combination of differentiation and integration of the organization's operations, in response to the level of uncertainty in its external environment. The expanding size of organizations gives rise to increasing subdivision of responsibilities, facilitates supervision and widens the span of control of supervisors, and simultaneously creates structural differentiation and problems of coordination that require supervisory attention. In times of high uncertainty, greater organizational effectiveness is achieved through high differentiation, coupled with high integration. In times of low uncertainty, low differentiation and low integration are more effective.

DIFFERENTIATION: as with flexibility, there are many aspects to differentiation. However, when considering differentiation and structure we focus mainly on the degree to which the tasks and the work of individuals, groups and units are divided up within an organization. Differentiation means that the organization is composed of many different units that work on different kinds of tasks, using different skills and work methods. Dimensions of differentiation may include:

~ differentiation of a formal organization into components in terms of several dimensions – spatial, occupational, hierarchical, functional
~ subdivision of responsibilities occurs amongst functional divisions (e.g. marketing, sales, production, HR, finance, etc.), enabling each one to concentrate on certain kinds of work
~ Local branches may be established in different places to facilitate serving clients in various areas
~ A business must decide if it wants to differentiate based on tasks or product offerings
~ The management of such a differentiated structure requires managerial responsibilities to be subdivided amongst managers and supervisors on different hierarchical levels
~ The more simple tasks are separated from various kinds of complex ones, the easier it is for unskilled employees to perform the routine duties and for skilled employees to acquire the specialized training and experience to perform the complex ones
~ members of an organization are formally divided into positions, as illustrated by the division of labour; or into ranks, notably managerial levels; or into subunits, such as local branches, headquarters divisions, or sections within branches or divisions
~ Increased specialization

A structural component is either a distinct official status (for example, employment interviewer or first-line supervisor), or a subunit in the organization (for example, one branch or one division). The term differentiation refers specifically to the number of structural components that are formally distinguished in terms of any one criterion. How differentiated is the organization? Measures used are number of branches, number of occupational positions (division of labour), number of hierarchical levels, number of divisions, and number of sections within branches or divisions.

SPECIALIZATION	✓	✓*	✓**
Are the following activities performed by specialists*?			
Purchasing			
Research and development			
Marketing			
HR			
Strategy			
How many specialist departments are there?	<5		>10

*Do they have specialist qualifications (2)? **Do they operate in a specialist function/department (3)? – score 1 point for first column. Add points (0–18). < 6 = 'low' specialization; 6-12 fairly specialized and > 12 specialized. One tick per row only.

INTEGRATION: As organizations differentiate their structures they also need to be concerned about integration and coordination of activities. Differentiation tends to enlarge the administrative component in organizations to effect coordination. Integration means that these differentiated units are reintegrated so that work is coordinated into an overall product. Coordination mechanisms – achieving unity.

~ Coordination by plan: clear, formal and well communicated mission and goals

~ Culture: shared problems and assumptions through broad participation
~ Assurance through cross-functional committees with good visibility (through information) of the current situation
~ KPIs and feedback mechanisms
~ Use of cross-functional teams
~ Cross-functional (senior) Process managers and MBWA (management by walking around)
~ Coordination by mutual adjustment (informal communication)
~ Coordination by standardization; to improve coordination, organizations may also use formalization (rules and regulations governing how people in the organization interact)

STANDARDIZATION	L	M	H
To what extent is work done in the same way each time?			
How closely defined is a typical work task (work procedures)			
How detailed is the marketing policy			
How detailed are the inventory management procedures			
To what extent are external standards utilized			
To what extent would this company conform to quality standards			
Are HR practices (recruitment, selection and discipline) standardized?			

*L = little/low, M = moderate, medium, and H = high. Score 1 point for first column, then 2 for the second and 3 for the third. Add points (0–18). < 6 = 'low' standardization; 6–12 fairly standardized and > 12 high degrees of standardization. One tick per row only.

4. CENTRALIZATION VERSUS DECENTRALIZATION

Centralization concerns the degree to which decision-making is concentrated at a single point in an organization – where decision-making power (authority) resides in the organizational structure. A centralized organization is a company in which senior managers delegate very little authority to the lower levels of the organization or rely on specialist departments to make decisions on behalf of the company. Decentralization on the other hand is where specific delegation is given to subunits or groups within an organization such that they enjoy a measure of autonomy or independence.

An organization can be more or less centralized, i.e. managers must decide what to centralize, the choice between centralized or decentralized is not an either/or choice. Most large businesses necessarily involve a degree of decentralization when it starts to operate from several locations or it adds new business units and markets. The main advantages and disadvantages of centralization are:

Advantages	Disadvantages
Easier to implement common policies and practices for the business as a whole, greater uniformity	Local or junior managers are likely to be much closer to customer needs
Easier to coordinate and control from the centre – e.g. with budgets	Reduces motivation, commitment and satisfaction
Economies of scale and overhead savings easier to achieve	Might result in delays in decision-making; customer service does not benefit from flexibility and speed in local decision-making
Greater use of specialization	Hinders diversification
Duplication of functions and facilities is minimized which in turn reduces costs	

Organizations may also decide that a combination of centralization and decentralization is more effective. For example, functions such as accounting and purchasing may be centralized to save costs, whilst tasks such as recruitment may be decentralized as knowledge of local law, benefits, terms and conditions may be required. Organizations that pursue a global strategy (treat the world as one) tend to centralize more whilst organizations pursuing a multi-domestic strategy value local decision-making and therefore decentralization.

5. FORMALIZATION

Formalization is the degree to which rules, instructions, procedures and communications, etc. are written down; the concept is related to standardization. It may also go hand in hand with centralization as formalization can enable aspects of decentralization. Furthermore it is typically increased with age – as the company matures it has opportunity to lay down more written rules etc. and is correlated with specialization – specialists create written policies etc. However, it is often negatively correlated with increased environmental uncertainty i.e. less is written down when business challenges are in a constant state of flux. Once again, given that the extent of formalization can vary, organizations may ask how formal they are or should be. Examples of formalization include:

~ **Belief system (formal)** – the explicit set of organizational definitions that senior managers communicate formally and reinforce systematically to provide basic values, purpose and direction for the organization.
~ **Formal communication** involves presenting information in a structured and consistent manner. Such information is normally created for a specific purpose, making it likely to be more comprehensive, accurate and relevant than information transmitted using information communication.
~ **Formal management controls** include a firm's budgeting and reporting activities which serve to inform those further up the firm's organizational chart about the actions taken by people lower down in the organizational chart.
~ **Formal reporting structure** a description of who in the organization reports to whom
~ Organization charts, meeting agendas and minutes, job descriptions, handbooks, manuals, procedures, forms.

FORMALIZATION	Y*	M	H
What and how much is written down?			
Is there a detailed employee handbook or rulebook?			
Is there an organizational chart (for the company, departments)?			
Are there detailed job descriptions or work specifications?			
Have business processes been mapped?			
Have detailed work procedures been written down?			
Overall, considering manifestations such as written agendas, minutes of meetings, etc. would you regard this as a formal organization?			

*Y = Yes (simple), M = medium detail and H = high. Score 1 point for first column, then 2 for the second and 3 for the third. Add points (0–18). < 6 = 'low' formalization; 6–12 fairly formalized and > 12 high degrees of formalization. One tick per row only.

Section Six
Contemporary Approaches to Management Theory

CHAPTER 10
VALUE-DRIVEN RESPONSIVE ORGANIZATIONS – TOWARDS INTEGRATION AND A UNIFIED APPROACH

Key Concepts

- Value
- Value configuration
- Business process orientation
- Learning organization
- Postmodern organization

Learning Outcomes   Having read this chapter, you should be able to:

- explain how management theory has evolved to date
- discuss why and how companies add value
- explain the process view of management
- explain what is meant by a learning organization
- describe the characteristics of the postmodern organization.

1.   In our quest to identify management theories throughout this first part of the book we have identi-fied four broad approaches: classical, human relations, systems and contingency approaches; collectively these approaches may define modern management. However, the term modern management is synonymous with the 1970s and 1980s and is not so resonant with managers of the present day. In this chapter we discuss how these approaches have evolved more recently and will also consider the tenets of a postmodern management theory. Since the 1990s and as a result of a variety of changes, a more recent view of organiza-tions and management is captured under the banner of postmodernism.

2.   Advocates of postmodernism are likely to reject rational approaches and question the possibility of any kind of complete and coherent theory of management. It may be argued that postmodernism is less a specific approach and more a generalized concept. In many ways it can be seen as a healthy challenge to traditional approaches. Today, interest in the management of organizations is as lively as it was throughout the twentieth century. The search has never been stronger for better and more efficient ways of utilizing people's knowledge and skills in providing goods and services for domestic and global markets. The desire to understand the external world of the organization and to learn how best to cope with change in the environment is more challenging now than it has ever been.

3.   This chapter explores how systems thinking, differentiation and integration evolved with the challenge to be more responsive as an organization. In particular we focus on integration through the concept of the value chain and later through a business process orientation. We also consider the learning organization and summarize current issues for management.

10.1 VALUE – VALUE ADDING ACTIVITIES AND CONFIGURATIONS

4.   As was discussed in the previous section, organizations differentiate and then must consider how to integrate and unify the parts they have created to perform different work tasks. Integration is about linking and coordinating. The value configuration of a company outlines the set of interdependent activities to deliver value profitably and create a competitive advantage.

5.   Towards the end of the twentieth century, influenced by the work of management thought leaders such as Porter, many companies focused on the concept of added value. Value is the construct that encapsulates the regard that something is held to be worth, typically although not always in financial terms; the perception of the benefits associated with a good, service, or bundle of goods and services in relation to what buyers are willing to pay for them. Perceived value is a customer's assessment of the extent to which a product or service can satisfy their needs. Similarly, a **value proposition** is a concept indicating what the customer gets for their money. A customer can evaluate a company's value proposi-tion on two broad dimensions: *relative performance*, what the customer gets from the vendor relative to a competitor's offering, and *price*, what the customer pays to acquire the product or service, plus the access cost.

6.   **Added value** is the value added to a product or service by an organization through the work (transfor-mational process) which they perform. In the 1980s, companies began to focus on **value added activities** - activities that customers perceive as adding usefulness to the product or service they purchase. If activities did not add value they were often ceased.

7.   **Value analysis** is a systematic interdisciplinary examination of factors affecting the cost of a product or service, in order to devise means of achieving the specified purpose, most economically, at the required standard of quality and reliability. It is a term used to describe an analytical approach to the function and costs of every part of a product with a view to reducing costs whilst retaining the functional ability; sometimes known as value engineering.

8.   The **Value chain** is a model for analysis of how work activities can add value to products and services delivered to the customer and thus add a margin of value to the organization; the set of activities that must be accomplished to bring a product or service from raw materials to the point that it can be sold to a final customer. The value chain encourages managers to view a firm as a series, chain or network of basic activities which add value to its products and services and thus add a margin of value to the firm. Porter's renowned value chain highlights a main sequence of five (primary) value adding activities: inbound logis-tics, production, outbound logistics, marketing and sale, and after-sale.

INBOUND LOGISTICS → PRODUCTION → OUTBOUND LOGISTICS → MARKETING/SALE
→ AFTER-SALE → VALUE

Primary activities are the five direct activities within the value chain necessary to bring materials into an organization, to convert them into final products or services, to ship them out to customers, and to provide marketing and servicing facilities. Secondary activities, procurement, technology, human resource management and firm infrastructure support the primary activities.

9. Porter's value chain analysis is a method for decomposing the firm into strategically important activities and understanding their impact on cost and value. However, some have criticized the overall value-creating logic of the value chain believing it invalid for some industries (e.g. service provision). Porter argued it was important to focus on how value could be added within each primary activity (reducing cost and differentiating the product or service) but also the importance of integrating and 'linking' (coordinating and unifying) activities.

10.2 BUSINESS PROCESSES

10. The value chain of the 1980s inspires organizations to focus holistically and systematically on the work that is undertaken, the transformational process and the resources utilized and how they are managed. During the 1990s, coupled with developments in database and networking technologies, management theory evolved to focus further on integration and responsiveness, replacing much of the bureaucratic, hierarchical and functional aspects of management theory with a horizontal, flatter, more coordinated way of managing. This approach became labelled a horizontal approach to management and was based upon a process orientation.

11. The concept of business process orientation (BPO) is based upon the work of Deming, Porter, Davenport, Hammer and others. This body of work suggests that firms could enhance their overall performance by adopting a 'process view' of the organization. BPO helps reduce conflict and encourages greater connectedness within an organization, whilst improving business performance; it is associated with customer satisfaction, product quality, delivery speed and time-to-market speed. Its champions argue it is a new approach to management replacing the rigid hierarchies of the past with much flatter structures that are more cooperative and more process (customer)-oriented.

12. A **process** is a structured set of activities designed to produce a specified output for a particular customer or market; an approach for converting inputs into outputs. It is the way in which all the resources of an organization are used in a reliable, repeatable and consistent way to achieve its goals. The term may also be used to describe a lateral or horizontal organizational form that encapsulates the interdependence of tasks, roles, people, departments and functions required to provide a customer with a product or service. In many ways it is a more detailed and specific version of the value chain. Similar to the value chain where the organization is conceived of several major activities, organizations are conceived as several core and numerous supporting processes. A process may describe a set of related activities within (1) a specific department or function (e.g. procurement) (2) an organization i.e. cross-functional or (3) inter-organizational (e.g. supply chain management – discussed in the next chapter).

13. **Cross-functional processes** span multiple functional areas of the enterprise in a purely sequential fashion, involving reciprocal or simultaneous interactions between two or more functional areas. An easy example of a cross-functional process is the fulfilment process (see Figure 10.1), which may include activities such as: order processing (the receipt and transmission of sales order information), procurement, production, warehouse picking and packing followed by shipment and finally accounting (invoicing and receivables). In this sense the process is seen as the end-to-end activities required to meet a specific goal – in this case to provide the customer with the goods or services they require.

14. A 'business process culture' is a culture (collective way of working) that is cross-functional (horizontal in its outlook as opposed to hierarchical and vertical), customer-oriented, along with process and system thinking. Teams tend to be emphasized above individuals and as a consequence, management style, methods of motivation and reward differ from traditional perspectives. Commitment to process improvement is reflected in the quality literature which also emphasizes the role of culture within

FIGURE 10.1 Cross-functional (fulfilment) process

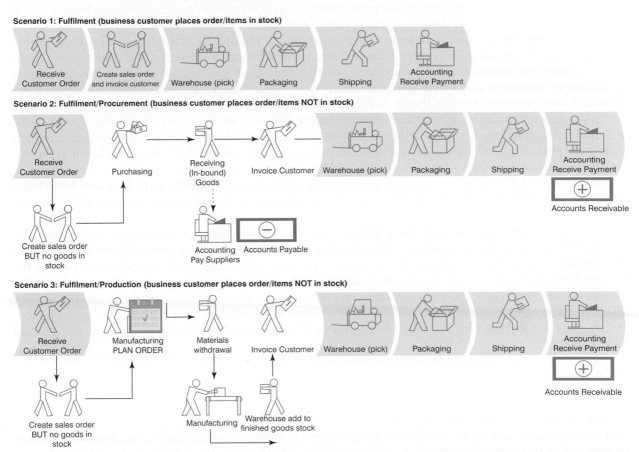

organizations in enhancing performance through improved customer satisfaction. Technology plays a key role in supporting the BPO and defining the culture through the way work is carried out.

15. In summary, contemporary organizations are likely to view management as a set of activities which add value whilst enhancing performance through being responsive. A BPO, based upon systems and contingency theory, differentiation and integration is seen as one way to accomplish this. Another key management approach, based on systems thinking, contingency theory and culture is that of the learning organization.

10.3 THE LEARNING ORGANIZATION

16. We noted in the previous chapters that systems-thinking allows managers to consider businesses as bounded objects. Peter Senge is an American scientist and Director of the Centre for Organizational Learning at the MIT Sloan School of Management. He has had a significant impact upon the way we conduct business today. Senge believed in the theory of systems thinking which has sometimes been referred to as the 'cornerstone' of the Learning Organization (LO). We also noted in the previous section that, when faced with a dynamic or turbulent environment, companies need to learn faster than their competitors and to develop a customer-responsive culture. Such companies must understand what is happening in the external environment and produce creative solutions using the knowledge and skills of all within the organization. This requires cooperation between individuals and groups, open communication and a culture of trust. Some aspects of traditional and classical management are thought to conflict with such goals.

17. From a collective or cultural perspective, the learning organization is characterized by a clear shared vision. The development of a shared vision is important in inspiring employees to learn, as it creates a common identity providing focus and motivation for learning. The culture of a learning organization

encourages experimentation, trial and error (it does not have a blame culture often associated with the bureaucratic organization and predictable environment). Experimentation creates new knowledge which is then disseminated.

18. The learning organization is an underlying organizational philosophy that enables individual learning to create valid outcomes such as innovation, efficiency, environmental alignment and competitive advantage. Learning organizations value collective and not just individual learning; this may be reflected in more participative structures and a managerial emphasis on continuous learning (i.e. organizational improvement). This reflects open systems theory and the challenges identified by Emery and Trist.

19. A learning organization is capable of continual regeneration from the variety of knowledge, experience and skills of individuals within a culture which encourages mutual questioning and challenge around a shared purpose or vision. Whereas the traditional organization emphasized efficiency, the learning organization, in contrast, focuses on problem-solving and effectiveness and does this through broad participation (empowerment and employee involvement). Learning organizations typically have excellent knowledge management structures, allowing creation, acquisition, dissemination and implementation of this knowledge in the organization.

20. In summary, the basic rationale for organizations is that in situations of rapid change only those that are flexible, adaptive and productive will excel. For this to happen, it is argued, organizations need to discover how to harvest people's commitment and capacity to learn at all levels. Managers must create the climate for organizational learning to take place. They can do this by creating a shared vision; determining the policies, strategies and structures that translate guiding ideas into business decisions and creating effective learning processes which will allow for continuous improvement of the policies, strategies and structures. The Learning Organization contributes to our understanding of what it means to manage and be a manager.

10.4 POSTMODERNISM

21. Daft (2009) contrasts traditional work (modernism) with the contemporary workplace (postmodernism) suggesting that in the traditional world of work, management involved controlling and limiting people, enforcing rules and regulations, seeking stability and efficiency, designing a top-down hierarchy and achieving bottom-line results. He suggests the new workplace asks that managers focus on leading change, harnessing people's creativity and enthusiasm, finding shared visions and values and sharing information and power. Teamwork, collaboration, participation and learning are guiding principles that help managers and employees manoeuvre the difficult terrain of today's turbulent business environment. He therefore describes a new 'era of management'.

22. Where modernist organization was rigid, postmodern organization is flexible. Management thinking has shifted from a concern with mass forms of consumption to a focus on niches and the individual customer. Where modernist organization and jobs were highly differentiated, demarcated and deskilled, postmodernist organization and jobs will be highly de-differentiated, de-demarcated and multi-skilled. The postmodern organization is a networked, information-rich, delayered, downsized, boundary-less, high-commitment organization employing highly skilled, well-paid, autonomous knowledge workers.

23. The following are issues identified in management theories promoted during the latter part of the last century: the

- importance of establishing a vision, or mission, and sustainable competitive advantage for the organization
- clarification of organizational purpose and goals
- development of shared values in the organization (i.e. 'culture')
- continuing need for leadership that can see beyond the bounds of what is, to what might be
- development of organization structures that permit flexibility of action, but with relative stable core systems
- development of multi-skilled employees with relevant knowledge, skills and competence

- optimization of employee contribution through job challenge and empowerment

- continuing need to anticipate changes in the external environment – improvement of internal communication and decision-making channels

- use of new technology to communicate more effectively with markets and individual customers

- use of business processes and enterprise-wide information systems to integrate activity

- management of change in and about the organization

- development of standards of excellence throughout the organization

- development of a global strategy in the light of international trade

- need to balance global control and universal standards with the culture and practices of the local business unit.

In diagrammatic form, the above issues can be seen in relation to each other, as in Figure 10.2.

FIGURE 10.2 Key management issues – 1970 to 2000

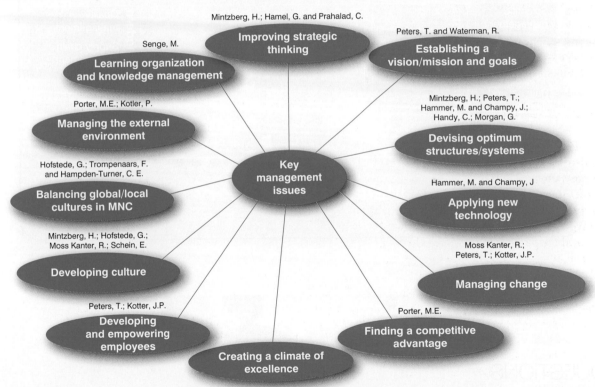

23. Of course, a diagram such as Figure 10.2 over simplifies the situation, but it does help to break down the complexity of the challenge facing management.

CONCLUSION

24. Management is complex. Throughout this part of the book we have tried to arrange and organize the major (popular) approaches to management, successful throughout the twentieth century, see Figure 10.3. We have presented an overview of the ideas, theories and management philosophies which have contributed to

making the workplace what it is today. The principles provide a foundation and framework for us to explore the practice of management and analyze organizations. In this chapter, we have considered more recent trends and approaches and built on our management understanding. Since no one management approach provides universally applicable principles of management, today's manager must take those ideas from the different approaches which best suit the particular requirements of their culture, organization and their job. In some cases the classical theories and principles along with systems theory and contingency approaches may be adopted whilst in other cases ideas from the human relations movement may be of more value. The different approaches are not generally in competition with each other and in many cases we can trace a progression of ideas, each building upon or complementing the other; all of the approaches discussed in this part of the book contribute to the blend that defines contemporary management. We should also recognize, particularly in complex and ever changing contexts, that many view management as much of an art as a science. There are many aspects to management and we will attempt to illuminate some of the more important ones over the following chapters of this book.

FIGURE 10.3 Evolution of management theory

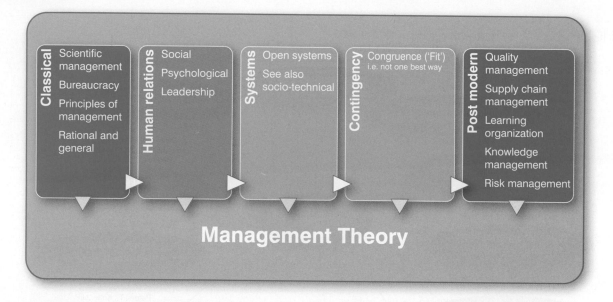

QUESTIONS

1 Critically evaluate the main traditional approaches to management (classical, humanistic, systems and contingency) and contrast them with postmodern ideas of management.

2 Explain how management theory has evolved over the past 100 years.

3 Discuss why it is important to understand both historic and contemporary theories of management.

4 Define what is meant by management – in your answer you should list and describe the popular approaches to management developed throughout the twentieth century and discuss the evolution of management theory. Are the different approaches complimentary or in competition with one another? Explain your answer.

USEFUL WEBSITES

Chartered Management Institute: **www.managers.org.uk**

Chartered professional body in the UK dedicated to promoting the highest standards in management and leadership excellence

REFERENCE

Daft, R.L. (2009) *New Era of Management*, 9th edn, Thomson Learning, SouthWestern Division.

CHAPTER 11
MANAGING THE SUPPLY CHAIN – A UNIFIED APPROACH TO MANAGEMENT

Key Concepts

- Logistics
- Operations management
- Supply chain management
- Supply chain
- Value system

Learning Outcomes Having read this chapter, you should be able to:

- define what is meant by a value system
- explain what is meant by supply chain management
- evaluate the importance of managing supply chain linkages
- explain why managers may seek to manage beyond the boundaries of the firm
- explain what is meant by the terms a 'unified organization' and a 'unified supply chain'.

Vignette

THE DELL CUSTOM FACTORY INTEGRATION (CFI) DIFFERENCE – 'ADDING VALUE, NOT COST'

Organizations, such as IT customers, could save time and resources if they had their (computer) systems configured before delivery. The organization could simply open the box and plug it in – this would be seen as a solution they could value. Dell has been developing its processes and offerings with the goal of presenting such value. Custom Factory Integration (CFI) delivers businesses the computers they need, already built to their specification during manufacture at Dell, ISO 9001 certified, factories. The process starts with capturing the customers' required specification(s); this is a direct business model, disintermediating the traditional supply chain. Once agreed, they build their systems, with no additional lead time. By automating the process, there is no limit to the number of computers that can be supplied. As every aspect of building and configuring systems is handled in one location, layers of complexity and human error due to multiple touches are eliminated. A well-defined and standardized production process ensures (global) consistency. Finally, the customer benefits from having systems arrive pre-configured as this frees IT staff from configuring individual systems, thus making them more efficient. Saving time, effort and manpower enables them to focus on business-critical projects.

The CFI process

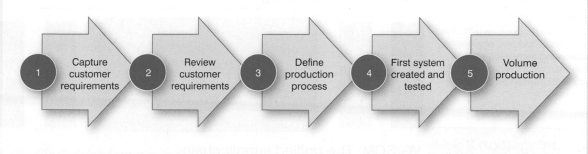

1. Since the 1980s there has been an evolutionary attempt towards more and more integration, starting with activities within the organization (value chain perspective) to beyond organizational boundaries – the value system perspective and the supply chain. Some scholars and practitioners discuss a staged approach to integration.

2. Whilst scholars vary in the number of stages (amount of detail) they identify, for simplicity we have shown three stages of integration in Figure 11.1. The fragmented, silo stage (or phase) models organizations for much of the twentieth century and was influenced by classical management theory in particular.

3. The previous chapter utilized the value chain (VC) framework and focused on intra-organizational linkages – unifying parts of the organization and its primary activities. This is represented as the second stage (Integration 1) in our diagram. In the next major stage of integration and unification, companies turn their attention to inter-organizational linkages in an attempt to unify their supply chains (value systems). This is the third stage (Integration 2) in our diagram. Organizations need to consider not only their own VCs, but how they are linked with suppliers and channels to customers, if they are to increase value yet further and develop competitive advantage based on time compression and differentiation. Furthermore, integration within the supply chain often enhances efficiency and leads to cost reduction. Much of this chapter will focus on stage 3 – supply chain integration.

11.1 VALUE REVISITED

4. In the previous chapter we defined value in terms of the perception of the benefits associated with goods, services, or a bundle of goods and services in relation to what buyers are willing to pay for them. Christopher (2010) defines customer value as the difference between the perceived benefits that flow from a purchase or a relationship and the total costs incurred.

FIGURE 11.1 A staged approach to integration

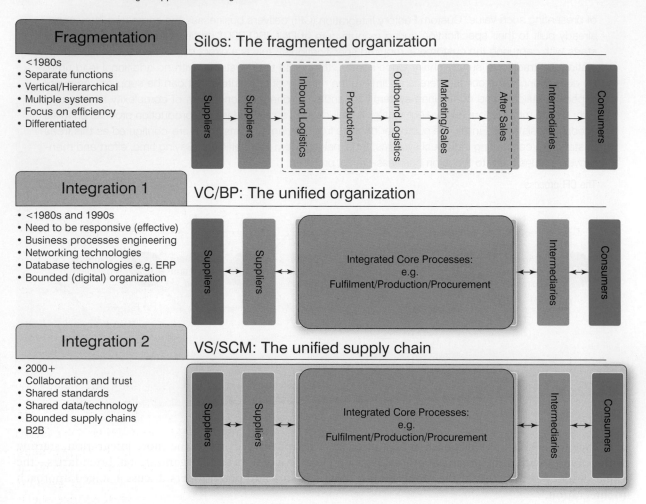

$$Customer\ value = \frac{Perceptions\ of\ benefits}{Total\ cost\ of\ ownership}$$

Christopher uses Total cost of ownership rather than price because in most transactions there will be costs other than the purchase price.

5.   Other scholars such as Johansson *et al.* (1993) cited in Christopher (2010) have defined value more specifically:

$$Customer\ value = \frac{Quality \times Service}{Cost \times Time}$$

In this case:

- Quality refers to the functionality, performance and technical specification of the offer.

- Service is the availability, support and commitment provided to the customer.

- Cost refers to the customer transaction costs, including price.

- Time is about the time taken to respond to the customer, e.g. delivery times.

Collectively, the definitions of value provided contribute towards helping us understand what we must do to add more value. Each of the four constituent elements above requires a continuous programme of improvement, innovation and investment to ensure continued competitive advantage. Companies must always consider quality, product features, technology, durability, reliability, time taken and ease of doing business if they are to win business. They must ask, regularly, what do our customers value? They must then translate such requirements into an offer (the value proposition referred to in the previous chapter).

6. A focus on creating value through operations and the supply chain starts with attention to the business processes discussed in the last chapter, which act as the parts to be linked. In linking up with their supply chain partners, organizations can forecast downstream demand and share it with upstream suppliers, enabling better planning and controlling (management) of the flow of goods and services throughout the supply chain. They use and share information system resources to enable this.

7. **Upstream** typically refers to the processes which occur before manufacturing or conversion into a deliverable product or service, usually dedicated to obtaining raw materials from suppliers. Whereas **downstream** in manufacturing refers to processes that occur later on in a production sequence or production line; processes dedicated to forwarding goods and services to customers and consumers. These processes usually involve warehousing and distribution, with subsequent transportation to retail outlets. A final key term used in supply chains is the **intermediary** – an independent business concern that operates as a link between producers and ultimate consumers or end industrial users. It renders services in connection with the purchase and/or sale of the product offering moving from producers to consumers.

8. Dell (see opening vignette) operates a direct model and a make-to-order production strategy. The direct model is based on disintermediation (the elimination of intermediaries; removing the layers of intermediaries between sellers and buyers typically through e-commerce technology) which firstly reduces cost but more importantly allows the company to be more responsive. Through the use of e-business/commerce technologies, direct model companies build a relationship with the customer and integrate customer requirement information immediately into their production process, enabling them to design products and services with value to the customer. Furthermore, they may require upfront payment thus improving cash flow. Aside from this demonstration of downstream integration, Dell also integrates its systems, information and processes upstream. This often requires suppliers to locate near to the Dell factory thus facilitating a JIT approach. Order information and forecasts are shared enabling suppliers to plan for meeting Dell's future needs. Thus the supply chain is integrated and responsive (see 'Integration 2' of Figure 11.1), providing competitive advantage. Historically, a business had to wait weeks for a new PC for an employee, whereas a 24-hour wait is now typical no matter where the employee is located in the world. The important question for any business student is this – why is it some companies can achieve this type of performance whilst others cannot?

11.2 OPERATIONS MANAGEMENT (OM) AND LOGISTICS

9. First we will revisit briefly the key aspects of the previous chapter where we introduced the value chain and the five primary activities (inbound logistics, production, outbound logistics, marketing and sale, and after-sale). Operations refers to the core activities of a business; the entire process of producing and delivering a product/service to a consumer. **Operations management** is the planning, scheduling, and control of the activities that transform inputs into finished goods and services (OM is traditionally thought of in the way the transformation process is represented in the diagrams of Chapter 8).

10. The VC starts with **inbound logistics** – the management of material resources entering an organization from its suppliers and other partners. Once goods have been produced the next primary activity is **outbound logistics** – the management of resources supplied from an organization to its customers and intermediaries such as retailers and distributors. **Logistics** then is the management of both inbound and outbound materials, parts, supplies and finished goods. **Logistics management**, broadly speaking, is the coordination of activities of the entire distribution channel to deliver maximum value to customers: from suppliers of raw materials to the manufacturer of the product, to the wholesalers who deliver the product, to the final customers who purchase it.

11.3 VALUE SYSTEMS

11.   In the previous chapter we considered the value chains as an intra-organizational system-based approach to integration; a means to unify the organization around specific goals. In this chapter we build on the ideas of value creation, integration and systems, but will consider the broader inter-organizational context-value systems.

12.   Porter and Millar (1985) note that the value chain for a company in a particular industry is embedded in a larger stream of activities they term the **value system**; the producers, suppliers, distributors and buyers (all with their own value chains). Linkages not only connect value activities within a company but also create interdependencies between its value chain and those of its suppliers and channels. A company can create competitive advantage (cost, differentiation, niche focus and time compression) by optimizing and coordinating such links with the outside.

13.   The value system concept extends the scope of management significantly. In considering the value system, managers may apply Fayol's managerial activities of forecasting, planning, organizing, controlling and coordinating beyond the boundaries of the firm. For example, a manufacturer might require the supplier of its parts to be located nearby its assembly plant – to minimize the cost of transportation and support JIT delivery. By exploiting the upstream and downstream information flowing along the value chain, the firms may try to bypass intermediaries, creating new business models, or in other ways creating improvements in its value system.

14.   Supply chain management emerged in the 1980s as a new, integrative philosophy to manage the total flow of goods from suppliers to the ultimate user and evolved to consider a broad integration of business processes along the chain of supply. The original focus was the 'management of a chain of supply as though it were a single entity, not a group of disparate functions'.

11.4 SUPPLY CHAIN MANAGEMENT (SCM)

15.   During the past two decades much confusion has occurred amongst supply chain researchers due to the many supply chain management definitions that have been proposed in the literature. Whilst most scholars have agreed that SCM includes coordination and integration, cooperation among chain members, and the movement of materials to the final customer; there are still varying conceptualizations of how SCM should be defined (Stock and Boyer, 2009).

16.   Stock and Boyer integrated 173 definitions and proposed the following encompassing definition of **SCM**:

> *The management of a network of relationships within a firm and between interdependent organizations and business units consisting of material suppliers, purchasing, production facilities, logistics, marketing, and related systems that facilitate the forward and reverse flow of materials, services, finances and information from the original producer to final customer with the benefits of adding value, maximizing profitability through efficiencies, and achieving customer satisfaction.*

17.   Despite its detail and precision, the above definition is a little lengthy. A more concise version might read as: all of the activities related to the acceptance of an order from a customer and its fulfilment. In its extended format, it also includes connections with suppliers, customers and other business partners.

18.   Supply chain and value chain are complementary views of an extended enterprise with integrated business processes, enabling the flows of products and services in one direction, and of value as represented by demand and cash flow in the other.

19.   As SCM integration becomes more widespread, sophisticated and technically enabled and the whole supply chain bounded, organizations and their partners aim to develop the **agile supply chain**. This concept captures the desired ability of firms in a supply chain to respond rapidly to frequent changes in consumer preferences and levels of demand. Other scholars refer to responsive supply chains which focus on flexibility and responsive service and are able to react quickly to changing market demand and requirements. Such firms will often pursue simultaneously **efficient supply chains** designed for efficiency and low cost

by minimizing inventory and maximizing efficiencies in process flow. See also the lean supply chain, an integrated approach which emphasizes the elimination of waste at every stage in the supply chain.

11.5 SCM LINKAGES

20.   Organizations in the supply chain are linked together through physical, information and monetary flows as depicted in Figure 11.2. Technology plays a significant role in supporting these linkages. With regard to flow of goods, RFID technology (technology that enables identification of a product by receiving a radio signal from a tag attached to the object – supported by database systems) can be used to track products through the supply chain.

21.   Sophisticated databases, combined with networking technologies are available throughout the organization to integrate parts and facilitate information flows. Technologies such as enterprise and customer relationship management (CRM) systems are good examples of this. Common standards now make data exchange between organizations much easier. e-Commerce and business applications aid the flow of monetary resources and link supply chain partners. RFID and other manufacturing technologies will be discussed in more detail in Chapter 36.

22.   In order to manage SCM linkages, businesses must build trust relationships with the partners with whom they collaborate and develop a better understanding, not only of their own, but also of their partners' processes. Those firms that manage linkages successfully can enjoy responsiveness and efficiency-based advantages. They may be able to reduce delivery times to their customers thus becoming preferred suppliers. Furthermore, reduction in delivery times along with efficient supply chains translates into less inventory and therefore cost. Such firms are also likely to collaborate with partners on new products and ways to bring them to market more quickly.

FIGURE 11.2 Physical, information and monetary flows

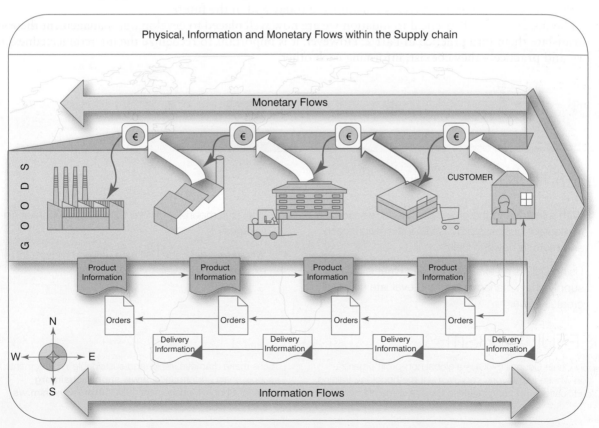

CONCLUSION

23.   This chapter considered how organizations have transformed supply chains into integrated value systems, thus creating a unified approach and perspective. This level of integration and unification is made possible through a business process approach and the integration of value chains through technology.

24.   Towards the end of this section about management theory we traced the evolution of integration, showing how management theory and organizations have evolved from fragmented structures (a result of differentiation) through to integrated structures; not only within but between organizations operating within a supply chain. This management approach has been enabled by process management and technology and embraces systems and contingency theory at its foundation. The approach delivers efficiency, effectiveness and competitive advantage. In particular it enables time compression advantage, supporting customers in their desire for products and services 'right-here-right-now'.

25.   With the evolution and development of management theories it is possible to contrast styles in terms of traditionalists (the scientific, classical managers) at one end of a spectrum and the unionists at the other. Of course, any simple such classification is ambiguous and of little use; not all theories fall within the same scale and some theory options are not dichotomous or mutually exclusive. Given the range of management theories and their eclectic nature, there are many possible patterns and interpretations of management within organizations around the world.

26.   Whereas the management theory of the twentieth century concerned the management of the organization, firms in the twenty-first century no longer consider it enough to simply manage their own business. They also seek to manage the supply chain. This enables them to meet demands for ever greater levels of value, particularly in terms of responsiveness.

27.   This part of the book should have provided you with a management theory toolkit and arguments to aid selection, rejection or adaptation. It should help you evaluate what constitutes management and its meaning in different contexts. By now, you should also understand why management is not the same, nor should it be, in the many organizations around the world. And finally, you should appreciate why management theories from the past 100 years remain valid today and in the future.

28.   Having created a theoretical foundation we are now well placed to develop our management theories and translate them into practice in Part 2. However, it is important to recognize the interconnectedness of theory and practice – they coexist, informing each other.

QUESTIONS

1   With reference to the opening vignette, discuss the (expected) business processes, information, cash and material flows at Dell.

2   Using Dell as an example, explain what is meant by supply chain management, and evaluate how Dell creates value.

3   Why is it important for Dell to manage supply chain linkages?

4   Would you describe Dell as a unified organization – explain your answer.

USEFUL WEBSITES

Supply Chain Council (SCC) is a global non-profit organization whose framework, improvement methodology, training, certification and benchmarking tools help member organiza-tions make dramatic, rapid, and sustainable improvements in supply chain performance: **www.supply-chain.org**

Institute for Supply Management (ISM): **http://www.ism.ws**

REFERENCES

Christopher, M. (2010) *Logistics and Supply Chain Management*, 4th edn, Financial Times/Prentice Hall.

Porter, M.E. and Millar, V.E. (1985) 'How information gives you a competitive advantage', *Harvard Business Review*, 63(July–August): 149–174.

Stock, J.R. and Boyer, S.L. (2009) 'Developing a consensus definition of supply chain management: a qualitative study', *International Journal of Physical Distribution & Logistics Management*, 39(8): 690–711.

SKILL SHEET 5   **SCM and Processes Modelling**

Use this sheet in conjunction with Chapters 10 and 11 and case sheet 5.

Regardless of your specific role on a team or project, the work you do is part of a larger process. Understanding — and sometimes improving — that process is an important agenda item for both management and team members who seek efficiency and opportunities to add value. A diagram of your business process can provide team members with a common frame of reference when discussing changes and improvements. Modelling has many benefits such as enabling communication, coordination, control, quality management, process optimization and re-engineering, standardization, benchmarking and process outsourcing. There are different types of model such as process flows, workflows, decision/data and information flow diagrams, Geo Maps (describes material flows in a geographic context), material flow diagrams and more. In this skills sheet we consider how to create a simple process chart in Section 1 and then build on this when considering supply chain modelling. It is important to note that there is no single way of modelling and that many approaches and models/diagrams are acceptable. That said, there are a few basic guiding rules that will be outlined.

Processes Modelling

A Business Process Model (BPM) is commonly a diagram (notation) representing a sequence of activities (*see* also business process diagrams (BPDs)). Business process mapping refers to activities involved in defining what a business entity does, who is responsible, to what standard a business process should be completed, and how the success of a business process can be determined. One of the main purposes behind business process mapping is to assist organizations in becoming more efficient. A flowchart is a primary type of business process mapping. This type of flow chart is sometimes referred to as a 'detailed' flow chart because it includes, in detail, the inputs, activities, decision points and outputs of any process. A 'process map' visually describes the flow of activities of a process. A process flow can be defined as the sequence and interactions of related process steps, activities or tasks that make up an individual process, from beginning to end. As a visual representation such models make use of symbols with universal meaning:

Common process mapping symbols/shapes

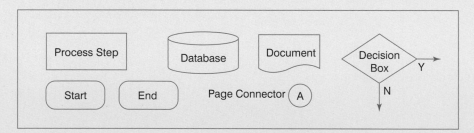

Terminator –signifies the start and finish points of a process (an event).

Process (step) – represents a step or activity in the process.

Decision – shows where a decision is made e.g. Yes or No – usually subsequent steps are shown in the process map for each decision that could have been made.

Document –a step in the process that results in a document.

Data/Database – shows data that is entering or leaving the process.

Connector –arrows/lines are used to join one step of a process to another – arrows show the direction the process is following.

Swim lanes are a visual mechanism of organizing and categorizing activities, based on cross-functional flow charting, e.g. all of the activities undertaken by Department A will be in the Department A swim lane;

other departments will have their own swim lanes (see example below).

There are two main types of BPM: (1) the 'as is' or baseline model (the current situation) and (2) the 'to be' model (the intended new situation).

How to Create a Business Process Chart/Model

Generally people approach the task in the following way:

A. **Ascertain** the process e.g. procurement, fulfilment

B. **Bring to light**, gain a full understanding of ALL steps involved

C. **Chart** a visual presentation ('As Is') of the steps involved

D. **Document** (create supporting procedures/ guidance) Continuous Improvement:

E. **Evaluate –** review and analyze the 'AS IS' model determine where costs may be reduced/value added and time compressed

F. **First draft** of improved process model

G. **Generate** the 'To Be' model.

The following information will be required before the model is constructed:

- the desired outcome of the process
- the start and end points
- the activities/tasks that are performed
- the order (sequence) of activities
- the people/ functions who perform the activities
- the documents used and exchanged between functions.

Example: Draft an 'As-Is' cross-functional process (Fulfilment)

MPhones4U – a mobile phone handset retailer sells online. You have been asked to create an 'As-Is' model/ chart of their fulfilment process. Having spoken with the Sales and then the Warehouse Manager you ascertain that online orders (containing customer, product and payment information) are *received* by the sales team who process them manually. The sales employee will first *check* the item is in stock (if not, email the customer) and then *process payment* – if the phone is available in the warehouse. Should payment be authorized the warehouse will *pick*, *pack* and *ship* the goods; if payment is *declined* an *email* is sent to the customer requesting an alternative form of payment. The process ends when the goods have been shipped.

(TIP: underline the activities and circle the decisions in the above text then list them in sequence before attempting your first draft chart/model)

Mobile phone handset stock item fulfilment (MPhones4U)

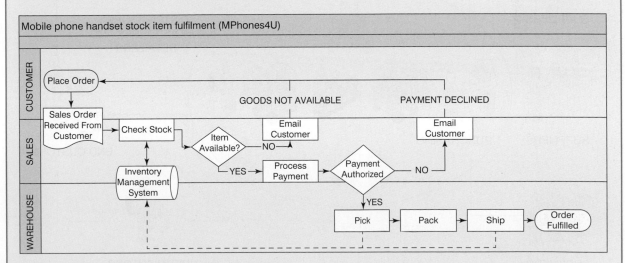

Software: There are many software applications to aid in the creation of process diagrams. Simple tools are presented in MS PowerPoint (click on the 'Insert' tab, then the 'shapes' button and scroll down to 'Flow chart'). Alternatively use MS Visio. On load, select the template category 'Flow chart' then basic, cross-functional or workflow.

Remember, the aim of modelling is to illustrate a complete process; enabling managers, consultants and staff to improve the flow and streamline the process (manage). The focus of the improvement is on 'value added' actions that make customer service and experience better, and reducing wasted time and effort. The outcomes of a business process modelling project are (1) value for the customer and (2) reduced costs for the company.

When utilizing process charts to aid continuous improvement it is advisable to create the As-Is chart and then annotate with KPIs and show current performance/benchmark data. Then create a performance improvement team to discuss the process and brainstorm ideas for improvement. Improvements typically take the form of step (activity or task) removal when not adding value; application of new technologies to reduce cost/differentiate or reduce time/error, etc.

Supply Chain Modelling

A number of different techniques may be used to model the supply chain. Techniques vary in terms of model purpose, detail and scope.

The Supply-Chain Operations Reference (SCOR) model has become the cross-industry standard diagnostic tool for SCM. It is a process reference model for SCM, spanning from the supplier's supplier to the customer's customer. Process reference models integrate the well-known concepts of business process re-engineering (Capture the 'As-Is' state of a process

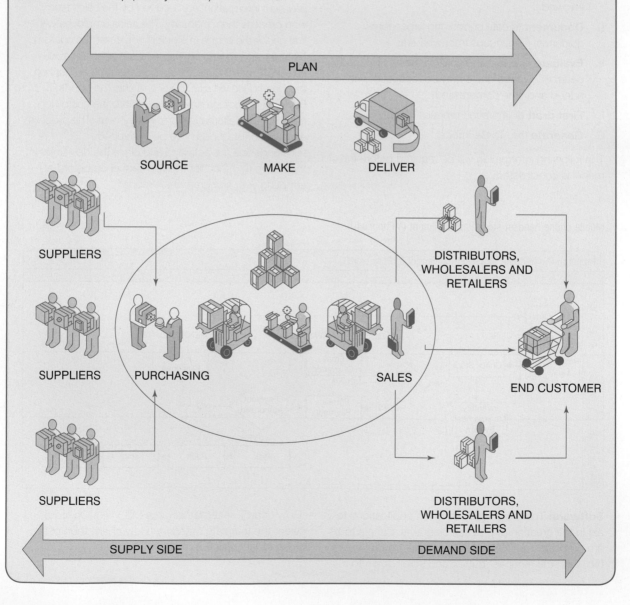

and derive the desired 'To-Be' future state), benchmarking (quantify the operational performance of similar companies and establish Internal targets based on 'best-in-class' results) and process measurement into a cross-functional framework.

A Process Reference Model Contains:

- Standard descriptions of management processes.
- A framework of relationships among the standard processes.
- Standard metrics to measure process performance.
- Management practices that produce best-in-class performance.
- Standard alignment to features and functionality.

SCOR is a model providing a language for communicating amongst supply-chain partners. SCOR[1] contains three levels of Process Detail:

1. Top Level (Process Types) – SCOR is based on Five Distinct Management Processes (Types) – collectively these define the supply chain's configuration:

    1. PLAN: Processes that balance aggregate demand and supply to develop a course of action which best meets sourcing, production and delivery requirements.

    2. **SOURCE**: Processes that procure goods and services to meet planned or actual demand.

    3. **MAKE**: Processes that transform the product to a finished state to meet planned or actual demand.

    4. **DELIVER**: Processes that provide finished goods and services to meet planned or actual demand, typically including order, transportation and distribution management.

    5. RETURN: Processes associated with returning or receiving returned products for any reason. These processes extend into post-delivery customer support.

Each Basic Supply-Chain is a 'Chain' of Source, Make, and Deliver Execution Processes. Each inter-

section of two execution processes (Source-Make-Deliver) is a 'link' in the supply chain. Execution processes transform or transport materials and/or products. Each process is a customer of the previous process and a supplier to the next. At the next level of detail there are,

2. Configuration Level (Process Categories)

    1. PLANNING: A process that aligns expected resources to meet expected demand requirements.

    2. EXECUTION: A process triggered by planned or actual demand that changes the state of material goods. Example Make level 2 processes: › Make-to-Stock, › Make-to-Order and › Engineer-to-Order.

    3. ENABLE: A process that prepares, maintains or manages information or relationships on which planning and execution processes rely.

3. Process Element Level (Decompose Processes) Level 3 processes describe the steps performed to execute the level 2 processes. The sequence in which these processes are executed influences the performance of the level 2 processes and the overall supply chain. Example Make-to-Order level 3 process: › Schedule Production Activities, › Issue Product , › Produce and Test, › Package, › Stage, › Dispose Waste, › Release Product (as was described in the previous section 'Process modelling').

Level 4 processes describe the industry-specific activities required to perform level 3 processes. Level 4 processes describe the detailed implementation of a process. SCOR does not detail level 4 processes. Organizations and industries develop their own level 4 processes. Example 'Issue Product' level 4 processes: › Print Pick List › Pick Items › Close Pick Order.

A set of standard notation is used throughout the Model. **P** depicts Plan elements, **S** depicts Source elements, **M** depicts Make elements, **D** depicts Deliver elements and **R** depicts Return elements. SR = Source Return and DR = Deliver Return. An **E** preceding any of the others (e.g., EP) indicates that the process element is an Enable element associated with the Planning or Execution element (in this case, EP would be an Enable Plan element).

[1] Source: The complete SCOR-model and other related models of the SCC are accessible through the members' section of the www. supply-chain.org website.

Different levels of SCOR

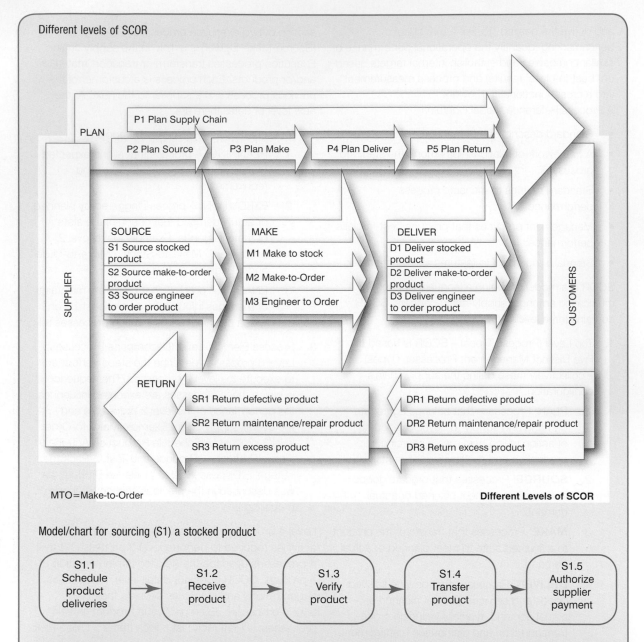

MTO=Make-to-Order

Different Levels of SCOR

Model/chart for sourcing (S1) a stocked product

| S1.1 Schedule product deliveries | S1.2 Receive product | S1.3 Verify product | S1.4 Transfer product | S1.5 Authorize supplier payment |

Example

The chart could be exploded in parts to show more detail such as tasks (for each process element) and activities for each task.

Steps to Establish SCOR Process Models (Workflows)

1. Obtain generic descriptions (this is what people describe).
2. Map these generic descriptions to SCOR process IDs (normalize).
3. Create swimming lanes to reflect organizational boundaries.
4. Create workflow with these SCOR processes.
5. Add description to workflows to reflect inputs/outputs of the processes.
6. Optionally add other relevant information.

SCOR® is typically used to identify, measure, reorganize and improve supply chain processes. Measuring the performance of the supply chain and comparing against internal and external industry goals. Supply chain performance is focused on **responsiveness** – the time it takes to react to and fulfil customer demand and **Agility** – the ability of supply chain to increase/decrease demand within a given planned period for example. Realigning supply chain processes and best practices to fulfil unachieved or changing business objectives. This realignment is achieved through a combination of: Classic process re-engineering from 'As-Is' to 'To-Be', Lean Manufacturing, Six-Sigma, ISO-9000, etc.

Process Classification Framework[SM]

The American Productivity and Quality Centre's (APQC) Process Classification Framework[SM] (PCF[2]) is a taxonomy of cross-functional business processes intended to allow the objective comparison of organizational performance within and amongst organizations. The PCF was developed by APQC and its member companies as an open standard to facilitate improvement through process management and benchmarking, regardless of industry, size or location. The PCF uses 5 levels: Level 1 **Category** – represents the highest level of process in the enterprise, such as Manage customer service, Supply chain, Financial organization, and Human resources; Level 2 **Process Group**

[2] The PCF was developed by non-profit APQC, a global resource for benchmarking and best practices, and its member companies, as an open standard to facilitate improvement through process management and benchmarking, regardless of industry, size or geography. The PCF organizes operating and management processes into 12 enterprise level categories, including process groups and over 1000 processes and associated activities. To download the full PCF or industry-specific versions of the PCF as well as associated measures and benchmarking, visit **www.apqc.org/pcf**.

– indicates the next level of processes and represents a group of processes e.g. Perform after-sales repairs, Procurement, Accounts payable, Recruit/source, and Develop sales strategy are examples of process groups; Level 3 **Process** – a series of interrelated activities that convert inputs into results (outputs); processes consume resources and require standards for repeatable performance; and processes respond to control systems that direct the quality, rate and cost of performance; Level 4 **Activity** – indicates key events performed when executing a process. Examples of activities include Receive customer requests, Resolve customer complaints and Negotiate purchasing contracts; Level 5 **Task** – tasks represent the next level of hierarchical decomposition after activities. Tasks are generally much more fine grained and may vary widely across industries. Examples include: create business case and obtain funding and design recognition and reward approaches.

To further support process definition, benchmarking and content management activities, APQC provides definitions and key performance indicators (KPI) for many of the process elements in the PCF. For example – the process group 'Market and Sell Products and Services' includes all processes required to research and understand customers, the market and the organization's related opportunities. Key Performance Indicators:

Current market share; average monthly sales forecast error within a product family; current customer wallet share and percentage of customers who would recommend product/service.

PART II
MANAGEMENT IN PRACTICE

This part of the book comprises four sections, each is outlined below:

THE CONTEXT OF MANAGEMENT

Having examined some of the key theoretical aspects of management, we now turn to the practice of management. This section of the book considers some of the important contextual issues that lie behind the day-to-day operation of work organizations. Chapter 12 takes a closer look at the national, international and global environment as a context for management. Chapter 13 focuses on the organization as a group of people who work together. Before discussing the different major types of business organization from a legal perspective, we will first consider the organization at a high level, as a social system. This is followed in Chapter 14 which builds upon our concepts of the organization, environment and business context by exploring the internal environment in the form of the organization culture. We define culture and explore its impact upon organizations (and their performance). Finally in Chapter 15 we continue to explore and analyze the internal environment from a human capital perspective and its relationship with the external environment. We will continue to develop an understanding of how an organization's internal environment may differ (examining diversity) and evaluate consequences in terms of strengths and weaknesses.

STRATEGY (PLANNING)

The following five chapters provide a basic introduction to the fundamental management activity of planning and formulating and implementing strategy. No enterprise can be undertaken in a vacuum. It must have some purpose in mind, and the means to at least make a start towards achieving that purpose. Chapter 16 acts as a foundation chapter by considering decision-making – the process of making choices. Decisions may be made at any organization level. Strategy is often about making decisions with a long-term impact. In Chapter 17 we start by asking what is meant by the term strategy and how strategy is created. We build upon this by exploring strategy development and strategic management. Next we identify generic strategies pursued by all companies and how companies compete (business level strategy – how the firm competes). A number of approaches to strategy creation will then be discussed. Chapter 18 focuses on the way organizations translate strategy into action, through policy and more detailed planning (budgets) in particular. Chapter 19 is also concerned with transforming strategy into action. It is therefore concerned with how to manage strategy. This chapter turns attention to implementation issues, strategic control.

ORGANIZING FOR MANAGEMENT

If strategy and planning are considered as providing the route map for the journey, then organizing is the means by which we arrive at our chosen destination. Plans, as we saw earlier, are statements of intent, direction and resourcing. To translate intentions into effect requires purposeful activity, and this is where the role of the organizing function of management is introduced. Organizing is concerned, above all, with activity. It is a process for: determining, grouping and structuring activities; devising and allocating roles arising from the grouping and structuring of activities; assigning accountability for results and determining detailed rules and systems of working, including those for communication, decision-making and conflict-resolution. The next seven chapters concentrate on key aspects of the process of organizing. In particular, Chapter 20 deals with organizing the workforce: organization structures and designs, Chapter 21 is about organizing work, Chapter 22 explains why innovation is needed and how to accomplish it by organization and design, Chapter 23 focuses on organizing for engagement. A common theme throughout the chapter is the attainment of goals and performance through design and organization with an emphasis on the discretionary work effort of employees; Chapter 24 recognizes the constant need to reorganize – to transform, rearrange, restructure, adjust and change the way in which the workforce and transformational resources are organized and used. In Chapter 25 we explore how organizations can strengthen relationships through internal communication, and in Chapter 26 we discuss how to organize yourself in the manager's role.

CONTROL IN MANAGEMENT

The control function in management rounds off the POMC process referred to at the outset of this book. Once the planning, organizing and motivating activities are underway, then they must be monitored and measured, i.e. controlled. The primary aim of the control function of management is to measure performance against aims, objectives and standards with a view to enabling corrective actions to be taken, where necessary, to keep plans on course. Control is essentially a question of developing feedback systems throughout the organization. It may be implemented both quantitatively and qualitatively. There are three chapters in this section of the book. We start by asking why control is seen as a key aspect of management in Chapter 27. This is followed by a chapter (Chapter 28) explaining key terms and concepts associated with quality and consider why quality is so important to every organization today. In Chapter 29, we extend the scope of control into the management of risk and the attempt to control the future and uncertainty by anticipating events that might hinder the organization in its attempts at goal attainment.

Section Seven
The Context
of Management

CHAPTER 12
THE BUSINESS ENVIRONMENT

Key Concepts

- Culture
- Globalization
- Macro-environment
- Micro-environment
- PESTEL
- Opportunity
- Threat

Learning Outcomes Having read this chapter, you should be able to:

- analyze the business environment using the PESTLE framework
- analyze the competitive environment within which a business operates
- explain what is meant by globalization
- distinguish differences between the domestic and global business environment.

FIGURE 12.1 The external environment

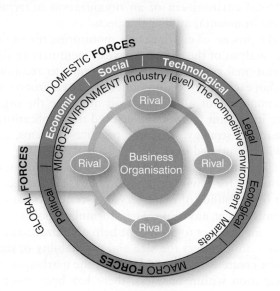

1.   In Chapter 9 we introduced the contingency approach and emphasized the role of the environment in determining management problems and challenges. This chapter takes a closer look at the national, international and global environment as a context for management. The business environment is divided into the external and internal environment. The internal environment consists of all resources and capabilities found within the organization which influence the organization's ability to act (to create outputs). This chapter will focus mainly on the external environment; we will consider the internal environment in chapters to follow. Analysis of the business environment allows organizations and their employees to understand the context within which they operate and appreciate how strategy is developed and implemented. It is important to note, however, that environments are not static but constantly changing. Understanding the business environment and its economic, social and political influences is crucial to success in today's business world. Since the comments of Emery and Trist, almost 50 years ago, we have witnessed great change in the environment of many industries and organizations.

2.   One of the first challenges is to recognize the enormity of factors in the business environment and therefore decompose it into manageable parts. Environmental variables are factors which affect the organization, but are beyond the direct or positive control of the organization. The external environment (see Figure 12.1) may be divided into layers: the macro-environment is the wider environment of social, legal, economic, political and technological influences (forces). The macro-environment contains the more general factors likely to affect organizations in a similar manner, whereas, at the industry level, the factors are of more specific concern to a specific set of organizations. The micro-environment is the immediate (industry) environment, including customers, competitors, suppliers and distributors. One of the main factors affecting most organizations is the degree of competition faced. Greater influence is likely to come from the actions of competitors and the behaviour of customers or prospects. Markets change rapidly through the entrance of new competitors, technologies, legislation and evolving customer needs. Next we consider how to analyze the macro-environment before examining the competitive environment in more detail. In this chapter we present an overview of the business environment; readers can find a more detailed analysis of the contemporary environment in Kelly and Ashwin (2013).

12.1 ANALYZE THE MACRO BUSINESS ENVIRONMENT

3.   Making sense of the macro-environment poses a significant challenge. However, there are diagnostic frameworks to help break it down into more manageable components (environmental variables) which can

of value (and supply) chain fragmentation whereby organizations may 'separate' activities and then locate them around the world. The extent of internationalization and the way organizations see the world can be used to categorize companies – as domestic, domestic with an export department, global, multi-domestic and transnational. Whatever the company type, globalization means that the internal workforce is likely to be diverse and employees are likely to come into contact with customers, suppliers, partners and subsidiary employees, etc. who are different. We therefore discussed practical implications of working and conducting business in other countries. Finally, we recognized that management styles are not universal and practices may need to be adapted when working in other countries.

QUESTIONS

1   Evaluate the impact of globalization on the domestic organization.

2   Use the PESTLE framework to analyze the external environment of a company with which you are familiar.

3   How has globalization and Internet technology impacted the company discussed in question 2?

4   To what extent would you expect the company to be a global organization (as opposed to a multi-domestic organization) – should it see the world as one marketplace or many different marketplaces?

5   Discuss the process of internationalization at the company.

USEFUL WEBSITES

International Monetary Fund: **www.imf.org** The International Monetary Fund (IMF) is an organization of 185 countries, working to foster global monetary cooperation, secure financial stability, facilitate international trade, promote high employment and sustainable economic growth, and reduce poverty around the world.

UNESCO: **www.unesco.org** United Nations Educational, Scientific and Cultural Organization – Topics include: Publications; Statistics; UNESCO partners; Information services

World Trade Organization: **www.gatt.org** World Trade Organization official site

United Nations: **www.un.org**

Geert Hofstede™ Cultural Dimensions: **www.geert-hofstede. com/** On each country page you will find the unique Hofstede graphs depicting the Dimension scores and other demographics for that country and culture – plus an explanation of how they apply uniquely to that country.

EUROPA: **europa.eu/pol/socio/index_en.htmeuropa.eu/ pol/socio/index_en.htm** EUROPA is the portal site of the European Union (europa.eu). It provides up-to-date coverage of European Union affairs and essential information on

European integration. Users can also consult all legislation currently in force or under discussion, access the websites of each of the EU institutions and find out about the policies administered by the European Union World Trade Organization (WTO): **www.wto.org** European Union information service: **www.europa.eu.int** UN Global Compact: **www.unglobalcompact.org** The UN Global Compact is a strategic policy initiative for businesses who are committed to aligning their operations and strategies with ten universally accepted principles in the areas of human rights, labour, environment and anti-corruption. By doing so, business, as a primary agent driving globalization, can help ensure that markets, commerce, technology and finance advance in ways which benefit economies

OECD – Public Employment and Management: **www.oecd.org** The work of the Directorate for Public Governance and Territorial Development on public sector employment and management supports productive managerial change and improved personnel policies in the public service, integrating them with budgetary and other reforms to improve the responsiveness of government and the efficient delivery of public services.

REFERENCES

Hampden-Turner, C.M. and Trompenaars, F. (2000) *Building Cross-Cultural Competence – How to Create Wealth from Conflicting Values*, Wiley.

Hofstede, G. (1984) *Cultures Consequences – abridged*, Sage.

Kelly, P.P. (2009) *International Business and Management*, Cengage Learning EMEA.

Kelly, P. and Ashwin, A. (2013), *The Business Environment*, 1st edn, Cengage.

13.1 ORGANIZATIONS

4.   The process of management discussed in Part 1 does not take place within a vacuum but within the context of the organization; as an open system the organization exists within the wider environment discussed in the previous chapter. An **organization** is a social arrangement for achieving controlled performance in pursuit of collective goals. Thus, organizations are about groups of people with a common goal. We will focus on goals before reviewing common features of organizations.

5.   The theory of the firm consists of a number of economic theories which describe the nature of the firm (company or corporation), including its existence, its behaviour and its relationship with the market. The traditional 'theory of the firm' assumes that profit maximization is the goal of the commercial organization. More recent analyses suggest that sales maximization or market share, combined with satisfactory profits, may be the main purpose of large industrial corporations. Furthermore, whilst traditional views recognized only the shareholder as the focus of organizational goals, more recently, organizations have considered society as a key stakeholder. Organizations exist in a wider environment, where they compete with other organizations for revenue. If the costs of doing business are less than the amount customers are willing to pay for the organization's goods and services, the organization makes profit which may be retained or distributed to shareholders.

6.   Amongst the performance measurements for organizations is the triple bottom line. The triple bottom line (or 'TBL', '3BL', or 'People, Planet, Profit') captures an extended range of values and criteria for measuring organizational success; economic, environmental and social. The concept of TBL demands that companies should be responsible to 'stakeholders' rather than shareholders. In this case, 'stakeholders' refers to anyone who is influenced, either directly or indirectly, by the actions of the organization.

    i.   People (Human Capital) pertains to fair and beneficial business practices towards labour and the community and region in which a corporation conducts its business

    ii.   Planet (Natural Capital) refers to sustainable environmental practices, and

    iii. Profit (not limited to the internal profit made by a company or organization) is the bottom line shared by all commerce – the economic benefit enjoyed by the host society.

7.   The triple bottom line idea proposes that an organization's licence to operate in society comes not just from satisfying stakeholders through improved profits (the economic bottom line), but by also improving its environmental and social performance. As such, it encompasses environmental responsibility, social awareness and economic profitability.

8.   Returning to the concept of the organization we have noted it to be about groups of people with common goals. There are, arguably, two other aspects to organizations, particularly but not exclusively business organizations. Organizations tend to have structure (Section 9) and some process of management. It is management, as we saw in Part 1, who direct and control the activities of organizational members, in pursuit of goal(s). Goal setting and planning are the management activities associated with strategy, to be discussed in the next section of the book.

9.   Fundamentally there are two types of organization: formal and informal. The **formal organization** is the collection of work groups that has been consciously designed by management to maximize efficiency and achieve organizational goals. The **informal organization** on the other hand is the network of relationships between members of an organization that form of their own accord, on the basis of common interests and companionship.

10.   Organizations can be viewed in many ways, with different *components*. Many scholars and practitioners separate the organization into the operating (production work) and the administrative components. Others decompose the organization further recognizing senior (strategy) and middle (coordination and integration and tactics) management.

11.   Another common way to distinguish organization type is in terms of the private and public sector. This method of classification is based on company ownership which may be shareholders versus government respectively. Similarly, goals may differ as profit or not-for-profit. However, as discussed earlier, profit is no longer the only goal for private sector organizations.

12.   Organizations may also be categorized according to whether they are production or service organizations. Whilst a product may be regarded as anything that is capable of satisfying customer needs, some

business scholars distinguish it from a service – the application of human and mechanical efforts to people or objects in order to provide intangible benefits to customers; an intangible product involving a deed, a performance or an effort that cannot physically be possessed.

13. As discussed so far we can classify organizations in many ways: according to purpose (economic/public service), prime beneficiary (members, owners, public) and the primary activity – generating products or services. The type of organization impacts upon various aspects of the internal environment and context.

14. Organizations may also be classified according to their size. Within the EU the category of micro, small and medium-sized enterprises (SMEs) is made up of enterprises which employ fewer than 250 persons and which have an annual turnover not exceeding 50 million euro, and/or an annual balance sheet total not exceeding 43 million euro.

15. In the EU (2010), there are over 20 million SMEs providing around 130 million jobs and representing 99 per cent of all enterprises. They provide two out of three of the private sector jobs and contribute to more than half of the total value-added created by businesses in the EU. Moreover, SMEs provide the foundation for the European economy as they are responsible primarily for wealth and economic growth, next to their key role in innovation and R&D. What is even more intriguing is that nine out of ten SMEs are actually micro enterprises.

16. A micro-enterprise (company) has a headcount of < 10 and an annual turnover < €2M; a small company has a headcount of < 50 and an annual turnover < €10M; and a medium-sized enterprise has a headcount of < 250 and an annual turnover < €50M. A large enterprise is a business which has both the following: Over 250 full-time equivalent employees and an annual turnover > €50M.

17. A further way of classifying organizations is based on their legal status. We will devote the remainder of this chapter to this topic as it influences organization and management. The most common types of business organization are as follows:

- limited companies

- sole traders, and

- partnerships.

The following paragraphs summarize the principal features of these businesses, together with the main advantages and disadvantages for the parties concerned. This is the first of three chapters that explore the internal environment. Taken with the previous chapter, they provide the context which may determine key aspects of management as considered by the contingency theories of management discussed in Chapter 9.

13.2 LIMITED COMPANIES

18. A limited company is a type of business entity; it is the most common form of business 'structure'. When a limited company is formed, it is said to have become 'incorporated', i.e. endowed with a separate body, or person. The corporation so formed is treated in law as a separate entity, independent of its members; a company with its own legal identity. The corporation, or 'company', as it is generally called, is capable of owning property, employing people, making contracts and of suing or being sued. Another important feature of a company is that, unlike a sole trader or a partnership, it does have continuity of succession, as it is unaffected by the death or incapacity of one or more of its members. Limited companies can be found in most countries, although the detailed rules governing them vary widely.

19. A limited company then is an organization owned by its shareholders. The key feature of a 'limited' company is that, if it fails, it can only require its members (shareholders) to meet its debts up to the limit of the nominal value of their shares (what they have invested). The principle of legally limiting the financial liabilities of persons investing in business ventures was introduced in the 1850s to encourage the wealthy to give financial support to the inventors, engineers and others who were at the forefront of the Industrial Revolution. Without the protection of limited liability, an investor could find himself stripped of his home and other personal assets in order to meet debts arising from the failure of any company in which he had invested his money.

20. Since the turn of the twentieth century, various laws have determined the principles and procedures to be followed in the conduct of business organizations. These rules intended to minimize the risk to suppliers and customers as well as to shareholders, and to a lesser extent employees, arising from gross

mismanagement of, or deliberate restriction of information about, a company. Within the UK, for example, legislation was consolidated into one Principal Act – the Companies Act 2006. The Act provides a comprehensive code of company law for the UK, and made changes to almost every aspect of the law in relation to companies. The Act codifies certain existing common law principles, such as those relating to directors' duties and introduces various new provisions for private and public companies but otherwise amends or restates almost all of the Companies Act 1985.

21.   Within the EU, harmonization of the rules relating to company law and corporate governance, as well as to accounting and auditing, is essential for creating a single market for Financial Services and products. In the fields of company law and corporate governance, objectives include: providing equivalent protection for shareholders and other parties concerned with companies; ensuring freedom of establishment for companies throughout the EU; fostering efficiency and competitiveness of business; promoting cross-border cooperation between companies in different Member States; and stimulating discussions between Member States on the modernization of company law and corporate governance.

22.   EU company law and corporate governance rules for companies, investors and employees must be adapted to the needs of today's society and to the changing economic environment. In December 2012, the European Commission published plans to modernize European company law and corporate governance. They believe that European company law and corporate governance should ensure that companies are competitive and sustainable. They seek to encourage and facilitate long-term shareholder engagement, by increasing the level of transparency between companies and their shareholders and by simplifying cross-border operations of European undertakings. Their action plan foresees merging all major company law directives into a single instrument. This would make EU company law more accessible and comprehensible and reduce the risk of future inconsistencies.

23.   Limited liability companies fall into two categories: public limited companies (plcs) and private limited companies. The Memorandum of a plc must state that the company is a public company (i.e. its shares are available for purchase by the public) and the company name must end with the words 'Public limited company'. A private limited company, by comparison, may not offer its shares to the public, and is even restricted in the transfer of its shares between the private shareholders. The name of a private limited company must end with the word 'Limited'. Both kinds of company must have at least two members and one Director. Once registered, a private company can begin trading without further formality. A public limited company must obtain a certificate of trading from the Registrar of Companies.

24.   All limited companies must fulfil certain procedures before they can be incorporated. These include the filing of two particularly important documents: (a) the Memorandum of Association (purpose of the company etc.) and (b) the Articles of Association which regulate the internal affairs of the company. Companies are required to submit annual returns to the Registrar, and these are available for public inspection.

25.   The main advantages of limited liability can be summarized as follows:

- in the event of business failure, shareholders are protected against the loss of more than the nominal value of their shareholding

- the separate legal person of the company exists independently of the members

- shares (in plcs) are readily transferable.

The disadvantages are primarily as follows:

- because liability is limited, it may be difficult for small companies to borrow money as extensively as desired, since banks and other financial institutions may be unable to recover their funds if the business fails

- there are legal procedures involved in setting up a company, as well as the procedures incurred in publishing the various financial accounts of the company.

26.   The European Company Statute, more commonly known by its Latin name 'Societas Europaea' or SE, was adopted on 8 October 2001 (IP/01/1376, MEMO/01/314), after more than 30 years of negotiations. The Statute for a European Company (Council Regulation (EC) No 2157/2001) creates the legal form of 'European public limited-liability company'. It contains a set of rules directly applicable in all Member States, in particular on the formation and the structure of an SE. The legal regime of the SEs is completed

with cross-references to the national legislation applicable to public limited-liability companies (see para 23). The Council Regulation on the Statute for a European Company 2157/2001 is an EU Regulation containing the rules for a public EU company, called a Societas Europaea, or 'SE'. An SE can register in any member state of the EU and transfer to other member states.

27. The SE is a European Public Limited-Liability Company. An SE may be created on registration in any one of the Member States of the European Economic Area (EEA). Article 10 of the Regulation requires Member States to treat an SE as if it is a public limited company formed in accordance with the law of the Member State in which it has its registered office. Regardless of the currency in which it is expressed, an SE is required to have a minimum amount of subscribed share capital equivalent to at least EUR €120 000. The Statute for a European Company (Societas Europaea or SE) gives companies operating in more than one Member State the option of establishing as a single company under EU law. This allows them to operate throughout the EU with one set of rules, including a unified management and reporting system.

13.2.1 Company Directors

28. Thus far we have defined the organization and considered certain organizational types but have not considered who is ultimately responsible for their management. The directors of an organization are the persons who are members of its board. A *board of directors* is a body of elected or appointed members who jointly oversee the activities of a company or organization. Directors may also be employees (sometimes referred to as an Executive Director), officers, major shareholders or persons similarly connected to the organization. On the other hand, an 'outside' or non-executive director is a member of the board who is not otherwise employed by or engaged with the organization. Outside directors bring outside experience and perspective to the board. They keep a watchful eye on the inside directors and on the way the organization is run. However, in some countries, a director is simply someone who supervises, controls or manages.

29. Executive directors are usually full-time employees, whereas non-executives usually work part-time for 1 or 2 days a month. Some non-executive directors serve on several different boards, and this has raised questions as to whether there should be restrictions on the number of such posts held by any one individual. Recently, non-executive directors have been encouraged to take the leadership of key board committees, such as the audit and remuneration committees. This means they, rather than their executive colleagues, are monitoring the company's financial audits and establishing the remuneration of the board members. There are a few who argue that the UK's so-called unitary boards are *de facto* two-tier boards, where one section is composed of full-time executive directors, fully in the picture about what is happening in the company, whilst the other, smaller section comprises the part-time non-executives, who are remote from most of the day-to-day events in the company.

30. The directors of the company are, in law, its agents, and are accountable for the conduct of the company's affairs; they must act within their powers and abide by the terms of the **company's memorandum and articles of association** and decisions made by the shareholders. They are appointed by the shareholders/members to use their best endeavours to achieve the company's objectives. Every director has a duty to act honestly in the best interests of the company (fiduciary duties), to avoid possible conflicts of interest, and not to make a personal profit from the directorship other than what the company is prepared to pay by way of salary and fees, for example. Directors must act in a way that benefits the shareholders as a whole, but additionally must have regard for other matters such as the interests of employees, the impact on the community and the environment, etc.

31. The principal director is usually the *Chairman* of the board, who may be full or part-time. The senior executive director is the person who holds the title of Managing Director or **Chief Executive Officer (CEO)** and who is responsible for overall day-to-day operations, as well as for board duties. The CEO is responsible for implementing policies and strategy, as well as helping to formulate them. He, or she, is responsible for building and motivating the senior management team, and for installing appropriate systems to ensure the smooth-running of the business. The chief administrative officer of the board is the Company Secretary, who is responsible for ensuring that the legal requirements are adhered to when running meetings, appointing directors, voting and executing other procedures. The Company Secretary may, or may not, be a director. In a small company the CEO may act as Company Secretary.

32. Directors' responsibilities include determining and subsequently monitoring the company's strategic goals and the policies under which they are to be achieved. Directors are also responsible for preparing and

publishing the company's financial accounts for the shareholders/members. These accounts (see Chapter 44) must include the balance sheet, showing the company's assets and liabilities at the end of the trading year. They must include a profit and loss account (or income and expenditure account), showing the income received from trading activities, the cost of sales, the amount of profit, taxation, dividends paid and profits retained in the business. Most accounts also include a cash flow statement.

33.   Accounts may need to be audited by an external and independent firm of accountants, in order to confirm that the accounts represent 'a true and fair view of the state of affairs of the company'. Otherwise, the auditors may qualify the accounts. It is the responsibility of the directors to recommend the appointment of the company's auditors, and to satisfy themselves the auditors are fulfilling their duties properly. In particular, directors need to pay attention to the way the company treats such issues as depreciation, stock valuation and financial provisions.

13.3 CORPORATE GOVERNANCE

34.   Businesses around the world seek to attract funding from investors in order to expand and grow. Before investors place their funds in a particular business, they want to be sure that the business is financially sound and will continue to be so in the foreseeable future. Investors therefore need to have confidence that the business is being well-managed and will continue to be profitable. The financial crisis which came to a head in 2008–09 along with several corporate scandals during the beginning of the millennium triggered widespread reappraisal, locally and internationally, of the governance systems which might have alleviated it.

35.   The manner in which company directors promote and control their company's operations, that is the way they exercise their stewardship, is not just a matter of interest to their shareholders/members, but is a matter of public interest too. Around the world and in the UK a number of codes of good practice have been developed over recent years, following criticisms of the behaviour of some boards and individual directors. In the USA the federal government passed the Sarbanes-Oxley Act in 2002, intending to restore public confidence in corporate governance. Similar corporate failures in other countries stimulated increased regulatory interest.

36.   The UK Corporate Governance Code 2010 ('the Code') is a set of principles of good corporate governance aimed at companies listed on the London Stock Exchange. The Code is essentially a consolidation and refinement of a number of different reports and codes concerning opinions on good corporate governance. The purpose of corporate governance is to facilitate effective, entrepreneurial and prudent management in order to deliver long-term success of the company. The Code's function should be to help boards discharge their duties in the best interests of their companies.

37.   The first version of the UK Code on Corporate Governance was produced in 1992 by the Cadbury Committee. Its paragraph 2.5 is still the classic definition of the context of the Code: Corporate governance is the system by which companies are directed and controlled. Boards of directors are responsible for the governance of their companies. The shareholders' role in governance is to appoint the directors and the auditors and to satisfy themselves that an appropriate governance structure is in place. The responsibilities of the board include setting the company's strategic aims, providing the leadership to realize these aims, supervising the management of the business and reporting to shareholders on their stewardship. The board's actions are subject to laws, regulations and the shareholders in general meeting. Corporate governance is therefore about what the board of a company does and how it sets the values of the company, and is to be distinguished from the day-to-day operational management of the company by full-time executives.

38.   The Code is not a rigid set of rules. It consists of principles and provisions. The Listing Rules (publicly listed companies have to abide by additional regulations called the 'Listing Rules'; traditionally set by the Stock Exchange itself but now administered by the Financial Services Authority (FSA) and effectively have the force of law) require companies to apply the main principles and report to shareholders on how they have adhered to these principles. The main principles of the code focus on:

  i.   LEADERSHIP – every company should be headed by an effective board which is collectively responsible for the long-term success of the company

  ii.   EFFECTIVENESS – e.g. the board should be supplied, in a timely manner, with information in a form and of a quality appropriate to enable it to discharge its duties

iii.   ACCOUNTABILITY – the board is responsible for determining the nature and extent of the significant risks it is willing to take in achieving its strategic objectives. The board should maintain sound risk management and internal control systems

iv.   REMUNERATION – formal and transparent procedures on executive remuneration etc., and

v.   RELATIONS WITH SHAREHOLDERS – e.g. the board should use the AGM to communicate with investors and to encourage their participation.

13.4 SOLE TRADERS

39.   The sole trader is the simplest form of business organization – one person in business on their own. In the UK, over 3.6 million individuals are classed as 'enterprises with no employees' – they represent three out of four businesses. The legal requirements for setting up such a business are minimal, but the owner is fully liable for any debts incurred in running the business, since the owner literally is the business. Ownership and control are combined. All profits made by the sole trader are subject to income tax rather than the corporation tax levied on company profits. Apart from the need to maintain accounts for controlling the business and for dealing with the Inland Revenue, there are no formal accounts to be published.

40.   The main advantages of operating as a sole trader are:

-   easy to start

-   complete autonomy to run the business as the individual wishes

-   the profits of the business belong to the trader

-   various business expenses are allowable against income tax

-   no public disclosure of accounts (except to Inland Revenue).

The main disadvantages are as follows:

-   the sole trader is entirely responsible for the debts of the business

-   the individual as owner and manager has to be responsible for all aspects of the business (marketing, product development, sales, finance, etc.).

13.5 PARTNERSHIPS

41.   A partnership is a type of business entity in which partners (owners) share with each other the profits or losses of the business. Partnerships are often favoured over other business forms for taxation purposes. However, owners of a partnership may be exposed to greater personal liability than they would as shareholders of a corporation. The legalities required to set up a partnership are minimal, although it is advisable to have a formal partnership agreement drawn up by a solicitor. Such an agreement can specify the rights and obligations of individual partners, and can make provision for changes brought about by death or retirement of partners.

42.   As with a sole trader, the members of a partnership are owners of its property and liable for its contracts. Therefore they are fully responsible for meeting their debts to third parties. Partners are not automatically entitled to a salary for the services they provide for the partnership, but are entitled to their proper share of the profits of the business. However, many agreements do allow for salaried partners. UK partnership law refers to the rules under which partnerships are governed in the UK. The principal sources of law are the Partnership Act 1890 and the Limited Partnership Act 1907. Most professional persons, and especially accountants and solicitors, maintain partnership as their form of business in order to preserve the principle of individual professional accountability towards the client.

43. The main advantages of partnership are:

- few formalities required for starting up

- sharing of partners' knowledge and skills

- sharing of management of business

- no obligation to publish accounts (except for Inland Revenue purposes)

- sharing of profits (or losses!) of business.

The disadvantages are primarily these:

- each partner is liable for the debts of the partnership, even if caused by the actions of other partners

- risk that the partners may not be able to work together at a personal level

- the death or bankruptcy of one partner will automatically dissolve the partnership, unless otherwise provided for in a partnership agreement.

CONCLUSION

44. In Part 1 we explored management and organizational theory, discussing how organizations should be managed. Whilst in Chapter 2 we stated, in broad terms, what is meant by the term 'organization', we did not explore types of organization in practice. That was the focus of this chapter. Different types of company can exist in law and each has different advantages and disadvantages and rules within which they must comply. In this chapter we explored the main types of organization (limited companies, sole traders, partnerships) and how they evolve.

45. We recognized that in some cases the owners and investors may not be employed by the company, typically in public limited companies. In such situations there is a need for mechanisms to ensure that the board, directors, managers and employees act in the best interests of the shareholders. We introduced the concept of corporate governance, explicit 'rules' and principles to guide the management of such companies by their directors.

QUESTIONS

1 After completing your business studies, you and several friends decide to set up a consultancy company. Evaluate the types of business organization and select the one you believe is most suited to your venture. Explain your choice.

2 Review each of the main types of organization (limited companies, sole traders, partnerships and cooperatives) and discuss the role of corporate governance (rules and principles) in managing the company.

3 Discuss why corporate governance is important for contemporary UK listed companies. Evaluate the role of governance codes in organizations.

USEFUL WEBSITES

The Management Standards Centre **http://www.management-standards.org**

Institute of Directors **http://www.iod.com**

The UK Corporate Governance Code **http://www.frc.org.uk/documents/pagemanager/Corporate_**

Governance/UK%20Corp%20Gov%20Code%20June%202010.pdf

The Companies House website **http://www.companieshouse.gov.uk/index.shtml** Companies House is a registry of corporate information.

CHAPTER 14
ORGANIZATIONAL CULTURE

Key Concepts

- Culture
- Organizational culture
- Organizational climate

Learning Outcomes Having read this chapter, you should be able to:

- explain what is meant by organizational culture
- list factors that may be a source or manifestation of organizational culture
- differentiate several dimensions of organizational culture
- evaluate organizational culture as strength or weakness
- describe how and why managers attempt culture change.

Vignette

SHIFTING TO A DIGITAL CULTURE

Contemporary organizations will not succeed in this digital age by simply adopting digital processes and systems, argue Chitkara and Davidson (2013). The workforce must also adopt new ways of working. Chitkara and Davidson believe an organization must develop a culture that does not simply tolerate digitization but embraces it. 'Culture is an organization's self-sustaining pattern of behaving, feeling, thinking, and believing. It gives an organization its personality and shapes both its internal processes and the way it is seen by the outside world.' Apple's corporate culture is one of innovation, simplicity and elegant design and Ikea's frugal culture is embodied in every aspect of the company's day-to-day operations, from product development to store design. It is instilled in all employees who are recruited and trained by the company. However, developing the right culture cannot be accomplished overnight. 'Changing culture takes a very long time. It is not something that changes with a memo from managers trying to convince people of the merits of digitization.' Chitkara and Davidson provide advice on the process of evolving to a digital culture.

They argue a need to 'Match strategy to culture … the particular strategy an organization employs will only be successfully executed if it is supported by appropriate cultural attributes.' They also argue that there is no such thing as all good or all bad culture. There will be aspects that are considered a strength and should be preserved whilst there will be aspects ('limitations') that may not assist the organization in its mission. Chitkara and Davidson advise that leaders should support the adoption of digital culture not merely through commands but through actions.

1.   In the previous chapter we identified with organizations and noted that when a limited company is formed, it is said to have become 'incorporated', i.e. endowed with a separate body, or person. The corporation so formed is treated in law as a separate entity, independent of its members; a company with its own legal identity. In the opening vignette the authors suggest that culture gives an organization its personality. Thus, we might suggest that not only does the entity become endowed with a separate body but also a collective mind and this is the culture of the organization. But how does the culture form and develop?

2.   Part 2 opened with a chapter about the business environment where we made use of the PESTEL framework to decompose the macro (external) environment, creating manageable components. Amongst the PESTEL components is the social factor, itself strongly associated with culture. Culture at this level is about nations and countries, i.e. the values and beliefs common to a particular race or society. We suggested that culture describes the shared ways of thinking and behaving (uniformity) within a group of people. In para. 32 we noted that 'two main types of culture, of interest to readers of this book, are national (country level) and organizational'. We also stated that we would review the literature on organizational culture in this chapter. Whereas national culture is mainly seen as an external factor (influencing customer preferences etc.), it nevertheless permeates the workforce, contributing to shared ways of thinking and behaving within the workplace. It is less likely to be a significant factor when comparing two or more domestic companies than when comparing companies from different countries. In such cases it may be viewed, relative to specific goals, as a strength or weakness. As has been previously noted, it is an integrative mechanism that can unify the workforce.

3.   In the previous chapter we discussed organizations, noting them to be about groups of people with common goals. In many ways this could also be a definition of culture. Yet culture is more than this as will be seen by the end of this chapter. Culture also seeks to encapsulate shared ways of thinking and behaving. However, it is important to realize that shared ways of thinking and behaving will often be driven by goals.

4.   We have already made repeated reference to (organizational) culture on a number of occasions throughout Part 1 of this book. In Chapter 3 we noted how Handy (1999) described bureaucracies as 'role cultures' based on logic and rationality. In Chapter 10 we argued a 'business process culture' is a culture (collective way of working) that is cross-functional (horizontal in its outlook as opposed to hierarchical and vertical), customer oriented along with process and system thinking. Later in that chapter we discussed a customer responsive culture and a culture of trust. Furthermore, we noted that the culture of a learning organization encourages experimentation, trial and error. We discussed culture as shared values (Chapter 10, para. 23). Throughout Part 1 we were discussing organizational culture, a construct we explore in more detail here.

5.   In this chapter we define culture and explore its impact upon organizations (and their performance). Leading scholars believe culture to be extremely difficult to define and one of the most contentious concepts in business! Even if we could define culture it may prove either impossible or very difficult to develop or change as some scholars see culture as something an organization 'is' rather than something it has. Despite this, many organizations see culture as a means to unify (integrate) employees, leading to cost efficiencies since employees are almost self-regulated (self-controlled) as opposed to being controlled through tight supervision and excessive bureaucracy. When culture is used as a unifying mechanism and when employees are more homogenous in their collective ways of thinking and behaving, we can say that a strong culture exists. Strong cultures are seen as efficient and more appropriate for stable environments but in a dynamic environment the organization may emphasize the importance of creativity. It has been argued that this is a more likely outcome from weaker, more heterogeneous cultures (weak culture).

6.   Culture has many functions (and dysfunctions) and deals with how things are done in a company (**practice** – behaviour) therefore impacting upon many aspects of the organization, including its performance. It can help with motivation, recruitment, retention, sales and investment. In this chapter we start by explaining what we mean by culture at the organizational as opposed to the national level; we also identify how managers recognize culture in the workplace. We then develop our concept of culture by considering leading thinkers' (such as Edgar Schein) ideas on the matter. Having explored what is meant by culture we then evaluate organizational culture as strength or weakness. Finally, we discuss the development of organizational culture, asking whether it is possible and why organizations might try to change their culture and how they might go about the task.

14.1 WHAT IS CULTURE AND HOW DO WE RECOGNIZE IT?

7.   For many, the 1980s was the 'decade of organizational culture'. There was a great deal of academic and practitioner interest and activity around this time. The concept became in-vogue as a result of increasing competition, both nationally and globally, and turbulence in the external environments of many organizations. Towards the end of the 1980s strategists moved from a focus on external positioning strategies (recall Porter's five forces) to a concern with the use of internal resources to gain sustainable competitive advantages. Culture became the intangible strategic weapon that competitors found difficult to imitate. Consequently, any associated advantages were enduring. During this period many definitions of the construct emerged along with a plethora of prescriptive advice on its management.

8.   In the opening vignette culture was defined as an organization's self-sustaining pattern of behaving, feeling, thinking and believing. Some readers may find this definition a little unfocused. There are many definitions of culture and as a socially defined construct this is only to be expected. The best way to gain an understanding of its meaning is to review several leading definitions and identify common aspects. Culture is always about groups and shared thinking or behaviour.

9.   Whilst there are several types (levels) of culture they tend not to be defined in the same way. When defining national culture we should consider how members of a country or society can share ideas and practices from an early and formative age whilst members of organizations tend to be adults when they work together. For this reason, definitions of organizational culture tend to be different. Schein (1996) notes the importance of culture which he refers to as shared norms, values and **assumptions** in how organizations function. Buchanan and Huczynski (2010) define organizational culture as 'the collection of relatively uniform and enduring values, beliefs, customs, traditions and practices that are shared by an organization's members, learned by new recruits and transmitted from one generation of employees to the next'. The important point about culture is that whilst there may be striking differences between organizations, there is a shared understanding within them. The culture does not become established until this shared understanding achieves dominance in the collective thinking of the members of the organization.

10.   Having considered definitions of culture, for now we need to deliberate what it looks like within organizations. When all has been said and done about the theoretical side of culture, the practical question remains: 'Where, and how, do managers come to recognize the dominant culture in their organization?' Where should they look, and what questions should they ask? Johnson (1988) described a cultural web, identifying a number of elements that can be used to describe (or influence) organizational culture. At the centre of the web is the **paradigm**, the set of beliefs and assumptions held relatively common through the organization. Surrounding the paradigm are the:

- Organizational structures
- Power structures
- Symbols
- Routines
- Rituals and myths
- Control systems.

11. Many respected writers on culture discuss similar components. *Symbols* are things that can be experienced with the senses and used by members of an organization to make meaning. They represent one 'tool' for interpreting culture. Examples include logos, uniforms, how employees dress, cars (types provided to executives), offices (space and layout), etc. Symbols can also be used to indicate status within a culture. This includes clothing, office decor and so on. Status symbols signal the correct behaviour to be directed at others in the hierarchy; they prescribe behaviours that are appropriate for their status and position.

12. *Routines* are the organizationally specific 'ways we do things around here' which tend to persist over time and guide people's behaviour. *Rituals* are the series of actions or types of behaviour regularly and invariably followed by employees (see for example management meetings, reports). Another word for ritual is *rite* though some people use the word more specifically as any customary observance or practice. People often discuss *rites of passage*, generally changing an individual's social status, such as graduation or induction into a new job. They may also discuss rites in terms of enhancement (awards and promotion), renewal (training and development) or integration (developing bonds and relationships). What is important is that organizations develop their shared way of doing such things and that the way things are done codifies shared assumptions and beliefs within the organization.

13. Corporate *slogans* and *stories* also encapsulate and communicate aspects of organizational culture, like 'customer first'. Stories are narratives frequently shared amongst employees. Often told to new employees they can inform them about the organization. Often about company heroes (role models) they serve as models or ideals for cultural norms and values. Slogans, stories, symbols, routines, rituals and rites are all means by which organizational culture can be transmitted to members. We will revisit them later in the chapter when discussing methods to develop organizational culture.

14. The idea of culture existing at different levels has been applied in two key ways. We have already discussed levels of culture when contrasting national with organizational culture. People also discuss the professional level or even sub-cultural (departments within an organization) level. The idea of levels is also used within a specific type of culture. A number of experts on culture describe organizational culture on two levels: surface and underlying. On the surface are the visible artefacts (phenomena accessible to the senses, including architecture, myths, rituals, logos, type of personnel employed and so on, which signify the values in an organization's culture) and observable behaviour. The visible elements of organizational culture reflect deeper values, assumptions, ways of thinking and beliefs in the minds of employees. Many believe this to be the true but invisible culture.

15. Schein extends our understanding of culture when he suggests it is generated not only by sharing values and traditions, but even more by sharing the assumptions that emerge about the best way of handling problems. He describes espoused values, which may or may not be practised throughout the organization. We could say at this level that individuals may experience a certain amount of 'lip-service' being paid to selected values. Attention to customer care, for example, may be a value that is proclaimed in mission statements and departmental objectives, yet may be placed on one side when the organization is busy or when some other operational factor demands managers' attention.

16. According to Schein's perception of culture, it is only as these second-tier values become absorbed into the organization's subconscious, and become implicit assumptions about behaviour, that they truly deserve to be termed the organization's culture. Thus, in this example, attention to customer care becomes so much a way of behaving that no one would compromise it, even when operational difficulties occurred.

17. A similar construct to organizational culture is that of the institution. Institutions have been defined as 'rules, norms and beliefs that describe reality for the organization, explaining what is and is not, what can be acted upon and what cannot' (Hoffman, 1999: p. 351). As taken-for-granted, culturally embedded understandings, they specify and justify social arrangements and behaviours, both formal and informal.

18. Other scholars have introduced the concept of the organizational climate – the prevailing atmosphere surrounding the organization – the level of morale and strength of feelings or belonging, care and goodwill among members – organizational climate is based on the perceptions of members towards the organization. It paves the way for the notion of organizational culture. It is a set of properties of the work environment, perceived directly or indirectly by the employees, that is assumed to be a major force in influencing employee behaviour. In a similar way, culture can play an important role in creating an organizational climate that enables learning and innovation. We have summarized the key concepts used so far in Figure 14.1.

FIGURE 14.1   Culture – key concepts

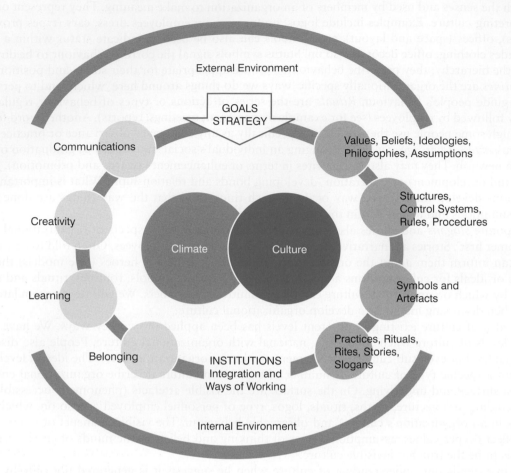

19.   On a more specific level, scholars have discussed the communication climate – the prevailing organizational atmosphere in which ideas and information are exchanged; an open climate promotes collaborative working, which is discouraged by a closed communication climate. Climate, culture and the institutional constructs are important aspects of the overall internal context, environment or situation. Although culture and climate are related, climate often proves easier to assess and change.

20.   The external environment, customers, competitors, suppliers and other external stakeholders will all exert some influence on what the organization chooses to do, and how it will do it. Figure 14.1 illustrates some important interrelationships that both produce and are deeply affected by the organization's culture.

21.   To identify and interpret culture requires us to make inferences on observable artefacts. As Figure 14.1 shows, there are several factors that are both a source of culture, and a manifestation of it. Examples of some of the ways in which managers learn about their culture are: mission statements, corporate aims, policy statements, organizational rituals (induction programmes for newcomers, retirement parties/leaving speeches, reward ceremonies for key sales staff, etc.), organizational logos, procedures/rules, management attitudes, organizational structure, behaviour that is rewarded or punished, etc.

22.   Hofstede found that the major cultural differences between organizations lay in their practices rather than in their values. He examined cultural practices in terms of six dimensions, presenting them as a means to analyze and compare organizations and their culture. He believed organizations differ according to whether they focus more on the way work is done (method) or the results; what Hofstede labelled as a *Process versus results orientation*. Some organizations favour a concern for people versus an emphasis on completing the job (the task) – *Employee versus job orientation*. In some organizations individual employees identify themselves more with their organization whilst others with their profession – *Parochial versus*

professional. Hofstede also commented on aspects of the climate, distinguishing an *Open versus closed (social) system* – whether the organizational culture favoured openness to newcomers and outsiders, or had an inward-looking, almost secretive attitude towards its members. In some organizations strict adherence to matters of cost and timeliness are found, whilst others prefer a more relaxed approach to these issues, *loose versus tight control*. In some organizations the culture expects people to conform to rules, while others expect employees to act flexibly in order to meet customers' wants or achieve targets.

23.   In summary there have been many definitions of organizational culture. This is to be expected and any attempt to focus on one seems to limit the construct. That said, from a pragmatic standpoint, it is helpful to have a simple understanding in mind. For us it is the *customary and traditional way of thinking and doing things shared by employees within the organization*. As a complex set of interdependent factors it is something the organization 'is' rather than 'has'. However, it is possible to tease out some of the factors (components) for manipulation by management. It is, however, far from a perfect science and not a case of simply pulling a few levers to bring about change. In the next section we learn about why organizational culture is considered to be such an important management construct.

14.2 CULTURE TYPES, PURPOSE AND ORGANIZATIONAL PERFORMANCE

24.   The purpose of organizational culture is to integrate, unify and provide employees with a sense of organizational identity and a fundamental rationale, ideology or philosophy. This becomes an inner compass for employees, to guide all kinds of work behaviours. When this leads to success it becomes self-perpetuating and institutionalized. We can decompose the purpose into two discrete and critical functions; one with an external and the other an internal focus.

1)   ADAPTATION (External) – survival challenges

2)   INTEGRATION (Internal) and a reason for being

Culture helps employees interpret the challenges of the external environment, shaping the lens through which they view the world and guiding their activities to meet goals and work together productively. It directs employee decision-making in the absence of written rules or policies.

25.   Most management scholars now believe that the organizational culture (type) is contingent on the external environment and on the strategy. At this point you may recall that systems theory suggests many management variables are interconnected and interdependent. This point is reflected in the well-known McKinsey 7S Framework, a management model developed by business consultants Robert H. Waterman, Jr and Tom Peters. The model is based on the theory that, for an organization to perform well, seven elements need to be aligned and mutually reinforcing. The basic premise of the model is that there are seven internal aspects of an organization that need to be aligned if it is to be successful. The seven interdependent elements are:

Strategy | Structure | Systems | Shared Values | Skills | Style | Staff

26.   We know that environments vary on a continuum from stable to dynamic (requiring flexibility). Consequently we might expect some cultures to perform better than others according to their alignment with the environment. Historically and traditionally, we might have expected to observe a **bureaucratic culture** prevalent in stable and predictable environments where employee behaviour is governed by formal rules, standard operating procedures and hierarchical control. Such a culture has an internal focus that supports a methodical approach to doing business. This culture emphasizes cooperation, tradition, and following established policies and practices as ways to achieve goals. The culture is about consistency and conformity, i.e. efficiency. Contrast this with what has been termed an **adaptability culture** which encourages entrepreneurial values, norms, beliefs. Such a culture is likely to embrace change and encourage risk taking, experimentation, trial and error. Innovation, creativity and risk taking are valued and rewarded. Technology companies, in particular, tend to have such a culture.

27. Scholars and practitioners now recognize many organizational culture types. Recall the opening vignette for this chapter where the authors identified with a 'digital' culture. They also discussed Apple's corporate culture as one of innovation. Stephen Maguire, Associate Professor of Strategy and Organization at McGill University, defines an Entrepreneurial Organizational Culture (EOC) as a system of shared values, beliefs and norms of members of an organization, including valuing creativity and tolerance of creative people, believing that innovating and seizing market opportunities are appropriate behaviours to deal with problems of survival and prosperity, environmental uncertainty, and competitor threat, and expecting organizational members to behave accordingly.

28. If organizational culture is defined as a variable then it might seem reasonable to suggest that some cultures may outperform others given a context and set of goals. Although little empirical research exists to support the link between organizational culture and performance, there is little doubt among scholars and practitioners that such a relationship exists. Research suggests several outcomes to be associated either directly or indirectly with organizational culture. Indeed the success of a number of high profile and superior companies has been attributed, at least in part to their culture. The organizational culture may provide various benefits, including the following:

- Competitive advantage derived from innovation and customer service

- Consistent, efficient employee performance

- Team cohesiveness

- High employee motivation and engagement

- Strong company alignment towards goal achievement.

14.3 EVALUATE CULTURE AS STRENGTH OR WEAKNESS

29. Organizational culture is considered to be functional when it is aligned with strategy and the external environment. In such cases it helps the organization achieve its goals and perform. Culture can become a significant problem for the mature organization when it becomes 'set' or 'rigid' and dysfunctional. If the environment changes, the organization may fail to adapt; the existing values may become detrimental to future performance. An organization may have existed for some time in a stable environment. Consequently it may have derived success from a strong bureaucratic culture. In such a case the resultant efficiency gains will have manifested themselves as cost savings. However, as has already been noted, the dynamic environment may necessitate an adaptive, flexible and entrepreneurial culture.

30. How then might we 'objectively' evaluate culture? Enid Mumford, a Professor at Manchester University and Senior Fellow of the Manchester Business School, and Geert Beekman (1994), a Dutch consultant, adopt a socio-technical approach to business change. They argue the 'organizational architect must always take account of the informal organization; the norms, values and behaviour patterns that employees collectively support and believe in.' They believe attitudes, norms and culture do not just 'happen' to an organization. 'They evolve over time, become an accepted way of behaving and are very difficult to change. Yet if they are dysfunctional or inappropriate for the future business mission and objectives of the organization, changing them must be an important part of the design and rebuilding task.'

31. Thus a starting point for evaluating culture may be to understand the organization's survival problem (challenges posed by the external environment) and what the organization is trying to achieve – its goals, mission and objectives. Next, we could consider the organizational attributes that may be seen as beneficial to attaining the goals. To what extent do we need to be efficient, creative, innovative, different and responsive? Next, map desirable behaviours and ways of working to the goal – do you need to focus on quality? Would a horizontal process orientation be preferable to a bureaucratic vertical orientation? Is the environment dynamic – does the organization face a need of continual adaptation? Finally, audit the culture as it is now against the desired philosophies, orientations and behaviours. Are there any shortfalls or deficiencies – does the current culture appear dysfunctional? If there are shortfalls then these act as triggers for culture change.

32. There are a variety of 'off-the-shelf' tools to measure organizational culture; see for example, The Organizational Culture Inventory. Some practitioners suggest its use as a part of a cultural audit – a study and examination of an organization's cultural characteristics (such as its assumptions, norms, philosophy and values) to determine whether they hinder or support its vision and mission.

33. There are dangers, however, in 'judging' cultures – particularly national cultures. The danger is inherent in the criteria used to judge which may well be based upon the evaluator's own culture. This is suggesting that the evaluator's culture is right and the other culture wrong! Ethnocentrism is a tendency to regard one's own ethnic group, nation, religion, culture or gender as better than or more correct than others. It is a belief in the superiority of one's own culture over other cultures. In business, this can mean a tendency for many Western global businesses to assume that the norm to aspire to is a Western cultural model. As suggested by Kelly (2009) to be ethnocentric means using one's own set of standards and customs to judge all people, often unconsciously. It is an unquestioning belief that one's own national culture and ways of doings things are the best. However, placing the dangers of ethnocentrism and the issues with cultural audit tools to one side, if a culture is seen as dysfunctional it needs to be developed, a matter we address in the final part of this chapter.

14.4 DEVELOPING ORGANIZATIONAL CULTURE

34. As was noted earlier in the chapter, some scholars take the view that culture is something an organization 'has' whilst others believe it is something the organization 'is'. Scholars of the latter school believe that managers cannot control culture in the way that many management writers advocate because it is so diffuse. Trice and Beyer (1993: p. 12) also argue that cultures can be dysfunctional but suggest that 'there is less agreement on whether cultures can be deliberately changed' (p. 16). They differentiate between 'changing' and 'creating' cultures. Cultures change incrementally; they emerge and may be shaped intentionally. We discuss these two mechanisms in the following and final paragraphs.

35. Starting with the values and actions of founding members, culture develops in response to organizational problems. The nature of the technology available, and the way it is implemented in the organization, will play a part in the development of culture and, of course, the organizational structures, mechanisms and procedures that are a major part of the organization's fabric. The latter analogy is illuminating because it helps to think of the culture as being woven inbetween all the other factors, linking them together and producing a whole tapestry.

36. Treating organizational culture as a whole other than the sum of the parts is advocated in Gestalt theory. Gestalt psychologists find it is important to think of problems as a whole. They believe the configuration or pattern of elements (dimensions of culture, embedded) so unified as a whole that its properties cannot be derived from a simple summation of its parts, i.e. it has properties as a whole.

37. Aside from the manager, there are many factors that may influence and shape culture. As was discussed earlier, culture develops in response to challenges and business problems. Depending on their relative power in a particular situation, the behaviour of stakeholders such as customers, suppliers, creditors (e.g. banks) and competitors may also influence the organization's culture. Competitors, in particular, can introduce changes into their marketing strategy and organization, which not only change their own culture, but also contribute to change in others, who may be forced to follow their lead in order to retain market share.

38. Managers seeking to develop culture should first consider the aspects of culture discussed in para. 10 to 13 in particular. They should also be mindful of Hofstede's comments that the major cultural differences between organizations lie in their practices. Organizational practices are learned through socialization at the workplace. Work environments (the climate) reinforce culture on a daily basis by encouraging employees to exercise cultural values. Amongst possible culture change tactics are:

(1) recruit like-minded people

(2) socialize to instil and sustain ideologies (e.g. induction and orientation programmes)

(3) cultural communications; symbols, rites and rituals, stories

(4) resource allocation methods

(5)   criteria used to promote, reward and punish employees

(6)   organizational design and structure, systems and procedures

(7)   design of physical space, buildings etc., and

(8)   formal statements of organizational philosophy, values, goals and mission (See for example the **Belief system (Formal)**).

39.   Trice and Beyer (1993) emphasize the role of leadership in bringing about cultural change. It is what leaders pay attention to that focuses the thoughts and actions of others. Senior management have a key role to play in providing examples of the behaviours they want employees to replicate. What leaders pay attention to, the behaviours they demonstrate, stories they tell, behaviours they reward and punish, and what they measure sends messages to employees about what they desire. Another set of 'tools' leaders can use to shape culture is the formal structure and systems of the organization.

40.   Schein (1997) also emphasizes the role of leaders, noting them to be a source of beliefs, values and assumptions – as role models they transmit and embed culture. Whilst we have discussed tools and tactics so far, Schein discusses culture 'embedding mechanisms'. Schein's primary embedding mechanisms revolve around the role of the leader. What the leader pays attention to, measures and controls on a regular basis; how leaders react to incidents; allocate resources; role model; allocate rewards; and the observable criteria used by leaders to recruit, promote and terminate employees. As with other scholars, Schein believes that such mechanisms create the 'climate' of the organization. In the case of younger organizations, 'the climate created by the founding leaders precedes the … culture' (1997: p. 230). At a later stage 'climate will be a reflection and manifestation' of culture.

CONCLUSION

41.   In this chapter we introduced and defined culture, noting it to have many functions but also arguing that it can be dysfunctional, ultimately impacting upon organizational performance. It is a very important but indistinct concept as it exists in many levels and is diffused throughout the organization. Culture is always about groups and the way they behave; in some cases we might also consider the way they think and their assumptions about the problems they face. Culture can be strong or weak and this is a measure of the similarity of thinking and behaviour within the group. We noted that strong culture may be more appropriate in stable or predictable environments where efficiency is emphasized but that weak cultures may encourage the creativity and constant challenging attitude of employees needed to question their goals and ways of achieving them. Cultural differences encourage a contingency approach to management and cultural changes should reflect environmental changes and demands. Culture change is difficult, tending to be incremental rather than radical and relying heavily on organizational leaders to shape it.

QUESTIONS

1   Distinguish between national and organizational culture whilst considering the relationship between the two.

2   Discuss why organizations may seek to change organizational culture and identify the possible tactics they may use.

3   Why is culture such an important concept in business? You should discuss the functions and dysfunctions of organizational culture. In your opinion, is it better to have a strong or a weak organizational culture?

USEFUL WEBSITES

CIPD **www.cipd.co.uk/research/_visionandvalues.htm_**
Vision and values: organizational culture and values as a
source of competitive advantage

New Paradigm consulting **www.new-paradigm.co.uk/ Cul-
ture.htm** Organization Culture – Links & Articles

Geert Hofstede™ **www.geert-hofstede.com** Hofstede's five
Cultural Dimensions (national culture)

REFERENCES

Buchanan, D. and Huczynski, A. (2010) *Organizational Behaviour*, 7th edn, Financial Times Press.

Chitkara, P. and Davidson, V. (2013) 'Shifting to a digital
culture - Government agencies need to create a culture that
not just tolerates digitisation but embraces it', CIO magazine,
Copyright 2013 IDG Communications. www.cio.com.au/
article/523036/shifting_digital_culture/ [Accessed
August 2013].

Hampden-Turner, C.M. and Trompenaars, F. (2000) *Building
Cross-Cultural Competence – How to Create Wealth from
Conflicting Values*, Wiley.

Handy, C.B. (1999) *Understanding Organizations*, 4th edn,
Penguin.

Hoffman, A.J. (1999) 'Institutional evolution and change: environ-
mentalism and the US chemical industry', *The Academy of
Management Journal*, 42(4): 351–371.

Hofstede, G. (1980) 'Motivation, leadership and organization: do
American theories apply abroad?', *Organizational Dynamics*,
Summer: 42–43.

Hofstede, G. (1984) *Cultures Consequences – abridged*, Sage.

Hofstede, G. (1997) *Cultures and Organizations*, McGraw-Hill.

Hofstede, G. (1998) 'Attitudes, values and organizational culture:
Disentangling the concepts', *Organisation Studies*, 19(3):
477–492.

Johnson, G. (1988) 'Rethinking incrementalism', *Strategic Management Journal*, 9(1): 75–91.

Kelly, P.P. (2009) *International Business and Management*, Cengage Learning EMEA.

Mumford, E. and Beekman, G.J. (1994) *Tools For Change &
Progress*, CSG Publications.

Peters, T. and Waterman, R. (1982) *In Search of Excellence*
(1995 edn), HarperCollins Business.

Schein, E. (1999) *The Corporate Culture Survival Guide*, Jossey
Bass.

Schein, E. (1997) *Organisational Culture and Leadership*, 2nd
edn, San Francisco: Jossey Bass.

Schein, E. (1996) 'Three cultures of management: The key to
organizational learning', *Sloan Management Review*, 38(1): 9.

Trice, H.M. and Beyer, J.M. (1993) *The Cultures of Work Organizations*, Prentice Hall.

CHAPTER 15
DIVERSITY

Key Concepts

- Discrimination
- Diversity
- Human capital
- Inclusion
- Multicultural
- Social capital
- Talent

Learning Outcomes Having read this chapter, you should be able to:

- explain what is meant by diversity and multiculturalism in the workplace
- explain, with reference to social identity, stereotyping, generalizing and perception theory why some employees may be treated differently from others
- discuss the organizational consequences of discriminatory behaviours
- critically evaluate the impact of diversity upon organizational performance
- discuss what organizations may do to create an inclusive climate and make diversity a strength.

Vignette

Accenture is a global management consulting company, with over 250 000 workers serving clients in more than 120 countries. The consultancy collaborates with clients to help them become high-performance businesses. Recognizing the need to manage diversity challenges within the UK and Ireland (UKI), they employ a Human Capital and Diversity (HCD) Senior Executive. This person is responsible for driving the human capital strategy and agenda across UKI and working with the leadership team to achieve diversity and inclusion goals. They also lead corporate citizenship activities, focus on employee engagement and seek to use the HCD programmes as a way to extend Accenture's footprint with clients. The Chairman and CEO believes that the companies' *diversity makes [it] a better company ... [able] to bring together multiple perspectives, backgrounds, cultures and skills – reflecting the clients served around the world.'* He also believes it is extremely powerful in driving innovation and being relevant to clients' needs. Accenture take the widest possible view of inclusion and diversity, going beyond abilities, age, ethnicity, gender, religion and sexual orientation and gender identity and expression to create an environment that welcomes all forms of differences. Inclusion and diversity are fundamental to their culture and core values, fostering an innovative, collaborative and high-energy work environment. They believe that by embracing an inclusive culture which supports diverse talent, their people collaborate successfully and enable the company to compete effectively in the global marketplace.

1. The annual reports of many companies in Europe, North America and Asia state that their human capital (HC) and intellectual property are their most important assets. Many of the companies believe that succeeding in this new era requires organizations to put people at the heart of performance. Indeed Accenture argue 'the importance of an enterprise's human capital has risen dramatically'. As could be seen from the opening case, like numerous other companies, Accenture have appointed senior executives to assure diversity and inclusion goals are met.

2. In this chapter we continue to explore and analyze the internal environment from a human capital perspective and its relationship with the external environment. In the previous chapter we discussed culture which, together with managing diversity and talent, form key components of most HC strategies. We will continue to develop an understanding of how an organization's internal environment may differ and evaluate consequences in terms of strengths and weaknesses. One important area of difference in contemporary organizations concerns the extent to which they are diverse (heterogeneous) and the impact upon organization performance. In many ways we are discussing the human capital of the firm; the knowledge, skills and other attributes of labour that contribute to the development of a business.

3. In Chapter 8 we discussed the transformation process (refer back to Figure 8.2). Amongst the key resources used for input or transformation are people, the employees of the company. When considering work and the transformation process we may pay attention to each and every individual employee and their productive contribution or we may consider the organization as a group of people (refer back to Chapters 13 and 14 and Gestalt theory). **Human capital** (to include cultural and social capital and other related intangibles herein) refers to the stock of competencies (combined ability), knowledge, talents and capabilities and personality attributes embodied in the ability of the workforce to perform work so as to create value and contribute to the process of production. In this sense, human capital is vitally important for an organization's success. There is strong evidence that organizations that possess and cultivate their human capital outperform other organizations lacking human capital.

4. The term 'social capital' became widely used in the late 1990s and refers to features of social organization, such as networks, norms and trust that facilitate coordination and cooperation for mutual benefit. The construct addresses the way we relate to each other and participate in work activities. In many ways it describes the extent of cohesion (unity) within the workforce. A concept that encompasses the strength of relationships between people that enable participants to act together more effectively to pursue shared objectives. Clearly, social networks that include people who trust and assist each other can be a powerful asset.

5. The human capital of a firm has many attributes and can be described in a number of ways. Two of the more important aspects of HC are culture (as discussed in the previous chapter) and diversity. Diversity and culture are related concepts as will be seen throughout this chapter. We noted in the previous chapter that culture refers to groups and the extent to which they share aspects of thinking and behaving. We also noted that new employees can both shape and be shaped by organizational culture. They are a source of values and beliefs but are also flexible to some extent, adopting new ways of thinking and behaving. Finally, we discussed culture strength in terms of the extent to which employees *share* the same values, beliefs and ways of working. Diversity, on the other hand, is about the extent of difference within the workforce.

6.   Globalization, along with shifting social values and demographics - amongst other external factors, is altering the nature of the workplace. Changing patterns of migration and mobility in Europe and around the world are making national sentiments and feelings about belonging to a particular nation more diffuse and complex. Increased immigration and the general free movement of people across borders results in more heterogeneous populations – a country's population will have proportions of people from other national cultures residing there. Through migration, domestic populations are becoming more diverse.

7.   Immigration, changing demographics, globalization, increased international business and technology impact upon today's workforce which is older, more racially diverse, more female and more varied. The twenty-first century workplace typically has a diverse (heterogeneous) workforce. This changing internal environment brings new challenges and a potential for new strengths and weaknesses. Organizations face challenges such as managing discrimination and assuring fairness at work, recruiting talent from across society, creating an inclusive climate and work environment and integrating employees who are different. These are challenges associated with managing diversity.

15.1 WHAT DOES DIVERSITY MEAN?

8.   There is no question that today's workforce is more diverse. As with any social construct there are many definitions of **diversity**. It has been described as the heterogeneity of attitudes, perspectives and backgrounds amongst group members; valuing, respecting and appreciating the differences (such as age, culture, education, ethnicity, experience, gender, race, religion and sexual orientation, amongst others) that make people unique or, more simply, as all the ways in which we differ.

9.   Two general approaches to defining workforce diversity seem to dominate: the first, the narrow view, defines workforce diversity only as a term related to equal employment opportunity; the second argues that workforce diversity is a broader concept that includes all the ways in which people can be different. The narrow view typically adopts categories of race, colour, religion, sex and national origin whilst a broader definition makes use of additional categories such as teaching, education, sexual orientation and differences in values, abilities, organizational function, tenure and personality. Taking a broader view, diversity management initiatives attempt to maximize the potential of all employees, increasing the firm's human capital, for the direct benefit of the organization.

10.   Race can therefore be a factor that may make a group diverse. Organizations that have employees from different races may be described by some scholars as **multicultural**. In the literal sense, a multicultural organization is an organization that contains many different cultural groups and values diversity. Multiculturalism in the organizational studies context is another term for (national) cultural differentiation or the existence of subcultures in an organization. However, it has been argued that the mere presence of a mixed race workforce does not in itself create a multicultural organization. To be a **multicultural organization** there should be minimal prejudice, discrimination, subgroup differences and conflict; true multicultural organizations are characterized by integration and an inclusive climate i.e. the subcultures are unified. We return to such issues later in this chapter.

11.   When management practitioners discuss diversity within organizations they will often discuss talent as well. **Talent** concerns skills and abilities (natural aptitude) of a higher quality. Talented employees can do certain work well. Successful organizations in the twenty-first century compete through their people (workforce) and therefore seek to attract and develop the best people for the job. **Talent management** refers to the process of developing and integrating new workers, developing and retaining existing workers, and attracting highly skilled workers to work for a company. The organization seeks to manage talent in order to develop capabilities (HC) and gain sustainable competitive advantage. Such advantages typically derive from knowledge and creativity, enabling the organization to meet customer needs. It is a strategic and integrated approach to developing a skilled and competent workforce, involving targeted recruitment, development and retention.

12.   Talent management presents key arguments regarding why organizations become diverse. Organizations become diverse for many reasons. Society is becoming more culturally and racially diverse; legal forces are shaping equal opportunities; and there is a widespread recognition that talent can be found in every

walk of life regardless of race, gender, age or sexual orientation. Consequently, if organizations want the most creative, knowledgeable and capable employees they must recruit them from the whole population as opposed to creating a homogeneous workforce comprising all white males for example. We revisit talent management in section 13, later in the book – when we consider the contribution of HR to the organization. 13. Next in this chapter we consider the theoretical background to explain challenges associated with diverse organizations. In particular we draw on social identity theory to explain how we come to label groups (such as those associated with gender, race, age, etc.) and how people identify with them. We then consider how people from diverse groups perceive themselves and others and the implications of such thinking on their behaviour towards each other (discrimination). Drawing on people perception theories, we discuss problems in generalization and stereotyping. Next we evaluate diversity within organizations, asking whether it is a strength or weakness, before considering what organizations may do to create an inclusive climate. We discussed organizational climate in the previous chapter and the creation of an inclusive climate is seen as essential by many management scholars (refer back to the opening case) if the challenges of diversity are to be overcome and the organization is to benefit from diversity as a strength.

15.2 THEORETICAL BACKGROUND

TABLE 15.1 United Kingdom Council for Access and Equality (UKCAE) HELPING BUILD INCLUSIVE ORGANIZATIONS Equality and diversity facts and figures

DISCRIMINATION AT WORK CAN BE EXPENSIVE
236 100 claims at employment tribunals in 2009-10
Women accounted for 12 % of directors in FTSE 100 companies (2009), dropping to 7% for FTSE 250
Only 7% of managerial positions in the UK are held by people from an ethnic minority group
The gap between men's and women's hourly rates of pay is 22%
People with a disability or long-term illness are over twice as likely to face bullying or harassment in the workplace as non-disabled people
EQUALITY AND DIVERSITY - HOW ORGANIZATIONS CAN BENEFIT COMMERCIALLY
Better use of women's skills in work could be worth in the region of £15 – 23 billion for the economy per annum. People from ethnic minorities and religious groups are significantly less likely than average to be in work, and when in work are paid significantly less than average, and this could be worth £8.6 billion a year to the UK economy
It is expected that ethnic minority spending power will soon exceed £300 billion

14. Discrimination towards minority groups has existed in society for decades, and though in recent years these negative attitudes have declined, many barriers and disadvantages still exist for those who belong to different minority groups in the workplace. Diverse organizations contain people who are different. Those people who share some characteristic or attribute are likely to form subgroups. There is a tendency for people to favour the people within their group and negatively discriminate against people not in their group but employed by the organization. Thus if a group controls organizational resources and has power they may abuse this in an unfair manner. In such cases there will be winners and losers. Discrimination is the prejudicial and/or distinguishing treatment of an individual based on their actual or perceived membership in a certain group or category. In many cases (see Table 15.1) such treatment or behaviour is either unlawful or generally looked down upon. There are many types of discrimination such as: ageism, disability and employment discrimination, racial, gender or religious discrimination, and discrimination against sexual minorities. A key organizational problem accompanying discrimination is the associated lack of unity, harmony and sense of fairness required of productive human capital.

15. Social identity theory is best described as a theory that predicts certain intergroup behaviours. Belonging to groups whether they are professions, organizations, gender-based or location-based, for example,

affects the way we think about and see ourselves (who we are) and the way others think about and see us. Such thinking impacts upon behaviour, the way we behave and the way others behave in relation to ourselves and the groups to which we may belong.

16.   How we view ourselves (self-concept) is determined in part by the groups to which we belong (social identity). Thus, social identity defines the person and appropriate behaviours for them. This typically happens through social comparison – individuals not only compare themselves with other individuals with whom they interact, but they also compare their own group with similar, but distinct, out-groups.

17.   We all see ourselves as members of various social groupings, which are distinguishable and hence different from other social groupings. According to social identity theory (SIT), people tend to classify themselves and others into various social categories, such as organizational membership, religious affiliation, gender and age cohort. As these examples suggest, people may be classified in various categories, and different individuals may utilize different categorization schemas. Categories are defined by typical characteristics abstracted from the members; the consequence is that by identifying with certain groupings but not others, we come to see the world in terms of *us* (in-group) and *them* (out-group).

18.   For example, we may categorize ourselves as students, lecturers, IT professionals, 'Brits', European, etc. In doing so we might have a reference model of how students or lecturers (or whatever the reference group is) should behave. There are many groups we might associate with and therefore categorize ourselves. We may then use this identity to guide our own behaviour.

19.   Whilst group membership may have its benefits (self-esteem, privilege) it can also be a source of conflict and could, through generalizations and stereotypes determine inappropriate (discriminatory) behavioural responses. Social identity theory has been used to explain why some people prefer to work with others like themselves, favouring homogeneity to diversity. Indeed the concept of the idea that the more similar people are in background variables such as socioeconomic status or attitudes, the more attracted they are likely to be to each other (at least initially), is a phenomenon that when observed in friendship patterns is called homophily bias.

20.   One reason for this phenomenon is that people who are similar in backgrounds may have similar values and share common life-experiences; they therefore, find the experience of interacting with each other positively reinforcing. Group heterogeneity, thus, may have a negative impact on individual feelings of satisfaction through decreasing an individual's sense of identification or social integration within the group. Research repeatedly suggests the presence of a systemic problem, namely, that groups and organizations will act systematically to push out individuals who are different from the majority, unless this tendency to drive out diversity is managed. This finding is a manifestation of the tendency of people to identify with particular groups and then define these groups as the in-group and all other groups as out-groups. In the context of organizations, such processes will tend to create what has been referred to as homosocial reproduction; resulting in the creation of very homogeneous groups that are not representative. This tendency to drive out diversity is an extremely serious and systematic force which organizations who value diversity will have to develop mechanisms to counteract.

21.   Earlier we touched on the issues of stereotypes and generalizations. In order to understand discrimination (and poor decision-making) in the workplace we need to explore these concepts in more detail. When we think about such concepts we are really considering how the brain processes information when making decisions about how to behave (towards others) in the workplace. Perception theory, the process of selecting, organizing and interpreting information inputs to produce meaning, is a useful theory to explore at this point.

22.   Two people can observe the same thing but perceive it in quite different ways – why should this be so? An answer to this question may be found in the perception process. Through our senses (especially sight) the brain receives incoming raw data from the outside world (stimuli). We are not able to pay attention to everything so we filter out less relevant or important information through perceptual filters; this allows us to focus on what we see is important (selective attention); we concentrate on the matters of particular interest and importance to us. Individual predispositions control what we see. No two people will select exactly the same information to focus upon. Consequently, people may 'see' different aspects of the same reality.

23.   Following selective attention, we organize the filtered incoming stimuli in systematic and meaningful ways; we classify or group similar stimuli together. During this activity (top-down processing) we may fill in the gaps of incomplete or ambiguous information (see the principle of closure). We make

sense of a situation and then respond through our actions; our perceptions (the meanings we attach to incoming information) shape our actions. Such activities are susceptible to problems (see stereotyping to be discussed later).

24.   Classification or categorization helps us make sense of the world; for example, we categorize people as male or female, black or white – such categories are social constructs which we learn and what we learn is often culture bound. We classify people who resemble each other (the similarity principle); for example the person(s) may be of a similar ethnic origin. A related concept is the proximity principal where we assume people are similar just because they are near to each other – possibly living or working in the same location. One of the problems with 'closure' is that we may take incomplete information about someone or an event and then draw inferences from it (see the problem of generalization). For example, we might only know a person's country of origin or gender but may then assign traits to them based on our learned knowledge of people from that country i.e. once we know or assume a person's apparent group membership (categorization) we may then attribute a range of qualities to them based on stereotypes and generalizations. In some cases such generalizations may prove convenient in other cases they could be wrong.

25.   Bias in person perception may take place during perceptual organization when we group together people who seem to us to share similar characteristics – stereotyping. Stereotypes are over-generalizations which enable us to shortcut the evaluation process and make predictions about an individual's behaviour. The way we are categorized and the generalizations made about the group we are associated with may result in others treating us more or less favourably.

26.   Women, racio-ethnic minorities and other groups have historically been excluded from the middle and upper levels of many Western organizations and whilst some improvement has been made in upward mobility, it is well documented that institutional racism and sexism persist in the workplace. Throughout life we become conditioned to thinking in ways that generalize and stereotype others. Such thinking may result in behaviours categorized as prejudice, privileged or oppressive. Such thoughts and the behavioural consequences have significant implications for the organization. Although usually rooted in some truth, stereotypes often do more harm than good. Stereotypes arise when we act as if all members of a group share the same characteristics. There are many indicators of group membership such as race, age, gender that may be used by the observer. In some cases the assumed characteristics are respected (positive stereotype) and in other cases may be disrespected (negative stereotype).

27.   Social identity theory, stereotyping, generalizing, perception and attribution theory explain why some people may be treated differently (discriminatory behaviour) from others. In some cases certain groups may be discriminated against. Prejudice and other discriminatory behaviours have consequences in the organization. If people feel that they are not being treated fairly, their motivation and performance is likely to be affected; people may leave the organization or be absent from work. This will impact upon productivity and ultimately performance.

15.3 DIFFERENCES, DISCRIMINATION AND CONFLICT AT WORK

28.   The theories discussed thus far can explain why some employees may be treated more or less favourably than others in the workplace. They can also explain why some organizations are successful in attracting, retaining, engaging and maximizing the potential of talented employees – a strength - whilst others are not. An understanding of why discrimination may occur can help managers avoid the negative consequences that may be associated and ultimately help them develop diversity as an organizational strength. Discrimination can take place during recruitment and selection and promotion processes in particular but may manifest in all aspects of work. All groups, be they based upon gender, race or other categories can experience discrimination.

29.   Numerous studies show a continuing problem for women and minority groups who aspire to senior management positions (refer back to the equality and diversity facts and figures). In business, any minority group member may be promoted less frequently, may work in less prestigious firms or receive less favourable terms and conditions. Disparities exist even when men and women or employees of minority groups hold equivalent qualifications. Fiona Wilson is Professor of Organizational Behaviour (OB) in the

Department of Business and Management, University of Glasgow. She believes that every prestigious or highly paid occupation in Britain is dominated by men, both numerically and in terms of who wields power (Wilson, 2002).

30. Wilson notes that women in the UK hold just one in five of all management positions. Studies on the relationship between gender, and the likelihood that a candidate will be recommended for hiring, find an advantage in favour of men. Gender stereotyping of women remains evident at work. Although women make up the majority of the local authority workforce, they tend to be concentrated in lower grades and are underrepresented at senior management level. The phenomenon of overrating men and underrating women job candidates appears to be widespread. Women fare worse than men in salary, promotion and ability to reach the top, regardless of occupation.

31. There have been numerous research studies into possible differences between men and women in aspects of workplace behaviour such as motivation, attitudes to work, ability to motivate teams and in work performance generally. The overall results demonstrate clearly that on these points there are no major differences between the sexes. The difficulties faced by women, in attempting to break into what has been, and still is, mainly a man's world, has been referred to as 'the glass ceiling' (see for example Pichler, Simpson and Stroh 2008), an analogy which attempts to describe the subtly transparent barrier that prevents women (or any discriminated against group) from gaining access to the more senior roles in their organizations. Stereotyping occurs when individuals are judged not on their unique characteristics or merits, but on generalized characteristics associated with the group to which they belong.

32. Sex stereotypes have been disadvantageous to women in selection, placement and promotion decisions, especially for managerial jobs. The sex type of a job is determined by two factors: the gendered characteristics believed to be required for that job and the proportion of men (or women) occupying the job. Stereotypes also describe how men and women should be – that is, what behaviours are (and are not) appropriate, based on one's gender. When women demonstrate masculine behaviour or succeed at male-type tasks, they meet with opposition and are not accepted, ultimately resulting in biased performance evaluations. Sex bias stemming from such stereotypes has contributed to the glass ceiling. More specifically, when a woman exhibits stereotypically feminine behaviour, she is considered a poor fit for most managerial jobs, and when a woman exhibits stereotypically masculine behaviour, she is typically perceived as being unnecessarily aggressive and hostile.

15.4 EVALUATING DIVERSITY: STRENGTH OR WEAKNESS

33. For reasons discussed earlier, both the marketplace and workplace are becoming more diverse; particularly form a national culture perspective. A diverse workforce is not simply a goal but a reality for most companies today. Whereas some organizations have harnessed benefit from diversity others have not. It is only a strength if the benefits outweigh the costs.

34. Proponents of diversity maintain that different opinions provided by culturally diverse groups make for better-quality decisions. Heterogeneity in decision-making and problem-solving styles produces better decisions through the operation of a wider range of perspectives and a more thorough critical analysis of issues. Orlando (2000) examined the performance impact cultural diversity has on organizations; benefits include skills transfer and insight and cultural sensitivity pertinent to reaching different market segments as companies enter new markets or their existing markets change and develop. Furthermore, cultural diversity can provide organizations with diverse experience and knowledge. A diverse workforce, with established customer relationships is an example of a difficult to imitate resource that can confer a sustainable competitive advantage for the firm.

35. There are, however, a number of counterarguments that may be presented, suggesting that diversity may actually be counterproductive for the firm. Research has shown that although diversity in human resources may contribute to the quality of ideas, it also creates additional costs stemming from increased coordination and control requirements; diverse groups require more effort to integrate. Minority members of groups may feel alienated and pushed out. Employees are more likely to want to work with people like themselves. Differences amongst employees (diversity) can manifest as different analyses of the situation (see perception theory), unproductive communications, disagreement about goals, investment, methods

and procedures. Furthermore, from a national culture perspective, people tend to be ethnocentric, using their own culture as the standard for defining 'normal'. Consequently, we should expect greater conflict and disagreement in the multicultural organization.

36.   In summary it is costly to manage a diverse workforce which requires intervention in the form of policies, procedures, training, discipline and specialist staff to maintain. Further costs may also have to be met by the organization should employees make claims of unfair treatment. Finally, organizations that fail to manage diversity and an inclusive climate are likely to fail to attract, get the most out of or lose talented employees. On the other hand, diverse companies are likely to be more effective, creative and adaptable when diversity is managed to ensure fairness and HC becomes a sustainable competitive advantage. Engaged employees will cooperate to achieve the organization's goals.

15.5 NURTURING AN INCLUSIVE CLIMATE

37.   Organizations can be diverse, but that is not an automatic lever to improved performance. When individuals feel that they cannot be themselves at work, they will not engage fully as part of the team or in assigned work; if they do not feel valued they are unlikely to add value. It is widely accepted that diversity will thrive if the internal environment (climate) is open, fair and inclusive. We saw in the chapter opening case that Accenture embrace an inclusive culture. An inclusive environment is one that creates a sense of belonging and encourages and supports its members. Inclusion is engaging in diversity to create a culture of belonging in which differences are valued. Today's managers are looking to make the workplace a better environment by modifying HR practices to reach a more diverse audience, to engage and support employees successfully.

38.   If talent is to be cultivated and diversity is to become an organizational strength then managers should be aware of the glass ceiling problem and attempt to remedy its causes. As Meyerson and Fletcher (2000) note, valuing gender diversity often involves sensitivity or diversity training. This type of training could be used to explain sex discrimination and associated biases. Although these three approaches to gender diversity management can help support the inclusion of women in the workplace, as well as their advancement into senior management, even in combination they may not be enough to remove the invisible barriers which form the glass ceiling. As Meyerson and Fletcher (2000) noted, the exclusion of women from senior management roles is related to biases entrenched in institutionalized organizational systems, such as performance appraisals; therefore, these systems must also be changed. Removing gender bias from such organizational systems as selection decisions and performance evaluation is essential to increasing gender diversity in organizations, especially at the highest levels of management.

CONCLUSION

39.   In this chapter we considered the importance of treating employees fairly, creating an inclusive climate and managing diversity. We explained causes of discriminatory behaviour with a reference to SIT, perception, stereotyping and other cognitive processes. Such theories help explain why minorities in the workplace may operate under a glass ceiling which reduces their career progression and opportunities. Given that some individuals might prefer homogeneity over diversity and the institutional discrimination that permeates policies, practices and the subconscious of many managers, organizations must manage diversity actively if it is to become a strength and advantage. Managing diversity and talent develops the firm's HC and therefore a source of sustainable advantage. However, this is not without cost. Despite this, we recognized that firms are diverse whether they want to be or not and that a lack of diversity management could make diversity a weakness, increasing costs and reducing the productive capacity of human capital. Many scholars believe that as organizational tasks and challenges become more complex, the value of diversity increases.

QUESTIONS

1   Explain why sex discrimination remains a significant business problem despite management efforts (over the past 10 to 20 years) to overcome it.

2   Why is it important for organizations to embrace diversity and pursue equal opportunity – what is the business/social case? In your answer you should present arguments for and against diversity within organizations.

3   Identify how women may be discriminated against in the workplace and then discuss the organizational consequences of such discriminatory behaviour. What is the glass ceiling problem and what are the main approaches to the management of gender diversity in organizations?

USEFUL WEBSITES

Chartered Management Institute: **www.managers.org. uk/ practical-support/management-community/ professional-networks/women-management** Women in Management (WiM) Network. WiM Network is a national organization addressing the key issues affecting women managers today

Discrimination – In England: **www.adviceguide.org.uk/index/ your_rights/discrimination.htm** Information on discrimination because of age, disability, race, religion or belief, sex and sexuality; when is discrimination lawful or unlawful; taking action; discrimination in providing goods, services...

Discrimination at work: **www.direct.gov.uk/en/Employment/ ResolvingWorkplaceDisputes/DiscriminationAtWork/ index.htm** An introduction to what discrimination is, the types of discrimination

EHRC: **www.equalityhumanrights.com** Promote equality in the areas of disability, gender and race

Catalyst: **www.catalyst.org/home** Catalyst is a non-profit membership organization working globally with businesses and the professions to build inclusive workplaces and expand opportunities for women and business

REFERENCES

Meyerson, D.E. and Fletcher, J. (2000) 'A modest manifesto for shattering the glass ceiling', *Harvard Business Review*, 78(1): 127–136.

Orlando, R. (2000) 'Racial diversity, business strategy, and firm performance: A resource-based view', *Academy of Management Journal*, 43(2): 164–177.

Pichler, S., Simpson, P.A. and Stroh, L.K. (2008) 'The glass ceiling in human resources: Exploring the link between women's representation in management and the practices of strategic human resource management and employee involvement', *Human Resource Management*, 47(3): 463–479.

Wilson, F.M. (2002) 'Management and the professions: how cracked is that glass ceiling?', *Public Money & Management*, 22(1): 15–20.

SKILL SHEET 6 **Analyzing the Environment**

This skills sheet provides a set of tools to help the reader understand the relevant context for management within their organization. The external environment is divided into the macro- (PESTEL) and micro-environments (market concentration and five forces). The internal environment is analyzed using the value chain, the McKinsey 7S framework and a set of questionnaires to explore the organization climate and culture. Finally, analysis of the environment is consolidated in the SWOT analysis.

Use this sheet in conjunction with Chapters 12–15 and case sheet 6.

1. EXTERNAL – MACRO (PESTEL) ANALYSIS

A PESTEL analysis is a framework or tool used to analyze and monitor the (external) macro-environmental factors impacting upon an organization. The results of this analysis are used to identify opportunities and threats (OT) which are used in SWOT analysis. The process of carrying out the analysis should involve as many managers as possible. It includes the following steps: **(1)** Gather information about political, economic, social and technological changes and any other factor(s). Consider researching and also brainstorming the changes happening around you.

POLITICAL		SOCIO-CULTURAL	
P1.	Government stability	S1.	Health consciousness
P2.	Government policies	S2.	Education level
P3.	Government term and change	S3.	Attitudes toward imports
P4.	Bureaucracy	S4.	Attitudes toward work, leisure, career and retirement
P5.	Corruption level		
P6.	Tax policy (rates and incentives)	S5.	Attitudes toward product quality and customer service
P7.	Freedom of press		
P8.	Regulation/deregulation	S6.	Attitudes toward saving / investing
P9.	Trade control	S7.	Emphasis on safety
P10.	Import restrictions/Tariffs	S8.	Lifestyles
		S9.	Buying habits
P11.	Competition regulation	S10.	Religion and beliefs
P12.	Government involvement in trade unions and agreements	S11.	Attitudes toward 'green' or ecological products

P13.	Wars and conflicts	S12.	Attitudes towards and support for renewable energy
		S13.	Population growth rate
		S14.	Immigration and emigration rates
		S15.	Age distribution/life expectancy
		S16.	Average disposable income level
		S17.	Social classes
		S18.	Family size and structure
		S19.	Minorities

ECONOMIC		ENVIRONMENTAL (ECOLOGICAL)	
Eco1.	Growth rates	Env1.	Weather
Eco2.	Inflation rate	Env2.	Climate change
Eco3.	Interest rates	Env3.	Laws regulating environment pollution
Eco4.	Exchange rates		
Eco5.	Unemployment trends	Env4.	Traffic safety
		Env5.	Air and water pollution
Eco6.	Credit availability		
Eco7.	Level of disposable income	Env6.	Public health
		Env7.	Recycling
Eco8.	Monetary policies	Env8.	Waste management
Eco9.	Fiscal policies	Env9.	Attitudes toward 'green' or ecological products
Eco10.	Current deficit		
Eco11.	Price fluctuations		
Eco12.	Stock market trends	Env10.	Attitudes towards and support for renewable energy
Eco13.	Energy cost		
Eco14.	National income		

TECHNOLOGICAL		LEGAL	
T1.	Legislation regarding technology	L1.	Anti-trust law
		L2.	Discrimination law
T2.	Spending on research and development	L3.	Copyright, patents/Intellectual property law
T3.	Communication infrastructure	L4.	Consumer protection and e-commerce
T4.	Access to newest technology	L5.	Employment law
		L6.	Health and safety law
T5.	Internet infrastructure and penetration	L7.	Data protection
		L8.	Judicial system
T6.	Transportation infrastructure	L9.	Environmental Law

Examples of such factors are provided in the table above. It is a good idea to code each factor (e.g. P1 Government stability) as we have done as this helps with cross-referencing later. **(2)** You should consider local, national and global factors. Listing PESTEL factors does not, in itself, tell you very much. You need to think about which factors are most likely to change and which ones will have the greatest impact. **(3)** Rate each factor in terms of intensity of importance.

1 Lowest | 3 Moderate Importance | 5 Important | 7 Very Important | 9 Highest

Example:	Local	National		Global	
Political		P1 P2	5 7		
Economic		Eco1 Eco2 Eco3	7 7 5	Eco4	9
Social		S12	7	S12	7
Technological		T1	9		
Environmental		Env1	7		
Legal		L8	7		

(4) It is also a good idea to add a table column labelled 'Impact on Business' (record free text comments in the column) and to classify the outcome type (positive, negative or unknown). Some analysts classify the impact in terms of low, medium or high.

POLITICAL			
Factor	**Impact On Business**	**Importance**	**Outcome Type**
P1. Government stability	New government likely to be more interventionist, leading to… (Medium)	5	Negative

Then, **(5)** Identify which of the factors represent specific opportunities or threats. Additionally, review factors holistically and brainstorm opportunities and threats. Finally, refer back to skills sheet 4 where the measurement of environmental uncertainty was explained.

2. MICRO (COMPETITION) ANALYSIS

Two methods are used to quantify the extent of rivalry/competition within the industry to be analyzed:

METHOD 1 – THE MARKET CONCENTRATION RATIO

The *n-firm concentration ratio* is the market share of the *n* largest firms in an industry; it can be expressed as:

$$CR_m = s_1 + s_2 + \ldots + s_m$$

where s_i is the market share and m defines the ith firm

Analysts will typically consider the largest 3–5 firms. Concentration ratios, especially the four-firm concentration ratio, are designed to measure industry concentration, and by inference, the degree of market control. For example, consider the number of firms manufacturing skateboards in France. Imagine there were only four companies. If market shares (%) were 32, 26, 10 and 32 respectively, then the concentration ratio of the three largest firms would be CR3 90. Concentration ratios range from 0 to 100 per cent. At the lower end (no concentration) the largest firms in the industry would not have any significant market share (perfect competition), i.e. competition that is EXTREMELY competitive, whilst at the other end, 100 per cent means an extremely concentrated oligopoly (total concentration). Generally, below 50 per cent is low, 50–80 is medium and > 80, high. Thus, in our example above, we might describe the French skateboard market as highly concentrated from oligopoly toward monopoly.

METHOD 2 – HERFINDAHL–HIRSCHMAN INDEX (HHI)

HHI is a measure of the size of firms in relation to the industry and an indicator of the amount of competition amongst them. The index involves taking the market share of the respective market competitors, squaring it, and adding them together:

$$H = \sum_{i=1}^{N} S_i^2$$

Where S_i is the market share of firm *i* in the market and *N* is the number of firms.

Example (fictitious): Contrast skateboard manufacturers in France with those in North America. Hypothetically, in both cases the six largest manufacturers could account for 90 per cent of the market. France: All six firms have 15 per cent each, and in North America: One firm has 80 per cent whilst five others share 2 per cent each. Assume that the remaining 10 per cent of output is divided amongst ten equally sized manufacturers. The six-firm concentration ratio would equal 90 per cent for both France and North America. However, France would promote significant competition, whereas America approaches monopoly. The Herfindahl index for these two states of affairs makes the lack of competition in the second case patently clear:
France Herfindahl index =
$6 * 0.15^2 + (10 * 0.01^2) = 0.136$ (13.6 per cent)

– A HHI index below 0.15 indicates an unconcentrated index – indicating a competitive industry with no dominant players; whilst in the **North America** example, the Herfindahl index =

$0.80^2 + (5 * 0.02^2) + (10 * 0.01^2) = 0.643$ (64.3 per cent) – A HHI index above 0.25 indicates high concentration. A HHI index < 0.01 (or 100) indicates a highly competitive index.
< 0.15 (or 1500) indicates an unconcentrated index.
0.15 to 0.25 (or 1500 to 2500) indicates moderate concentration.
> 0.25 (above 2500) indicates high concentration.
For help go to www.unclaw.com/chin/teaching/antitrust/herfindahl.htm or www.amosweb.com/cgi-bin/awb_nav.pl?s=wpd&c=dsp&k=Herfindahl+index

3. MICRO (COMPETITION) ANALYSIS: FIVE FORCES

The five forces framework is used to identify whether new products, services or businesses have the potential to be profitable and helps us understand both the strength of current competitive position, and the strength of a position a company may be considering moving into. By thinking about how each force affects the company, and by identifying the strength and direction of each force, we can assess the strength of our position and our ability to make a sustained profit in the industry.

This tool was created by Michael Porter, to analyze the attractiveness and likely profitability of an industry. The classic article which introduces it is 'How Competitive Forces Shape Strategy' in *Harvard Business Review* 57, March – April 1979, pages 86–93.

The approach involves the following steps:

1) PROBLEM DEFINITION (RESEARCH): Gather information about each of the five forces
2) Brainstorm the relevant factors for your market
3) Create table (see below – partially completed)
4) ANALYZE: Indicate the strength of the force (+++) force strongly in your favour to (– – –) force strongly against.
5) Comment on how the force affects you/the market
6) FORMULATE STRATEGIES
Brainstorm competitive strategies (e.g. cost leadership, price change; differentiate, distribution channels, etc.)
Higher profits are more likely when: suppliers and customers are weak, there are high entry barriers

FORCE	Value	Strength	Comments (how it affects)
Threat of new entry T1 Time to enter (months) T2 Cost to enter – capital (€) T3 Specialist knowledge/learning curve T4 Economies of scale T5 Cost advantages T6 Technology protection T7 Barriers to entry T8 Brand Identity/power T9 Access to distribution T10 Ability to retaliate T11 Government regulation	 6M 250K -	 +++ ++ ----	Ease for new competitors to enter market then drive prices down (establish new warehouse) Little required
Overall:		++	
Threat of Substitution TS1 Switching costs TS2 Substitute performance TS3 Buyer propensity to substitute			The extent to which different products/services can be used
Overall:			

Supplier Power			The power of suppliers to drive up prices of inputs (costs)
SP1 Number of suppliers			
SP2 Ease of supplier change			
SP3 Differentiation of inputs			
SP4 Threat: vertical integration			
SP5 Importance of volume			
SP6 Suppliers hold scarce resources			
Overall:		O	
Buyer Power			The power of customers to drive down prices
BP1 Prospects (N)			
BP2 Order size (€)			
BP3 Price sensitivity			
BP4 Buyer substitute ability			
BP5 Buyer concentration			
BP6 Buyer volume			
BP7 Buyer information			
Overall:		--	
Rivalry			The strength of competition
R1 Number of competitors			
R2 Concentration ratio/HHI	14		
R3 Quality differences	0.19	O	Moderate concentration
R4 Customer loyalty			
R5 Industry growth			
Overall:			

and few opportunities for substitute products and there is little rivalry. **Lower profits** are typically observed with strong suppliers/customers, low entry barriers, many opportunities for substitution and intense rivalry.

4. INTERNAL ENVIRONMENT ANALYSIS

We now shift attention from opportunities and threats presented by the external environment to analysis of the internal environment (resources) where we focus on strengths and weaknesses. Various frameworks seek to consider the integrated aspects of the internal business environment, such as the 7S framework, others focus on work activities (VCA) or on the human capital of the firm (diversity, people, culture and climate).

THE McKINSEY 7S FRAMEWORK is a management model most often used as a tool to assess and monitor changes in the internal situation of an organization. The basic premise of the model is that there are seven internal aspects (Strategy, Structure, Systems, Shared Values, Skills, Style and Staff) within an organization requiring alignment if the company is to be successful. The 7S framework provides a useful diagnostic tool for analyzing the strengths and weaknesses of an organization. Having clarified the organization's goals, each of the seven internal aspects is rated (overall) as strength or weakness (see table below) to decide where attention should be directed. Various questions (one or two are suggested below) may help determine the overall rating.

VALUE CHAIN ANALYSIS describes the *activities* that take place in a business and relates them to an analysis of the competitive strength of the business. Value chain analysis (VCA) can be broken down into a three sequential steps:

Instructions: rate the degree to which **you** agree or disagree with the following statements. Scoring (add up the score for the boxes you ticked. Column 1 = 1 point, Column 2 = 2 points … Column 5 = 5 points	Strongly Agree	Agree	Undecided	Disagree	Strongly Disagree
Strategy: The firm has a clear strategy The strategy is known and understood by staff Everyone is aligned with the strategy					
Overall rating of strategy as strength/weakness:					
Structure: The number of management layers is appropriate Decision-making authority is devolved where necessary					
Overall rating of structure as strength/weakness:					
Systems: The company systems add value The company systems create advantage					
Overall rating of systems as strength/weakness:					
Shared Values: Employees share the same guiding values					
Overall rating of shared values					
Style: The leadership style is appropriate					
Overall rating of current style as strength/weakness:					
Staff: The company has hired able people, trained them well and assigned them to the right jobs					
Overall rating of current staff as strength/weakness:					
Skills: Employees have the skills needed to carry out the company's strategy					
Overall rating of current skills as strength/weakness:					
Ratings are determined relative to the organization's goals. For example, if goals required flexibility then under structure, autonomy (devolving decision-making) would be considered strength.					

1) **Activity Analysis**: Decompose the organization listing its key activities under each of the major headings in the model; Identify the firm's primary and support activities. You may use Porter's generic VC activity headings (refer to main text) or key business process activities.

2) **Value Analysis**: Assess the potential for adding value via cost advantage or differentiation (or responsiveness etc.). Identify cost drivers for each activity, identify links between activities and identify opportunities for reducing costs. Use this to identify strengths and weaknesses.

3) **Evaluation**: Evaluate whether it is worth making changes, and then plan for action

ACTIVITY	VALUE FACTORS	CHANGES NEEDED
Procurement		
Order taking	Response time (answering phone/accessing email etc.) Know the customer (CRM) Understand needs Manage expectations	

Technology and the value chain: The framework can also be used to determine where to invest in IT etc. see Porter and Millar (1985), 'How information gives you a competitive advantage', *Harvard Business Review*, July-August 63, pp. 149–174

5. ANALYSIS: PEOPLE – HC, CULTURE AND CLIMATE

Human capital (HC) is one of several elements (refer back to social and organizational capital) making up intellectual capital which describes the knowledge and productive assets available to an organization. HC is critical to organizational success and is often the subject of analysis when considering organizational strengths and weaknesses.

PRODUCTION-ORIENTED PERSPECTIVE OF HUMAN CAPITAL

The value (strength) of HC is inherently dependent on its potential to contribute to the competitive advantage or core competence of the firm. Measuring HC has always been viewed as challenging; measuring HC is not just about measuring skills or even contribution in the form of productivity; it is also about measuring how successfully that knowledge and contribution translates into organizational value.[1] Organizations may measure HC in terms of current capabilities or may assess the extent of investment in development (e.g. training) which will enhance future HC. In measuring HC we are concerned with core competencies (strengths) in terms of productivity. HC measurement can be used to suggest policies regarding HR. Firm or task specific HC is usually accumulated through

education, training and work experience. There is no single measure or set of measures that can uniformly provide a value for HC. HC reporting aims to provide quantitative, as well as qualitative, data on a range of measures. However, the evaluation of HC remains difficult for most companies as the contribution of people is difficult to isolate (and measure) from other factors.

DIFFERENT TYPES OF DATA, USEFUL IN MEASURING HC

INPUTS (multiple raters advisable)

~ Levels of expenditure on training – Analysts adopt a **Cost-based approach** – measuring the stock of HC through summing costs invested in people. This figure can then be benchmarked against competitors.
~ Workforce composition demographic data: age, gender and ethnicity profile.
~ Experience and talent development: length of service, competence levels, days of training provided, number of individuals on development programs or acquiring professional qualifications, etc.

Although data in each of these areas may give some useful insights into the value of HC, it is the outcome measures or rather the impact HC makes on performance that will have the greatest value to managers i.e. productivity and profitability data for a particular business unit (OUTPUTS). Analysts measure aspects of HC that are relevant to the strategy (e.g. the need for specific competencies) and the emphasis of measurement has moved away from absolute measures towards understanding the specific situation for a given company. In the absence of statistical and objective data, analysts may turn to measuring the organization's **perceived human capital**.[2]

It is generally agreed that engaged employees are more likely to perform better and many organizations also measure employee attitudes in the organization. Measures of engagement help rate the strength of HC of the firm.

[1] Baron, A. (2011), 'Measuring human capital', *Strategic HR Review*, Vol. 10(2):– 30–35.

[2] Wright, P. and McMahan, G C. (2011), 'Exploring human capital: putting "human" back into strategic human resource management', *Human Resource Management Journal*, –21(2): 93–104.

Instructions: (to be completed by departmental managers) rate the degree to which **you** agree or disagree with the following statements. Scoring (add up the score for the boxes you ticked. Column 1 = 1 point, Column 2 = 2 points … 5 = 5 points	Strongly Agree	Agree	Undecided	Disagree	Strongly Disagree
(a) Our employees hold suitable education for accomplishing their job successfully					
(b) Our employees are well trained to accomplish their jobs successfully					
(c) Our employees hold suitable work experience for accomplishing their jobs successfully					
(d) Our employees are well skilled professionally to accomplish their jobs successfully					
All our employees are …					
highly skilled					
widely considered to be the best in our industry					
creative and bright					
experts in their particular jobs and functions					
Department: *Overall HC rating*					

CULTURE

As was observed in the main text, organizational culture may be viewed as strength or weakness (functional or dysfunctional) dependent upon its impact on goal achievement. Organizational culture may be decomposed into many dimensions (factors) to be measured such as: leadership, risk taking (creativity, entrepreneurialism or innovation), control (rule orientation or bureaucracy), reward systems, communications, etc. In some cases there is a focus on effectiveness and in other cases on efficiency. We have provided sample questions to help you evaluate the organization culture below:

LEADERSHIP

The head of this organization is mostly considered to be:

- a mentor, a wise, or a father or mother figure
- an entrepreneur, an innovator, or a risk taker
- a coordinator, an organizer, or an administrator
- a producer, a technician, or a hard driver.

GOAL ORIENTATION[3] Is this a results/goal-oriented company? How competitive are we? How important is the bottom line (profit)? Do we do things quickly? How often…

is competitiveness in relation to other organizations measured?
is individual appraisal directly related to the attainment of goals?

[3] See for example the competing values model (after Quinn, 1988).

Does management specify the targets to be attained? Is reward dependent on performance?

SUPPORTIVE/COLLABORATIVE ORIENTATION Is there an emphasis on the well-being and development of people? Do employees do things together? Is there an emphasis on long-term development? How often…

do managers show concern about employees' personal problems?
are new ideas about work organization encouraged?
do management practices allow freedom in work?

INNOVATION ORIENTATION Is this a creative and innovative organization? Do we do things first? Do managers seek to encourage creativity? How often…

does the organization search for new markets for existing products?
is there a lot of investment in new products?
do unpredictable elements in the market environment present good opportunities?
does the organization search for new opportunities in the external environment?
does the company make the best use of the employee skills to develop new or better products/services?

CONTROL/RULES ORIENTATION Is there a preference for structure or flexibility? How important is it to do things right? How important is stability? How often…

are instructions written down?
are jobs performed according to defined procedures?

Do management follow the rules themselves?
Are people held accountable for their actions?

MARKETING CULTURE

In describing the marketing culture, consider responses to the following questions:

~ What is the commitment of senior management to providing quality?
~ To what extent do employees focus on customer needs?
~ Customer satisfaction: do employees get positive customer feedback?

ADDITIONAL CULTURE ASSESSMENT QUESTIONS

Do employees have an action orientation – the pace is quick and things get done on time (to what extent are employees expected to meet all deadlines on time)?
How quickly does the company make decisions?
Is there a teamwork spirit?
Are employees consulted and listened to – does management pay careful attention to employee suggestions?
Is work–life balance supported?
Is this a fun place to work?
Can employees trust what management tells them?
Do employees always behave in an ethical manner?

Are the mission, goals, objectives and strategies clear and do employees know what must be done? Is there a shared commitment and collective mission, i.e. are employees unified in embracing the same objectives and strategies?
Are employees encouraged to learn from experience or do they fear blame when things go wrong?

ORGANIZATIONAL CLIMATE

As was discussed in the core text, there is a relationship between organizational culture and climate. Analyzing the climate provides both a reflection of the prevailing organizational culture and can reveal how it may develop in the future. The sample questions provided below will help reveal aspects of the organizational climate. Ultimately, the climate will need to be evaluated as a strength or weakness in terms of goal achievement.

Instructions: rate the degree to which **you** agree or disagree with the following statements. Answer for your company. Scoring (add up the score for the boxes you ticked. Column 1 = 1 point, Column 2 = 2 points … 5 = 5 points	Strongly Agree	Agree	Undecided	Disagree	Strongly Disagree
Participation, openness and honesty is the norm					
Employees work well together, valuing each other					
There is a sense of cooperation across boundaries/levels					
People are optimistic about the future					
Managers show confidence and trust in subordinates					
Subordinates feel free to talk to supervisors about work					
Managers often seek and use ideas from subordinates					
All employees feel responsibility for realizing firm goals					
Employees feel part of a team cooperating to reach goals					
Information flows up and down in this organization					
Managers know the problems subordinates face daily					

Decisions are made at all levels, staff act autonomously		
Organizational goals are established through consensus		
Employees regulate their own work in this company		
This is a very personal place. It is like an extended family		
This company is dynamic, entrepreneurial and risk taking		
This is a bureaucratic company: formal and structured		
A major concern is with getting the job done. People are not very involved personally		
Overall Climate rating		

Climate description: *Include an evaluation of climate as strength or weakness relative to organizational goal accomplishment.*

6. ANALYSIS: DIVERSITY AND INCLUSION

In this final section about the internal environment we consider analysis of HC from a diversity perspective. How can we determine the degree of diversity within the organization? Not only do analysts seek to measure diversity but they will also seek to ascertain whether the internal environment is *inclusive*. It is widely accepted that diversity will thrive if the internal environment (climate) is open, fair and inclusive.

QUANTITATIVE MEASUREMENTS OF DIVERSITY

Representation: What is the **workforce profile? E.g.** UK

Headcount		
Average age (~39) industry specific		
(%) Female (e.g. 40–45%)		
(%) Female senior managers		
(%) by Race (4–5% minority staff)		
(%) Ethnic minority senior managers		

% with Disabilities (4–5%)[4]		
Average Length of Service (5yrs)		

– are the percentages and numbers of the workforce aligned with the local area?

Recruitment and Promotion: Are certain groups less represented in the recruiting and hiring process? Are the rates similar for men and women? Are the rates similar for whites and ethnic minorities? Pay equity: are groups paid the same?

Representation of senior managers: Identify the percentage of men and women, by ethnic group, in senior management/executive roles. Are percentages consistent with the rest of the organization? Which groups are under-represented? What is the visible diversity of the people most likely to replace the senior managers?

QUALITATIVE MEASUREMENTS OF DIVERSITY COMMITMENT

Overall assessment: Is this a diverse organization? _____

Comments: (subtract 5 from the total score. A score

Instructions: rate the degree to which **you** agree or disagree with the following statements. Scoring (add up the score for the boxes you ticked. Column 1 = 1 point, Column 2 = 2 points … 5 = 5 points	Strongly Agree	Agree	Undecided	Disagree	Strongly Disagree
This company is committed to diversity					
This company respects individuals and values differences					
A vision of diversity is published and communicated					
Diversity matters are communicated frequently					
There are diversity champions throughout the structure					
Total Diversity Commitment Score					

close to zero indicates a greater commitment to diversity)

INCLUSION CLIMATE

As with other constructs, the inclusion environment may be quantitatively or qualitatively assessed. In the case of the former, analysts make use of the results of employee satisfaction surveys. Alternatively, they may make use of employee perceptions – the perceived level of inclusion felt by all employees – to create a qualitative assessment of the inclusion climate. Use the following questions to assess inclusion:

Overall assessment: Does this organization promote inclusion? ____
Comments: (subtract 10 from the total score. A score close to zero indicates a more inclusive climate)

Instructions: rate the degree to which **you** agree or disagree with the following statements. Scoring (add up the score for the boxes you ticked. Column 1 = 1 point, Column 2 = 2 points … 5 = 5 points	Strongly Agree	Agree	Undecided	Disagree	Strongly Disagree
All employees are treated with respect and dignity					
All employees are provided with equal opportunities					
Racist or sexist jokes etc. are rarely heard					
Discrimination is rarely observed in this company					
Employees feel positive about diversity in this workplace					
All group members are used when solving problems					
All employees feel included in the organization					
All employees are treated with respect					
Senior management support diversity initiatives					
Staff can talk openly with managers about diversity issues					
Total Inclusion Score					

7. SWOT ANALYSIS

The aforementioned tools can be used to develop an understanding of opportunities, threats, strengths and weaknesses. The SWOT analysis brings this range of tools and analytical steps together, in order to describe the overall situation. Undertaking a SWOT analysis is a simple process that can offer powerful insight into the potential and critical issues affecting a business. Use the analysis discussed in Sections 1–3 to determine opportunities and threats. This is the first part of your SWOT analysis. When considering opportunities and threats PESTEL Analysis can help to ensure you do not overlook external factors, such as new government regulations, or technological changes in your industry. A useful approach when looking at opportunities is to look at strengths (see Sections 4–6) and ask whether these open up any opportunities. Alternatively, look at organizational weaknesses and ask whether opportunities could be realized by eliminating these weaknesses.

1) The SWOT analysis begins by conducting an inventory of internal strengths and weaknesses in the organization. Next,
2) Note the external opportunities and threats that may affect the organization.

	Helpful	Harmful
	to achieving goals	
INTERNAL	**Strengths**	**Weaknesses**
EXTERNAL	**Opportunities**	**Threats**

Strengths: characteristics of the business that give it an advantage over others

Weaknesses: characteristics that place the business at a relative disadvantage

Opportunities: elements that the business could exploit to its advantage

Threats: elements in the environment that could cause trouble for the business

When evaluating strengths and weaknesses it is important not to simply ask what the firm is good at but what is it better at than the competition. Similarly, it is a good idea to relate strengths and weaknesses to critical success factors where possible. Other aspects of the internal environment (strengths) may include all productive assets (land, facilities, machinery and brands), customer relationships and customer satisfaction, competitive advantage and strategy, leadership, quality, access to finance/funding, patents and flexibility.

TOWS MATRIX

An alternative way of structuring the SWOT is the more elaborate 'TOWS Matrix'. With a TOWS analysis, threats and opportunities are examined first and weaknesses and strengths are examined last. After creating a list of threats, opportunities, weaknesses and strengths, managers examine ways the company can take advantage of opportunities and minimize threats by exploiting strengths and overcoming weaknesses. The TOWS Matrix indicates four conceptually distinct alternative strategies, tactics and actions. In practice, of course, some of the strategies overlap or they may be pursued simultaneously.

1) Create TOWS Matrix (see opposite)
2) Populate the O1, O2, O_n; S1, S2, S_n, etc.
3) Brainstorm strategies and record in appropriate cell/quadrant
4) Identify, in brackets, the relevant strengths, weaknesses, etc. for the strategy

Internal ⟍ External	**STRENGTHS** S1. Xxx S2. Xxx	**WEAKNESSES** W1. Xxx W2. Xxx
OPPORTUNITIES O1 Xxx O2 Xxx	Opportunity-Strength (OS) Strategies (Maxi Maxi) Use strengths to take advantage of opportunities 1) 'strategy 1' (S_x, O_y) 2) 3)	Opportunity-Weakness (OW) Strategies Overcome weaknesses by taking advantage of opportunities (Maxi Mini) 1) 2)
THREATS T1. Xxx T2. Xxx	Threat-Strength (TS) Strategies Use strengths to avoid threats (Maxi Mini) 1) 2)	Threat-Weakness (TW) Strategies Minimize weaknesses and avoid threats (Mini Mini) 1) 2)

Understanding strengths, weaknesses, opportunities and threats is important to many aspects of the practice of management to be discussed throughout this book.

Caution: we have presented a number of tools within this skills sheet. There are many problems associated with any instrument that seeks to diagnose management problems. Issues such as whether the right data exist, whether something can be measured, problems with perceptions and the fundamental issue of being sure you are measuring what you think you are measuring! Consequently we advise against using the tools to make statements such as this is a diverse company or not etc. but recommend that the questions be used to stimulate thinking about specific areas of management to determine focal areas – where attention may be needed and why. They should be used more to trigger thoughts and discussion, less to classify and categorize. In the case of the latter, they will be of more use when used consistently to compare and contrast firms.

Section Eight
Strategy (Planning)

ent starting point and approach for strategy creation. The Market (opportunity) driven approach seeks to exploit opportunities in the market by developing and deploying resources with customer needs in mind; the resource-based approach determines organizational strengths (internal focus) and then seeks to exploit these by pursuing suitable market opportunities; and competitor-influenced approaches analyze what rivals are doing and use this as a basis for strategy creation, countering competitor threats. We next consider the approaches in more detail.

17.5 THE EXTERNAL ENVIRONMENT – STRATEGIC POSITIONING

26.   Mintzberg (1987) discusses strategy as 'position', a means of locating an organization in its environment. He suggests that strategy is about creating situations where revenues may be generated and sustained. Organizations with a profit goal realize that profit will be impacted by the intensity of competition, value of the product to the customer and bargaining power of producers relative to suppliers. This was encapsulated within Porter's five forces framework discussed in Chapter 12. This framework is used to classify and analyze the factors that determine the intensity and levels of competition at the industry level. It helps strategic analysts understand how industry structure drives competition and determines industry profitability. Such analysis can be used to forecast future profitability, position the firm in relation to the competitive forces it faces and find ways to change industry structure. The positioning perspective is a perspective that emphasizes the external environment and opportunity as the starting point for strategy development. Recognizing and understanding organizational competitive forces allows positioning of your firm where competitive forces are weakest. Strategic positioning is about performing activities which differ from the activities of rivals or performing similar activities in different ways (Porter, 1996).
27.   There are many examples of positioning. Consider the music industry wherein CD sales fell when digital downloads, a substitute product (external threat), emerged. If you were working for an established music business, reliant on CD sales, how might you have prepared or reacted through changing position? You might have analyzed the industry and concluded that it was segmented, with the young more likely to download, contrasted with older folk who were more likely to stay with the CD. You could therefore have positioned your CDs to make yourself more attractive (through the type of music offered) to the older group. In other, more recent examples, Apple has positioned itself in a lucrative smartphone segment of the mobile phone industry whilst operators engage in price wars. Effective positioning obliges the organization to anticipate future developments in the competitive forces and industry.

17.6 THE INTERNAL ENVIRONMENT – LEVERAGING RESOURCES

28.   Earlier (para. 25) we noted there were three main approaches to strategy creation and we now consider the resource-based (internal/strength) perspective. Scholars and practitioners alike strive continuously to perfect the knowledge of what makes some organizations perform better than others. *Leverage* reflects the extent to which resources are utilized in the organization. The idea of looking at organizations as a broader set of resources returns to the seminal work of Penrose (1959). Wernerfelt (1984) argued that we can identify types of resources which can lead to high profits. He discussed resources and profitability; by a resource he meant anything which could be thought of as a strength or weakness of a given organization. More formally, an organization's resources at a given time could be defined as those (tangible and intangible) assets which are tied semi-permanently to the organization.
29.   Examples of resources are brand names, in-house knowledge of technology, talented people, trade contacts, machinery, efficient procedures, capital, etc.
30.   The resource-based view (RBV) is the perspective on strategy stressing the importance of capabilities (sometimes known as core competencies – those capabilities fundamental to the organization's strategy and performance; a bundle of skills and technologies that enables a company to provide a particular benefit to customers) in determining sustainable competitive advantage. The fundamental principle of the RBV is that the basis for organizational competitive advantage lies primarily in the application of the bundle of valuable resources at its disposal. The bundle of resources, under certain conditions, can assist the organization, sustaining above average returns. Such resources must be valuable and must enable the achievement of goals.

31.   Which resources matter? Resources within the RBV are broken down into two fundamental categories: 1) tangible and 2) intangible resources. The central proposition of the RBV is that not all resources are of equal importance in contributing to organizational performance. The resource-based literature describes resources in terms of their

value

rareness

inimitability, and

non-substitutability (VRIN see also **VRIO Framework**).

32.   Organizational assets may be [intangible] assets that can resist the imitation efforts of competitors. Organizational assets (e.g. culture, HRM policies and organization structure) contribute order, stability and quality to the organization. Some scholars suggest that without strong organizational assets, the organization will weaken productivity, deliver poor quality products and services and will have inferior human talent. Organizational assets may be difficult to duplicate. Although not legally protected by property rights, reputation is argued to be an important and sophisticated asset; reputation is built, not bought, suggesting that it is a non-tradable asset that may be far more difficult to duplicate than tangible assets.

33.   Capabilities, as ultimately reflected by the organization's know-how, are what the organization can do and are argued to be the principal source of organizational performance; the productivity and performance of any organization is solely dependent upon the know-how of its employees. Lastly, the ability to build and maintain relationships external to the organization is not only essential for competitive success; it is largely reflective of the knowledge-generating, knowledge-sharing and learning ability of the organization. In other words, building and maintaining external relationships is critical for the organization and largely consists of a 'collective', organization-wide effort of the know-how of a variety of employees and managers. Although intangible assets may be resistant to competitor duplication, capabilities are viewed as a 'superior' intangible resource.

17.7 SUCCESS FACTORS

34.   The concept of the key or critical success factor features heavily in the strategy literature and is considered more important by some scholars and practitioners than others (see for example Ghemawat who believes key/critical success factors do not supply a stable foundation for strategy). Of concern are those factors within the firm's market environment that determine the firm's ability to survive and prosper – if they can be identified. They have also been referred to as the small number of key factors executives consider critical to the success of the enterprise. These are key areas where effective performance will assure the success of the organization and attainment of its goals; those few things that must go right in order to ensure the organization's survival and success.

35.   In order to identify the success factors we must ask questions constantly such as: Who are our customers? What do they want and how do they choose between competing offerings? What drives competition and how can we obtain a superior competitive position? Thus if consumers choose on the basis of price then cost efficiency will be the primary basis for competitive advantage. There are many examples of success factors but they will vary from industry to industry and segment to segment. For example, having fast order delivery times, regular and reliable deliveries, controlled costs and so on.

36.   In summary, organizations will use strategic analysis to create their competitive offering. This offering and the resources used to create it will reflect (1) the success factors for the relevant industry and the needs of customers and (2) distinctive competencies and capabilities which yield competitive advantage. Earlier we discussed three major approaches to strategy creation: an external focus (market pull and opportunity), an internal focus (resources and strengths enabling the exploitation of opportunity) and competitor influenced. In many organizations strategy will be created with (simultaneous) attention to all three areas but one may dominate.

CONCLUSION

37.   Strategy is often defined as the match between what a company can do (organizational strengths and weaknesses) within the universe of what it might do (environmental opportunities and threats). Much strategy focuses on competition and advantage. As was noted, dominant theories about the sources of competitive advantage cluster around the internal or external environment. The dominant paradigm in the 1980s was the competitive forces approach, developed by Porter, which focused on the external environment. The key aspect of the firm's environment is the industry or industries within which it competes. Industry structure strongly influences the competitive rules of the game as well as the strategies available to firms. In the competitive forces model, five industry-level forces – entry barriers, threat of substitution, bargaining power of buyers and suppliers and rivalry amongst industry incumbents – determine the inherent profit potential of an industry. The approach can be used to help the firm find a position in an industry from which it can best defend itself against competitive forces or influence them in its favour. Such an approach is often referred to as a model of strategy emphasizing the exploitation of market power. Later, the 'resource-based perspective', was proposed, with an internal focus, emphasizing firm specific capabilities as the fundamental determinants of organizational performance. This perspective represents a strategy model emphasizing efficiency. The RBV approach sees organizations with superior systems and structures being profitable not because they engage in strategic investments that may deter entry and raise prices above long-run costs, but because they have markedly lower costs, or offer markedly higher quality or product performance. Organizations which are able to accumulate resources and capabilities that are rare, valuable, non-substitutable and difficult to imitate will achieve a competitive advantage.

38.   The different approaches to strategy and the attainment of superior and sustainable organizational performance discussed thus far, view differently the sources of wealth creation and the essence of the strategic problem faced by organizations. The competitive forces framework sees the strategic problem in terms of industry structure, entry deterrence and positioning. Resource-based perspectives have focused on the exploitation of firm-specific assets. Each approach asks different, often complementary questions. The approaches discussed are considered to be complementary and practitioners must work out which frameworks are appropriate for the problem in hand. Mindless devotion to one approach to the exclusion of all others is likely to generate strategic blind spots. Winners in the global marketplace are organizations who can demonstrate timely responsiveness and rapid and flexible product innovation, coupled with the management capability to coordinate and redeploy internal and external competencies effectively.

QUESTIONS

1   Explain how the RBV may complement the positioning view of strategy.

2   Review the significance of the external and internal environment for strategy formulation.

3   Use a case study of your choice to explore what is meant by strategy. You should discuss corporate and business level strategy and make use of the Ansoff and Boston matrices in your answer.

REFERENCES

Grant, R. (2007) *Contemporary Strategy Analysis*, 6th edn, Blackwell Publishing.

Kelly, P and Ashwin, A. (2013) *The Business Environment*, Cengage.

Mintzberg, H. (1987) 'The Strategy Concept I: Five Ps for strategy', *California Management Review*, 30(1): 11–24.

Penrose, E.G. (1959) *The Theory of the Growth of the Firm*, New York: Wiley.

Porter, M.E. (1996) 'What Is Strategy?', *Harvard Business Review*, 74(6): 61–78.

Wernerfelt, B. (1984) 'A Resource-based View of the Firm', *Strategic Management Journal*, 5(2): 171–180.

CHAPTER 18
STRATEGY IN PRACTICE (IMPLEMENTATION) — CONTROLLING BEHAVIOUR THROUGH POLICY, PLANS AND BUDGETS

Key Concepts

- Budget
- Business ethics
- Business model
- Business plan
- Corporate social responsibility
- Policy

Learning Outcomes Having read this chapter, you should be able to:

- discuss the role of corporate objectives
- review the role of policy in strategy implementation
- identify and discuss the application of ethics to managerial decision-making and business conduct
- explain what is meant by corporate social responsibility (CSR) and the reasons organizations pursue CSR strategies
- describe the budgeting process as a part of corporate and strategic planning.

1.   Much of the previous chapter was concerned with creating strategy and making strategic choices (corporate and business level strategy) and the organization's position in the environment (analyzed using tools presented in Section 7 of the book). There is a need to control the implementation of strategy. This chapter focuses on the way organizations translate strategy into action, through policy and more detailed planning (budgets) in particular. Planning involves decisions about ends (specific and detailed objectives) as well as means, and decisions about conduct as well as results. This chapter is concerned with translating the organizational purpose (explored in the previous chapter and communicated through the mission, vision and corporate objectives) into action and the associated need to define expectations of outcome and the behaviours used to attain such outcomes. Resources must be allocated and employees aligned with the new mission if it is to be accomplished.

2.   Organizations convert strategy into action in many ways. Once corporate or high-level goals and objectives have been set, via the process of corporate planning, the rest of the organization (subsidiaries, departments, etc.) must be aligned, coordinated and controlled to assure attainment. The organization is likely to reorganize, adapting structure to fit strategy and will allocate financial resources through a budgetary process to ensure managers throughout the organization have the necessary resources to achieve the specific targets and goals they have been set. The budgetary process, as triggered by objectives and the strategic plan, is discussed at a high level at the end of this chapter but will be discussed in more detail in Chapter 45, in the financial management section of the book. Organization and structure is discussed in the next section of the book.

3.   The organization also makes use of policy, culture, CSR and ethics when seeking to control employee behaviour during the implementation of strategy. There are informal behaviour control mechanisms such as culture and more formal mechanisms such as objectives, policy and codes of conduct (ethics). Whilst the business plan, with the mission and objectives, may define 'what' needs to be done, the aforementioned mechanisms guide 'how' employees and the organization will conduct themselves in attaining goals and fulfilling their purpose. The existence and sophistication of budgetary processes and policies to guide strategic behaviours will depend upon company size, resources and degree of formalization.

4.   Whereas policy is developed within the frame of the objectives and details the 'how', 'where' and 'when' in terms of the course of action which must be followed to achieve the objectives, business models may be used in order to communicate how corporate and strategic goals may be achieved. We start the chapter by outlining what encompasses the term business models, their components and purpose. We then consider the hierarchy of planning – how the organization translates the company-wide, corporate objectives into more specific unit level objectives. Next we focus on controlling behaviour through policy when seeking to assure plans are implemented consistently and as intended. We also consider the role of ethics at this level and the idea of corporate social responsibility. The chapter finishes with a brief introduction to budgeting – the more detailed and action-oriented aspect of planning.

18.1 BUSINESS MODELS

Vignette

Wonga is a digital finance company based in London, providing microfinance loans. Whilst sometimes criticized on moral grounds, the payday lender's business model has proved effective with the company's post-tax profits rising 36 per cent in 6 years. This has been achieved as 1 million customers take out nearly 4 million payday loans, making Wonga a significant UK lender. Wonga's business model (easy-access payday lending – short-term loans) has four key elements: (1) efficient assessment of credit risk kept default rates to 7.4 per cent in 2012 – a rate that would disgrace a mainstream lender but is easily tolerable for Wonga with its relatively high rates of interest, (2) Wonga manages to provide its customers with what they want, processing loans rapidly. This is not a service mainstream banks have mastered; the company has clearly identified an appetite for instant loans, (3) Wonga is a capital-efficient business. The company makes only £15 net profit per loan, however as they turn over their capital several times each year, the 'same' £200 might earn £15 six or seven times in the space of 12 months. Wonga's return on shareholders' equity is about 30 per cent and after-tax profit margins are 20 per cent and (4) the company's customers are prepared to borrow at very high interest rates. Payday lenders profit from people's tendency to discount the future, i.e. distant rewards are worth less than immediate ones.

5. The business plan informs us what needs to be done and, to some extent, how and when. Additionally, the **business model** concept may be used to communicate *how* corporate and strategic goals may be achieved. Most business models show *how* the organization will meet customer needs (value proposition); *how* the organization will earn money (revenue model) and *how* the organization will compete and be structured. Business models may also be used to create and communicate new strategic alternatives (used in the strategy creation process – refer back to Figure 17.2).

6. Thompson and Martin (2005) suggest the business model provides an explanation of an organization's recipe for success (see the vignette as an example), and it contains those factors which essentially define the business. It is, they argue, the vehicle for delivering the purpose or mission. The business model of a profit-oriented organization explains *how* it generates revenue and profit consistently. The business model may be described more precisely with attention to specific model components.

7. Osterwalder and Pigneur (2010) discuss how to generate business models ('blueprints for strategy'). They identify nine building blocks (components of a business model):

Customer Segments – which customers are served (who are most important)

Value Propositions – what the customer gets (product benefits, needs satisfied)

Channels – how value propositions are delivered to customers (distribution etc.)

Customer Relationships – how to acquire, retain and upsell

Revenue Streams – how revenue is made (item sale, usage fee, subscription, etc.)

Key Resources – what key resources the value propositions and model need

Key Activities – what are the most important things the company must do

Key Partnerships – who are the key partners/suppliers, what do they provide

Cost Structure – what are the major costs, whether the firm is cost/value driven

8. Today, 'business model' and 'strategy' are among the most carelessly used terms in business; they are often stretched to mean everything – and end up meaning nothing (Magretta, 2002). Business models are, at heart, stories that explain how enterprises work. Magretta believes they answer certain questions: Who is the customer? How do we make money? What underlying economic logic explains how we can deliver value to customers at an appropriate cost? Every viable organization is built upon a sound business model, but a business model is not a strategy, even though many people use the terms interchangeably. Business models describe, as a system, how the pieces of a business fit together. But they do not factor in one critical dimension of performance: competition. That is the purpose of strategy, argues Magretta.

18.2 TOWARDS DETAILED PLANS AND OBJECTIVES

9. Following creation of the corporate strategy (and possibly a business model), parts (units such as subsidiaries, divisions or departments) of the organization must formulate specific (shorter-term) plans

identifying what will be done by whom and when. In parallel, they will engage in the budget process (discussed at the end of this chapter) to ensure they are allocated the required resources to meet objectives. Once objectives, targets, plans and budgets have been agreed, the organization (through its parts) can engage in implementation and action to fulfil objectives. This whole process is subjected to monitoring and control.

10. In the previous chapter we discussed the corporate mission and strategic management. *Business planning* – the theme of this section – follows on from the setting of the organization's key objectives and policies. Plans state how the organization intends to move forward over a given period, usually between 1 and 5 years. At the forefront of such planning the strategic or corporate plan is created which identifies the broad direction the organization will take over the next 2 to 5 years, or in some cases up to 10 years, and the resources to be deployed to ensure that the plan is implemented. The resources are expressed in financial terms, sufficient to cover anticipated expenditure on people, buildings, machinery, etc. Because of the number of variables at work in the external environment, most business organizations tend to work on a rolling 3 to 5-year plan basis, in which only the next year's budgets are expressed in detailed terms, and the remaining years are set out in flexible terms, allowing for a range of unexpected contingencies. The value of the business plan has been called into question, particularly in smaller entrepreneurial firms. On the one hand it can be argued that they help provide focus, communicate goals and intentions (therefore motivate action), and force managers to be explicit about assumptions (which can be critically analyzed by others) yet on the other hand they may stifle creativity, provide an illusion of control and take time and company resources to complete.

11. Objectives are statements of specific outcomes that are to be achieved. They exist at many levels within the organization: corporate (goals of the organization) and strategic, divisional or subsidiary level strategic objectives, tactical and operational. Objectives tend to be more generalist at the corporate level, becoming more specific towards the operational level. Overall objectives tend to be stated in general terms, and are intended to be relatively permanent. The clarification and definition of key objectives is vital for any organization since objectives provide it with a sense of direction and a mission. The primary purpose of objectives is to align, coordinate, guide and motivate employee action. SMART objectives are objectives that are specific, measurable, attainable, realistic and time bounded.

12. The objectives set for an organization are determined mainly by the owners or senior management (board) and are based upon the organization's prime purpose. Thus, the objectives of a business organization will be based around concepts such as profitability, growth, customer service, shareholder satisfaction and employee motivation. The objectives of a public service are likely to focus on the efficient delivery of a service (e.g. health or education) to the community.

13. In the traditional (shareholder) view of the firm, the organization has a fiduciary duty to place the needs of the shareholders (the owners) first, to increase value for them. Another theory of the firm has been called the stakeholder theory. Stakeholder theory argues there are other parties involved, including governmental bodies, trade associations, trade unions, communities and the public. A stakeholder is a member of a group who has a vested interest in or whose support is necessary for the organization to exist. Over the past two decades we have seen a gradual rejection of the 'management serving the shareowners' model, and a greater acceptance of stakeholder theory based either on broad theories of philosophical ethics, such as utilitarianism, or on narrower 'middle-level' theories derived from the notion that a 'social contract' exists between corporations and society. Stakeholder theory suggests the role of the organization is to satisfy a wider set of stakeholders, not simply the owners. The theory is used to interpret the function of the corporation, how things should be, including the identification of moral or philosophical guidelines for the operation and management of corporations.

14. Where this theory is held, strategic objectives are set not only for the good of the business, but also for the good of these other groups as well. An example would be where a pharmaceutical company sets objectives relating to the safety aspects of its products, both in relation to its own employees and to its consumers. Apart from small, owner-managed enterprises, most organizations tend to adopt the stakeholder theory, if only in response to external pressures. Stakeholder management requires, as its key attribute, simultaneous attention to the legitimate interests of all appropriate stakeholders, both in the establishment of organizational structures and general policies and in case-by-case decision-making. This requirement holds for anyone managing or affecting corporate policies, including not only professional managers, but shareowners,

the government and others. The theory does, however, not imply that all stakeholders (however they may be identified) should be equally involved in all processes and decisions.

18.3 POLICIES

15.   Once an organization has established its corporate objectives, it may then determine in what manner it intends these to be achieved. Policy statements are made to indicate to those concerned just what the organization will and will not do in pursuance of its overall purpose and objectives – it frames the objectives. Such statements are one expression of the organization's culture and belief system. Policies are not the same as objectives or plans, even though they are frequently confused with them. Objectives state an aim or goal, i.e. they are ends; plans provide a framework within which action can take place to attain objectives, i.e. they are means; policies, on the other hand, are neither ends nor means, they are statements of conduct – principles designed to influence decisions and actions. Policies cause managers to take action in a certain way; they are not actions in themselves. Policies both reflect and contribute to organizational culture. Examples of different kinds of policies are as follows:

– It is our policy to ensure this place of work is free from negative, aggressive and inappropriate behaviours, and that the environment is aimed at providing high-quality products and services in an atmosphere of respect, collaboration, openness, safety and equality.

– The company is an equal opportunity employer and makes employment decisions on the basis of merit.

– Customer care will be provided in a professional manner across the company by well trained and knowledgeable staff.

– It is our policy to achieve for all our operations, best practice in our standards of business integrity. This includes a commitment to maintaining the highest standards of corporate governance and ethics.

16.   Policies may either state what the organization will do or what it will positively not do. Some policies relate to marketing issues, others relate much more to ethical and philosophical issues. The variety can be considerable, but the intention is the same: to guide the organization's managers in the conduct of its affairs. Policies are typically disseminated through official written documents and handbooks. They are formal and seek to assure consistency and standardization, to guide employee behaviour. To that end, they are essentially aspects of a bureaucratic system of management (see Chapter 3).

17.   **Policy** documents typically contain standard components including a purpose statement (why the organization is issuing the policy, and what the desired effect or outcome of the policy should be); an applicability and scope statement (describing who the policy affects and which actions are impacted by the policy); an effective date; a responsibilities section (indicating which parties and organizations are responsible for carrying out individual policy statements) and policy statements which indicate the specific regulations, requirements or modifications to organizational behaviour the policy intends to create. Some policies may contain additional sections, including a background section which may point out the reasons and intent (motivating factors) that led to creation of the policy. This information is often helpful when policies must be evaluated or used in ambiguous situations. Finally, definitions for terms and concepts may also be found in the policy document. Typically accompanying the creation of policies is the need to establish new roles and responsibilities and allocate resources to assure action and policy conformance.

18.4 ETHICS

18.   When seeking to fulfil objectives, aside from considering policy, employees might ask, 'what is acceptable business practice?' they may answer with a view from the organization, their own or a range of stakeholder perspectives. Ethics (see also morals and morality) considers what is right and wrong and **business ethics** concerns the accepted principles (beliefs and values) of right or wrong governing the conduct of business people. Ethical principles can be used by individuals to make choices which guide their behaviour.

Unethical behaviour can cost a company its reputation and its customers and therefore revenues and hard cash; it can also result in a loss of investors and may lead to a reduction in share price. Furthermore, employees do not like working for unethical companies and suppliers and other value-system players do not like to do business with such companies. If loss of revenue were not incentive enough, corporate wrong-doings may be dealt with in the courts with directors, employees or the organization receiving punishment. It is no longer sufficient for organizations to simply follow a profit-only goal and recognize investors as the only stakeholders who matter.

19.   The principal aspects of a business likely to produce moral dilemmas include:

- the way certain activities or decisions are reported in the annual accounts

- the gaining of sales contracts in highly competitive markets, where inducements or trade-offs may be suggested (bribery and corruption)

- the acquisition of competitors' plans, designs and other critical information by underhand means (industrial espionage)

- the deliberate suppression of facts that might compromise the safety or effectiveness of a product.

20.   Other ethical issues may arise from the exploitation of women or child labour either directly, or by suppliers. Multinational enterprises in particular may have to confront local practices involving vulnerable groups working long hours for low wages. There are also many environmental matters that can be directly influenced for good or worse by business corporations. The world is increasingly endangered by pollution, destruction of rainforests and other ecosystems and the problem of global warming. The boards of large enterprises can contribute positively to alleviating such problems by minimizing pollution, reducing waste and developing eco-friendly methods of production. In some cases they are encouraged to act positively by national laws and international agreements, but where no such laws or agreements exist, the responsibility for creating a healthier environment lies with the leaders of such enterprises and the ethical standards to which they adhere.

21.   Over time, a variety of general principles have been proposed to describe what is meant by ethical behaviour. Individuals should keep promises (fidelity), be fair (justice), not harm others, put right any wrong caused (reparation), show gratitude to others and improve the lives of one's self and others (beneficence). Other principles include fiduciary obligations (not putting self-interest above the overall interests of the organization), reliability (fulfilling promises), transparency (openness and honesty), dignity (respecting others), fairness (not taking bribes or colluding with others), citizenship (respecting the law and the environment), responsiveness and respecting property. When people and organizations adhere to a moral code they are said to possess integrity. As integrity is eroded, unethical and illegal behaviour follows.

22.   Managing the organization ethically may mean following laws and regulations, ensuring equal opportunity or dealing with social responsibility issues. In many cases it is about ensuring ethical decision-making and resultant action. In order to do this, the organization must ensure employees understand ethical and moral values and can use this understanding to make sense of business problems. In considering options for action, the organization needs its employees to show good ethical judgement, being able to evaluate different options and determine which are more acceptable, based on the moral values and beliefs of the decision-makers and the organization as a whole.

23.   The organization may create and adopt a number of statements to communicate the corporation's view on the subject of ethics. A code of ethics is a written document that states explicitly what constitutes acceptable and unacceptable behaviour for all employees in the organization. Common issues to be included in business ethics are accountability (transparency and reporting), business conduct (compliance with the law, competitive conduct, corruption and bribery, conflicts of interest), community involvement (community economic development and employment of locals), corporate governance (investor rights), environment (policy, code of conduct and management systems to protect the environment), human rights (health and safety, child labour, forced labour, freedom of association, working hours, wages and benefits), consumer protection (marketing, product quality and safety, consumer privacy) and labour (workplace/employee) relations.

24.   The existence of a code of practice in ethics, supported by senior management and made a natural feature of a company's culture, will enable better distinctions to be made between what is acceptable business practice and what is sharp practice (behaviour that is technically within the rules of the law but borders on being unethical – unscrupulous). It is often suggested that leadership by example is the most effective way to improve business ethics. Leaders must therefore be honest and trustworthy, with high integrity. To be perceived as an ethical leader, it is not enough to just be an ethical person. An executive ethical leader must also find ways to focus the organization's attention on ethics and values and to infuse the organization with principles that guide the actions of all employees.

18.5 CORPORATE SOCIAL RESPONSIBILITY

25.   We shall now consider one important area for policy development – that of 'social responsibility'. Being 'socially responsible' implies playing more than just an economic role in society. Corporate social responsibility (CSR) is a concept whereby organizations consider the interests of society by taking responsibility for the impact of their activities on customers, suppliers, employees, shareholders, communities and the environment in every aspect of their operations and decision-making; it is about good business citizenship.

26.   Central to the CSR approach is that the organization should use resources responsibly (sustainable, no waste, to produce the goods and services for society in a profitable manner) and should comply with relevant laws and regulations. In addition to the moral issue, there are many arguments in favour of CSR. A CSR programme can be seen as an aid to recruitment and retention, particularly within the competitive graduate student market. Reputations and brands that take time and resources to build up can be ruined in hours through unethical decisions manifest in incidents such as corruption scandals or environmental accidents. These events can also draw unwanted attention from regulators, courts, governments and media. Building an ethical culture of 'doing the right thing' can offset these risks. Furthermore, by taking voluntary action, organizations can persuade governments and the wider public that they are taking seriously issues such as health and safety, employee relations or the environment and so avoid intervention.

27.   What does it mean for a corporation to be socially responsible? The main components are: legal – they obey the law; ethical – they do the right thing (see previous section); they are efficient and profitable – they use resources efficiently; and finally such companies show good judgement, they are charitable and philanthropic. Four key arguments have been offered to encourage organizations to act in a socially responsible manner: (1) **MORAL OBLIGATION** – companies have a duty to be good citizens and to 'do the right thing'; they should achieve commercial success in ways that honour ethical values and respect people, communities and the natural environment, (2) **SUSTAINABILITY** – emphasizes the environment by meeting the needs of the present without compromising the ability of future generations to meet their own needs, (3) **LICENCE TO OPERATE** – every company needs tacit or explicit permission from governments, communities and numerous other stakeholders to do business and (4) **REPUTATION** – through this argument, attempts are made to justify CSR initiatives on the grounds they will improve a company's image, strengthen its brand, boost morale and even raise the value of its stock.

18.6 DETAILED PLANNING AND CONTROL PROCESSES: BUDGETING

28.   In this final section we will consider the role of budgeting within the planning process. As suggested within Figure 18.1 the implementation of strategy typically follows the creation of objectives. As was discussed earlier in this chapter a hierarchy of objectives exists within the larger firm. Starting with corporate objectives, objectives must also be developed for the different parts (units) of the organization. Once strategies have been agreed upon (a strategic plan has been created) and appropriate courses of action planned, strategies should be implemented.

FIGURE 18.1 Strategic planning and budgetary process

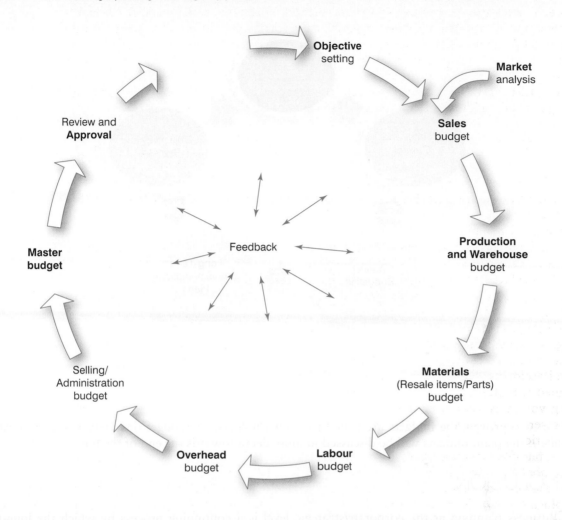

29.   According to Drury (2013) **budgeting** is the implementation of the long-term plan for the year ahead through the development of detailed financial plans and a **budget** is a financial plan for implementing management decisions. Budgets are used to aid coordination within the firm, communicate plans, motivate and control action. Whereas long-term plans indicate the broad direction the organization intends to follow, budgets – depicting a shorter time frame – tend to be more precise and detailed. Organizations typically instigate an annual budgeting process.

30.   There are two key perspectives on the budgeting process: top-down budget setting means imposing budgets and targets from above, without the participation of the individuals involved and bottom-up budget setting means allowing individuals to participate in the setting of budgets and targets. Firms establish procedures and typically a budget committee (high level executives) for approving budgets. Larger organizations will also appoint a budget officer (normally an accountant) to coordinate the different budgets within the organization.

31.   The important stages of the budgeting process are depicted within Figure 18.2. Organizations usually start with the sales budget preparation since demand or production capacity typically restricts performance (revenue goal) in many organizations. Budgets are drafted by units and then examined and negotiated through broad participation. When all the budgets are in harmony with each other they are summarized into a master budget (a document that brings together and summarizes all lower level budgets and which consists of a budgeted profit and loss account, a balance sheet and cash flow statement – to be discussed in Chapter 44).

FIGURE 18.2 Budgetary process

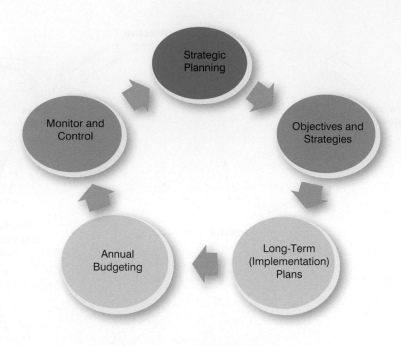

32.   Once approved, the budgets are issued to budget holders; the budget then acts as the authority to implement the plan. Budgets will be discussed in more detail towards the end of the book.

CONCLUSION

33.   Business planning at the corporate/strategic level is a continuing process by which the long-term objectives of an organization may be formulated, and subsequently attained, by means of long-term strategic actions designed to make their impact on the organization as a whole. Corporate planning also involves deciding the policies, or code of conduct, of the organization in pursuit of its objectives. Thus business aims and ethical considerations are brought together. The typical planning process adopts a contingency perspective and is based upon analysis of the environment. However, the process is not entirely mechanical and rational/economic and affords plenty of scope for choices to be made which are influenced by the values and beliefs of managers and other stakeholders.

34.   High level corporate plans and objectives drive the creation of more specific subsidiary, business unit and departmental plans and ultimately budgets. Budgets are used to aid coordination within the firm, communicate plans, motivate and control action.

QUESTIONS

1 Review the role of policy in strategy implementation.

2 Explain what is meant by corporate social responsibility and the reasons organizations pursue CSR strategies.

3 Select an organization with which you are familiar and then document and evaluate the business model.

USEFUL WEBSITES

The Centre for Ethics and Business: **cba.lmu.edu/ academicprograms/centers/ethicsandbusiness.htm**
Provides an environment for discussing issues related to the necessity, difficulty, costs and rewards of conducting business ethically

Institute of Business Ethics: **www.ibe.org.uk**
Raises public awareness of the importance of doing business ethically

REFERENCES

Drury, C. (2013) *Management Accounting for Business*, 5th edn, Cengage Learning.

Magretta, J. (2002) 'Why business models matter', *Harvard Business Review*, 80(5): 86–92.

Osterwalder, A. and Pigneur, Y. (2010) *Business Model Generation: A Handbook for Visionaries, Game Changers, and Challengers*, Wiley.

Thompson, J.L. and Martin, F. (2005) *Strategic Management*, 5th edn, Cengage Learning EMEA.

CHAPTER 19
MANAGING STRATEGY: STRATEGIC CONTROL AND ORGANIZATIONAL PERFORMANCE MANAGEMENT

Key Concepts

- Dashboard
- Management by objectives
- Metric
- Performance management
- Scorecard
- Strategic control

Learning Outcomes Having read this chapter, you should be able to:

- appraise the role of performance management systems and processes in transforming strategy into action
- explain management by objectives (MBO)
- discuss how scorecards are used to transform strategy into action
- explain how measurements and performance indicators can be used in the process of strategic control
- contrast traditional with contemporary approaches to organizational performance management.

Vignette

THE BALANCED SCORECARD, STRATEGY MAPS AND DASHBOARDS: WHY ARE THEY DIFFERENT?

Gary Cokins believes that senior management teams are disposed to focus excessively on short-term financial results and use historic information for control, reported 'after the damage is done'. The balanced scorecard on the other hand gives management a broader, more holistic view of the organization by incorporating non-financial operational measures – metrics that are related to customers; internal processes; and employee innovation, learning and growth. These influential non-financial measures are reported during the period when adjustments can be made and small problems can be addressed before they become large issues. These actions in turn lead to better performance. Cokins suggests organizations think more deeply about what measures drive value and achievement of goals.

1.   Having dedicated the past three chapters to strategy creation and planning, we now consider two critical questions posed by Harvard Business Professor, Robert Simons (2000):

(1) *How can we be sure that people understand what we are trying to achieve?* And (2) *How can we ensure that we are reaching our strategic goals?*

Simons believes that business strategy is at the root of effective performance measurement and control. Performance measurement and control systems provide the analytical discipline and communication channels to formalize business strategy and ensure that strategic goals are communicated throughout the business. Such systems are also the primary vehicle to monitor the implementation of strategy (Simons, 2000: p. 16).

2.   The main focus of this chapter is on transforming strategy into action. It is therefore concerned with how to manage strategy. Previous chapters have considered how strategy is created. This chapter turns attention to implementation issues, **strategic control**. As with many aspects of management theory we have witnessed a shift in thinking from a traditional concern with historic financial indicators, towards strategic management systems that also have a present and future orientation, and consider a broader range of metrics, typically consolidated in a scorecard or dashboard (refer to opening vignette).

3.   Organizations require mechanisms to ensure strategy cascades down the organization and leads to action. Johnson, Scholes and Whittington (2006) discuss converting strategy into action and the relationship between overall business strategy and strategies in resource areas such as people, information and technology. They discuss strategy and people and the ways in which human resource activities can help enable the strategy. In particular they recognize the important role of goal setting and performance management (p. 449).

4.   Once organizational strategies and objectives have been defined, unit level managers, in conjunction with senior management, create unit level objectives and plans. Along with respective budgets, they ultimately influence team and individual performance expectations and job descriptions. The behaviour, results and developmental plans of all employees must be aligned with the vision, mission, goals and strategies of the organization and the unit within which they work. This leads to improved coordination, unification and motivation of the workforce.

5.   Performance is a term used to consider an action, task, goal or operation, seen in terms of how successfully it was performed or accomplished. It may be evaluated from the individual to the corporate level. Organizational (corporate) performance comprises the actual output or results of an organization as measured against its intended outputs (goals and objectives). Specialists in many fields such as strategy, quality and HR are concerned with organizational performance. Individual performance, on the other hand, describes the actual effort displayed by the employee whilst undertaking their role at work. Performance relates to the person's ability to perform all of the tasks and duties required for a specific job. Clearly the sum of individual performance can be used as an indicator for corporate performance.

19.1 METRICS, MEASUREMENTS AND PERFORMANCE INDICATORS

6.   In Chapter 17 we discussed the creation of mission and vision statements yet Brown (1996: p. 161) suggests that the development of such statements will do nothing to change or improve the organization unless other changes follow. People need to understand how they can contribute to the vision. Indicators and other measurements can be used to translate such statements into more meaningful information. Information that can drive performance towards targets and goals. Metrics are simply measurements that facilitate the quantification of some particular characteristic (like an objective or goal); they quantify results. They may also be methods of evaluation. Business metrics define business progress in measurable terms. Performance metrics quantify the unit's performance. The terms metric, indicator and measurement are often used interchangeably in management.

7.   We discussed the measurement of performance and performance indicators (KPIs and success factors) in the first skills sheet, Efficiency and Bureaucracy, and then again in Chapter 17 (see 17.7 Success Factors). Indeed there is a relationship between the accuracy of an organization's measurement system and the quality of an organization's decision-making (see Chapter 16). Consultant Mark Brown's book 'Keeping Score' (1996) is about using the right metrics to drive world-class performance. In this sense a metric is a system or standard of measurement. Similarly Marr (2012), discusses KPIs and argues that 'what gets measured gets done' and 'if you can't measure it, you can't manage it'. Interestingly, he also introduces the concept of the Key Performance Question (KPQ) – a management question that seeks to capture exactly what it is that managers need to know and precedes KPI selection or design.

8.   Brown (1996: p. vii) argues that measuring the right variables will ensure success. He believes that metrics should focus on the past, present and future and be linked to key success factors (and ultimately the company vision); changing as the situation and strategy changes. Multiple measures are typically combined into several indices of performance. Marr (2012) also discusses the grouping of KPIs, suggesting that dashboards and scorecards (to be discussed later in this chapter) are used by companies to group KPIs together into displays or reports so they provide at-a-glance overviews of business (or business unit) performance.

9.   Organizations should begin by defining their mission and vision for the future (future goal), (Brown 1996: p. 10). Next they should identify key success factors, i.e. what the organization needs to focus on to beat competitors and achieve the vision. From this, the organization can develop performance metrics, short-term goals and appropriate strategies (activities to achieve the goals). Typical measurement systems will be organized into data categories such as: financial, supplier or process performance, customer or employee satisfaction and quality.

10.   In designing the measurement system, some organizations adopt a top-down approach, first developing a set of macro metrics for the entire organization and then developing related but more detailed metrics for the different business units. Alternatively, organizations may adopt a bottom-up approach, beginning with the business unit and eventually consolidating with the organizational system.

11.   Brown (1996: p. 171) also comments on what is important when reviewing data (measurements and indicators). Organizations need to assess their level of performance and will therefore compare achievement of their goals with past performance, with competitors' performance and with benchmark organizations. Benchmarking is one of the best methods of establishing realistic stretch goals. We return to measurement, scorecards and dashboards later in the chapter. First we consider a more traditional top-down approach to aligning employees with the corporate strategy.

19.2 PERFORMANCE MANAGEMENT: TRADITIONAL APPROACHES

12.   **Performance management** has been defined in many ways, often dependent upon the level of analysis, i.e. companywide or individual employee. In the context of this part of the book we might consider it to be a strategic and integrated approach to increasing the effectiveness of organizations. However, a broader and more employee-centric definition is provided by Aguinis (2009) who describes a continuous process of identifying, measuring and developing the performance of individuals and teams and aligning performance

with the strategic goals of the organization. It ensures that employee activities and outputs are congruent with the organization's goals. Performance management systems usually measure both employee behaviours and the outcomes of such behaviour.

13.   The performance management system has several purposes: it may be used to help senior management achieve strategic business objectives, encourage behaviours consistent with the attainment of organizational goals; make decisions about employee compensation (interlinked with the reward system); it is a communication device to set goals, provide feedback and drive action, identifying training needs, etc.

14.   Performance management systems should be congruent with strategy and provide information that allows for the identification of effective and ineffective performance; the measures of performance should be valid, consistent and reliable and the system perceived as fair by all participants. A good system is operated transparently and in a consistent manner. The performance management system is typically integrated with budgetary and HR systems and may also be used in conjunction with wider aspects of human resource management.

15.   The performance management process, a continuous process, is made of several key activities:

1.   PLANNING – determining what needs to be done, objectives and required behaviours/competencies

2.   EXECUTION – employee undertakes the work

3.   ASSESSMENT – evaluating the extent to which the desired behaviours have been displayed and results achieved

4.   REVIEW – appraisal.

It is dependent upon both strategic goals and those cascaded downwards as departmental and individual objectives.

16.   In measuring employee results, the organization typically identifies the areas where an employee is accountable, then sets objectives (measurable outcomes) and performance standards (acceptable performance). An emphasis on objectives and standards should allow employees to translate organizational goals into individual goals. This is a key aspiration of **management by objectives**. The term 'management by objectives' was first popularized by Peter Drucker in his 1954 book 'The Practice of Management'. The essence of MBO is participative goal setting (refer back to motivation), the measurement and comparison of actual employee performance with the standards set.

FIGURE 19.1 **MBO process**

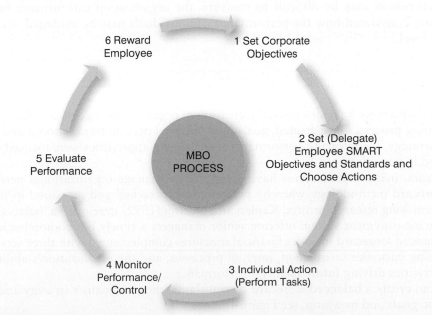

17.   The MBO process is outlined in Figure 19.1. Accountabilities are determined from the job description and are based on the requirements of the individual's job. For example, where the jobholder manages a team there may be team-building, coaching or supervisory accountabilities. After the accountabilities have been identified, the next stage is to determine the specific objectives. Typically these will be specific, measurable, achievable, results-based and time specific (SMART, see previous chapter). For example, the jobholder may have an objective to deliver team training sessions throughout the year. Having developed objectives, the next step is to define performance standards. When managing performance, we need to determine how well the objectives were achieved (quality), how much was produced (quantity) and whether deadlines were met; ideally standards will include an action, the desired result, a due date and some type of quality or quantity indicator. They describe satisfactory performance. Standards should be specific and measurable, meaningful, realistic and achievable and will be reviewed regularly.

18.   MBO is a means of integrating organizational goals, such as profit and growth, with individual managers' needs to contribute to the organization and to their own self-development. A system of management by objectives, therefore, seeks to achieve a sense of common purpose and common direction amongst the management of an organization in the fulfilment of business results. The most important features of MBO are as follows:

- it focuses on results (system outputs) rather than on activity (system processes)

- it develops logically from the corporate planning process by translating corporate and departmental objectives into individual managerial objectives, and

- it seeks to improve management performance.

19.   The cycle of events demonstrates the links between the organization's strategic plan, the objectives and key tasks of individual managers, and the vital review of performance which provides important feedback for other parts of the system. The performance review provides feedback to the operating system (plans and objectives), and to the training and development system (training needs and succession plans). The potential review feeds back to the training and development system.

20.   Evaluating the MBO approach, Mullins (2010) acknowledges the MBO system is attractive with much to recommend it and that it has been adopted in a wide range of organizational settings. However, he questions its relevance today. MBO appears to have suffered a decline in popularity as it is difficult to specify and measure targets for some important aspects of work. Consequently, these areas may become neglected. Despite this, many present-day methods are very similar to MBO in their approach and results. When results may be difficult to measure, the organization can measure behaviour as an alternative. Having considered how the performance of individuals may be managed, we now return to the organization level.

19.3 MEASURING CORPORATE PERFORMANCE: SCORECARDS

21.   In previous chapters we have discussed the creation of organizational goals and the use of budgets in the detailed planning process. Once created, goals (and budgets) need to be monitored and measured – an essential part of strategy. Traditionally, performance management approaches were focused solely on financial indicators and historic data.

22.   In recent years, many organizations have attempted to manage organizational performance using the balanced scorecard methodology whereby performance is tracked and measured in multiple dimensions. During a year-long research project, Kaplan and Norton (1992) developed a 'balanced scorecard', a new performance measurement system offering senior managers a timely but comprehensive view of the business. The balanced scorecard includes financial measures complemented with three sets of operational measures addressing customer satisfaction, internal processes, and the organization's ability to learn and improve- – the activities driving future financial performance.

23.   Managers can create a balanced scorecard by translating their company's strategy and mission statements into specific goals and measures, see Figure 19.2.

CHAPTER 20
ORGANIZING THE WORKFORCE: ORGANIZATION STRUCTURES AND DESIGNS

Key Concepts

- Contingency approach to organization design
- Functional, area and product structures
- Horizontal design
- Organizational design
- Organizational structure
- Tall hierarchical (vertical) structure

Learning Outcomes
Having read this chapter, you should be able to:

- explain how organizations provide structure to their workforce
- define and discuss the nature of organization design
- identify factors likely to determine the design of organizations
- explain the basic parts of organizations
- evaluate common organization designs (structural forms)
- compare centralization and decentralization
- contrast vertical and horizontal organizations.

20.1 INTRODUCTION

1.   In the previous section we discussed strategy. Alfred Chandler, back in the 1960s, famously argued that 'structure-follows-strategy'. This means that a corporate structure is created in order to implement a given corporate strategy. He described corporate strategy as the determination of long-term goals and objectives, the adoption of courses of action and associated allocation of resources required to achieve goals; he defined structure as the design of the organization through which strategy is administered. Since Chandler's thesis there have been alternative arguments suggesting strategy follows structure. It is now more common, following Mintzberg, to view strategy and structure as reciprocal. An organization must consider simultaneously its goals and the way it organizes resources and work. Thus this section of the book is closely linked with the previous section.

2.   There are many work tasks to be carried out in any organization and consequently the work must be divided up and allocated (discussed further in the next chapter). Employees performing similar work are often grouped together in order to manage interdependencies and work activity. Once work has been allocated and differentiated there is then a need to integrate the various parts of the organization (refer back to Chapter 9, 9.3), ensuring parts pull together to achieve the corporate goals (discussed in Chapters 17–19). The overall pattern of structural components and configurations used to manage the total organization is termed the **organization design**.

3.   A number of fundamental design questions may be proposed for managers of organizations: should jobs be broken down into narrow areas of work (specialization) or do we, for flexibility, require generalists? Should there be a tall or flat hierarchy, i.e. how many levels of management do we need? How should jobs and therefore people be grouped together (by function, geography or product)? How should employee groups be differentiated and integrated? Within this chapter we seek answers to such questions and consider aspects of organizational design and structure, noting Duncan (1972) who suggested that organizational structure is more than boxes on a chart; it is a pattern of interactions and coordination linking technology, tasks and human components of the organization (refer back to Figure 9.2) to ensure the organization accomplishes its purpose.

4.   The study of organization design and structure (the words will be used interchangeably throughout this chapter) has been a major source of interest for classical theorists (see Section 2), the inspiration for Weber's theory of bureaucracy, and a key element in the work of the theorists of complex organization – the contingency school (Chapter 9). This chapter summarizes the structural issues facing modern organizations and identifies the most important practical options available to senior management.

5.   In the opening part of the chapter we explore what organizational design means and ask about its purpose. We then consider elements of structure (the building blocks) before discussing how they may be configured. We outline the common designs to be found within organizations before a discussion of the determinants of structure. Finally, we recognize that the traditional (vertical) and hierarchical structure of organizations was criticized at the end of the twentieth century as business process management and associated technologies revolutionized aspects of organization design. Arguments were then presented for a horizontal design and philosophy that will be discussed at the end of the chapter. Finally, organization design entered a new era where outsourcing and fragmentation of the value chain became commonplace – thus creating boundaryless organization designs.

20.2 DESIGN PURPOSE

6.   An organization is a group of people who work together. The group share a unifying purpose, i.e. they have common goals (see vision, mission, goals and objectives). As companies (organizations) grow there is a need to arrange and cluster workers together according to the business-related activities they undertake, i.e. the group must be decomposed into smaller, more manageable groups. One of the most challenging tasks of a business may be organizing the people who perform its work. A business may start small but as the business grows, the amount and type of work performed increases, and more people are needed to perform various tasks. In order to avoid duplication and ensure all necessary work is undertaken, companies typically

allocate work to individuals (see next chapter) and group the individuals who perform similar work. Through this division of work, individuals can become specialists at a particular job (and therefore more efficient). However, no one person will typically transform all of the raw materials into the finished product or create and deliver the complete service to the customer. Consequently, the outputs of one person's work may form the inputs of another, i.e. different individuals and parts of the organization become dependent upon each other. Because there are many people – often in different locations – working towards a common objective, there must be a plan showing how the employees and work will be organized. The plan for the systematic arrangement of people and work is the formal organization structure (and associated business processes).

7.   An organization structure describes the way in which the interrelated groups of an organization are constructed – the way in which employees are formally divided into groups for coordination and control. The primary purpose of design is to divide and allocate work and then coordinate and control that work so that goals are met. An appropriate design might yield benefits such as efficiency and scale, the ability to access specialized and location-embedded resources, enhanced innovation through operations across markets and the creation of operational flexibility with which to respond to factors outside a firm's control. The design can impact upon performance through employee motivation, commitment and loyalty and has the ability to link interdependent activities. The design may also impact upon the sharing of resources, including information and knowledge.

20.3 ELEMENTS OF STRUCTURE

8.   Structure is a complex term and there are many aspects to it. We introduced some of the elements of structure in Chapters 2 and 3 (and skills sheet 4) when we discussed specialization, **centralization**, formalization and standardization as dimensions of bureaucracy. Organization **structure** (also termed design) comprises functions, relationships, responsibilities, authorities and communication of individuals within each part of the company. In this section we explore the dimensions, tools and elements of **organizational structure** before considering how such dimensions and elements may be configured in overall organizational designs.

9.   Tools used to add structure include:

Organizational chart – a plan of formal relations which the company intends should prevail within it.

Job definitions/description (often accompanied by a person specification profile of the candidate required for the work) – the task requirements of a particular job in the organization.

Span of control – the number of subordinates who report directly to a single manager or supervisor.

Authority – the right to guide or direct the actions of others.

Responsibility – an obligation placed upon a person, who occupies a certain position in the organization structure, to perform a task, function or assignment.

Accountability – responsibility for some activity.

10.   Aside from considering the aforementioned elements of structure there are other constructs, tools and frameworks that may be utilized during the design process. Mintzberg, at the strategic level, identified five basic parts of an organizational structure (Figure 20.1), summarized as follows:

A 'strategic apex' comprising the chief executive and directors; then, proceeding down the operational line,

a 'middle line' of operational management, followed by the 'operating core' of those directly involved in supplying the firm's goods and services; on either side of the operational line (traditionally called 'the line' in classical thinking) are

(i)   the 'techno-structure' comprising functional specialists and advisors, and

(ii)   the 'support staff', who provide corporate services (and who in classical terms would be seen as 'staff' employees).

FIGURE 20.1 The basic parts of organizations – Mintzberg's model.

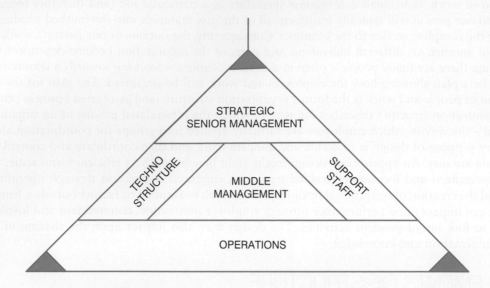

11.   Mintzberg's model looks, on the surface, as though it is the hierarchical model we associate with bureaucracy, but he uses it flexibly to develop five different configurations of structure. These configurations reduce the separate influences of key organizational features into manageable concepts that can be used in the study of organizations. In Mintzberg's own words 'In each structural configuration, a different one of the coordinating mechanisms is dominant, a different part of the organization plays the most important role, and a different type of decentralization is used.' The five configurations are as follows:

1)   Simple structure (basically no structure).

2)   **Machine bureaucracy** (dominated by technical/specialist priorities) a type of organization which possesses all the bureaucratic characteristics. The important decisions are made at the top, whilst at the bottom, standardized procedures are used to exercise control.

3)   Professional bureaucracy (dominated by skills of core staff). A decentralized form of organization that emphasizes the operating level and standardization of skills.

4)   Divisionalized form (dominated by products/outputs). A moderately decentralized form of organization that emphasizes the middle level and standardization of outputs.

5)   **Adhocracy** A form of organization structure typified by few levels of management; little formal control; decentralized decision-making; few rules, policies and procedures; specialization of work function.

12.   When establishing the structure, designers typically start by defining larger groups, then decomposing them into smaller units. Departmentalization is a process of grouping together employees who share a common manager and resources, who are jointly responsible for performance and who tend to identify and collaborate with each other. The organizational chart usually shows the departments within an organization. The chart also shows relationships between departmental staff in the organization which can be line (direct relationship between superordinate and subordinate); lateral (relationship between different departments on the same hierarchical level), staff and functional.

13.   Organization structure is as much about power and authority as it is about grouping activities and deploying key roles. The inevitable push towards specialization in all but the smallest of organizations leads to the diffusion of authority and accountability. The need to structure activities develops logically into the need to allocate appropriate amounts of authority to those responsible for undertaking those activities. Thus, every organization, regardless of size, has to consider what degree of authority to delegate from the

centre, or the top. Only the small entrepreneurial organization can effectively retain authority at the centre. Most organizations have to decide how, and how much, to delegate to managers and others throughout the job hierarchy.

14. The concept of centralization, as it is being considered here, is not referring to the physical dispersal of an organization, but to the dispersal of the authority to commit the organization's resources. The physical deployment of an organization may or may not reflect genuine power sharing. In our definition, therefore, a highly decentralized organization is one in which the authority to commit people, money and materials is widely diffused throughout every level of the structure. Conversely, a highly centralized organization is one where little authority is exercised outside a key group of senior managers (or experts). In practice, some functions are more easily decentralized than others. So, even highly decentralized organizations tend to reserve certain key functions to the centre. As well as planning and research, it is usually the finance and IT functions that are least decentralized, because of the need to maintain procedural consistency and legal and other standards. However, the arguments for centralization are more complex in the international organization. For example, we might expect HR to be centralized within the domestic firm but decentralized within the MNC. Arguments for or against centralization in the MNC tend to be influenced by the strategy. Where there is a pursuit of standardization and the world is perceived as a single boundaryless marketplace we might expect greater centralization. When the company emphasizes the need to think local and a strategy of differentiation we might expect greater degrees of decentralization.

15. The advantages of decentralization are chiefly, it:

- prevents senior management overload

- speeds up operational decisions by enabling line units to take local actions

- enables local management to be flexible in their approach to decisions in the light of local conditions, and thus be more adaptable in situations of rapid change

- focuses attention on important cost and profit centres within the total organization, which sharpens management awareness of cost-effectiveness as well as revenue targets

- can increase motivation, engagement and commitment.

16. The main disadvantages of decentralization are that it:

- requires an adequate control and communication system if major errors of judgement are to be avoided on the part of operational management

- requires greater coordination by senior management to ensure that individual units in the organization are not working against the interests of the whole

- can lead to inconsistency of treatment of customers, clients or the public, especially in service industries

- may encourage parochial attitudes in subsidiary units

- does require a plentiful supply of capable and well-motivated managers, able to respond to the increased responsibility which decentralization brings about.

17. On balance, there are clear advantages and disadvantages associated with centralization which may suit some strategies but not others. Organizations vary in the extent of decentralization which may be viewed more as a grey scale than a binary choice. It is worth recalling at this point the University of Aston's study conclusion (see Chapter 9) that large size tends to lead to less centralization, but relatively more specialization, more rules and more procedures (formalization).

18. Organizations can be tall or flat in relation to their total size and number of management levels. The main features of a **tall organization** are shown in Figure 20.2. Tall (traditional/hierarchical) organization structures tend to have many authority levels with narrow spans of control. The advantages of tall structures arise mainly from their ability to sustain a very high degree of specialization of functions and roles.

FIGURE 20.2 Chart of a tall organization structure

They can also provide ample career and promotion opportunities for employees. Their principal disadvantages are connected with long lines of communication and decision-making. Thus tall structures seem to go hand in hand with formality and standardization, which may discourage initiative and risk-taking at operational levels.

19. Flat organizations tend to have few authority levels and a wide span of control. In recent times, as flatter structures become more common, there have been major efforts to delegate authority throughout the system by empowering workforce teams in a way not thought possible or desirable some years ago. A flat organization is less likely to provide career development opportunities than a taller structure. On the other hand, a flat organization has fewer problems of communication and coordination, does encourage delegation by the managers involved and can motivate rank-and-file employees to take greater responsibility for their output. See Figure 20.3.

20. The major factors in determining the number of levels for any one organization are likely to be the size of the operation; nature of operation, especially in relation to the complexity of production; and the dominant management style. As a general rule, the smaller the organization, the more likely it is to have no more than three or four levels, and the larger it is, the more likely it is to have seven or eight levels (though many contemporary medium to large organizations will aim for five management levels). Factors such as the technology employed can offset the influence of size alone.

21. Two other concepts important to organization structure are authority and responsibility. **Authority** is the legitimate power to act in certain ways; it emanates from the top, and can be delegated to subordinates. Relatively few people in an organization are endowed with authority. Line authority is the authority that every manager exercises in respect of his or her own subordinates. Thus specialist managers, such as chief accountants and HR managers, exercise line authority over their own staff. In this role they are not different from so-called line managers, such as production managers and sales managers. Line authority, then, is not dependent on line functions. It is the central feature of the total chain of command throughout the entire organization structure.

22. Responsibility is the obligation to perform certain functions on behalf of the organization. Responsibility may range from the very specific to the very broad; it is commonly called accountability; unlike

FIGURE 20.3 Chart of a flat organization structure

authority it cannot be delegated. Every job holder has some level of responsibility for their work. Both of the above concepts can be distinguished from power, which is the ability to implement actions, regardless of considerations of formal authority or responsibility.

20.4 COMMON (BUREAUCRATIC) STRUCTURES – DESIGNS

23.   Organizations face choices when designing the formal organization. The formal organization is the collection of work groups that has been consciously designed by senior management to maximize efficiency and achieve organizational goals as opposed to the informal organization – the network of relationships that establish themselves spontaneously between members of an organization on the basis of their common interests and friendships. The formal organization is the planners' conception of how the intended conse-quences of the organization may best be achieved. The organizational design or **structure** must be a solution to many problems. When grouping activities and people the designer must consider how much to take account of specialization (how narrow the work will be); whether the organization should be tall or flat (span of control) and how to group people (by specialism, product or area). Degrees of control must also be determined along with centralization and formalization and the mechanisms to be used for **integration**.
24.   Perhaps the first major design challenge – typically considered by senior managers and supported by HR professionals – concerns the manner in which employees are grouped together (by geographical area, function/specialism, product or process worked on). Arguments for the alternative grouping approaches typically consider the type of knowledge that is most important when adding value and undertaking the organization's primary activities – is it more important to know about the function such as accounting, the geographical area worked in or the product created?
25.   The most common forms of 'designed' structure are as follows:

1)   Functional organization – based on groupings of business functions such as production, marketing, finance or HR.

2)   Product-based organization – based on individual products, or product ranges, where each grouping carries its own functional specialisms.

3)   Geographical organization (**area structure**) – centred around appropriate geographical features, e.g. regions, nations, subcontinents.

4) Divisionalized structure – usually based on products, or geography, or both and with certain key functions such as planning and finance reserved for headquarters.

5) Matrix structures – based on a combination of functional organization with project-based structures, and thereby combining vertical and lateral lines of communication and authority.

These structures are considered in the following paragraphs, commencing with functional organization.
26.   In a functional organization structure, tasks are linked together on the basis of common functions. Thus, all production activities, or all financial activities, are grouped together in a single function which undertakes all the tasks required of that function. A typical chart of a functional organization is as shown in Figure 20.4. The main advantages of functional organization are that by grouping people together on the basis of their technical and specialist expertise, the organization can facilitate both their utilization and their coordination in the service of the whole enterprise. Functional grouping also provides better opportunities for promotion and career development.

FIGURE 20.4 Functional organizational structure

The disadvantages are primarily the growth of sectional interests which may conflict with the needs of the organization as a whole, and the difficulties of adapting this form of organization to meet issues such as product diversification or geographical dispersal. **Functional structures** remain common and are probably best suited to relatively stable environments.
27.   Another frequent form of grouping is by **product** as shown in Figure 20.5. This is a popular structural form in large organizations having a wide range of products or services. The advantages of a product organization as shown are that it enables diversification to take place, it can cope better with problems of technological change by grouping people with expertise and their specialized equipment in one major unit. The main disadvantage is that each general manager may promote his or her own product group to the detriment of other parts of the company. In this situation senior management must exercise careful controls, without, at the same time, removing the motivation to produce results within the product managers.
28.   Another familiar form of organization structure is the one grouped on a geographical basis. This is usually adopted where the realities of a national or international network of activities make some kind of regional structure essential for decision-making and control. An example of this form of organization is shown in Figure 20.6. As in a product organization, the geographically based organization tends to produce decentralized activities, which may cause additional control problems for senior management. Hence it is usual with such structures to find groups of senior functional managers at headquarters in order to provide direction and guidance to line managers in the regions or product groups.

FIGURE 20.5 Example of a product-based structure

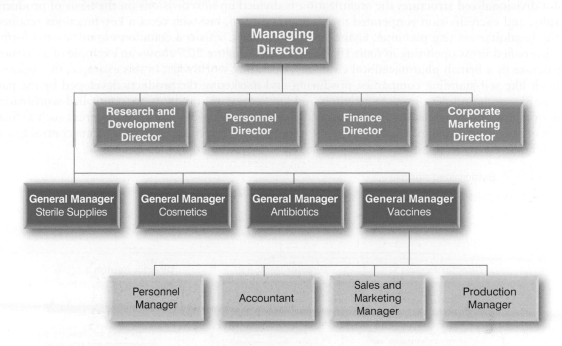

FIGURE 20.6 Geographically based structure for a road transport company

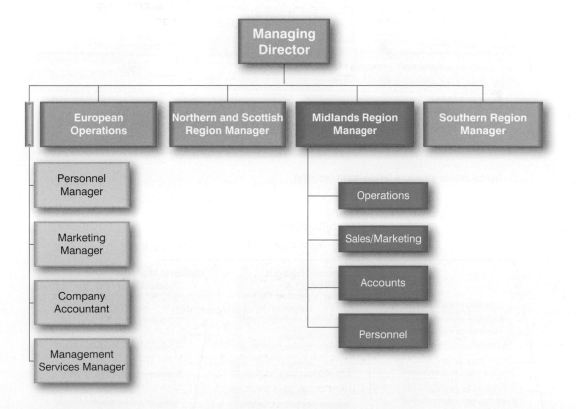

29. With increasing complexity and size, many companies are opting for a mixed structure, which may combine the benefits of two or more of functional, product and geographical forms of organization. Two

such mixed structures will be looked at briefly: divisionalized structures and matrix structures. In the case of a **divisionalized structure**, the organization is divided up into divisions on the basis of products or geography, and each division is operated in a functional form, but with certain key functions retained at company headquarters (e.g planning, finance and HR policy). This is a common organizational form for highly diversified firms operating in more than one country. Figure 20.7 shows an example of a divisionalized structure in a British pharmaceutical company, operating worldwide. In this example, the regions act very much like self-standing companies, producing and marketing the products developed by the parent company. Research and development activities and key corporate standards are controlled worldwide via the functional divisions, whilst the headquarters division provides group policy in key areas such as finance and human resources. A balance can therefore be maintained between necessary corporate control from the centre and desired divisional independence at the regional and functional levels.

FIGURE 20.7 Divisionalized structure

FIGURE 20.8 Typical matrix structure (engineering industry)

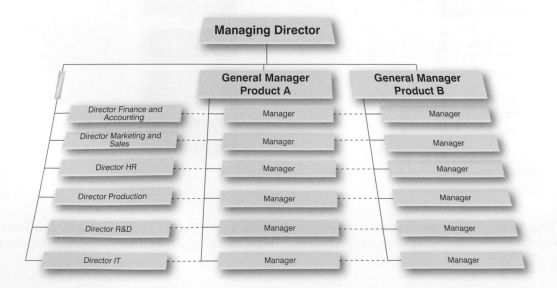

30.   Matrix structures are organizational forms which have evolved as a result of coordination problems in highly complex industries such as aircraft manufacture, where functional and product types of structure have not been able to meet organizational demands for a variety of key activities and relationships arising from the required work processes. A matrix structure usually combines a functional form of structure with a project or product-based structure, as demonstrated in Figure 20.8. The main feature of a matrix structure is that it combines lateral with vertical lines of communication and authority (see also matrix management). This has the important advantage of combining the relative stability and efficiency of a hierarchical structure with the flexibility and informality of an organic form of structure. However, like all organizational forms, matrix structures do have their disadvantages. The key disadvantages are: the potential conflicts that can arise concerning the allocation of resources and the division of authority; the relative dilution of functional management responsibilities throughout the organization; and the possibility of divided loyalties.

20.5 DETERMINANTS OF DESIGN

31.   So far we have highlighted the common types of structure and listed the elements of structure that can be configured to create unique designs. The search for a good design is continual. But what makes a good design – what rules might designers draw upon when configuring the organization's structural variables? In Chapters 8 and 9 we advocated the need to ensure the structure 'fits' the strategy and therefore, an appropriate design might enable the achievement of strategies such as cost leadership, differentiation, focus and responsiveness.

32.   Designing the organization involves configuring necessary structures, processes, practices and policies and allocating resources to achieve a desired business strategy. 'There is not one best organization design, or style of management or method of working. Rather, different patterns of organization and management will be most appropriate in different situations', Nadler (1980) cited in Mabey and Mayon-White (1993).

33.   Nadler points out that 'often changes in the environment necessitate organizational change (discussed further in Chapter 24). For example, factors related to competition, technology or regulation shift and thus necessitate changes in organizational strategy'. Contingency theory research has clearly demonstrated the correlation between structure and the environment and central to the contingency approach is the basic notion that organizational performance depends upon taking management action which is consistent with the situation. It is now widely accepted that there is no single best way to organize, structure or manage the firm. Contingency theory, in the context of organization structure, argues that an organization, to be effective, must adjust its design/structure in a manner consistent with its environment, technology and other contextual factors.

34.   The key organizational issues or variables featuring recurrently in discussions about what determines organization structures are basically as follows (see Figure 20.9):

1)   Purpose/goals (the fundamental aims and goals of the group)

2)   People (those who make up the organization)

3)   Tasks (those basic activities required to achieve organizational goals)

4)   Technology (the technical aspects of the internal environment)

5)   Culture (the dominant values guiding the organization)

6)   External environment (the external market, PESTLE factors affecting the organization's activities).

35.   Environmental determinism theory states that internal organizational responses are wholly or mainly shaped, influenced or determined by external environmental factors. Externally, the contemporary turbulent environment calls for flexible, adaptable and responsive structures; historically, a more predictable

FIGURE 20.9 **Major variables in establishing organization structure**

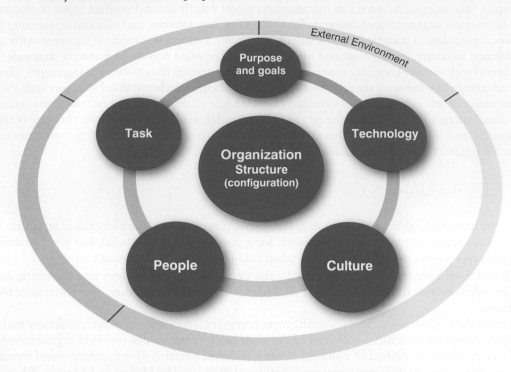

environment favoured the bureaucratic approach. Environmental variables include: cultural, social, techno-logical, educational, legal, political, economic, ecological and demographic factors. Specific environmental variables might include customers/clients, suppliers (including labour), competitors, technology and socio-political factors.

36.   When undertaking any enterprise, the design of a suitable structure must begin with some idea of what the organization is there for, and where it intends to go. In other words, the prime purpose, or raison d'etre, of the group plays a key role in directing the members towards the kind of structure required. In making this step the group must take account of the external environment, and the nature of that environment in terms of change or stability. The next step is to identify the key tasks that must be accomplished if the group is to succeed in its purpose. This leads on to a consideration of people, especially the skills and talents of current members, and the identification of any gaps in their portfolio of skills and knowledge, which may have to be bridged by training, or the employment of newcomers. The question of technology must also be addressed. What production systems are already in operation, or planned? What equipment will be necessary? What are the demands of new software systems on people and work processes? How well do existing staff cope with new technology? Lastly, there is one other important variable, which must be taken into account, and that is the organization's culture (or value system). Given the dynamic nature of organizations, it is likely that there will be pressures to adapt the structure somewhere in the organization, even if not overall. Thus structuring and restructuring is a continual process in the life of many organizations.

20.6 HORIZONTAL AND ALTERNATIVE DESIGNS

37.   Organizational structure within an organization clarifies employee roles, facilitates communication and establishes a chain of responsibility; it deals with task allocation, coordination and supervision, which are directed towards the achievement of organizational goals. Bureaucratic structures, vertical hierarchies (see previous designs), have been at the core of business since the industrial revolution; they have a struc-ture, with power emanating from the top, down. There are, however, many associated problems: the verti-cal design fosters fragmented tasks, overspecialization, empires, and turf wars, delays in decision-making

FIGURE 20.10 Evolution of design developments

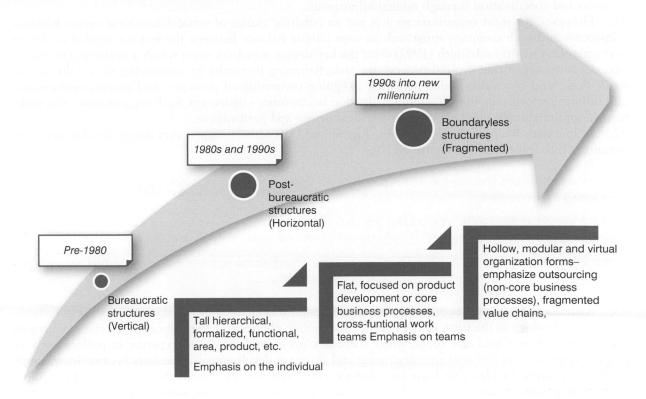

and other negatives that inhibit responsiveness. There is general agreement that vertical structures are too rigid and slow. An excessive level of authority reduces communication and coordination of activities.

38.   Since the 1980s there have been a number of post-bureaucratic structures described. However they tend to retain certain aspects of bureaucracy; rather than make a fundamental shift away from bureaucracy they tend to remove aspects that make bureaucracies rigid or slow to act; they may also shift emphasis from individuals to teams. Contemporary organizations will still be formal to some extent, are likely to have specialists in some parts of the organization and may centralize certain work areas. However, in some organizations there may be more determined attempts to base decisions on dialogue and consensus rather than authority and command. Indeed the organization may be seen more as a network rather than a hierarchy. Many contemporary organizations will aim to facilitate broader participation, involvement and engagement in their design efforts.

39.   Horizontal organizational structure is a design in which decision-making is spread amongst employees along horizontal lines, as opposed to a vertical and hierarchical structure. The philosophy behind this form of management is that a collaborative model improves engagement, productivity and creativity. It is a method often used in organizations that are heavily focused on product development or core business processes. Cross-functional work teams are a common feature of a horizontal organizational structure.

40.   A horizontal organization has a less-defined chain of command and tends to be a flatter organization. An alternative way of grouping individuals and their activities is based on business processes (see next chapter) which cut horizontally across traditional functional areas, i.e. horizontal grouping. There is real performance leverage in moving towards a flatter, more horizontal mode of organization, in which cross-functional, end-to-end workflows link internal processes with the needs and capabilities of both suppliers and customers. Whereas functional groupings may be task-centred, the process groupings are more customer-oriented. The primary focus for functional groupings is on the 'what', whereas process groupings focus on 'how'. Functional organizations value specialists whereas process organizations value generalists. The functional organization may have a parochial perspective whereas the process organization has a more

holistic perspective. Workers involved with a particular process are grouped together to facilitate communication and coordination through mutual adjustment.

41.   However, for most organizations it is not an either/or choice of vertical/functional versus horizontal/process and each company must seek its own unique balance between the features needed to deliver performance. Ostroff and Smith (1992) distil the key design principles upon which a horizontal organization depends: organizing around process not task; flattening hierarchy by minimizing the subdivision of work flows and non-value-added activities; assigning ownership of processes and process performance and linking performance objectives and evaluation to customer satisfaction. Such organizations also make teams, not individuals, the basis of organizational design and performance.

42.   In line with the previous paragraphs, Anand and Daft (2007) suggest that design developments are organized into three eras (see Figure 20.10).

Era 1 was dominant until the late 1970s and included the use of traditional, functional and divisional structures, including matrix overlays.

Era 2 started in the 1980s and includes the designs that organize around horizontal processes, such as re-engineering.

Era 3 came into its own in the 1990s when corporations embraced the hollow, modular and **virtual organization** forms that open the organization to outside sourcing partnerships.

43.   Anand and Daft's third era of organizational design was enabled by rapid improvements in communication technology in the form of the Internet and mobile phones and coincides with the rise of emerging economies such as China and India, where there is a 'great pool' of skilled expertise in performing very specific tasks such as low-cost manufacturing and software development. Managers became increasingly comfortable with the idea that their organization could not perform efficiently all of the tasks required to make a product or service. They therefore outsourced aspects of their work (fragmenting their value chains). The phenomenon became most noticeable in the shifting of the manufacturing function to cheaper areas of production in Asia.

44.   There are a number of principles governing the design of the hollow organization. Such organizations typically identify core and non-core business processes in the organization. Typically, core processes are critical to business performance, they create competitive advantage, and they are likely to drive future growth and rejuvenation. Non-core processes become likely candidates for outsourcing. With increasing globalization and installation of high-touch informational technology systems, it is possible to offshore work to places that are not only cheaper, but also of higher quality. The main advantage is in the cost savings that emerge from utilizing a lesser amount of capital expenditure and in carrying a less administrative overhead. This design also provides greater organizational flexibility. Firms can focus on what they do best, whilst unleashing the best sources of specialization and technology outsourcers can offer.

45.   There are also downsides to the hollow design. There is a loss of in-house skills, and with that possibly the reduced capacity to innovate; furthermore, the costs of transitioning to a hollow state are likely to be high. Also, if the supplier is distant both geographically and culturally, then there may be additional costs in terms of increased monitoring or switching to another supplier. Hollow organizations have less control over the supply of their products because of dependence upon outsourcing partners.

CONCLUSION

46.   An organization's structure dictates who is in a position of authority, how work is divided and how employees are assigned duties. It seeks to help the organization accomplish its goals and fulfil its purpose. This chapter focused on how to (organize) make efficient and effective use of human resources in order to attain goals through design and structure. We identified the purpose of design – to divide up organizational activities, allocate resources, tasks and goals and to coordinate and control activities so that goals can be achieved. An appropriate design might yield benefits such as efficiency, access to specialized and location-embedded resources, enhanced innovation and the creation of operational flexibility; the design can impact

upon performance through employee motivation, commitment and loyalty and has the ability to link inter-dependent activities.

47.   The tools used to structure organizations include: organizational charts, job definitions, span of control, authority, responsibility and accountability descriptions. A key concept in contemporary design is decentralization, where specific delegation is given to subunits or groups within an organization such that they enjoy a measure of autonomy or independence.

48.   Whereas bureaucratic structures, i.e. vertical hierarchies, dominated much of the twentieth century, the pursuit of flexibility, creativity, responsiveness and an engaged workforce has driven many organizations to post-bureaucratic and boundaryless structures. Contemporary organizations are more likely to adopt designs that are flatter, emphasize teams and cross-functional work groups, outsource non-core processes and promote participation and autonomy.

QUESTIONS

1   Evaluate the advantages and disadvantages of a tall/hierarchical structure.

2   Contrast vertical and horizontal organizations.

3   Select an organization with which you are familiar and identify factors likely to determine the design of the organization.

4   Explain the basic parts of organizations.

USEFUL WEBSITE

Organizational Structure Net: **organisationalstructure.net**
This site is dedicated to the enhancement and awareness of organizational structure.

REFERENCES

Anand, N. and Daft, R.L. (2007) 'What is the right organization design?', *Organizational Dynamics*, 36(4): 329–344.

Duncan, R. (1972) 'Characteristics of organizational environments and perceived environmental uncertainty', *Administrative Science Quarterly*, 17(3): 313–327.

Mabey, C. and Mayon-White, B. (1993) *Managing Change*, The Open University.

Ostroff, F. and Smith, D. (1992) 'The horizontal organization', *McKinsey Quarterly*, 1: 148–168.

CHAPTER 21
ORGANIZING WORK

Key Concepts

- Business process management
- Coordination
- Division of labour
- Flexible working
- Interdependence
- Job design

Learning Outcomes Having read this chapter, you should be able to:

- recount the purpose of job design
- discuss the strengths and weaknesses of early ideas on the design of work
- identify contemporary approaches to the design of work
- understand secondary design challenges: the need to coordinate and integrate
- explain how processes are used to coordinate and organize work activities.

Vignette

THE GRIM REALITY OF LIFE ON ZERO HOURS CONTRACTS

Zero hours contracts are divisive since, for business, they provide the ultimate flexibility, allowing them to employ and let staff go at will. Yet for workers they provide no job security, no guaranteed hours, no benefits, and jobs that can be cancelled at the drop of a hat. 'Zero hours contracts lead to a huge turnover of staff. How can you provide good quality staff when they don't know how much they will earn?'

1.   As the opening vignette suggests, it is highly important that employers design jobs and work with both organizational and employee goals in mind. **Job design** is the systematic and purposeful allocation of tasks to individuals and groups within an organization. The purposes of job design include:

1) To organize the work of employees so that corporate goals and objectives are attained through the efficient and effective utilization of human resource.

2) To improve the performance of employees by enhancing motivation, job satisfaction and employee engagement by making work meaningful, interesting and challenging.

3) To reduce stress and improve work–life balance and the quality of working life.

2.   Organizations are often troubled by how to organize, particularly when a new strategy is developed. Organizing is the management function that usually follows after planning (previous section). It involves the assignment of tasks, the grouping of tasks into departments and the transfer of authority and distribution of resources through the organization. Organization is employed to achieve the overall objectives of the firm, focusing individual attention towards such objectives.

3.   As seen in the previous chapter, individuals form groups and these groups (teams, sections, departments, units) form the organization. Thus, the organization is the composition of individuals and groups. Individuals are grouped into departments (structure) and their work is coordinated and directed towards organizational goals. The organization divides the entire work and assigns tasks to individuals in order to achieve organizational objectives. Work specialization (also called **division of labour** or job specialization) is the degree to which organizational tasks are subdivided into individual jobs. It may increase the efficiency of workers, but with too much specialization, employees may feel isolated and bored. Coordinating and linking these tasks at the final stage is called integration (discussed in Chapter 9).

4.   The entire philosophy of organization is centred on the concepts of specialization (refer back to Chapters 2 and 3) and division of work. The division of work is assigning responsibility for each organizational component to a specific individual or group. It becomes specialization when the responsibility for a specific task lies with a designated expert in that field. The efforts of the operatives are coordinated to allow the process at hand to function correctly. To make optimum use of resources (including people) it is necessary to design an organization properly.

5.   The contemporary organization needs people to work willingly, effectively and productively to achieve organizational goals and contribute to organizational success. No one can do all of the work of the organization and there is therefore a need to differentiate work and consider how work should be designed to meet organizational goals. **Jobs** are interdependent and must be designed to make a contribution to the organization's overall mission and goals. As we will see in this chapter, however, there are numerous approaches to designing jobs. Job design involves determining the specific job tasks and responsibilities, the work environment and the methods by which the tasks will be carried out to meet operational goals.

6.   Job design requires knowledge of classical management theory (scientific management) and human relations theories (motivation) in particular – refer back to Part 1 of the book. According to Daft (2009: p. 518) job design is the application of motivational theories to the structure of work in order to improve productivity and satisfaction. This chapter examines some of the key issues involved in designing work for people, and outlines several important approaches which have been adopted in the search for the best ways of combining people's needs and aspirations with the constraints and opportunities offered by technology and work processes.

7.   Aspects of the job design process are shown in Figure 21.1 which will provide structure for the remainder of the chapter. Having already discussed the inputs (corporate goals) we will move on to identify and explain several approaches to job design. Many were developed in the first three-quarters of the twentieth century. These approaches started with scientific management and were followed with approaches borne out of the human relations school and theories of motivation. We refer to them as traditional approaches; examples include job simplification, enlargement, enrichment and the job characteristics model. We will then move on to identify several more recent approaches to job design – where flexibility and work–life balance goals are reflected. Finally, we consider the secondary design challenges: the need to coordinate and integrate and explain how processes are used to coordinate and organize work activities.

FIGURE 21.1 Job design process

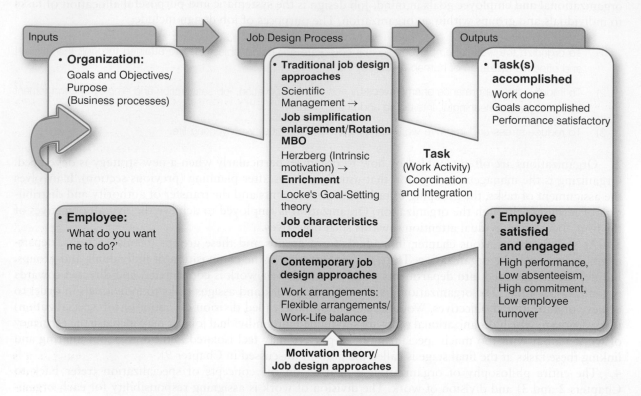

21.1 EARLY TRADITIONAL WORK DESIGN AND JOB SIMPLIFICATION

8.   One of the major legacies of 'Scientific Management' (see Chapter 2) is that work has generally been designed around technology and technical processes, rather than attempting to fit the latter around the needs and preferences of employees and their managers. Thus, the most important criteria for designing work have tended to include the following:

–   maximizing the degree of job/task specialization

–   minimizing the time required to do a specific job/task

–   minimizing the level of skill required to perform the job/task

–   minimizing the learning/training time in the job

–   maximizing the use of machines and technology

–   minimizing the individual worker's discretion over how work should be done.

9.   **Job simplification** (job engineering), drawing on the principles of scientific management, is an approach to job design based on a minimization of the range of tasks into the smallest convenient size to make the job efficient and cost-effective. Job simplification typically reduces the number of tasks completed by an employee and as a consequence the employee requires less training and can master the task quickly. The consequences, criticisms and implications are discussed next.

10.   Despite the theoretical arguments in favour of simplifying industrial jobs, it is clear that industrial nations have experienced far fewer benefits than expected. Indeed Daft (2009: p. 518) suggests that as a motivational technique, job simplification failed. People dislike routine and boring jobs and react in a number of negative

ways including sabotage, absenteeism, high labour turnover, lateness and poor attention to quality. Studies into motivation and job satisfaction (see Chapters 4 and 5) have demonstrated clearly that employees at all levels seek some degree of self-control and self-direction at work.

11.   Numerous management scholars have argued that job simplification, the fragmentation of work tasks and various principles of scientific management lead to the deskilling of work and demotivation of employees. Consequently, the twentieth century was characterized by two contradictory trends in work design. The first half of the century placed greater emphasis on scientific management and job simplification without full regard for the needs of the employee. The second half of the century witnessed a reaction against Taylorism, adopting more people-oriented approaches, with emphasis on the quality of working life.

12.   In the latter part of the twentieth century two key debates ensued: deskilling and upskilling. Deskilling was arguably a consequence of scientific management principles (the separation of task conception from task execution, standardization, predictability, control and efficiency) and the adoption of technology. Organizations that seek to provide customers with a uniform, standardized product or service, ultimately limit the discretion employees have when undertaking work tasks.

13.   However, various criticisms were levelled at the deskilling thesis. Aside from its treatment of employees as passive, it ignores alternative management strategies. Furthermore, it fails to recognize the potential for hybrid approaches which draw upon classical and human relations theories. Aside from the critique of the deskilling thesis, some management scholars have argued an upskilling position as a result of technology adoption. They argue that the increasing use of technology and need for flexibility requires higher levels of skill amongst employees. Technology may replace jobs involving boring repetitive work, enabling employees to focus on more interesting work. Consequently, many scholars now agree that some work may become deskilled as a result of the application of job simplification whilst other work may become upskilled in the face of new technology.

14.   Jobs may vary according to whether they create products and services directly or support others that do. Jobs also vary in the amount of tacit knowledge (skill and ability) or judgement required. It may therefore be helpful to categorize jobs when considering the different approaches to design. For example, jobs may be categorized according to the range of work, which may involve performing a small number of tasks (narrow) through to a wide range of tasks. Jobs may require little or large amounts of discretion. They may be specialized or general. If we redesign jobs to adapt technology to meet the motivational needs of employees, then it is important to know which elements of their work employees find demotivating. A range of factors have been shown to make work boring, such as carrying out uninteresting, undemanding, repetitive or meaningless tasks. Boredom may also arise from the lack of any sense of completion of the task, i.e. the belief that however much work is achieved in a day, there is always more to come.

21.2 LATER MOTIVATIONAL APPROACHES TO JOB DESIGN

15.   So far we have evaluated traditional approaches to work design (job simplification) and commented on the resultant shift towards the adoption of human relation theories of work design. The tasks to be undertaken in an organization need to be combined into specific jobs that make sense for people to undertake. Job design must take account of a variety of contextual factors (concerns and drivers) such as those shown in Figure 21.2.

16.   We can draw upon a variety of studies to suggest the crucial characteristics required in order that a job may satisfy human needs. Studies suggest that employees require a degree of autonomy over the way tasks are to be achieved; individuals need to be responsible for their own work, and for the resources they use (e.g. equipment); an element of variety should be present in the job in order to permit variations in task, pace and method; task repetition should be reduced to a minimum; feedback needs to be available on job performance; wherever practicable, the job should enable the completion of an entire item; there should be some degree of social contact available to the jobholder; learning opportunities should be built into the job in order to provide an element of challenge, as well as the opportunity to extend individual repertoire of knowledge and skills; roles should be clear so that jobholders and others know what is expected from the job and every job should have some definite goals for which to aim.

17.   There are three main approaches to achieving increased job satisfaction at work through task restructuring. These are (1) job enlargement, (2) job enrichment and (3) autonomous work groups.

FIGURE 21.2 **Determinants of job design**

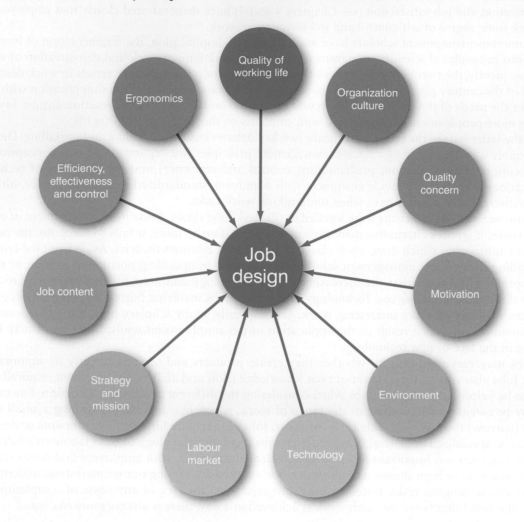

Each of these approaches embodies several, if not all, of the characteristics referred to in the previous paragraph. There are, of course, other methods of enhancing employee job satisfaction, for example by improving consultation or permitting participation in decision-making, but here we concentrate on the three principal approaches. The different methods of job design are not necessarily separate approaches. They are interrelated and there is some overlapping between them. The process of vertically increasing the responsibilities of a job, by the addition of motivators, e.g. more discretion, improved job interest, etc.

18.   **Job enlargement** emerged in the 1950s and is the horizontal extension of jobs (not to be confused with the horizontal organization) – extra tasks of the same level as before are added. It simply means 'to add one undemanding job to another!' **Job rotation** – the moving of a person from one job or task to another in an attempt to add variety and help remove boredom (it may also give the individual a holistic view of the organization's activities and be used as a form of training) – is a form of job enlargement. Such a step does increase job variety to a certain extent, and may create more meaningful tasks. What it does not achieve is any real increase in responsibility. The approach nevertheless has many supporters, not least because it often works in practice to bring about improved morale or productivity.

19.   The term 'job enrichment' is usually applied to the vertical extension of job responsibilities. It implies taking tasks from those both senior and junior to the jobholder in order to enable a jobholder to have more responsibility than before. Herzberg (see Chapter 4) saw job enrichment in terms of building motivators

into a job. His view was that opportunities for achievement, recognition and responsibility need to be included in a person's work. For individual employees the main benefits of job enrichment are felt in terms of increased job satisfaction resulting from increased intrinsic rewards in the job. Organizations tend to benefit by a reduction in overhead costs caused by absenteeism, lateness, lack of attention to quality and other negative features of poor morale. One of the difficulties associated with job enrichment is that it will lead to changes throughout a job hierarchy. Some jobholders may find their jobs are threatened by a job enrichment programme. Supervisors, in particular, may find that many of their duties have been handed down to members of their team. Any attempt at job enrichment must take account of such consequential changes on the overall structure of jobs.

20.   The **job characteristics model** is a model of job enrichment based on the need to incorporate a number of core job dimensions (skill variety, task identity, task significance, autonomy and feedback) within the design of a job. Skill variety concerns performing a number of diverse activities; task identity is about performing the whole job; task significance is the degree to which the job is perceived as important; autonomy is the degree to which the worker has freedom and discretion and feedback – output that is returned to the appropriate members of the organization to help them evaluate or correct work behaviours. The model assumes that the more the five core characteristics can be designed into the job, the more employees will be motivated and performance, quality and satisfaction will be higher.

21.   Following the application of intrinsic motivation theory, goal-setting theory (refer back to the work of Locke) also had an influence on job design. Goal setting is the process of developing, negotiating and formalizing the objectives which employees must accomplish. Later this led to the concept of management by objectives (MBO) – see Chapter 19 then key performance indicators (KPIs).

22.   A work team with delegated responsibility for a defined part of an organization's activities, with the freedom to organize its own resources, pace of work and allocate responsibilities within the group is often termed an **autonomous work group**. The idea behind autonomous work groups is that **job satisfaction** and hence employee morale can be enhanced if employees work together in a group to achieve their production goals. An autonomous group is a self-organized work group which is held responsible for the rate and quality of its output. This approach to work design resulted from the efforts of the socio-technical systems theorists from the Tavistock Institute (see Chapter 8). The first reported autonomous work groups were those established in the British coalmining industry under the 'composite longwall method'. Subsequent experiments in Norway and Sweden, especially the work at the Volvo car plant, have shown that such groups can improve quality and reduce overheads as well as providing greater job satisfaction for employees concerned.

21.3 CONTEMPORARY WORK DESIGN

23.   More recent job design approaches have also embraced the idea of removing or avoiding factors leading to job dissatisfaction. Such approaches have emphasized work location and working hours as variables within which the organization can be more flexible. The approaches have emerged at a time when family lifestyles have undergone significant change, e.g. both parents working etc. The approaches therefore seek to accommodate a desirable **work–life balance** – the balance between work, family, personal and leisure activities. Recent approaches also take account of stress, ageing populations and changes to retirement age.

24.   Advances in technology (Internet and telecommunications) have enabled remote, teleworking and homeworking. Additionally, flexibility in working hours has led to **flexible working** – an arrangement whereby the start and finish times of a worker may be varied whilst not exceeding the daily/weekly hours of a normal working day/week over a predetermined period; **flexitime** (flexible working hours) is a system enabling employees to vary their working hours in a particular period, provided they do attend during certain 'core hours', e.g. 10:00 hours to 16:00 hours; **job sharing** is an arrangement that allows two or more individuals to split a traditional 40-hour-a-week job; and **zero-hours contracts** are arrangements whereby an employer can offer to provide work but without actually guaranteeing any. Organizations may also design jobs with a compressed work week – allowing a full-time job to be completed in fewer than the standard 5 days.

21.4 COORDINATING AND INTEGRATING WORK: TASK INTERDEPENDENCE AND BUSINESS PROCESSES

25. Job design is typically undertaken by jobholders and/or their line managers or supervisors. In some cases the job design precedes the organization design whilst in other cases it may be undertaken simultaneously or afterwards. However, job design and specialization does create a second design challenge. In business, people and departments must rely on one another and the specialized work they do. Indeed the output of one unit may become the input for another unit (they act as if they were in some kind of chain). People in the early part of the chain tend to be more independent but the people in the latter part of the chain may be highly dependent on the first part. As a part of organization there is a need to manage sequential interdependence. In some work there may also be a need to manage chains where the output and input of activities flow both ways between units (reciprocal interdependence). Thus, there are interactions within the organizational structure discussed in the previous chapter. Indeed the unit groupings of the organization structure and design seek to coordinate work within groups but in doing so create a challenge for the management of interfaces between groups. The study of interdependence helps managers understand how the different departments or units within their organization depend on the work and performance of others. The job of managing interdependencies is becoming more challenging as organizations become more complex.

26. Tasks divided amongst a group of individuals must be synchronized and integrated in some way so as to achieve the overall objectives of the group. Jobs must fit into a coherent flow of work. Coordination is the process of linking and integrating functions and activities of different groups (assuring resources work well together towards the common goal); it provides the appropriate linkage between different task units within the organization. Companies and their managers employ various coordination mechanisms (meetings, liaison roles, etc.) to achieve integration amongst different units within their organization.

27. So far we have discussed the division of labour and task allocation to individuals and groups. In para. 3 we noted a subsequent need to coordinate and link tasks (the final stage); this is called integration. Work is activity (a collection of tasks) directed at making or doing something. In the case of the organization, work activities transform inputs into outputs (products and services) for the benefit of customers, adding value along the way. A collection of related work tasks and activities is typically labelled as a business process. Business processes are used by organizations to coordinate and organize work activities – to integrate. Indeed a process is a set of logically related tasks performed to achieve a defined business outcome. Processes encapsulate the interdependence of tasks, roles, people, departments and functions required to provide a customer with a product or service.

28. Commenting on the 1990s, Tom Davenport – an American academic and author specializing in business process innovation – suggested the contemporary business world abounds with references to the concept of process – a noun denoting how work is done (Davenport, 1994). Davenport defined the term 'process' as a structured set of activities designed to produce a specified output for a particular customer or market. It has a beginning, an end and clearly identified inputs and outputs. A process is therefore a structure for action, for how work is done. Processes (refer to skills sheet 5 and Chapter 10) are therefore the structure by which an organization does what is necessary to produce value for its customers. Typical business processes include product development, selling products, receiving orders, delivering services, distributing products, invoicing and accounting for money received. Processes are used to manage the flow of goods, products and services, information and money. They organize work as flows of related activities. An example was provided in Figure 10.1.

29. Business process design considers the challenge of how to do things in the best way – effectively and efficiently, i.e. do the right things right. Associated with the business process approach and higher degrees of interdependency where more extensive integration may be needed, companies often create cross-functional teams with end-to-end responsibility for a process (refer back to the horizontal organization).

30. Also in the 1990s, the late Michael Hammer, a former Professor of Computer Science at the Massachusetts Institute of Technology (MIT), known as one of the founders of the management theory of business process re-engineering (BPR), challenged what he termed the 'centuries-old' notions about work. He argued that for many organizations, their *job designs*, *workflows*, *control mechanisms* and *organizational structures* came of age in a different competitive environment and before the advent of the computer. Such organizations were geared

towards efficiency and control. According to Hammer, commenting on twentieth century organizations, rules of work design are based on assumptions about technology, people and organizational goals that are no longer valid. He suggested that business processes and structures were outmoded and obsolete and had not kept pace with the changes in technology and business objectives. Companies had typically organized work as a sequence of separate tasks and employed complex mechanisms to track its progress. Conventional process structures emphasized differentiation but as a result were fragmented and piecemeal, and they lacked the integration necessary to maintain quality and service.

21.5 BPR AND BUSINESS PROCESS MANAGEMENT (BPM)

31. Organizations should seek to improve business processes continuously in order to enhance the organization's performance and benefit its interested parties. There are two fundamental ways to conduct process improvement: a) breakthrough projects which either lead to revision and improvement of existing processes or the implementation of new processes (typical of BPR); and b) small-step ongoing improvement activities conducted within existing processes by people (typical of TQM). In the 1970s and 1980s organizations generally turned to continuous process improvement programmes whilst, later, in the 1990s, the same organizations turned to more radical process change approaches.

32. The need for BPR was essentially born out of the lack of alignment between traditional organizations and the new environment of the 1990s in which they operated. This environment was more turbulent and required flexibility, innovation, adaptation and efficiency. Hammer (1990) argued that re-engineering enabled companies to break away from the old rules about how they organize and conduct business. Re-engineering requires looking at the fundamental processes of the business from a cross-functional perspective. At the heart of re-engineering is the notion of discontinuous thinking – of recognizing and breaking away from the outdated roles and fundamental assumptions that underlie operations.

33. Re-engineering need not be haphazard and Hammer (1990) suggested several guiding principles. He argued a need to organize around outcomes, not tasks. In most organizations, those who do the work are distinguished from those who monitor the work and make decisions about it. Instead, he suggests the people who do the work should make the decisions and the process itself can have built-in controls. In rethinking a key business process, such as ordering, a company employing the BPR approach must place its existing arrangements mentally to one side, and then question everything about the process – for example, how the customer orders, what it is he wants, why he wants it that way, who deals with the customer, how and in what order. The idea is to go back to basic principles and completely rethink the process in question. The re-engineering process tends to lead to the following changes in the way work is undertaken:

- several jobs or tasks becoming combined with related jobs/tasks

- workers become more involved in decision-making (i.e. empowerment)

- a reduction in the number of checks and controls during the process

- a single person as point of contact with the customer ('empowered')

- work structures move from functional departments towards process teams

- the focus for performance and payment shifts from activities to results, from individuals to teams

- a culture change will occur in which the typical employee will see the customer as more important than the boss

- organizational structures are likely to become flatter and less hierarchical.

34. Information technology (IT) plays an important role in the re-engineering concept. The role of IT in BPR is crucial as the horizontal approach necessitates information flows across departments and processes. Empowered employees require access to company information. It is considered a major enabler for new forms of working and collaborating within an organization and across organizational borders. Technological innovations throughout the 1990s, especially in the form of database and Internet technologies, led to

the creation of enterprise resource planning systems and broader enterprise-wide systems (see Section 15). Such systems enable empowered employees by making data and information immediately available.

35.   Whilst there are many examples of companies having achieved dramatic performance improvements by moving towards a more horizontal structure, there are also failures. Research conducted by Stalk and Black (1994) found that much of what people label the 'Horizontal Organization' or 'Organizing Around Processes' is labelled incorrectly. What really happens is the modification of traditional structures to make process management easier. Stalk and Black also found that different processes have fundamentally different characteristics – and they thrive in different structures and that 'one size does not fit all'.

36.   Critics claim that BPR dehumanizes the workplace, increases managerial control, and is or has been used to justify downsizing. The most frequent critique against BPR concerned the strict focus on efficiency and technology and the disregard for people within organizations subject to re-engineering initiatives. Re-engineering treated the people inside companies as if they were just interchangeable parts to be re-engineered. But no one wants to 'be re-engineered'. Other criticisms and problems associated with BPR include implementation of generic (best-practice) processes that do not fit specific company needs and that many organizations simply perform BPR as a one-off project with limited strategy alignment and long-term perspective.

37.   The goal of process management is not to replace vertical structures with horizontal ones. Rather, it is to intertwine and reinforce the best aspects of both – strong functional expertise and flexible, responsive processes. **Business process management** can be considered as a successor to the BPR wave of the 1990s. BPM is intended to align business processes with strategic objectives and customers' needs but also requires a change in a company's emphasis from functional to process orientation. BPM has been defined as a systematic, structured approach to analyze, improve, control and manage processes with the aim of improving the quality of products and services.

38.   BPM differs from BPR in that it does not aim at one-off revolutionary changes to business processes, but at their continuous evolution. The activities which constitute BPM can be grouped into three categories: design, execution and monitoring. Whereas TQM emphasized continuous improvement in a traditional (vertical) structure and BPR advocated transformational change within the horizontal organization, BPM embraces both types of change but within a more horizontal design.

39.   The term Business Process Management as a field of study is still in its infancy, yet the interest in BPM has grown steadily over recent years Hung (2006). Principles of BPM include:

–   a holistic view (BPM addresses the interdependence of strategy, people, processes and technology in achieving business objectives)

–   strategic imperative

–   enabled by IT

–   corporate-wide impact, BPM affects every aspect of an organization, from its structure (organized around processes) to its management (process leaders versus functional heads), and

–   emphasizes cross-functional process management.

It is therefore a continuous attempt to improve business effectiveness and efficiency.

40.   Jeston and Nelis discuss what Davenport claims in Jeston and Nelis (2014). He argues that BPM is an amalgam of a number of previous approaches. The idea that work can be viewed as a process, and then improved, is hardly new, he argues. 'It dates at least to Frederick Taylor at the turn of the last century'. The next great addition to process management was created by the combination of Taylorist process improvement, and statistical process control by Shewart, Deming, Juran and others. Their version of process management involves measuring and limiting process variation, continuous rather than episodic improvement and the empowerment of workers to improve their own processes. According to Davenport the next major variation on BPM took place in the 1990s when there was an emphasis on radical rather than incremental improvements and a use of IT to enable new ways of working. The most recent additions to BPM, however, have revolved around six Sigma and lean approaches. Consequently, we might view BPM as an eclectic set of management theories spanning over a century.

CONCLUSION

41.   Organizations achieve organization, typically following strategy but in some cases beforehand, through a range of tools that provide structure. This includes designing the organization by grouping people that perform similar or related work and through job design. Once labour has been divided and becomes specialized, a second organization challenge emerges as a result of work and departmental inter-dependencies. Organizations will then organize through coordination and various integration mechanisms. These have evolved over the past two decades where the use of business processes has come to the fore.

42.   Designing and redesigning jobs is not easy. However, when work can be redesigned effectively, the rewards are twofold. For individuals, there is the opportunity to find personally challenging and satisfying work. For firms, there is the opportunity to achieve lower costs, better quality and improved productivity through a more effective match between the needs of people and the requirements of technology. The approach to work structuring and job design embodied in some aspects of business process re-engineering focuses on key business processes rather than on tasks and operational structures in designing work. This may lead to job losses for some, but also to more interesting and challenging jobs for others. Organizations employing BPR/BPM may enjoy reduced costs of production and improved customer relations.

QUESTIONS

1   Evaluate theories of motivation and their contribution to job design.

2   Select a job with which you are familiar and redesign it with the approaches discussed in mind. Explain what you may change and why.

3   List and describe the various approaches to work design.

4   Why should managers be concerned with job design? Why are they unlikely to give it the full attention it may deserve?

5   How might technology affect the organization of work?

6   Why, despite criticisms, is job simplification so popular amongst job designers?

7   Evaluate job simplification as an approach to job design.

8   Discuss the impact of human relations theories on work design. List and describe three main approaches to achieving increased job satisfaction.

9   What is a business process? You should provide examples to support your answer.

10   Contrast two methods used by organizations to improve their business processes.

USEFUL WEBSITES

EDUCAUSE: **www.educause.edu/node/645/ tid/17023?time=1286377022**
Business Process Reengineering – Resources BPM:
   www.bpm.com

Articles, news, research and white papers on business process management and workflow

REFERENCES

Daft, R.L. (2009) *New Era of Management*, 9th edn, Thomson Learning SouthWestern; International edition.

Davenport, T. (1994) 'Managing in the new world of process', *Public Productivity & Management Review*, 18(2): 133–147.

Hammer, M. (1990) 'Reengineering work: don't automate, obliterate', *Harvard Business Review*, 68(4): 104–112.

Hung, R. (2006) 'Business process management as competitive advantage: a review and empirical study', *Total Quality Management*, 17(1): 21–40.

Jeston, J. and Nelis, J. (2014),*Business Process Management*, 3rd edn, Routledge.

Stalk, G. and Black, J. (1994) 'The myth of the horizontal organization', *Canadian Business Review*, 21(4): 26–30.

CHAPTER 22
ORGANIZING FOR INNOVATION

Key Concepts

- Creativity
- Entrepreneurship
- First-mover advantage
- Innovation
- Learning organization
- Risk taking

Learning Outcomes   Having read this chapter, you should be able to:

- discuss the meaning of innovation and its related concepts

- explain why it is important for companies to organize for innovation

- evaluate traditional (classical) designs and the argument that they may stifle creativity and innovation

- discuss why a contemporary firm may require both an operating organization and an innovating organization

- discuss structures for the innovating organization

- evaluate the role of leadership, culture and climate in developing an innovative organization.

Vignette
WORLD'S MOST INNOVATIVE COMPANIES

Google is a well-known technology innovator which has long dominated the top ten most innovative companies in Boston Consulting Group's (BCG) survey of the world's most innovative companies. Google was number two every year between 2006 and 2012, losing one place to Samsung in 2013. Apple has been number one every year since 2005. The list of top-50 innovators continues to be significantly slanted towards technology and tele-communications companies, including Apple, Google, Samsung and IBM. Many management scholars have asked why Google or Apple or Samsung are consistently so good at innovation and why they innovate.

1.   In the previous chapter we discussed job design as the systematic and purposeful allocation of tasks to individuals and groups within an organization. The purposes of job design included to organize the work of employees so that corporate goals and objectives are attained. In Section 8 we discussed strategy and throughout this unit have noted how firms must *organize* to accomplish strategic goals. It is therefore worth noting that many organizations have goals that involve some aspect of innovation or entrepreneurship. This point is supported by Johnson, Whittington and Scholes (2011: p. 17) who discuss strategic choices. They argue that 'most existing organizations have to innovate constantly simply to survive'. They go on to add, 'a fundamental question, therefore, is whether the organization is innovating appropriately'. They note that companies may seek to be pioneers or followers (2011: p. 295) and that innovation is a key aspect of strategy with implications for cost, price and sustainability. Pioneers may experience a **first-mover advantage** which exists where an organization is better off than its competitors as a result of being first to market with a new product, process or service.

2.   The drivers for innovation (strategies) include technological advances, changing customers and their needs, the changing business environment and increased competition. Companies innovate continuously or radically in order to gain advantage through reduced costs, differentiated products and services or means to make them more responsive to their customers. The importance of understanding innovation was first recognized in the early part of the twentieth century by the Economist Joseph Schumpeter who introduced the term 'creative destruction' to describe the pattern in which small, entrepreneurial new entrants unseat large, incumbent corporations. He considered innovation to be about *new* products, *new* methods, *new* markets, *new* sources of supply or *new* forms of competition.

3.   In a turbulent environment, innovation is an important driver of the organic growth necessary to generate sustained, above-average returns. Organizations may have the goal to create value from ideas. In order to do this innovation may take a variety of forms: from incremental changes in existing products to entirely new offerings for customers. Companies also use knowledge to increase efficiency and lift profits.

4.   Innovation can be systematically managed if one knows where and how to look, argues Drucker (1998). He also notes that most innovations, however, especially the successful ones, result from a conscious, purposeful search for innovation opportunities. The **innovating organizations** – designed to do something for the first time – are those that recognize and formalize the roles, processes, rewards, and people practices which naturally lead to innovations. Jay Galbraith (1982), a leading expert on organization design, argues that the organization that purposely designs these roles and processes is more likely to generate innovations than is an organization that does not plan for this function. Such a purposely designed organization is needed to overcome the barriers to innovation. Because innovation is destructive to many established groups, it will be resisted and overlooked. These and other obstacles are more likely to be overcome if the organization is designed specifically to innovate.

5.   Galbraith (1982) describes the components of an organization geared to producing innovative ideas. He contends the basic components of the innovating organization are no different from those of an operating organization. That is, both include a task, a structure, processes, reward systems and people (each component must fit with each of the other components). Interestingly, Galbraith refers to the same design variables as those introduced in the previous two chapters when we discussed organizing people and work. However, he argues that the task of the innovating organization is fundamentally different from that of the operating organization. The innovating task is more uncertain and risky, takes place over longer time periods and assumes that failure in the early stages may be desirable. Therefore, the organization that performs the innovative task should also be different; a firm that wishes to innovate needs both an operating organization and an innovating organization.

6.   Having argued a need to organize for innovation we start the chapter by defining key concepts. Following this we reveal shortfalls and the dysfunctional aspects of traditional (classical) designs. Recognizing that traditional designs may well work against innovation we then explore what organizations can do to manage innovation. Aside from introducing the process of innovation we will also explore the role of leadership commitment, culture and climate. Having studied the chapter, the reader should be better placed to explain why innovation is needed and how to accomplish it by organization and design.

22.1 KEY CONCEPTS

7.   So far we have mentioned concepts like entrepreneurship, innovation and creativity. We will now define the terms along with several related constructs. Entrepreneurship refers to a certain kind of activity. At the heart of that activity is innovation: the effort to create purposeful, focused change in an enterprise's economic or social potential (Drucker, 1998). **Entrepreneurship** concerns the identification and exploitation of previously unexploited opportunities. It often requires the organization to be both creative (the ability to produce novel and useful ideas) and innovative (implementation of new ideas). Creativity and innovation can lead to new products and services, novel applications and cost savings. Most companies continue to rank innovation as a top strategic priority. More than three-quarters of companies taking place in a survey placed innovation as either number one or among the top three (BCG, 2013).

8.   **Creativity** is 'the connecting and rearranging of knowledge – in the minds of people who will allow themselves to think flexibly – to generate new, often surprising ideas that others judge to be useful', Plsek (1997: p. 28). It is the ability to produce novel and useful ideas and can lead to new products and services, novel applications and cost savings. A creative environment develops from a trusting, open culture with good communication and a blame-free atmosphere. Conversely, creativity is inhibited by lack of trust or commitment and fear of the consequences of change.

9.   **Innovation** is 'the first, practical, concrete implementation of an idea done in a way that brings broad-based, extrinsic recognition to an individual or organization', Plsek (1997: p. 30). Michael Porter defined innovation in terms of improvements and better ways of working. As we have already indicated, innovation can take place in products, services, processes and business models (dimensions of innovation). Furthermore, there are different degrees of innovation which may be dramatic and a breakthrough, radical or incremental.

10.   Plsek (1997) argues that creativity and innovation are related: Creativity is about the production of ideas whilst innovation is the step beyond this where the ideas are implemented; the innovator is not necessarily the creator. Others also decompose innovation into two parts, separating idea generation (invention) from implementation (exploitation) thus:

INNOVATION = IDEA (INVENTION) + IMPLEMENTATION (EXPLOITATION)

11.   Drucker (1998) emphasizes the relationship between innovation and opportunity; closely associated with the seizing of opportunity is risk taking. **Risk taking** is really about a person or groups' degree of willingness to take chances. In a corporate sense, risk is the probability and consequences of the failure of a strategy. It is the possibility of suffering harm or loss in pursuit of a desired outcome; the chance of something happening that will have an impact upon objectives and goals. People and employees or managers are often categorized as either Risk averse (a person who prefers the certain prospect to any risky prospect); Risk neutral (the risk neutral person exhibits a reaction to risk in line with its statistical probability) and Risk seekers (who choose among the risks that have negative consequences). Individuals or groups may engage in risk avoidance – decisions not to become involved in, or action to withdraw from, a risk situation. As was noted earlier, it is not just individuals that can take risks. Bozeman (1998) defines **Risk culture** as an organization's propensity to take risks as perceived by the managers in the organization.

12.   Entrepreneurship then is about finding, creating and exploiting opportunity through innovation and risk taking. It is not surprising that organizations seek to develop an entrepreneurial orientation – directing structures, process, practices, decision-making activities and systems toward the exploitation of opportunity. Indeed companies typically want employees to behave like entrepreneurs whilst working within a large organization. An **intrapreneur** has been defined as 'a person within a large corporation who takes direct responsibility for turning an idea into a profitable finished product through assertive risk taking and innovation'.

ENTREPRENEURSHIP = INNOVATION + RISK TAKING + OPPORTUNITY

22.2 TRADITIONAL DESIGNS (BUREAUCRACY) – DYSFUNCTIONS AND CRITICISMS

13.   Throughout Section 2 we discussed the classical theories of management and the idea of bureaucracy and throughout the book have repeatedly noted the influence of such theories in contemporary organizations.

Despite this, many aspects of bureaucracy have been attacked by scholars and practitioners alike (see, for example, Child, 2001: p. 1135, 'Many have argued that [the attributes of bureaucracy] are maladaptive when massive change, environmental dynamism and considerable uncertainty are the norm: bureaucracy is characterized as slow to adapt when a change is necessary.').

14.   The features of bureaucracy, a rational model for organization structure, include specialization or division of labour, a hierarchy of authority, written rules and regulations and the rational application of rules and procedures. The primary purpose of bureaucratic control is to 'standardize and control employee behaviour' according to Daft (2001: p. 293). The concept of bureaucracy effectively dehumanizes the organization and makes it machine-like, focusing on routine.

15.   Daft (2001: p. 292) claims 'excessive bureaucracy can impede effectiveness and productivity' and Huczynski and Buchanan (2001: p. 491) discuss 'dysfunctions of bureaucracy'. They start by discussing degrees of bureaucracy, referencing the influential work of Pugh *et al.* in the 1960s and 1970s. They state that research recognized that 'bureaucracy should be treated as a continuum'. In their summary of weaknesses in bureaucracy they include: maintenance costs, slowness to adapt (rules introduce delays); a failure to make maximum use of innovative resources (rules stifle initiative and creativity); demotivated employees; prevention of employee contribution to decisions (hierarchy) and people not recognizing or caring about problems outwith their domain. We would also add difficulties in creating and maintaining rules in the face of constant change. One interesting specific empirical study involving conclusions that attacked bureaucracy was conducted by Bozeman (1998) who argues that formalization reduces employee risk taking.

22.3 INNOVATION STRUCTURE, PROCESS AND MANAGEMENT

16.   It is largely accepted that a firm's entrepreneurial orientation has five attributes:

1)   Innovative (adopts creative processes, supports experimentation, new ideas)

2)   Risk taking (commits resources in the pursuit of opportunity)

3)   Proactive (takes the initiative, introduces new technologies)

4)   Competitive (challenges rivals)

5)   Adopts autonomous work (encourages independent action of individuals/teams).

17.   Galbraith (1982) contrasts components of operating and innovating organizations. Operating organizations are designed for efficiency – to process the millionth order or serve the millionth client. An organization that is designed to do something well for the millionth time is not good at doing something for the first time. Therefore, organizations wanting to innovate or revitalize themselves need two organizations, an operating organization and an innovating organization. In addition, if the ideas produced by the innovating organization are to be implemented by the operating organization, they need a transition process to transfer ideas from the innovating organization to the operating organization. The operating organization has a traditional, more bureaucratic structure, that divides labour and emphasizes departmentalization and span of control. Its processes focus on planning and budgeting, measuring performance and integrating departments.

18.   The structure of the innovating organization, on the other hand, is different. It includes new roles such as the 'Idea generator', 'Sponsor' and 'Orchestrator' (see Figure 22.1). It also has processes for funding, obtaining ideas, and managing programmes. Virtually everyone in the organization can be an idea generator, and all middle managers are potential sponsors. However not all choose to play these roles. People vary considerably in their innovating skills.

19.   Every innovation starts with an idea generator. The idea generator is typically a low-level employee who recognizes a problem and develops a solution to it. The low status and authority level of the idea generator creates a need for someone to play the next role. Often ideas need at least one sponsor to promote them. To carry an idea through to implementation, a manager has to discover it and fund the increasingly disruptive and expensive development and testing efforts that shape it. One of the sponsor's functions is to lend their authority and resources to an idea to carry it closer to commercialization. The sponsor must

FIGURE 22.1   Innovation roles

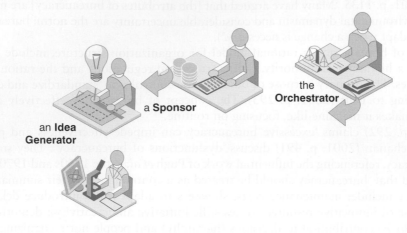

also recognize the business significance of the idea. In any organization there are numerous ideas floated at any one time. The sponsor must select those that might become marketable. Sponsors are usually middle managers who may be anywhere in the organization; they may run divisions or departments. They must be able to balance the operating and innovating needs of their business or function.

20.   Finally, an orchestrator is necessary because the management of ideas is a political process; they destroy investments in capital equipment and people's careers. The problem is that the political struggle is biased toward those in the company who have authority and control of resources. Orchestrators are the organization's senior managers, and they must design the innovating organization. The orchestrator must balance the power to give the new idea a chance. They must protect ideas people, promote the opportunity to try out new ideas, and back those whose ideas prove effective. This person must legitimize the whole process. A person orchestrates by funding innovating activities and creating incentives for middle managers to sponsor innovating ideas.

21.   Thus key structural questions focus on whether to create dedicated departments tasked to innovate (e.g. R&D, product development, market development and new process technology); and whether to create new roles or add responsibilities to existing roles for the innovation tasks and processes. In the innovating organization's role structure the chief executive or another senior manager functions as an orchestrator. Divisional managers are the sponsors who work in both the operating and the innovating organizations.

22.   One key structural problem is whether to separate the creative function physically, financially, and/ or organizationally from the day-to-day activities (operations) that are likely to disrupt it. Furthermore, consideration should be given to how creative functions are structured and managed. Should such functions be freed from staff controls designed for the operating organization? The effect of too much control was discussed earlier. Controls based on operating logic reduce the innovating organization's ability to rapidly, economically and regularly test and adapt new ideas.

23.   The key processes discussed by Galbraith include idea generation (getting and blending ideas), funding and programme management. Whilst idea generation is often a chance occurrence, Galbraith argues that the odds of match-ups between idea generators and sponsors can be improved by organization design. Network-building actions such as company-wide seminars and conferences facilitate matching. In addition a process to fund new ideas is required. Finally, program management is necessary to implement new products and processes within divisions. At this stage of the process, the idea generator usually allocates the idea to a product/project/program manager. The product or process is then implemented across the functional organization within the division. The point is that a program management process and skill is needed. The aforementioned processes are basic components of the innovating structure. Even though many of these occur naturally in all organizations, Galbraith (1982) argues that the odds for successful innovation can be increased by explicitly designing these processes and by earmarking corporate resources for them.

24. BCG (2012) conducted interviews with some of the most innovative industrial companies to understand what helps drive innovation performance. They identified a set of emerging ways in which leading industrial companies are focusing attention so as to maximize the value of their innovation efforts:

– cultivate a deep customer understanding (strong customer focus)

– use market understanding to find opportunity (know supply and demand)

– senior leadership commitment to innovation as a competitive advantage

– inclusiveness, broad involvement and participation, having people committed full-time to innovation and product development

– insist on strong processes.

These are not individual drivers of success, notes BCG; they are interconnected and reciprocally reinforcing.

25. Whereas some ideas are formed spontaneously and some may be generated for continuous improvement, some writers on the subject describe phases of innovation and an innovation process (see Figure 22.2). For example, Goffin and Mitchell (2010: p. 17) identify three key phases of an innovation ('the development funnel'). In the first phase ideas are generated (ideas phase). Some of the ideas are immediately filtered out (prioritization) whilst others may be further developed into concepts (phase 2). Finally, in phase 3 (project phase) a selected concept will be implemented and innovation will have taken place. Goffin and Mitchell (2010: p. 27) build on the development funnel, adding two extra elements: innovation strategy and people and organization (they name their new model the innovation pentathlon). This emphasizes the link between the portfolio of projects to the overall strategy of the organization. Goffin and Mitchell argue that underlying innovation are many issues related to the organization of human resources; 'these include hiring and training policies, job design and creating effective organizational structures'. Furthermore, they recognize a need to create a culture of innovation. We will focus on the organization of people for innovation in the remainder of the chapter.

FIGURE 22.2 **Innovation process phases**

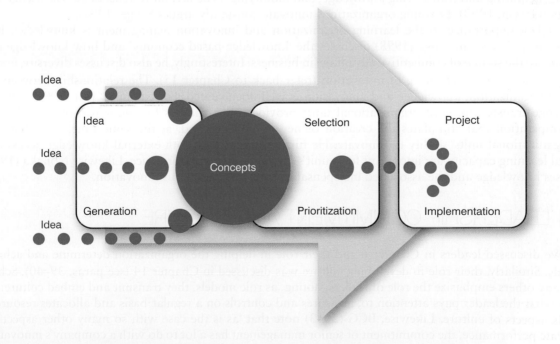

26.   The ability of the innovating organization to generate new business ideas can be increased by systematically recruiting, selecting and developing those people who are better at innovating than others. Job design (see previous chapter) is also of importance when organizing for innovation. The work of 'innovative' employees may be reflected in their job descriptions, some of which will be written for employees in dedicated innovation departments such as R&D. In other cases it may be beneficial to add responsibility for continuous improvement through the generation and implementation of new ideas within the company. In previous chapters we have also discussed the need to align employee objectives with those of the organization (see MBO for example, but also goal-setting theory). Managing innovation performance typically includes the cascading of innovation goals to employees.

27.   The desirable attributes of innovative roles must be identified. The psychological attributes of successful entrepreneurs include a great need to achieve and to take risks. However, to translate that need into innovation, several other attributes are necessary. Prospective innovators have irreverence for the status quo. They often come from outcast groups or are newcomers to the company; they are less satisfied with the way things are and have less to lose if change occurs. Previous start-up experience is also desirable (Galbraith, 1982). The innovating organization must also attract, develop, train and retain people to manage the idea development process. Likely prospects for such positions should have a management style that enables them to handle ideas people. Such employees do not take very well to being supervised. Idea generators often gain their satisfaction by having 'done it their way'. The intrinsic satisfaction comes from the ownership and autonomy. However, ideas people also need help, advice and sounding boards. More than the idea generators, the sponsors need to understand the logic of innovation and to have experienced the management of innovation. Again, the ability to recognize business ideas and to shape partial ideas into business ideas is needed.

28.   At this stage we might well ask how ideas are actually generated within the organization. We have already recognized that ideas may be generated in groups with a specific role to innovate but also argued that every employee of the company may generate ideas for improvement and innovation. The latter is actively encouraged as a part of a quality culture (to be discussed later). Ideas may simply come to individuals at any time or in a meeting arranged specifically for that purpose. Such meetings will typically encourage brainstorming and the use of similar creative thinking techniques. Many companies tap into the creative potential of their workforce through the use of new idea and suggestion schemes (boxes). They also give autonomy to teams to free them up from constrained thinking. Others encourage experimentation and promote a learning organization culture. A **learning organization** is an organization skilled at creating, acquiring and transferring knowledge, and modifying its behaviour to reflect new knowledge and insights (Garvin, 1993). Learning organizations innovate constantly argues Senge (1991).

29.   Of key importance to the learning organization and innovation management is **knowledge**. In a subsequent publication, Senge (1998) discusses the 'knowledge-based economy' and how knowledge and learning are the source of competitive advantage in business. Interestingly, he also discusses diversity, noting that difference is the wellspring of innovation (refer back to Chapter 15). The relationship between the learning organization, knowledge and innovation is well documented. For example, Tsai (2001) suggests knowledge transfer amongst organizational units provides opportunities for mutual learning and inter-unit cooperation that stimulates the creation of new knowledge and, at the same time, contributes to the organizational units' ability to innovate. He further argues that both external knowledge access and internal learning capacity are important for a unit's innovation and performance. Likewise Nonaka (1991) discusses knowledge and the associated indispensable tools for continuous innovation.

22.4 LEADERSHIP COMMITMENT AND CULTURE

30.   We discussed leaders in Chapter 6 and their role in helping the organization determine and achieve its goals. Similarly, their role in developing culture was discussed in Chapter 14 (see paras. 39–40). Schein and many others emphasize the role of leaders, noting, as role models, they transmit and embed culture. He argues what the leader pays attention to, measures and controls on a regular basis and allocates resources, embeds aspects of culture. Likewise, BCG (2013) note that 'as is the case with so many other aspects of corporate performance, the commitment of senior management has a lot to do with a company's innovation

track record'. Companies rated as strong innovators were more likely to cite the CEO as the driving force behind the company's innovative efforts.

31.   In Chapter 14 we noted a similar construct to organizational culture is that of the institution. In para. 19 we noted that 'Climate, culture and the institutional constructs are important aspects of the overall internal context'. BCG (2013) take a similar stance when they discuss 'Institutionalizing Innovation'. They note that corporate history is cluttered with companies that were once renowned for their inventiveness but could not maintain their ability to innovate. Yet more than half of the most innovative companies on the 2013 list are more than 50 years old; 'they have continued to create value, jobs and growth because of their ability to institutionalize innovation'.

32.   A creative environment develops from a trusting, open culture with good communication and a blame-free atmosphere. Conversely, creativity is inhibited by a lack of trust or commitment and fear of the consequences of change. Organizations may have dedicated idea generators, organizational units, such as R&D groups that are totally devoted to creating new ideas for future business; these are havens for 'safe learning'. When innovating, one wants to maximize early failure to promote learning. Thus there may be a need for a different culture and way of working. Such a culture may be less likely to emphasize efficiency.

33.   The relationship between rewards and culture development is well documented (see for example, Schein, 1997: p. 85). The innovating organization, like the operating organization, needs an incentive system to motivate innovating behaviour (Galbraith, 1982). Because the task of innovating is different from that of operating, the innovating organization needs a different reward system. The innovating task is riskier, more difficult, and takes place over longer time frames. These factors call for some adjustment to the operating organization's reward system, the amount of adjustment dependent upon the level of innovation within the operating organization and the attractiveness of outside alternatives. Galbraith believes the functions of the reward system are threefold: (1) the rewards must attract and retain ideas people to the company, (2) the rewards must provide motivation for the extra effort needed to innovate and (3) successful performance deserves a reward. These rewards are primarily for idea generators. However, a reward system for sponsors is equally important.

22.5 THE WORK ENVIRONMENT AND THE IMPORTANCE OF PLACE

34.   Having discussed culture in the previous paragraphs it is worth noting that outward manifestations of culture include dress codes and the physical layout of workspaces. An organization's ability to sustain innovation depends, in large part, on its work environment. We have already discussed culture and leadership as important aspects of the work environment. Previously we noted that culture and climate are closely related constructs. Key aspects of the culture and climate include (1) degrees of involvement and participation (see next chapter), (2) autonomy, (3) trust, (4) high idea-support, (5) whether debate is encouraged and (6) the tolerance of uncertainty and ambiguity – and the risk-taking culture. In addition consideration may be given to the design of workspace to foster innovation.

35.   Workspace design takes account of several basic functions of workspace: Workspace is often used for thinking, communicating and working. Space is not neutral and workspace must be consciously designed to optimize innovation. Companies use large, mobile whiteboards to facilitate creativity and idea sharing; technology to enable and enhance conversations and decision-making; furniture on wheels to create a fluid workspace that adapts to the needs of the participants. Companies have been known to combine coffee-shop and office atmospheres; use furniture that allows employees to reconfigure their desks to work individually or collaboratively; create curve-shaped rooms that promote collaboration because of their lack of corners; use bright colours and create offices without walls or barriers; incorporate brew stations and staff pantries on every floor; and open work areas to promote collaboration. However, if employees are happier and get most of their big ideas outside the office, the firm must ask how important is it to be physically present?

36.   Desirable behaviours and the organizational culture goals should also be reflected in the office design. We have already discussed design for collaboration and autonomy but what about trust? Is it better to gather around a table or use a conference call? Can you read non-verbal communication when not in the same

physical space as your colleagues? How can you stimulate spontaneous encounters? Physical proximity, touching, eating and drinking together can show commitment and build trust.

37.   Companies have made use of practices such as the dress code as a means to stimulate creativity and make the culture more innovative. Such companies typically believe that employees may be stifled with a dress policy. Employers institute dress codes to maintain the company's professional image. Dress codes may be written but more often are unwritten rules with regard to clothing. Clothing has a social significance, with different rules and expectations being valid, depending upon the situation. Employees are sometimes required to wear a uniform or certain standards of dress, such as a business suit or tie. Casual dress may make people more excited to go to work, and make them feel more comfortable in the work environment. Additionally, some companies set aside days – generally Fridays ('dress-down Friday', 'casual Friday') – when workers may wear casual clothes.

CONCLUSION

38.   Innovation is increasingly seen as a key strategic priority due to its potential to create sustainable competitive advantage. Innovative organizations are more able to mobilize the knowledge, skills and experiences of people, and create new products, services and processes successfully to get things done faster, better and at lower cost. When customers buy the outcome of innovations, companies increase their turnover. Although creativity is innovation's precursor, both are key concerns for organizational survival and growth. By recognizing the need for innovation roles, developing employees to fill them, giving them opportunity to use their skills in key processes, and rewarding innovating deeds, the firm can do considerably better than simply allowing a spontaneous process to work. The sponsors and managers who manage the idea development process must be recruited, selected and developed. The skills that these people need relate to their style, experience, idea-generating ability, deal-making ability and generalist business acumen. People with these skills can either be selected or developed.

QUESTIONS

1   Discuss the meaning of innovation and its related concepts.

2   Explain why it is important for companies to organize for innovation.

3   Evaluate traditional (classical) designs and the argument that they may stifle creativity and innovation.

4   Discuss why a contemporary firm may require both an operating organization and an innovating organization.

5   Discuss structures for the innovating organization.

6   Evaluate the role of leadership, culture and climate in developing an innovative organization.

USEFUL WEBSITES

Stanford Social Innovation Review – an award-winning magazine and website that covers cross-sector solutions to global problems. **www.ssireview.org**
Innovation Management Community for Practitioners – **www.incrementalinnovation.com**

Department for Business Innovation & Skills – Find tools and guidance for business, **www.gov.uk/government/ organisations/department-for-business-innovation-skills**

REFERENCES

BCG (2012) 'The Most Innovative Companies 2012', available at **www.bcgperspectives.com/content/articles/growth_ innovation_the_most_innovatinn_companies_2012/?ch apter=2#chapter2**, accessed 19 October 2013.

BCG (2013) 'The Most Innovative Companies 2013', available at **www.bcgperspectives.com/content/articles/ innovation_growth_most_innovative_companies_2013_ lessons_from_leaders/**, accessed 19 October 2013.

Bozeman, B. (1998) 'Risk culture in public and private organizations', *American Society for Public Administration*, 58(2): 109–118.

Child, J. (2001) 'Organizations unfettered: organizational form in an information-intensive economy', *Academy of Management Journal – Briarcliff Manor*, 44(6): 1135–1148.

Daft, R.L. (2001) *Organization Theory and Design*, 7th edn, South-Western.

Drucker, P. (1998) 'The discipline of innovation', *Harvard Business Review*, 76(6): 149–157.

Galbraith, J. (1982) 'Designing the innovating organization', *Organizational Dynamics*, 10(3): 4–25.

Garvin, D. (1993) 'Building a learning organization', *Harvard Business Review*, (July/August): 78–91.

Goffin, K. and Mitchell, R. (2010) *Innovation Management: Strategy and Implementation using the Pentathlon Framework*, 2nd edn, Palgrave Macmillan.

Huczynski, A. and Buchanan, D. (2001) *Organizational Behaviour: An Introductory Text*, 4th edn, Financial Times Prentice Hall.

Johnson, G., Whittington, R. and Scholes, K. (2011) *Exploring Strategy: Text & Cases*, 9th edn, Prentice Hall.

Nonaka, I. (1991) 'The knowledge-creating company', *Harvard Business Review*, 69(6): 96–104.

Plsek, P.E. (1997) *Creativity, Innovation and Quality*, ASQC Quality Press.

Schein, E. (1997) *Organizational Culture and Leadership*, 2nd edn, San Francisco: Jossey Bass.

Senge, P.M. (1991) 'Learning organizations', *Executive Excellence*, 8(9): 7.

Senge, P.M. (1998) 'The knowledge era', *Executive Excellence*, 15(1): 15–16.

Tsai, W. (2001) 'Knowledge transfer in intraorganizational networks: Effects of network position and absorptive capacity on business unit innovation and performance', *Academy of Management Journal*, 44(5): 996–1004.

CHAPTER 23
ORGANIZING FOR ENGAGEMENT

Key Concepts

- Delegation
- Employee engagement
- Employee involvement
- Empowerment
- Engagement culture
- Participation

Learning Outcomes Having read this chapter, you should be able to:

- contrast micromanagement with an empowerment style of management
- evaluate when and why to delegate, empower and engage employees within the organization
- discuss good practice (how to) in delegating and empowering employees
- evaluate arguments for and against greater empowerment and engagement in contemporary organizations
- explain what is meant by an engagement culture.

23.1 INTRODUCTION

1.   In this chapter we continue to examine how management theory is translated into practice, again focusing on how managers organize their resources to meet strategic goals. Central to the design of work is the attainment of organizational goals through people and technology. One of the key challenges for management is therefore to get the most out of their human resources within the context of their organization. The external context includes the degree of predictability in the environment and the internal environment includes the strategy and the degree to which it emphasizes standardization and one best way of working.
2.   Earlier in this book we discussed certain aspects of structure and organization such as power, authority, responsibility and control. Each is a management variable and can be used to describe management style. Managers and organizations vary in accordance with how much power they share with employees and how they seek to control. For some time it has been thought that there are patterns or configurations of such variables and that some patterns are more applicable than others for certain contexts (see contingency theories).

3. In the second section of the book we examined the classical, scientific and calculated aspects of management and in the third section turned to the human relations theories (motivation theory). The school of human relations helped by scholars such as Mayo, Herzberg, Vroom, Likert and Maslow, amongst others (see Chapters 4 and 5), has drawn conclusions from their various studies that positive motivational factors brought about by such methods as employee involvement may develop a more creative, interested and therefore more productive workforce.

4. In this chapter we examine the practical application of such theories in organizing people at work. We start by reviewing traditional management as a (micro)management style and consider its impact on employees. We then consider arguments as to why aspects of this style are not adequate for a dynamic environment and, influenced by human relations theories of motivation, introduce concepts associated with empowerment and job redesign. Towards the end of the chapter we discuss the more recent concept of employee engagement and the characteristics of the engagement culture. A common theme throughout the chapter is the attainment of goals and performance through design and organization with an emphasis on the discretionary work effort of employees.

23.2 TRADITIONAL MICROMANAGEMENT: BUREAUCRACY, STANDARDIZATION AND THE DISEMPOWERED EMPLOYEE

5. Lashley (1999) discusses manufacturing industry models of control which minimized the significance of individual idiosyncrasies. Based on essentially Taylorist views of job design, they establish standardized procedures and one best way of doing each task. In many cases this extended to scripting the interaction with customers and left little to the discretion of the individual employee. The consequence of this has been the rapid growth of organizations specializing in high volume, mass produced, standardized services which minimized the significance of labour inputs. This has been referred to as the Command and Control style (micromanagement): employees are subjected to external control, have low discretion, undertake simple routine tasks in a high predictability environment. Their involvement is described as calculative. Whilst this strategy was tremendously successful over the two decades preceding 1990, many companies now see the limits of standardization and this style of control. Apart from high labour turnover which has been endemic in many of these firms, even the most standardized operation encounters occasions when customer needs are difficult to predict and a quick response is needed at the touch point. The intangible element of any service encounter requires some form of employee participation, even in highly standardized and Tayloristic situations.

23.3 EVOLUTION OF MANAGEMENT – TOWARDS THE EMPOWERED EMPLOYEE

6. Empowerment, a situation where employees are allowed greater freedom, autonomy and self-control over their work, and the responsibility for decision-making, is often described as the opposite of micromanagement. It has been hailed as a management technique which can be applied universally across all organizations as a means of dealing with the needs of modern business, and is said to benefit all organizations. The fast moving global economy requires that organizations learn and adapt to change quickly, and employees have a key role to play here. However, empowerment is not a simple concept and there are different managerial perceptions of it. A range of managerial meanings have been applied based on different perceptions of business problems, motives for introducing empowerment and perceived benefits to be gained from empowerment. Empowerment can be used as a term to describe different initiatives. Companies may, to differing extents, require employees to exercise discretion; the offering may be highly standardized and require employees to practise delivery in 'the one best way' or it may be differentiated requiring customization to meet customer service needs. This may call into question the somewhat simplistic claims for the universality of empowerment, and the supposed benefits which ensue. Lashley (1999) investigated different approaches to empowerment in an attempt to establish a framework for understanding. This framework of analysis suggests that there is a need to approach the study of empowerment in a systematic manner.

7.   Drivers for empowerment may include:

- requirement to be more responsive to the marketplace

- reduction in number of levels in structures – so-called delayering (see BPR)

- need for lateral collaboration and communication amongst work teams with minimal supervision

- allows senior management to concentrate on longer-term (strategic) issues

- need to make best use of all available resources (especially human resources)

- pressure to meet the higher expectations of a better-educated workforce

- the development of 'learning organizations'.

23.4 DEFINITIONS OF EMPOWERMENT

8.   Prior to defining empowerment we will first consider a number of related concepts. Earlier we noted that empowerment resulted in employees having more power. Empowerment is more than this but for now we consider one of the earlier power-sharing concepts – delegation. Delegation is a distinct type of power-sharing process. It occurs when a manager gives subordinates responsibility and authority for making certain decisions previously made by the manager and involves the assignment of new and different tasks or responsibilities to a subordinate. Sometimes delegation involves the additional authority and discretion associated with tasks and assignments already performed by the subordinate. The extent to which a subordinate must check with the boss before taking action is another aspect of delegation.

9.   The benefits derived from delegation will be dependent upon situational factors that may include improved decision quality and enhanced subordinate commitment. Through delegation, work can be made more interesting, challenging and meaningful (enriched). However, delegation may have negative consequences should the subordinate not desire additional responsibility or lack the necessary skills or resources to discharge responsibilities. From the manager's perspective, delegation is a time management tool and a means to develop subordinates. In the process of delegating tasks with their commensurate authority, it is important to ensure that the amount of authority is defined, or prescribed, in an unequivocal way. The principal options open to a manager, ranging from tight to lose control, are shown in Figure 23.1.

We will revisit delegation in Chapter 26, with time management and personal effectiveness.

FIGURE 23.1   Delegation – the main options

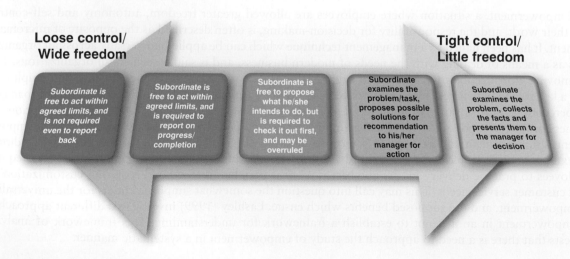

Loose control/ Wide freedom

Tight control/ Little freedom

Subordinate is free to act within agreed limits, and is not required even to report back

Subordinate is free to act within agreed limits, and is required to report on progress/ completion

Subordinate is free to propose what he/she intends to do, but is required to check it out first, and may be overruled

Subordinate examines the problem/task, proposes possible solutions for recommendation to his/her manager for action

Subordinate examines the problem, collects the facts and presents them to the manager for decision

10.   In Figure 23.1 we made attempts to distinguish between categories of participation. In a similar manner, Marchington and Wilkinson cited in Sisson and Bach (1999), provide a simple stage model which distinguishes between the major categories of involvement, focusing on the extent of influence. Starting with no involvement, where managers make all the decisions, organizations at the other extreme may be controlled by employees. The next stage after no involvement is more about communication and the exchange of information between the employer and employees; information sharing may be witnessed in team briefings, news sheets, attitude surveys and suggestion schemes. Following this, in the next stage (consultation) information may be exchanged through formalized channels and management may make use of information provided by employees before making decisions; it is important to note that there may be, in some situations, a legal duty to consult (see, for example, redundancy, pension changes or in the event of one organization being taken over by another). In the next stage, before employee control, there is joint decision-making (co-determination). Generally this stage is less common within the UK where important decisions tend to be made by managers.

11.   Throughout the second half of the twentieth century numerous management trends emerged. From command and control or micromanagement managers gradually recognized the need to arouse discretionary work effort from employees through initiatives that were influenced by motivation theories. Thus the literature starts with delegation and then discusses participation and involvement (see previous paragraphs). Yet most attention was given to the concept of empowerment which we turn to next.

12.   **Empowerment** on the other hand, is more than simple delegation and must be seen through the eyes of the employee, asking whether they feel empowered and not powerless. It is concerned with issues to do with (1) management style and (2) employee participation. As a motivational construct, empowerment is individual and personal, it is about discretion, autonomy, power and control. This motivational aspect to empowerment becomes the defining feature of the initiative. The empowered must feel a sense of personal worth, with the ability to effect outcomes and having the power to make a difference; it helps firms to enthuse and enable employees to take responsibility. Ultimately empowerment is said to enable companies to gain competitive advantage through improved service quality and differentiation or through cost reduction (as a direct consequence of delayering or through the creative thoughts of employees directed at continuous improvement of work practices). The feelings of the empowered are fundamental to understanding the concept of empowerment and variations in form and application. Most definitions of the state rather than the form of empowerment stress the need for the individual to feel in control, have a sense of personal power together with the freedom to use that power and a sense of personal efficacy and self-determination.

13.   The argument that employees can give much more to the customer and their company is based upon generating feelings of commitment. When committed and with the appropriate amount of power and the freedom to use that power, the employee can meet customer needs as they arise. Advocates of empowerment, argue how empowered employees willingly take responsibility, respond more quickly to customer needs, complaints and changes in customer tastes. The organization will experience lower labour turnover; there will be high staff morale and employees will take responsibility for their own performance and its improvement. Employees' inherent skills and talents will be put to work for the organization so as to produce more satisfied customers and greater profits.

14.   The various concepts discussed so far have been summarized in Table 23.1 and in Figure 23.2 (dimensions of empowerment).

TABLE 23.1 Empowerment and related constructs

ACCOUNTABILITY	Accountability is answerability and is closely associated with responsibility; it is about responsibility for decisions, actions and results.
AUTHORITY	A right conferred on some members of an organization to act in a certain way over others (this term was also considered in Chapter 4). It can be regarded as a defined amount of power granted by the organization to selected members (legitimate power).
AUTONOMY	The degree to which a job provides substantial freedom and discretion to the individual in scheduling the work and in determining the procedures to be used in carrying it out.

(Continued)

COMMITMENT	The degree of identification and involvement which employees have with their organization's mission, values and goals. This translates into: their desire to stay with the organization; belief in its objectives and values; and the strength of employee effort in the pursuit of business objectives.
CONTROL	A process which brings about adherence to a goal through the exercise of power or authority – there are different types of control (see next section).
DELEGATION	The degree to which the authority to commit resources was diffused throughout the organization by means of the formal allocation of roles within a structure. In fulfilling their responsibilities, a person may delegate (i.e. hand down) some of their own authority to act, but they cannot pass off their responsibility (accountability). This is why there is always an element of risk attached to delegation, for if things go wrong, the delegator cannot blame the person to whom he or she assigned certain tasks. The delegator alone is accountable.
DISCRETION	The freedom to decide what should be done in a particular situation; the power to decide or act according to one's own judgment.
INVOLVEMENT	Employee involvement is a participative, employer-led process that uses the input of employees and is intended to increase employee commitment to an organization's success.
LOCUS OF CONTROL	The degree to which an employee believes that they are subjected to outside control (work decisions are controlled by factors which they cannot influence) as opposed to having internal control (the employee believes they have control) over the forces influencing their work.
MICROMANAGEMENT	Involvement in the detailed control of the activities in one's area of responsibility; a management style whereby a manager closely observes or controls the work of subordinates or employees.
PARTICIPATION	The action of taking part in some aspect of work; participative management is a style in which employees at all levels are encouraged to contribute ideas towards identifying and setting organizational goals, problem-solving, and other decisions that may directly affect them. Also called consultative management.
POWER	The ability of individuals or groups to persuade, induce or coerce others into following certain courses of action.
RESPONSIBILITY	An obligation placed upon a person who occupies a certain position in the organization structure to perform a task, function or assignment. Another word for responsibility is 'accountability', which in some respects is a more helpful term, since it implies that one person is accountable to another for a given task.
TRUST	The degree of confidence that one person (or organization) has in another to fulfil an obligation or responsibility.

23.5 MANAGERIAL INTENTIONS FOR EMPOWERMENT

15.   Empowerment has been used to describe a number of specific initiatives (see Table 23.2) such as the use of quality circles; suggestion schemes; employee involvement; autonomous work groups and removal of levels of management (delayering); and the delegation of greater authority. Indeed 'there is considerable overlap between employee empowerment, employee participation, employee involvement and even employee commitment. Often these terms are used interchangeably (Lashley, 1999). Thus quality circles, autonomous work groups, suggestion schemes and various employee share ownership programmes are frequently discussed under these different headings without defining the boundaries between them. Employee involvement is intended to improve communication with employees, generate greater commitment and enhance employee contributions to the organization. This might equally be said of the intentions for employee empowerment.

FIGURE 23.2 Dimensions of empowerment

TABLE 23.2 Empowerment initiatives

AUTONOMOUS WORK GROUPS	A process whereby management gives formal groups the right to make decisions on how their work is performed on a group basis, without reference to management; a team of workers allocated to a significant segment of the workflow, with discretion concerning how the work will be carried out, and how tasks and responsibilities will be allocated, shared and rotated.
BONUS SCHEMES	Alternative term for incentive scheme – A scheme by which an employee will receive extra pay or other rewards if certain targets or objectives are achieved. Motivation schemes can build long-term engagement.
BPR	The redesign of business processes in an effort to reduce costs, increase efficiency and effectiveness, and improve quality.
DELAYERING	Reducing the number of layers (levels) in a job hierarchy. (See also Downsizing.)
EMPLOYEE SHARE OWNERSHIP	An employee-owner scheme that provides a company's workforce with an ownership interest in the company. (See share option schemes etc.)
JOB ENLARGEMENT	The horizontal increasing of job responsibility.
JOB ENRICHMENT	The process of vertically increasing the responsibilities of a job, by the addition of motivators, e.g. more discretion, improved job interest, etc.
JOB REDESIGN	The changing and restructuring of individual's jobs primarily through job rotation, job enlargement or job enrichment.
PROFIT SHARING	A system in which the people who work for a company receive a direct share of the profits.

(Continued)

QUALITY CIRCLES	A group of people within an organization who meet (often with management) together on a regular basis to identify, analyze and solve problems relating to quality, productivity or other aspects of day-to-day working arrangements using problem-solving techniques. When matured, true quality circles become self-managing, having gained the confidence of management.
SUGGESTION SCHEMES	Giving staff the opportunity to provide suggestions as to improvements, without risking their job security.
TEAM BRIEFINGS	Regular meetings with a team which allow the provision of accurate updates on policies, projects, priorities and staffing issues to key people, all at the same time; a powerful method of making possible communications up and down the management structure of any organization.
WORKS COUNCILS	Representative bodies organized at workplace level, which give employees rights to information and consultation in personnel and other business related issues within the firm.

16.   A view frequently expressed by line managers is that empowerment of subordinates will result in a loss of control. In reality, empowerment as an employment strategy is concerned with both commitment and control of employees. It is more a shift in the locus of control. The locus of control is a continuum between externally imposed control of the individual to internally generated self-control. Employee empowerment, in its more participative form, is more reliant on internalized self-control, where the employee works to the desired standard and controls his or her own performance accordingly.

17.   In some cases empowerment is defined as 'management strategies for sharing decision-making power' (a shift in authority) whilst others may define it in terms of 'the act of vesting substantial responsibility in the people nearest the problem' (a shift in responsibility). Thus there are different managerial intentions for empowerment. Empowering through participation is chiefly concerned with empowering employees with decision-making authority in some aspect of the work which had been formerly the domain of management; use of semi-autonomous work teams provides a good example. Empowerment through involvement is chiefly concerned with gaining from the experiences and expertise of employees through consultation and joint problem-solving. Employees have little authority to make decisions, managers continue to make the decision but with inputs from employees. Attempts at empowerment through commitment overlap and interrelate with both these categories. Whilst the three foregoing intentions are typically concerned with employees, particularly front line personnel, some initiatives empower managers within the management hierarchy. This may be called empowerment through delayering. Here the intention is greater managerial focus on the source of organizational profits, greater responsiveness to customer needs, reduced management costs and the encouragement of entrepreneurialism. In this case, empowerment of the unit managers means they are not as closely supervised by those above them in the chain of command and are 'left to get on with it'. The aforementioned managerial intentions are not mutually exclusive and managerial actions can be driven by a mixture of motives. Consequently, there are different managerial perceptions about empowerment and the benefits it will deliver.

23.6 THE FORM AND DIMENSIONS OF EMPOWERMENT

18.   Whatever the intentions of managers, initiatives which claim to be empowering will be translated into concrete practical arrangements which set the limits and boundaries within which the empowered operate. These arrangements will clarify just what the empowered have the authority to do and for what they will be responsible. Lashley (1999) has identified five dimensions of empowerment which provide a means of describing, analyzing and locating the form of empowerment being introduced in a particular company:

1)   The **task dimension** (of empowerment) considers the discretion which is allowed to the empowered in performing the task for which they were employed.

2) The **task allocation dimension** considers the amount of responsible autonomy an individual employee or group of employees have in carrying out their tasks. To what extent are they directed, or need to ask permission to complete their tasks? To what extent do company policies and procedures lay down what has to be done and then let them get on with it? A 'one best way' approach involves close supervision.

3) The **power dimension** is concerned with the feelings of personal power which individuals experience as the result of being empowered. To what extent do management efforts to share power foster feelings of empowerment in employees?

4) The **commitment dimension** explores the assumptions about the source of employee commitment and organizational compliance in a particular form of empowerment. To what extent do they follow patterns in traditional organizations which assume that commitment is calculative and based on material extrinsic rewards? To what extent does the initiative assume a moral commitment, as the individual takes a personal sense of ownership in their activities and work? To what extent is there recognition that individuals may differ in their attachments and needs from work?

5) The **culture dimension** examines the extent to which organizational culture fosters feelings of empowerment. To what extent can it be typified as being oriented towards openness, learning, and employee contributions and creating a climate of trust? To what extent can the culture be described as bureaucratic, role, task or control-oriented? To what extent is the initiative to empower a part of a broad organizational culture, or just 'bolted on'?

19.   Each form of empowerment is likely to represent different sources of satisfaction to employees and represent different benefits to employers. Lashley (1999) also identifies four different managerial meanings of empowerment:

Empowerment through participation: autonomous work groups, job enrichment, works councils

Empowerment through involvement: quality circles, team briefings, suggestion schemes

Empowerment through commitment: employee share ownership, profit sharing, bonus schemes, quality of working life programmes (job rotation, job enlargement

Empowerment through delayering: job redesign, autonomous work groups, job enrichment, BPR. (BPR was discussed in Chapters 20 and 21 and has enormous implications for employee involvement as its supporters advocate stripping away unnecessary layers of management and empowering the workforce to seek better process solutions in the drive towards greater efficiency.)

20.   Thus far we have been discussing empowerment and a range of related constructs. A relatively new concept is **employee engagement**. This concept describes an individual's involvement and satisfaction with, and enthusiasm for, the work they do. Buchanan and Huczynski (2010: p. 286) suggest that engagement means more than just motivation or job satisfaction. Engaged employees are open to new ideas, willing to change, have a customer focus and are confident in their ability. We discuss employee engagement and an engagement culture in the final part of this chapter.

23.7 WHAT IS ENGAGEMENT?

Vignette

WHAT IS EMPLOYEE ENGAGEMENT?

'Adopting innovative practices is essential and without staff engagement, this is not going to be possible' says Jan Sobieraj (Managing Director, NHS Leadership Academy). In a panel discussion on improving employee engagement within the National Health Service (England) participants were asked: what is employee engagement? Tim Shepherd, Head of Sector for Healthcare, Unipart: 'At the simplest level we believe it is when an employee is a) aligned and engaged with the organization's goals and b) willing to put discretionary effort into their work in the form of time, thought and energy to achieve those goals.' He advocates a need to share information openly and regularly with all employees. Team members can then start to be empowered to manage their own performance. Sue Morris, Executive Director of Corporate Services, Sussex Partnership NHS Foundation Trust, said she saw employee engagement 'as creating the culture where people can give their best, which means feeling a sense of control of their working day.' She also believes that line manager relationships with direct reports often have the most significant impact on the level of satisfaction and engagement with the organization. Paul Sweetman, Head of Employee Engagement, also discusses culture, suggesting there must be a more proactive and consistent focus on establishing cultures that visibly value and celebrate the contribution made by employees in all areas and at all levels of an organization. Likewise, Nicky Westwood, University Hospitals Birmingham NHS Trust, declared that 'celebrating good practice, shouting about what we do really well, encouraging staff to view their achievements positively and to make them feel valued and appreciated goes a long way to engaging, and more importantly, empowering staff.'

21.   Over recent years there has been been a significant shift in the employee–employer relationship (contract), as was highlighted in the previous chapter. Organizations demand people put in extra effort and generate innovative ideas to improve products and services and ways of working and reducing costs. Managers need to recognize this shift and refrain from using an autocratic management style, which is likely to disengage employees who seek more collaborative and empowering management and challenging work, and inhibit innovation and a readiness to apply more effort (Bates, 2004). Mike Rude VP of HR at Stryker Corp., a manufacturer of surgical and medical products, cited in Bates (2004) suggests engagement is a mutual contract between employer and employee; the company is responsible for building a meaningful workplace. Employees have a responsibility for contributing to an engaging workplace.

22.   Studies have shown (see Harter, Schmidt and Hayes, 2002) that high levels of engagement are associated with high levels of customer satisfaction, productivity, profits and low levels of employee turnover; organizations reporting high levels of employee engagement are more likely to attract and retain high performing employees. Engagement has been viewed as an outcome, a performance construct, an attitude; many see it as a step higher than satisfaction or motivation. It is generally agreed that engaged employees feel a sense of attachment towards their organization, investing themselves not only in their role, but in the organization as a whole.

23.   Research (see Robertson-Smith and Marwick, 2009: p. 28) most frequently highlights the following key drivers of engagement:

- **Work design**: it is important to have challenging, creative and varied work

- **Meaningful and purposeful work:** work should be seen by employees as important; employees understand how they contribute

- **Developmental opportunities**

- **Timely recognition** and rewards

- **Good relationships** between co-workers, especially between employee and manager

- **Inspiring leaders and managers** inspire confidence in individuals, giving them autonomy to make decisions.

24.   Speaking at the Employee Engagement Summit in 2009, John Purcell (cited in Robertson-Smith and Marwick, 2009: p. 39), Strategic Academic Advisor at ACAS National, suggested six key factors that limit or damage engagement:

- Job insecurity

- Unfairness, particularly in reward and pay systems

- Jobs with no space, i.e. repetitive work with short cycle times

- Highly stressful jobs with very little flexibility or autonomy

- Poor line management behaviour and bullying

- Working for long periods of time without a break.

We may also add:

- a lack of trust.

Such factors could lead to disengagement.

23.8 ENGAGEMENT CULTURE

25. In the previous chapter we emphasized the importance of innovation to business. Employers rely on ideas from their employees, customers and partners to help drive the organization forward. Engaged employees are most likely to contribute those innovations, according to a Gallup Management Journal (GMJ) survey of US workers (Gallup, 2006). Gallup research has shown that engaged employees are more productive, profitable, safer, create stronger customer relationships and stay longer with their company than less engaged employees. Gallup's employee engagement research has consistently shown a connection between employee engagement and customer engagement. Gallup's research into the relationship between employee engagement and innovation strongly indicates that engaged employees are far more likely to suggest or develop creative ways to improve management or business processes. They are also far more likely to find creative ways to solve customer problems or to involve their customers in creating service innovations.

26. Many practitioners and management scholars agree that workforce engagement is one of the most crucial issues in culture development today. As has previously been noted earlier, culture is about shared ways of thinking and behaving within the organization. The fact that they are shared means that the culture can be used as an informal control of employee behaviour – guiding decision-making and action. In the vignette we recognized a need to develop an engagement culture within organizations. An engagement culture (see Figure 23.3) is one where the majority of employees feel valued and are committed to

FIGURE 23.3 Engagement culture

EMPLOYEES	
DISENGAGED	**ENGAGED**
Indifferent or disinterested in work	**Passionate about work**
Disloyal to the organization	**Commitment to the organization**
Passive	**Active**
Respond slowly	**Respond promptly**
Complain about work	**Enjoy their work**
Typically late or more likely absent	**On time, dependable**
Low participation	**High participation**
Shirkers, Loafers, Clock-watchers	**Volunteers, Attentive, Team players**
	go the extra mile

the organization and its goals; they participate and feel involved in, are enthusiastic about and satisfied with their work. Such organizations typically have an open communications climate where information is widely shared, employees are listened to and trust their managers and leaders. Such organizations have values that emphasize clearly the importance of accessing the potential of every employee.

27.   Dimensions of an engagement culture (see Figure 23.4) can easily be recollected through the acronym – 'ESCAPE ROT'. First, employees should feel empowered. Information should be shared so that they are enabled to make decisions and act autonomously. Not only should goals be clear but employees should share and be aligned with them. Employees should have the power, freedom and discretion to plan and undertake their work and in determining the procedures to be used in carrying it out. When employees participate in making decisions, they feel more engaged in the organization. Decision-making tends to be pushed down to the lowest possible level. Employees need to understand how their job contributes to the organizational objectives and mission and what they must do more of and do differently to help the business succeed. Celebrating their contribution will make them feel more valued and committed. The communication climate should be open and allow for two-way feedback. Where there is an engagement culture there are mechanisms for employees to communicate upwards on a regular basis. Finally, there is trust in leadership and in management. Senior managers build trust by developing a clear vision of the organizations' future and communicating this to all employees. Organizations that value engagement are also likely to nurture an innovative environment (see previous chapter) and deliver challenging work assignments.

28.   Winning the hearts and minds of employees is a goal of those seeking to develop a culture of engagement. The hearts of employees may be won through the organization purpose. Purpose is the belief that what

FIGURE 23.4 Dimensions of an engagement culture

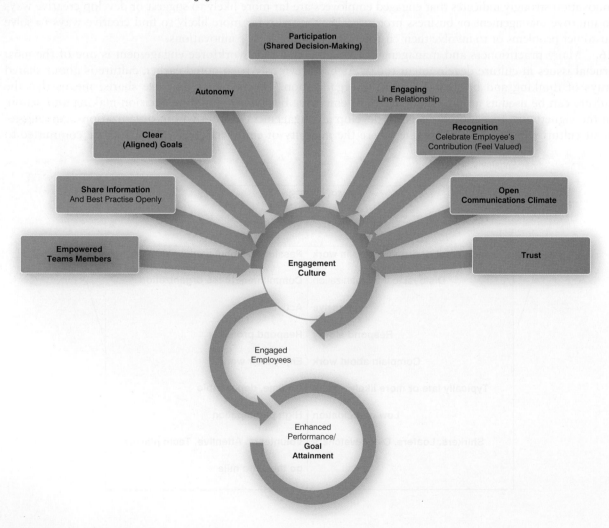

we are doing is meaningful and worthwhile; that we are contributing to more than just the bottom line. Managers play an important role in building and supporting this sense of purpose. Aside from communicating the mission they can connect with, recognize and appreciate employees. They can engage minds through autonomy, and by providing challenges to employees, stretching them so that they have the opportunity to develop. Managers can then provide direction to focus employee energy, letting people know what is important and providing them with continual information regarding expectations and their performance.

CONCLUSION

29.   In this chapter we discussed various forms of employee involvement (participation) and engagement. In turbulent environments and where work is surrounded by uncertainty, employees typically require greater freedom, autonomy and self-control over their work and responsibility for decision-making. We discussed delegation as the process of allocating authority and responsibility to others throughout the various levels of the organization. Whereas managers occasionally used delegation throughout the twentieth century, in the twenty-first century empowerment and engagement became the norm. As environments became more dynamic and turbulent, empowerment and engagement (more than simple delegation) became a necessity in many organizations. Like empowerment, a 'one size fits all' approach to enabling engagement is ineffective, because levels of engagement and its drivers vary according to the organization, employee group, the individual and the job itself.

QUESTIONS

1   Compare and contrast the related concepts of delegation, empowerment and employee engagement.

2   Contrast three companies with which you are familiar and discuss the extent of empowerment you might expect to witness within the organizations. Explain your expectations.

3   Whilst visiting a company, a manager informs you of her intent to further empower employees in her department. She would like your advice on the techniques and practices associated with empowerment. You should list and describe five common approaches. You should also discuss the prerequisites for enabling empowerment strategies.

4   What are the general arguments for empowering employees within contemporary organizations?

USEFUL WEBSITES

IPA: **www.ipa-involve.com/employee-engagement**
    Employee engagement

REFERENCES

Bates, S. (2004) 'Getting Engaged', *HR Magazine*, 49(2): 44–51.
Buchanan, D. and Huczynski, A. (2010) *Organizational Behaviour*, 7th edn, Financial Times Press.
Gallup (2006) 'Gallup Study: Engaged Employees Inspire Company Innovation', *Gallup Business Journal*, October 12, 2006 available online at **http://businessjournal.gallup. com/content/24880/gallup-study-engaged-employees-inspire-company.aspx**.
Harter, J.K., Schmidt, F.L. and Hayes, T.L. (2002) 'Business-unit-level relationship between employee satisfaction, employee engagement, and business outcomes: a meta-analysis', *Journal of Applied Psychology*, 87(2): 268–279.
Lashley, C. (1999) 'Employee empowerment in services: a framework for analysis', *Personnel Review*, 28(3): 169–191.
Robertson-Smith, G. and Markwick, C. (2009), 'Employee Engagement – A review of current thinking', Institute for Employment Studies (Report 469) available from University of Sussex.
Sisson, K. and Bach, S. (1999) *Personnel Management*, Blackwell Publishers.

CHAPTER 24
REORGANIZING: MANAGING CHANGE

Key Concepts

- Change model
- Continuous change
- Episodic change
- Force-field analysis
- Organizational change
- Readiness for change
- Resistance to change

Learning Outcomes   Having read this chapter, you should be able to:

- describe the main theoretical foundations of change management
- explain the planned and the emergent approach to change
- discuss the common change management models
- understand resistance to change
- evaluate the role of leaders, managers and change agents in the change process.

1.   The chapters in this section have been about the management activity of organizing (as a part of the POMC approach); adding structure, determining, designing and coordinating efficiently the work activities of business units and departments and allocating responsibilities and resources for the achievement of plans. The aim has been to construct a workforce and transformational resources into an orderly, functional, structured whole, able to fulfil its purpose and attain goals. This is never a one-off management activity and there is a constant need to reorganize – to transform, rearrange, restructure, adjust and change the way in which the workforce and transformational resources are organized and used. This is for the purpose of updating and improving, competing, seizing opportunity and averting threat, surviving and attaining goals. Change is fundamental in order to guarantee long-term success within an organization. In our previous discussions about contingency theory we noted that the organization must align itself with its environment. We only have to look briefly at today's environment to note constant change. Most contemporary management scholars and practitioners agree that the amount, pace, unpredictability and impact of change are

greater than ever before. New products, processes and services have appeared at an ever-increasing rate. Local markets have become global markets and industries have been opened up to competition.

2.   Within organizations we have observed restructuring, delayering, value chain fragmentation, outsourcing, culture change programmes, business process re-engineering, the implementation of enterprise systems, empowerment and engagement strategies, the development of competencies and capabilities, new business models and the introduction of new products and services. Yet perhaps the major **organizational changes** observed over the past 20 years may be better known for their failure than their success. Changes can take longer to implement than planned (time problems); may not live up to expectations (quality problems) or may cost more to implement than was budgeted (cost overrun problems). There is little doubt then that managing change is very difficult and risky. Change management requires an interdisciplinary perspective and an understanding of organization, strategy, change, systems, psychological and sociological theories.

3.   Before attempting to change something, managers must understand what it is they intend to change. They must also be aware of intervention strategies, alternative solutions and how to overcome **resistance to change**. We start by defining change and exploring what it is that can and usually is changed within organizations. Several change types are identified and the need for change discussed further. In recognition of the absence of a single universal change theory we explore a number of related theories used in change management. A variety of **change models** are discussed. Later in the chapter we consider the role of the change agent and the challenges associated with implementing change, particularly in the face of resistance and the context of complexities associated with contemporary organizations.

24.1 UNDERSTANDING CHANGE

4.   To change something implies altering it, varying or modifying it in some way. Organizations change, or adapt, what they want to achieve and how they wish to achieve it. Some organizations change mainly in response to external circumstances (reactive change); others change principally because they have decided to change (proactive change). Some organizations are conservative in outlook, seeking little in the way of change; others are entrepreneurial in outlook, ever seeking new opportunities and new challenges. Some organizations are constructed (even constricted!) so that change, i.e. adaptation, is a slow and difficult process; others are designed with an in-built flexibility, enabling adaptation to take place regularly and relatively easily.

5.   Change is a process which is rarely contained by functional or specialist boundaries. Change in one part of an organization invariably affects people and processes in another part (refer to Section 5, Systems Theory). As Figure 24.1 illustrates, organizational change can influence, and be influenced by, several important features of organizational life – the organizational mission and strategy, its structure, products and processes, its people and culture, and the nature of the technology employed. These features of the organization are themselves affected by the nature of the external environment.

6.   It is true that a successful organization's practices and behaviours, having worked for decades, can cease to be right? The realities (environment) faced by each organization change quite dramatically, though assumptions about them may not. Whereas reality may change, the theory of the business (assumptions about the environment, the mission and the core competencies needed) may not change with it – in some organizations. Planned change is usually triggered by the failure of people to create continuously adaptive organizations. Thus, organizational change routinely occurs in the context of failure of some sort. Drucker (1994) suggests each organization should challenge every product frequently, every service, every policy, every distribution channel with the question: If we were not in it already, would we be going into it now? Without this self-challenging approach, an organization will be overtaken by events.

7.   Organizational change concerns the alteration of organizational components (such as the mission, strategy, goals, structure, processes, systems, technology and people) to improve the effectiveness or efficiency of the organization. Change may take place in any part and at any level of the organization. When we think of organizational change, we may think of significant changes aimed at making the organization more effective such as mergers, acquisitions, buyouts, downsizing, restructuring, launch of new products and the outsourcing of major organizational activities. Examples of smaller (efficiency-based) changes include: departmental reorganizations, the implementation of new technologies and systems. The primary needs for change derive from the need for alignment between the organizations' internal and external environments.

FIGURE 24.1 Organizational change and key organizational features

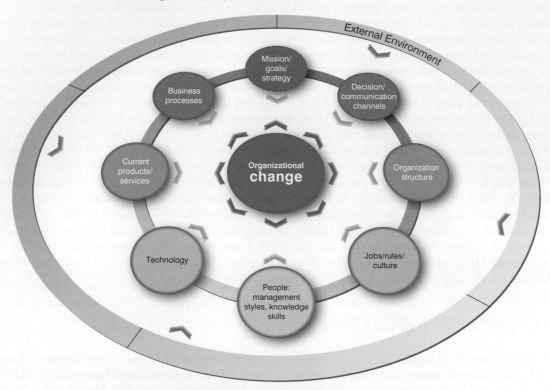

8.   Change can be triggered by any number of external and internal factors. External triggers may include:

-   changes in demand for the organization's products or services

-   threatening tactics of competitors

-   arrival of a newcomer with a competing product or service

-   takeover of the business by a more powerful enterprise

-   merger of the business with another

-   failure of a key supplier to meet the organization's requirements

-   development of new technologies now available for application

-   political changes.

9.   An important point concerning these external triggers is that some are less predictable than others, and therefore less open to planned (i.e. proactive) change. Internal triggers, which should, in theory, be more predictable indicators of change, include the following:

-   planned changes in strategy

-   efforts to introduce cultural changes

-   need to improve productive efficiency/make better use of resources

-   need to improve the quality of products or services

-   need to respond to the development of new products/services

    –   need to improve standards/systems for dealing with suppliers

    –   need to deploy people (the human resources) where they are most effective.

10.   In facing up to these internal **triggers of change**, management must plan how best to respond to them. Some changes will have been announced well beforehand, and in these cases planning is proactive. Some changes will, however, be brought about by a crisis of some kind (e.g. the failure of a new product or supplier or even a key manager). In these latter cases, it may be impossible to plan in any detail, but only to respond reactively and urgently. Where key individuals or products are concerned, however, well-organized enterprises will usually have a fallback position in the shape of a 'contingency plan'. This may not be the ideal response, but at least it will prevent a crisis from turning into a tragedy of major proportions. Having looked inside and outside the organization, it must ask if they are still in the right business and doing the right things or whether there is a need for change. If a need for change is identified, the organization must also consider how ready it is for such change. This will mean examining culture and then determining whether they are locked into particular ways of doing things.

11.   There are many types of change such as discontinuous versus **continuous** and revolutionary versus evolutionary. The phrase **episodic change** is used to group together organizational changes that tend to be infrequent, discontinuous and intentional. Such changes arise as a result of the organization's inability to respond adequately to external environmental changes. Change may be planned or unplanned – planned change is a deliberate, conscious decision to improve the organization in some manner. Furthermore, change may take place at a variety of levels. At the total system level, the emphasis is on organizational purpose, mission, strategy, structure of culture. In some cases there will be a need for significant (transformational) and in other cases less significant (transactional) change.

24.2 BUILDING THE NEED FOR CHANGE

12.   In many cases, the need for change will derive from an evaluation of organizational outputs (products and services), where the organization operates, what it does (primary activities) and how it performs such activities (work). Some people may consider the current way of working to be ineffective or inefficient or may consider that such ways of working will become ineffective or inefficient in the future. The need for change is the pressure for change in the situation – sometimes the pressure is high (typically a problem of ineffectiveness), other times lower (a problem of inefficiency). This need can be viewed as a 'real need', demonstrated by data and facts, or a 'perceived need' seen by change participants. The need for change will often be based upon the analysis of internal and external data or the perspectives of the various stakeholders, the concerns of senior managers and change leaders in particular.

13.   The need for change may arise from a crisis, commanding a reactive approach or from proactive thinking. In some cases it will result from new opportunities to do things differently and in other cases will be driven by threat, the failures of some existing system or approach to work. It is important to make such distinctions as they will impact upon the ease with which the argument for change can be based, the need for change being clearer in the case of a crisis. Once a need for change has been identified by a change initiator, it will then become important to direct the organization's attention to change (change awareness) and gain support for it. In many cases there is likely to be confusion and disagreement over the need for change, what needs changing, when and how to bring about change.

24.3 CHANGE MODELS

14.   A variety of models exist to help managers develop a sense of what needs to change in their organization; such models enable the organization to be analyzed and consider the organization's strategy, how it fits with the changing environment and how the various components of the organization also fit with the strategy and the environment. We develop an appreciation of what to change, through the use of models of organizational analysis such as the McKinsey 7S model, the Nadler and Tushman congruence framework and the Burke-Litwin model.

15.   The organizational system (diamond) model proposed in the 1960s by the late Dr Harold Leavitt, a long-time business professor at Stanford University, is made of four major components: task (the organization's purpose), people (those who carry out the task), technology (tools and computers, etc.) and structure. The components are interdependent and a change in any one of the components will result in change amongst the other three, he argues. The Leavitt model adopts a systems theory perspective but does not incorporate open systems theory, i.e. takes no account of the external environment.

16.   A decade later, Nadler and Tushman developed their model (refer back to Figure 9.2 Congruence model of organizational behaviour). Recognizing the organization is influenced by its environment, their model took account of both systems and open system theory. Nadler and Tushman divided their model into inputs, process and outputs. Their (transformation or internal) process contained similar components to the model proposed by Leavitt. Inputs came from the environment including organizational history and current strategy which help define how people in the organization behave. Nadler and Tushman also argued a need for the transformational process components to be congruent or 'fit' with each other. Nadler and Tushman did however recognize that such congruence may present advantages and disadvantages. In the short term, a system with high congruence is an effective and performing system. However, such a system may be resistant to change. Their model suggests there is no one best way to organize. Rather, the most effective way of organizing is determined by the nature of the strategy as well as the work, the individuals who are members of the organization, and the informal processes and structures (including culture) which have emerged over time. One criticism of this model is that a system which is highly congruent may in fact be resistant to change as it develops ways of insulating itself from outside influences.

17.   One way of thinking about organizational components and their alignment with the environment can be found in the McKinsey 7S model explained by Peters and Waterman (1982: p. 10). The components of this model include strategy, structure, systems, style, staff, shared values and skills. The underlying thesis of the model is that organizational effectiveness is a function of the degree of 'fit' achieved amongst these factors and the environment. When organizations experience change, the degree of 'fit' is affected, and the challenge of change management is to make changes so that high levels of 'fit' can be achieved amongst the seven elements. Changes to one of the components can affect all the other components. The strengths of the 7S model are its description of organizational variables which convey obvious importance – strategy, structure, systems, etc. – and its recognition of the importance of the interrelationships amongst all of these seven variables or dimensions. The 7S model, on the other hand, does not contain any external environment or performance variables. The model is a description of these seven important elements and shows that they interact to create organizational patterns but there is no explanation of how these seven dimensions are affected by the external environment. Nor do we know how each dimension affects the other or what specific performance indices may be involved.

18.   More recently Burke and Litwin (1992) presented a complex model of organizational performance and change. Their model conforms to the open system way of thinking, with the external environment represented as an input. The authors go beyond description and suggest causal linkages that hypothesize how performance is affected and how effective change occurs. Change is depicted in terms of both process and content, with particular emphasis on transformational compared with transactional factors. Transformational change occurs as a response to the external environment and directly affects organizational mission and strategy, the organization's leadership and culture. In turn, the transactional factors are affected – structure systems, management practices and climate. These transformational and transactional factors together affect motivation, which, in turn, affects performance. Through their model, Burke and Litwin attempt to provide a causal framework that encompasses both the what and the how – what organizational dimensions are key to successful change and how these dimensions should be linked causally to achieve the change goals. Burke and Litwin incorporated dimensions from earlier models, in one form or another, to develop their model. Interestingly, both the 7S and the Burke and Litwin models were informed by consulting practice.

24.4 GENERIC CHANGE MODEL

19.   Figure 24.2 (taken from Kelly, 2009) also shows the environment as a driver for change – a source of opportunity and threat, mediated through individuals who then see a need to change aspects within the organization. In some cases the change initiators are the senior managers (top-down change) and in other

FIGURE 24.2 Generic change model

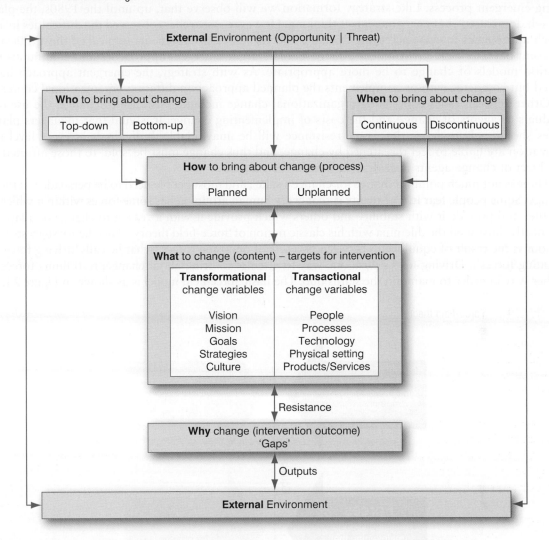

cases may be managers, professionals or employees from lower levels within the organization (bottom-up change). Change may also be initiated by external consultants or other employees. Change may occur as a 'one-off' activity or may be viewed as a constant process of alignment and pursuit for efficiency. In some cases the change will be formally planned, typically using rational tools and techniques and in other cases will simply emerge from the day-to-day activities and decisions of the organizational members. As we said earlier, there are many aspects of the organization that can be changed – some more fundamental than others. Change managers differentiate between major or transformational change or less major **transactional change**. Examples of transformational and transactional targets for intervention are shown in Figure 24.2. Change is initiated for a reason – there is a need for the change. In some cases the need is more obvious than other cases. In the case of the model shown in Figure 24.2 we could have shown the 'Why change' box directly beneath the environment. We have shown it further down the model to emphasize a need to demonstrate the need for change in order to overcome resistance, particularly emanating from the recipients of change.

24.5 RESISTANCE TO CHANGE

20.   Two main approaches to change management have been suggested in the literature: a planned and an emergent approach. The former tends to see change management as a formal, top-down, rational and

pre-planned process whilst the latter sees change management as a disordered, bottom-up, less rational and ongoing emergent process. Like strategy formation we will observe that, up until the 1980s, the planned approach dominated change management thinking. However, researchers observed the difficulties in applying such approaches in ever increasing dynamic and turbulent environments (typical of the 1990s and of the present day). In such environments, many scholars argue emergent approaches and continuous transformation models of change to be more appropriate. As with strategy, the emergent approach has not replaced but competes with or complements the planned approach in differing organizational contexts.

21.   Other general issues concerning organizational change include resistance to change, the use of key individuals as agents of change and the costs of implementing change. It is vital that managers planning changes should acknowledge that some resistance will be unavoidable. Individuals at every level in the organization are liable to feel threatened by change, and thus change must be 'sold' to those affected by it. The subject of change agents is dealt with later in the chapter.

22.   There is not much point in 'change for change's sake', and most people need to be persuaded of the need to change. Some people fear it. The reality is that every human grouping has some forces within it which keep it together and provide it with stability and others which provide it with a reason to change or adapt. Kurt Lewin neatly illustrated the dilemma with his classic notion of 'force-field theory'. This theory suggests that all behaviour is the result of equilibrium between two sets of opposing forces (what he calls 'driving forces' and 'restraining forces'). Driving forces push one way to attempt to bring about change; restraining forces push the other way in order to maintain the status quo. The basic force-field model is as shown in Figure 24.3.

FIGURE 24.3 **Force-field theory**

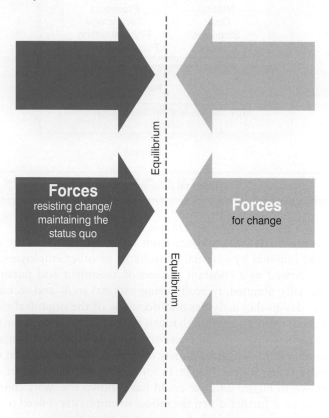

23.   Generally speaking, human beings tend to prefer to use driving forces to bring about change. They want to 'win' by exerting pressure on those who oppose them, but, as Lewin's model suggests, the more one side pushes, the more the other side resists, resulting in no change. The better way of overcoming resistance, therefore, is by focusing on the removal, or at least weakening, of the objections and fears of the resisting side. Thus the initial policy should not be 'how can we persuade them of our arguments for change?', but rather 'what are their objections/fears, and how can we deal with them?'

24. Lewin developed a three-stage approach to changing behaviour, which was later adapted by Edgar Schein. This comprises the following three steps:

1) Unfreezing existing behaviour (gaining acceptance for change)

2) Changing behaviour (adopting new attitudes, modifying behaviour)

3) Refreezing new behaviour (reinforcing new patterns of thinking/working).

The unfreezing stage is aimed at ensuring people see that change is not only necessary but desirable. The change stage is mainly a question of identifying what needs to be changed in people's attitudes, values and actions, and then helping them to acquire ownership of the changes. The role of a change agent (i.e. a person who is responsible for helping groups and individuals to accept new ideas and practices) is crucial at this stage. The refreezing stage is aimed at consolidating and reinforcing the changed behaviour by various support mechanisms (encouragement, promotion, participative management style, more consultation, etc.).

24.6 IMPLEMENTING CHANGE

25. We now turn to the action side of change – making it happen. Change is about replacement – one system for another, one process for another, one strategy or mission for another. There are two dominant approaches to change implementation: the planned and the emergent. There are many prescriptions for the planned approach and we start by describing a generic change process. Many change management scholars suggest the planned approach to change is closely associated with the practice of organizational development (Carnall, 2007). Despite this approach originating during the middle of the twentieth century it has evolved to present an integrated framework of theories and practices capable of solving or helping to solve most of the important problems confronting the human side of organizations. Organization development (OD) represents an enormously influential mode of thinking about and practice in the change management field; it is about planned change, ensuring individuals, teams and organizations function better. We therefore describe this approach immediately after describing the generic change process. Whilst linear models and plans have the merit of simplicity they are not without criticism. Recognizing criticisms of the planned approach (that it is impossible to plan in a constantly changing world), in the final part of this chapter we briefly describe emergent approaches to change.

26. Williams, Woodward and Dobson (2002) raise the following practical questions relating to the implementation of change: do we need external consultants for the implementation process? How do we motivate people to implement change? What kinds of leadership are best when implementing change? How can we help staff cope with the stress of change? And how do we help individuals to adopt mental sets compatible with the changes being introduced? In addition we might have further questions such as: should change be a top-down or bottom-up approach, planned or emergent? What tools and techniques may be appropriate? We will consider a number of these questions throughout the remainder of this chapter.

24.7 PLANNED APPROACHES TO CHANGE

27. We have outlined a generic 'planned' approach to change (change process) in Figure 24.4. Working around the model, a number of circumstances may trigger change such as performance problems and new opportunity or threat – competition will drive organizations and individuals to innovate and change. Performance feedback and benchmarking is used to identify areas in need of attention. Such triggers will create forces for change. The forces act upon the status quo, however there will also be forces for stability. There then follows an initial analysis or diagnosis phase. A range of tools and techniques may be applied. We have already discussed tools such as PESTLE, SWOT and attitude surveys. Additionally, organizational and industry data may be gathered, analyzed and presented to define the change problem.

FIGURE 24.4 Change process

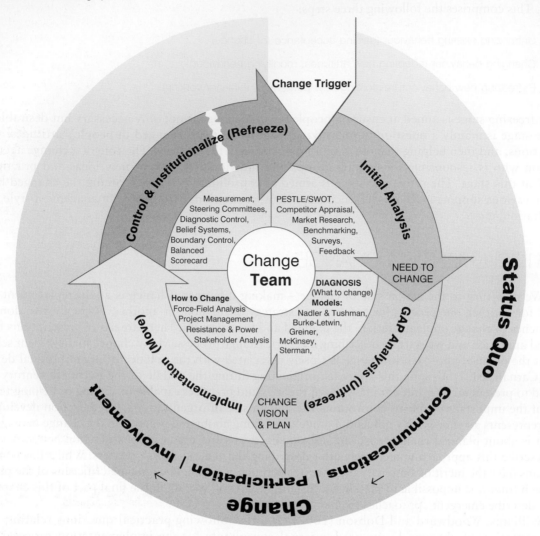

28.   Having analyzed and diagnosed the present ('as-is') situation, organizations must decide where they want to be in the future (vision) and how to get there, i.e. what to change. Additionally, they must establish and communicate the need for change and overcome pre-change problems, the organization must then execute the actions that will bring about the change. Implementing the change involves translating the change vision into specific actions undertaken by employees. The plan outlines targets and dates and considers contingencies. Programme and project management tools and techniques are typically adopted to ensure the change plan is executed as intended.

29.   Change requires decision-making and resource allocation and is therefore dependent on the will of the organization's power holders. Successful change managers build a change team, develop detailed communication plans and understand how to manage the change transition. Change agents and the change team (see centre of Figure 24.4) specify who does what, when and how and may manage planned change through the use of project management tools and techniques. There is a need to mobilize commitment to change (through joint diagnosis and the development of a shared vision and fostering consensus), reduce resistance, communicate and manage the change. We have previously mentioned the need to educate and communicate with others so that they can see the need and logic for the change. There is also a need to get others involved and participating and to allocate resources, training or time to support the change. Change agents attempt to create willingness for change by making people aware of the pressures for change.

30.   Aside from considering the forces for change, the organization will seek to understand people's fears and concerns that may bring about resistance to change. Openness helps people to understand the need for change. There is a need to gain support (see **coalition building**) from people and as a consequence, many organizations develop an involvement strategy. Communication and involvement are essential to gain people's understanding of the need for change and to develop their commitment to such change. Successful change requires attention to many areas but it is generally thought there is a need to establish a sense of urgency; create a guiding coalition; develop a vision and strategy; communicate this with others; empower action; generate short-term wins; consolidate gains and produce more change and anchor new approaches in the culture – see Kotter's (2007) 'Eight Steps To Transforming Your Organization'.

31.   Finally, measures are critical components of the control system which guide the change and integrate the initiatives and efforts of various parties. There are many ways to control change projects and care must be taken in selecting the methods of control and the variables to measure; noting the belief that what gets measured gets managed. Typically, a change champion will fight for the change and senior executives will act as sponsors, fostering commitment to the change and helping to make it happen. In larger change initiatives, it is common to establish a steering and a design and implementation team. The steering team provide advice to the champion regarding the direction of the change in light of other events and priorities in the organization. The steering team plays an advisory and navigational function for the change project and is the major policy determining group. The design and implementation team focuses on the tasks that must be accomplished and deals with the stakeholders who have primary responsibility for implementation. Typically, the design and implementation team will often have a Change Project Manager who tracks the change efforts and the team's progress towards change targets.

24.8 ORGANIZATION DEVELOPMENT (OD)

32.   As was noted earlier, the planned approach to change is closely associated with the practice of **organizational development** (Burnes, 2009). In the USA at least, OD has become a profession with its own regulatory bodies, to which OD practitioners must belong, with its own recognized qualifications, a host of approved tools and techniques and its own ethical code of practice. Organization development is a generic term which embraces a wide range of planned intervention strategies which are aimed at the development of individuals, groups and the organization as a total system. More specifically, it is a strategy and systematic process for improving organizational effectiveness by means of behavioural science approaches, involving the application of diagnostic and problem-solving skills (typically by an external consultant) in collaboration with the organization's management. OD is a methodology or technique used to effect change and managed from the top. Furthermore, it is an organization-wide process that takes essentially a systems view of the organization and utilizes the techniques and approaches of the behavioural sciences.

33.   OD is utilized when senior management recognize that the key components of the organizational system are not working harmoniously together. In other words, when the complex mix of objectives, people and structure is failing to produce the fruits of organizational activity, then is the time to consider revitalizing the entire enterprise. This situation could be due to rapid expansion of the business, or radical changes in markets or technology, or to internal social pressures for change.

34.   The success of any OD programme depends largely upon the part played by the change agent. The change agent must be a good relationship builder able to establish credibility and gain trust and respect in order to obtain the commitment required. The roles required by the third party range from the highly directive, leader type of role to a non-directive counselling role. In the first mentioned role, the third party will tend to prescribe what is best for clients; at the other extreme they will tend to reflect issues and problems back to clients without offering any judgement. In between these extremes are several other possible roles, as indicated in Figure 24.5.

35.   The desirable qualities, values and abilities required of change agents include the ability to listen diagnostically, and to apply rational approaches to problems and situations, plus handle conflict openly and constructively. Change agents also require good communication skills such as interviewing and presentation skills and the ability to establish and maintain comfortable relationships with a wide cross-section of people.

FIGURE 24.5 Range of roles for third party

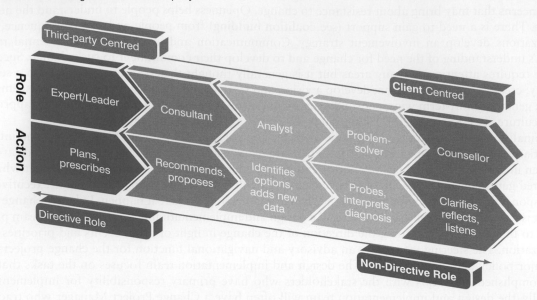

36.   The most significant benefits of an OD programme are indicated below. The relative importance and relevance of any one benefit obviously depends upon the needs of the organization at the commencement of the programme. However, in general terms, the benefits of OD can be summarized as follows:

–   it enables an organization to adapt to change with the full commitment of employees

–   it can lead to structures that facilitate employee cooperation and the achievement of tasks

–   it releases latent energy and creativity in the organization

–   it can improve understanding of organizational objectives by employees

–   it can improve decision-making processes and skills

–   it provides opportunities for management development in the context of real organizational problems

–   it may stimulate more creative approaches to problem-solving throughout the organization

–   it usually increases the ability of management groups to work as teams.

24.9 DIFFICULTIES IN IMPLEMENTING CHANGE

37.   Kotter (2007) identifies eight typical mistakes made by senior management in relation to organizational change:

1)   They allow too much complacency

2)   They fail to create a sufficiently powerful guiding coalition

3)   They underestimate the power of vision (the sense of an end-goal)

4)   They greatly under-communicate the vision to be attained

5)   They permit obstacles to stand in the way of the vision

6)   They fail to create short-term wins

7) They declare victory too soon

8) They neglect to anchor changes in the organization's culture.

38. The result of such errors is to reduce the positive effects of new strategies or schemes, producing fewer outcomes over a longer than expected period, with greater costs than forecast. Kotter's answer to the above problems is to establish an eight-stage process of creating major changes, as follows:

1) create, and sustain, a sense of urgency about the future

2) create and empower a leadership team (a 'guiding coalition')

3) develop an end-goal (a 'vision') and a strategy for achieving it

4) constantly communicate the new vision and set out the required changes in behaviour

5) empower employees to help change happen by removing obstacles

6) generate benefits in the short-term so that people can see tangible improvements

7) consolidate short gains and produce more change by continuing the actions

8) embed the new approaches in the organization's culture ('anchoring') so as to avoid eventual regression into previous practices.

24.10 EMERGENT APPROACHES

39. Supporters of emergent change tend to be united more by their disbelief in planned change than by a commonly agreed alternative. Nevertheless, there does seem to be some agreement regarding the main view of what constitutes emergent change. It is a continuous process of experimentation and adaptation, aimed at matching an organization's capabilities to the demands of a dynamic and uncertain environment and such change is typically achieved through many small to medium-sized incremental changes. Over time these can lead to a major reconfiguration and transformation of an organization. Change is a multilevel, cross-organizational process that unfolds in an iterative and disordered fashion, over a period of years and comprises a series of interlocking projects.

40. Proponents of the emergent approach believe change is a political-social process and not an analytical-rational one. The role of managers is not to plan or implement change but to create or cultivate an organizational structure and climate which encourages and sustains experimentation, learning and risk taking and to develop a workforce that will take responsibility for identifying the need for change and implementing it. Managers are expected to become facilitators and hold responsibility for developing a collective vision or common purpose that provides direction to their organization. The key organizational activities which allow these elements to operate successfully are: information gathering – about the external environment and internal objectives and capabilities; communication – the transmission, analysis and discussion of information; and learning – the ability to develop new skills, identify appropriate responses and derive knowledge from their own and others' past and present actions.

41. The emergent approach is founded on the assumption that organizations operate in a dynamic environment where they have to transform themselves continuously in order to survive. Only by continuous transformation will organizations keep aligned with their environment and thus survive. Similarly, when the pace of environmental change is so rapid and complex it is not possible for a small number of senior managers to identify, plan and implement the necessary organizational response. There is a need for a bottom-up response. Organizations wishing to create a climate for change must enable a bottom-up approach by empowering employees (see previous chapter). There is a need for openness, broad participation and the sharing of information, particularly about the external environment, benchmarking and measurements about targets. Managers need to encourage experimentation and occasionally diverging views. Organizations seeking such an approach will also have a strong customer focus, a strategy of continuous learning and will be oriented toward the environment.

CONCLUSION

42.   Organizational change concerns the alteration of organizational components to improve the effectiveness or efficiency of the organization. Change may take place in any part and at any level of the organization. The primary needs for change derive from the need for alignment between the organizations' internal and external environments. Diagnosis is used to motivate and determine what to change. Having established the need for change, change initiators then consider whether the organization is in fact ready for change. Two dominant approaches to change, planned and emergent, were described; the planned approach dominated management for much of the twentieth century. However, planned change has faced increasing levels of criticism due to the changing organizational context, i.e. from predictable to turbulent environments. In such environments, change must be a continuous process and in many cases it is difficult to determine what must be done and then create a sophisticated plan to achieve it. The emergent approach tends to see changes driven from the bottom-up rather than from the top-down and stresses change as an open-ended and continuous process of adaptation to changing conditions and circumstances. Various people are responsible for making change happen; leaders need to be persuasive and political and overcome resistance. They must monitor the environment, identify and establish the need for change and provide clear direction for organizational change effort. They must also communicate that need and initiate activities.

QUESTIONS

1   Discuss the need for change in organizations, listing possible reasons (with examples) why change occurs. Next, comment on how and why managers build the need for change.

2   Discuss how managers overcome resistance to change, commenting on force-field analysis and Lewin's three-stage approach to changing behaviour.

3   Discuss what is meant by planned and emergent approaches to change.

4   Identify and describe the typical stages/steps and activities in a planned approach to change.

5   Why do supporters of the emergent approach not favour the planned approach?

USEFUL WEBSITES

IFAL: **http://www.ifal.org.uk/** Action learning involves working on real problems, focusing on learning and actually implementing solutions. It is a form of learning by doing

CIPD: **www.cipd.co.uk/subjects/corpstrtgy/changemmt** Change management resources

Local Government Improvement and Development: **www.idea.gov.uk/idk/core/page.do?pageId=5829768** Information and downloads

Institute for employment studies: **www.employment-studies. co.uk/consult/index.php?id=org&tab=work** OD, change and organizational effectiveness

REFERENCES

Burke, W.W. and Litwin, G.H. (1992) 'A causal model of organizational performance and change', *Journal of Management*, 18(3): 523–545.

Burnes, B. (2009) *Managing Change*, 5th edn, Financial Times Press.

Carnall, C. (2007) *Managing Change in Organizations*, 5th edn, FT Prentice Hall.

Drucker, P. (1994) 'The theory of the business', *Harvard Business Review*, 72(5): 95–104.

Kelly, P.P. (2009) *International Business and Management*, Cengage Learning EMEA.

Kotter, J. (2007) 'Leading change', *Harvard Business Review*, 85(1): 96–103.

Peters, T. and Waterman, R. (eds.) (1982) *In Search of Excellence*, Harper Collins Business.

Williams, A., Woodward, S. and Dobson, P. (2002) 'Managing change successfully: using theory and experience to implement change', Thomson Learning.

CHAPTER 25
ORGANIZING
COMMUNICATIONS

Key Concepts

- Communication process
- Corporate communication
- Formal and informal communication
- Identity, image and reputation
- Strategic communication

Learning Outcomes Having read this chapter, you should be able to:

- discuss the purpose of communications for organizations
- contrast traditional with social models of business communication
- list key responsibilities of the corporate communications function
- evaluate common corporate communication tools and methods.

The most important thing in communication is to hear what isn't being said.

– Peter Drucker

1.   In Chapter 23 we argued a need for an engaged workforce and in this chapter we explore how organizations can strengthen relationships through internal communication. In the previous chapter we discussed change management and recognized the benefits of communication to the change process – keeping people informed in order to remove uncertainty and anxiety whilst building trust. Communication is required to reveal the need for change, capture feedback and inform of changes and successes. We also noted that communication and the communications climate was critical to the development of organizational culture in Chapter 14. Indeed much of what we have discussed in the planning, organizing and controlling section is reliant on effective communication. Communication is central to understanding organizational behaviour. Managers help develop culture through communication. They must communicate values, the mission and organizational purpose, goals and the expected way of doing things. They tell stories, issue rewards and sanction punishments. Communication also plays a major role in strategy, performance management and decision-making in particular. Interpersonal communication is important in building and sustaining relationships at work.

There is also a significant need for external communications: marketing to customers, investor relations, brand image and reputation management to include CSR. Thus there are many purposes for communication in organizations.

2.   Philip Clampitt, a Business Professor at the University of Wisconsin, defines communication as the transmission or reception of signals through some channels that humans interpret, based on a probabilistic system that is deeply influenced by context. We transmit by talking, writing, texting, illustrating and touching. We receive by listening, reading, watching or feeling. Signals can be verbal, non-verbal or visual and we use an ever-changing array of channels, including face-to-face, mobile phones and emails to send messages and information to others.

3.   As with many areas of management a review of the literature and communications theory reveals a traditional and more contemporary approach to communications. Companies have moved away from top-down, one-way communications using mass communication channels directed principally at employees, to engagement systems with a wide range of stakeholders, utilizing digital technologies as well as face-to-face meetings that encourage dialogue, participation and involvement – a more open communications climate. Employees are less likely to be in the office and may be scattered around the globe, often only reached through new communications technologies. Such technologies aid collaboration and can enable virtual teams. Communications are now considered to be of strategic importance; the (employee) communications function has moved out of HR and now typically reports directly to the CEO, reflecting greater significance and influence both internally and externally. Such functions embrace technology and a range of methods in order to engage rapidly within the global village.

4.   The communication that takes place in an organization is an important influence in the success of that organization (Clampitt, 2010). In the 1990s it was increasingly recognized by many employers and managers that the creation of effective communication is an extremely important aspect of the efficient running of organizations. Communication is a complex series of processes operating at all levels within organizations, ranging from the 'grapevine', to formalized systems. These can operate at many levels and can be one or two-way, top-down or bottom-up as well as across the organization. Formal communication involves presenting information in a structured and consistent manner. Such information is normally created for a specific purpose, making it likely to be more comprehensive, accurate and relevant than information transmitted using informal communication. Despite this, there are always unofficial, or informal, methods of communication within organizations, usually described as the 'grapevine', which refers to information passed on by individuals with no authority, and which gives rise to rumour and gossip. Sometimes such informal communication represents strongly felt opinions from amongst the workforce, and may eventually be recognized as legitimate, and be placed in the formal communication chain.

5.   Mintzberg (2011) discusses the job of managing and the role of communicating. He argues the job of managing to be significantly one of information processing, essentially through a great deal of listening, seeing and feeling, as well as a good deal of talking. Managers take in information through monitoring activities and send their information out through disseminating activities. Managers spend much of their time communicating – 'the medium through which managerial work is constituted'. We revisit Mintzberg's thoughts on the role of the manager in the next and final chapter of this section. Managers and the organization must understand how they can make the communication process and enabling technologies work for them. In order to do this they must understand the importance of communication, how communication takes place, how technology may enable communication, and must understand the barriers to communication if they are to become competent communicators, able to persuade and motivate others and build trusting relationships. Such matters and related theories, tools and techniques will be explored in this chapter. We start with the communication process.

25.1 COMMUNICATION PROCESS

6.   The transmission (exchange or sharing) of information between people and systems defines the communication process, see Figure 25.1. The transmitter (source) and receiver are entities (people or electronic devices) and the message (the content of communication – ideas, facts, opinions and feelings) may be communicated verbally or non-verbally through a variety of channels such as face-to-face, telephone,

FIGURE 25.1 Communication process

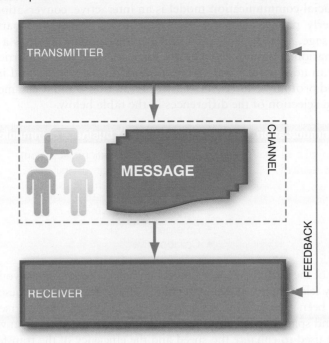

email, text or video conference. **Feedback** is used to detect how the message has been received and may be used to then modify the message. **Communications** may be formal or informal, verbal or non-verbal, written, electronic, synchronous or **asynchronous**. Furthermore, communication may be enabled by technology, discussed later. Skills often associated with communication include report-writing, chairing meetings, interviewing, interpersonal, persuasion, group work, marketing and selling.

7.   Paul Argenti, a Professor of Management and Corporate Communication at the Tuck School of Business at Dartmouth (2013: p. 40) suggests that delivering messages effectively involves two steps. A company must decide how it wants to deliver the message (choose a communication channel) and the approach to take in structuring the message itself. He lists several communication channels and categorizes them as old (spoken word, letter and printed media) and new (email, blogs, podcasts, text messaging, Internet, voice-mail, RSS feeds, Facebook, Twitter, etc.). Messages must be structured correctly, he argues, distinguishing direct from indirect approach. Direct structure means revealing your main point first and then explaining it whilst indirect means giving the context first and then revealing your main point.

8.   We stated that the content of communication (the message) may typically be classified as ideas, facts, opinions and feelings. Whether information is supplied in written, electronic or audio-visual forms, its essential purpose is to convey some message. In a work organization the message is usually factual, supplying information about internal policies and procedures, reporting on issues or providing details of meetings.

9.   This brings us on to the form in which communications are sent. Many of these have not changed much over the past decades. Internal memos, letters, formal reports, minutes of meetings, statements of accounts, invoices, bulletins and a variety of notices are still the principal form of formal communications, and have been unaffected by changes in technology. And, of course, we must not overlook the countless conversations that take place between individuals as they grapple with problems and situations at work. Written forms of communication tend to be more considered than face-to-face forms, and have a permanence that is lacking in the latter, which are usually spontaneous. Written forms are less susceptible to misinterpretation and, being visible, are less easy to deny, or qualify, than oral communications. This is one reason why written minutes of meetings are so important, because they attempt to capture the spoken words and put them on record. Written forms, of course, take longer to prepare, and are only as good as the powers of expression of the writer. Oral communication, whilst transient, nevertheless has the advantage of enabling the communicator to see the immediate **non-verbal** reactions of the recipient, such as facial expression, gestures and body posture.

10.   Bovee and Thill (2014: p. 53) discuss a new approach to business communication. In contrast to traditional models the **Social communication model** is an interactive, conversational approach to communication in which formerly passive audience members are empowered to participate fully. Instead of transmitting a fixed message, a sender in a social media environment initiates a conversation by sharing information. This information is often revised and reshaped by the web of participants as they share and comment on it. People can add or take from it, depending on their needs and interests. Bovee and Thill comment on the 'deep and profound' differences between traditional and social models of business communication. We have listed a selection of the differences in the table below.

Traditional business communication	Social models of business communication
• Monologue (lecture) • Unidirectional (one:one/one:many) • Control (hierarchical) • Few channels • Static • Planned • Unconnected	• Dialogue (conversation/discussion) • Multidirectional (many:many) • Influence (egalitarian) • Many channels • Dynamic • Emergent • Collaborative

11.   Until the last decade of the twentieth century, most internal communications would have been conducted in face-to-face meetings or by telephone, or presented in hard copy written format. These methods of communicating are still vital but have been enhanced by technology. Virtual markets, the dispersed organization, groups or teams separated in time and space depend upon tools to bring them together when working towards common goals. Technology may be used to enhance the speed and the efficiency of the transfer of information/message content. Technological advances such as electronic mail (email), web pages and intranets and mobile phones, high speed data connections and voice-over-IP have changed lifestyles around the world. What the electronic revolution has enabled is communication on a faster and more global basis than before. Items of news or information can be sent to colleagues on the other side of the world in an instant; such is the effectiveness of the Internet. Bovee and Thill (2014) recognize instant messaging, interactive websites and wikis as technologies that help with collaborating and sharing information; web-based meetings, video conferencing, voice technologies and mobile applications help professionals that are out of the office; blogging and podcasting keeps the organization connected with stakeholders and social networking, gaming technologies, community sites and microblogging can be used to build communities, see Figure 25.2

FIGURE 25.2   Communication tools

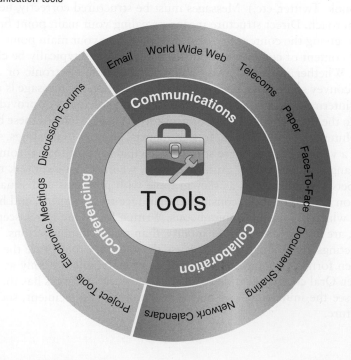

12.   When undertaking a review of the various communication technologies and tools it is clear that there have been a number of significant developments over the past 50 years. Interestingly, Bell and Smith (2010: p. 8) discuss the 'communications revolution' in phases. We have adapted their stage model in Figure 25.3. Whilst the developments depicted in the figure have brought many benefits they have also brought many new challenges, such as more words, information, documents, and less time to create, digest and respond.

FIGURE 25.3 Communication revolution – stage model

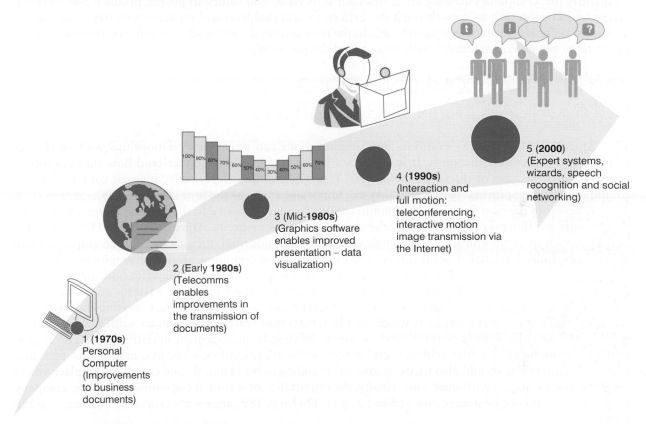

13.   The vast array of choices regarding communication content and channel demands employees understand the strengths and weaknesses of each within a specific context. Clampitt (2010: p. 98) offers a model for selecting appropriate communication technologies. He suggests that we consider our objectives as the sender of a message (e.g. to educate, motivate, persuade, inform and impress); the attributes of the message (length, timing, formality, complexity); the channel (email, telephone, face-to-face, text message) and the characteristics of the receiver (location, occupation, access and age). Traditionally there was a trade-off between the richness of information (amount, quality and interactivity) and the reach (number of people involved in the information exchange): typically, the richer the information the smaller the reach. New technologies mean that information exchange is open and virtually cost-free.

25.2 THE CORPORATE COMMUNICATIONS FUNCTION

14.   Corporate communication is a management function or department dedicated to the dissemination of information to key stakeholders, the implementation of corporate strategy and the development of messages for a variety of purposes for inside and outside the organization. Argenti (2013: p. 47) introduces the corporate communications function (formerly public relations). He lists several key responsibilities of corporate communications: investor relations, corporate website and advertising, marketing communications, community relations, employee communications and the corporate intranet.

15.   Having recognized the function he then debates whether or not it should be centralized or decentralized. A centralized model helps the organization achieve consistency and control whilst the decentralized model enables flexibility. Preferences are often dependent upon company size, geographical dispersion and the diversity of products and services. The function typically reports to the CEO but in some organizations may report to the Head of Marketing. In more sophisticated organizations, the corporate communications function may have specialists or departments that focus on image, reputation and public relations, crisis management, employee communications and marketing.

16.   Argenti (2013: p. 58) argues the most critical part of any corporate communications function focuses on identity (the companies defining attributes such as its vision and values, its people, products and services), image (the corporation as seen through the eyes of its stakeholders) and reputation strategy (the sum of how all stakeholders view the organization). In the next section we will discuss internal communications in more detail before commenting briefly on external communications.

25.3 INTERNAL COMMUNICATIONS: THE FLOW OF COMMUNICATIONS IN ORGANIZATIONS

17.   Argenti (2013: p. 175) examines how organizations can strengthen relationships with employees through internal communications. It is important for each employee to understand how they contribute to the ultimate success of the organization (2013: p. 177). Ultimately, effective internal communications should reinforce employees' beliefs that they are important assets to the firm (2013: p. 178).

18.   Whereas in the past the internal communications function reported to the Head of Human Resources, increasingly the function is falling under the communications umbrella. Argenti (2013: p. 181) argues the best approach to communicating with employees is through informal discussions between employees and supervisors. Indeed in smaller organizations the ideal method of communicating with employees is one-on-one or in meetings with small groups of employees. It is important to communicate both up and down. Respecting employees as well as listening to and interacting with them forms the basis for an effective internal communication program. Argenti suggests managers make time for face-to-face meetings but recognize the advantages of company intranets which enable managers to reach (make contact with) their employees quickly and broadly with important news or events relating to management initiatives; it is also important to communicate visually (video, social media, websites, television, webcasts, multimedia presentations). Organizations should also focus on internal branding to build morale and create a workplace where employees are engaged with their jobs. Finally, the importance of informal communications (the company grapevine) should not be underestimated and Argenti (2013: p. 189) argues it is crucial for managers to 'tap into it'.

19.   The (traditional) communications network of most organizations consists of vertical lines of communication providing downwards, and to some extent upwards, means of transmitting information, with integrating mechanisms such as committees built across these lines. Some organizations also provide lateral lines of communication, which are seen as having equal importance with the vertical. Mechanistic (bureaucratic) organizations tend to adopt vertical lines of communication and interaction, whereas organic (and horizontal) organizations tend to adopt lateral lines. Management communicates policies, plans, information and instructions downwards, and employees communicate ideas, suggestions, comments and complaints upwards. Common methods of downward communication include the company newspapers or magazines, intranet, newsletters, team briefings. The downwards communication is achieved by means of the management chain, whilst the upwards communication is achieved through surveys, quality circles and by work-group meetings, joint consultation and grievance procedures. The flow of information across the organization (lateral communication) is used for coordinating (and integrating) the efforts of more than one department or section, and this may be done by means of interdepartmental meetings or committees (and cross-functional information systems/business processes). This is a rational and controlled approach to the problem of integration.

20.   Research work carried out on groups at work suggests that, for simple problems, the quickest and most accurate results will be obtained by means of centralized (leader-dominated) channels of communication. Conversely, for complex problems, the most acceptable results are likely to come from decentralized

communication channels, where there is greater encouragement to share facts, views and feelings. The most frequent channel alternatives that have been tested are shown in Figure 25.4. The wheel represents the most centralized communication channel with its obvious leader or coordinator at the centre of relationships. By contrast, the circle and, especially, the all-channel networks rely on decentralized channels with shared leadership. The chain and 'Y' networks are basically hierarchical and not decentralized. Organic organizations would show a preference for all-channel networks, mechanistic organizations would tend to use the chain, the 'Y' and the wheel.

FIGURE 25.4 **Communication networks**

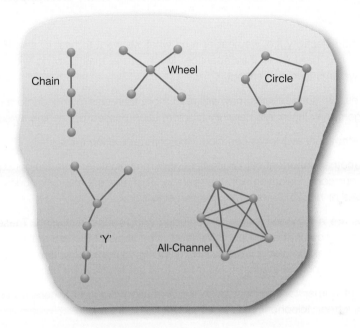

25.4 EXTERNAL COMMUNICATIONS: MARKETING COMMUNICATIONS

21.   Communication with external stakeholders is now viewed as a highly important aspect of the corporate communications function. Whilst Section 11 (see Chapter 33 Promotion in particular) considers marketing management, we will introduce aspects of marketing communication here. Chris Fill is internationally recognized for his contribution to **marketing communications** (formerly promotion and one of the marketing 'P's); he considers the scope, role and tasks. At a fundamental level, marketing communications are used to develop brand values and to help shape the behaviour of a target audience (Fill, 2013: p. 9). Planned marketing communications incorporate three key elements: tools (advertising, sales promotion, PR, direct marketing and personal selling), media and messages (informative or emotional). Similar to the HR role, the (strategic) primary role of marketing communications is to develop relationships with and engage audiences. At a more detailed level, the tasks of marketing communications are easily remembered through the DRIP elements:

Differentiate

Reinforce

Inform, and

Persuade (Fill, 2013: p. 15).

25.5 BARRIERS TO COMMUNICATION

22.   Many managers and employees must now communicate in the global marketplace. Similarly, the workplace is becoming increasingly diverse and heterogeneous, presenting communication challenges. The aspects of the communication content and context that can impair effective communication in the workplace are referred to as barriers to communication. There are many barriers to communication. Aside from culture and language, there are also geographical and time barriers, language and technology barriers, legal constraints, gender and power differences to consider. All may impair communications. In many cases the receiver's understanding may not be the same as the speaker's meaning.

23.   There are numerous barriers to communication, and some of the most important ones are discussed briefly below:

- Individual bias and selectivity, i.e. we hear or read what we want to hear or see. People are often unaware of their bias until it is brought to their attention. Much of the bias is to do with cultural background and personal value systems (see perception).

- Status differences, i.e. subordinates may well read more than was intended into a manager's message. By contrast, managers may listen less carefully to information passed up the line by subordinates.

- Fear and other emotional overtones can cloud the communication message.

- Lack of trust is another important barrier to effective communication. If we are not sure of someone, we tend to hold back in our communication with that person. This mistrust may arise because of doubts about the recipient's motives or his ability to grasp what is being said.

- Verbal difficulties are a frequent source of confusion and misunderstanding. These may arise because of the sheer lack of fluency on the part of the sender, or because of the use of jargon, or perhaps because of pitching the message at too high a level of understanding. In terms of written words, the barriers are usually those associated with long-windedness, i.e. a failure to get to the point quickly and concisely.

- Another important barrier to communication is information overload (where a person is overloaded with memos, reports, letters, telephone messages, etc.).

Additional barriers such as physical, perceptual, emotional, motivational and organizational are recognized by Bell and Smith (2010: p. 35–37). Overcoming or at least reducing the effects of barriers to communication mainly consists of finding answers to the issues raised in the paragraph above.

25.6 COMMUNICATIONS STRATEGY AND ETHICAL ISSUES

24.   Communication can take place to further operational, tactical or strategic goals; it may occur in an ad hoc or organized manner. Whereas **strategic communication** is communication aligned with the company's overall strategy (Argenti, 2013), **communication strategy** refers to the macro-level communication choices we make based on organizational goals and judgements about others' reactions, which serve as a basis for action (Clampitt, 2010). It recognizes that communication is central to engagement and performance. We have previously identified popular communication methods and an effective communication strategy should:

- Target communications to the audience (select the most apt method)

- Utilize mixed methods (a single method is often less effective)

- Be clear and consistent

- Be culturally sensitive

- Ensure communication is two-way (dialogue and feedback)

- Foster a climate of freedom of expression (without fear but with responsibility).

25.   Communication methods include (some methods can be used as both a one or two-way mechanism):

Top-Down (One-way)	Two-Way
• Chain of command	• Suggestion schemes
• Team briefings	• Open door policy
• Company intranet	• Quality circles
• Newsletter etc.	• Surveys
• Noticeboards	• Interactive systems
• Conferences and seminars	• Team meetings
	• Workshops

26.   We discussed ethics in Chapter 18. Every communication decision has an ethical dimension to it, argues Clampitt (2010: p. 47). Choosing to disclose information, motives or feelings to others inevitably involves an ethical element. Company directors, managers and employees must make ethical judgements in choosing what, when and how to communicate. Managers may face many ethical dilemmas. For example, should they keep information secret or communicate with others? What should a manager or employee do when they disagree with organizational policy, procedure, practice or decision? Should they share their concerns and engage in constructive debate and dialogue or remain quiet through fear of possible retaliation? Should they blow the whistle and communicate with the media about corporate abuses or safety hazards? Should we engage in rumour and gossip which could have a disastrous effect on organizations and people? Ethical communicators must consider what is fair, right and wrong. However, many ethical challenges are complex, with no clear-cut solution.

CONCLUSION

27.   Throughout this chapter we have recognized that communication affects organizational performance and is central to an understanding of organizational behaviour. Effective communication is required to ensure that the goals, feedback and other management messages to employees are received as intended. Trust and clarity help ensure efficiency and effectiveness. Through effective communication, managers can develop productive employees. Effective communication requires an understanding of the communication process, an ability to select the correct channel, deliver the right message in the right form, in the right place and at the right time. This chapter has explored a number of concepts, tools and techniques to assist with these issues. Aside from a need for day-to-day communications, there is also a strategic need; communications are used to transmit goals and establish organizational purpose. We have also recognized a more strategic and external role for corporate communications which must enhance the company's image and reputation.

QUESTIONS

1   Contrast traditional with social models of business communication.

2   Describe the communication process and distinguish between formal and informal communication.

3   Identify and describe important barriers to communication. Why should we focus on such barriers?

USEFUL WEBSITES

Article: **www.roxbury.net/images/pdfs/mc4ch1sample.pdf**
The Communication Process CIPD: **http://www.cipd.co.uk/
subjects/empreltns/comconslt/** Communication and
consultation resources
Article by Gerard M Blair: **www.see.ed.ac.uk/~gerard/
Management/art7.html?** Explanation of aspects of
communication as a management skill

Newcastle University: **lorien.ncl.ac.uk/ming/Dept/Tips/
present/comms.htm** Communication Skills – making oral
presentations

REFERENCES

Argenti, P. (2013) *Corporate Communication*, 6th edn, McGraw-
    Hill International Edition.
Bell, A.H. and Smith, D.M. (2010) *Management Communication*,
    3rd edn, Wiley.
Bovee, C. and Thill, J. (2014) *Business Communication Today,
    Global Edition*, 12th edn, Pearson.

Clampitt, P.G. (2010) *Communicating for Managerial Effective-
    ness: Problems | Strategies Solutions*, 4th edn, Sage.
Fill, C. (2013) *Marketing Communications: Brands, Experiences
    and Participation*, 6th edn, Pearson.
Mintzberg, H. (2011) *Managing*, Financial Times/Prentice Hall.

CHAPTER 26
ORGANIZING YOURSELF – THE MANAGER'S ROLE

Key Concepts

- Controlling role
- Disseminator role
- Figurehead role
- Linking role
- Management style
- Time management

Learning Outcomes
Having read this chapter, you should be able to:

- evaluate what makes an effective and efficient manager
- discuss the importance of time management by individuals at work
- discuss the main factors affecting time management
- identify factors that might lead to the ineffective or inefficient use of time
- explain why it is important for managers to understand their role if they are to be effective.

1. So far in this section on organizing, we have been considering organizational and group issues. Ultimately, however, the effectiveness of organizations comes down to the effectiveness of individual managers, which is the concern of this chapter. Managers must organize their own time and behaviours, leading some to be more effective than others. Effectiveness is dependent upon the managers' predispositions, the context, their skills and knowledge and perception of their role. Consequently we explore such matters – the manager's job, in this chapter. We start with a review of the work of Mintzberg on the manager's role. Mintzberg combines roles, to create a 'think-link-lead-do' model – where management is a form of thinking and leading by doing. Next we consider the management of time as an issue which is fundamental to the manager's job performance. Later in the chapter we focus on time management and personal effectiveness. In the final part of the chapter we consider the views of Drucker, Kanter and Buckingham on the contemporary manager's role.

2.   In the first part of this book we explored management theory, asking what is meant by the term management. We now build on this work, focusing on the role of the manager and the manager's effectiveness. In the 1970s, Mintzberg conducted a study into how managers actually spend their time. He concluded that if managers want to be more effective, they must recognize what their job really is and then use the resources at hand to support rather than hamper their own nature. Understanding their jobs as well as understanding themselves takes both introspection and objectivity on the managers' part. Following the study he set out to break away from Fayol's words and introduce a more supportable, and what he believed to be a more useful, description of managerial work. The managers' job can be described in terms of various 'roles', or organized sets of behaviours identified with a position. That is to say, the managers' effectiveness is significantly influenced by their insight into their own work. Performance depends upon how well the manager understands and responds to the pressures and dilemmas of the job. Thus managers who can be reflective about their work are likely to be effective at their jobs.

3.   Mintzberg argues that the best-known writers of management all seem to emphasize one aspect of the job: Tom Peters tells us that good managers are *doers*; Michael Porter suggests that they are *thinkers* whilst Abraham Zaleznik and Warren Bennis think they are really *leaders* (Mintzberg, 1994). Yet, for much of the twentieth century, the classical writers – Henri Fayol and Lyndell Urwick, among others – told us that good managers are essentially *controllers*. Heeding the advice of any one of them must lead to the lopsided practice of managerial work (Mintzberg, 1994). That is why it is important to consider all of the components of managerial work in a single model. Mintzberg argues a need to consider all aspects of the managerial job/role to achieve managerial effectiveness, 'only together do they provide the balance that seems so characteristic of effective management'. For example, too much leading and there is insufficient action. Likewise, the manager who only communicates or only conceives, never gets anything done whilst the manager who only 'does' ends up doing it all alone. Mintzberg combines the roles, to create a 'think-link-lead-do' model – where management is a form of thinking and leading by doing.

26.1 THE EFFECTIVE MANAGER – THE MANAGER'S JOB

4.   As discussed in the previous paragraphs, Mintzberg concluded that if managers want to be more effective, they must recognize what constitutes their job. They must also recognize that the job is influenced by their predispositions and the context of the work. An individual comes to a managerial job with a set of values, a body of experience, a set of skills or competencies – a base of knowledge. Each manager has some kind of frame for the job, the mental set the incumbent assumes to carry it out. They have a purpose, namely what the manager is fundamentally seeking to do with the unit he or she is supposed to manage. Mintzberg outlines the actual behaviours that managers engage in to do their jobs. Managers can manage action directly, they can manage people to encourage them to take the necessary actions, and they can manage information to influence the people in turn to take their necessary actions. In other words, the ultimate objective of managerial work, and of the functioning of any organizational unit, the taking of action, can be managed directly, indirectly through people, or even more indirectly by information through people. Managers may be categorized as:

- 'Doers' who prefer direct action

- 'Leaders' who prefer working through people, and

- 'Administrators' who prefer to work by information.

Each of the categories will now be discussed in more detail.

5.   Mintzberg (1994) identified three key ways that managers could get work done within their organizations. They could do the work themselves (hands-on), lead others or control others through information (administrators) – see Figure 26.1. The preferred approach to managing is influenced by the managers' predispositions and the context within which they operate. Clearly, there are infinite possible contexts within which management can be practiced. A model such as the one presented by Mintzberg (1994) can help to order them.

FIGURE 26.1 The integrated job of managing

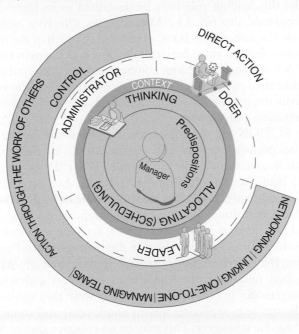

6. 'ADMINISTRATORS' – MANAGING BY INFORMATION: To manage by information is to sit two steps removed from the purpose of managerial work (Mintzberg, 1994). The manager processes information to drive other people who, in turn, are supposed to ensure that necessary actions are taken. In other words, here the managers' own activities focus neither on people nor on actions per se, but rather on information as an indirect way to make things happen. This was the classic perception of managerial work for the first half of the twentieth century. The managers' various informational behaviours may be grouped into two broad roles: (a) communicating and (b) controlling. Communicating (discussed in the previous chapter) refers to the collection and dissemination of information. Managers 'scan' their environments, monitor their own units and disseminate the information they collect (*disseminator role*). Such information may be formal (structured) or informal – such as gossip and hearsay – and even non-verbal information, namely what is seen and 'felt' but not heard. What can be called the *controlling role* (refer back to Section 2 and later in the next section) describes the managers' efforts, not just to gain and share information, but to use it in a directive way inside their units; to evoke or provoke general action by the people who report to them. They do this in three broad ways: they develop systems, they design structures and they impose directives. Each of these seeks to control how other people work, especially with regard to the allocation of resources, and so what actions they are inclined to take. First, managers implement systems for planning and performance control (such as budgeting). Second, managers exercise control through designing the structures of their units. By establishing responsibilities and defining hierarchical authority, they again exercise control rather passively, through the processing of information. People are informed of their duties, which in turn are expected to drive them to carry out appropriate actions. Third is imposing directives; managers make specific choices and give specific orders, usually in the process of 'delegating' particular responsibilities and 'authorizing' particular requests. In effect, managers manage by transmitting information to people so that they can act.

7. 'LEADERS' – MANAGING THROUGH PEOPLE: Other people may become the means to get things done (*leader role*). Managers may lead on the individual level, 'one on one'. They encourage and drive the people of their units – motivate them, inspire them, coach them, nurture them, push them and mentor them. Managers may also lead on the group level, especially by building and managing teams (team meetings, and team building). Finally, managers may lead on the unit level, especially with regard to the creation and maintenance of culture (refer back to Chapter 14). Managers, for example, engage in many acts of a symbolic nature ('figurehead' duties) to sustain culture. If the communicating role describes the manager as the nerve centre of the unit, then the leading role must characterize him or her as its 'energy centre'; the

leader unites his or her people, galvanizing them into action to accomplish the unit's mission and adapt it to a changing world. Whilst this leading role may be described as an internal role, managing through people also includes an external role, described by Mintzberg as a '*linking*' role. The manager is both an advocate of its influence outside the unit and, in turn, a recipient of much of the influence exerted on it from the outside; the manager acts as a kind of valve between the unit and its environment. All managers appear to spend a great deal of time 'networking' – building contacts and intricate coalitions of supporters beyond their own units, whether within the rest of the organization or outside, in the world at large. To all these contacts, the manager represents the unit externally, promotes its needs and lobbies for its causes. Contacts are expected to provide information and support.

8. 'DOERS' MANAGING ACTION: If managers manage passively by information and affectively through people, then they also manage actively and instrumentally by their own direct involvement in action. Mintzberg refers to this involvement as the '*doing role*'. What 'doing' means to Mintzberg is getting closer to the action, ultimately being just one step removed from it. Managers as doers manage the carrying out of action directly, instead of indirectly through managing people or by processing information. In effect, a 'doer' is really someone who gets it done: 'doing deals', 'championing change', 'fighting fires', 'juggling projects'. In the terms of decision-making introduced earlier, here the manager diagnoses and designs as well as decides: he or she gets deeply and fully involved in the management of particular activities. 'Doing' is also concerned with changing the unit itself, both proactively and reactively. Managers champion change to exploit opportunities for their units, and they handle its problems and resolve its crises, often with 'hands-on' involvement. Managers 'do' in two other respects as well: they substitute, sometimes doing the routine work of their subordinates (e.g. replacing absent employees) and some managers continue to do regular work after they have become managers. This may be an effective way of 'keeping in touch' with the unit's work and finding out about its problems.

9. **Management style**: Managerial work does vary, according to the needs of a particular job and the approach of its particular incumbent. Different managers emphasize different aspects in different ways. Style is considered to impact upon managerial work in three ways: (1) which roles a particular manager favours, (2) how he or she performs these roles and (3) what kind of relationship exists amongst these roles. First, and most obviously, managers in different contexts have to emphasize different roles. For example, the managers of autonomous professionals, as in hospitals or universities, tend to favour linking over leading (let alone controlling), since professionals tend to come to their work naturally empowered. In other words, they need little encouragement or supervision, although they do require support. However, when experts must work in teams, leadership becomes critical. Entrepreneurs, in contrast, who run their own businesses, tend to emphasize doing, as they involve themselves deeply in specific issues; interestingly, the same thing tends to be true of first-line managers. Senior executives of large diversified firms, conversely, give more attention to controlling, chiefly through their systems of performance control and their decisions to authorize major capital expenditure. Of course, regardless of the context, individual managers are often personally predisposed to favour particular roles or aspects of the job. Even in how they respond to requests, managers can exhibit subtle yet significant variations in style. Asked for advice by an employee, for example, a manager may respond as a communicator ('Payroll has some data on this'), a controller ('Don't do it') or a leader ('How do you feel about it?'). Of course, the doer may say, 'Just leave it with me!' (Mintzberg, 1994).

10. The point made by Mintzberg is widely supported. Rees and Porter (2008) similarly argue the first essential requirement for effective managers is to define their job carefully and accurately. They note that effectiveness depends upon the accomplishment of appropriate objectives rather than just being busy. Careful identification of the job is also a necessary foundation for effective **time management**. The main factors affecting a person's use of time are set out in Figure 26.2. These factors and the key issues arising from them form the subject of the remainder of the chapter. The principal issues of time management can be grouped under three headings. Those related to the:

- nature of the job
- personality and attributes of the jobholder, and
- people who make up the jobholder's role-set.

FIGURE 26.2 Main factors affecting time management

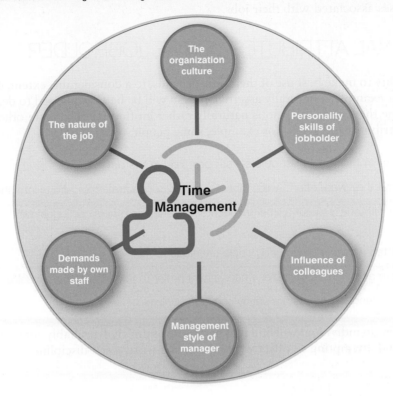

26.2 TIME MANAGEMENT, PRIORITIZATION AND NATURE OF THE JOB

11.   The scheduling of time and the prioritization of issues are obviously of great concern to all managers, and, in fact, are themselves significant consumers of managerial time. Accordingly, a great deal of attention has been devoted to these concerns, including numerous courses on 'time management' (Mintzberg, 1994). The nature of a person's job is fundamental to the amount of control over time that is both desirable and necessary. For example, a person whose job involves regular contacts with others is always going to be under greater pressure from interruptions than someone whose work is of a solitary nature. Similarly, a person who is employed in a new and developing job is more likely to suffer from conflicting priorities and unpredictable events than someone working in an established position, where predictability and routine are the order of the day.

12.   An important issue for any jobholder is the identification of the priorities in the job. In cases where management-by-objectives (see Chapter 19) or some form of target-setting is practised, then individuals will have experience of identifying and working towards priorities, or key result areas, in the job. However, by far the great majority of managerial and professional employees do not work under such systems, and are therefore unused to a systematic approach to prioritizing key tasks. A useful method is to encourage individuals to identify (a) the tasks they alone are responsible for and (b) the tasks that either require the greatest effort, or produce the greatest return (see pareto effect). Once individuals have identified what they see as their key tasks or responsibilities, they can discuss these with their immediate manager. It is not enough, however, just to consider job priorities. It is also important to consider what the individual jobholder has to do in order to fulfil them. Some jobs call for administrative skills and a sound knowledge of organization procedures, others demand social skills and sensitivity to people-needs, and yet

others require technical and specialist knowledge and the ability to apply it. Individuals, therefore, need to examine the processes associated with their jobs.

26.3 PERSONAL ATTRIBUTES OF THE JOBHOLDER

13.   A person's ability to make best use of their time depends, to a considerable extent, on their personality and inclinations. For example, a naturally assertive person will be better equipped to deal with people who trespass on their time than someone who is naturally rather inoffensive. There are other important differences in personal attributes and styles, for example, some people:

- work best early in the day, whilst others work best later in the day

- like to pace out their work effort, whilst others prefer to concentrate their efforts into short, intensive periods

- can only deal with one issue at a time (monochronic), whereas others can juggle with several simultaneously (polychronic)

- are task-oriented whereas others are people-oriented

- like to delegate as much as possible, where others prefer to keep tasks to themselves

- are tidy and methodical, others are untidy and disorganized.

In the final analysis, an individual will find that better use of time will probably come about by developing personal strengths and attempting to offset weaknesses, in a word – self-discipline.

26.4 THE JOB CONTEXT

14.   The context of a person's job consists of the:

- members of his or her role-set (boss, own staff, colleagues, etc.)

- physical surroundings (office, location of others, etc.), and

- culture of the organization (the dominant values that prevail).

The implications of these three job context factors will be considered briefly.

15.   The people who work alongside an individual – their role set (see Figure 26.3) – are always an important influence on that person's use of time. An interfering boss, for example, can be very disrupting. By contrast, a boss who is an effective delegator can be a positive source of help in identifying job priorities. Subordinates' abilities to work effectively on their own, rather than seeking advice from their manager all the time, can enable the latter to work on personal tasks without undue interruptions. Colleagues can be a frequent cause of wasted time, especially when they call into the manager's office at a time when they themselves are less busy, or want a short break from what they are working on. Senior or experienced members of any group will find that they are regularly sought out by junior members wishing to clarify a point or discuss an immediate problem. All these activities have their benefits, but at the cost of any one individual's time.

16.   Physical surroundings may help or hinder a person's efforts to make better use of his or her time. Clearly, if the manager does not have an office, then there are no real physical barriers that can be erected between the manager and all those who, however well-intentioned, wish to interrupt the manager's work. Managers who do have an office of their own can always shut the door, even at the risk of a certain amount of unpopularity. Whilst an 'open door' policy for staff communication is generally recommended, there are still occasions when it would be better to suspend this policy temporarily in the interests of personal work efficiency. The location of furniture and equipment can also affect the use of time. For example, if the photocopier and the computer terminal are located on different floors or are at the opposite end of the building, then a good deal of time can be wasted walking to and from these machines.

FIGURE 26.3 Role set for customer service manager

17. Another major physical influence on an individual's work pattern is that of travelling. The location of colleagues, customers and suppliers invariably means that an individual has to spend some time in travelling between appointments. This time can often be completely wasted, unless, for example, the individual travels by train or has a chauffeur-driven car, in which case it is possible to carry out work tasks whilst travelling.

18. The final aspect of the job context that we shall consider is the organizational culture. Some cultures favour strict adherence to procedures and protocol, which discourages informal contacts and 'short cuts'. Others encourage an open access policy on all aspects of communications, which can be very stimulating but also very wasteful of individual time. Organizations that set great store by accuracy and quality are implicitly requiring their members to take more time over their work, compared with organizations which are always working to tight deadlines and thus have to risk the occasional error or inaccuracy. In yet other organizations, the speed with which decisions are reached is more important than the thoroughness of those decisions. Such an attitude clearly has considerable implications for an individual's personal work standards.

26.5 TIME MANAGEMENT

19. Managers are typically busy each and every day and find it almost impossible to do everything. They must develop ability and methods to help them decide what to do and when to do it. They must also consider what to delegate (refer back to Chapter 23). This means establishing priorities in terms of task importance and urgency. They must find the balance between manager-imposed, system-imposed (routine administrative tasks) and self-imposed work. Working on the wrong or unnecessary tasks is a waste of time and the manager must identify the right things to work on (effectiveness) and how to work efficiently. There are several ways in which managers can improve their own and others' use of time. These are broadly the following, by:

– personal priority and action planning, to-do lists

– target-setting

– work sequencing

- negotiation with key members of their role set

- delegating tasks to own team members

- developing appropriate skills (e.g. faster reading, writing, handling meetings and being assertive)

- developing an appropriate strategy for self-development.

20.   Personal priority and action planning entails sitting down with one's manager, and subsequently one's work-team, in order to agree job priorities, and in particular, those things that the others will look to you for completing. Prioritizing implies having a clear idea of the principal responsibilities of the job. It may lead to people setting targets for their own staff and for themselves. Managers always do well to consider the '80-20' rule – that is identifying the 80 per cent of their activities that are only likely to produce 20 per cent of the required outcomes, and focusing on the 20 per cent of the job that delivers 80 per cent of the results.

21.   One aspect of time management requires us to deal with time-wasters at work. Whilst a high level of interaction between people at work can normally be considered as a healthy phenomenon, there are nevertheless potential disadvantages for any one individual's personal effectiveness. These arise from the following:

- prolonged, or unnecessary, meetings with colleagues

- interruptions from own staff, colleagues or boss (however well-intentioned)

- idle conversations (in the sense of casual chit-chat)

- unnecessary memos and other paperwork.

22.   One way for managers to make better use of their time is to delegate some of their work to subordinates. DELEGATION was considered earlier (Chapter 23). The first step is to explain what is required of the employee concerned, both in terms of what is to be achieved and to what standard. Unless the person concerned is extremely inexperienced or the task truly warrants it, the manager should not normally explain in detail how the job should be done. It will be enough to give general guidance initially and then be available to assist if necessary. This gives the subordinate an opportunity to learn from the experience. Part of the help that the manager must supply is to define the limits of the person's authority to commit the organization's resources (e.g. people, materials and money). Any authority delegated can only be within the authority of the manager. The next stage is for the manager to devise a simple control procedure for ensuring that progress is being made and that any difficulties are identified and dealt with. Part of this control procedure will embrace an opportunity for counselling, or coaching, the employee. In some cases special training may be required as part of the resourcing involved. In order that the delegation is seen to be taken seriously, the manager should ensure that the task is completed, or the responsibility fulfilled, to an acceptable standard. If a task is delegated, but then forgotten by the manager, the credibility of the process comes into question. Finally, the employee should be thanked. Good practice is discussed in the skills sheet (Organizing for Management) at the end of this section.

23.   Assertiveness can contribute to the better use of managers' time by enabling them to deal more effectively with interruptions. Assertion is the ability to express ideas, opinions or feelings openly and directly without putting down ourselves or others. The right to say 'no' is difficult for most people to accept. They feel that they ought not to say 'no' because it is uncooperative, selfish, etc. Assertiveness training attempts to emphasize the importance for individual rights of the capacity to say 'no' without feeling guilty about it, and points out that in saying 'no' we are rejecting the request not the person. Making better use of one's personal rights can enable managers to fend off many of the interruptions inflicted on them by others, and thus create more space for themselves at work. Similar considerations apply to the right not to feel obliged to take responsibility for other people's problems. In this case managers can learn, by assertiveness training, to improve their ability to tactfully, but firmly, pass back to colleagues, team members and even superiors, problems which are the latter's responsibility.

26.6 THE MANAGER'S JOB – A CONTEMPORARY PERSPECTIVE

24.   Rosabeth Moss Kanter (cited in Jossey-Bass, 2004: p. 112) discusses the 'new managerial work', believing the 'old bases of managerial authority are eroding' and that 'the new managerial work consists of looking outside a defined area of responsibility'. The new managers' role involves communication and collaboration across functions, divisions and companies. Kanter argues that 'rank, title or official charter will be less important factors in success at the new managerial work than having the knowledge, skills and sensitivity to mobilize people and motivate them to do their best'. She advocates examining what managers must now do to achieve results in the change adept organization. Relationships of influence are shifting from the vertical to the horizontal, from chain of command to peer networks. The distinction between managers and those managed is diminishing, especially in terms of information, control over assignments and access to external relationships. Consequently, every manager must think cross-functionally and spend more time working across boundaries if they are to be effective. Their role must become more collaborative; they must serve as integrators and facilitators. Furthermore, they are encouraged to develop alliances, establish trust and make partnerships work.

25.   More recently Drucker (2004) has added to the body of knowledge concerned with managerial effectiveness. He argues every effective executive follows eight simple practices. They ask (1) what needs to be done, (2) what is right for the enterprise, they develop (3) action plans, they take responsibility (4) for decisions and (5) communicating, (6) they focus on opportunities rather than problems, (7) they run productive meetings and (8) they think in terms of 'we' rather than 'I'. The first two practices generate the required knowledge; the next four convert this to action and the final two practices ensure the whole organization feels responsible and accountable. Commenting on managerial decisions he impresses a need to: make a person accountable for carrying it out (name the responsible person); include a deadline and identify the people who will be affected by and should be informed about the decision.

26.   Finally, Buckingham (2005: p. 70) asks what makes a great manager – what they do. Recognizing there to be as many styles as there are managers he argues one quality sets managers apart – 'they discover what is unique about each person and then capitalize on it'. The job of a manager is to turn one person's particular talent into performance. Their job is to challenge each employee to excel in their own way. This is about managing diversity and talent. Indeed Buckingham (2005: p. 73) discusses 'capitalizing on differences'. He argues that identifying and capitalizing on each employee's uniqueness saves time and makes employees more accountable whilst building a sense of team. Finally, Buckingham suggests three key factors managers need to be aware of in order to manage direct reports well: (1) strengths – by spending time with employees managers can observe and learn their strengths, (2) triggers that activate strengths and good performance – such as recognition and (3) how they learn – such as by analyzing, doing or watching.

CONCLUSION

27.   Like management theory itself, the manager's role and job is somewhat eclectic. Managers are typically busy each and every day and find it almost impossible to do everything. The management of time is therefore an issue which is fundamental to job performance. Managers wanting to be more effective must recognize the true purpose of their job. That is to say, the manager's effectiveness is significantly influenced by insight into their own work. The manager's job can be described in terms of various 'roles', or organized sets of behaviours identified with a position. Performance depends upon how well the manager understands and responds to the pressures and dilemmas of the job. Thus, managers who can be reflective about their work are likely to be effective at their jobs. They must develop ability and methods to help them decide what to do and when to do it. They must also consider what to delegate. Assertiveness can contribute to the better use of managers' time by enabling managers to deal more effectively with interruptions. Assertion is the ability to express ideas, opinions or feelings openly and directly without putting down ourselves or others. Finally, a manager's use of time can be made more productive if personal communication skills are improved.

QUESTIONS

1 Explain why it is important for managers to understand their role if they are to be effective.

2 Evaluate how the nature of the job, personal attributes of the jobholder and the job content impact upon the control a person may have over time.

3 Evaluate methods used by managers to manage their time.

4 Contrast traditional with contemporary views of the manager's job.

USEFUL WEBSITES

The Association for Project Management (APM) **www.apm.org. uk** Articles, resources, etc.

Project Management Institute in the United Kingdom **www.pmi. org.uk** Active in promoting project management to industry and government organizations and publishes a bimonthly newsletter for members

Mind Tools **www.mindtools.com/pages/main/ newMN_HTE. htm** Time Management articles and tools

Time Management **www.timemanagement.com** Section for managers: project management tools, effective meetings, etc.

Personal Time Management Guide **www.time-management-guide.com** Time Management articles and tools

REFERENCES

Buckingham, M. (2005) 'What great managers DO', *Harvard Business Review*, 83(3): 70–79.

Drucker, P. (2004) 'What makes an effective executive', *Harvard Business Review*, 82(6): 58–63.

Jossey-Bass (Editor), (2004), 'Management Skills: A Jossey-Bass Reader', Ed 1, Jossey-Bass Publishers.

Mintzberg, H. (1975) 'The manager's job: folklore and fact', *Harvard Business Review*, 53(4): 49–61.

Mintzberg, H. (1994) 'Rounding out the manager's job', *Sloan Management Review*, 36(1): 11–26.

Rees, W. and Porter, C. (2008) *Skills of Management*, 6th edn, Cengage Learning EMEA.

SKILL SHEET 8 **Organizing for Management**

This skills sheet provides a set of tools to help the reader organize for management. Use this sheet in conjunction with Chapters 20–26 and case sheet 8. The reader may benefit from revisiting skills sheet 5 where the skill of process modelling was outlined. Similarly in skills sheet 7 the creation of the mission, vision and goals was discussed; such instruments clarify organizational purpose and therefore organize the workforce.

THIS SHEET HAS BEEN ORGANIZED INTO THE FOLLOWING SECTIONS:

1. **ORGANIZING THE WORKFORCE: ORG CHARTS**
2. **CREATING A JOB DESCRIPTION**
3. **ORGANIZING WORK: DELEGATION PRACTICE**
4. **ORGANIZING FOR ENGAGEMENT**
5. **ORGANIZATION DEVELOPMENT (OD)**
6. **FORCE-FIELD ANALYSIS**
7. **COMMUNICATION SKILLS**

1. Organizing the Workforce: Org Charts

An organization chart graphically represents the management structure of an organization, such as departments within a company. It can be any manager's role to create such charts. Charts may show the company 'as is' or 'to be'. There are many ways to draw the chart, which consists of boxes and lines. here is one simple way:

a. Start, at the top of the page, with the CEO/MD
b. List (brainstorm) all of the divisions, departments, units that report to the CEO (e.g. Operations, R&D, Finance, etc.)
c. Draw a vertical line from the top of each box in b) to the bottom of the CEO box.
d. Next, select one of the boxes from b) and list all of the departments, groups that report to the manager and then repeat step c.
e. Repeat the steps above until you have a chart showing the preferred amount of detail. Charts may reflect the whole company, particular units, groups headed by managers only or all groups. Add a title for the chart.

See example

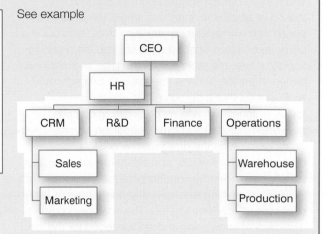

Tips:

a) Aside from the matrix structure there should only be one line emerging from the top (or left) of any box on the chart. This signifies a 'line relationship' (or chain of command) in this chart between the CEO and the managers of CRM, Finance, etc. The CEO has direct responsibility for these managers. Similarly, the Warehouse Manager reports directly to the Operations Manager.
b) Try to place managers of a similar grade/level along the same 'virtual' horizontal line. The higher up the chart, the more authority and responsibility. Typically senior managers (Directors, Vice Presidents, etc.) are at the top and first line managers at the bottom.
c) Some organizations place job holder names on the chart, others do not as people and their roles frequently change.
d) It is a good idea to put the chart creator's name, position and date in the footer.
e) You can draw it on paper, or use org chart software like Visio – with Microsoft office, if you want to illustrate the reporting relationships in your company or organization, you can create a SmartArt graphic that uses an organization chart layout, such as Organization Chart, or you can use Visio to create an organization chart.
f) Various shapes can be used to indicate different roles. Colour can be used both for shape borders and connection lines to indicate differences in authority and responsibility, and possibly formal, advisory and informal links between people.

2. Creating a Job Description (JD)

Whereas the org chart shows the intended groupings within the company, the JD (see also job specification and related person specification) focuses on the individual employee; it defines where the job is positioned in the organization structure. A JD sets out the purpose of a job, where the job fits into the organization structure, the main accountabilities and responsibilities of the job and the key tasks to be performed. A JD is a list that a person might use for general tasks, or functions, and responsibilities of a position. It may often include to whom the position reports, specifications such as the qualifications or skills needed by the person in the job, or a salary range/grade. It is usually developed by conducting a job analysis, which includes examining the tasks and sequences of tasks necessary to perform the job. The analysis considers the areas of knowledge and skills needed for the job. A job usually includes several roles. Normally written by the job holder's manager, HR may help in the creation of the JD as it provides essential information to potential recruits; though it is more likely that HR will simply issue policy and templates to help managers and staff create the JD to a house style. The JD is also used in performance management and individual objectives can be set based on the job description. In some cases the job description forms an important part of the legally binding contract of employment. The process of writing a job description requires having a clear understanding of the job's duties and responsibilities. Consider using a template similar to this:

JOB DESCRIPTION <insert title – this indicates the role/function that the job plays within an organization, and the level of job within that function>
Company Name:
Job Title: <brief and accurate description of the job>
Department:
Location: <place of work>
Reporting responsibilities: <the direct boss of the jobholder>
Subordinates: <who reports directly to the jobholder?>
Job Grade:
Effective Date: <the date that the JD is effective from >
Revision Date: <the date the JD was created >

Job Purpose: <an accurate and concise statement summarizing the overall purpose of the job. This statement should be brief and should not normally be more than 2 or 3 sentences in length>
Position Overview/Main Responsibilities/ Duties: <describe the key areas in which results must be achieved in order to fulfil the overall purpose of the job. These are the key outputs of the job>
Essential Job Functions
- **<define the main duties and responsibilities of the job>**
Non-essential Job Functions
- **<insert>**
Knowledge, Skills and Experience Needed
- **<describe the knowledge, skills and experience needed to perform the job at the required level. This should include only the knowledge, skills and experience required to carry out the job at a fully satisfactory level; try to phrase in a manner that allows measurement>**
Key Contacts/Relationships
- **<briefly describe the significant types of internal and external relationships that are important in getting the job done>**
NOTE: This job description is not exhaustive. The jobholder may perform other related duties appropriate to the grade, as required, to meet the future development needs of the company.

Tips:

- The level of detail employers provide will vary. A job description may include relationships with other people in the organization: Supervisory level, managerial requirements and relationships with other colleagues
- The JD should be a clear, factual record of what the jobholder is required to do
- Do not under-state or over-state the requirements of the job – try to describe it objectively and accurately
- Describe the requirements of the job, not the person in it. Describe the skills and qualifications required for the job, not those of the current jobholder
- Summarize the functions of the job; avoid writing a list of the tasks that are carried out by the jobholder. JDs should usually be no more

than 2 pages long. The JD should describe the core of the job in broad terms; fine details are not necessary. Also, take care not to repeat the same information in different sections

- The person specification matches the right person to the job. It describes the desirable personal attributes required of the jobholder. It is a profile of the candidate required for the work. Elements of a person specification include: Knowledge, Skills and Preferences. It might contain the educational qualifications, previous experience, general intelligence, specialized skills, interests, personality and physical requirements.

3. Organizing Work: Delegation Practice

Delegation is a skill that can be used to manage time whilst developing and motivating employees. Good delegation practice is likely to include the following principles:

- ensure that the objective to be achieved is made clear
- indicate the standard of performance that is required (what, when, etc.)
- decide what level of authority to grant
- allocate adequate resources (staff, equipment, expenses, etc.)
- ensure that clear reporting arrangements are made
- encourage subordinate to request further help if needed
- inform subordinate that early mistakes will be used as learning opportunities
- ensure that the task is completed according to agreed standards, and
- thank the individual for their efforts.

4. Organizing for Engagement

Ensure employees:

- know what is expected of them at work
- have the materials and equipment they need to do their work properly
- have the opportunity to do what they do best every day
- receive recognition or praise for doing good work
- receive encouragement for development
- realize that someone at work cares about them as a person

- opinions count
- feel that their job is important
- have someone at work who talks to them about their progress
- have opportunities at work to learn and grow.

5. OD

Here we consider the means by which OD programmes are carried out. Most of the activities in a programme can be classified in three ways: those aimed at 1) changing people's behaviour, 2) changing organization structures and 3) problem-analysis. Examples of typical activities for each of these three classifications are briefly described below.

Activities designed to change behaviour at work include:

- coaching and counselling to help individuals, usually on a one-to-one basis
- team building to improve team relationships and task effectiveness
- inter-group activities, to improve the level of collaboration between interdependent groups
- training and development to improve key areas of employee knowledge and skill.

- **Activities aimed at changing structures** include:

- role analysis – i.e. focusing on what is expected of people rather than on their present job description, and devising new configurations of jobs and tasks
- job re-design/job enrichment – reassessing current jobs in terms of their range and type of tasks, reallocating tasks and redefining jobs, including vertical job enlargement.

- **Activities aimed primarily at problem-analysis** include:

- diagnostic activities utilizing questionnaires, surveys, interviews and group meetings
- planning and objective-setting activities, designed to improve planning and decision-making skills
- process consultation, where the third party helps clients to see and understand the human processes that are taking place around him (e.g. leadership issues, communication flows, competition between individuals or groups, power struggles, etc.), and
- business process re-engineering.

6. Force-Field Analysis

Force-Field Analysis helps businesses make decisions by analyzing the forces for and against change, and then assists with communicating the reasoning behind business decisions. It can be used for two purposes: to decide whether to proceed with the change; and to increase the chances of success, by strengthening the forces supporting change and weakening those against it.

Proposed Change			
Forces for Change	Score	Forces Against Change	Score
Total		**Total**	

- It is important to identify as many as possible of the factors that will influence the change. Where appropriate, involve (through meetings, workshops, etc.) other people, such as team members or experts in the organization.
- The first step is to agree the area of change to be discussed. This might be written as a desired policy goal or objective.
- Use a blank sheet of paper or whiteboard and list all of the factors (forces) for and against the decision or change (use the table above to structure your analysis). What business benefit will the change deliver? Who supports the change? Who is against it? Why? How easy will it be to make the change? Do you have enough time and resources to make it work? What costs are involved? What other business processes will be affected by the change? What are the risks?
- Then score each factor based on its influence e.g. 1 (weak) to 5 (strong), and sum the scores for and against change to find out which of these is greater.
- Review the forces. Decide which have some flexibility for change or which can be influenced.
- For a visual representation of the influence exerted by each force draw arrows around them. Use larger arrows for the forces that will have a greater influence on the change, and smaller arrows for forces that will have less of an influence.
- If appropriate, use the analysis to decide whether or not to move forward with the change or to think about how you can strengthen the forces

that support the change and weaken the forces opposing it, so that change is more likely.

- Create a strategy to strengthen the driving forces or weaken the restraining forces, or both. If each force has been rated how can you raise the scores of the Driving Forces or lower the scores of the Restraining Forces, or both?
- Prioritize action steps. What action steps can you take that will achieve the greatest impact? Identify the resources needed and decide how to implement the action steps.
- Throughout the process, rich discussion, debate and dialogue should emerge. This is an important part of the exercise and key issues should be allowed time.

7. Communication Skills

'No other skill can help your career in as many ways as communication' (Bovee and Thill,[1] 2014, p. 39). The quality of communications in any organization is as good as the people who contribute to the process. It takes skill to write a good report or lead an effective meeting. It takes skill to sell services over the telephone or interview prospective staff. Sometimes there is tendency to assume that these skills are present in everybody, and that people just need a little practice to improve them. Most business enterprises soon discover that this attitude is not enough – employees need to be trained to develop appropriate skills. Fortunately, any communication skill that is improved is likely to remain with the individual for life, because communication is a need we can exercise in every interpersonal relationship we encounter. There are several areas of communication where skills are particularly called for: report writing, chairing meetings and committees, giving presentations and face-to-face meetings:

A. Communication Skills: Report Writing

In a work organization the commissioning of a report is a frequent response to dealing with a problem that has occurred, or an issue that needs to be faced. Asking for a formal report gives those concerned the opportunity to delegate the essential fact finding and analysis to another member of staff (or external consultant) before they themselves are required to make a judgement on the matter. The first skill of report writing is to

[1] Bovee, C. and Thill, J. (2014) *Business Communication Today, Global Edition*, 12th edn, Pearson.

understand what sources of information and data are worth consulting in order to provide the basic material for the report. Some of the required information will be available in written form from internal and external sources. Other information must be gleaned from interviews with appropriate personnel. Some information may be available via the Internet. Whatever the outcome, one thing is sure – the report writer will end up with far more information than can be utilized within the report. A process of distillation must take place before any kind of summary material can emerge. This is often the most difficult part of writing a report because it forces the writer to decide what to include in the final document and what to omit.

Once the raw material has been refined to the point where it can be considered suitable for inclusion in the report, the writer must then decide how to present the information. At this stage, meeting the needs of the readers must be the foremost requirement. What are these? The first need surely is for clarity of expression, closely followed by logic of argument. Readers will want to be able to see readily the thrust of the report and the supporting evidence. They will want to know what the implications of the research are, and to see some alternative solutions for dealing with them. Report writers are not usually expected to come up with one right answer, but it is very helpful if they can point to possible scenarios that will stimulate ideas amongst readers. The point of most reports is to provide evidence and argument that will enable other people to make better decisions.

Experience has shown that the headings likely to be helpful to report writers when considering how to set out their findings are as follows:

TITLE OF REPORT
Date of report
Terms of reference (as given by the entity requesting the report)
Executive summary (a one or two page outline of key points, including analysis and recommendations in cases where the report is lengthy or complicated)
Contents page (in cases where the report is lengthy)
Introduction (setting the scene; spelling out aims, purpose and scope; explaining the methodology, outlining the report structure)
Main findings (reporting the main facts)
Implications of the findings (may be combined with findings)

Conclusions (in the light of findings and implications)
Recommendations or proposals
Appendices
(supplementary/illustrative material to support main findings)

A clear, well-argued report will be received far better than one that is over-complicated and badly expressed, however relevant its content. Employees who can write good reports are well sought after in work organizations from chief executives down to junior managers.

B.   Communication Skills: Chairing Meetings

All managers are called upon to chair meetings at some time or another. Senior managers, in particular, may find that most of their time is taken up in this way but even junior managers will be called upon to conduct meetings of their own team. Learning how best to manage a meeting is an important skill, and one that can be improved by training and subsequent experience. Of course there are always exceptional individuals who consistently have the capacity to bring out the best in a group, but these are a minority. Most managers have to work at chairing a meeting and there are a few important guidelines that, if followed carefully, will enable them to do so relatively successfully. Pointers for formal committees are referred to later, but for less formal management meetings, helpful guidelines are likely to include the following:

1. **Ensure there is an agenda (typically circulated in advance)**
2. **Be as well briefed as possible beforehand**
3. **Bring relevant reports/documents (may be circulated in advance)**
4. **Explain purpose of the meeting**
5. **Set out any procedures to be followed**
6. **Where possible, take account of personality and experience of group members**
7. **Encourage participation/questions/ideas when appropriate**
8. **Summarize progress as appropriate**
9. **Record minutes of the meeting**
10. **Ensure list of action points where appropriate**

C. Communication Skills: Committees

Committees abound in practically every kind of organization. They are an integral part of the operation of every public sector organization, and are almost as popular in the private sector. What are committees? The first thing that can be said about them is that they are formal groups with a Chairperson, an agenda and rules of conduct. Committees invariably have a specific task or set of tasks to achieve. These tasks are frequently, although not always, associated with decision-making. Some committees meet regularly, others meet for ad hoc purposes only. The formality of a committee is expressed by the following features:

–   A Chairperson who is responsible for ensuring (a) that the committee is conducted in accordance with the rules and (b) that it is supplied with the necessary resources, particularly with the written information it requires to carry out its work effectively.
–   A Secretary, who is responsible for taking the minutes of meetings, sending out the agenda and other papers, and generally acting as the administrative link with the members.
–   An agenda, which sets out the agreed subject matter of the meeting. Part of the Chairperson's job before the meeting is to approve the agenda. The agenda enables committee members to know what is to be discussed, and in what order, and this enables them in turn to prepare adequately before the meeting.
–   The minutes of the meeting, which are the official record of what has taken place. They serve to remind members of important issues or decisions debated at the time.
–   Committee Papers and Reports, which provide the committee with the quality of information to enable it to make well-informed decisions or proposals.
–   Rules of procedure, designed to promote the smooth running of a committee and to ensure that consistency and fair play are maintained. Such rules include procedures for speaking in a debate, proposing motions, voting, adding emergency items to the agenda and other issues relating to the operation of the committee as a communication medium. The rules enable both sides in an argument to state their case, they help to minimize the effect of bullying tactics, and they ensure that a proper record of the proceedings is kept. In the light of all this formality, what are the benefits and disadvantages of committees? The advantages can be summarized as follows:

Advantages

Decisions or proposals are based on a group assessment of facts and ideas, and not just on one powerful individual's preferences.
Committees can encourage the pooling of special know-how and talents possessed by individual members.
Committees are very useful for achieving coordination and collaboration between work groups.
Committees act as a useful focal point for information and action within organizations.

Disadvantages

Decision-making is an altogether slower process when dominated by committees. It is also true that committee decisions may often represent compromise solutions rather than optimum solutions.
Managers may be tempted to hide behind committee decisions, where these have proved unpopular, and thus abdicate their personal responsibility.
Committees sometimes have a tendency to get bogged down in procedural matters, which reduces the time available for the discussion of substantive issues.
Committees do not exist between meetings, and thus cannot act quickly and flexibly to meet sudden changes in a situation.

On balance, committees are probably best suited to large-scale bureaucracies and organizations which have a high degree of public accountability. Smaller-scale enterprises, on the other hand, would probably benefit more from the greater flexibility obtainable from less formal processes of decision-making, such as informal management meetings and temporary project groups.

D. Communication Skills: Presentations

Most managers are called upon from time to time to make a presentation to their colleagues or more senior employees. Presentations are widely used in selling situations, and in management-planning exercises; they are also used when formally introducing major reports or when introducing new ideas or proposals to colleagues. There are three key elements in any presentation:

– Preparation | Content | Delivery

Preparation is a vital prerequisite for any presentation. The person making the presentation needs to consider the content of a talk and its delivery. So far as **content** is concerned, this is primarily a question of considering what to include and what to leave out, taking into account the needs and prior knowledge of the audience. Senior management groups, for example, are mainly interested in the salient features of an idea or proposal, together with a summary of its principal benefits and disadvantages. Operational levels of management generally require more detailed information and will respond to a more technical approach than their senior counterparts. The question of how to **deliver** the presentation again depends largely on the nature of the audience and culture of the organization. Some groups will not be satisfied with anything less than a brilliant display of wit and ingenuity, others will be quite satisfied with a low-key, but extremely relevant, demonstration. One point that is always helpful, whatever the audience, is the use of visual aids. There is hardly a presentation that does not benefit enormously from visual illustration. Visual aids that are most frequently employed include PowerPoint, flipcharts, films and models or physical examples of an item. A code of good practice in the making of presentations could be as follows:

Consider the venue, your audience and their needs.
Assemble your facts and ideas in the light of the above and the complexity of the material.
Develop sufficient and suitable visual aids.
Consider what other information should be made available (drawings, specifications, reports, etc.).
Tell your audience what you are going to tell them, tell them, and then tell them again!
Be enthusiastic (unless this would be inappropriate, e.g. the announcement of a redundancy plan).
Be natural, i.e. if you are a quiet person, then be quietly enthusiastic.
Maintain eye contact with your audience.
Be prepared for questions both during and at the end of your presentation.

Tips: When using PowerPoint

1. Consider including Title, Aims, Introduction and Conclusion slides.
2. Create a theme (consistent colour, style, layout, font type).
3. Ensure high contrast (font and background colour).
4. Keep it simple; don't attempt to entertain – don't overuse clipart, sound or animation.
5. Ensure all diagrams/text can be read easily from the rear.
6. Don't have too many slides (approx. one slide/2–5 mins).
7. Avoid reading from notes or the screen; don't have too many words/bullets (approx. < 20/slide).
8. Allow time for questions – tell the audience whether questions will be dealt with at the end or as you present.
9. Remember not to add anything to the conclusion that was not discussed during the main presentation.
10. If appropriate, include citations and a references slide.

E. Communication Skills: Non-Verbal

When communicating face-to-face, we can use our own gestures, facial expressions and tone to deliver a message and we can also use the gestures, facial expressions and tone of the recipient as feedback. Consequently, non-verbal communication (NVC) can either enable or hinder the communication process dependent on whether the NVC is accurately interpreted. Amongst the forms of NVC to be considered are:

– Kinesics: body language, including winking, head nodding, hand gestures and arm movements.
– Facial and eye behaviour: which give clues about truthfulness, can enhance reflective listening, showing the message sender that you are listening?
– Paralanguage: variations in speech such as pitch, tone, loudness, tempo, also act as communication cues.
– Proxemics: when either person varies the physical distance that separates the two.

Note that non-verbal communication is culture-bound.

Section Ten
Control in
Management

CHAPTER 27
ORGANIZATIONAL
CONTROL

Key Concepts

- Agency theory and the problem of cooperation
- Behaviour control
- Controller and controllee
- Coordination
- Control mechanism
- Control system
- Control target
- Formal management controls
- Informal management controls

Learning Outcomes Having read this chapter, you should be able to:

- distinguish the concepts of coordination and control
- explain the nature and importance of control
- evaluate common techniques/mechanisms for control
- identify the targets of control mechanisms and systems
- contrast traditional with contemporary perspectives of control

1.   We start by asking why *control* is seen as a key aspect of *management*. Organizational control is a fundamental aspect of organizing – dealt with in the previous section. Control systems have long been recognized as a vital feature of all organizations through which managers seek to align employee capabilities, activities and performance with organizational goals and aspirations. Motivation (Section 3) and control are tightly linked concepts. Both are closely associated with strategy and goal attainment (Section 8). However, in order to understand such concepts we must revisit organization purpose and the demands it places on organizational resources, especially people.

2.   Weibel (2010), in discussing 'high motivation control mechanisms', believes formal management controls are thought to solve the *cooperation problem* (see also **agency problem**) which stems from employees having different and often conflicting goals, and these individual goals often conflict with the

goals of the organization. Thus it can be argued that one of the main managerial objectives is to solve the problem of cooperation (2010: p. 434). One way to handle the problem of cooperation is to achieve goal alignment by drawing on employees' extrinsic motivation. In this case, employees' cooperative efforts are 'bought'. Goal alignment can also be achieved by inciting employees' intrinsic motivation (to cooperate voluntarily). Cooperative behaviour is intrinsically motivated when employees cooperate for their own sake. In management science, the purpose of formal managerial control is to influence the probability that people behave in ways which lead to the attainment of organizational goals by regulating activities through hierarchical authority.

3.   For some scholars and practitioners, the primary aim of the control function of management is to measure performance against aims, objectives and standards with a view to enabling corrective actions to be taken, where necessary, to keep plans on course. We discussed control in Chapter 18 when we considered the challenge of translating strategy into practice (implementation) – controlling behaviour through policy, plans and budgets (revisited at the end of this chapter). However, as will be seen later in this chapter, it is not only employee behaviour that is a target for control.

4.   We start by introducing key terms and concepts before contrasting coordination and control as integrative processes. After outlining traditional perspectives of control we move on to discuss what should be controlled, and how, within the organization. Next, we consider aspects of 'controlling' as the final step in the management process. In this section we describe control processes, and systems. This chapter should be considered in conjunction with the next two chapters where we focus on quality and quality control and the control of risk.

27.1 KEY TERMS AND CONCEPTS

5.   What then do we mean by **control**? Control has been defined by many scholars. For example, Kelly (2009) defined it as ensuring plans are properly executed; assuring the organization functions as planned; Drury (2013) defined it as the process of ensuring that a firm's activities conform to its plan and that its objectives are achieved; and Sitkin, Cardinal and Bijlsma-Frankema (2010) defined it as any process whereby managers direct attention, motivate and encourage organizational members to act in ways desirable to achieving the organization's objectives. All focus on making sure organizational goals are attained. A detailed analysis of control definitions reveals a number of key words; such as objectives, achieving, monitoring and authority. A tag cloud (word cloud or weighted list in visual design) is a visual representation for text data. This format is useful for quickly perceiving the most prominent terms and to determine relative prominence. Words like 'process', 'organization', 'objectives', 'planned', 'ensuring', 'activities' and 'system' are most prominent within the analyzed definitions of control.

6.   The term 'control' is used in many related management concepts – selections are represented in the table shown in Figure 27.1. In many cases the target of control is a key concept (e.g. *inventory* control, *access* control, *input* control, *behavioural* control, *financial* control, etc.) whilst in other cases the mechanism or type of control becomes the concept (e.g. formal control, management control, process control, diagnostic control, bureaucratic control, peer control and cultural control). Finally, attributes of control may form the concept (e.g. loose control, span of control, tight control, etc.).

27.2 TRADITIONAL PERSPECTIVES ON CONTROL

7.   In common with previous chapters it is possible to distinguish two broad sets of theory associated with control: traditional (much of the twentieth century) and contemporary (1980/90s onwards). Traditionally, 'control' is seen as one of the four primary functions of management (the others are planning, organizing and motivating). The traditional view focuses on the manager as the developer and implementer (controller) of organizational controls. Theories have posited various ways by which organizational control might be achieved, including: leadership and the development of formal policies, the application of rational-legal authority and rules, activation of cultural norms and rituals, adherence to incentive systems, reliance on direct supervision, or through the design of work environments such as assembly lines. Control theorists have generally built their ideas on the fundamental premise that managers apply organizational controls to

FIGURE 27.1 Control–related management concepts

Inventory control	Access control	Administrative control	Behavioural control
	Biometric controls	Bureaucratic control	Capital controls
Control loop	Control mechanisms	Control process	Control systems
Control targets	Controller	Controlling	Cultural control
Data control	Diagnostic control system	Feedback control	Financial control
Formal control mechanisms	Formal control system	Formal control tools	Formal management controls
Functional control	General controls	Identity-based control	Implementation controls
Informal control mechanisms	Input controls	Integrated control systems	Internal controls Quality control
Locus of control	Lose control	Loss control	Management control
Management control system	Monitoring and control	Open-loop control system	Operational control
Out of control	Output or results controls	Peer control	Planning and control
Process control systems	Project control	Pull control	Push control
Risk control	Span of control	Statistical process control	Strategic control
System of internal control	Tight control	Uncontrolled work	Work performance control

address the agency problem; subordinates may be incapable or unwilling to fully and effectively cooperate in the pursuit of objectives.

8.   From the earliest research on organizations, the act of controlling subordinates has been recognized as a primary managerial function. Since that time, researchers have identified various mechanisms by which managers exercise control in their organizations including the development and implementation of formal policies, rational-legal authority and rules, cultural norms and rituals or incentive systems, direct supervision, and or work designs (see also job descriptions of formal job specifications). Also, rewards and other sanctions are often introduced to encourage employees to adhere to organization standards. Traditional control theory focuses primarily on how managers exercise their power through applications of such controls. Ultimately, managers seek to cultivate high levels of superior-subordinate cooperation; over time organization owners and managers identify rules to standardize how tasks are done, usually with the aim of having them done more efficiently.

9.   **Managerial authority** refers to a person's (manager's) right to exercise power based on the belief that his or her actions are legitimate and in alignment with accepted standards and appropriate conduct. Bureaucratic control systems emphasize the specification, monitoring and enforcement of rules and primarily applied formal control mechanisms. Thus traditionally, control is seen as a process by which organizations or their representatives channel individual and group efforts towards the attainment of organizational objectives. Traditional control assumes that the employee will not act in the best interest of the organization. In such situations, control is attempted through mainly formal and partly informal mechanisms.

10.   In previous chapters we have discussed various attacks on bureaucracy (stifling creativity, intrapreneurship and demotivating) and the formal control aspect has not been without criticism. Underlying this is the recognition that the employee might not have diverging interests and may become less motivated in the face of certain control mechanisms. A number of studies suggest that in order to achieve organizational control, it may not always be necessary to monitor work so closely (typical of bureaucratic control). Consequently, organizational control, as actually practised, seems to reflect theories from the traditional, human relations and process perspectives. Furthermore, certain controls are inconsistent with the ideas of empowerment and autonomy. Cardinal, Sitkin and Bijlsma-Frankema (2010: p. 51) observe 'control theory research spans many decades'; though traditional organizational control theories are viewed as less relevant today. After contrasting control with coordination we will discuss contemporary views on organizational control.

27.3 COORDINATION AND CONTROL

11.   For any large complex organization a central and continuing concern is the problem of ensuring that its constituent parts act in accordance with overall policy, purpose and goals. The division of labour (the design process discussed in previous chapters) creates dependencies. Dependency concerns the extent to which an individual or unit's outcomes are controlled directly by or are contingent upon, the actions of another individual or unit. Dependencies typically cause problems that are overcome through *coordination mechanisms*. The specialization of subunits, which allows the organization to undertake complicated tasks, requires a system of integration to bind them into an operational whole. Integration processes include coordination and control. The integration of subunits into large organizations depends mainly on the manipulation of the two processes.

12.   Henri Fayol identified organizing, commanding, coordinating and controlling as key managerial activities. The need for coordination is dependent upon the extent of interdependence amongst the organization's groups. A given group may rely upon mutual assistance, support, cooperation, or interaction amongst constituent members within its group, between other groups in the organization or with various partner organizations. In some cases they simply cannot exist or survive without each other (interdependent). Interdependence drives a need for cooperation and communication within and between the parts of the organization. Coordination, then, is the process of linking and integrating the functions and activities of different groups, units or divisions; it is about assuring that segments of the organization are operating in compatible ways, i.e. one role of management is to bring organizational parts together and cause them to work efficiently as a united entity.

13.   Groups and individuals may be dependent upon one another in differing ways. Tasks may be worked on jointly and simultaneously, or work may be passed back and forth between entities. As dependency increases, the amount of coordination increases. Typical *mechanisms* (to coordinate work and workflow) include: departmentalization, centralization or decentralization, through the hierarchy of formal authority, formalization (written policies, practices, rules, procedures, instructions, job descriptions and communications), standardization, mutual adjustment, liaison, line and staff roles, informal networks and workflow systems.

14.   In summary, coordination is seen as a response to problems caused by dependencies. Communication and information are integral to all of the coordination mechanisms discussed. The two integration processes (control and coordination) described provide very different solutions for the problem of binding subunits into the larger organization. We focus on control for the rest of this chapter and the next two chapters. We start by asking what should be controlled.

27.4 WHAT SHOULD BE CONTROLLED (CONTROL TARGETS)?

15.   Having developed the mission, goals and strategy, the organization must ensure appropriate action (employee behaviour and decision-making). It must translate the strategy into a comprehensive set of performance measures which provide the framework for a strategic measurement and management system. Additionally, managers need to keep track of the organization's financial and other resources. A primary goal of most commercial organizations will be profit maximization and many organizations, profit or not-for-profit, must consider the management of costs. To achieve such goals, managers need financial controls – considered later in this chapter.

16.   Controls may be applied to many aspects of organization: assuring strategy implementation and the attainment of goals; the management of finances and use of financial resources; the management of risk, protection of assets; the behaviour of employees in terms of performance and goal attainment; operations management in terms of transformational processes, inventory and quality and organizational change, including the management of projects. Strategic control seeks to ensure progress in executing the corporate plan.

17.   Control targets typically include specific elements of organizational transformation processes (i.e. inputs, behaviours (process) or outputs), to which control mechanisms are intended to be applied. In short, control targets include inputs, behaviour and outputs. More specifically it is the resources (people, financial

and physical assets and the collective work they do). Having discussed what should be controlled we will next consider the specific methods (mechanisms) used to control.

27.5 HOW SHOULD WE CONTROL (CONTROL MECHANISMS)?

18. **Control mechanisms** are the individual, molecular units of organizational control (e.g. standards, policies, norms) that are applied in control processes (Sitkin, Cardinal and Bijlsma-Frankema, 2010); control mechanisms include rules, norms, direct supervision or monitoring. We have already discussed traditional control and specified associated formal control mechanisms. Hellriegel and Slocum (1973) describe six management control strategies (mechanisms) to exercise control over individuals on the basis of power. They describe control through organization structure, policies and rules, recruitment and training, rewards and punishment, budgets and machinery. The category of formal mechanisms is shown on Figure 27.2.

19. In 'Levers of Control', Robert Simons (1995) proposes a control framework to assure organizational goals are correct and achieved (effectively and efficiently). For Simons, control is about getting people to do what you want them to do in the way you want them to do it and minimizing the risk of them doing something that you do not want them to do. There are five control types (levers) proposed by Simons:

- **Belief systems** (values, vision, mission and purpose)

- **Boundary systems** (formal rules, codes of conduct and operational guidelines)

- **Diagnostic control systems** – essentially feedback control, reliant on data

- **Interactive systems** enable adaptation, renewal and change

- **Internal control systems** are used to safeguard assets.

20. Ouchi and Wilkins (1983) also considered the problem of how to control employees, suggesting three broad organizational control strategies: traditional/formal (bureaucratic) and informal ('clan' or 'cultural') control. They also discuss market control – examples of intra-organizational market control systems include intracompany transfer prices, commission-based incentives, and results-based performance programs to align the motivations and actions of employees with organizational goals. We have added Ouchi's control categories (systems) to Figure 27.2.

21. Bureaucracy is used to control employee behaviour through standardization, formalization, specialization and centralization. Clan control systems emphasize informal control mechanisms; managers use traditions and beliefs to motivate members to align their values with those of the collectives with which they are affiliated. Clan or culture as control is essentially based on peer pressure (discussed later) and the observation of 'the way things are done around here'.

22. Ouchi and Wilkins proposed a general theory of clan control, based on goal congruence – the idea being that if both the employee and employer are pursuing common goals or at least not mutually exclusive goals, the employee will naturally act in the best interest of the organization, thus removing the costly requirement for 'close monitoring' typical of bureaucracy. Under clan control, the employee is committed to the organization and this becomes a source of motivation to cooperate.

23. Ouchi and Wilkins discuss a variety of determinants and consequences of control mechanism/system. Clan control is argued to be more adaptive, processing information rapidly and requiring less supervision. They argue that clan control should be preferred when goal congruence and uncertainty (in the environment) is high. In contrast, they describe bureaucratic control, legitimate authority rules and close monitoring argued to make organizations more efficient in stable environments where goals may be incongruent.

24. The control mechanisms, systems and targets of Figure 27.2 may be summarized as follows. Clan control systems rely highly on informal controls but have a low reliance on formal controls. Bureaucratic systems, on the other hand, have a high reliance on formal controls and low reliance on informal controls. Market systems tend not to be targeted at input or behaviour (favouring outputs) having a low reliance on formal and informal controls. Integrated control systems have a high reliance on both formal and informal

FIGURE 27.2 **A contingent system of control**

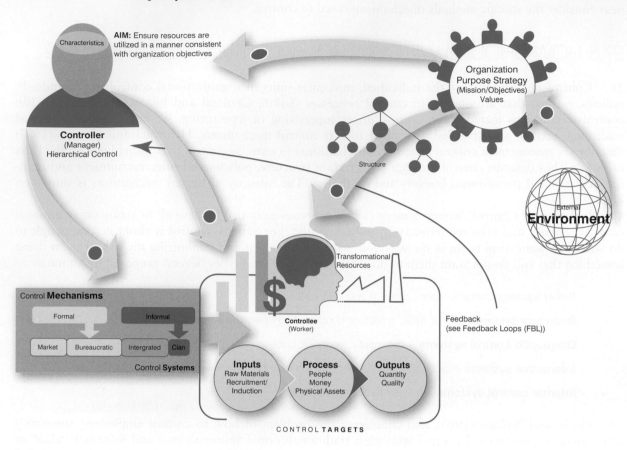

mechanisms which may be targeted at inputs, behaviour or output. The figure shows the external environment influencing control systems (mediated through strategic choices) in line with the comments of Ouchi and Wilkins who align control system type with environmental uncertainty. In this sense we present a contingent system of control. Control selection is not only dependent upon the environment and strategy but also the predispositions of managers who as controllers make choices about preferred control mechanisms and systems. We will return to the issue of control choice later, after first discussing a specific category of control (feedback) in more detail.

27.5 DIAGNOSTIC/FEEDBACK CONTROL

25. In previous paragraphs we discussed how organizations accomplish control. Continuing with this we now consider what is arguably the most important basis of control. According to the cybernetic hypothesis, the feedback loop is the fundamental building block for action. Inputs or outputs are analyzed and tested against a standard; if the comparison reveals a discrepancy, an error signal is generated, and the system takes some action via the effector to reduce the discrepancy. Feedback loops are used in organizations to enable adaptive responses and continuous improvement. A key issue concerns what to measure – given the cliché what gets measured gets managed. Thus, the basic elements of this control are as follows:

– Establish standards of performance

– Measure performance

–   Compare actual results against standards

–   Take corrective action where required.

This sequence of events can be demonstrated diagrammatically in a simplified form, as in Figure 27.3.

FIGURE 27.3 **The control sequence**

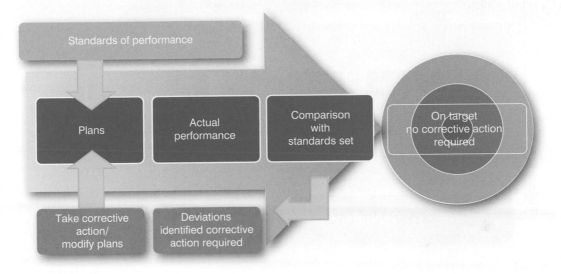

26.   Several comments can be made about Figure 27.3. First, standards of performance need to be verifiable and clearly stated, for example in units of production or sales volumes. Second, the measurement of performance depends heavily upon the relevance, adequacy and timeliness of information. The supply of such information comes from a variety of sources within the organization. For example, the accounting department is responsible for the regular production of operating statements, expenditure analyses, profit forecasts, cash flow statements and other relevant control information. Third, when comparing actual against target performance, most organizations only require action to be taken when the deviation against standards is significant. Otherwise no action is taken and no upward referral is recommended. This is sometimes called the 'management by exception' principle. Fourth, control is not just a matter of identifying progress; it is also a matter of putting right what may have gone wrong. Hence the importance of directing part of the control process to the implementation of appropriate corrective action. Feedback controls can be applied throughout the transformational process as shown in Figure 27.4.

27.   The information necessary to execute the control function effectively is produced from a variety of sources and often in a variety of forms. The raw data is the basic facts and figures of operational life, such as output figures, hours worked, invoice values, part numbers, etc. This data may be stored on manual or computer systems. The data itself may not have great meaning. Taken together and assembled into relevant groupings, it becomes information, which is data that has been analyzed, summarized and interpreted for the benefit of the potential user, in this case a manager. A variety of computer-based information systems are useful to management concerned with control at the tactical level.

28.   The application of a management information system (MIS) to key management functions, assists control in a variety of ways, as the following examples suggest. In marketing/sales, information may be used to clarify current order position, identify profitability of particular products, identify selling costs, produce customer analysis and provide analysis of markets. In HR/personnel management, information is used to provide wage and salary analysis, identify sickness absence trends, analyze manpower statistics and for the production of labour turnover reports. Finally, MIS outputs can be used in management accounting to enable the production of operating and budget statements, analysis of costs/expenditure, investment appraisal analysis, profit forecasts and cash flow projections/statements.

FIGURE 27.4 Feedback in the control system

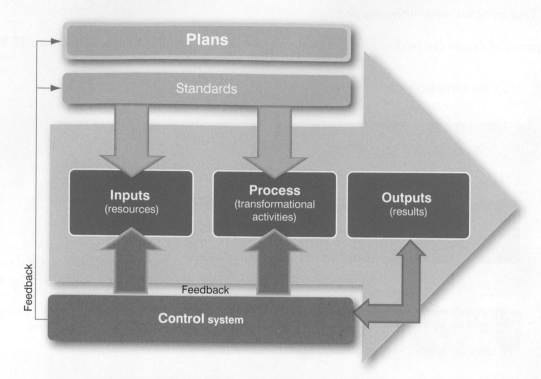

29.   An important consideration for diagnostic/feedback control designers is to whom the information should be targeted: the manager (controller) or employee. Under the traditional view the manager as controllee would receive MIS outputs, identify performance gaps and then determine appropriate (formal) controlling action. Clearly this takes some time, is costly and may demotivate employees. Under the clan or integrated control system the information is supplied to employees who may then self-regulate (a much faster, cheaper and motivational process).

27.6 CONTROLLING BEHAVIOUR

30.   Having identified types of control and what should be controlled we now turn our attention to controlling behaviour specifically, where we will also consider how controllers select (choose) control mechanisms and systems to achieve their goals. A useful way to understand control choices is to consider the nature of the relationship between controller and controllee (see Figure 27.2). If outcome (work outputs and results) can be measured then outcome controls can be used. Similarly, if a controller understands the transformation process (and if behaviours are observable directly through monitoring or revealed through information systems) then behavioural controls may be used. Finally, if the controller does not understand the process nor can they measure outcomes, then only clan control is viable. In the cases of a hierarchical (superior-subordinate) relationship formal control may be utilized. If a manager expects a subordinate to exercise self-control, the manager may structure an employee's environment so that it is conducive to self-control.

31.   The fact that there are a number of strategies (mechanisms) for controlling people presents a problem for managers who must make choices; they must determine how to achieve control within their organizations. Such choices reflect the national and organizational culture (see Chapter 14) – organizations may be described on a continuum from loose to tight control. Ouchi suggested the control approach will be determined by the environment. Likewise, Pugh noted that internal context will determine aspects of control; company size in particular. As an organization increases in size, it increases in differentiation, which creates a control problem of integrating the differentiated subunits.

32.   In Chapter 9, when we discussed contingency theory we also noted the role of managers in determining organizational arrangements, i.e. they make choices based on their values, attitudes and beliefs. We have previously noted that managers vary in their attitude towards people as employees. Managers may consider employees generally to be responsible (Theory Y) or not to be trusted (Theory X). People who subscribe to Theory X believe that individuals will pursue their own goals, unless controlled, and that their goals will be incongruent with the organizational goals. Subscribers to Theory Y, on the other hand, treat people as responsible beings who, if treated as such, will strive for the good of their work organization.

33.   The amount and type of control adopted within organizations varies considerably. One explanation for this finding is given by Pugh (1997) who discusses the 'organizers' and 'behaviouralists', with the former believing in greater and the latter in less control within organizations. Organizers believe 'more and better control is necessary for efficiency' whilst behaviouralists believe that 'the continuing attempt to increase control over behaviour is self-defeating', that 'increased efficiency does not necessarily occur with increased control'. Pugh indicates that behaviouralists' beliefs are aligned with environmental turbulence and the organizers are more prevalent in predictable environments where bureaucracy is favoured.

34.   Figure 27.5 emphasizes the importance of understanding the motivational orientation of the worker when selecting appropriate controls. Korsgaard, Meglino and Jeong (2010) discuss 'motivational orientation'. They suggest that organizations exert control through two distinctly different motivational mechanisms; that is, by appealing to employees' rational self-interest or through indirect social influence processes that de-emphasize the self. They discuss two key factors: (A) the *motive* where the individual may look out for themselves (self-interest) or others and (B) the *mode* of reasoning (see reasoning process in the figure), the method of making judgements; this may be through a rational process or heuristically driven.

FIGURE 27.5 Shaping employee behaviour

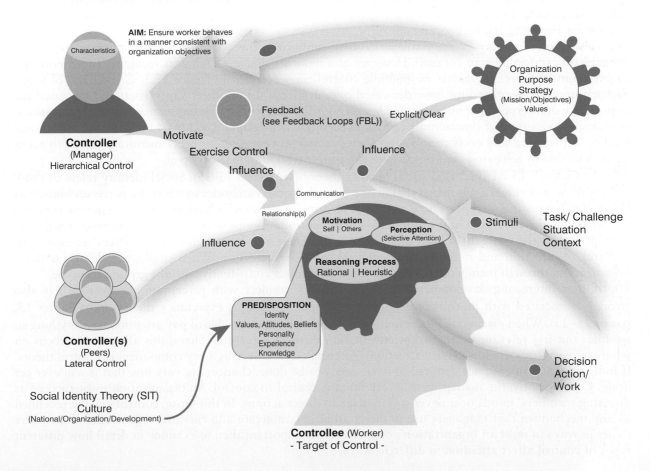

35.   Motivational theory suggests that an employee's choices and actions are mediated by a consideration of anticipated personal consequences (pay, promotion, discipline, etc.). Thus the success of certain organizational controls is heavily dependent on employees being motivated by self-interest and engaged in a rational, deliberative choice process. On the other hand, Korsgaard, Meglino and Jeong (2010) note certain forms of organizational control that do not require rational deliberations by the employee. In some cases responses are motivated through a process of indirect social influence. Thus we need to understand both the motive and judgement processes underlying an individual's actions if we are to understand and apply control theory more effectively.

36.   There seem to be two broad judgement/decision-making approaches adopted within our brains. It is important that we understand these when contemplating control. *Rational reasoning* refers to thinking and acting in a manner that is expected to lead to an optimal or maximum result for a person based on a consideration of the person's values and risk preferences (a deliberative process that considers the consequences of one's actions). *Heuristic reasoning,* on the other hand, is the application of existing knowledge structures (i.e. rules, norms, scripts) as a means of determining choices and behaviour (a rapid, relatively effortless process largely outside of the actor's conscious control – i.e. does not require the systematic evaluation of anticipated consequences).

37.   Rational and heuristic reasoning are considered distinct modes of processing. Combining motive and mode of reasoning, Korsgaard, Meglino and Jeong (2010: p. 231) distinguished four different orientations: (1) rational self-interest – a focus on personal gain in pursuance of self-serving goals in a manner that maximizes expected personal outcome, (2) mindless self-interest – individuals may pursue self-interest without engaging rational reasoning (spontaneous and impulsive behaviour), (3) collective rational – in this case individuals may be motivated to serve their own interests as well as the interests of others (for example when belonging to a group) and formulate intentions in a rational manner and finally (4) other, individuals may act subconsciously (without rational reasoning) in the interests of others (for example, group members). Individuals with a rational self-interested orientation are more responsive to controls involving behaviour-consequence contingencies, whereas individuals with an 'other' orientation are more responsive to controls involving indirect social control.

38.   The controller may be the manager (formal authority), the board (through explicit goals) or the organization (informal clan control). However, at a more specific level, scholars recognize the importance of **peer control** where there may be multiple controllers – depicted in Figure 27.5. Greater use of teams and self-managed workgroups have decreased organizational use of direct supervision and increased the importance of interpersonal influence and lateral coordination to direct or motivate work in organizations. Peer control is a type of (horizontal) control occurring when people who are of the same organizational level or in the same field exert control over their peers; a process whereby peers encourage others to act in ways desirable to achieving the objectives of the people who initiate the control.

39.   In Chapter 15 we discussed social identity theory (see paras. 15–19). Social identity refers to those aspects of an individual's self-image that derive from the social categories to which he perceives himself as belonging. Interestingly, scholars now argue that identity is a driver of behaviour and consequently the basis of control. Identity is thus a non-traditional way of controlling employees. Control is the process whereby managers align the interests of both organizations and their members, such that employees' actions, both in terms of direction and intensity, are beneficial to the organization. When employees identify with an organization, through membership, they are motivated to act consistently with the group prototype.

40.   Other interesting developments of control theory connect with perception theory which is also strongly associated with motivation theory (see Chapter 5 para. 2, expectancy theory and Chapter 15, paras. 21–23). When discussing perception we noted that we are not able to pay attention to everything so we filter out less relevant or important information through perceptual filters; this allows us to focus on what we see as important (selective attention). Attention is now seen as a key component of control theory. If individual attention is not directed at what needs to be done, chances are very low that it will ever get done. Consequently, the management of attention is central to control. An organization must succeed at directing members' minds or it never will manage to direct actions. In this sense, control may be redefined as any mechanism that managers use to direct attention, motivate and energize organizational members to act in ways to meet an organization's objectives. It is important then to examine in detail how different types of control affect attention in different ways.

27.7 FINANCIAL CONTROL: BUDGETS

41. Earlier we discussed the need to control capital, the financial resources of the organization. Controlling capital is also about controlling decision-making and behaviour – both of managers and employees. In this final part we turn our attention to financial control through budgets. The process of budgeting was outlined in Chapter 18 (see 18.6 Detailed planning and control processes: budgeting). In Chapter 18 we defined budget and budgeting (see para. 29) as plans used to *control* decisions and action. Budgetary control takes the targets of desired performance as its standards, then systematically collates information which relates to actual performance (usually on a monthly or quarterly basis) and identifies the variances between target and actual performance. Thus, whereas budgets in themselves are primarily tools of planning, the process of budgetary control is both a planning device and a control device.

42. The steps by which a budgetary control system is constructed are as follows:

1) Forecasts for key aspects of the business are prepared. These are statements of probable sales, costs and other relevant financial and quantitative data.

2) A sales budget is prepared based on an analysis of past sales and a forecast of future sales in the light of a number of assumptions about market trends. The resulting budget is an estimate of sales for a given budget period.

3) A production budget is prepared on the basis of the sales budget. This involves an assessment of the productive capacity of the enterprise in the light of the estimates of sales, and a consequential adjustment of either, or both, to ensure a reasonable balance between demand and potential supply. Production budgets will include output targets, and cost estimates relating to labour and materials.

4) A capital expenditure budget is drawn up to cover estimated expenditure on capital items (fixed assets) during the budget period.

5) A cash budget is prepared by the accountant to ensure that the organization has sufficient cash to meet the ongoing needs of the business. This budget reduces the organization's transactions to movements of cash and indicates shortfalls or excesses of cash at particular periods of time.

6) Departmental budgets are drawn up in the wake of the sales and production budgets.

7) Finally, the budgets are collected into one master budget, which is effectively a statement of budgeted profit and loss together with a projected balance sheet.

8) Production of period budget statements, which inform management about their performance against budget in the immediately preceding period and indicate any variances.

9) Action by management, as appropriate.

CONCLUSION

43. Organizational control is, in practice, a complex and dynamic phenomena. No amount of planning and organizing will assure that goals are attained. Control is therefore the essential final step in the management process to ensure that all proceeds as planned, or that unrealistic plans and targets are revised, where appropriate. As the final step in the management process, controlling provides the critical link back to planning. There are many purposes for control such as assuring goals are attained, employees empowered and motivated and organizational resources protected. There are also many business aspects that can be controlled, from plans, through behaviour to the raw materials and transformational resources of the organization. This chapter has emphasized the control of employee behaviour and performance in relation to organizational goals but made reference to other targets for control. A key aspect of control is to enable the organization to function as planned, to minimize disruption, enable coordination and integration and help the organization to adapt to its environment.

QUESTIONS

1   Select two organizations with which you are familiar; explain how and why control strategies may vary between the organizations. You should state whether you would expect an emphasis on formal or informal control and explain why.

2   Discuss the purpose of control in organizations, identifying what should or may be controlled.

3   Explain how feedback loops could be used in (a) traditional and (b) clan or self-control.

REFERENCES

Drury, C. (2013) *Management Accounting for Business*, 5th edn, Cengage Learning.

Hellriegel, D. and Slocum, J.W. (1973), 'Organizational design: A contingency approach. A model for organic management design', *Business Horizons*, 16(2): 59–68.

Kelly, P. (2009) *International Business and Management*, Cengage Learning EMEA.

Korsgaard, M., Meglino, B. and Jeong, S. (2010) 'The Role Of Motivational Orientations in Formal and Informal Control', in Sitkin, S.B., Cardinal, L.B. and Bijlsma-Frankema, K.M., *Organizational Control* (pp. 222–247), Cambridge University Press.

Ouchi, W.G. (1977) 'The relationship between organizational structure and organizational control', *Administrative Science Quarterly*, 22(1): 95–113.

Ouchi, W.G. and Wilkins, A.L. (1983) 'Efficient cultures: exploring the relationship between culture and organizational performance', *Administrative Science Quarterly*, 28(3): 468–481.

Pugh, D.S. (1997) *Organization Theory*, 4th edn, Penguin.

Simons, R. (1995) *Levers of Control*, Harvard Business School Press.

Sitkin, S.B., Cardinal, L.B. and Bijlsma-Frankema, K.M. (2010) *Organizational Control*, Cambridge University Press.

Weibel, A. (2010) 'Managerial Objectives of Formal Control: High Motivation Control Mechanisms' in Sitkin, S.B., Cardinal, L.B. and Bijlsma-Frankema, K.M., *Organizational Control* (pp. 434–462), Cambridge University Press.

CHAPTER 28
MANAGING QUALITY

Key Concepts

- Business process management (BPM)
- Quality assurance
- Quality management
- Quality management system (QMS)
- Six Sigma
- Total quality management (TQM)

Learning Outcomes Having read this chapter, you should be able to:

- review what is meant by quality and quality management
- define the key concepts associated with quality
- discuss the importance of quality to contemporary organizations
- Identify key quality standards and frameworks and discuss their benefits
- list the eight quality management principles defined in ISO 9000.

1.   Customers, wherever they are, want satisfaction. If they are buying a product they obviously want it to be fit for purpose, safe, reliable, probably durable too and they are influenced by price. For example, most people want a car, but not everyone wants a top-of-the-range or an expensive executive model. They are quite happy with a standard middle-range vehicle, but they want it to be reliable, safe and economical. In the past many manufacturers were unable even to guarantee these three features. Nowadays, all manufacturers have to provide these, and many other standard features, in order to maintain their sales against the competition. In the case of a service, people are looking for factors such as availability, reliability, effectiveness (fitness for purpose) and courtesy. They may also be influenced by price. In summary we are discussing quality – from the customer's perspective.

2.   The subject of quality has been referred to throughout this book and in the previous chapter where we focused on control, and is further mentioned in the chapters on Marketing and Production in Part 3. The concept of quality is omnipresent throughout management theory and practice. Indeed quality is a matter of concern for everybody from the board of directors down to the humblest employee. We therefore start this chapter by explaining key terms and concepts associated with quality and consider why quality is so important (rationale) to every organization today. Evans (2011) argues that many quality principles are based on management theories that are familiar to students and we will make links with strategy, organization design, leadership, marketing, production, organization behaviour, culture, decision-making, information systems,

business processes and continuous improvement. From the outset we recognize quality to be a complex construct, used to describe inputs (raw materials), processes and transformational resources and outputs. It is relevant to value creation through the organization's value chain and its value system. It is a stakeholder perception and may therefore be defined in many ways. Having considered what is meant by the term quality and why it is so important, we then focus on the management of quality in organizations, considering basic principles and methods and then **quality standards**.

28.1 QUALITY AND MANAGEMENT – KEY CONCEPTS AND RATIONALE

3.   What is 'quality'? It is difficult to find agreement on this, since much depends on the perspective of those concerned. For example, an engineer will tend to see quality in terms of how well the product or component fulfils its purpose, an accountant might judge the product in terms of its cost-effectiveness, whilst a customer may judge it in terms of its reliability. The point is, however, that 'quality' is seen as something good and worth having, whatever one's perspective. Most definitions of quality emphasize the degree to which something such as a product or service, or part thereof, fulfils requirements. Whilst the scope of quality is vast, there is one useful way of distinguishing between different sorts of quality, and that is to separate out the quality of the original design (the intention) from the quality of the conformance to that design (the implementation).

4.   Much of traditional quality control has been directed towards the latter, i.e. to ensure that the production process delivered components or finished goods which conformed to their specification (or within close tolerances). This has been described as the internal view of quality, and has been a feature of Western production systems for decades. In contrast to this approach, the emphasis today is more on the former perspective, i.e. to focus on the original design, which the customer ordered or expressed a preference for. This has been described as the external view of quality, and has been typified in recent years as the Japanese approach to quality.

5.   Another distinction drawn between the approaches to quality lies in the different attitudes towards specifications. In traditional quality control systems, based on the internal view, there is an underlying assumption that there will always be faulty parts, components, etc. and that allowance (tolerances) must be made in the production process. This viewpoint is not accepted in a total quality control approach, based on the external view, which expects that every part or component will be fit for its purpose, that everything will be 'right first time'. Such an approach places considerable responsibility on suppliers to provide exactly the right specifications. If, as in total quality systems, every person or unit in a production process is seen as a supplier of goods (or services) to others, then there is a clear pressure on all concerned to ensure they pass on a perfect product or service to their colleagues (who are, in effect, their customers).

6.   There are many reasons why organizations pursue and seek to manage quality. Quality may be associated both with organizational effectiveness, delivering what customers want, and efficiency through continuous improvement, a reduction in error and associated costs. The pursuit of quality and excellence is a strategy, enabling differentiation (see competitiveness) and impacts upon the organization (operations and tactics). Operational effectiveness (and efficiency) is about performing similar activities better (through operational improvements) than rivals perform them. Improvements can be made in productivity, quality or speed. Such initiatives change how organizations perform activities in order to eliminate inefficiencies, improve customer satisfaction and achieve best practice. Some companies are able to get more out of their resources than others because they eliminate wasted effort, employ more advanced technology, motivate employees better or have greater insight into managing particular activities or sets of activities.

7.   **Quality management** refers to systematic policies, methods and procedures used to ensure that goods and services are produced with appropriate levels of quality to meet the needs of customers. Quality management may be viewed as a proactive or reactive approach. In some organizations it means continuously improving the product or service and aiming for the prevention of errors whilst others may rely on inspection to correct mistakes and/or to reject faulty components.

8.   Many organizations adopt frameworks for achieving a recognized level of quality. Achievement of a quality standard (discussed towards the end of this chapter) demonstrates that an organization has met

the requirements laid out by a certifying body. In many cases they adopt a systematic approach to proactively managing quality, based on documented standards and operating procedures. The best known quality management systems are those based on the ISO 9000 series of quality standards. See also Six Sigma – an approach to improvement and quality management that originated in the Motorola Company, originally based on traditional statistical process control, it is now a far broader 'philosophy of improvement' that recommends a particular approach to measuring, improving and managing quality and operations performance generally; the Malcolm Baldrige National Quality Award envisioned as a standard of excellence to help US organizations achieve world-class quality; and lean manufacturing systems and techniques of production enabling companies to reduce waste, leading to greater flexibility in production processes and products.

9.   To summarize, quality and its management is a company and value-system-wide concept that ripples through almost every aspect of the organization and its activities. When managing quality it is essential to adopt a system-wide and holistic approach. We have used the transformation process in Figure 28.1 to indicate the scope of quality and the important stakeholders. Quality goals are articulated through the corporate strategy. Through leadership an appropriate quality culture will be developed to ensure a customer and continuous improvement orientation by all employees.

10.   At the functional level (see Part 3), operations may set specifications for products and services and manage operations to assure the products and services delivered meet such specifications; marketing will manage communications with customers to ensure expectations are met and the customer is satisfied. The quality of outputs is affected by the quality of the inputs and transformational resources. Thus suppliers and partners also play a key role in assuring quality.

FIGURE 28.1 **The scope of quality**

28.2 BASIC PRINCIPLES AND METHODS

11.   Having considered what is meant by quality and quality management and why organizations strive to improve quality, we now briefly turn our attention to the practical aspects of quality, i.e. how quality is managed – the main principles, methods, tools and techniques. We present only a brief explanation of quality principles and methods as the matter is revisited in Part 3 when we consider production and marketing in more detail. We start by tracing the history of quality management and consider the significant influencers of the approach.

12.   The greatest influence on the total quality approach to management has been exercised by Deming, Juran and Ishikawa. The late William Edwards Deming and Joseph Juran, both Americans, applied and developed earlier techniques such as statistical process control to the post-war industries of Japan. They showed that, by paying attention to the continuous improvement of production processes and gaining employee commitment to the idea of quality at every stage of production, it was possible to achieve consistently high standards of finished goods at a price the customer was more than willing to pay in order to secure reliability and acceptable performance. Juran argued for a proactive approach, that it is essential to look further ahead in order to prevent problems occurring in the first place. In essence, he was urging management to stop trying to cure the symptoms of production problems, and concentrate instead on identifying and tackling their underlying causes.

13.   Deming is arguably the godfather of Japanese industrial success witnessed in the second half of the twentieth century. In the immediate post-war period, after Japan had suffered great devastation of its industries, Deming persuaded the Japanese Union of Scientists and Engineers (JUSE) to try his approach of looking at products from the customer's point of view, and then meeting customer requirements in close collaboration with suppliers. A further key point in Deming's approach was to gain both managerial and employee commitment to engage in a process in which quality was paramount. Thus the total quality approach was born – an approach based not just on statistical process control but on a positive attitude towards quality at every level in the organization.

14.   Deming's initial work led him to promote Fourteen Points for Total Quality Control. These give considerable insight into his arguments for a total quality approach, and can be summarized as follows:

1)   Create and publish a statement of the company's mission (aims and objectives).

2)   Everyone must aim to continuously improve customer satisfaction.

3)   Provide the means to improve customer satisfaction.

4)   Introduce participatory leadership style in order to achieve employee cooperation.

5)   Develop climate of trust between management and employees, and between groups.

6)   Develop an across-the-board approach to cooperation and teamwork.

7)   Ensure adequate training of employees and suppliers (so they know what is expected).

8)   Continuously aim to improve the production system.

9)   Remove numerical quotas for production in favour of methods for improvement.

10) Use inspection primarily for improvement rather than for detecting and correcting errors.

11) Award business to suppliers on the basis of consistent quality and reliability.

12) Remove barriers to workmanship by providing adequate training and equipment.

13) Encourage education and self-improvement at every level.

14) Create a climate where quality improvement is embedded in the organization's culture.

15.   In view of the above statements it is not surprising that Deming's approach emphasizes senior management commitment; the development of a longer-term rather than short-term view towards quality; the need for management to persist in the face of initial setbacks on the road to total quality, the encouragement of developing quality at source and a ban on emphasizing output at the expense of quality. Deming's approach tends to lead to a three-tier system of quality management with (1) senior management responsible for the quality of the aims, objectives and fundamental strategy of the organization, (2) middle management responsible for the implementation of those aims and objectives in accordance with the overall policy towards quality and (3) the work group responsible for results within a continuous programme of improvements to production processes.

16.   The Japanese influence on quality came especially from Professor Ishikawa, who in the early 1960s introduced the idea of quality circles. This idea arose from his interest in the training of supervisors in the quality process, where he realized that if the work groups themselves participated in the process it would

provide a means of securing quality standards at the workplace, and provide a system for giving feedback to supervisors and managers on quality problems. The strongly participative nature of quality circles aids the process of gaining every employee's commitment to quality. However, such groups are not intended to be ends in themselves but are an integral part of a total quality control approach.

17.   In a quality approach, especially where 'just-in-time' (JIT) systems are being implemented, an important lesson for quality circles is that their output is not passed on to the next process group until it is asked for. They in turn are not required to accept components, parts, etc. from their 'suppliers' until they are ready for them. Thus, each work group has to learn to react to the needs of their 'customers'. This idea of everyone being a supplier and a customer of someone else in the organization is a key feature of a total quality approach.

18.   In summary, **Total Quality Management (TQM)** – dominant in the 1970s and 1980s – is an integrated management philosophy and set of practices that emphasizes, amongst other things, continuous improvement, meeting customers' requirements, reducing rework, long-range thinking, increased employee involvement and teamwork, process redesign, competitive benchmarking, team-based problem-solving, constant measurement of results and closer relationships with suppliers. TQM may produce value, through a variety of benefits such as: the improved understanding of customers' needs; improved customer satisfaction; improved internal communication; better problem-solving; greater employee commitment and motivation; stronger relationships with suppliers; fewer errors; and reduced waste. Despite TQM and related philosophies emerging in the 1980s the tools and techniques remain useful for contemporary organizations.

19.   As was noted earlier in this book, TQM was followed by BPR in the 1990s. BPR was used to change traditional organizations radically and align them with the new demands of the twenty-first century. However, once realigned with their environments, radical change occurs less frequently in such organizations. They then return effort and focus on continuous (incremental) improvement. Whilst many companies continue to adopt many of the principles of TQM, **business process management (BPM)** has emerged to align business processes continually with strategic objectives and customers' needs. BPM requires a change in a company's emphasis from functional to process orientation.

20.   BPM may be defined as a systematic, structured approach to analyze, improve, control and manage processes with the aim of improving the quality of products and services. BPM differs from business process re-engineering in that it does not aim at one-off revolutionary changes to business processes, but at their continuous evolution. Whereas TQM emphasized continuous improvement in a traditional (vertical) structure and business process re-engineering (BPR) advocated transformational change within the horizontal organization, BPM embraces both types of change but within a more horizontal design. The roots of business process management can be traced back to the 1980s and that of TQM philosophy, and in the 1990s of BPR. The primary principles of BPM include:

–   a holistic view

–   strategic imperative

–   enabled by information technology, and

–   emphasis on cross-functional process management.

We now consider quality standards, what they are, their role and their benefits to organizations.

28.3 QUALITY STANDARDS

21.   Quality improvement has been defined as actions taken throughout the organization to increase the effectiveness and efficiency of activities and processes, resulting in added benefits to both the organization and its customers. Quality improvement is achieved by improving processes. The continual improvement of the organization is considered within a number of quality standards. The International Organization for Standardization widely known as ISO, is an international standard-setting body composed of representatives from various national standards organizations. The organization disseminates worldwide proprietary industrial and commercial standards. ISO 9000 is a family of standards for quality management systems. A **quality standard** is a framework for achieving a recognized level of quality within an organization. Achievement of a quality standard demonstrates that an organization has met the requirements laid out by a certifying body.

FIGURE 28.2  World distribution of ISO 9001 certificates in 2012

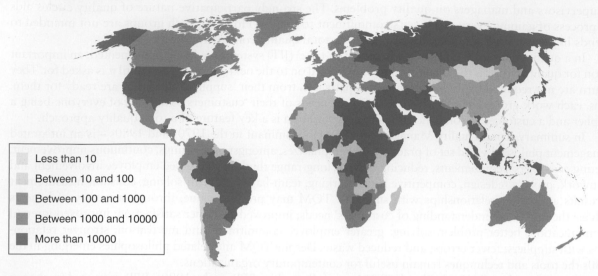

Less than 10

Between 10 and 100

Between 100 and 1000

Between 1000 and 10000

More than 10000

22.   The ISO 9000 family is amongst ISO's most widely known standards (see Figure 28.2). ISO 9000 standards are implemented by over 1 million organizations in 184 countries. (Data from **http://www. iso.org/iso/home/standards/certification/iso-survey.htm**, reproduced with the permission of ISO.) The top three countries for the total number of certificates issued were China, Italy and Spain, while the top three for growth in the number of certificates in 2012 were Spain, China and Romania. ISO 9000 has become an international reference for quality management requirements in business-to-business dealings. The ISO 9000 family is primarily concerned with 'quality management'. This means what the organization does to fulfil:

– the customer's quality requirements, and

– apply regulatory requirements, whilst aiming to

– enhance customer satisfaction, and

– achieve continuous improvement of its performance in pursuit of these objectives.

23.   In adopting the standards, organizations are required, amongst other things, to establish a set of procedures that cover all key processes in the business; monitor processes to ensure they are effective; keep adequate records; check outputs for defects, with appropriate and corrective action where necessary; review processes regularly and the quality system itself for effectiveness; and facilitate continual improvement. Developing a quality management system and meeting requirements of the standard can take months or years to do. Organizations may simply comply with the spirit of the standards as best practice or may elect to be audited by an independent and accredited certification body (not ISO). A company or organization that has been independently audited and certified to be in conformance with ISO 9001 may publicly state that it is 'ISO 9001 certified' or 'ISO 9001 registered'. ISO 9000 certification may be a requirement for doing business with certain other companies in the supply chain.

24.   Written procedures, instructions, forms or records (formalization) help ensure that everyone is not just 'doing his or her own thing', and that the organization goes about its business in an orderly and structured way. This means that time, money and other resources are utilized efficiently. To be efficient and effective, the organization can manage its way of doing things by systemization. This ensures that nothing important is left out and that everyone is clear about who is responsible for doing what, when, how, why and where. Large organizations, or ones with complicated processes, may not function well without management systems. ISO's management system standards make this good management practice available to organizations of all sizes, in all sectors, everywhere in the world.

25. To keep customers satisfied, the organization needs to meet customer requirements. The ISO 9001:2008 standard provides a tried and tested framework for taking a systematic approach to managing the organization's processes so that it turns out products which satisfy customers' expectations consistently. ISO 9001 is a useful basis for organizations to be able to demonstrate that they are managing their business in order to achieve consistent (good!) quality goods and services.

26. As stated earlier, ISO 9001 can be used as a supply chain tool to ensure that suppliers understand what is expected from them, and are capable of providing a consistent, conforming product. Suppliers often refer to being 'ISO 9000 certified', or having an 'ISO 9000-compliant QMS'. This will normally mean that they are claiming to have a QMS meeting the requirements of ISO 9001.

27. One objective of ISO 9001 is to provide a set of requirements that, if implemented effectively, will provide an organization with confidence that its suppliers can provide goods and services that meet the needs and expectations of the organization consistently and comply with applicable regulations. The requirements cover a wide range of topics, including senior management commitment to quality, customer focus, adequacy of resources, employee competence, process management, quality planning, product design, review of incoming orders, purchasing, monitoring and measurement of processes and products, calibration of measuring equipment, processes to resolve customer complaints, corrective/preventive actions and a requirement to drive continual improvement of the QMS. ISO 9001 does not, however, specify requirements for the goods or services purchased by a procuring company. It is up to the buyer to define requirements by making clear the needs and expectations for the product.

28. ISO 9001:2008 provides a set of standardized requirements for a quality management system, regardless of the user organization's type of business, its size or whether it is in the private or public sector. It is the only standard in the family against which organizations can be certified. The other standards in the family cover specific aspects such as fundamentals and vocabulary, performance improvements, documentation, training, and financial and economic aspects. The quality management system standards of the ISO 9000:2008 and ISO 9000:2000 series are based on eight quality management principles. These principles can be used by senior management as a framework to guide their organizations towards improved performance.

29. The eight quality management principles are defined in ISO 9000:2005, Quality Management Systems Fundamentals and Vocabulary, and in ISO 9004:2000, Quality Management Systems Guidelines for Performance Improvements:

1) Customer focus – organizations depend on their customers and therefore should understand current and future customer needs, should meet customer requirements and strive to exceed customer expectations.

2) **Leadership** – leaders establish unity of purpose and direction of the organization. They should create and maintain the internal environment in which people can become fully involved in achieving the organization's objectives (refer back to Chapter 6).

3) Involvement of people – people at all levels are the essence of an organization and their full involvement enables their abilities to be used for the organization's benefit (see Chapter 23).

4) Process approach – a desired result is achieved more efficiently when activities and related resources are managed as a process (see Chapter 21).

5) **System approach** to management – identifying, understanding and managing interrelated processes as a system contributes to the organization's effectiveness and efficiency in achieving its objectives (see Chapter 8).

6) Continual improvement – continual improvement of the organization's overall performance should be a permanent objective of the organization.

7) Factual approach to decision-making – effective decisions are based on the analysis of data and information (see Chapters 16).

8) Mutually beneficial supplier relationships – an organization and its suppliers are interdependent and a mutually beneficial relationship enhances the ability of both to create value.

30. On the face of it, it may appear that the standards promote bureaucracy and to some extent they do. However, it is important to distinguish bureaucracy from red tape. The latter has rules for rules sake whilst the former has its focus on efficiency. As was mentioned earlier in the book, bureaucracy should be

viewed as a continuum and not all bad. We also recognized that formalization and standardization were two key dimensions of bureaucracy. The requirements for a quality system have been standardized – but many organizations like to think of themselves as unique. So how does ISO 9001:2008 allow for diversity? The answer is that ISO 9001:2008 lays down the requirements a quality system must meet, but does not dictate how they should be met in any particular organization. This leaves great scope and flexibility for implementation in different business sectors and business cultures, as well as in different national cultures.

CONCLUSION

31.   Quality is an extremely important omnipresent strategic, tactical and operational management concept, associated both with differentiation and cost reduction strategies. It focuses on effectiveness and efficiency. Quality management typically begins with a consideration of customers, be they internal employees, other businesses or members of the public. Their wants and needs must be translated into specifications of one kind or another. These specifications need to be developed and tested. Resources and operational plans have to be drawn up. Then production (or delivery, if a service) can begin. The process of production (or delivery of a service) must be assessed and monitored at every stage in order to see where improvements can be made and ensure that outputs meet customer needs. Once the customer has received the goods or service, procedures need to be in place to deal with after-sales problems or queries, and to assess the level of customer satisfaction. Then the quality process can begin all over again – in a total quality management system it is a cyclical process which never stops. Organizations may use standards to help them develop their quality management systems. Certification of compliance with a standard such as ISO 9001:2008 can bring many benefits and may help a company win business.

QUESTIONS

1   Evaluate why quality is fundamental to business operations – in your answer you should define the concept of quality and quality management, discuss its goal and business benefits.

2   Briefly discuss the role of culture in quality management.

3   Discuss the ultimate purpose of quality systems within organizations.

4   Identify and describe two fundamentally different strategies used to bring about improvement within organizations.

USEFUL WEBSITES

International Organization for Standardization: **www.iso.org/iso/home.html**

ISO (International Organization for Standardization) is the world's largest developer and publisher of International Standards. Management system refers to what the organization does to manage its processes, or activities, so that its products or services meet the objectives it has set itself, such as: satisfying the customer's quality requirements, complying with regulations or meeting environmental objectives. Management system standards provide a model to follow in setting up and operating a management system. This model incorporates the features on which experts in the field have reached a consensus as being the international state of the art. The ISO 9000 family addresses 'Quality management'. This means what the organization does to fulfil: the customer's quality requirements, and applicable regulatory requirements, whilst aiming to enhance customer satisfaction, and achieve continual improvement of its performance in pursuit of these objectives.

REFERENCES

Evans, J. (2011) *Quality Management, Organization, and Strategy*, 6th edn, South Western.

CHAPTER 29
MANAGING RISK

Key Concepts

- Audit
- Business continuity and crisis management
- Risk
- Risk management
- Uncertainty

Learning Outcomes   Having read this chapter, you should be able to:

- define threat, hazard, vulnerability, risk, uncertainty and related constructs
- discuss the risk management process and its contribution to corporate governance
- explain how organizations attempt to 'control' risk
- contrast traditional with 'new' risk (management) thinking
- discuss the role of audit and business continuity management in managing risk.

Vignette
WINNING WITH RISK IN AN UNCERTAIN WORLD

Varunee Pridanonda is PwC Thailand's leader for governance, risk, compliance and internal audit services. Commenting on the PwC Global CEO Survey in 2013 she notes, 'The threats facing Chief Executive Officers are coming from all directions; they're coming harder and faster; ... Confronted with this changing risk landscape, CEOs recognize that traditional risk management techniques aren't enough.' There is a need 'to fuse strategy more closely with risk ... the board is well equipped to embed the right risk culture and behaviours ... The resulting awareness and scrutiny of risk at all levels in every business decision will help to protect the organization's reputation and further enhance its resilience in an uncertain world.'

only authorized people access systems for the right purpose is a key area for system control.

Identification, Authentication and Logical Access

When unauthorized users access information a confidentiality breach occurs and when unauthorized users add, delete or modify data, integrity and availability concerns arise. A user should be authorized before being allowed access to a specific system. Logical access controls are the means to do this. Logical access control essentially consists of three components: *Identification* and *Authentication* of the user and/or the equipment and *Authorization,* i.e. restrictions on what the user is able to do. Identification and authentication are the first two steps. A user will then be allowed to use the system as permitted by their authorizations. The identification and authentication of a user may make use of three classes of basic techniques. These classes may be used either on their own or in combination, they are: something known exclusively to the user (user ID and passwords, etc.), something possessed (such as tokens, keys, swipe card, etc.) or a unique physical attribute (biometric techniques). Cryptography is now widely used to authenticate equipment and users. Once authenticated the user may make use of the system according to their privileges. Users should only be provided with the functions necessary to perform their role.

Physical Control

Physical controls normally encompass the use of physical barriers such as building materials, perimeter fences, gates, guards, etc. Physical entry controls ensure that only authorized people are allowed access to organization resources. Many organizations ensure that all employees wear some form of visible identification (typically a pass card) and that they challenge anybody failing to display valid identification. The visitor management procedure typically goes hand in hand with this approach. Physical controls may include:

1. Site location and Site perimeter. If you can choose a site, evaluate the risk the location presents, e.g. proximity to natural hazards such as rivers that may flood or closeness to likely terrorist targets. Site access and visibility should also be considered. The site perimeter is generally the first line of physical control.
2. Building construction/Building shell.
3. Internal construction.
4. Access control and Guarding. This should be used to authenticate people who have access to the various parts of the building/site.
5. Intruder Detection System (IDS) and CCTV.

3. Control of Processes and Quality

Business processes (and quality) have characteristics that can be measured, analyzed, controlled and improved. Six Sigma has been adopted by many organizations that strive for near perfection; it is a disciplined, data-driven approach and methodology for eliminating (controlling) defects in any process. The fundamental objective is the implementation of a measurement-based strategy that focuses on process improvement and variation reduction through the application of Six Sigma improvement projects. A Six Sigma process is one in which 99.99966% of the products manufactured are statistically expected to be free of defects (3.4 defective parts/million) or any process activity that will deliver the specified output (e.g. orders fulfilled on time).

Six Sigma

The main purpose of a Six Sigma project is to solve a given problem in order to contribute to an organization's business goals (ISO, 2011).[3] Six Sigma (a trademark of Motorola, Inc.) is a set of techniques and tools for process improvement/control. It seeks to improve the quality of process outputs by identifying and removing (controlling) the causes of defects (errors) and minimizing variability in manufacturing and business processes. Each project follows a defined sequence of steps (see Figure 2) and has quantified value targets, such as reduce process cycle time, reduce costs, increase customer satisfaction and increase profits. ISO standard 13053:2011 deals exclusively with the application of Six Sigma to improve existing processes: Part 1 describes the five-phased methodology DMAIC (Define, Measure, Analyze, Improve and Control), and Part 2 describes tools and techniques to be used at each phase of the DMAIC approach. The key activities associated with each step of the DMAIC approach are shown in Figure 2.

[3] ISO (2011), 'BS ISO 13053-1:2011 Quantitative methods in process improvement. Six Sigma. DMAIC methodology', BSI.

of measure could be a count of the number of returns etc. by specified period of time.

4. **Comparison step** – the results of the measurement step (3) then have to be compared to a reference point (best practice metric).

5. **Action** – corrective action is then used to reduce any variance between the actual performance and reference point.

Root Cause Analysis (RCA)

Control often necessitates a deep understanding of the causes of a business problem. Feedback systems may draw attention to a problem area but they do not always establish the cause (detail). RCA (see also fishbone diagram) is a class of problem-solving methods aimed at identifying the root causes of problems or events; it is also an important quality management tool. Such analysis tries to explain the variations in a particular process (performance). This analysis may then be used to focus on the most important issues (see Pareto analysis) and may drive BPR. When analyzing process (work activity) problems (manifest through measurements of various indicators and targets) it is necessary to first find the *causes* of variation and to quantify the effect.

Step 1: Identify the Problem: define the problem faced; create a succinct summary of the problem and write it in a box half way down and on the right of a blank piece of paper or whiteboard (you can also use MSVisio which has a template to help) – see Figure 3 Cause effect (Fishbone) example. In the example we focus on the problem of on-time delivery i.e. the company is not always delivering goods to customers when the customer wants them (a quality problem in need of control).

FIGURE 3 Cause effect (Fishbone) example

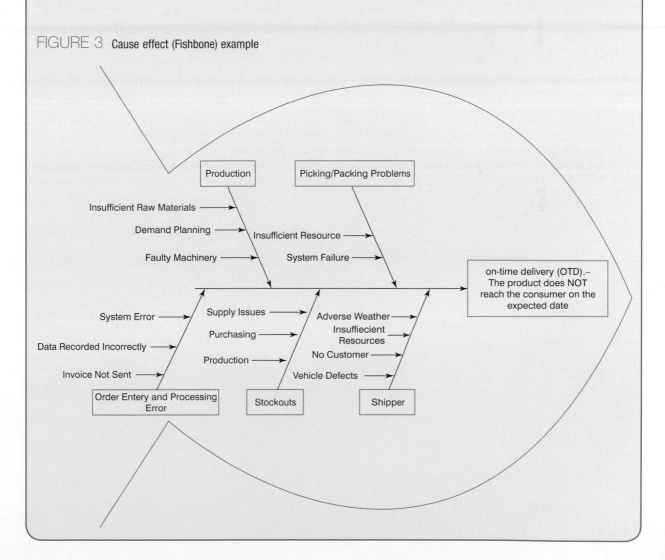

Step 2: Determine the Major Factors Involved: identify (typically through a brainstorming workshop) the factors that may be part of the problem. Create a 'spine' line across the page to the problem box highlighted in step 1. Then draw a line off the 'spine' of the diagram for each factor. For example, a major factor in delivering to customer's on-time might be the supplier (courier) or production, etc.

Step 3: Identify Possible Causes: for each of the factors considered in step 2. Brainstorm possible causes of the problem that may be related to the factor. Show these possible causes as shorter lines coming off the 'bones' of the diagram. Where a cause is large or complex, then it may be best to break it down into sub-causes. Show these as lines coming off each cause line. For example, in our diagram, we show 'insufficient resources' as one cause/reason why the distributor might not deliver goods on time.

Step 4: Analyze the Diagram: further investigate the most likely causes; discuss as a group and identify recommendations for solutions. Finally, select the (most critical) causes and solutions that you may seek to control in some way and implement the controls. Utilize change management skills (Section 9) at this point.

PART III
FUNCTIONAL MANAGEMENT – MARKETING, PRODUCTION (OPS), HRM, FINANCIAL AND IS/IT

There are five sections to the third part of this book: Marketing, Production (Operations), HR, Financial Management and Information Systems and Technology (IS/IT). Whilst this part of the book is about management functions, the reader should be aware of the debate regarding silo (fragmented) organizations and the need for integrated management – a matter dealt with in various parts of the book.

MARKETING MANAGEMENT

Marketing has to be concerned with what is going on outside the organization as well as with what is happening internally. Marketing fundamentals are introduced in Chapter 30. This is followed by three chapters which explore traditional (transactional) marketing in the form of the marketing mix. Following this, in Chapter 34, we explore the changes in marketing philosophies, approaches, strategies and tactics. Marketing thinking has progressed from a functionality based 'make and sell' philosophy to an enterprise-wide view on delivering customer value to target market segments. We outline the development of the marketing discipline; consider the evolution from transaction marketing to relationship marketing, to customer relationship marketing (CRM) and customer management and a more holistic marketing perspective. We will also consider direct and database marketing which paved the way for relationship marketing approaches.

PRODUCTION (OPERATIONS) MANAGEMENT

The production function of an organization exists in order to make available the goods or services required by the customer. Production management, in particular, is concerned with the provision of goods. It is the central part of the manufacturing process. Its responsibility is to plan, resource and control the processes involved in converting raw materials and components into the finished goods required to satisfy the needs and wants of the organization's existing and potential customers.

The transformation processes and activities (operations) start with the procurement of raw materials and transformational resources. Chapter 35 considers managing the procurement function: sourcing inputs. In this chapter we start by discussing sourcing strategies, considering issues such as insourcing and outsourcing (make or buy) and supplier selection; we will then describe the day-to-day purchasing process. Procurement or purchasing usually initiates the flow of materials through an organization. Purchased raw materials and parts to be used in the production process must be stored within a warehouse (inventory) before being transformed into the outputs (company's products and services) which will also be stored prior to distribution. Thus, Chapter 36 follows immediately from the previous chapter, considering the management of the logistics function. This is followed logically by Chapter 37 where we will focus on the transformational process – creating outputs (products and services); activities involved in creating a product. Finally, in Chapter 38 we are concerned with the application of technology to the different operations processes (work) and the manufacturing organization holistically.

HR MANAGEMENT

This section comprising five chapters on HR emphasizes people as the critical resource for organizations. It also identifies the contemporary role of the HR function within organizations. The emphasis throughout is on the activities of specialists within HR. Chapter 39 acts as a foundation chapter for the section and explores what HR management (HRM) is, how it has developed and its function within the organization. Specific HR activities are then explored. In Chapter 40 we consider resourcing: recruitment, selection and appointment and in Chapter 41 Performance Management (PM) and HR Development (HRD). Building successful employment relationships is important and makes good business sense as organizations with good employment relationships tend to be more successful. The employment relationship describes the dynamic, interlocking economic, legal, social and psychological relations that exist between individuals and their work organizations and is explored in Chapter 42. Since the early 1990s there has been a growing interest in International HRM (IHRM), reflecting the growing recognition that the effective management of human resources internationally is a major determinant of success or failure in international business. In Chapter 43 we establish the scope of IHRM, define key terms in IHRM and outline the differences between domestic and IHRM.

FINANCIAL MANAGEMENT

This section of the book contains two chapters. Chapter 44 provides an introduction to accounting, the accounting process, financial statements and different types of cost. The next chapter will focus more on management accounting, budgeting and the use of financial information in internal decision-making.

TECHNOLOGY MANAGEMENT

There are two chapters in the final section of this book part. Technology is considered broadly as a general means to enable employees and work towards the achievement of organizational goals and then more specifically in the management of information resources.

Section Eleven
Marketing
Management

CHAPTER 30
MARKETING
FUNDAMENTALS

Key Concepts

- Marketing
- Marketing audit
- Marketing concept
- Marketing mix
- Marketing orientation
- Marketing planning and plan

Learning Outcomes Having read this chapter, you should be able to:

- outline the marketing concept
- identify what is meant by the marketing mix
- evaluate generic competitive strategies
- explain the marketing planning process
- discuss ways of organizing the marketing department.

1.   This part of the book is about functions. A 'Functional' approach generally refers to an organizational structure based on business functions, such as Manufacturing, Finance, HR, Accounting, Sales and Marketing. Such functions, through their specific expertise, typically carry out a part of the mission of an organization; they are responsible for certain business activities. Some organizations may also classify 'core' (primary activities) or 'support' functions (secondary activities). Organizations may also refer to the 'Functional Manager', a manager who leads a particular function within a firm and 'Functional level strategy', i.e. long-range plans made by the functions of the business which support the competitive advantage pursued by the business level strategy.

2.   Marketing is the one function of management which must be particularly concerned with what is going on outside the organization as well as with what is happening internally. Marketing activities are conducted across the external and internal boundaries of the organizational system, and they are undertaken by managers of all functions, not only by marketing specialists. The idea of the 'marketing concept' is introduced in this chapter. Managers frequently pose questions such as how might we communicate with and relate to customers?; what is the role and value of the brand?; how do I identify markets and then

enter them?; what products should we offer and what should be the content of the business and product portfolio and, how do we price offerings? We address such issues in this part of the book.

3.   Every business or public organization has its market, that is to say the group of existing and potential buyers (prospects) or users of its goods and services. A market may consist of a mere handful of people, or it may consist of millions. Clearly, relationships with the market are also an important ingredient of strategy. Organizations have developed several different ways of regarding their existing and potential customers. The most notable options are as follows:

- **Production orientation** – in this situation, the organization concentrates its attention on production efficiency, distribution and cost in order to attract customers to its products. This works well when demand is well ahead of supply, and where lower costs will encourage people to buy.

- **Product orientation** – in this case the organization stands or falls by the quality of its products. The thinking behind this orientation is that customers buy products or services rather than solutions to problems. Examples of product orientation are to be found in education, the arts and journalism, where the inference is often that the supplier knows best what the customer needs.

- **Sales orientation** – here the dominant concept is that people will not buy until they are persuaded to buy by positive selling. Thus the focus of attention is more on the skills of selling, than on the needs of the buyer. Several life-insurance companies have adopted this approach over the years.

- **Market orientation** – a market-oriented organization is one which focuses on the needs of its customers. Its primary concern is to identify customer needs and wants so that these may be met with the highest level of customer satisfaction. In this situation, production responds to the demands of marketing rather than the other way round. Aside from having a customer orientation, the market orientation is also characterized as having a competitor orientation and a company-wide approach to marketing. This approach to marketing is called the 'marketing concept' and its perspective is radically different from the approaches of production, product and sales-oriented organizations.

4.   Few business organizations have total control over their markets. On the contrary, most businesses find they are in fierce competition with others wanting to serve the same group of buyers. In recent times, competition has become more widespread, as foreign competitors join domestic competitors in offering similar goods or services to the same market. Lower trade barriers, better worldwide transport systems and access to the Internet, digital technologies and social networks mean that new competitors can enter markets previously the preserve of just one or two key players. Suddenly, the world seems a smaller place, and major firms decide on their marketing strategies in a **global** context, both in terms of markets and suppliers. Thus '**globalization**' and 'competitiveness', especially in terms of competitive advantage, become increasingly important concepts to modern companies.

30.1 MARKETING AND THE MARKETING CONCEPT

5.   Baines, Fill and Page (2010) recognize the concept of marketing has changed over the years. **Marketing** is the management process responsible for identifying, anticipating and satisfying customer requirements profitably. The marketing concept is the philosophy that an organization should try to provide products which satisfy customers' needs through a coordinated set of activities that also allow the organization to achieve its goals. It takes the view that the most important stakeholders in the organization are the customers. This does not necessarily mean that the customer is always right, but it does mean that the customer forms the starting point for the organization's strategy. Organizations adopting the marketing concept also tend to see marketing as a very diffuse activity, shared by many and not just the preserve of a specialist group called marketing and sales. This is a very important consideration, for, as we shall see shortly in the discussion of the marketing mix, there are certain key issues, such as pricing, which must be considered and agreed on a shared basis.

6.   Adrian Palmer, Professor of Marketing, also considers what is meant by the term 'marketing'. He distinguishes between marketing as a fundamental philosophy (customer focus lying at the heart) and

marketing as a set of techniques. The marketing philosophy is reflected in company values (refer back to Chapter 17 and skills sheet 7). Such values influence employee behaviour throughout the organization. Marketing techniques include 'pricing, the design of channels of distribution, and new product development' (2012: p. 6). Taken together, the philosophy and techniques establish marketing as an activity that brings together buyers and sellers.

7.   Key marketing concepts include: customers, needs, value, exchange and markets, (Palmer 2012: p. 15). The 'customer' has been defined by many scholars. For example ISO (2011) defined it as an organization or person that receives a product; Baines, Fill and Page (2010) defined customer as the person who purchases and pays for (or initially requests and specifies, in the case of a non-financial transaction) a product, service, or other form of offering from a company or organization; and Palmer (2012) defined it as a person who buys a firm's products (although they may not be the actual consumers of the product). The value concept was introduced in Chapter 10 where we discussed why and how companies add value. Similarly, markets and competitiveness were discussed in Chapter 12, The Business Environment. The exchange concept refers to the provision or transfer of goods, services and ideas in return for something of value.

8.   Reference was made earlier to customer needs and wants. How do customer needs and wants differ? One way of distinguishing between them is to define needs as basic physical and psychological drives arising from being human (e.g. need for food, clothing, self-esteem, etc.), and to define wants as specific desires directed towards fulfilling the basic needs. A need for food, for example, could be transformed into a specific desire (want) for curried chicken, or for bread and cheese or countless other variations of food. The point is that human beings have relatively few needs, but can generate an enormous number of wants. Not surprisingly, therefore, most marketing efforts concentrate predominantly on satisfying people's wants. In addition to this, some marketing is directed specifically at creating or changing people's wants.

9.   The marketing role in an organization is carried out by numerous individuals. First, senior managers and their advisers, contributing to the organization's corporate plan, are fulfilling a marketing role by examining the marketplace and assessing the organization's ability to meet current and future demands on its resources. Second, many middle managers also carry out a marketing role when dealing with issues relating to their public. Finally, there is the marketing department. Their people are specifically charged with marketing duties – assessing customer wants, gathering market intelligence, obtaining customer reactions and organizing sales and distribution.

10.   Central to (traditional) marketing management is the concept of the **marketing mix** (Palmer 2012: p. 20). The marketing mix, shown in Figure 30.1, is a conceptual framework which highlights the important

FIGURE 30.1 **The marketing mix**

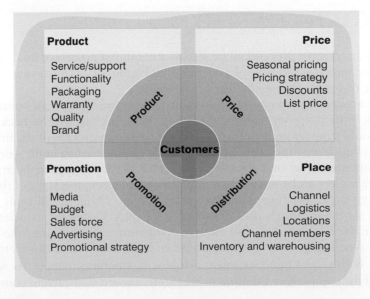

decisions made by marketing managers. Whilst there has been much debate about what should be included in the marketing mix, it is traditional to include the four elements of product, price, promotion and place (4Ps). Other scholars have added elements such as people, process and physical evidence – these will be discussed in more detail in the final marketing chapter of this book section. Product decisions are important because products are the means by which organizations satisfy customer needs. Pricing is a critical element of the marketing mix of most companies as it determines the revenue that will be generated. Place decisions include deciding how to transport (logistics) and where to distribute products (channels). Finally, promotion is used by companies to communicate the benefits of their products to their target markets. The following three chapters explore the marketing mix in more detail. Before considering detailed aspects of marketing, it will be helpful to look briefly at marketing planning and organization, since they are of such significance within modern marketing practice.

30.2 ORGANIZATION, STRATEGY, PLANNING AND IMPLEMENTATION

MANAGING THE MARKETING CONTRIBUTION

11. Having discussed what is meant by marketing, we now consider the challenges of marketing in practice: planning, organizing, implementing and controlling the marketing effort. Through the remainder of this chapter and section we will consider the marketing manager's activities such as: determining which markets to operate in, identifying competitors and the marketing strategies used by them and finally determining the organization's marketing goals, resource requirements and strategies.

12. Larger organizations will design marketing strategies, programmes and plans that meet customer and market needs. **Marketing planning** is a systematic process of assessing marketing opportunities and resources, determining marketing objectives and developing a thorough plan for implementation and control (Dibb *et al.*, 2006). It is a structured process that leads to a coordinated set of marketing decisions and actions, for a specific period, through analysis of the current marketing situation; clear marketing direction, objectives, strategies and programmes (Wood, 2010). The output of the process is the **marketing plan** which has been defined by many scholars. For example, Dibb *et al.* (2006) defined it as the written arrangements for specifying, implementing and controlling an organization's marketing activities and marketing mixes; and Wood (2010) defined it as an internal document outlining the marketplace situation, marketing strategies and programmes that will help the organization achieve its goals and objectives during a set period, usually a year.

THE MARKETING MANAGEMENT PROCESS

13. The marketing management process can be seen as a continual process of analysis, goal-setting, strategy, implementation, monitoring and control as depicted in Figure 30.2. This process helps to integrate the efforts of a wide range of people throughout the organization.

14. In Chapter 9 we argued that an organization must understand its strategic context. First, the organization must take stock of its purpose, mission, vision and corporate goals (refer back to Chapter 17). The marketing strategy should support and reinforce the corporate strategy. One of the first steps in marketing planning is an analysis which may include a SWOT analysis or a **marketing audit** – defined as a systematic examination of the marketing function's objectives, strategies, programmes, organization and performance to assess strengths, weaknesses and areas needing improvement. During this stage of the process the organization gains a thorough understanding about the target market. Other useful tools include the PESTLE analysis and the other tools and frameworks discussed in Chapter 12 and the associated skills sheet.

15. During this stage the marketer will also analyze competitors, determining who the competitors are, their strengths and weaknesses, goals and strategies. When customers have a choice, the organization must compete for business. With this in mind we might ask how companies compete. As was noted in Chapter 12, Porter's analysis of the competitive situation facing firms showed that current competitors were not the

FIGURE 30.2 The marketing management process

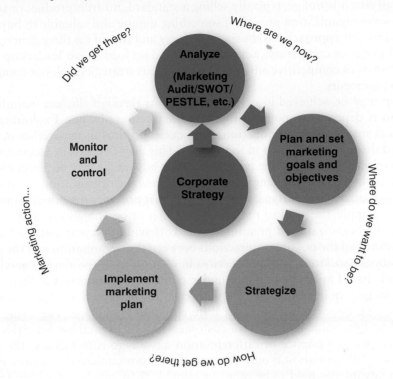

only competitive forces at work in the external environment. Suppliers and buyers also made an impact on the competitive situation, as did the actions of potential newcomers and the possibility of substitute products. Competitiveness, according to Porter and others, is primarily about delivering enhanced value to customers.

16. In the second stage of the process the organization asks where it wants to be. Marketing objectives and goals are then established. Marketing objectives include (1) Growth – business growth strategies (BGS) focus on how to develop/grow a business, i.e. win larger market share (e.g. through Market Penetration, Market Development, Alternative Channels, Product Development, New Products for New Customers), refer back to Chapter 17, para. 17 and Figure 17.2. In some cases niche objectives will be selected – a small sub-segment of a market which can be targeted with a distinct marketing strategy, (2) Hold – is another strategic objective based on defending against attacks from aggressive competitors, (3) Harvesting – is a strategic objective based on maximizing short-term profits and stimulating positive cash flow, often used in mature markets as firms/products enter a decline phase and (4) Divesting – is a strategic objective that involves selling or killing off a product when products continue to incur losses and generate negative cash flows.

17. There are many ways in which the marketing objectives and goals can be accomplished and a variety of strategies are identified and selected. Competitive advantages exist in relation to rivals operating within an industry as factors that enable an organization to earn a higher rate of profit. Such advantages emerge from the actions of organizations (internal sources) or from changes in the external environment (external sources). With regard to external sources, an organization may be more capable or better equipped to exploit changes in customer demand, technology, political or economic factors. An external change may create opportunity for profit. Consequently, organizations must be able to identify and respond to opportunity. As markets become increasingly turbulent, so responsiveness to external change has become increasingly important as a source of competitive advantage.

18. There are two fundamental, internal sources of competitive advantage (see **generic routes to competitive advantage**): cost and differentiation. An organization may compete by offering customers what they want at the lowest price/cost or may differentiate their products and services in such a way that the

customer is prepared to pay a premium price for them. Cost leadership requires the organization to find and exploit sources of cost advantage, typically selling a standard, no-frills product or service whilst differentiation necessitates the organization providing something unique and valuable to buyers. They represent two fundamentally different approaches to business strategy and two of the three generic strategies referred to by Porter. A third source of competitive advantage is based on focus. Cost leadership and differentiation are industry-wide sources of competitive advantage whilst focus strategies seek out competitive advantages for particular market segments.

19. Cost leadership may be achieved in many ways such as through efficient manufacturing processes, whilst differentiation is dependent upon creativity and marketing abilities. Exploiting new technologies and business processes may improve production techniques and thus increase efficiency. Cost advantages may also be obtained through a reduction in input costs. This may come from access to raw materials and location advantages (global sourcing). One form of location advantage may be a reduction in labour costs.

20. Differentiation is about understanding customers and how the organization can meet customer needs. The organization differentiates itself from competitors when it provides something unique and valuable to those customers; for example, the product may perform better or be of higher quality. In return, customers are prepared to pay the organization a premium price. Differentiation may manifest itself in product or service features and in any of the possible interactions between the organization and the customer in selling, delivering and providing associated customer services in relation to the product or service offered.

21. Differentiation is based much more on an understanding of customers and their needs. Establishing differentiation advantage requires creativity. As with cost advantages, the value chain provides a useful framework for analyzing opportunities to gain differentiation advantage. The value chain enables the organization to analyze how value is created for customers and focus on those activities which can be used to achieve differentiation. The essence of differentiation advantage is to increase the perceived value of offerings to customers. Differentiation is only effective if it is communicated to customers.

22. Differentiation advantages tend to be more sustainable than cost-based advantages. This is because cost-based advantages are much more vulnerable to change as a result of external forces. Advantages based on low labour costs, technology or business processes can disappear quickly.

23. Whilst we have presented two core generic strategies, they are not presented as an either/or choice and organizations tend not to consider differentiation strategy in isolation from cost based strategies. All organizations must consider efficiency goals. Interestingly, however, differentiation adds costs. Differentiation costs include higher quality raw materials and other inputs, specialized production machinery and skilled employees. Organizations which differentiate are likely to spend more on packaging, marketing and sales channels. In pursuit of differentiation strategies, organizations will still seek out cost efficiencies as a prerequisite of profitability.

24. Companies that are more responsive may also have an advantage over their sluggish rivals. Responsiveness is enabled through resources (information) and capabilities (flexibility). Speed of response as a source of competitive advantage is termed time-based competition. Technological improvements in communications, and business process improvements, coupled with manufacturing technologies, have enabled organizations to be both flexible and responsive, reducing cycle times drastically.

25. Once established, competitive advantage is subject to erosion by competition. The durability of the advantage is related to the ability of competitors to either imitate or substitute factors leading to advantage. Imitation necessitates competitor identification and diagnosis of the source of competitive advantage and must be both able and motivated to acquire or develop the resources and capabilities necessary for imitating the advantage. Organizations seek out sustainable competitive advantages where barriers exist to imitation. For example they may secure exclusive access to key raw materials, develop proprietary standards, act in secrecy or take steps to persuade rivals that imitation will be unprofitable. In some cases there may be a first mover advantage whereby the initial occupant may gain access to resources and capabilities that a follower cannot match, for example through a patent or copyright.

26. Having chosen a strategy, the next step is implementation, typically through a 12-month marketing plan. In order to organize the marketing function there is a need to design the internal and external relationships, establish policies and procedures as well as create the means and methods by which different participants in the marketing function can carry out their responsibilities in an effective and efficient manner. Three important questions should be addressed when organizing the marketing resources: should the organization be (1) vertical or horizontal, (2) centralized or decentralized and (3) bureaucratic or flexible.

MARKETING ORGANIZATION

27.   We discussed the horizontal organization in Chapter 10 (paras. 10–12) and again in Chapter 20 where we also considered vertical structures. In Chapter 20 we also presented various organizational forms: functional, product, area or customer base organizations and discussed the concept of centralization (para. 14). If marketing is centralized, then headquartered marketing managers are responsible for most of the important decisions. When marketing is decentralized the local marketing manager will have more autonomy and control over the marketing decisions. A decentralized approach can be used to motivate marketing managers at a local level. Such managers are generally seen to be closer to the customer and therefore able to factor their requirements into speedier decisions. The bureaucratic marketing organization relies on rules and procedures for making decisions or solving problems. However, whilst this may ensure consistency and a standardized approach (possibly strengthening the brand) it can make the company less responsive to changing customer needs.

28.   Marketing management needs to be integrated with other management functions. Some organizations and marketers have even questioned whether they should have a marketing department at all in the belief that this may hinder a true customer centred marketing orientation. Indeed Drucker believed marketing to be so basic that it could not be considered to be a separate function. By placing all marketing activity with a specific department other employees may feel no responsibility for attracting and retaining customers.

29.   In many organizations, however, the marketing department will coordinate other functions and take responsibility for activities such as advertising, sales management and pricing. The marketing manager must work closely with production to shape the product offering in terms of value, cost and volume. The marketing manager must work with HR in order to recruit the right talent and develop an appropriate innovative and customer-oriented culture. Marketing managers must also work with finance who will allocate funding and may also become involved with customer management decisions, particularly in terms of credit management.

30.   There are a variety of types of marketing organization. In some cases marketing and sales are separate departments whilst in other cases they may report to the same manager. In some larger organizations there may be centralized and local marketing functions. The smaller organization may consider outsourcing some aspects of its marketing operation and yet others may well resource marketing activities through the use of cross-functional teams.

31.   Finally, a range of monitoring and control systems are utilized to assure goals are attained using the resources allocated. Consideration must also be given to the marketing budget and ultimately, control of the marketing plan. A marketing budget will indicate how much is to be spent on marketing activities and is an important aspect of the marketing manager's job. The purpose of a marketing budget is to consolidate revenues and costs into one comprehensive document. We discussed the control of behaviour through budgets in Chapter 18 (refer back), presenting the budgetary process in Figures 18.1 and 18.2. We will also consider budgets in Section 14 of this book. The process involves making forecasts (of sales and related expenditures) based on the proposed marketing strategy and programmes. Such forecasts are used to construct profit and loss statements which can be used by various parts of the organization for planning purposes.

30.4 GLOBALIZATION AND INTERNATIONAL MARKETING

32.   In the preceding paragraphs we described the marketing planning process. As mentioned earlier, the tendency for firms to operate in a global market, both for sales and supplies, has accelerated over the past two decades. It is no longer unusual for major manufacturing firms to be investing in substantial operations overseas, whilst maintaining similar facilities in their domestic market. Adopting a global approach to marketing strategy provides two distinct ways in which firms can gain a competitive advantage, or at least offset a domestic disadvantage. These are (1) a global firm can spread activities among nations to serve the world, and this not only enables business expansion but also helps to offset poor returns in domestic or other select markets and (2) a global firm can coordinate dispersed activities, for example where marketing, distribution and after-sales are located in the buyers' nation, but manufacturing and supply can be located

anywhere. Global presence makes available to the firm's managers five value-creation opportunities: (1) to adapt to local market differences, (2) to exploit economies of global scale, (3) to exploit economies of global scope, (4) to unleash optimal locations for activities and resources and (5) to maximize knowledge transfer across locations.

33.   Companies must simultaneously capture global-scale efficiency, respond to national markets and cultivate a worldwide learning capability for driving continuous innovation across borders. **Internationalization** is the gradual process of taking organizational activities into other countries. Such companies may then be described as global, **multidomestic** or transnational in their orientation. The global organization trades internationally as if the world were a single and boundaryless entity whilst the multidomestic organization trades internationally as if the world were a collection of many different (country) entities. Transnational enterprises (TNE) operate a balanced combination of the multidomestic and **global strategies**.

34.   There are several alternatives open to companies wishing to globalize their operations, as follows:

-    By exporting their goods and services to foreign countries, which is the easiest option.

-    By entering into joint ventures with companies in the target nation through licensing agreements or joint ownership, for example.

-    By direct investment in new plant and manufacturing facilities in the foreign country. Worldwide operations will imply that the organization's marketing mix (see following chapters) will have to be adapted to meet conditions in the foreign countries in which the firm is operating. It will also be necessary to have an appropriate marketing organization to support its overseas activities, ranging from an export sales department (at the very least) through an international division to the establishment of a full international subsidiary company.

International marketing involves the organization making one or more marketing mix decisions across national boundaries.

CONCLUSION

35.   This chapter sets the scene for the marketing section of the book. We defined marketing, discussing both a philosophy and set of techniques and the marketing concept and then contrasted marketing from a domestic and global standpoint. We recognized that when customers have a choice, the organization must compete for their business. With this in mind we outlined how companies compete. We then explored the marketing planning process which starts with a consideration of the corporate strategy and an analysis of the environmental context. It culminates in a detailed plan. This plan must be implemented and controlled and the marketer must organize resources if marketing and corporate goals are to be attained.

QUESTIONS

1   Organizations have developed several different ways of regarding their existing and potential customers. Evaluate the most notable options.

2   Explain what is meant by a) product orientation, b) sales orientation, c) production orientation and d) a market orientation.

3   Explain the marketing process in your own words.

4   Evaluate how globalization might impact upon the marketing operation/function.

USEFUL WEBSITES

European Marketing Academy: **www.emac-online.org** European Marketing Academy – a website that provides a society for persons professionally concerned with or interested in marketing theory and research

Michael Porter: **www.isc.hbs.edu** Based at Harvard Business School, the Institute studies competition and its implications for company strategy; the competitiveness of nations, regions and cities; and solutions to social problems.

American Marketing Association Site: **www.marketingpower. com/Pages/default.aspx** Provides a 5-step overview to marketing planning

Academy of Marketing: **www.academyofmarketing.org** Academy of Marketing (UK) – a Learned Society catering for the needs of marketing researchers, educators and professionals

Chartered Institute of Marketing: **www.cim.co.uk** A leading international body for marketing and business development.

Knowledge Wharton: **http://knowledge.wharton.upenn.edu** Leading business school publishes a bi-weekly online magazine that often includes articles on marketing

A. T. Kearney Globalization Index: **www.atkearney.com/index. php/Publications/globalization-index.html**

REFERENCES

Baines, P., Fill, C. and Page, K. (2010) *Marketing*, 2nd edn, Oxford University Press.

Dibb, S., Simkin, L., Pride, W.M. and Ferrell, O.C. (2006) *Marketing: Concepts and Strategies*, 5th edn, Houghton Mifflin International Inc.

Palmer, A. (2012) *Introduction to Marketing – Theory and Practice*, 3rd edn, Oxford University Press.

Wood, M.B. (2010) *Essential Guide to Marketing Planning*, 2nd edn, FT/Prentice Hall.

CHAPTER 31
THE MARKETING MIX: PRODUCT AND PRICE

Key Concepts

- Brand, branding and brand equity
- Price
- Product and product mix
- Product life cycle

Learning Outcomes Having read this chapter, you should be able to:

- discuss what is meant by branding
- explain the process by which new products are developed and adopted by markets
- understand how the management of products and services changes over the different stages of the life cycle
- identify internal and external pricing influences
- understand pricing strategies and how to price products and services.

1.   Once a company determines its target market and establishes a position within that market, it is ready to begin its marketing. The tools used for this are the controllable variables of the marketing mix (Barringer and Ireland, 2010) introduced in the previous chapter. The mix is effectively the tactical 'toolkit' of the marketing programme; product, place/distribution, promotion, price (and people) variables, as illustrated previously in Figure 30.1. Baines, Fill and Page (2010) deem it to be the list of items a marketing manager should consider when devising plans for marketing products. The marketing mix is a key component of a **marketing plan**. The offer made to the customer can be altered by varying the mix elements. Each aspect of the marketing mix is described in this section of the book, starting in this chapter with the product and price.

31.1 PRODUCTS AND BRANDING

2.   New product or service development is an essential part of business (refer back to Chapter 22 where we discussed innovation, see Figure 22.2). Any discussion about the marketing mix must begin with the product. The '**product**', in this context, means anything that is offered to a market for its use or consumption.

The product can be a physical object or a service of some kind. The marketer must also assess what constitutes the product from the customer's perspective.

3.   *Product decisions* include determining the brand name, functionality, level of quality, warranty, accessories and ancillary services. Product design can be thought of as the characteristics or features (including quality) of a product or service that determine its ability to meet the needs of the user. In contrast the product development process is the overall process of strategy, organization, concept generation, product and marketing plan creation and evaluation and commercialization of a new product. In order to reach a final design of a product or service, the design activity must pass through several stages. However, stages are not necessarily followed in a linear fashion.

4.   Whilst there are many ways to describe the product development process, the first phase of a product development effort is typically termed the concept development phase. Here a company identifies ideas for new or revised products and services. Ideas for new products or services can come from many different sources inside and outside the organization. New ideas may come from customers, competitors, front office staff or the research and development department. The second (screening and planning) phase of a product development effort begins to address the feasibility of a product or service. Organizations will assess the ability of an operation to produce a product or service (feasibility), the acceptability of the product or service (will customers want it?) and the associated risks. Having created a feasible, acceptable and viable product or service concept, the next stage is to create a preliminary design. The company invests heavily in the development effort and builds and evaluates prototypes (design and development phase). Preliminary designs are evaluated and improved upon. In the fourth phase of a product development effort (commercial preparation phase) the organization invests heavily in the operations and supply chain resources (infrastructure) needed to support the new product or service. The final phase of a product development effort is termed the launch phase. For physical products, this usually means 'filling up' the supply chain with products. For services, it can mean making the service broadly available to the target marketplace. Once a product has been designed, operational managers must make important decisions concerning processes for producing those goods or services. The choice of production process is discussed in Section 12.

5.   Once designed and developed, branding is used to help customers differentiate between the various offerings in a market – to distinguish the goods of one producer from another. Buyers use information from a variety of sources in order to evaluate the product they may wish to purchase. A brand is more than a product argues Keller (2012: p. 31). A **brand** is a name, term, design, symbol or any other feature that identifies one seller's good or service as distinct from those of other sellers. Marketers often refer to branded products. These are products that are easily recognized and associated with a particular seller/manufacturer, e.g. Kellogg's corn flakes or the Dyson vacuum cleaner. Brands matter because if consumers recognize a brand it can be used to simplify the purchase process. Examples of strong and valuable brands include Coca-Cola, IBM, Microsoft, Google, Apple, McDonalds and Disney.

6.   The design, performance and quality of the product itself provide intrinsic cues (signals) whereas brand names present extrinsic cues. Companies may choose from several branding strategies: (1) all branding may occur at the organizational level-corporate brand (see for example Disney or Virgin). A corporate brand increases the attractiveness of the entire company, building trust, loyalty and even commitment amongst stakeholders. Through a corporate brand, a consistent appearance is maintained. This approach is common amongst related product lines but may be problematic as product variety and market diversity increases, (2) when products or customer expectations vary, an alternative branding approach, house branding, may be adopted. In such cases, the company name may be used in conjunction with the product name and (3) finally in some cases it may be beneficial to engage in separate branding.

7.   Wood (2010: p. 126) argues that, in planning for a brand, you should identify ways to increase brand equity. In simple terms this is the marketing and financial value associated with a brand's strength in a market. It is the brand's assets (or liabilities) linked to a brand's name and symbol that add to (or subtract from) a product/service. Attributes of brand equity include the extent to which customers are aware of the brand; customer associations with the brand; customer feelings about the brand and ultimately the customer's relationship with it. Wood believes that higher brand equity contributes to sustained competitive advantage. It can build long-term loyalty. Keller (2012: p. 57) believes brand equity to be one of the most popular and potentially important marketing concepts to arise in the 1980s.

8.   Consequently, in order to increase brand equity, the marketer will seek to make customers in the targeted segment aware of their brand identity. In shaping associations with the customer, they will define and communicate what the brand stands for. When customers understand what the brand stands for they can short cut purchase decisions. Ideally, marketers will want their customers to believe in the brand, trust it and perceive associated positive qualities, possibly even forming an emotional connection with it. Finally, the marketer will want to encourage strong and enduring brand relationships because loyal customers tend to buy more and are less likely to switch to competing brands. Furthermore, they may be willing to pay a premium price for the brand.

9.   Products, strongly branded or not, need to be packaged. **Packaging** is an important factor in the presentation of a product to the market. It has both a functional and communication role. Similarly, labels deliver information about product use and help promote the brand. Not only does packaging provide protection for the product, but it can also reinforce the brand image and the point-of-sale attraction to the buyer. The protective aspect of packaging is vital in respect of certain items. Some goods may not need such protection, but other considerations apply, such as the appearance of the goods on the shelf, or the possibility of seeing the contents through the packaging. Other aspects of packaging may emphasize the convenience of the pack, as for example in cigarette packets which may be opened and reopened several times, or beer cans, which can be opened safely by pulling a ring.

10.   Some products are sold with a very strong emphasis on after-sales service, warranties, guarantees, technical advice and similar benefits. Mail-order firms invariably have an arrangement whereby, if customers are not satisfied with the goods received, they may return them at the firm's expense without any questions being raised. Car retailers sell vehicles with various kinds of warranties concerning replacement of faulty parts at the supplier's expense. In recent years the growth of 'consumerism' or consumer protection lobbies has led to many organizations taking action to improve the service to the customer after the sale has been concluded.

11.   Since most, if not all, of the organization's revenue is going to be obtained from the sale of its products, it is important that the range and quality of the **product mix** is frequently evaluated and amended. Organizations need to develop and maintain a competitive combination of products and/or services – a **product portfolio**. Portfolios will vary in terms of the number of product lines, the age structure of products and the number of variations of the total products. The marketer must ensure a sufficiently large number of products exist in order to generate sufficient cash flow to finance new product development or penetration and expansion strategies. In order to maintain a balanced portfolio, new products are developed continually and introduced into markets. However, the marketer must be careful to ensure **product cannibalization** risk is minimized. Cannibalization occurs where one product within a company's range reduces sales of other products in its range (Palmer, 2012) – *see also* channel cannibalization.

12.   The process of managing groups of brands and product lines is called portfolio planning. The business portfolio is the collection of businesses and products that make up the company. The best business portfolio is one that fits company strengths and helps exploit the most attractive opportunities. The company must (1) analyze its current business portfolio and decide which businesses should receive more or less investment and (2) develop growth strategies for adding new products and businesses to the portfolio, whilst at the same time deciding when products and businesses should no longer be retained.

13.   The **Boston Matrix** is a well-known tool for the marketing manager – it is an approach to product portfolio planning (see **product portfolio analysis**). The matrix analyzes the success of a company's products or services by looking at the percentage of sales they have in the market and how fast the sales are growing. It has two controlling aspects, namely relative market share plotted on the X-axis and market growth, plotted on the Y-axis. Typically each axis is divided in two with a low and high category thus making a 2×2 matrix, see Figure 31.1. Market share is the percentage of the total market serviced by the company, measured either in revenue terms or unit volume terms. Market growth is used as a measure of a market's attractiveness. Markets experiencing high growth reflect expansion of the total market share available, with plenty of opportunity for all to make money. By contrast, competition in low growth markets is often bitter and whilst a company may enjoy high market share in the short term, given a few months or years, the situation might be very different; this makes low growth markets less attractive.

14.   Having considered relative share and growth rates, the organization may consider one of four possible strategies: (1) build share: the company can invest to increase market share, (2) hold: the company

FIGURE 31.1 **The Boston Matrix**

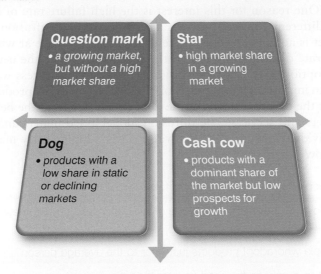

invests just enough to remain in its present position, (3) harvest: the company reduces the amount of investment in order to maximize the short-term cash flows and profits and (4) divest: the company can divest – in order to use the resources elsewhere. Thus, product management includes the introduction of new products, marketing of existing products and the elimination of others. Resources and the marketing system may not cope with the introduction of too many products over a short space of time.

15.   Emphasis on the make-up of the product is not only vital because of the need to sell benefits to potential customers, but also to take account of another key factor, the '**product life cycle**'. Studies have shown that most products pass through a series of stages – their life cycle – from the time they are introduced until the time they are withdrawn. A product will typically pass through five major stages in its life. These are shown in Figure 31.2. The consequences of these stages of the product life cycle are as follows:

–   Introduction: costs are high (because they include the development costs), sales and profits are low. Few competitors. Price relatively high.

–   Growth: sales rise rapidly. Profits at peak level. Price softens. Increasing competition. Unit costs decline. Mass market appears.

–   Maturity: sales continue to rise, but more slowly. Profits level off. Competition at its peak. Prices soften further. Mass market.

–   Saturation: sales stagnate. Profits shrink. Measures taken against remaining competition. Prices fiercely competitive. Mass market begins to evaporate.

–   Decline: sales decline permanently. Profits low or even zero. Product is withdrawn from the market.

FIGURE 31.2 **Product life cycle**

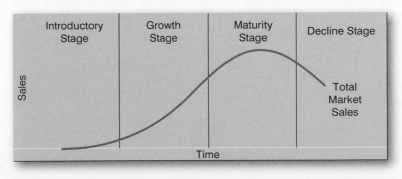

16. Marketing managers within organizations have long been concerned with how to launch new products more efficiently. One reason for this interest is the high failure rate of new consumer products. Products are adopted by different consumer groups at different times. Diffusion is the process by which a new idea or new product is accepted by the market; the extent and pace at which a market is likely to adopt new products. The rate of diffusion refers to the speed with which the new idea spreads from one consumer to the next. Adoption is similar to diffusion. The adoption process was first described almost 50 years ago but remains an important marketing tool. This extension of the product life cycle simply looks at who adopts products at the different stages of the life cycle. It describes the behaviour of consumers as they purchase new products and services. The diffusion model aided understanding of the consumption of new products. The individual categories of innovator, early adopter, early majority, late majority and laggards are described below:

- Innovators – first people to adopt a new product; they want to be ahead,

- Early adopters – enjoy being at the leading edge of innovation and buy into new products at an early stage, are key opinion leaders

- Early majority – people who adopt products just prior to the average person

- Late majority – tend to purchase the product later than the average person, sceptical but eventually adopt because of economic necessity/social pressure

- Laggards – the last people to adopt, suspicious of new products and oriented towards the past.

Various scholars and practitioners argue the marketer should focus on one group of customers at a time, using each group as a base for marketing to the next group. The most difficult step is making the transition between early adopters and early majority (so-called the chasm). If a successful organization can create a 'bandwagon' effect then momentum builds and the product becomes a de facto standard.

31.2 PRICE

17. Of the marketing mix variables, many managers regard *pricing decisions* (**price variable**) to be the most difficult decisions. Pricing decisions are closely intertwined with product decisions. After all, the price often determines the attractiveness of a company's offer. In this section we explain the importance of pricing decisions and the factors which influence the final price. Product pricing is important because it may be used by the buyer to judge quality, attractiveness and general value (cues). Pricing may be used as a competitive strategy and will interact with distribution. In short, proper pricing of goods and services can be a key to success for the organization.

18. Figure 31.3 shows a selection of pricing strategies and the internal and external influences. Five major internal (5Cs) influences are shown:

Costs – the cost to produce products needs to be recouped from the price. Fixed costs remain constant for a specified time period and are not affected by the volume of activity. Variable costs are those expenses which vary according to the number of units of product made or service sold. For instance, variable costs in the drinks market would include plastic bottles in which to place the liquid. The breakeven point refers to the volume level for a business at which total revenues cover total costs.

$$\text{Breakeven point} = \frac{\text{Total fixed costs}}{\text{Unit Price}-\text{Variable costs per unit}}$$

Example: How many units of product must be sold at price €10 where the total fixed costs are €10 000 and a unit's variable costs are €5?

$$? = \frac{10\ 000}{10-5}$$

= 2000 units, i.e. if the company sells more than 2000 units it will gain profit; sales below this figure will result in a loss.

FIGURE 31.3 **Pricing**

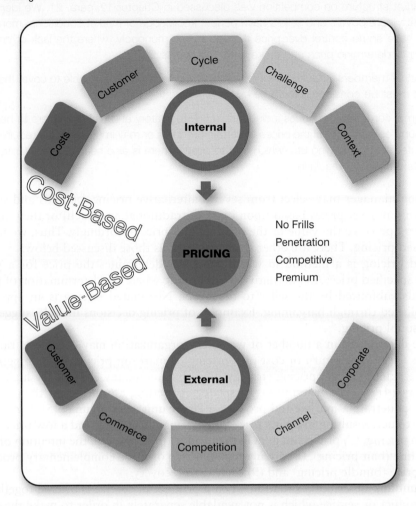

Customer – pricing decisions should be consistent with the customer segment targeted (are they bargain hunters, affluent, etc.).

Cycle – pricing decisions will change during the product life cycle. An organization may start with either a market skimming, premium or market penetration pricing strategy. Competition is likely to increase during the growth state and pricing may reflect a need to stimulate higher demand for greater economies of scale. Thus, as competition varies at each stage of the product life cycle so too might the price.

Challenge – price will be influenced by various organizational goals and targets, particularly in terms of revenue generation, market share, etc. The company may be intent on profit maximization, sales growth or simply survival.

Context – pricing is also influenced by the other marketing mix decisions.

19. The five major external (5Cs) are:

Customer – whereas the choice of customer segment was deemed an internal influence, customers themselves constitute a significant external influence on price. The offer price must be within what the customer considers an acceptable range.

Commerce – price will also be affected by demand and other factors within the marketplace where commerce takes place. The marketer must be sensitive to concepts such as the elasticity of demand. When demand is elastic a small change in price will usually produce a large change in quantity demanded. Similarly, when demand is not elastic a small percentage change in price will usually produce a small change in quantity demanded.

Competition – customers will evaluate the costs and benefits of competing products when considering value. The effects of the market structure on competition was discussed in Chapter 12, para. 21. We identified the perfectly completive market where buyers and sellers have perfect knowledge of market conditions; monopolistic competition where firms have some control over price through to the monopoly, where the lack of competition enables the dominant firm to determine price and make abnormal profits.

Channel – all channel members (supply chain entities/intermediaries) have to be able to cover their own costs; thus all of these costs must be considered to some extent when setting the price.

Corporate – external corporate influences include the legal, regulatory and ethical matters to be considered when pricing. Some countries may control the prices of certain products or may impose certain requirements with regard to product attributes and packaging etc. which add to costs. There is also need to consider taxes (such as VAT) and other aspects of industry regulation.

20.   The marketing manager may select from several alternative pricing methods and strategies. Fundamentally, a company may set prices based upon costs (a traditional approach) or they may seek to determine how customers perceive the value of the product and price accordingly. Thus, we might distinguish cost and value-based pricing. There are other strategies such as those discussed below.

21.   Administered pricing is a method in which the seller determines the price for a product and the customer pays the specified price. An alternative is bid pricing where the determination of prices is through sealed or open bids submitted by the seller to the buyer. Negotiated pricing is an approach where the final price is established through bargaining. Examples of pricing decisions include: suggested retail price, discounts and seasonal pricing.

22.   Price may be determined in a number of ways. The organization may consider a range of objectives for pricing such as (1) rate of return or cost plus pricing or mark-up pricing, (2) competition-led pricing, (3) market or price-skimming is a pricing strategy whereby a company charges the highest possible price that buyers will pay, (4) market penetration – a strategy of setting a price below the prices of competing brands in order to penetrate a market and produce a larger unit sales volume, (5) demand led – the level of demand for a product, resulting in a high price when demand is strong and a low price when demand is weak, (6) premium pricing, (7) pricing an item in the product line low, with the intention of selling a higher-priced item in the line (bait pricing), (8) pricing together two or more complementary products and selling them for a single price (bundle pricing) and (9) early cash recovery.

23.   Pure price bundling describes a situation when a product or service is offered together with another complementary product or service which is not available separately in order to make the original product or service seem more attractive (e.g. a CD with a music magazine or a mobile phone package with text messages and international call packages included in the price). It refers to the practice of charging a combined price for a number of products, rather than setting prices for each individually. In some cases, organizations may choose later to unbundle the offering.

24.   The marketing manager may have less influence over pricing of some products than others. Commodities and commoditized products have an established market price – the mechanisms of supply and demand dictates that price when products are undifferentiated. A variety of factors influence price setting. Costs determine a product's lower-price limit. The attractiveness of a product to the target customers determines the theoretical price ceiling in a given market. However, the purchasing power of customers, itself influenced by income distribution, exchange rates and inflation will drive price down. Furthermore, additional costs must be accounted for when selling in another country.

25.   Few products stand still in terms of their costs. Labour costs increase from year to year; material costs and energy costs may be subject to less regular, but sharper, increases; interest rates may be extremely variable, and hence the cost of financing products fluctuates. Many costs can be offset by productivity savings. Therefore, the costs which are the most crucial are those which represent sudden and substantial increases, which cannot be absorbed by improving productivity. In this situation, price increases are inevitable, and the question is 'by how much should we increase them?'. In certain situations, it may be possible to gain a temporary advantage over competitors by raising prices by the lowest possible margin, and offering some other advantage such as improved after-sales service or credit terms.

26.   Competitor activity has an important bearing on pricing decisions. The most obvious example is when a competitor raises or lowers prices. Assuming your product offers no particular advantages over a rival and the rival drops their price, you may be forced to follow suit; however, price wars are often destructive. If, on the other hand, there are other advantages to be offered in your marketing mix, there may be no pressure at all to reduce your price. If a competitor raises their price, perhaps because of rising costs, it may be possible to hold yours steady, provided rising costs can be contained. Pricing is a very flexible element in the marketing mix and enables firms to react swiftly to competitive behaviour.

27.   Payment terms also reflect important decisions for the marketing manager. The organization desires payment as quickly as possible due to the impact upon cash flows and subsequent non or late payment risks. Payment methods regulate the way goods or services are exchanged. Alternatives include payment in advance, deposits, letters of credit and payment against documents (invoices). Companies may manage payment risks through the use of terms and conditions (transferring liabilities, identifying preferred currency), guarantees and insurance. Companies may also conduct customer risk assessment and credit risk assessment before making offers.

28.   Whilst a company may set a price for its product it may, under certain circumstances, adapt that price. For example, discounts may be given for a variety of reasons; customers may be allowed to trade in and receive credit towards purchases of new products; prices may be marked down during certain seasons or periods in order to attract sales when they are normally sluggish and finally prices may be adapted for customers according to their segment, for example, age.

CONCLUSION

29.   Products (including services) must be developed and launched in order to generate revenue for the organization. They then pass through various stages, as reflected in the product life cycle. Organizations rarely rely on a single product and the process of managing groups of brands and product lines is called portfolio planning. We introduced the Boston Matrix to help consider management of the portfolio. Products must compete with similar rival offerings and brands help customers to differentiate between offerings. Packaging and labelling can help contribute to the success of a product/brand. Before a product is offered, the organization must determine the offer price. This is important because price determines profitability and revenue generation. Price, costs, quality and value are interconnected. There are a variety of pricing policies and strategies and the marketing manager must consider many factors when setting price. Whilst competitor pricing must be considered, price wars can devastate companies and there are ways to avoid them.

QUESTIONS

1   What is the product life cycle?

2   What are the two main strategies for new product introduction?

3   New products and services have to offer benefits that meet customer needs. How might companies identify customer needs? Identify sources of new product ideas.

4   An effective development process for products or services should be divided into a number of key stages. Define what is meant by 'product development process' then brainstorm and describe the key stages and activities of the process.

USEFUL WEBSITES

IDSA: **www.idsa.org** The Industrial Designers Society of America (IDSA) is the world's oldest, largest, member-driven society for product design, industrial design, interaction design, human factors, ergonomics, design research, design management, universal design and related design fields

Product Development and Management Association: **www.pdma.org** A comprehensive glossary of new product development terms

www.cim.co.uk/marketingplanningtool/tech/tech4.asp Overview of planning for the marketing mix, including pricing, from the Chartered Institute of Marketing.

www.themanager.org/Knowledgebase/Marketing/Pricing. htm Articles about pricing

REFERENCES

Baines, P., Fill, C. and Page, K. (2010) *Marketing*, 2nd edn, Oxford University Press.

Barringer, B.R. and Ireland, D. (2010) *Entrepreneurship: Successfully Launching New Ventures: Global Edition*, 3rd edn, Pearson Higher Education.

Keller, K.L. (2012) *Strategic Brand Management: Global Edition*, 4th edn, Pearson.

Palmer, A. (2012) *Introduction to Marketing – Theory and Practice*, 3rd edn, Oxford University Press.

Wood, M.B. (2010), *Essential Guide to Marketing Planning*, 2nd edn, FT/Prentice Hall.

CHAPTER 32
THE MARKETING MIX: DISTRIBUTION

Key Concepts

- Disintermediation
- Distribution channel
- Intermediary
- Logistics
- Place or distribution
- Reverse channel

Learning Outcomes Having read this chapter, you should be able to:

- explain the purpose of distribution as a variable in the marketing mix
- define what is meant by a channel of distribution (including functions) and key considerations in channel strategy and decision-making
- discuss the types and roles of intermediaries
- explain the importance of logistics and supply chain management (SCM)
- discuss the role, function and importance of retailers in distribution
- evaluate the role of Internet technologies in distribution.

1.   Having looked at two major elements in the marketing mix – product and price – we can now turn to place/distribution. This chapter focuses on aspects of the marketing mix that deal with making products available in the quantities desired, to as many customers as possible and keeping the total inventory, transport and storage costs as low as possible. **Place or distribution** is essentially about how to place the optimum amount of goods and/or services before the maximum number of members of your target market, at times and locations which optimize the marketing outcome, i.e. sales. However, distribution embraces a broader concept than just the delivery of goods (Baines, Fill and Page, 2010: p. 440). It includes understanding the strategic importance of distribution channels, member roles in the channel, and the rising importance of customer service. The distribution system exists for two prime reasons: (1) to distribute goods and services and (2) to establish and maintain customer relationships. The marketer needs to design an appropriate channel structure, select the channel members and specify their roles in order to meet objectives.

2.   In a society that expects everything to be right here, right now, 24 hours per day and 365 days per year, the marketing mix variable of place has evolved considerably. Compare for example, developments in banking – how we now manage our money (ATMs and Internet banking); how we buy tickets for entertainment, shows or travel and how we buy food (fast-food restaurants, drink and snack dispensing machines). Distribution channels are important because they enable sales and therefore revenue generation and permit the company to deliver offerings that meet customer expectations. Distribution activities help the organization add value – however, distribution may be costly. Consequently, the marketing manager must make many trade-offs when deciding upon the best strategy.

3.   The organization must understand what customers want from distribution activities. They may want speedy delivery and order fulfilment, reliability, choice, availability, convenience and support and all at a good price. Such an understanding is likely to improve the quality of distribution channel management strategies and decisions.

4.   Distribution ranges from production and manufacturing to logistics, warehousing and the final delivery of goods to the customer. In this chapter we first consider and evaluate distribution channels before discussing logistics and supply chain management. Finally, we evaluate, briefly, the impact of Internet technologies on distribution. As with all marketing mix decisions, distribution and channels are also dependent upon the target market.

32.1 MARKETING (DISTRIBUTION) CHANNELS

5.   Distribution channel (or marketing channel) refers to a group of individuals and organizations that direct the flow of products from producers to customers. Distribution channels are needed because producers are separated from prospective customers. The most common function of a marketing channel member is to resell the product into a market that could not be reached as efficiently or effectively by the original seller. In general, there are two ways to distribute goods; the organization may deal with the customer directly (integrated) or indirectly (through the use of intermediaries). Direct channel structure is where the product goes directly from the producer to the final customer. In contrast, the indirect channel structure is where the product goes from the producer through an intermediary, or series of intermediaries, such as a wholesaler, retailer, franchisee, agent or broker to the final customer. However, it is quite common for an organization to operate both distribution methods simultaneously. A hybrid channel structure is where some products go directly from producer to customers and others go through intermediaries. The three options are shown in Figure 32.1.

FIGURE 32.1 Channels of distribution

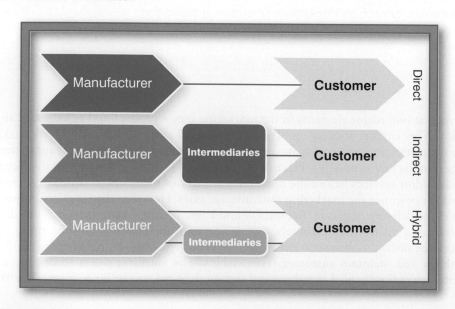

6.   Marketing channels can be classified as channels for consumer products and services, or channels for industrial, business to business products and services. We may also categorize channels according to length. Channel length refers to the number of intermediaries a product passes through before it reaches the final consumer. Thus a longer channel may include several intermediaries. Channel length will have implications in terms of price in particular.

7.   Channel functions have evolved considerably. They may be required to distribute products and services, manage customer relationships including undertaking research, promote, price and assemble the product, negotiate the sale, manage credit arrangements and provide financing and service options. When determining the channel strategy it is important to consider who will perform such functions; it is also important to consider whether the channel needs to provide access to exclusive, selective or mass markets.

8.   The marketer must also consider how many intermediaries to use. Intensity of channel coverage refers to the number of intermediaries used (Baines, Fill and Page, 2010). Intensity on distribution is typically considered along a continuum that ranges from the intensive (mass) through to the exclusive. With intensive coverage, distribution is through every reasonable outlet in the market. When distribution is through a single intermediary channel, coverage is classified as exclusive; between these extremes is selective distribution, using multiple but not all reasonable outlets in the market.

9.   In an integrated distribution system the organization's own employees generate sales, administer orders and deliver products or services. In the case of indirect channels, two fundamental types of intermediary are encountered: agents and merchants – the agent operates in the name of the organization and does not purchase the products being distributed; merchants (distributors and wholesalers) typically buy, handle and sell the goods and services on their own account (see also franchisees and retailers). The benefits of intermediaries include improved efficiency, accessibility and the provision of specialist services. There are however, disadvantages, a loss of control (and power) and cost in particular.

10.   Retailing means all transactions in which the buyer intends to consume the product through personal, family or household use. It is all the activities related directly to the sale of goods and services to the ultimate end consumer for personal and non-business use. This is also called the retail trade. Retailers are intermediaries who purchase products and resell them to final consumers. They are a business, purchasing products for the purpose of reselling them to ultimate consumers – the general public – often from a shop or store. The primary purpose of a retailer is to provide customers with access to products. They do this conveniently, i.e. they enable speedy access and an easy way for consumers to obtain products. Examples of retailers include departmental stores, convenience stores, supermarkets, speciality shops, etc.

11.   Intermediaries (middlemen) may perform a variety of functions such as the physical handling of products (from import through assembly and inventory to delivery); product promotion, sales and customer acquisition; the development and management of business relationships and may also assume certain business risks. The distribution of power between the organization and its intermediaries varies from one country to another and from one product market to another. Power relationships impact upon the organization's ability to control the implementation of marketing mix decisions in the channel.

12.   Accepting there to be a range of channel options we might ask, how then does the organization select its channel strategy? Three main factors: commercial, coverage and control are considered when making decisions about channels for distribution (see Figure 32.2).

FIGURE 32.2 Channel strategies 3Cs

From a *commercial* and economic standpoint it is important to consider the associated costs and revenues to be generated with each channel in order to maximize profit; associated with revenue is the issue of availability and being able to reach large numbers of customers (*coverage*) and it is important to retain as much *control* as is necessary over the product and the way it is marketed. This control factor will normally be balanced against cost and coverage considerations. For example, a desire for coverage may necessitate the use of intermediaries and therefore a reduction in control. As with many managerial decisions, channel management is often a balancing act, optimizing variables to meet organizational goals.

13. Channel design must consider the customer. The size, geographic distribution, shopping habits, outlet preferences and usage patterns of customer groups must be taken into account when making distribution decisions. Product characteristics such as size, shape, weight, value, perishability, etc. also play a key role in determining the distribution strategy. Transportation and warehousing costs of the product are critical issues.

14. When considering options it is worth noting that the direct channel requires capital (and has an opportunity cost), resources and knowledge to establish and operate. Furthermore, customers may shun such a channel due to the low variety of products typically offered by a single manufacturer. In contrast, the indirect channel structure allows the manufacturer/provider to focus on production whilst relying on the skills and infrastructure of one or more intermediaries for distribution. This has the benefit of reach and allows the manufacturer to do what they do best. The main disadvantages include the reduction of control and the need to share profits. Hybrid approaches also increase reach whilst providing greater control and allowing for the optimization of margins whilst developing direct relationships with customers and prospects. Such approaches are prone to conflict however.

15. The use of multiple channels creates the possibility of channel conflict and cannibalization. Channel conflict is where one channel member perceives another channel member to be acting in a way that prevents the first member from achieving their distribution activities. There may be price differences etc. A further source of channel conflict comes from the sharing of control between the producer and the intermediary. In some cases the distribution structure may also create conflict with customers who may not understand which channel they should use. **Channel cannibalization** means the decrease in sales through an existing channel due to the introduction of a new channel. This may be a particular problem when an established physical channel operated by an intermediary suddenly has to compete with a new online and direct channel offered by the manufacturer. Compare, for example, the physical travel agent with the online cheap fares website.

16. Organizations should also consider the need for a **reverse channel** which allows for returning goods, parts or packaging (Wood, 2010). The reverse channel describes a flow that moves backwards through the supply chain. In some cases the provision of such a channel may be a legal necessity. For example, European manufacturers and retailers must comply with Waste Electrical and Electronic Equipment (WEEE) regulations. EU legislation to promote the collection and recycling of such equipment has been in force since August 2004.

17. The WEEE Directive aims to tackle improper treatment of waste electrical and electronic equipment. This is the fastest growing waste stream in the EU, producing approximately 9 million tonnes in 2005, growing to 12 million tonnes of WEEE by 2020. When WEEE is treated in the EU without proper procedures, environmental harm arises, in particular from release of heavy metals like mercury from compact fluorescent lamps and flat-screens, and lead from TVs. Cooling and freezing equipment will release an average of over 6 720 tonnes of ozone-depleting greenhouse gases annually over 2011–20 causing climate damage monetized at around €1 billion each year.

32.2 SUPPLY CHAIN MANAGEMENT AND LOGISTICS

18. Dibb *et al.* (2006: p. 411) note that an important function of the marketing channel is the joint efforts of all channel members to create a **supply chain**. They note that the key tasks in **supply chain management** include planning and coordinating of marketing channel partnerships; sourcing necessary resources, goods and services to support the supply chain; facilitating delivery; and relationship building in order to nurture ongoing customer relationships.

19. The supply chain is a network of manufacturers and service providers working together to convert and move goods from the raw materials stage through to the end user. These manufacturers and service

providers are linked together through physical, information and monetary flows. Supply chain management involves the active management of supply chain activities and relationships in order to maximize customer value and achieve a sustainable competitive advantage. It represents a mindful effort by an organization or group of organizations to develop and run supply chains in the most effective and efficient way possible. Internationalization, globalization, increasing competition, EC and relationship management has increased the importance of SCM to managers working within organizations. Major SCM activities include: running overseas plants or coordinating international activities, selection of transformation processes; forecasting; capacity planning; inventory management; planning and control, purchasing and logistics.

20.   The management of the physical flow of products from the point of origin as raw materials to end users as finished products is termed logistics. Logistics is that part of the supply chain process that plans, implements and controls the efficient, effective flow and storage of goods, services and related information, from the point of origin to the point of consumption, in order to meet customer requirements. Logistics covers a wide range of business activities such as: transportation, warehousing, material handling, packaging and inventory management.

21.   Logistical operations impact upon costs, flexibility and delivery performance and are critical to many organizations. Transportation modes include the roads, water, air, rail and pipeline. Each has its own advantages and disadvantages. Road transport is flexible but costly, water transport is typically slow but cheap and air transport is both the quickest and most expensive. Many organizations adopt a multimodal system, i.e. they seek to exploit the strengths of multiple transportation modes through physical, information and monetary flows that are as seamless as possible.

22.   The logistics strategy is a functional strategy ensuring an organization's logistic choices – transportation, warehousing, information systems and even form of ownership are consistent with its overall business strategy and support the performance dimensions most valued by targeted customers. As logistics becomes more globalized and information-intensive, more organizations are outsourcing the logistics function to specialists, most notably third-party logistics providers (3PLs).

23.   Transportation systems represent just one part of the physical flow of goods and materials – the other is warehousing; any operation that stores, repackages, stages, sorts or centralizes goods or materials. Organizations use warehousing to reduce transportation costs, improve operational flexibility, shorten customer lead times and lower inventory costs. The organization must identify where its customers are located and in what quantity; they need to consider export volumes, the value density of their products and whether or not customers require rapid delivery. Such factors will influence distribution channel, transportation and storage decisions.

32.3 INTERNET, DISTRIBUTION AND SCM

24.   Having described traditional approaches to supply chain management we now turn to how e-commerce can be used to make enhancements. SCM incorporates both e-procurement, upstream activities and sell-side e-commerce, downstream activities; it involves the coordination of or supply activities of an organization from its suppliers and delivery of its products to its customers. The objectives of supply chain management include (1) maximize efficiency and effectiveness of the total supply chain for all players and (2) maximize the opportunity for customer purchase by ensuring adequate stock levels at all stages of the process. Internet and associated technologies are vital to SCM since managing relationships with customers, suppliers and intermediaries is based on the flow of information and the transactions between these parties.

25.   Organizations seek to enhance the supply chain in order to provide a superior value proposition (quality, service, price and fulfilment times), which they do by emphasizing cost reduction, increased efficiency and consequently increased profitability. Not only can we conceive the supply chain as an opportunity to increase profits, it may also be viewed as a sequence of events intended to satisfy customers. Typically, it will involve procurement, manufacture and distribution, together with associated transport, storage and information technology.

26.   The 1960s and 1970s were typified by a focus on the management of finished goods (stock management, warehousing, order processing and delivery) using manual (paper-based) information systems. The just-in-time (JIT) philosophy was the philosophy of the 1970s and 1980s. Efficiency was seen to derive from

flexibility: holding limited stock whilst ensuring customer orders were met in a timely manner. Undersupply and oversupply can impact significantly upon an organization's profitability. In the 1980s and 1990s we witnessed much closer integration between the supplier, customer and intermediaries. During this period, the Internet became an enabling technology, especially for smaller players who could now source raw materials globally and therefore improve competitiveness. During this period, new integrated information systems such as enterprise resource planning systems helped manage the entire supply chain.

27.   Technology enabled the introduction of faster, more responsive and flexible ordering, manufacturing and distribution systems. Early supply chain thinking was manufacturing-led whereby the first consideration was product development, followed by market identification (push supply chain). An alternative approach focuses on customer needs and starts with analysis of their requirements. This latter approach relies on greater communication within the supply chain (pull supply chain).

28.   Marketing is about identifying, anticipating and satisfying customer requirements profitably; it includes the creation, distribution, promotion and pricing of goods, services and ideas. Traditional marketing-communications-media included TV, print and radio that were pushed towards customers with no or limited interactivity. Customer needs were either assumed, addressed collectively en-mass or determined using costly and time-consuming market research questionnaires and face-to-face interviews. e-Marketing refers to the use of any technology to achieve marketing objectives. Digital media (Internet, interactive TV and wireless mobile communications) have all impacted upon marketing activities.

29.   Internet-based marketing may include the use of websites, banner advertising and direct email to win new customers and build relationships with existing customers. New media is considered to be more interactive (two-way) – the customer usually initiates contact, seeking information (pull); it allows low-cost and timely intelligence (market research) gathering; allows greater individualization (personalization); can be integrated with and complement other channels and can extend reach.

30.   Distribution channels are affected through the process of disintermediation (the elimination of intermediaries; removing the layers of intermediaries between sellers and buyers) as the Internet makes direct contact between end-users and producers more feasible. As more information about products and services becomes instantly available to customers, and as information goods are transmitted over the Internet, traditional intermediary businesses and information brokers are circumvented (disintermediated) and the guiding logic behind some traditional industries begins to disintegrate. At the same time, new ways of creating value are opened up by the new forms of connecting buyers and sellers in existing markets (reintermediation).

CONCLUSION

31.   Distribution or place is the marketing mix variable referring to activities which aim to make products available to customers when and where they want to purchase them. It ranges from production and manufacturing to logistics, warehousing and the final delivery of goods to customers. Activities are organized within distribution channels which may be direct, indirect or hybrid. In the case of the direct channel, the manufacturer distributes products and services to the end consumer. In the case of the indirect channel, the manufacturer makes use of intermediaries as a link between themselves and the ultimate consumer. Each channel has differing advantages and disadvantages, particularly in terms of economics (commerce), coverage and control.

32.   The distribution channel is responsible for many functions and their joint efforts may be captured under the general banner of supply chain management. This latter concept promotes the coordination of all business entities engaged in the activities of providing customers with the products or services demanded. Internet technologies have impacted upon the supply chain to enable both e-procurement, upstream and e-commerce downstream. Such technologies reduce transaction costs and enable two-way communication with consumers. They also enable manufacturers to adopt direct channels or hybrid models that can lead to channel conflict and cannibalization.

33.   Organizations must decide on the best way to store, handle and move their product so that it is available to customers in the right quantity, at the right time and in the right place. Logistics includes the activities that relate the flow of products from the manufacturer to the customer or end consumer. Logistical activities include order processing, inventory control, warehousing and transportation. We will revisit the challenges of logistics and inventory management in Chapter 39.

QUESTIONS

1   Explain the purpose of the distribution variable in the marketing mix.

2   Explain how Internet technologies have enabled marketing, particularly distribution. You should discuss supply chain management, channels and disintermediation in your answer. You should also contrast e-marketing with traditional marketing.

USEFUL WEBSITES

Institute of Supply Chain Management: **www.ism.ws** ISM is a not-for-profit association that provides opportunities for the promotion of the profession and the expansion of professional skills and knowledge

Electronic Retailing Association: **www.retailing.org** ERA serves as the cohesive voice for multi-channel marketers

British Retailing Association: **www.brc.org.uk** The British Retail Consortium (BRC) is the lead trade association representing the whole range of retailers, from the large multiples and department stores through to independents, selling a wide selection of products through centre of town, out of town, rural and virtual stores

National Retailing Federation: **www.nrf.com** The world's largest retail trade association, with membership that comprises all retail formats and channels

REFERENCES

Baines, P., Fill, C. and Page, K. (2010) *Marketing*, 2nd edn, Oxford University Press.

Dibb, S., Simkin, L., Pride, W.M. and Ferrell, O.C. (2006) *Marketing: Concepts and Strategies*, 5th edn, Houghton Mifflin International Inc.

Wood, M.B. (2010) *Essential Guide to Marketing Planning*, 2nd edn, FT/Prentice Hall.

CHAPTER 33
MARKETING MIX: PROMOTION (MARKETING COMMUNICATION)

Key Concepts

- Buying behaviour
- Marketing communication
- Promotion
- Promotional mix

Learning Outcomes Having read this chapter, you should be able to:

- understand the role, purpose and aims of marketing communications (promotion) in the marketing mix
- explain how marketing communications works
- discuss and evaluate the principal methods of promotion
- identify the stages of the simple buying process and the importance of marketing communications at each stage
- discuss multi-mode buying and the implications for marketing.

1. So far in this marketing section we have discussed a necessity to understand the needs and wants of customers, target particular customers and then develop the offering (product, price and place) for them. This aspect of the exchange process is shown in Figure 33.1. Next there is a need to make the target audience aware of the offering. Every product needs to be promoted, that is to say it needs to be drawn to the attention of the marketplace (people), and its benefits identified.

2. **Promotion** is another ingredient of the marketing mix that is concerned with decisions about marketing communications. Many definitions have been offered for the marketing term of promotion. It has been defined as all types of **marketing communication**; one of the four Ps in the marketing mix and the use of communications to persuade individuals, groups or organizations to purchase products and services.

FIGURE 33.1 Exchange process

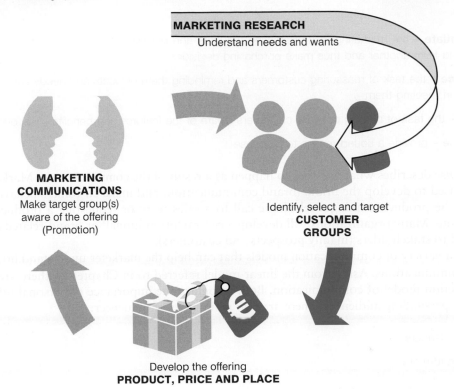

MARKETING RESEARCH
Understand needs and wants

MARKETING COMMUNICATIONS
Make target group(s) aware of the offering (Promotion)

Identify, select and target
CUSTOMER GROUPS

Develop the offering
PRODUCT, PRICE AND PLACE

3. Marketing communication is the transmission of persuasive information about goods, services or an idea, aimed at key stakeholders and consumers within the target **market segment**. Marketing communication aims to raise product visibility and awareness and, at the same time, differentiate the company's products and services from its competitors. Baines, Fill and Page (2010: p. 369) suggest that marketing communications, as a concept, has superseded 'promotion'; we use the terms interchangeably throughout the chapter and book.

4. When discussing *promotion* or marketing communication, many marketing textbooks start with an overview of the communications process. This will be discussed next. Following this we ask how marketing communications work. We outline the main promotional tools of advertising, personal selling, sales promotion, public relations and direct marketing. In addition to this mix of tools we discuss, briefly, the media used for delivering advertising messages to target audiences. The chapter ends with an understanding of how customers 'shop' and 'buy' which can help marketers to encourage and facilitate a prospect's buying behaviour. Throughout the chapter we consider the customer, i.e. the organization or person that receives or uses a product and the 'prospect' – a potential customer.

33.1 THE COMMUNICATIONS PROCESS AND MARKETING

5. Communication is concerned with a sharing of meaning through the transmission of information. Communication was covered in Chapter 25 (refer back to Figure 25.1). Originally, adopting a relatively short-term perspective, marketers made use of (mass) one-way communications to persuade people to buy products and services – they promoted their product and services. This traditional perspective has now been superseded and it is more common to think in terms of marketing communications.

6. The new perspective comprises three main aspects, remembered through the 'EAR' acronym:

- **Engagement** – the audiences' communication needs and how they can be involved/encouraged to participate
- **Audience** – who to communicate with
- **Response** – what we want to happen as a result of the communication

7.   Baines, Fill and Page (2010: p. 386) offer the DRIP (four separate tasks) model as a means to *engage* audiences:

- **Differentiate** – the marketing task of creating thoughts and positive attitudes to help customers distinguish one brand from another and thus make purchasing decisions

- **Reinforce** – the task of reassuring customers and reminding them of wants and needs and the benefits of a product in meeting them

- **Inform** – the task of making potential customers aware of the features and benefits of an offering(s)

- **Persuade** – provide a sound reason to purchase

8.   The *response* describes what we want to happen as a result of the communication. Marketing communications are used to develop the brand (brand communication) and make customers behave in particular ways: buying the product, making a telephone call to a sales team or requesting a product brochure or visiting a website. Many organizations will develop a central 'promotional' or brand-related message to be communicated to stakeholders (mainly prospects and customers).

9.   There are a variety of communication models that can help the marketer understand how to go about marketing communications. Aside from the linear model referred to in Chapter 25 there are the two-step and the interaction model of communication. Both recognize the importance of personal influences when informing and persuading audiences. There are two main types of influencer:

- Opinion leaders

- Opinion formers

10.   **Opinion leader** has been defined by many scholars. For example, Baines, Fill and Page (2010) defined them as people who are predisposed to receiving information and then reprocessing it in order to influence others. They belong to the same peer group as the people they influence, they are not distant or removed; Wood (2010) defined the opinion leader as a person who is especially admired or possesses special skills and therefore exerts more influence over certain purchases made by others; and Clampitt (2010) defined them as informal leaders, respected for their insight and expertise, who serve a vital and influential role in the employee social structure.

Opinion formers on the other hand are people who exert personal influence because of their profession, authority, education or status associated with the object of the communication process. They are not part of the same peer group as the people they influence (Baines, Fill and Page, 2010: p. 374–9). Marketers do not simply rely upon communicating directly with their target audience. They will also target their communications at opinion leaders and formers in order to penetrate the market more quickly.

11.   Marketing communications encompasses three components: a set of tools, the media and messages. Within the marketing function, the term promotional mix is often discussed. This refers to the specific combination of communication tools an organization uses to promote a product, including: advertising, personal selling, publicity and public relations, sales promotion; and direct marketing. The scope of marketing communications is vast. In addition to the aforementioned tools there are a range of media which will be outlined towards the end of this chapter.

33.2 HOW MARKETING COMMUNICATIONS WORK

12.   At this point we might ask how marketing communications work. Traditional thoughts were directed at the sales process where the 'AIDA' model is often cited. First there is a need to create *awareness*. Following this, *interest* is generated and then *desire* is stimulated. From this, *action* (a sale) emerges. Throughout the latter part of the twentieth century a number of similar models, breaking the selling/marketing communication process down into steps, were produced. Various advertising theories have also been proposed. The strong theory of advertising suggests that advertising is capable of persuading people to buy a product

they have not already purchased – thus increasing a firm's sales. However, the weak theory of advertising takes a different view and suggests that choices are based more on purchasing habit than by exposure to promotional messages. According to this theory, advertising is used to reinforce existing attitudes. Others have argued the ATR framework (awareness – trial – reinforcement) as a model to explain how advertising and marketing communication works.

13.   An aggregated summary of such theories is presented in Figure 33.2. The model attempts to explain how marketing communications work. Whilst it is possible to conceive numerous steps, for simplicity we identify three: first the consumer must learn and gain knowledge about the entity – brand, company, product, etc.; this influences attitude formation and generates feelings and emotions towards the entity. Should these be positive the consumer may then engage in the desired behaviour such as contacting the company or one of its agents or purchasing the product(s). We have presented the model in a circular manner to reflect ideas from the strong and weak theories – but any of the three steps may be possible start points.

FIGURE 33.2 How marketing communications work

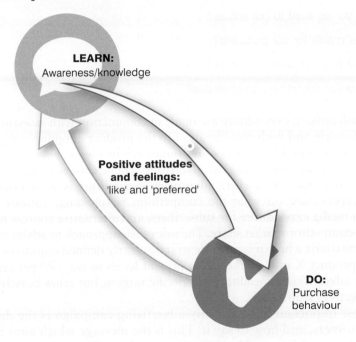

LEARN:
Awareness/knowledge

Positive attitudes and feelings:
'like' and 'preferred'

DO:
Purchase behaviour

33.3 TOOLS OF MARKETING COMMUNICATIONS

14.   Thus far we have emphasized the process of communication and its application in marketing. Communication theory encompasses aspects of the message, the channel between the message originator and intended recipient and the specific contact points where information may be exchanged. A touchpoint (point of contact) describes the interface of a product or brand with customers before, during and after a transaction.

15.   In this section we outline the main promotional tools of advertising, personal selling, sales promotion, public relations and direct marketing. In addition to this mix of tools there is the media used to deliver advertising messages to target audiences. The scope of marketing communications is vast. In addition to the aforementioned tools there is a range of media. In his book 'Essentials of Marketing Communications', Jim Blythe (2006) discusses print media advertising, active media, TV, radio and cinema, outdoor advertising, public relations and corporate image, branding, packaging and merchandising, managing exhibitions and trade events, direct and database marketing, sales promotion, personal selling and sales management

and twenty-first century marketing communications. In addition Kotler *et al.* (2008) add building customer relationships and more recently, De Pelsmacker, Geuens and Van Den Bergh (2013), in their book on marketing communications, add sponsorship and coverage of e-communication, including e-marketing, mobile marketing and interactive television.

TOOLS – ADVERTISING

16.   **Advertising** is the process of communicating persuasive information about a product to target markets by means of the written and spoken word, and by visual material. By definition the process excludes personal selling. The principal media of advertising are as follows: the press – newspapers, magazines, journals, commercial television, direct mail, commercial radio, outdoor hoardings, transport advertisements, Internet and the World Wide Web.

17.   Whatever the medium a number of questions must be decided about an organization's advertising effort. These are as follows:

-   How much should be spent on advertising?

-   What message do we want to put across?

-   What is the best media for our purposes?

-   When should we time our advertisements?

-   How can we monitor advertising effectiveness?

18.   Decisions about advertising expenditure are made in conjunction with assessments about the position of the product in its life cycle and with consideration to the product adoption process. If the product is at the introductory stage, a considerable amount of resources will be invested in advertising. Conversely, if the product is in decline, little or no expenditure on advertising will be endorsed. Some organizations decide to adopt a 'percentage-of-sales' approach, where advertising expenditure is related to sales revenue. Another approach is to base expenditure on what the competition is spending. Various organizations provide regular information on media expenditure for subscribers, and alternative sources provide information on other key facts such as competitor market share. The sales-task approach to advertising expenditure can be particularly useful in situations where it is possible to state clearly defined objectives for advertising, e.g. 'to increase awareness of product X in Y market from present levels to (say) 70 per cent'. This approach has the merit of allocating advertising expenditure to specific targets, but relies heavily on the organization's ability to define its objectives realistically.

19.   Probably the most important aspect of any advertising campaign is the decision about what to say to prospective customers, and how to say it. This is the message which aims to make people aware of and desire the product and favourably inclined towards it. The entire process is the fundamental one of turning customer needs into customer wants. Advertising aims to achieve one or more of the following:

-   increase customer familiarity with a product

-   inform customers about specific features or the key benefits of a product

-   establish the credibility of a product

-   encourage potential customers to buy the product

-   maintain loyalty of existing customers.

20.   In setting out to achieve such aims, advertisers must abide by a series of laws and codes of practice. Most countries exert some degree of state control over the content and form of advertising. Issues such as obscenity, blasphemy, racial prejudice and sheer misrepresentation figure high on the list of prescriptions.

21.   What is the best way of transmitting a message? This is an important question at this stage. The content and the form of the advertisement have been dealt with, and now the key point is to get the message over to the customers. The choice of media depends upon the organization's requirements in terms of the:

–   extent of coverage sought to reach customers

–   characteristics of the target market

–   characteristics of the product

–   customer access to the advertising media (e.g. will they have broadband?)

–   frequency of exposure to the message

–   effectiveness of the advertisement

–   timing of the advertisement

–   costs involved.

22.   This brings us to the question of how organizations assess the effectiveness of their advertising. There are two main ways of looking at the question of advertising effectiveness – the first is to consider the results of the advertising in achieving target improvements in specific tasks, e.g. increasing brand awareness in a specific market; the second is to consider the impact of advertising on sales generally. It is extremely difficult to assess the impact of advertising on sales as a whole, because so many other factors, internal and external, are at work in the marketing process of an organization. It is easier to assess the impact of specific advertising campaigns on sales in specific product areas.

TOOLS – PERSONAL SELLING

23.   However vivid the message transmitted by advertising, there is little substitute for the final face-to-face meeting between the buyer and the seller or representative – this is more true of specialist products but less true in the case of commodities or commoditized products. Advertising creates the interest and the desire, but personal selling clinches the deal. In industrial markets, personal selling plays an even more extensive role. For the moment, let us consider the basic sales process. This is understood to encompass five immediate aims, plus a follow-up, as shown in Figure 33.3.

24.   So far as consumer markets, and especially mass markets, are concerned, advertising must play a vital role in the first three stages of the process. After that, advertising becomes rapidly less important, and personal selling takes over. By comparison, advertising plays a much less important role in industrial markets, where even the first stage is dominated by personal selling. Personal selling is the most expensive form of promotion and ranges from the mere taking of an order in a shop or a sales office, to the creation of new sales in a highly competitive market. Companies who utilize an aggressive sales policy, based on personal selling, are said to be adopting a **push strategy**. The tasks of a sales representative, except in the routine order-taking role, include other duties than making sales. These other duties can comprise:

–   after-sales servicing (dealing with technical queries, delivery matters)

–   gathering information (feedback on customer reactions, competitor activities)

–   communicating regular information to buyers (new catalogues), and

–   prospecting (looking out for new selling opportunities).

25.   In order to fulfil these duties a sales representative needs to have relevant information about:

–   his or her own organization (policies, resources available, organization structure)

–   the products on offer (goods, services, ranges)

FIGURE 33.3 **Personal selling**

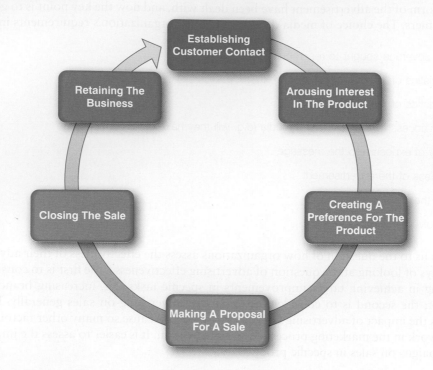

- sales and profit targets
- customers (size, type, location)
- sales plan for his/her area
- promotional material (brochures, catalogues), and
- techniques of selling (creating interest, dealing with objections, closing a sale).

26. Whilst many organizations still see the primary role of the sales representative as that of generating sales, there is an increasing trend which sees the representative in a wider marketing role, which emphasizes the profit responsibility of the position. If sales are pursued regardless of costs, other factors, such as reputation and the value of the sales volume obtained, can be severely reduced, e.g. if costs have been excessive and/or the organization's image has been tarnished by over-zealous representatives. If, on the other hand, representatives are trained to place themselves in their customers' shoes, i.e. develop a market-oriented approach, they are less likely to favour immediate sales gains before the prospect of much larger market opportunities in the future. This, of course, assumes that they are rewarded on this basis as well. In a sales-oriented approach the sales representative is focusing on his or her needs as a seller. By comparison, a market-oriented approach to selling concentrates on the needs of the buyer.

27. We should note that personal selling is costly. There are direct costs of wages, commissions, royalties, bonuses, etc. to pay, as well as infrastructure costs including rent for retail outlets, utilities, etc. Such costs may be relatively low for some highly differentiated products but when competing more on price, such costs may need to be reduced or eliminated. For this reason, many organizations have turned to e-commerce.

TOOLS – SALES PROMOTION

28. Sales promotion activities are a form of advertising designed to stimulate sales mainly by the use of incentives; they refer to communication tools that seek to encourage people to buy now rather than at some

point in the future. Sales promotion activities tend to be planned and funded by the organization's own resources. They can take a number of different forms, as, for example:

- coupons

- twin-pack bargains (two for the price of one 'BOGOF')

- temporary price reductions and special discounts

- point-of-sale demonstrations

- frequent user incentives and loyalty cards

- money refunds

- consumer competitions, and

- free merchandise.

29. Reference was made earlier to 'push' and 'pull' strategies. Sales promotion falls into the first category. It aims to push sales by offering various incentives at, or associated with, the point-of-sale. Its use is most frequent in the field of consumer products. The objectives of a promotion directed at consumers could be to:

- draw attention to a new product or line

- encourage sales of slow-moving items

- stimulate off-peak sales of selected items

- achieve higher levels of customer acceptance/usage of a product or product-line, and

- persuade dealers/retailers to devote increased shelf space to an organization's products.

TOOLS – PUBLICITY AND PUBLIC RELATIONS

30. **Publicity** is news about the organization or its products, reported in the press and other media, without charge to the organization. Publicity differs from the other promotional devices mentioned in this chapter in that it often does not cost the organization any money! Of course, although the publicity itself may be free, there are obvious costs in setting up a publicity programme, but these are considerably lower than for advertising, for example. Publicity usually falls under the heading of **public relations**, which is concerned with the mutual understanding between an organization and its public; managing and controlling the process of using publicity effectively. It is the planned and sustained effort to establish and maintain goodwill and understanding between an organization and its target publics.

31. **Sponsorship** is a marketing communications activity, whereby one party permits another an opportunity to exploit an association with a target audience in return for funds, services or resources. Sponsorship events in the arts and sports are becoming an increasingly popular form of publicity. Again, although the publicity itself is free, the costs of sponsorship are not. Nevertheless, such activities can contribute significantly to an organization's public image.

TOOLS – DIRECT MARKETING

32. Direct marketing refers to the use of non-personal media, the Internet or telesales to introduce products to customers, who then purchase the products by mail, telephone or the Internet. Common direct marketing approaches include: direct mail, telemarketing, door-to-door personal selling and the Internet. New technologies may enable direct marketing. For example advances in automated call centres may enable telemarketing. Direct marketing may be used to avoid dependence on intermediaries and may also enable the organization to focus marketing communications on specific segments and targeted customers.

33.3 BUYING BEHAVIOUR

33.   In previous chapters we have discussed various channels used by customers. Earlier in this chapter we discussed (see Figure 33.2) how marketing communications works – leading to purchasing behaviour. We introduced the idea of the touchpoint. Touchpoint management allows companies to optimize all the interactions with existing and potential customers. We have also discussed the media used to communicate with customers and prospects. Understanding how customers 'shop' and 'buy' can help marketers to encourage and facilitate prospects' buying behaviour.

34.   **Buying behaviour** describes the decision processes and actions of people involved in buying and using products; the way in which customers act, and the processes involved in making a purchase decision. A way or manner in which something occurs or is experienced, expressed or done is referred to as a mode. Kelly (2009: p. 545) discusses multi-mode buying and the idea that customers will use different channels and touchpoints for different stages of the buying process. Companies who understand how customers use a range of media in their purchase decision-making can develop integrated communications strategies which support their customers at each stage of the buying process, see Figure 33.4.

FIGURE 33.4 **Buying behaviour**

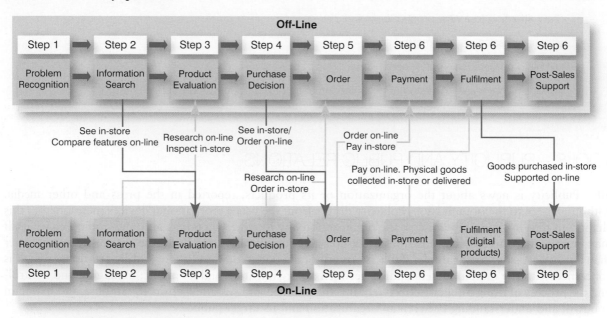

35.   The simple buying process may be broken down into stages of problem recognition, information search, evaluation, decision, purchase and post-sales support. Companies must consider how they can support each stage. Aside from differences in buying behaviour in target markets, we might consider the differences between B2C (business-to-consumer) and B2B (business-to-business) buying behaviour. There tend to be far fewer but larger buyers in business-to-business. Business purchases typically involve a more complex decision-making process since more people are involved (users, influencers, buyers, deciders and the gatekeepers).

33.4 DEVELOPING A MARKETING COMMUNICATIONS PLAN

36.   The SOSTAC Model developed in the 1990s by P.R. Smith is a widely used marketing tool based on the generic problem-solving process. The framework can be used in the specifics of marketing communications

planning or more broadly, to plan marketing – as a marketing planning model. SOSTAC is an acronym for the six basic elements of the marketing plan:

Situation Where are we now? (PESTLE, SWOT, EAR, Competitor analysis, Segments)

Objectives Where do we want to get to? (SMART, Marketing metrics)

Strategy How are we going to get there? (AIDA, Communications theory, Life cycle)

Tactics How are we going to get there? (Communications tools)

Actions Who is going to do what and when? (Resource allocation, Gantt charts)

Control How can we monitor performance? (Metrics, KPIs, Review)

CONCLUSION

37. The primary role of promotion is to communicate with a range of stakeholders with the aim of directly or indirectly facilitating exchanges. Promotion is often referred to as marketing communications. To gain maximum benefit from promotional efforts, marketers must make every effort to plan, implement, coordinate and control (manage) communications properly. An important purpose of promotion is to influence and encourage prospects and customers to access or adopt goods and services. The major promotional methods include advertising, personal selling, public relations and sales promotion and may include sponsorship, direct marketing and the use of Internet technologies such as the World Wide Web.

QUESTIONS

1   Identify and describe the main promotional tools of marketing communications.

2   Explain the role, purpose and aims of marketing communications (promotion) in the marketing mix.

3   Explain how marketing communications works.

4   Identify and describe the stages of the simple buying process and the importance of marketing communications at each stage.

5   Discuss multi-mode buying and the implications for marketing.

USEFUL WEBSITES

Brand Channel: **www.brandchannel.com** Valuable source for information about brands and branding strategies Adage: www.adage.com Online sources for advertising and media news

Interbrand: **www.interbrand.com** Interbrand is a web link that brings together a diverse range of insightful thinkers to discuss, create and design branding strategies.

Warc: **www.warc.com** Provide data on trends and forecasts of advertising expenditure for all major economies, which are used by media researchers worldwide

Brand Republic: **www.brandrepublic.com** Latest news for marketing, advertising, media and PR

eMarketer Inc: **www.emarketer.com** Market research on e-business and online marketing Direct Marketing Association: **www.dma.org.uk/content/home.asp** Regulation, news and information on direct marketing

Institute of Sales Promotion: **www.isp.org.uk** Information on sales promotion industry and various items such as award winning campaigns.

All About Branding: **www.AllAboutBranding.com** For brands design and creation

Brand Strategy Insider: **www.brandingstrategyinsider.com** A website dedicated to helping marketing-oriented leaders and professionals build strong brands

REFERENCES

Baines, P., Fill, C. and Page, K. (2010) *Marketing*, 2nd edn, Oxford University Press.

Blythe, J. (2006) *Essentials of Marketing Communications*, 3rd edn, Financial Times Press.

Clampitt, P.G. (2010) *Communicating for Managerial Effectiveness: Problems, Strategies, Solutions*, 4th edn, SAGE.

De Pelsmacker, P., Geuens, M. and Van Den Bergh, J. (2013) *Marketing Communications: A European Perspective*, 5th edn, Pearson.

Kelly, P.P. (2009) *International Business and Management*, Cengage Learning EMEA.

Kotler, P., Armstrong, G., Wong, V. and Saunders, J. (2008) *Principles of Marketing – European Edition*, 5th edn, Financial Times Press.

Wood, M.B. (2010) *Essential Guide to Marketing Planning*, 2nd edn, FT/Prentice Hall.

CHAPTER 34
CUSTOMER-ORIENTED MARKETING APPROACHES

Key Concepts

- Customer relationship marketing (CRM)
- Customer loyalty
- Customer satisfaction
- Direct and database marketing
- Lifetime customer value (LCV)
- Relationship marketing (RM)
- Transactional approach

Learning Outcomes Having read this chapter, you should be able to:

- understand the difference between the transactional and the relationship approach to marketing
- discuss how database marketing helps improve customer understanding and management
- understand how trust, commitment, customer satisfaction and loyalty are interlinked
- describe the different stages of the customer relationship life cycle
- evaluate the benefits of customer retention
- explain what is meant by CRM.

1. Whilst we have discussed the traditional approach to marketing, introduced halfway through the twentieth century through the marketing mix, there are indeed many ways of 'doing' marketing. Over the past two or three decades we have witnessed significant changes in marketing philosophies, approaches, strategies and tactics. Indeed, marketing thinking has progressed from a functionality-based 'make and sell' philosophy to an enterprise-wide view on delivering customer value to target market segments. We will contrast and explore a number of approaches in this final chapter of the marketing section. In this chapter we outline the development of the marketing discipline, consider the evolution from transaction marketing to relationship marketing, to CRM and customer management and a more holistic marketing perspective.

We will also consider one or two additional marketing approaches, such as direct, digital and database marketing which appeared in the final quarter of the twentieth century.

2. Price, Promotion, Product and Place – discussed in the previous chapters – have been among the traditional marketing instruments for decades. Marketers believed that pulling such levers would lead to increased demand for the company's offerings. However, '4Ps' marketing has been criticized by professionals and academics for a lack of any meaningful consideration of customers. Indeed some dismiss the usefulness of these 'old' concepts and argue that customer-centric analysis and marketing is the only way forward. Ettenson, Conrado and Knowles (2013) suggest that the 4Ps have served consumer marketers well for half a century. They argue that 'it's not that the 4Ps are irrelevant, just that they need to be reinterpreted to serve contemporary marketers'. They suggest a new model that shifts the emphasis from products to solutions, place to access, price to value, and promotion to education – SAVE, for short. Finally they note that in adopting the SAVE model, management must encourage a solutions mindset throughout the organization. An alternative framework is the SIVA Model (Solution, Information, Value and Access). In this model the Promotion 'P' is substituted for 'Information'.

3. Baines, Fill and Page (2010) also suggest that the marketing mix (4Ps) concept is considered by some to be both an outdated and inappropriate explanation of how marketing works. In order to compensate for deficiencies within the 4Ps, some marketers have recognized '7Ps' – People, Process and Physical evidence added later. Indeed some have termed the expanded mix as the relationship marketing mix.

4. Marketing may also be regarded in terms of interactions with individuals (prospects and customers). Traditional marketing places emphasis on the marketing mix and individual transactions whereas relationship marketing focuses on winning and retaining customers. Similarly, Dibb *et al.* (2006) discuss the 'relationship marketing era' as the current period, in which the focus is not only on expediting the single transaction but on developing ongoing relationships with customers. Relationship marketing requires a different philosophy in the organization and is reliant upon database technologies to support customer acquisition, retention and continued selling activities.

5. The (traditional) transactional approach to marketing is a business strategy that focuses on solitary, 'point of sale' transactions; it is focused on a single objective, and that is making the sale and a sale is a one-time/one-off event. Exchanges are seen as being independent of any other or subsequent exchanges. The emphasis is on maximizing the efficiency and volume of individual sales rather than developing a relationship with the buyer. Value is seen to be embedded in the product and its price (Chapter 31). Products are the main focus and price the key mechanism to exchange. Under the transactional approach, the marketing process is one of matching the market mix with market forces, external opportunities or threats in the markets the organization engages. This is essentially the marketing programme. Under this approach the marketing mix elements are focused on customer acquisition and are not relationally oriented. In short, the mix elements are about making the offer.

6. In the 1980s an alternative to the transactional model, relationship marketing, emerged. This approach emphasizes *customer retention* and future interaction with the company. Relationship marketing has broader, longer-term goals than transactional marketing. It is based on the principle that there is a history of exchanges and there will be exchanges in the future. Relationship marketing focuses on developing long-lasting relationships with clients to secure sales well into the future. Trust and commitment, to be discussed later, underpin these relationships; the importance of price is replaced by customer service and the quality of interaction between buyer and seller. However, whilst we have identified two different approaches, most organizations include components of both in their strategy. Having discussed many aspects of the transactional approach in previous chapters we will focus on the relationship approach, discussing customer relationship management and customer management throughout this chapter.

7. In the next section we consider early approaches that some consider as the forerunners of customer relationship approaches – direct and database marketing. Afterwards we identify the important business constructs associated with relationship marketing. We then define CRM and explore the concept, particularly as a company-wide and strategic approach. CRM components are discussed along with the customer life cycle. Finally we discuss problems and strategies associated with customer retention.

34.1 DIRECT AND DATABASE MARKETING

8.   In the opening paragraph we suggested that there were a number of approaches to ways of doing marketing. Direct (and digital and database) marketing is a rather complex collection of principles and practices that together make up an entirely 'self-contained' choice for marketers (Tapp, Whitten and Housden, 2013: p. 9). **Direct marketing** has been defined by many scholars. We will describe it here as the use of non-personal media, the Internet or telesales to introduce products to customers, who then purchase the products by mail, telephone or the Internet; Baines, Fill and Page (2010) defined it as a marketing communication tool that uses non-personal media to create and sustain a personal and intermediary-free communication with customers, potential customers and other significant stakeholders; and Wood (2010) defined it as the use of two-way communication to engage targeted customers and stimulate a direct response that leads to a sale and an ongoing relationship.

9.   Alan Tapp, Professor of Marketing at Bristol Business School, is regarded by some as a leading authority on direct marketing; joined by Ian Whitten and Matthew Housden, the trio bring great expertise across direct, database and digital marketing to provide comprehensive, compelling coverage of the key theory and debates of the fields. Tapp, Whitten and Housden (2013) suggest direct marketing is a method of marketing based on individual customer records held on a database. The records form the basis for marketing activities. According to the authors, the use of the database forces a natural focus on customers rather than products and 'encourages us to think in terms of customer relationships' (2013: p. 4). They note that as companies have become larger and more disconnected from their customers, certainly on a face-to-face basis, they find it more difficult to know them. Marketing databases fill this void, enabling segmentation and targeting in particular.

10.   Tapp, Whitten and Housden (2013) ask whether direct marketing is based on relationship marketing or the '4Ps' (the transactional approach/philosophy). If we go back to direct marketing's early development, it concentrated on prompting action from customers to make a sale. This approach is heavily influenced by the '4Ps' they argue. However, it is also recognized that direct marketing is developed as a powerful tool in customer loyalty strategies. Furthermore, relationship marketing starts with the premise that customer retention is critical to company profitability, which is also the starting point of modern direct marketing. By the mid-1990s, relationship marketers started to integrate direct marketing into thinking. Thus it can be argued that direct marketing draws from both philosophies whilst maintaining its own clear identity as an approach based on a customer database. Finally, Tapp, Whitten and Housden (2013: p. 4–5) declare that, 'there is a natural alignment between direct marketing and relationship marketing … In fact, the key to modern direct marketing is the capture of individual customer details at the first sale, so that the markets can begin a relationship with that customer.' Many writers now use the terms direct marketing and relationship marketing interchangeably (2013: p. 12). Having identified what is meant by database marketing we will next explore specific applications.

34.2 CUSTOMER DATABASE APPLICATIONS: SEGMENTATION

11.   Marketing databases enable easy manipulation of customer data. One of the fundamental methods of manipulation concerns the grouping of similar customers together into segments. Such segments then represent the more specific target market for marketers to devise initiatives and activities. **Market segmentation** has been defined by many scholars. For example Baines, Fill and Page (2010) defined it as the division of customer markets into groups of customers with distinctly similar needs; Dibb *et al.* (2006) defined it as the process of grouping customers in markets with some heterogeneity into smaller, more similar or homogeneous segments. The identification of target customer groups in which customers are aggregated into groups with similar requirements and buying characteristics; and Wood (2010) defined it as a process of grouping consumers or businesses within a market into segments based on similarities in needs, attitudes or behaviour that marketing can address.

12.   The purpose of market segmentation is to leverage scarce resources: to ensure that the elements of the marketing mix are designed to meet particular needs of different customers. Market segmentation is related to product differentiation, i.e. companies adapt to different offerings and variations of offerings to satisfy segments.

There are a number of ways to segment the market. The approach used for the consumer market is likely to differ from that of the business market as different variables (**segmentation variables or bases**) may be used to group customers. Segments should be distinct, accessible and profitable. The organization must decide which segments to serve, i.e. determine its target markets.

13.   Various types of data are used in segmentation. It is a description of a customer or set of customers that includes demographic, geographic and psychographic characteristics, as well as buying patterns, creditworthiness and purchase history. Marketers typically describe their customers using (1) Demographics – their age, gender, income, (2) Psychographics – their personality type, preferences and (3) Behaviour. Marketers will also (4) locate their customers and Geodemographic data are data about People who live in the same locality and are collected and categorized on the assumption that they are more likely to have similar characteristics than are two people chosen at random. Additionally, Marketers will want to understand a prospect or customer's purchasing process and behaviour. In the case of the latter they will typically mine customer orders in order to determine recency, frequency and monetary value (RFM) of purchases. Other marketing professionals and scholars refer to the FRAC score – the frequency, recency, amount and category.

14.   RFM, in consumer behavioural analysis, enables segmentation (Kahan, 1998). The RFM process, a widely recognized behavioural analysis technique (described in skills sheet 10), requires that base customer data, such as name and address, have been assigned a unique (database) reference key, such as a customer account number. Likewise, it requires that all order or sales data are stored electronically with the unique key included in each transactional record. This matter is easily attended to with the relational marketing database. By creating a score for each customer, based on the recency, frequency and monetary value of purchases, the customer base can be segmented according to the score awarded. Thus more profitable customers will be awarded a higher score and grouped together, just as the less profitable customers will become grouped.

15.   When implementing a new marketing campaign, instead of targeting the entire customer base, users may first target a percentage of each RFM segment. The response is then tested against breakeven rates. Following this, the marketer will roll out the campaign only to those RFM segments that are proven to achieve profitable response rates. This methodology allows marketers to test campaigns to smaller segments of customers, and direct larger campaigns only towards those customer segments that are predicted to respond profitably. Thus, database marketers can more effectively use electronically captured information leading to: (1) increase response rates, (2) lower cost per order and (3) generate greater profit. Thus segmentation is a key application of the marketing database. However, whereas much analysis is based upon the company's own data there are benefits to accessing external databases also. We will return to customer databases later when discussing CRM technologies but first discuss the relationship marketing constructs important to customer retention and the maintenance of an ongoing relationship.

34.3 TRUST, COMMITMENT, CUSTOMER SATISFACTION AND LOYALTY

16.   'On average, the CEOs of US corporations lose half their customers every 5 years' (Reichheld, 1996). Discussing loyalty and profits Reichheld states, 'In general, the longer a customer stays with a company, the more that customer is worth. Long-term customers buy more, take less of a company's time, are less sensitive to price, and bring in new customers. Best of all, they have no acquisition or start-up cost. Good long-standing customers are worth so much that in some industries, reducing customer defections by as little as five points – from, say, 15 per cent to 10 per cent per year – can double profits.' Reichheld further notes that 'What keeps customers loyal is the value they receive' (refer back to Section 6).

17.   When an exchange meets the needs and expectations of the buyer we declare the customer satisfied. **Customer satisfaction** also refers to a qualitative measure of marketing performance that involves surveying customers over time (Dibb *et al.*, 2006). An indication of dissatisfaction is **defection**, defined by Reichheld (1996) as the loss of any portion of that customer's business. **Customer loyalty** on the other hand is the feeling of attachment to or affection for a company's people, products or services. These feelings manifest themselves in many forms of customer behaviour (Jones and Sasser, 1995). More recently, Palmer (2012) defines loyalty as non-random repeat purchasing from a seller, with behavioural and attitudinal dimensions.

18.   Many benefits are derived from having loyal customers. Not only are they positive advocates, they also offer greater resistance to competitive offerings. Customer loyalty is seen as an important driver of long-term financial performance. Organizations will therefore seek out methods to ensure true customer loyalty. Satisfied customers are typically linked with the idea of loyalty. However, Jones and Sasser (1995) reported a tremendous difference in loyalty between merely and totally satisfied customers. In their article they provide advice on how to keep your best – i.e. most profitable – customers 'delighted and devoted'.

19.   In order to secure customer loyalty, Jones and Sasser (1995) suggest the following steps:

FIGURE 34.1   Steps to secure customer loyalty (adapted from Jones and Sasser, 1995)

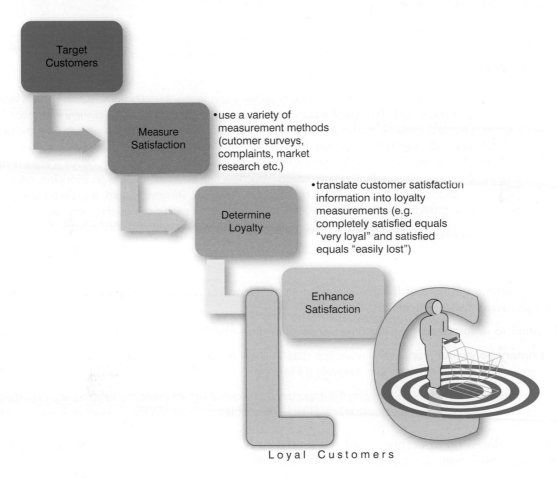

20.   At the heart of any successful strategy to manage satisfaction is the ability to listen to the customer. Jones and Sasser (1995) listed five major ways that businesses can listen to their customers: (1) customer satisfaction indices – surveying customers about their level of satisfaction; (2) feedback – customers' comments, complaints and questions; (3) market research; (4) frontline personnel – employees who have direct contact with the customer provide a means of listening; and (5) strategic activities.

21.   Relationships are also based on **trust** – a means of reducing uncertainty. It involves judgements about reliability and integrity and is concerned with the degree of confidence that exists between buyers and sellers, that each will fulfil their obligations and responsibilities. Trust may also be influenced by the reputation and perceived expertise of the company and its employees. The important concept related to trust is that of privacy – ensuring that personal information is not disseminated improperly. Trust helps establish customer satisfaction. If trust breaks down, the relationship is likely to be broken up. In addition to trust, **commitment** is also considered necessary for successful relationship marketing. Commitment is the construct that represents the consumers' desire to continue a relationship. It reflects dedication, allegiance and loyalty.

22.   Companies may make use of loyalty programs, typically enabled by the customer database, in order to build customer loyalty by rewarding consumers for their purchasing. **Loyalty programmes** are structured marketing efforts that reward, and therefore encourage, loyal buying behaviour – behaviour which is potentially beneficial to the firm. It is important to note that loyalty programmes require considerable investment, taking a number of years to deliver positive returns. Such programmes have the following aims:

- to retain customers (providing value and satisfaction)
- to stimulate repeat purchases
- to cross-sell other products.

Vignette

Tesco Clubcard is the loyalty card of the British supermarket chain Tesco. Its nationwide launch in 1995 was the foundation of Tesco's rise to become the dominant retailer in the UK and one of the biggest in the world. The Clubcard scheme operates in the UK and several other countries; it has been highly successful in the UK market in particular, with over 16.5 million members as of 2013. When shopping at Tesco, Clubcard holders receive one point for every £1 (1 point for every €1 in Ireland) they spend. The holder receives a statement and vouchers to the value of points they have saved. Vouchers can be spent in-store on shopping, on-line on grocery home shopping or direct, or used on Clubcard Rewards. The loyalty card, and particularly the database behind it, provides Tesco with an exceptional level of detail into whom its shoppers are and how they shop. Using the data from Clubcard, Tesco is able to predict consumer trends and react to them.

23.   The ultimate measure of loyalty is market share. However this may not always be easy to measure and so alternative measurements may be used:

(1)   **intent to repurchase –** ask customers about their future intentions to repurchase a given product or service

(2)   **primary behaviour –** analyzes transaction data to show actual repurchasing behaviour in terms of recency, frequency, amount, retention and longevity (RFM), and

(3)   **secondary behaviour –** recognizing the importance of word-of-mouth (customer referrals and endorsements) companies will often ask their customers whether they would recommend the product or service to others.

Having explored the concepts considered central to relationship marketing we will now explore the customer relationship marketing approach and philosophy.

34.4 CRM AND CUSTOMER MANAGEMENT

24.   At the beginning of this chapter we discussed the evolution of marketing concepts, philosophies and approaches. We discussed both relationship marketing and customer relationship marketing. At this point we might ask whether the two concepts are indeed different. Payne and Frow (2013: p. 4) suggest that the two terms have been used interchangeably; that CRM evolved from relationship marketing. They also recognized some subtle differences. One key difference focuses on the nature of relationships. Relationship marketing takes a broader view and considers relationships with all relevant stakeholders in the supply chain whilst some marketers suggest CRM focuses on the customer alone. Some marketers have taken this a stage further discussing 'customer management' as an approach. This is seen as a more tactical orientation to the management of customer interactions.

25.   Building on the relationship marketing approach and adopting greater use of technology, CRM emerged around the turn of the twentieth century into the twenty-first century. CRM has been defined by many scholars.

There is, however, no complete agreement upon a single definition. This is because CRM can be considered from a number of perspectives For example, Baines, Fill and Page (2010) defined it as software systems that provide all staff with a complete view of the history and status of each customer; Dibb *et al.* (2006) defined it as the use of technology-enhanced customer interaction to shape appropriate marketing offers designed to nurture ongoing relationships with individual customers within an organization's target markets; and Knights and Willmott (2007) defined it as a broad management approach that emphasizes the financial value of developing long-term relationships with and detailed knowledge of customers.

26. Organizations are now critically dependent upon marketing technologies to enable their marketing processes and activities (communication in particular). Technology facilitates the collection, analysis and dissemination of information for marketing purposes worldwide. Not only does technology make such processes faster but it also allows achievement at lower cost. Marketers now focus on technology, processes and philosophies associated with winning and retaining customers; such approaches seek to build a sustainable long-term business (relationship) with customers.

27. **Customer relationship management (CRM)** is the entire process of maximizing the value proposition to the customer through all interactions, both on-line and traditional. Effective CRM advocates one-to-one relationships and participation of customers in related business decisions. CRM may be described as a broad management approach or philosophy that emphasizes the financial value of developing long-term relationships with and detailed knowledge of customers. It refers to a learning relationship between an organization and its customer. Learning is enhanced as degrees of interaction increase. For example, through the use of information systems databases, it is assumed that customers can be 'captured' so that customized goods and services may be targeted appropriately at them. However, the term is generally taken to mean more than simply the application of technology but includes the corporate (customer-oriented) culture, beliefs and goals.

28. CRM has a strategic, tactical and operational orientation; typically directs relationship efforts to those with high customer lifetime values; seeks to provide the perfect customer experience through integrated channels; manages customer data from all touchpoints in order to learn more about each customer and thus produce the appropriate marketing response and seeks to measure customer acquisition, retention, satisfaction, loyalty, win-back and other related metrics. The tangible components of CRM include the integrated front-office (the area of an operation in which contact with customers normally takes place), customer touchpoints, call centres, salesforce automation and the Internet; back-office (the area of an operation in which there is normally no contact with customers) systems; business intelligence (BI) systems utilizing data warehousing and data mining and analysis tools. The basic architecture of a CRM system is shown in Figure 34.2.

29. The aim of CRM technology is to provide an interface between the customer and the employee – to replace or facilitate direct interaction. Ideal CRM systems support multichannel communications, needs of customers (product information, order placement, post-sales support) and the core needs of employees

FIGURE 34.2 **CRM components**

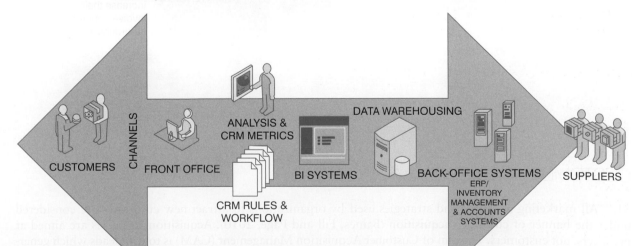

(placing orders received by telephone, fax, email or face-to-face and to answer a customer's questions). Databases lie at the heart of such systems. Baran and Galka (2013: p. 29) suggest that organizations without CRM capability will be at a serious competitive disadvantage. They believe that firms develop CRM systems in order to increase customer retention and loyalty; maintain competition; and in an attempt to differentiate themselves.

34.5 CUSTOMER LIFE CYCLE

30.   There are four phases of CRM and the customer life cycle: Customer Acquisition, Retention, Extension (CARE) and Decline are shown in Figure 34.3. Each is discussed in more detail below. Some marketing scholars have developed these stages into a customer relationship life cycle that is broadly similar to the product life cycle referred to in Chapter 31.

FIGURE 34.3   CARE (D) – the customer life cycle

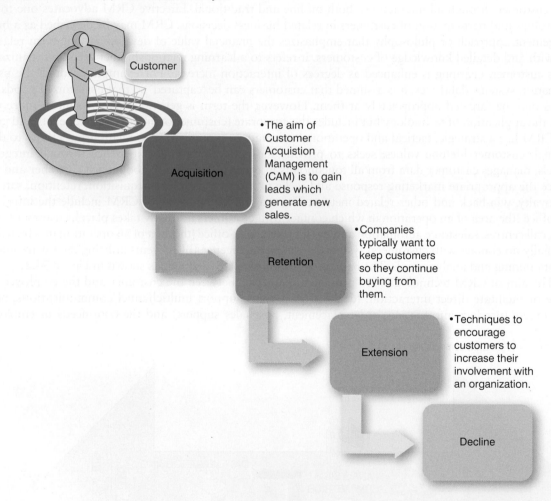

CUSTOMER ACQUISITION MANAGEMENT

31.   All marketing activities and strategies used by organizations to attract new customers are considered under the banner of **customer acquisition** (Baines, Fill and Page, 2010). Acquisition strategies are aimed at prospects, not customers. The aim of Customer Acquisition Management (CAM) is to gain leads which generate new sales. Marketers, however, know that 'having customers, not merely acquiring customers, is crucial'; many executives are concerned about the negative effects of **customer switching** (the action through which a customer changes supplier) on market share and profitability; switching costs businesses the customer's future

revenue stream. Other effects include costs associated with acquiring new customers which can add up to five times the cost of efforts that might have enabled the firm to retain a customer (Keaveney, 1995). The losses and costs associated with losing customers – referred to by some as **churn rate**, the proportion of contractual customers or subscribers who leave a supplier during a given time period – drives the marketer to seek out the reasons and counter initiatives in order to retain profitable customers. We discuss customer retention next.

CUSTOMER RETENTION AND CUSTOMER EXTENSION

32.   Companies want to keep profitable customers so they continue buying from them. This is a challenge for organizations as today's customers are more empowered, impatient, with short attention spans, facing lots of choice and able to switch easily from one supplier to another. In many industries, profitability is seen to be dependent on loyalty and loyalty on satisfaction. With reduced loyalty and satisfaction comes the threat of defection; worse still, dissatisfied customers may actually deter other prospects and customers from doing business with the organization. Consequently, it is important for companies to identify, measure and track loyalty-drivers and implement plans to make improvements.

33.   Keaveney (1995) reports results of a study conducted amongst more than 500 service customers. The research identifies many factors that caused customers to switch services. Customers' reasons for switching services were classified into eight general categories, see Figure 34.4.

34.   Keaveney (1995) later discusses the implications for managers – the actions firms or their employees can take to prevent customers switching from one service provider to another. Keaveney and others advocate the need to develop customer retention strategies. An important implication of her study for managers is that most of the switching factors are controllable. The categories suggest areas in which managers might take action to prevent customer switching:

- **Service failures** – a 'zero defects' philosophy (refer back to Chapter 28)

- **Failed responses to service breakdowns** – developing policies for effective service recovery (refer back to Chapter 29, see business continuity)

FIGURE 34.4 Customer switching causes

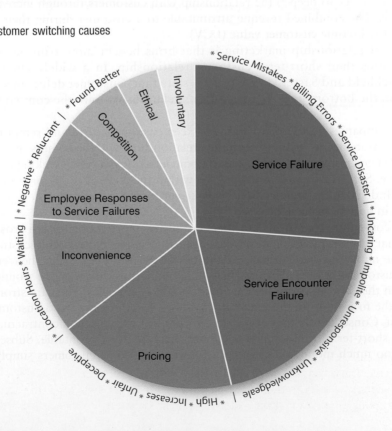

- **Inconvenience** – effective queue management, timely delivery of service and efficient management of reservations systems (refer back to Chapter 17, see time compression and time-based competition)

- **Unsatisfactory employee** – customer interactions – training employees to listen to customers, return telephone calls promptly, keep customers informed and explain procedures

- **Price-related reasons** – careful management of pricing policies, especially when service firms charge higher-than-competitive prices or are considering increases in fees, service charges or penalties (refer back to Chapter 31), and

- **Ethical problems** – develop behaviour-based control systems to reward ethical conduct and discourage unethical conduct amongst service contact employees (refer back to Chapter 18).

35.   A key prerequisite for customer retention and related CRM challenges is to know core customers. Unfortunately, identifying core customers is not always easy. Reichheld (1996) suggests asking three questions may reveal the answer:

(1) Which of your customers are the most profitable and loyal? Look for those who spend more money, pay their bills more promptly, require less service, and seem to prefer stable, long-term relationships

(2) Which customers place the greatest value on what you offer? ~ Some customers will have found that your products, services, and special strengths are simply the best fit for their needs, and

(3) Which of your customers are worth more to you than to your competitors? Some customers warrant extra effort and investment. Conversely, no company can be all things to all people: Customers who are worth more to a competitor will eventually defect.

36.   Customers generate revenue for companies from one-off or continued purchases. Continued purchases (referred to as extension selling) may be of the same or different (cross sales) products and services. Customer extension is about activities to deepen the relationship with customers through increased interaction and product transactions. The combined revenue attributable to a customer during their relationship with a company is termed the **lifetime customer value (LCV)**.

37.   A basic tenet of relationship marketing is that firms benefit more from maintaining long-term customer relationships than short-term customer relationship. In a widely cited *Harvard Business Review* article, Reichheld and Sasser (1990: p. 105) state that 'Customer defections have a surprisingly powerful impact on the bottom line. As a customer's relationship with the company lengthens, profits rise.'

38.   Not only do companies go to great lengths to keep customers loyal and retain them, they will also engage in win-back strategies in order to revitalize relationships with customers in decline or those who have already defected. Such strategies will be based upon *defection analysis* – seeking to identify the reasons why customers leave. Some of these reasons will be within the control of the organization (poor service, price, value, etc.). Indeed some organizations create win-back teams that are empowered to reactivate customers who are in decline or have defected.

39.   However, the contention that loyal customers are always more profitable is a gross oversimplification (Reinartz and Kumar, 2000). Long-life customers are not necessarily profitable customers. Reinartz and Kumar question the nature of the lifetime-profitability relationship. Based on their empirical study they suggest that some customers behave like butterflies: 'It is wonderful when they are around, yet unfortunately they leave easily. On the contrary, long-life customers are like barnacles: They are strongly attached to the firm but may cost the firm more in the long run.' In short, length-of-time as a customer does not always correlate with profit. Consequently they argue that loyalty, at least with non-contractual type sales may be overrated and that short-term transactional customers may be more profitable. Subsequently, companies should not spend too much money on certain customer types; some customers simply cost too much to serve.

34.6 CUSTOMER SERVICE

40.   At a simple level customer service refers to the assistance, activities and advice provided by a company to customers before, during and after a purchase and designed to enhance the level of customer satisfaction – that is, the feeling that a product or service has met the customer expectation. Providing good customer service is thought to help in the repeat purchase decision process and therefore continued sales. As good customer service is difficult to replicate it is considered a source of competitive advantage and an important aspect of customer management. CRM technologies, customer contact and call centres are all used to facilitate customer management and enhance customer service.

41.   Call centres and customer contact centres ensure that customers can communicate with people best placed to deal with any queries in a manner likely to improve efficiency, enhanced reputation and the quality of interaction with customers. This is a welcome alternative to the problem of shunting customers around the organization and thus provides a better customer experience. CRM applications typically consist of call management, lead management, customer record, and sales support and payment systems. It is important to recognize the good customer management requires attention not just to technology but also the organization's culture, training, strategy, propositions and processes.

CONCLUSION

42.   Contemporary marketers seem happy to combine a number of marketing philosophies and approaches in order to create a holistic approach to managing customers. The basic (traditional) marketing approach is presented around the marketing mix (4Ps) concept. However, some practitioners and scholars consider this to be both an outdated and inappropriate explanation of how marketing works. Marketing may also be regarded in terms of interactions with individuals (prospects and customers). Traditional marketing places emphasis on the marketing mix and individual transactions whereas relationship marketing focuses on winning and retaining customers. Relationship marketing requires a differing philosophy within the organization and is reliant upon database technologies to support customer acquisition, retention and continued selling activities. Relationship marketing is regarded more as a general philosophy and has a number of variations. Contemporary, relationship-oriented, marketing goals may be summarized as:

Strengthen **Trust** → Advance **Satisfaction** → Improve **Retention** → Grow **Profit**

QUESTIONS

1   Critically compare traditional with relationship marketing.

2   Explain what is meant by customer relationship management (CRM) and discuss the three phases of CRM.

3   Drawing upon a variety of resources, critically evaluate the Tesco Clubcard from the company's perspective – should Tesco continue with it?

4   Explain how trust, commitment, customer satisfaction and loyalty are interlinked.

5   Commenting on the role of database technology, discuss how segmentation enables effective marketing.

REFERENCES

Baines, P., Fill, C. and Page, K. (2010) *Marketing*, 2nd edn, Oxford University Press.

Baran, R.J. and Galka, R.J. (2013) *CRM – The Foundation of Contemporary Marketing Strategy*, Routledge.

Dibb, S., Simkin, L., Pride, W.M. and Ferrell, O.C. (2006) *Marketing: Concepts and Strategies*, 5th edn, Houghton Mifflin International Inc.

Ettenson, R., Conrado, E. and Knowles, J. (2013) 'Rethinking the 4 Ps', *Harvard Business Review*, 91(1): 26–26.

Jones, T.O. and Sasser, W.E. (1995) 'Why satisfied customers defect', *Harvard Business Review*, 73(6): 88–99.

Kahan, R. (1998) 'Using database marketing techniques to enhance your one-to-one marketing initiatives', *The Journal of Consumer Marketing Santa Barbara*, 15(5): 491–493.

Keaveney, S.M. (1995) 'Customer switching behaviour in service industries: an exploratory study', *Journal of Marketing*, 59(2): 71–82.

Knights, D. and Willmott, H. (2007) *Introducing Organisational Behaviour and Management*, Cengage Learning EMEA.

Palmer, A. (2012) *Introduction to Marketing – Theory and Practice*, 3rd edn, Oxford University Press.

Payne, A. and Frow, P. (2013) *Strategic Customer Management – Integrating Relationship Marketing and CRM*, Cambridge University Press.

Reichheld, F.F. (1996) 'Learning from customer defections', *Harvard Business Review*, 74(2): 56–69.

Reichheld, F.F. and Sasser, W.E. (1990) 'Zero defections: quality comes to services', *Harvard Business Review*, 68(5): 105–111.

Reinartz, W.J. and Kumar, V. (2000) 'On the profitability of long-life customers in a non-contractual setting: an empirical investigation and implications for marketing', *Journal of Marketing*, 64(4): 17–35.

Tapp, A., Whitten, I. and Housden, M. (2013) *Principles of Direct, Database and Digital Marketing*, 5th edn, Pearson.

Wood, M.B. (2010) *Essential Guide to Marketing Planning*, 2nd edn, FT/Prentice Hall.

SKILL SHEET 10 **Marketing Management**

This skills sheet provides a set of tools to help the reader engage in the practice of marketing.

1. Writing the Marketing Plan

A marketing plan includes factors such as: deciding which customers to target; how to reach them and how to win their business.
Recommended structure:

a. title page (specify target audience, author, relevant time period and date)
b. executive summary (a brief overview of the entire plan)
c. contents page
d. introduction (report purpose and context)
e. current situation (assessment of where the organization is now) – see the marketing audit below
f. marketing objectives and goals, see skills sheet 7
g. marketing strategies and programmes (outline what is to be done in order to reach the objectives and goals; identify the set of activities organized around the marketing mix plus those designed to manage relationships with customers)
h. marketing budget (present data on market share, sales, costs and other financial figures) – see section 7 of this skills sheet
i. implementation control (identify what will be measured and how control will be achieved) – see skills sheet 9
j. recommendations and conclusion.

The following sections can be used as stand-alone tools or methods to help write the detailed sections of the marketing plan.

2. Situation Analysis and the Marketing Audit

The first main section of the marketing plan will present the current situation. A marketing audit is a formal, detailed study of the marketing planning process and the marketing function to assess strengths, weaknesses and areas needing improvement; a systematic review of a company's marketing activities and of its marketing environment. Typical questions to ask about the current marketing situation include:

Q1. What is the firm's purpose, vision, mission, goal(s), etc. (see skills sheet 7)
Q2. Does the firm develop and implement formal marketing plans?
Q3. Is market research gathered?
Q4. Are marketing plans based on market segmentation?
Q5. What are the major market segments?
Q6. Are segments identified, measured and monitored/does the organization frequently analyze profitability of market segments?
Q7. What is the market size and is this changing?
Q8. What are market profit rates and how are these changing?
Q9. <PESTLE and Competition Analysis> see skills sheet 6
Q10. <SWOT Analysis> see skills sheet 6 Section 7
Q11. What are competitor's strengths and weaknesses within markets served?
Q12. What are competitor's strategies within your markets?
Q13. Is your present market segmentation approach effective?
Q14. Should your company withdraw from any business segment?
Q15. What are objectives for current product lines?
Q16. How do you gather, generate and screen new product ideas?
Q17. How do you manage the product portfolio: weed out unprofitable products and add new ones?

When structuring the situation-analysis of the marking plan consider organizing your examination under the following headings:

(1) **company** – vision, mission, goals, culture, product line, etc.
(2) **collaborators** and partners – information about suppliers, alliances and distributors
(3) **customers** – customer groups/segments (see Sections 3 and 4 below), market size
(4) **competitors –** list of competitors and their respective market shares in the relevant customer

grouping/segments; incorporate five forces analysis and micro-competition analysis (see for example, skills sheet 6 Sections 2 and 3), and

(5) **context** – PESTLE analysis (see skills sheet 6).

3. Market Segmentation

The purpose of market segmentation is to leverage scarce resources: to ensure that the elements of the marketing mix are designed to meet particular needs of different customers. Segments should be distinct, accessible and profitable. The organization must decide which segments to serve, i.e. determine its target markets.

The market can be divided up into sections or 'segments' based on any number of factors. Segments may be created in many ways using a variety of factors such as:

- **Demographics** – age, sex, income, education, race, marital status, household size, geographic location.
- **Psychographics** – personality and emotionally based behaviour linked to purchase choices; e.g. risk-takers or avoiders, impulsive buyers, etc.
- **Lifestyle** – hobbies, recreational pursuits, entertainment, etc.
- **Belief and value systems** – religious, political and cultural.
- **Life stage** – (e.g., pre-teens, teenagers, etc.)

Having identified a segment: estimate the number of individuals within; ensure it is a substantial, accessible, homogeneous group and the segment must be devised in such a way that it results in an action; it must have practical value.

B2B Segmentation

With B2B sales the decision-maker is often not the product user; B2B buyers are more rational; often buying more complex products; a small number of customers dominate sales (see the Pareto principle); and personal relationships and trust are often more important.

It is common to base segmentation on company (*Firmographics*) size, age, industry, company type (ownership) and the geographic scope of the market (e.g. a particular region, country).

Segmentation may also be based upon *product usage* in terms of volume, variety, frequency, RFM. You may also consider segments based upon the customer wants, i.e. price, value, quality, timing, warranty, payment options, service, etc. Segmentation variables will be combined in a manner that creates a meaningful segment with

practical value to the specific organization (seller). There is no generally accepted 'right way' to segment. The key issue is to better understand markets that can be successfully and profitably exploited.

In some cases it may be desirable to specify distinct product market segments. First list your products and then your customer groups. Multiply the two numbers together to determine how many business segments you serve. Next consider the regions or countries you sell into. Once again multiply the number of countries served by the number of customer groups and then by the number products in order to determine how many business segments you serve. Next, determine the sales by product market segment. Repeat this with data for each of the last 3 years. Then identify your largest segments. Finally, repeat the activity using profit contribution rather than sales contribution. However, as with any examination you should be cautious of paralysis through analysis. Concentrate on the few product market segments that truly drive your firm's profit.

As was explained in Chapter 34, marketing databases enable easy manipulation of customer data. One of the fundamental methods of manipulation concerns the grouping of similar customers together into segments. Such segments then represent the more specific target market for marketers to devise initiatives and activities, see RFM and FRAC below.

4. RFM and FRAC

RFM stands for

Recency – How recently did the customer purchase?
Frequency – How often do they purchase?
Monetary value – How much do they spend?

Once each of the attributes has appropriate categories defined, segments are created from the intersection of the values.

In the following example we extract four sample records from a customer order database. Each customer has a unique customer number e.g. Cxxxx. When sorted by recency, frequency or value the sequence number ('Rec') is inserted. There are 1000 customers in the example database. A summary table of each customer's transactional (order) history is queried to provide: (1) date of the last or most recent purchase (sort by date), (2) total number or frequency of purchases (count by customer) and (3) average amount spent per order (group by customer and then determine average). The analysis can begin once each account number has these three variables summarized:

Customer Ref Unique	Rec	Recency		Frequency		Average € value		RFM
		Last purchase 2014	R Score	Total	F Score	€	M Score	
C2495	001	30/11	1	18	1	€6000	1	3
C3657	002	29/11	1	17	1	€6500	1	3
C2275	501	30/06	3	14	2	€3000	3	8
C7693	999	30/01	5	2	5	€3000	3	13
Sample data (assume today's date is 31/12/2015)								

(1) Sort customers by purchase dates in reverse chronological order.

(2) Divide the customer list into five equal segments. For example, if you were starting with 1000 customers, each segment would contain 200 records.

(3) Tag those customers who have made the most recent purchases with a '1' indicating the top segment and work your way to the least recent purchases being tagged with a '5'. Segmenting into five equal groups is called quintiling.

(4) Next, sort your customers by number of orders (frequency) and apply the same methodology and tagging process.

(5) Finally, perform this sort on the average Euro (or UKP) amount of each order and perform the quintiling and tagging functions.

Add the R, F and M scores. You have now created RFM scores for each of your customers, from your best customer segment (3) to your worst (15). The major benefit of performing this analysis is the identification of your best customers.

An alternative methodology is to assign a scale of 1 to 10, whereby 10 is the maximum value and to stipulate the formula by which the data suits the scale. For example you could have:

Recency = 10 – the number of months that have passed since the customer last purchased; Frequency = number of purchases in the last 12 months (maximum of 10); Monetary = value of the highest order from a given customer.

FRAC scoring follows a very similar process and also uses a points system. For example, recency may be converted to points as follows: purchase within last quarter (24 points); last two quarters (12 points); last three quarters (6 points) and last year (3 points). Frequency points may be determined from the formulae: points = 4 × Number of purchases and monetary points derived from the combined purchase value with a ceiling of X points. Once a FRAC score has been determined, all customers are listed in a table and sorted from highest to lowest. Customers are then divided into groups. The top group are the most and the bottom group least responsive.

Having segmented the market, first assess the customer purchasing criteria and then use the marketing mix to compete within it.

5. Assessing Customer Purchasing Criteria

How do customers decide whether to purchase from you or one of your competitors?

1. Identify the (generic) decision-maker within a given segment, decision process and influencers. The decision-maker will not necessarily be the person who pays the bill nor even be the user.

2. Locate the value buyers wish to reap from your products or services (use criteria). Customers want products that lower cost, improve performance or otherwise satisfy their needs and wants. They use purchase criteria to make their decision. There are two types of purchase criteria: use and signalling. Use criteria derive from the ways a product or firm delivers value via lower costs or improved performance. Use criteria might include product quality, product features, delivery time, service and support.

3. Find out what influences the buyer's perception of your product or service (signalling criteria). Signalling criteria are factors that influence the buyer's perception of a firm or product's ability to add value in the areas that are most meaningful to the buyer, i.e. use criteria. Common signalling criteria include: Reputation, Advertising, Packaging and labels, Time in business, Customer list, Market share, Price (where price connotes quality), etc.

4. Reorganize your marketing programme (mix) with this knowledge.

The organization will need to satisfy the customer purchasing criteria. Many practitioners seek to identify key/critical success factors (KSFs or CSFs) to accomplish this. Success factors – product features that are particularly valued by customers, hence, where the organization must outrival competition – were discussed in Chapter 19. You must offer goods or services that are superior to those offered by your competitors.

6. Marketing Mix

Marketers adjust the 4Ps to match the needs of their customers in their target markets (refer to Chapters 31, 32 and 33). In determining the optimal mix and marketing decisions, the marketer will seek to:

(1) **product**: produce what customers want – this may mean new product development, the modification of existing products and elimination of products that are no longer attractive or profitable

(2) **place**: ensure products are available in the right quantities in the right place and at the right time; this will include inventory management, transport and storage decision-making

(3) **promotion**: inform customer groups about the organization and its products, and

(4) **price**: determine how much customers are willing to pay.

Tools to help with product and market choices include:

- Ansoff's product-market growth matrix: Ansoff's product-market matrix for determining competitive strategies: market penetration, market development, product development or diversification – see Chapter 17 and Figure 17.2

- The Boston Consulting Group designed the BCG Matrix, one of the best-known product portfolio planning tools, based on the concept of the product life cycle– see Chapter 17 and Figure 17.3. This matrix is based on three major variables: a firm's relative market share, the growth rate of its market(s) and the cash flows (negative or positive) generated by the firm's activities. The matrix can be used to identify the profit and growth potential of each business unit within the company.

7. Market Share

Market share is determined by measuring a company's sales revenues and incorporating them into the total sales for the industry:

1. Calculate total revenue (also called total sales) for the firm or a particular segment.
2. Calculate the total market sales. This is the total amount of sales (or revenue) made in the entire market; found through specific industry's trade associations or through a certified research firm.
3. Divide your company's total revenue by your entire industry's total market sales.

$$Market\ Share_{Company\ A} = \frac{Sales\ revenue_{Company\ A}}{Total\ industry\ sales\ revenue}$$

8. Marketing Budget and Spend Per Customer

The budget is one of the final parts of the marketing plan. Marketers spend money to attract AND retain customers – but how much should they spend in order to win and keep their customers?

First compute the LTV/LCV for each customer over a fixed period such as 5 years. Next imagine that the allowable spend for customer recruitment is €100/customer and the allowable spend for retention is €10 per customer per year. Having set such figures we can now determine the required marketing budget where (1) the acquisition budget is allowable spend for customer recruitment 'X' target number of customers. Should we require 1000 new customers then the acquisition budget = €100 × 1000, i.e. 100 000. This might fund a much larger mailshot to say 50 000 prospects and we would only need a 2 per cent response/acquisition rate. (2) The retention marketing budget = number of customers × allowable spend for retention (€10). Thus, for a customer staying for all 5 years of the LCV, the marketer would spend €100 + (4 × €10, i.e. 40) = €140. With this information it is possible to calculate the return on investment (ROI) for each customer = (LCV – spend) /number of years – thus determining the expected ROI per annum.

Section Twelve
Operations Management

CHAPTER 35
MANAGING THE PROCUREMENT FUNCTION: SOURCING INPUTS

Key Concepts

- Global sourcing
- e-Procurement
- Procurement process
- Purchasing
- Supply management
- Tendering (RFI, RFQ, RFP)

Learning Outcomes Having read this chapter, you should be able to:

- explain why purchasing is an important business function
- discuss sourcing strategies and the strategic sourcing process
- discuss what is meant by supply management
- explain, with reference to the transformational process, the relationships between the purchasing, logistics and operations functions
- explain the purchasing process
- discuss how organizations make reordering purchase decisions.

1.   In many organizations, acquisition or buying of services is called contracting, whilst that of goods is called purchasing or procurement. Purchasing has been discussed on a number of occasions throughout this textbook so far. In particular, we have discussed it as a part of supply chain management (refer back to Chapter 11, para. 16). In the previous marketing section we discussed purchasing from a consumer perspective but now consider the organization also as a consumer of goods – sometimes as a part of the production, manufacturing or service creation activity and other times in relation to assets and consumables that must be acquired to support the organization's existence.

2.   We also noted in the opening chapter that ScaterBoys has a Purchasing Manager and a procurement process (refer to the opening case study notes). At ScaterBoys, when inventory is running low or a customer orders goods not in stock, procurement place orders with suppliers. Goods are then received in-bound at the warehouse where the goods are stored and systems updated accordingly.

3.   What then is purchasing? **Purchasing** (supply management or sourcing) is the important organizational function, often part of the operations function, that forms contracts with suppliers to buy-in materials and services. Activities include identifying needs, locating and selecting suppliers, negotiating terms and following up to ensure supplier performance. **Procurement**, the act of getting possession of something from a supplier, is often used interchangeably with purchasing. Some people describe procurement as the purchasing (buying) process in a firm or organization. We will consider the day-to day purchasing activities reflected within the purchasing process after first introducing some of the strategic aspects of purchasing decisions.

4.   A further related concept is that of **supply**. Supply may refer to the action of providing what is needed or wanted (necessary goods and equipment) or a stock or amount of something available for use. The term **supply management** describes the methods and processes of corporate buying. This may be for the purchasing of supplies for internal use, referred to as indirect goods and services, purchasing raw materials for consumption during the manufacturing process, or for the purchasing of goods for inventory to be resold as products in the distribution and retail process.

5.   Earlier, we identified purchasing as an important organizational function. It is important because it can impact upon organizational performance. It can be linked with primary sources of competitive advantage (cost, differentiation and speed) through pricing, quality and delivery performance. In this chapter we start by discussing sourcing strategies, considering issues such as insourcing and outsourcing (make or buy) and supplier selection; we will then describe the day-to-day purchasing process. Many organizations have a dedicated and professional purchasing function and we will consider the typical roles and responsibilities of such a department. Finally, we will consider the specific problem of how they work with the operations function (logistics and warehousing) to manage inventory, stocking and restocking. Stockout's (shortages of products resulting from a lack of products carried in inventory, the inability to satisfy the demand for an item) can disadvantage the organization, leading to poor customer service, customer dissatisfaction and decline (refer back to the previous marketing section). Yet excessive stock ties up capital and is wasteful. The Purchasing Manager must work with the logistic function (see next chapter) in order to balance these two opposing challenges.

35.1 SOURCING STRATEGIES

6.   Much of what we have discussed so far may be categorized as **supply management** (used interchangeably with the terms sourcing or purchasing) – the broad set of activities carried out by organizations to analyze sourcing opportunities, develop sourcing strategies, select suppliers, and carry out all the activities required to procure goods and services (Bozarth and Handfield, 2012).

7.   Sourcing may take place within or outside the home country. **Global sourcing** is the process of identifying, evaluating, negotiating and configuring supply across multiple geographies. When evaluating global sourcing opportunities, the organization should consider the purchase price, transportation costs, inventory carrying costs, cross-border taxes, tariffs and duty costs, supply performance and risks. Operations may also seek to ensure they only deal with ethical suppliers.

8.   The strategic sourcing process is outlined in Figure 35.1. Whilst it is possible to break the process down into any number of stages, for simplicity we identify four key activity areas. The company must understand

FIGURE 35.1 Strategic sourcing process

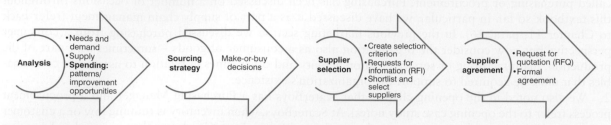

what materials (parts and components), products and services it is likely to need. The Purchasing Manager will determine how much is being spent with various suppliers, and spending patterns. They will also consider business needs and how such procured items are used and seek understanding of when products are required and who can supply them. Such insights will be of use when making sourcing decisions later.

9.   Earlier, when discussing the transformation process (refer back to Figures 8.1–8.3), we noted that the production system relied upon inputs (raw materials etc.). Each organization will consider whether or not to make or buy the raw materials and inputs. High-level, often strategic decisions regarding which products or services will be provided internally and which will be provided by external supply chain partners are referred to as sourcing (make-or-buy) decisions. **Insourcing** concerns the use of resources within the organization to provide products or services, as opposed to **outsourcing** where supply chain partners provide products or services.

10.   Such decisions are not without consequences. Insourcing provides for greater control and opportunity for scale advantages but may require high levels of investment and a loss of access to superior products. Outsourcing may enhance flexibility, improve cash flow and allow access to state-of-the-art products and services but creates communication and coordination challenges, reduces control and introduces the possibility of selecting an ineffective supplier.

11.   Having considered what is feasible and desirable to produce in-house, the Purchasing Manager must then determine the source of supply for parts or outsourced products and services. Several criteria are typically used when choosing suppliers. The price (cost) of goods and services is often near the top of the list. Additionally, the quality of goods provided along with reliability and delivery speed will be important for many companies (more important for companies seeking to offer differentiated products or services). Such matters are likely to impact upon the company's offering and ability to deliver good customer service. Other factors used for rating alternative suppliers include: the range of goods or services they may provide; dependability and responsiveness. In some cases it will be preferable to select more than one supplier (multi-sourcing) of any particular product or service required. This minimizes risk and dependency but may increase costs and reduce available discounts for volume and repeat purchases.

12.   In order to select an appropriate supplier, the Purchasing Manager requests further information from prospects. The **request for information (RFI)** is a request to vendors for general, somewhat informal information about their company and products. This information can be used to score prospective suppliers against the selection criteria established earlier. Suppliers with the highest scores can be shortlisted (just like the HR recruitment process) for more detailed evaluation and negotiation.

13.   Once the Purchasing Manager has a reasonable idea of the suppliers from which they wish to purchase, they will often request a quotation in order to determine costs and obtain promises about product or service quality and delivery. This activity is typically referred to as the **request for quotation (RFQ)** – a formal request for suppliers to prepare bids based on the terms and conditions set by the buyer. The RFQ will then form the basis of any agreement (contract). In some cases, the Purchasing Manager may also request proposals from suppliers. This is more likely when services are being purchased or when involving non-standard products that have yet to be created and where the purchaser may not fully understand the nature of the product or solution they wish to purchase. A **request for proposal (RFP)** then is a document specifying all the requirements and soliciting a proposal from vendors who might want to bid on a project or service.

35.2 PURCHASING PROCESS

14.   Once suppliers have been selected and approved through the strategic sourcing process, the organization can order and buy products and services routinely from them. This is what happens when repeat purchases are made from the supplier. However, in cases of one-off purchases, the purchasing and supplier selection process may be combined.

15.   The procurement process starts with the recognition of some need for particular products or services. This need may be generated through a stock check; a system generated stock reorder; it may be triggered through a customer order or an employee. In some cases the employee may source their own products or services whilst in other cases it will be left to the procurement professional.

16.   The procurement team will specify the particular requirement and then raise a **purchase order (PO)** – a document, sometimes referred to as a *requisition*, authorizing a supplier to deliver a product or service – which is sent to the preferred supplier. In most cases, the company then waits for the goods to be delivered (inbound logistics) or services provided. In some cases there may be a need to follow up (chase) the supplier if goods do not arrive when required/specified. The inbound goods must be inspected and receipted. In some cases they are stored in the warehouse or, in others, routed to the employee who triggered the purchase. Information Systems are updated to show receipt of goods or services.

17.   At some time between dispatch of the PO and receipt of the goods or services, an invoice from the supplier is received by the company. An Accounts function will raise payment at some time after the receipt of goods and invoice. Once again this is recorded in relevant Information Systems. We will return to the role of technology in enabling this process towards the end of the chapter.

18.   The Purchasing process, also referred to as the procurement process or the procure-to-pay cycle (see Figure 35.2), may vary, dependent upon the type of goods to be purchased. According to Owen (2001: p. 29) we may purchase direct or indirect (Maintenance, Repair and Operation (MRO) items) goods; the type of goods purchased will impact upon technologies and support processes. MRO goods are products, other than raw materials, necessary to ensure that the organization is able to continue functioning. They are often referred to as consumables. Direct goods represent a complex purchase since our decision may be determined by quality, price, payment terms, delivery and other factors. Consequently, we may need to evaluate suppliers, their products and then negotiate. The process may include data aggregation, demand forecast, RFQ management, supplier qualification, contract negotiation and award, purchase, shipping and receipt orders, invoicing, payments, tracking and customer service. The purchase of indirect goods is generally considered simpler with cost being one of the primary determinants of the purchase decision.

FIGURE 35.2 Procurement process

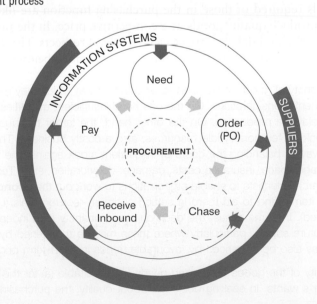

19.   In addition to MRO, the goods and services classified as indirect procurement are commonly bought for consumption by internal stakeholders (business units or functions). This may include the purchase of products or services such as: professional services, travel, IT related services (hardware, software), HR related services (recruitment agencies, training), utilities, capital goods (plant and machinery) and marketing related services. For example, most purchasing decisions can only be taken after due agreement with financial, production or marketing colleagues.

20.   Thus far we have considered procurement as the acquisition of goods, services or works from an outside external source. Organizations often define processes intended to promote fair and open competition for their business whilst minimizing exposure to fraud and collusion. Procurement may involve a bidding process known as **tendering**. Potential suppliers submit proposals of what they will provide and at what price. At that point the purchaser will usually select the lowest bidder deemed competent. In the EU, strict rules on procurement must be followed by public bodies, with contract value thresholds determining the processes required.

35.3 PURCHASING FUNCTION – ROLES AND RESPONSIBILITIES

21.   Purchasing is an important aspect of operations management. Purchasing costs, for example, often represent a substantial part of the total costs of production. At a time of extreme competitiveness in the marketplace, an efficient and cost-effective purchasing section can make all the difference between a competitively priced product and one that is comparatively more expensive.

22.   The primary responsibility of the purchasing/procurement department is to secure sufficient and suitable raw materials, components, other goods and services to ensure that the manufacturing process is fully supplied with all its materials, and to achieve this responsibility in a cost-effective and timely manner. To this end the purchasing department can be expected to be responsible for the following:

–   Appraisal and selection of and maintaining good relationships with suppliers.

–   Collation of up-to-date information on suppliers, prices, distribution methods, etc.

–   Negotiating the purchase of goods and services at prices which represent the best value to the business in the long-term (i.e. not necessarily the lowest prices at a given time).

–   Ensuring that suppliers are familiar with, and adhere to, relevant quality standards operated by the company.

–   Maintenance of adequate stock/inventory levels.

23.   The negotiating skills required of those in the purchasing function are likely to be crucial elements in a company's ability to produce quality goods at a competitive price. In the purchase of material goods, issues of quantity, quality, price and delivery are crucial in several respects. These could be described as the key elements of the 'purchasing mix'. Each item of the mix is described below:

–   QUANTITY. The quantity of goods to be ordered, and the time at which they need to be ordered, are major (inventory management) considerations. On the one hand insufficient quantities at a particular point in time will cause costly delays in production. On the other hand, the larger the quantity ordered, the more will have to go into stock as temporarily idle resources, also a costly business. The ideal to be aimed at is to find the optimum way of balancing the costs of insufficient stock against the costs of holding stock (e.g. tied-up capital, storage space, insurance costs, damage, deterioration, etc.). Techniques have been devised by operational research scientists to enable organizations to work out the **economic order quantity (EOQ)** for individual stock items, and to aid them in setting optimum reorder levels (i.e. the levels at which stock needs to be replaced). In some cases, the decision about quantity (and indeed time) may be dictated by considerations of future supply, particularly where these may be threatened by economic or political pressures. Decisions may also be influenced by favourable trends in short-term prices.

–   QUALITY. The quality of the goods purchased needs to be suitable (a) for the manufacturing process and (b) for the customer's wants. In seeking decisions about quality, the purchasing department have to work closely with both production and marketing employees to arrive at a suitable compromise. Inspection of goods received is vital to check the supplier is fulfilling the order to the correct specification.

– PRICE. Purchasing should ideally aim for a price which gives the best value to the organization, taking quality, delivery and relative urgency into account. This may not always be the lowest price available, but the one which represents the best value over a period of time.

– DELIVERY. A factor which must be considered by the purchasing department in the appraisal and selection of suppliers is the reliability of deliveries. The lead time between an order and a delivery is an important aspect of stock control. Where lead times are certain, they can be allowed for in stock calculations. Where they are uncertain, it makes stock control much more difficult. Not only is stock affected by the delivery situation, so is production. The latter is particularly vulnerable to delays in deliveries for items which are used continuously, and for which minimum buffer stocks are held. Buffer stocks are reserve stocks held for emergency shortages.

35.4 SUPPLY MANAGEMENT: STOCK

24. Several aspects of stock control have already been mentioned above, and these can be drawn together in a simplified graph of stock levels. Such graphs have a saw-tooth pattern, reflecting the outputs (usage) and the inputs (deliveries) to stock, as in Figure 35.3. The figure indicates how usage reduces stocks over a period of time, and invariably absorbs some of the buffer stock, unless planned deliveries are made on time. The lead time, as shown, is the time taken between the order being made and delivery taking place. As soon as the delivery is made, stocks shoot up again, until further usage reduces them, and this produces the saw-tooth effect on the graph. Should planned deliveries not take place, and should usage continue, then eventually a 'stockout' situation will be reached, where, in the short-term, the goods in question will be out-of-stock.

25. Working with the logistics and production function it is important for the purchasing department to identify optimum stock levels (preventing stockout whilst not tying up too much capital) and the reorder levels that will trigger purchases. Such decisions are also likely to be influenced by the finance function and once established may be automated. Such decisions are also likely to be influenced by the production strategy/policy: make-to-order or make-to-stock (discussed in Chapter 37).

FIGURE 35.3 Simple stock control graph

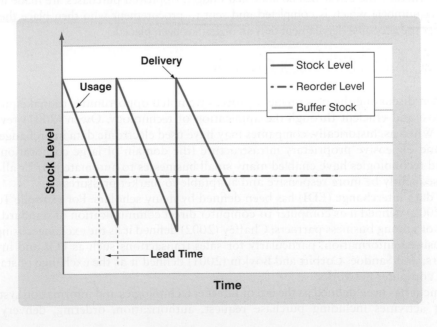

26.   The reorder point ('ROP') is the level of inventory when an order should be made with suppliers to bring the inventory up by the economic order quantity ('EOQ'). The reorder point for replenishment of stock occurs when the level of inventory drops down to a specified quantity. The two factors that determine the appropriate order point are:

(1)   the delivery-time-stock (the expected inventory usage between ordering and receiving inventory) and (2) the safety (or buffer) stock which is the minimum level of inventory held as a protection against shortages due to fluctuations in demand. The amount of safety stock is determined from the trade-off between the risk of stockout, resulting in possible customer dissatisfaction and lost sales, and the increased costs associated with carrying additional inventory. Therefore:

Reorder level = Normal consumption during lead-time + Safety stock

27.   Meredith and Shafer (2011: p. 264) suggest organizations that are highly effective in supply chain management purchasing follow three practices: (1) leverage their buying power, i.e. they typically centralize many aspects of procurement in order to gain benefits from scale and purchasing power, (2) they commit to a small number of dependable suppliers and (3) they will help suppliers reduce their total cost of production which is of mutual benefit.

35.5 LINE PURCHASING

28.   Up until now we have focused on the 'professional' aspects of purchasing – by the procurement function. However, many smaller organizations do not have a dedicated and professional resource for purchasing and even larger organizations often allow line managers and some non-managerial employees to make indirect purchases by themselves. The organization may supply company credit cards and/or a budget account for the manager/employee to use. Alternatively they may implement an expenses claims process whereby employees can be reimbursed for purchases made. This method is often used for travel and subsistence expenses but may be used for other types of purchase also. Budget holders are responsible for the authorization of expenditure within their budget allocation. Budget holders are also accountable for the types of purchases made and are often required to justify all over/underspending.
29.   Organizations use policy, budgets, procedure and processes to control this type of 'self'-authorized spending. A typical process is shown below, see Figure 35.4. In this example, ABC managers are allocated budgets and corporate credit cards for purchases under €1000. Approval is required for purchases exceeding this amount or for any purchase whereby the buyer has no allocated budget. Approved purchases are made using a PO (with unique identifying number) which is completed and sent to procurement who then place the order with the supplier and notify the accounts department that an order has been placed.

35.6 SOURCING TECHNOLOGIES

30.   Earlier, when discussing the procurement process we noted opportunities to make purchasing activities more effective and efficient through the application of technology. Owen (2001) reviews electronic trading models. Whereas, historically, companies may have used electronic data interchange (EDI), specialized networks and expensive proprietary infrastructure (the domain of large corporations), the Internet and Web-enabled technologies have enabled many small businesses to automate part or all of their supply chains, and consequently be more responsive and adaptable to market pressures.
31.   **Electronic data interchange (EDI)** has been defined by many scholars. For example Turban, McLean and Wetherbe (2002) defined it as computer-to-computer direct communication of standard business transactions between or among business partners; Chaffey (2002) defined it as the exchange, using digital media, of structured business information, particularly for sales transactions such as POs and invoices between buyers and sellers; and Sandoe, Corbitt and Boykin (2001) defined it as the exchange of standard business documents over computer networks.
32.   **e-Procurement** has been defined as the use of Internet technologies and information systems to manage all procurement activities including purchase request, authorization, ordering, delivery and payment

FIGURE 35.4 Simple self-authorized procurement process

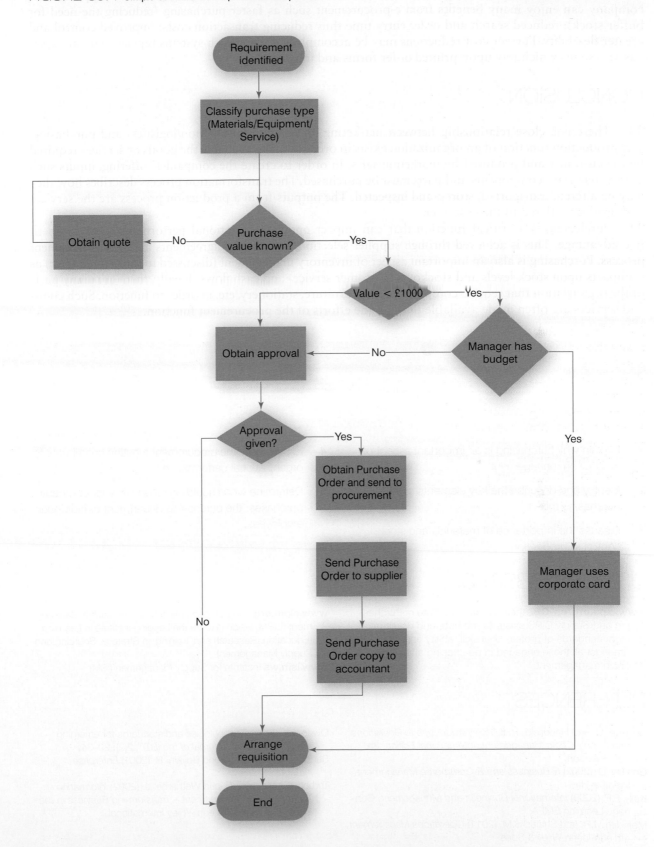

between a purchaser and a supplier, (Kelly, 2009); this may include identifying potential suppliers. The company can enjoy many benefits from e-procurement such as faster purchasing (reducing the need for buffer stock); reduced search and order entry time thus reducing transaction costs; improved control and greater flexibility. Further cost reductions may be accomplished when such systems replace manual paper-based systems which rely upon printed order forms and invoices, etc.

CONCLUSION

33. There is a close relationship between marketing, operations (production/logistics) and purchasing. The production function of an organization exists in order to make available the goods or services required by the customer and promised by marketing/sales. In order to create the companies' offering, inputs such as raw materials, components and parts must be purchased. The transformation process describes how they may be altered, transported, stored and inspected. The outputs from a production process are the services and products offered to the customer.

34. Purchasing is a critical function that can impact upon organizational performance and competitive advantage. This is achieved through supplier selection, contractual agreements and the procurement process. Purchasing is also an important aspect of inventory management (discussed in the next chapter) as it impacts upon stock levels and stockouts (customer service) and cash flows. Finally, there are many parts of the organization that require computers, office furniture, stationery, etc. in order to function. Such goods and services are often made available through the efforts of the procurement function.

QUESTIONS

1 Explain why purchasing is an important aspect of production management.

2 Identify and describe the key elements of the purchasing mix.

3 Discuss the importance of materials and stock control to production.

4 Explain how the procurement function contributes to organizational performance.

5 Determine who should be responsible for company purchases: the purchasing department or individual employees.

USEFUL WEBSITES

www.cips.org/en-GB/ the chartered Institute of Purchasing and Supply CIPS exists to promote and develop high standards of professional skill, ability and integrity amongst all those engaged in purchasing and supply chain management.

www.eipm.org The European Institute of Purchasing Management (EIPM) vision is to be the Leading Institute in Learning (Education, Research and Training) in Strategic Sourcing and Supply Management

www.ism.ws Institute for Supply Management(ISM)

REFERENCES

Bozarth, C. and Handfield, R. (2012) *Introduction to Operations and Supply Chain Management: International Edition*, 3rd edn, Pearson.

Chaffey, D. (2002) *E-Business and E-Commerce Management*, Prentice Hall.

Kelly, P.P. (2009) *International Business and Management*, Cengage Learning EMEA.

Meredith, J.R. and Shafer, S.M. (2011) *Operations Management*, 4th edn, John Wiley & Sons.

Owen, M. (2001) 'Technologies and standards for emerging e-trading models', *Journal of the IBTE*, 2(2): 29–34.

Sandoe, K., Corbitt, G. and Boykin, R. (2001) *Enterprise Integration*, Wiley.

Turban, E., McLean, E. and Wetherbe, J. (2002) *Information Technology for Management – Transforming Business in the Digital Economy*, 3rd edn, Wiley International.

CHAPTER 36
MANAGING THE
LOGISTICS FUNCTION

Key Concepts

- Logistics
- Inventory
- Materials handling
- Perfect order
- Picking and packaging
- Warehousing

Learning Outcomes Having read this chapter, you should be able to:

- explain how the logistics function can be a source of competitive advantage
- explain the different types of inventory and why organizations store products
- describe warehouse processes: receiving, putting away, picking and packing
- discuss what is meant by the perfect order
- explain how organizations make logistics facility location decisions.

1.   In the last chapter we discussed the role of the procurement function and described the procurement process. Procurement or purchasing usually initiates the flow of materials through an organization by sending a purchase order to a supplier. We also noted that the purchased raw materials and parts to be used in the production process must be stored within a warehouse (inventory) before being transformed into the outputs (company's products and services) which will also be stored prior to distribution. Thus, this chapter follows immediately from where we left things in the previous chapter.

2.   How much inventory to hold is one of the most fundamental decisions that must be made in a manufacturing organization (Bradley and Arntzen, 1999). In this chapter we focus on inventory decisions and management of the Logistics function (warehousing, materials handling and transportation). We consider aspects of the transmission process, inputs and outputs along with reverse Logistics. In the next chapter we focus more on the production function, i.e. the processes creating the organization's outputs.

3.   **Logistics** has been defined by many scholars. It has been defined as the management of both inbound and outbound materials, parts, supplies and finished goods; the process of transporting the initial components of goods, services and other forms of offering, and their finished products, from the producer to the

customer and then on to the consumer; and as a term in supply chain management broadly analogous to physical distribution management. We introduced logistics as a part of the marketing mix – place or distribution in Chapter 32. We also discussed reverse logistics and the supply chain. In this chapter we build upon Chapter 32 and the earlier Chapter 11 (Managing the Supply Chain).

4.   Procured goods need to be stored and we start this chapter with a discussion on inventory management. This is also relevant to the storage of work-in-progress and finished goods. Throughout the supply chain, including within the warehouse, goods must be moved around and when finished, goods that are ordered must be picked and packed. Consequently after explaining inventory management and the role of the warehouse we discuss materials handling in more detail. With reference to the fulfilment process, once the goods have been packed they must then be shipped to an intermediary or end consumer. Such activities are considered under the heading of transportation and distribution. In the final part of this chapter, recognizing the importance of the Logistics function to organizational performance, we consider the issue of location, asking where aspects of the operation should be located. Location, for example of warehousing, has an immediate impact upon costs (facility costs and transportation – proximity to customers) and time compression – speed of delivery and therefore competitive advantage (strategy). We will discuss factors and methods that influence location decisions. We will also highlight the risk challenges associated with this function. Having explained logistics processes we will be well placed to consider production and the transformational process in the following chapter.

36.1 THE ROLE OF THE WAREHOUSE, THE WAREHOUSE MANAGER AND INVENTORY MANAGEMENT

5.   Before proceeding further we first clarify a number of key concepts relevant to **inventory management** – planning, coordinating and controlling the acquisition, storage, handling, movement, distribution and possible sale of raw materials, component parts and subassemblies, supplies and tools, replacement parts and other assets needed to meet customer wants and needs. **Stock** refers to all items stored by organizations for future use and an **inventory** is simply a list of the items held in stock. One entry (distinct product) in the inventory is referred to as an **item** and a **unit** is a standard size or quantity of an item. Stocks are formed whenever an organization acquires materials, work-in process or finished goods for which it has no immediate need. Typical movements of stock are shown in Figure 36.1.

FIGURE 36.1 Stock movements

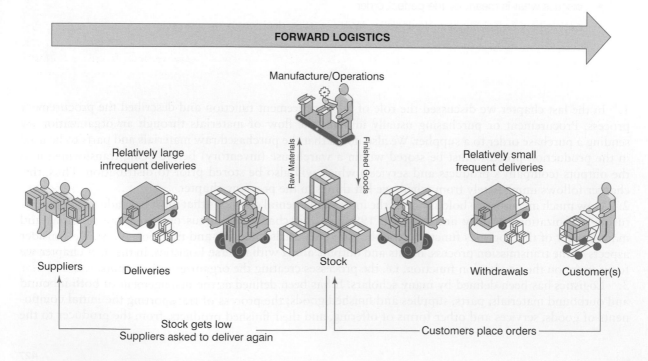

6.   In Chapter 16 we discussed decision-making in organizations and recognized many management scholars regard decision-making as the most important managerial activity. There are many examples of decision-making associated with the Warehouse Manager role. He/she must decide how much stock to hold, and when to reorder in particular. In this part of the chapter we consider the inventory management policy, the role of the warehouse, warehouse processes, forecasting, stock levels, with management policy, and material requirements planning. Holding stock is expensive – problems of inventory control are almost universal. Over the past decade organizations have been trying to improve customer service whilst lowering stocks and increasing the speed of material flow through their supply chains (Waters, 2003).

7.   **Warehousing** concerns the design and operation of facilities for storing and moving goods. Organizations use warehousing to reduce transportation costs, improve operational flexibility, shorten customer lead times and lower inventory costs. A **warehouse** is any location where stocks are held. In the case of raw materials storage the warehouse will often be located near to the point of manufacture which is likely to be near key suppliers. Warehouses will also store **finished goods** (product ready for sale – items that are ready to be moved to a customer), providing a buffer or safety stock.

8.   At this point we might ask why companies hold stock. **Inventory** has been defined as stock on hand; often divided between raw materials, work-in-process and finished goods; the stored accumulation of transformed resources in a process; those stocks or items used to support production (raw materials and work-in-process items), supporting activities (maintenance, repair and operating supplies) and customer service (finished goods and spare parts). In many cases the company will hold stock in order to manage uncertain and erratic demand patterns. They may also build up stock as a result of discounted bulk buying, to cover production shutdowns and shortages generally; safety stock is inventory needed to prevent stockouts.

9.   Within the warehouse, the manager is typically responsible for:

   a.   leadership and management of the warehouse team

   b.   provision of a responsive and cost-efficient warehouse aligned with the company's strategy

   c.   creation of the warehouse functional strategy

   d.   inventory management

   e.   materials handling

   f.   safety and security within the warehouse

   g.   warehouse processes, their quality and continuous improvement.

   The Warehouse Manager and supervisors/team leaders are expected to have good motivational, communication, problem-solving and teamwork skills. They should have an ability to delegate and empower, be flexible and customer-oriented. Furthermore they should have a comprehensive knowledge of relevant processes and procedures such as the core fulfilment, production and procurement and associated warehouse specific processes.

10   Whilst operating hours vary according to customer requirements, a classic warehouse shift pattern may run from 6 am until 2 pm and then 2 pm until 10 pm; in some cases there may be a nightshift and the working of weekends will vary; shift requirements will be dependent also on the volume of work and in some cases this may necessitate 24/7 working.

11.   The Warehouse Manager must balance pressures from marketing and sales to improve customer service, with pressure from finance to reduce cost. They can improve customer service through the perfect order and speeding up throughput (both of which are discussed later) and reduce cost with various stock controls, minimizing the amount of stock held and productivity improvements. The Warehouse Manager, through his team and operation, can be a source of competitive advantage. Their work can both differentiate and reduce cost in terms of Porter's generic strategies. Furthermore, they can ensure a fast, timely and accurate delivery, enabling the organization to compete as a reliable and responsive supplier. The Warehouse Manager's performance will be measured using the key performance indicators of the perfect order and order lead time – the length of time between placing an order and the receipt of the item by the customer.

12.   As highlighted above, cost management is a key challenge for the warehouse. There are two costs associated with ordering stock: the acquisition costs and the holding costs. Such costs have important implications for decisions about the optimum order size and frequency. We will first consider how much stock to order – the volume/quantity – decision. The optimal order size is often referred to as the **economic order quantity (EOQ)**.

13.   According to Waters (2003: p. 66), 'the EOQ calculation is the most important analysis in inventory control'. We introduced this concept in the previous chapter, refer back to Figure 35.3 'Simple stock control graph' and associated paragraphs and will elaborate further here. The variables used in the analysis include:

a.   **unit cost** (UC) – the price charged by the supplier for one unit of the item

b.   **reorder cost** (RC) – the cost of placing a routine order

c.   **holding costs** (HC) – the cost of holding one unit of the item in stock for one period of time (usually a year)

d.   **shortage cost** (SC) – the cost of having a shortage and not being able to meet demand from stock

e.   **order quantity** (Q) – the only variable directly under our control; when we set the order quantity this fixes the cycle length

f.   **cycle time** (T) – the time between two consecutive replenishments

g.   **demand** (D) – the number of units to be supplied. Any given time period

$$Economic\ Order\ Quantity = Q_0 = \frac{\sqrt{2} \times RC \times D}{HC}$$

$$Optimal\ Cycle\ Length = T = \frac{Q_0}{D} = \frac{\sqrt{2} \times RC}{D \times HC}$$

14.   In practice, software applications and spreadsheet programmes will be used for inventory control. A practical worked example is presented in the skills sheet for this section. There are a number of criticisms of the EOQ method (can cause too much capital to be tied up in stocks, suggests fractional values but products often come in discrete units, suppliers may not be willing to split standard package sizes and deliveries may be made by vehicles with mixed capacities). Consequently there are a number of adjustments to the model. However, a detailed review of methods is beyond the scope of this book.

15.   Having determined the quantity of a particular product to order, the organization (procurement or warehousing) must then determine *when* to place an order – the timing decision, i.e. the replenishment policy. Replenishment concerns placing materials into stock to replace units that have been used, (Waters, 2003). The reorder level (ROL) is the trigger level used which generates the ordering of a fixed amount (normally the EOQ). It is the stock level at which it is time to place another order for materials (generally the lead time demand plus safety stock, minus any stock on order).

16.   Aside from decisions on order quantity and frequency, the Warehouse Manager is responsible for designing a cost-efficient warehouse layout. Typical objectives will include making maximum use of space, minimizing movement and the amount of handling to which goods and materials are subjected. In order to increase **throughput** (number of units of product produced per unit of time) and productivity within the warehouse there is a need to reduce the amount of travel time and touchpoints, whilst also maximizing space utilization. The warehouse will be laid out to include spaces for the following: receiving goods, packing, dispatch and cross-dock area. In addition there will be the storage space and aisles. An example is provided in Figure 36.2.

17.   **Pareto analysis** is a type of analysis based on the observation that a very small proportion of items account for the majority of value; the principle that for many phenomena, 80 per cent of the consequences stem from 20 per cent of the causes (Pareto was an Italian economist, who observed that 80 per cent of income in Italy was received by 20 per cent of the population). It can be applied to many areas of management. When applied to inventory management problems, Pareto analysis may also be referred to as **ABC analysis**, which is a way of categorizing inventory items depending on value and use. The ABC system is used for ranking inventory into parts that require close control and parts that do not merit undue effort in

FIGURE 36.2 Warehouse layout

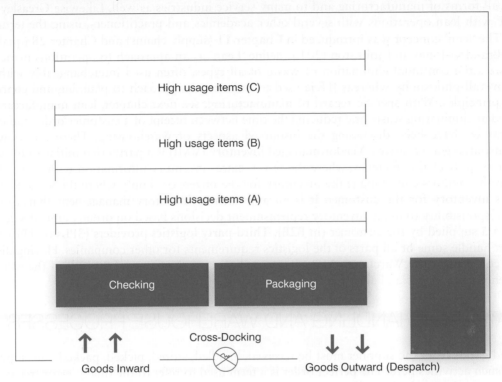

monitoring; a way of categorizing inventory items dependent upon value and use, not to be confused with Activity-Based-Costing (ABC).

18.   There are other cross-functional planning processes and associated decisions considered by the Warehouse Manager. **Material requirements planning (MRP)** is a planning process (usually computerized) that integrates production, purchasing and inventory management of interrelated products. It concerns the determination of component and materials requirements to support the production plan. MRP uses **bill-of-materials** data (BOM – a document/form stating the required quantity of materials for each operation to complete the product), inventory data and the production plan to determine when material needs to be produced or acquired (ordered). MRP is therefore about inventory control and includes a calculation of future need – including a set of calculations embedded in a system that helps operations make volume and timing calculations for planning and control purposes.

19.   Some scholars discuss MRP II – manufacturing resource planning (see for example, Waters, 2003). Similarly Paton *et al*. (2011), suggest MRP II to be an extension of MRP that not only identifies the amounts and times for delivery for components but also includes capacity checks, and extends the calculations to cover the scheduling of production, a matter we return to in the next chapter. Others (Greasley, 2009) suggest that it extends the idea of MRP to other areas in the firm such as marketing and finance; similarly, Turban, McLean and Wetherbe (2002), consider it a planning process that integrates production, inventory, purchasing, financing and labour in an enterprise.

20.   Thus far we have discussed demand forecasting and inventory management in the traditional sense. More recently, firms have sought out methods to reduce stock by establishing processes that ensure products are where they need to be, when they need to be. **Just-in-time** (mentioned in several previous chapters) is an approach in which processes are linked together in an extended chain to ensure good quality components are delivered to the user just-in-time (JIT) for them to be used. More specifically in the context of this chapter it refers to methods of managing inventory (stock) whereby items are delivered when needed in the production process instead of being stored by the manufacturer. Thus it can be viewed as an inventory scheduling system in which material and parts arrive at a workplace when needed, minimizing inventory, waste and interruptions. Indeed Bozarth and Handfield refer to it as a philosophy of manufacturing based

upon planned elimination of all waste and on continuous improvement of productivity. In the broad sense, it applies to all forms of manufacturing and to many service industries as well. Likewise Greasley (2009) discusses JIT with lean operations with several other academics and practitioners, using the terms interchangeably. The 'lean' concept was introduced in Chapter 11 (supply chains) and Chapter 28 (quality).

21.   Slack, Brandon-Jones and Johnston (2013) define 'Lean' as an approach to operations management that emphasizes the continual elimination of waste of all types, often used interchangeably with JIT; it is more an overall philosophy whereas JIT is used to indicate an approach to planning and control that adopts lean principles. With specific regard to manufacturing, see next chapter, lean manufacturing is a process aimed at eliminating waste and reducing the time between receipt of a customer order and delivery.

22.   Thus far we have been discussing the insourced aspects of warehousing. There are, however, a variety of outsourcing alternatives. **Vendor managed inventory** (VMI) is a partnering initiative for improving multi-firm supply chain efficiency, where the buyer shares inventory information with its vendors (or suppliers), so the vendors can manage the inventory for the buyer; or simply where the vendor monitors and manages inventory for the customer. It is an approach to inventory management that assigns the supplier the responsibility to make inventory replenishment decisions based on order, point-of-sale data or warehouse data supplied by the customer (in B2B). **Third-party logistics providers** (3PLs or TPL) are also suppliers that handle some or all parts of the logistics requirements for other companies. Having discussed the primary concerns of the Warehouse Manager we will discuss the day-to-day work of the warehouse, specific warehouse processes and activities next.

36.2 MATERIALS HANDLING AND WAREHOUSE PROCESSES

23.   Ordered goods from the supplier must be received, handled, stored, picked, packed and shipped and we focus on such activities here. The **perfect order** is a term used to refer to the timely, error-free provision of a product or service in good condition. Amongst other things, organizations adopt efficient and technically enabled warehouse processes such as receiving and putting away, picking, packing and staging in order to deliver the perfect order.

24.   **Material handling** is the function that physically moves materials around a warehouse or between operations – it refers to the physical handling of products. Material handling systems are the equipment and procedures needed to move goods within a facility, between a facility and a transportation mode, and between different transportation modes. In some cases the organization may deploy automated material handling systems (AMH) that have been designed to improve efficiency in the movement, storage and retrieval of materials.

25.   The receiving and putting away warehouse process is shown in Figure 36.3. This process, triggered by the PO, includes activities such as receiving, offloading, checking and putting away. In some cases, particularly where JIT inventory management is being practised, there may be a need for **cross-docking**. This is a technique used extensively in the retail industry where a product arrives at a warehouse or *distribution centre* (designed to move goods, rather than just store them) and is quickly processed and shipped to a retail store, i.e. goods arriving are moved straight away to a loading area ready to be sent to customers. In some cases it may be considered a form of warehousing in which large incoming shipments are received and then broken down into smaller outgoing shipments to demand points in a geographic area.

26.   In many cases there is a need to record data about the incoming goods on the organization's relevant information systems. This will often be done automatically from a reading of bar codes or radio frequency identification (RFID) tags. Once this information has been input to the system, in the case of finished goods, the product may then be offered for sale or allocated to customers, typically through e-commerce

FIGURE 36.3 Receiving and putting away process

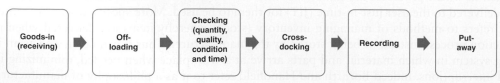

systems. In some cases, the recording of incoming goods may be cross-checked against open customer orders (automatically by the warehouse/fulfilment system). In such cases, open orders can then be fulfilled.

27.   If, as was discussed in the previous paragraph, a customer is awaiting the arrival of goods into the warehouse then the picking and packing process will be triggered. In other cases, if awaiting raw materials, the production process may be triggered. In the case of the picking and packing process, the new order is used to generate a paper list (or instructions on a handheld device) which will then be issued to a particular picker. Once the goods have been picked they will be placed in an appropriate carton/package along with the packing slip. A mailing label is placed on the package which is then moved to a dedicated location where it awaits collection by the carrier/shipper. In some cases, this is followed by the generation and sending of the invoice to the customer. Other organizations may do this as soon as the order is taken, in order to improve cash flow. The process is summarized in Figure 36.4.

FIGURE 36.4 Picking and packing process

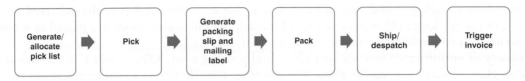

28.   Order picking is one of a warehouse's processes consisting of taking and collecting products in a specified quantity before shipment to satisfy customer's orders. It is a basic warehousing process and has an important influence on a supply chain's productivity. This makes order picking one of the most controlled logistic processes. Order picking is arguably the most costly activity within the warehouse. It is therefore essential to have a well laid out warehouse that minimizes travel time etc. (see previous paragraphs).

29.   In some warehouses the picking activity will be automated or robotics may be used. A variety of picking strategies may be observed such as (1) picking to order – the picker takes one order and travels through the warehouse collecting items until the whole order is picked and (2) cluster picking – in order to reduce overall travel time the picker can take a number of orders out into the warehouse simultaneously. Other strategies include batch or zone picking. Alternative order picking methods include making use of: (1) *paper pick lists* typically showing the order number, product and product code, location, description and quantity, (2) *barcode* scanning and (3) *radio frequency identification*.

30.   A barcode (see Figure 36.5) is an optical machine-readable representation of data relating to the object to which it is attached; typically the product number but could be a warehouse bay number or customer number. It can be thought of as a font. There are many different types of barcode. Their primary benefit is to reduce data input time and effort as the whole (product or customer) number can be entered into an information system through a single scan. The alternative would be to use a keyboard and manually enter each number. An EAN-13 barcode (originally European Article Number, but now renamed International Article Number) is a 13-digit (12 data and 1 check) barcoding standard.

FIGURE 36.5 Example of a barcode

31.   **Radio frequency identification (RFID)** is a wireless non-contact technology that enables identification of an object (such as product, vehicle or living creature) by receiving a radio signal from a tag attached to the object. The tags contain electronically stored information. RFID tags are used throughout the supply chains of many industries and are rapidly replacing barcode technology. RFID offers advantages over manual systems or barcodes. The tag can be read if passed near a reader, even if it is covered or not visible; it can be read inside a case, box or other container, and unlike barcodes, RFID tags can be read many at a time. In Chapter 38 we take a further look at operations technology, considering barcodes, RFID, warehouse management systems, ERP and other technologies associated with financial, information and physical flows throughout the supply chain.

32.   Once picked, the goods must then be **packed**. Packaging, from a logistics perspective, describes the way goods and materials are packed in order to facilitate physical, informational and monetary flows through the supply chain. Packaging is used to protect products and to communicate a message at the point of purchase; it can also be used to describe the way in which diverse products are offered in combination with each other. Typically a packing slip (itemized list of products, giving the quantity and description, prepared by the shipper and sent to the customer for accurate tallying of the delivered goods) will be included in the package. Once packed and addressed, the outbound goods are placed in a convenient location to load on to a vehicle for transportation (discussed later).

33.   A variety of performance metrics for picking and packing exist. KPIs include (%) on-time shipments with best-in-class typically aiming for above 99%; average time (hours) from order placement to shipment (generally less than 24 hours but often less than 8 hours) and order picking accuracy (>99.9%).

34.   Thus far we have discussed the warehouse processes associated with procurement (putting away) and fulfilment (pick, pack and ship). The warehouse must also have a process to pick the raw materials required by production/manufacturing. This is referred to as raw material issue and staging. When production authorizes a planned order and a production order has been created and authorized (see Chapter 37) the warehouse staff must locate and withdraw the parts/items required from the warehouse and stage them by production ready for assembly.

35.   A material withdrawal form/'pull list' is used to withdraw the components from the main storage location for movement to the issue storage location. If there are insufficient parts a PO is triggered (integrated process). The warehouse or production function may make use of **staging** areas, a location used to prepare items for use. Material staging is thus about transferring the material from the main store to a production location. Warehouse staff stage material needed for production at a certain time and in a particular quantity. Finally, once the operations function have transformed the raw materials into finished products they must be put away. This part of the process is analogous to putting inbound goods away.

36.   A final key process or set of warehouse activities to discuss are reverse logistics (returns), see Figure 36.6. **Reverse logistics** (returns) were discussed in Chapter 32 (see reverse channel, para. 16). They focus on bringing materials (defects, spare units, wrong deliveries, packaging, materials for recycling, containers, etc.) back from customers to suppliers. The items flow in a reverse direction, from the buyer back to the seller. A generic process map for reverse logistics is shown below.

36.3 TRANSPORTATION AND DISTRIBUTION

37.   In this part of the chapter we build upon principles discussed in the marketing section of the book. The channel strategy will have implications for transportation and distribution. **Transportation** is the process of moving a product from where it is made to where it is purchased and used. This may also be referred to as shipment of freight which is the action of shipping goods.

38.   Transport considerations and decisions include selecting the transportation mode, fleet management, routing and scheduling. **Transport modes** are methods of moving goods; these include railways, motor vehicles, inland waterways, airways and pipelines. Inter-modal transport is the combination and coordination of two or more modes of transport. Transportation modes are often evaluated in terms of cost, infrastructure, speed, safety and security, potential for delays, capacity, flexibility and versatility. Transportation inventory is inventory that is moving from one link in the supply chain to another.

FIGURE 36.6 Reverse logistics process

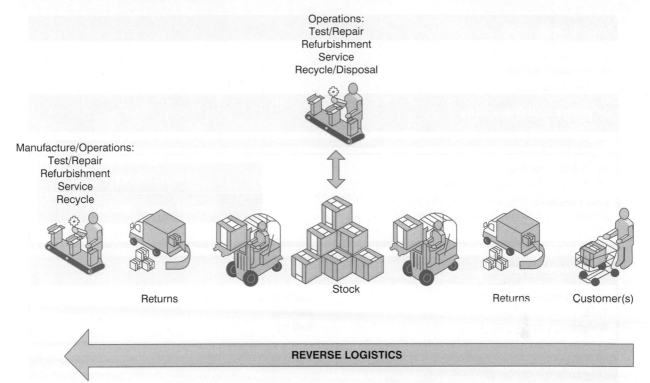

39.   A **shipper** (see also **freight forwarder** – companies who organize shipments), is a company that transports or receives goods. Shippers represent the owner of goods being transported by any mode of transport, whether consignors (the traditional meaning of shipper) or consignee. The definition of shipper has changed in line with the nature of international trade and transport: in today's global economy, shippers may contract third party logistics providers or freight forwarders to procure and manage their freight shipments.

40.   There are many companies (see for example DHL, UPS, FedEx, TNT, etc.) who offer safe and timely shipment. Sometimes the company may be referred to as a **courier**; a company that transports commercial packages. Couriers are distinguished from ordinary mail services by features such as speed, security, tracking, signature, specialization and individualization of express services and rapid delivery times. However, as a premium service, couriers are usually more expensive than standard mail services.

41.   **Package tracking** is the process of localizing deliveries at different points of time during sorting, warehousing, and package delivery to verify their origin and to predict and aid delivery. Packages may be tracked point-to-point as shown in Figure 36.7 or using GPS. With point-to-point the barcode or RFID scan at each point is used to update the database with entries organized according to the unique tracking number associated with the delivery. Tracking is a differentiating feature that improves customer service (the customer can arrange to be present to sign for the package with the minimum of inconvenience) and enables the warehouse to monitor shipments. As suggested by UPS, 'Clearly see, track, and manage what's coming and going, keeping your customers informed before they ask'. Furthermore, web-based package tracking has been used to automate customer service and as a cheaper alternative to phone-based call centres, providing the ability to track the status of a package 'within minutes'. This reduces cost at the same time as improving service and is a good example of the Warehouse Manager meeting what are normally viewed as conflicting goals! With smartphones, package tracking mobile applications are able to send tracking information to customers' phones. The popularity of such services has grown exponentially.

42.   Package tracking techniques and benefits are also explainable with **queuing theory**. This is a mathematical approach that models arrival and processing activities in order to predict the behaviour of queuing systems (also called waiting line theory). When seeking to improve customer service in this area, knowledge

FIGURE 36.7 Package tracking

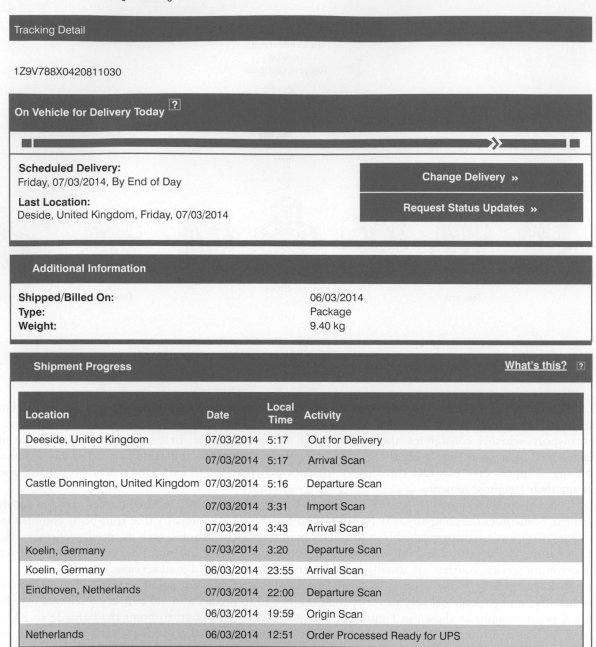

of how customers perceive queuing can assist. Customers perceive the wait before a service starts as more tedious than a wait within the process; uncertainty makes the customer think they have been waiting a long time; a wait of unknown duration is seen as more tedious than one whose duration is known; and an unexplained wait seems longer than one that is explained. With this in mind, imagine yourself – as a customer – awaiting delivery of a package. Evaluate the tracking detail shown in Figure 36.7. Do you feel it would help you perceive a faster delivery?

43. How then might the organization select the right shipper for their needs? Organizations may require the provision of a comprehensive range of services with a range of delivery options (express, next day, economy, etc.) to a broad range or narrow set of postal codes and countries. Needs may be domestic or global. In some cases there may be a need to transport items that are particularly heavy or large. Selecting the right service

is about understanding needs and options. Couriers are selected intentionally for door-to-door low-volume deliveries whilst the freight forwarder and shipper may be preferred for bulk movement of goods. Once again cost and service demands will influence shipper/courier selection decisions heavily.

36.4 LOGISTICS AND LOCATION AND RISK

44. The organization and the Logistics/Warehouse Manager must also make important decisions about where to place plants or warehouses. Such decisions are significant as they impact upon cost (facility, labour and transportation costs and risk) and speed/level of service (proximity to major customers). Thus a company's competitiveness may be affected by location.

45. The **weighted centre of gravity method** is a logistics decision modelling technique that attempts to identify the best location for a single warehouse, store or plant, given multiple demand points which differ in location and importance. It is a technique for comparing the attractiveness of alternative operational locations that allocates a weighted score to each relevant factor in the decision. It can be used to locate distribution centres and warehouses by minimizing costs and improving the timeliness of deliveries. The method assumes that distribution costs change in a linear fashion with the distance and the quantity transported. The coordinates (e.g. longitude and latitude) of customers (or suppliers) are collated and mapped. Each coordinate is then weighted in respect of variables such as order frequency. The ideal location is then identified according to the following formula:

$$X = \frac{\sum x_i Q_i}{\sum Q_i}$$

$$Y = \frac{\sum y_i Q_i}{\sum Q_i}$$

Where

Q_i = the weighted factor, e.g. order count or quantity of goods
X_i = x coordinates of destination i
Y_i = y coordinates of destination i
X = x coordinate of centre of gravity
Y = y coordinate of centre of gravity

This method will be explored in more detail in the skills sheet at the end of this section.

46. In Chapter 29 we discussed the management of risk and defined threat, vulnerability and related constructs. The risk management process is used to help an organization prioritize risk and make risk decisions through activities such as risk identification and analysis (probability and impact assessment). The logistics and warehouse functions may be exposed to a number of operational and physical risks such as fire, theft, flood, etc. All of which can impact upon business operations, leading to supply chain disruption and costs. Refer back to Chapter 29.5 'business continuity and crisis management' (paras. 31–36) and read about how an organization may minimize disruption and ensure business continuity. Typical risk controls and treatments include physical protection in the way of perimeter fencing, CCTV, access controls, intruder detection and guards but also include temperature and climate controls. It will also be important to conduct audits of inventory and warehouse, refer back to Chapter 29.6 'audit'.

CONCLUSION

47. The logistics function encompasses warehousing, materials handling, distribution, inventory management and transport. It works closely with marketing, purchasing and production and is central to core business processes such as the fulfilment, production and procurement process. As such it can be a source of competitive advantage in terms of differentiation, cost or speed. However, management must often deal with competing challenges, typically with marketing who call for improved customer service (product availability, delivery time and the perfect order) and finance seeking cost reduction (inventory management and stock control). Productivity gains are available through warehouse layout and location; in addition the use of technology and information systems and inventory management can all be used to minimize costs.

QUESTIONS

1   Create a job description for a Warehouse Manager in a company with which you are familiar. Draw on this chapter, wider reading and skills sheet 8 to inform the content and structure.

2   Create process maps for the logistics operations of a company with which you are familiar. Draw on this chapter, wider reading and skills sheet 5 to inform the content and structure.

3   Evaluate how the Warehouse/Logistics Manager can contribute to competitive advantage (optional: within a specific company).

4   Critically evaluate JIT as an approach within the integrated fulfilment, procurement and production processes.

5   For a specified company, create criteria for outbound shipper/courier selection and then compare and contrast each of three possible logistic companies and recommend one.

USEFUL WEBSITES

www.inventoryops.com source for information on Inventory Management and Warehouse Operations

www.inventorymanagement.com examples of Inventory management software

http://cscmp.org research and knowledge on supply chain management

REFERENCES

Bradley, J.R. and Arntzen, B.C. (1999) 'The simultaneous planning of production, capacity, and inventory in seasonal demand environments', *Operations Research*, 47(6): 795–806.

Greasley, A. (2009) *Operations Management*, 2nd edn, Wiley.

Paton, S., Clegg, B., Hsuan, J. and Pilkington, A. (2011) *Operations Management*, McGraw-Hill Higher Education.

Slack, N., Brandon-Jones, A. and Johnston, R. (2013) *Operations Management*, 7th edn, Pearson.

Turban, E., McLean, E. and Wetherbe, J. (2002) *Information Technology for Management – Transforming Business in the Digital Economy*, 3rd edn, Wiley International.

Waters, D. (2003) *Inventory Control and Management*, 2nd edn, Wiley.

CHAPTER 37
MANAGING THE OPERATIONS FUNCTION: PRODUCTION

Key Concepts

- Batch manufacturing
- Jobbing processes
- Mass production
- Production order
- Production process
- Production strategy

Learning Outcomes   Having read this chapter, you should be able to:

- discuss what is meant by operations management
- describe what the operations function is and does and why it is of critical importance to the organization
- list the basic elements of a typical production planning and control system
- discuss make-to-order and make-to-stock production planning policies
- describe the characteristics of the five classic types of manufacturing process.

1. Whereas the last chapter focused on the logistics aspects of operations, the inputs, storing and distribution of outputs, this chapter will focus on the transformational process – creating outputs (products and services); activities involved in creating a product. Production activity may be triggered by a customer order (make-to-order) or through planning as part of make-to-stock strategies – see Figure 37.1. The **production order** initiates the manufacturing process. Production orders are used to manage the conversion of purchased materials (refer back to Chapter 35) into manufactured items. Production orders (job or work orders) route work through various facilities on the **shop floor** (location in factories where industrial or

FIGURE 37.1 **Production process**

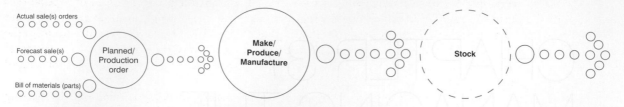

manufacturing workers are employed). A production order is an order to produce a specific quantity of material within a predefined time frame. It contains all of the relevant information required for completion of the process, including how much should be manufactured, and when, as well as information about the work site and all high level steps involved. The order includes the total planned raw material quantity that would be required for manufacturing the product, derived from the bill of material (see previous chapter) for the order quantity. It may also include the total cost required for manufacturing the order, derived by adding up the raw material cost, the operational activity costs and other relevant costs. Finally, the order is used for inventory reservation – to ensure the relevant parts will be available for the production team(s). Should any parts be unavailable the procurement process (Chapter 35) will be triggered as an integrated process.

2.   This chapter examines how the organization may undertake interrelated activities and processes associated with making and supplying goods and services. Several types of **production process** are described as alternatives for operations. Each is evaluated and strengths/weaknesses considered. First we ask what is meant by the term operations and then discuss the role of the operations function. We then consider operations planning and control before identifying and describing the common production processes. We end the chapter with a brief discussion about quality, lean manufacturing and the impact of globalization on operations.

37.1 OPERATIONS MANAGEMENT: THE FUNCTION

3.   The **Operations (production) function** is that part of the organization with responsibility for operations management. Also called operations it is the collection of people, technology and systems within an organization that has primary responsibility for providing the organization's products or services (Bozarth and Handfield, 2012). Others suggest that the operations function is one of the three core functions (including marketing and product/service development) of any organization (Slack, Brandon-Jones and Johnston, 2013: p. 6).

4.   The operations function is concerned with transformation processes that provide a firm's outputs: goods and services for its customers. **Operations management** are responsible for the planning, scheduling and control of the activities that transform inputs into finished goods and services and the management of the processes that produce or deliver goods and services. It has also been described as the science and art of ensuring that goods and services are created and delivered successfully to customers.

5.   As noted by Greasley (2013) operations management did not emerge as a field until the mid-part of the twentieth century. However, it draws from scientific management, the work of Frederick Taylor, Ford and others who led the era of mass production. Their work enabled production systems to offer goods to large numbers of customers at affordable prices. Following this, much of the theory surrounding the logistics management aspect of operations (see previous chapter) was instigated by the problems faced during the first and second world wars. This led to the development of operations research. More recently, technology advancements in the final quarter of the twentieth century saw the emergence of enterprise systems (enterprise resource planning (ERP) etc., see next chapter), business process re-engineering (BPR) and materials resource planning (MRP). Also significant were the quality movement, JIT and lean thinking. All have contributed to and shaped operations management thinking today.

6.   Given the importance and size of operations it is important to organize, plan, coordinate and manage the function so it makes a valued contribution to organizational goals. Strategy was discussed in Section 8 where we focused on corporate strategy but also introduced business and functional strategies (levels of strategy).

Evans and Collier (2007) suggest that the operations strategy describes how an organization will execute its chosen business strategies. The **operations strategy** is the overall direction and contribution of the operation's function to the business; the way in which market requirements and operational resource capabilities are reconciled within the operation (Slack, Brandon-Jones and Johnston, 2013). Similarly, but more broadly, the **operations and supply chain strategy** is a functional strategy that indicates how structural and infrastructural elements within the operations and supply chain areas will be acquired and developed to support the overall business strategy (Bozarth and Handfield, 2012).

7.   Operations may contribute to strategy through impact upon quality, speed, dependability (in meeting delivery times to a customer), flexibility and cost. Approaches to operations strategy have changed over time. Traditionally there may have been an emphasis on high volume and low cost. More recently an emphasis has been placed on flexibility, speed and reliability. The aforementioned variables are often used to set operations' performance objectives. To be successful, an operations strategy should support the competitive advantage pursued by the business strategy. The Operations Manager has responsibility for managing resources associated with the production and related processes.

37.2 PRODUCTION PLANNING

8.   Thus far we have stated what is incorporated within operations and operations management; we have discussed the relationship between the operations strategy and the corporate and business strategies. We now focus on operations' activities and processes – the work they do. Planning and control is about matching customer demand to the operations' capacity. As we know, demand is not always easily predicted however. There are a number of ways of dealing with unstable demand; some scholars refer to such ways as either production strategies or policies, see Figure 37.2. One way is to create the product or service in advance (see **make-to-stock**, a push strategy). A different way is referred to as **make-to-order** (a pull strategy). Make-to-stock (MTS) products require no customization. They are typically generic products and are produced in large enough volumes to justify keeping a finished goods inventory. Products customized only at the very end of the manufacturing process are termed assemble- or finish-to-order (ATO) products. Make-to-order (MTO) products, see Figure 37.3, are products that use standard components, but the final configuration of those components is customer-specific (e.g. a Dell computer). Finally, products that are designed and produced from the start to meet unusual customer needs or requirements are called engineer-to-order (ETO) products. They represent the highest level of customization. When customization occurs early in the supply chain, organizations have more flexibility to respond to customer needs but costs increase and lead times lengthen. When customization occurs late in the supply chain, flexibility is limited but lead times and cost may be less.

FIGURE 37.2 Production strategies

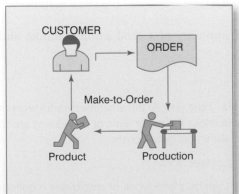
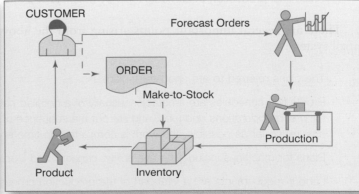

FIGURE 37.3 **Make-to-order process**

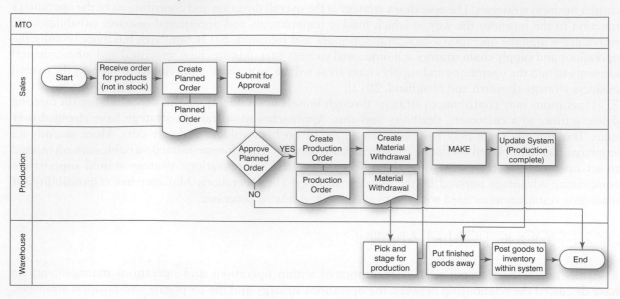

9. **Operations planning** are concerned with activities such as ensuring resources are in place, in anticipation of future events. The basic elements of a typical production planning and control system can be summarized as follows:

- Translate the customers' requirements, (production design, sales forecasts, specific sales orders), into production instructions (production and works orders)

- Prepare **production schedules** (statement of how many finished items are to be produced and when they are to be produced)

- Plan the supply of materials, parts, components, etc.

- Plan availability of machines, specify jobs, tools, etc.

- Allocate people/work-teams

- Set production and quality targets

- Maintain stock and purchasing records

- Progress orders throughout the factory

- Raise final production documents (delivery notes, invoices, etc.).

10. There are several important points arising from the above summary of a production planning and control system:

- The plans referred to are short-term plans.

- Production schedules are timetables, usually of a detailed nature. They specify the timetabled requirements for precise operations and jobs, and set out the sequence of priorities. The major aims of scheduling are to ensure, so far as possible, the work is completed on time and within budgeted costs.

- Plans for machines include the availability, capacity and loading of machines.

- Labour requirements are a vital part of the production process (numbers and types of employees required, pay and incentives, training and safety).

- All plans should set targets and will take into account considerations such as planned maintenance, product quality control and machine breakdowns.

- The progressing of orders through the production process is essentially a monitoring and reporting task, which also involves some 'chasing-up' of progress in situations where orders have fallen behind schedule. The main role of a progress chaser is to identify and report any deviations from schedule, and provide help in sorting out delays in production.

- Finally, the outputs of the production system need to be accounted for, invoiced and delivered (to the customer or into stock). Thus the final step is to ensure the appropriate information systems are updated.

11. Regardless of whether the organization adopts a MTO or MTS policy there will be a need to allocate orders and prioritize work. Loading refers to the amount of work that is allocated to a work centre (a collection of resources – people, machines, etc. – assembled together to undertake specific work tasks). Rules used to determine the order in which jobs should be processed when resources are limited and multiple jobs are waiting to be done are referred to as job sequencing rules. Examples of priority rules include: job with nearest customer due date; first come first served (see FIFO – first in first out); job that can be done quickest first (shortest operation time first – SOT) and job that takes the longest time to complete is done first (longest operation time – LOT). The critical ratio is determined according to the formula:

(Due date – Current date)/Days required to complete the work

If the ratio is less than 1 the job is behind schedule and should receive priority.

12. Scheduling is a term used in planning and control to indicate the detailed timetable of what work should be done, when it should be done and where it should be done. Backward scheduling is about starting jobs at a time so they should be finished exactly when they are due as opposed to forward scheduling which involves loading work as soon as it is practical to do so.

13. A key aspect of planning and control involves managers evaluating whether resources are adequate to meet demand. This is an issue of capacity. Capacity refers to the maximum production possible – the amount of work a production unit, whether individual or group, can accomplish in a given amount of time; the maximum goods or services that an operation can produce. Capacity concerns the capability of a worker, machine, work centre, plant or organization to produce output per time period. The manager must ask routinely how much capacity the organization needs and when they need it.

14. There are a number of capacity strategies the organization can follow (lead, lag and match) and various methods to evaluate the alternatives (based on demand, cost, expected value, etc.). One useful approach used in understanding process capacity is the theory of constraints (TOC). This is an approach to visualizing and managing capacity that recognizes that nearly all products and services are created through a series of integrated processes, and in every case, there is at least one process step which limits throughput for the entire chain. Thus, increasing the capacity of any other process step will not increase throughput for the entire process. The movement of materials through the process is analogous to the movement of liquid through a pipeline; the diameter of the pipe in its narrowest point is the bottleneck. This is what must be modified if capacity is to be increased. Thus there is a need to identify and remove the constraint.

15. One further concept worthy of note here is that of sales and operations planning. This is used to indicate how the organization will use its tactical capacity (size of workforce, inventory, number of shifts, etc.) resources to meet expected customer demand. (Bozarth and Handfield, 2012: p. 314) referred to this as a process to develop tactical plans by integrating marketing plans for new and existing products with the management of the supply chain. The process brings together all the plans for the business into one integrated set of plans (also called aggregate planning). Consequently the concept focuses on a cross-functional coordination. In the case of top-down planning, the process starts with the aggregate sales forecast which must then be translated into resource requirements (such as labour hours, equipment hours, raw material costs, etc.). Various production plans will then be evaluated and the proposed one selected. This analysis and planning may also be used to improve cash flow predictions and analysis. Once plans have been created the work must be done. Work activities are organized within production processes.

37.3 PRODUCTION PROCESSES

16.   The way businesses create products and services is known as the production process. Ultimately, the objective of the production process is to create goods and services that meet customer requirements. The needs of customers will be met if a business can produce the correct number of products, in the shortest possible time, to the best quality and at low cost.

17.   Two sets of resources are needed – the transforming resources (the facilities, machinery, technology and people to carry out the transforming processes), and the raw material inputs (procured parts). At each stage, value is added in the course of production. Adding value (refer back to Chapter 10) involves making a product more attractive to a consumer so they will pay more for it. Adding value is not restricted to operations, but may relate to all supply chain processes such as marketing etc. which make the final product more desirable. There are several key types of production process – project, job shop, batch, assembly line and continuous flow (project and job shop are often grouped together as are assembly line and continuous flow). We consider the production processes in more detail next.

18.   The essential feature of jobbing production is that it produces single articles or 'one-off' items. These products may be small, tailor-made components, huge pieces of equipment or large single items, such as a ship. Most products are made for a particular customer or to a particular order. Jobbing production is to be found in industries such as heavy engineering (e.g. production of electricity generating plant), shipbuilding and civil engineering (e.g. bridge construction). It is also to be found in most other industries, where it is employed to produce prototype models, spare parts, modifications to existing plant and countless other 'one-off', tailor-made pieces.

19.   Within jobbing production, because of the unique or individual nature of each article or item to be produced, planning is not easy and neither is control. Efficiency of operations has to give way to inventiveness and creativity. This can be illustrated by considering some of the key characteristics of jobbing production. These are as follows:

-   A wide variety of different operations to be performed under varying circumstances, i.e. no standardization.

-   Varying sequences of operations, also subject to varying circumstances

-   General-purpose machinery and equipment

-   Varied work layouts, depending on process and/or operation

-   Unpredictable demands on stores

-   Workforce with broad skill range

-   Adaptable and equally skilled supervision.

20.   Many of the above conditions make it extremely difficult to plan, integrate and control the types, sequence and timing of operations. It is difficult to avoid idle time for both employees and machines. Thus, the entire manufacturing process tends to be relatively expensive compared with other forms of production. Against this can be weighed the advantages of producing an article or item which is made especially to the customer's own specification.

21.   Batch production is the production of standardized units, or parts, in small or large lots (batches). It represents a halfway position between jobbing production and mass production (to be discussed next). The main distinction between batch and jobbing production lies in the standardized nature of the former. Unlike the varied operations and sequences of the unique 'one-off' products of jobbing production, the products of batch production are dealt with systematically in lots, or batches, only moving on to the next operation when each lot has been machined or processed in the current operation.

22.   Batches may be produced to order and forwarded direct to the customer, as in the production of subcomponents for another manufacturer, or they may be made for stock. One of the major problems associated with batch production is to determine the optimum size of batches, particularly where a generalized rather than specific demand for a product exists. If too many units are produced, stocks will lie idle or

go to waste; if too few are produced, the item will go out of stock, and it may be difficult to fit in further batches in the short-term.

23.   The key characteristics of batch production are as follows:

–   A standardized set of operations, carried out intermittently, as each batch moves from one operation to the next

–   General purpose machinery and plant, but grouped in batteries of the same type

–   Heavy shop-floor stores requirement

–   Narrower range of skills required

–   Emphasis on production planning and progressing

–   Relatively short **production runs.**

These characteristics lead to a well-controlled and efficient method of production, whose main disadvantage is the time-delay caused by the queuing effect of individual units waiting for the batch to be completed before moving on to the next operation. This problem can be overcome by changing to an assembly line operation which is a prominent feature of flow production, or mass production, as it is commonly called.

24.   **Mass production** dates from the time of Henry Ford, who was the first man to adopt the principle of the production line, when he used this approach to produce a restricted range of motor cars constructed in a flow-line process. In a unit mass production system, a small range of products are produced in large quantities by 'flowing' uninterruptedly from one operation, or process, to the next, until completion. This type of production requires careful and lengthy planning of plant and processes. The capital costs are high on account of the specialized nature of the machines required for the production line. However, once the line has been established, control is relatively simple. Mass production systems are dependent on the high demand created by mass markets, for it is only by making the fullest use of the capital equipment involved that a manufacturing organization can achieve its target profit levels. The key features of mass production are as follows:

–   Rigid product specifications, previously tested

–   Specialized machines and equipment, set out in a line formation

–   Highly standardized methods, tools and materials

–   Long production runs for individual products

–   Narrow range of skills, and specified range of operations required by workforce at any one point in the line.

25.   In purely rational terms, mass production is the most efficient way of producing large quantities of articles or items. Control can be exercised to a sophisticated level because of the standardized nature of the entire process. Its greatest drawback is that it requires human beings to adapt themselves to the production process, and in most Western countries, there has been a reaction against this requirement. Employees are seeking to counteract the tedium and monotony of the highly specialized work patterns in mass production by pressing for more integrated roles, requiring a wider range of skills and operations.

26.   Another form of mass production, usually called (continuous) **flow production** or process production, can be seen in continuous process industries such as steel-making, paper-making and cement production. In such industries the products literally flow from one process to the next, but, unlike in the mass production of individual products, this process is continuous for weeks or months on end. In flow processes, the supply of raw materials has to be planned to the highest standards in order to avoid complete plant shutdown owing to unforeseen shortages. In these situations, shortages have a much more serious effect than in unit mass production. Fortunately, the control mechanisms and procedures for flow processes are usually so sophisticated that the processes become automatically self-regulating. Another important difference between this form of mass production and unit mass production is that the former invariably requires a lower labour force than the latter.

27.   The **cycle time** is the time it takes a product to go from beginning to end of a production process; i.e., the time it is work-in-process; the length of time from start to completion of a product or service and is the sum of processing time, move time, wait time and inspection time; or simply the interval between successive outputs coming off the assembly line.

28.   Having discussed types of production process we now consider how the organization determines the optimal process. Process selection is influenced by product variety and volume. Generally, a job shop process is used in support of differentiation strategies and flow shops are used to support cost-based strategies. Other factors also influence process selection. Cost of labour, technology and facilities, energy and transportation may be considered. Furthermore, the stage of the product life cycle may be taken into consideration. A job shop may be more appropriate early in the product's life cycle but at maturity, when higher volumes are required, an assembly line may be more appropriate. Service processes vary also, with some devoted to producing knowledge-based or advice-based services, usually involving high customer contact and high customization, (such as management consultants) and those with a high number of transactions, often involving limited customization, for example, call centres. A comparison of production process attributes (degree of flow, flexibility, etc.) can be seen in Figure 37.4.

FIGURE 37.4   Production processes

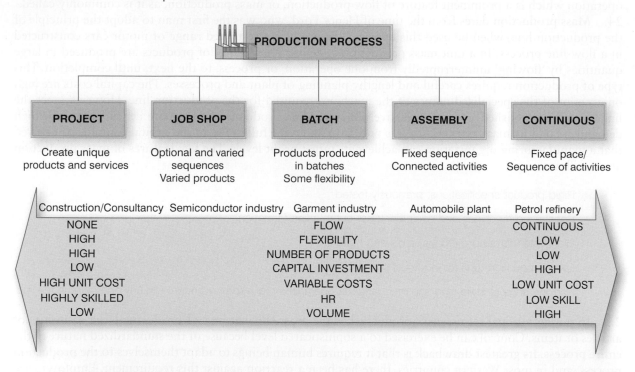

29.   The Operations Manager, like other functional managers, must also consider job and work design. Organizing work was discussed in Chapter 21. A further consideration is the layout of the operations area (facility). We discussed the warehouse layout in the previous chapter but there is an additional need to consider the layout of work space. A basic objective of layout is to ensure a smooth flow of work, material and information through the system. An effective layout can minimize material handling costs, result in a more efficient use of space and labour, eliminate bottlenecks, eliminate waste (unnecessary movement), facilitate communications and interaction between workers whilst enabling visual control and providing a safe and secure environment.

30.   Layout often correlates with the production process type. For example, the job shop often follows a **functional layout** – a type of layout where resources are physically grouped by function (e.g. welding or painting). This layout is used to group similar activities together in departments of

work centres according to the process or function that they perform. The **product layout** (assembly line) arranges activities in a line according to the sequence of operations that are needed to assemble a particular product. Each product will have its own line. Such layouts are suitable for mass production and repetitive operations. Whilst highly efficient, this layout is relatively inflexible. Finally, there is the fixed position layout. These are used when the product is too bulky or heavy to move. Originally the Boeing 737 aircraft adopted this approach but later moved to an assembly line/continuous flow layout. With the fixed position layout, workers, materials and equipment are brought to the production site.

37.4 LEAN OPERATIONS/MANUFACTURING

31. In the previous chapter we discussed the application of lean thinking to logistics. Likewise such a philosophy has also been applied to production and manufacturing. Lean manufacturing is a process aimed at eliminating waste and reducing the time between receipt of a customer order and delivery. As was discussed in the previous chapter, the concept often includes JIT and Six Sigma. In this context waste may include delay, duplication, unnecessary movements, incorrect inventory (e.g. stockouts), overproduction, unnecessary transport, missed opportunities and defective goods or errors.

37.5 INSPECTION, MONITORING, CONTROLLING AND MAINTENANCE

32.   Operations control seeks to ensure that the actual behaviour of the operations (production) system conforms to that required. Of particular concern is the control of quality (refer back to Chapter 29). This control and performance dimension begins with the sourcing and inspection of raw materials, continues with inspection during production, and ends with a final inspection before delivery to the customer. Objectives of operations will include:

- to turn out products which are satisfactory to the customer (quality, reliability, variety, etc.)

- to turn out products in a safe and socially responsible manner, and

- to attain the above within agreed levels of inspection and quality control costs.

33.   Garvin (1987) famously asked how a company competes on quality. He suggested that managers first have to divide the concept into manageable parts, that is, into the eight dimensions of quality by which consumers judge products: performance, features, reliability, conformance, durability, serviceability (easy to repair and maintain), aesthetics and perceived quality (reputation). Managers should research their potential markets carefully and the strengths of their competition to ascertain which of these eight quality dimensions can be emphasized in their goods and services – in effect, learn to compete within a quality niche. Garvin went on to suggest that it is a mistake to offer features consumers do not want.

34.   Having described the production system we finally turn our attention to **maintenance** – the activity of caring for physical facilities, systems and equipment (transformational resources) to avoid or minimize the chance of the system failing. Maintenance seeks to assure that production has the optimum availability of plant and machinery in the conduct of its operations, and that, if an unexpected breakdown occurs, it will be dealt with in the minimum possible time. There are several different kinds of maintenance, which may be preventive or corrective. The Operations Manager will adopt a planned programme of maintenance for each major piece of plant, building, system or machine. Planned maintenance means that routine servicing and overhaul arrangements are scheduled in advance and contingency plans drawn up for unexpected breakdowns. The effect of having planned maintenance is to minimize unforeseen faults or breakdowns. Thus maintenance can make an important contribution to containing machine running costs as well as ensuring optimum machine availability.

37.6 GLOBALIZATION AND PRODUCTION

35.   In the present-day environment, firms are more able to separate their operations internationally, locating each stage of production in the country where it can be done at the least cost, and transmitting ideas for new products and new ways of making products around the globe, see Figure 37.5. Kelly (2009) discusses the fragmentation process whereby different parts of goods and services are provided in different countries before they are combined in final goods. Companies now benefit from globalization and seek out location advantages such as lower wages and access to scarce raw materials. Kelly (2009: p. 23) also refers to value chain fragmentation (slicing up the value chain) in which different parts (activities) of the production process are located in different countries. This approach is enabled through forces of globalization (see Section 16) and advances in technology which will be discussed in the next chapter.

FIGURE 37.5 **Globalization and production**

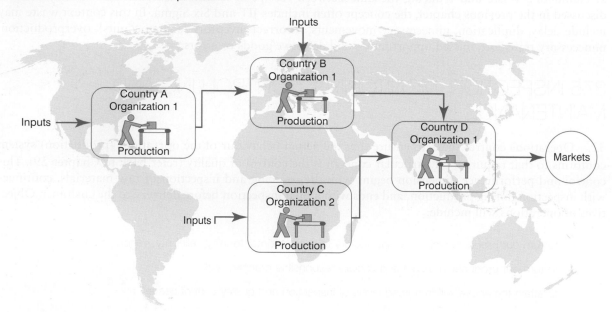

CONCLUSION

36.   We started by asserting the operations function is one of the three core functions of any organization, noting this function is responsible for the planning, scheduling and control of the activities that transform inputs into finished goods and services. Production activity may be triggered by a customer order (make-to-order) or through planning as a part of make-to-stock strategies. Regardless of whether the organization adopts a make to order (MTO) or make to stock (MTS) policy there will be a need to allocate orders and prioritize work. Various approaches to planning and control were discussed. We then considered production processes in more detail suggesting that process selection is influenced by product variety and volume in particular. We discussed lean manufacturing as a process aimed at eliminating waste and reducing the time between receipt of a customer order and delivery and noted the importance of quality to operations management generally. Finally we discussed the fragmentation process whereby different parts of goods and services are provided in different countries before they are combined in final goods. Companies now benefit from globalization and seek out location advantages such as lower wages and access to scarce raw materials. In the next chapter we consider the role of technology in operations.

QUESTIONS

1   Distinguish between types of production process.

2   Explain the main elements of a lean philosophy.

3   Draw the transformation process for a simple operations function (list the inputs, transformational resources and outputs).

4   With reference to a company you are familiar with, discuss the alternative production processes suggesting which you think may be most suitable.

USEFUL WEBSITES

The Institute of Operations Management (IOM): **www.iomnet. org.uk** OM learning resources

Technology & Operations Management: **www.sussex.ac.uk/ Users/dt31/TOMI/whatisom.html**

The portal provides information on a wide range of topics within the technology and operations management field, such as purchasing, product development, innovation management, manufacturing strategy, inventory control, logistics, quality and service operations

REFERENCES

Bozarth, C. and Handfield, R. (2012), '*Introduction to Operations and Supply Chain Management: International Edition*', 3rd edn, Pearson.

Evans, J. and Collier, D. (2007) *Operations Management Integrated Goods and Services Approach, International Edition*, 2nd edn, South Western.

Garvin, D. (1987) 'Competing on the eight dimensions of quality', *Harvard Business Review*, 65(6): 101–109.

Greasley, A. (2013) *Operations Management*, 3rd edn, Wiley.

Kelly, P. (2009) *International Business and Management*, Cengage Learning EMEA.

Slack, N., Brandon-Jones, A. and Johnston, R. (2013) *Operations Management*, 7th edn, Pearson.

CHAPTER 38
OPERATIONS
TECHNOLOGY

Key Concepts

- Automation
- Computer integrated manufacturing (CIM)
- Enterprise resource planning (ERP) systems
- Flexible manufacturing systems (FMS)
- Robot
- Technology

Learning Outcomes Having read this chapter, you should be able to:

- describe the physical, information and monetary flows within organizations
- describe the evolution of operations
- review the use of ERP and related information systems in manufacturing
- evaluate the role of technology in manufacturing
- explain what is meant by CIM and flexible manufacturing system (FMS).

1. Throughout this section of the book we have explored the meaning of operations and now consider how technology can support associated work. **Technology** has been defined by many scholars. It has been defined as the creation, usage and knowledge of tools, machines, crafts, techniques, systems or methods of organization in order to solve a problem or perform a specific job, in this case operations, manufacturing or service provision.

2. In Chapter 37 we discussed types of production (job shops, batch and mass production). Kalpakjian, Schmid and Kok (2010) also discuss the general types of production but additionally describe a wide range of specific manufacturing processes: methods to produce components for a product. For example, there are casting processes, bulk deformation, sheet metal forming, polymer processing, machining and finishing and joining processes. In this chapter we are concerned with the application of technology to the different operations processes (work) and the manufacturing organization holistically. We have already discussed a range of technologies such as barcodes and RFID in Chapter 36. Much of this chapter will be about the information systems, like enterprise resource planning (ERP), that support operations. We revisit technology management from a companywide perspective in Section 15.

3.   When considering the application of technology we may focus on the needs of management, knowledge and administrative workers or we may focus on the specific work tasks of those directly involved in creating goods and services. This chapter is therefore divided into two parts. The first considers new technology from a more general management and holistic business perspective and the second considers more specific technologies used to aid manufacturing tasks and methods.

4.   When considering the application of technology to manufacturing it is useful to consider general trends. Kalpakjian, Schmid and Kok (2010) suggest that product variety and complexity continue to increase, product life cycles are becoming shorter, markets are becoming more global and market conditions fluctuate widely, customers are consistently demanding high-quality and low-cost products and on-time delivery. The goals in manufacturing view operations activities in a holistic systematic manner. Organizations seek to build quality into the product at each stage of its production, adopt the most flexible, economical and environmentally friendly methods, aim for high levels of productivity, eliminate waste, provide dependable and on-time deliveries and seek continuous improvement. Manufacturers apply IT to all aspects of production. The trends and goals set the context for the aspirations of manufacturing and service-based organizations. Before we consider the management perspective in detail we will explore, briefly, the evolution of operations.

38.1 THE EVOLUTION OF OPERATIONS

5.   Throughout the twentieth century, operations and manufacturing evolved with changes in technology, mobility and transport, customer requirements, corporate strategies and competitive pressures. Scientific management and Taylorism were dominant influences in the first half of the century. Some companies used their low labour costs to gain entry to various industries (for example, industries with a high labour content such as textiles). As wage rates rose and technology became more significant, i.e. advantages and competitive edge eroded, companies shifted first to scale-based strategies (1950s) achieving high productivity and low costs by building the largest and most capital-intensive facilities technologically feasible; investment boosted workforce productivity – savings were achieved in the cost of production because the cost of initial investment could be spread across a greater number of producing units.

6.   The search continued for ways to achieve even higher productivity and lower costs. In the mid-1960s, it led companies to a new source of competitive advantage – the focused factory. Seeing the problem not as 'How can we increase productivity?' but as 'How can we compete?' scholars argued a need to consider the efficiency of the entire manufacturing organization, not only the efficiency of the direct labour and the workforce. A factory that focused on a narrow product mix for a particular market niche would outperform the conventional plant, which attempted a broader mission. Since its equipment, supporting systems and procedures concentrated on a limited task for one set of customers, its costs and especially its overheads were lower than those of the conventional plant. The focused factory did a better job because repetition and concentration in one area allowed its workforce and managers to become effective and experienced in the task required for success.

7.   Factory costs were very sensitive to the variety of goods a plant produced. Reduction of the product-line variety by half, for example, raised productivity by 30 per cent and cut costs by 17 per cent. In manufacturing, costs fall into two categories: those responding to volume or scale and those driven by variety. Scale-related costs decline as volume increases. Variety-related costs, on the other hand, reflect the costs of complexity in manufacturing: setup, materials handling, inventory and many of the overhead costs of a factory. In most cases, as variety increases, costs increase, usually at a rate of 20 per cent to 35 per cent per unit each time variety doubles. The sum of the scale- and variety-related costs represents the total cost of manufacturing.

8.   Traditional batch manufacturing has always had inherent limitations. Work in process levels are high and machine utilization is low. Jobs spend a high proportion of time waiting for something to happen to them, waiting for a machine to be set up, waiting to be moved or waiting for other jobs on the machine to be completed. Batch production often requires a mass of expediters or progress chasers in order to keep jobs flowing through the manufacturing facilities. It was recognized that some means of automatically routing jobs through the manufacturing system from one machine to the next was required and some

way of greatly reducing the set-up time of jobs on a machine. These requirements were met with the aid of computer and numerical control techniques and this led to the development of the basic concept of a flexible manufacturing system (FMS), to be discussed later in this chapter. Among the options for competition are price (cost), quality, delivery, service and flexibility.

9.   In the late 1970s variety became a competitive weapon. Japanese companies exploited flexible manufacturing to the point that a new competitive thrust emerged – the variety war. The advantage of flexible manufacturing – a flexible factory, enjoys more variety with lower total costs than traditional factories which are still forced to make the trade-off between scale and variety. In a flexible factory system, variety-driven costs start lower and increase more slowly as variety grows. Scale costs remain unchanged. Thus the optimum cost point for a flexible factory occurs at a higher volume and with greater variety than for a traditional factory. The advent of JIT production (see previous chapters) brought with it a move to flexible factories (1970/80s), as leading Japanese companies sought both low cost and great variety in the market.

10.   Thus far we have discussed competing through price (cost), quality, service, flexibility and variability. Since the 1980s, companies have capitalized on 'time' as a critical source of competitive advantage. They managed structural changes to speed up operational processes. Such companies competed with flexible manufacturing and rapid-response systems, expanding variety and increasing innovation. A company that builds its strategy on this cycle is a more powerful competitor than one with a traditional strategy based on low wages, scale or focus. Older, cost-based strategies require managers to do whatever is necessary to drive down costs: move production to or source from a low-wage country; build new facilities or consolidate old plants to gain economies of scale; or focus operations down to the most economic subset of activities. These tactics reduce costs but at the expense of responsiveness.

38.2 MANAGEMENT PERSPECTIVE

11.   Being responsive, lean and efficient drives a need for improvements in decision-making, planning, control and coordination – all of which are enabled through information flows. In Chapter 10 we described the value chain, citing the work of Porter and Millar (1985). Operations are typically conceived as the primary internal activities of the value chain. However, such activities rely upon raw materials, which may be sourced from upstream suppliers, and relationships downstream. The supply chain is a network of manufacturers and service providers who work together to convert and move goods from the raw materials stage through to the end user. These manufacturers and service providers are linked together through physical, information and monetary flows, see Figure 38.1. In this section we will focus on the information flows and how, through integrated systems, they can be managed efficiently to tie organizational parts together in a responsive manner.

INFORMATION SYSTEMS TECHNOLOGY

12.   Organizations historically developed **functional business (information) systems** to support different primary and secondary activities such as the manufacturing, order processing, accounting or HR systems. Functional systems serve the specific and local needs of parts of the organization and are developed using specific programming languages. Typically they have their own databases, data structures, operating systems and other idiosyncrasies.

13.   In the 1980s, Porter discussed the role of information in providing competitive advantage and the use of IT spread throughout the value chain. IT not only affects how individual activities are performed but, through new information flows it also greatly enhances a company's ability to exploit linkages between activities, both within and outside the company. Technology helps manage linkages between activities, allowing companies to coordinate their actions more closely with those of their buyers and suppliers. Information systems allow companies to coordinate value activities in far-flung geographic locations and create many new interrelationships amongst businesses.

14.   Whilst Porter and Millar (1985) noted the role of IT/IS in support of activities and linkages between such activities, the 1980s were characterized by a greater focus on the activities (a functional

FIGURE 38.1 Physical, information and monetary flows

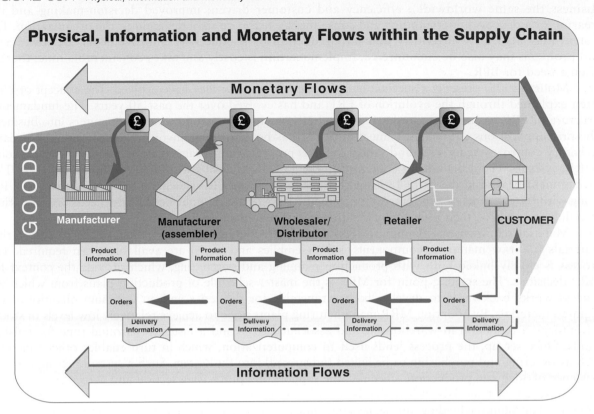

Physical, Information and Monetary Flows within the Supply Chain

Monetary Flows

GOODS

Manufacturer

Manufacturer
(assembler)

Wholesaler/
Distributor

Retailer

CUSTOMER

Product
Information

Product
Information

Product
Information

Product
Information

Orders

Orders

Orders

Orders

Delivery
Information

Delivery
Information

Delivery
Information

Delivery
Information

Information Flows

orientation), identifying ways in which systems could either replace or complement employee activity. Furthermore, the focus was much more intra-organizational rather than inter-organizational. The way IS/IT systems supported the functions of the traditional organization led to the creation of information islands or 'silos' within the organization. This in turn created coordination and control problems and contributed to problems associated with responsiveness and adaptation to the environment. Not only was the organization fragmented but, through outsourcing and global competition, so too was the supply chain.

15. In the 1990s the BPR movement focused on the linking of activities and company-wide processes through horizontal flows (process integration) – see Chapter 21. Organizations became flatter, more global in scope and employees more autonomous. Such changes drove a need for systems to better support the linkages of activities undertaken by various functions. There was a need for systems to support cross-functional processes and inter-organizational collaboration and deliver information widely throughout the organization. For example, consider the relationship between the procurement, fulfilment and production intracompany processes. As noted by Magal and Word (2009) in the real world, the three key processes are tightly integrated. Consider what happens when a customer places an order for something out-of-stock. The fulfilment process is paused and the production process may be activated. Similarly, if raw material inventories are running low, the procurement process may also be activated. In a similar manner, contemporary organizations must tie together intercompany processes. Consequently, enterprise systems (ES) evolved throughout the 1990s to replace the functional systems emanating in the 1980s.

16. **ERP systems** are information systems that integrate all manufacturing and related applications for an entire enterprise; they are applications used by organizations to manage inventory, resources and business processes across departments in the enterprise. More recently, ERP is considered as business software for running every aspect of a company including managing orders, inventory, accounting and logistics. Well known ERP software providers include Infor (formerly BAAN), Oracle (PeopleSoft),

and SAP. The advantages of an ERP system include the creation of a more uniform organization (does business the same worldwide); efficiency and customer driven; improved decision-making and the creation of a process understanding and consequently better control throughout the organization. The system may also drive inventory and staff reduction or productivity improvements. Disadvantages and problems may also be encountered. Implementation is costly and takes considerable time; there is often a need for BPR.

17. Møller (2005) presents a succinct overview of ES and how they have evolved. The concept of ES is often explained through the evolution of ERP and has evolved over the past 50 years. The fundamental structure of ERP has its origin in the 1950s and 1960s with the introduction of computers into business. The first applications automated manual tasks such as book-keeping, invoicing and ordering. The early inventory control systems (ICS) and similar systems progressively became material requirements planning (MRP) systems. The development continued in the 1970s and 1980s with the evolution of MRP II. This development peaked in the early 1990s with the advent of the ERP systems often embodied in SAP R/3 along with the other major vendors. Although the ERP systems were influenced by the needs of accounting, planning and control, their philosophy is entrenched in manufacturing.

18. Material requirements planning (MRP) is an internal production process designed to ensure that materials (i.e. raw materials, components, sub-assemblies and parts) are available when required. The process is closely linked both with production planning and purchasing, which provide the context for MRP decisions. The starting point for MRP is the master schedule of production plans from which the process works backwards to develop both a timetable for deliveries and an optimum quantity of the required materials. By adopting MRP, manufacturing plants hope to achieve relatively low levels of stocks (inventory), a reduction in warehousing and associated costs and a faster turnaround time for finished goods. Once set up, the process lends itself to computerization, which in turn enables other functions such as ordering and purchasing to be linked (integrated) into the system. Such a system presupposes the existence of adequate production schedules, the support of a purchasing section and agreement about the quality aspects of materials. Scheduling is the allocation of a start and finish time to each order whilst taking into account the loading and sequencing policies employed (Greasley, 2009). Computer-based information systems such as ERP software provide great assistance not only to the operations manager but to many functions of the organization.

19. ERP is standardized software designed to integrate the internal value chain of an enterprise; based on an integrated database, the ERP consists of several modules each designed for specific business functions. ERP is a method for the effective planning and controlling of all the resources needed to take, make, ship and account for customer orders in a manufacturing, distribution or service company.

20. In the new millennium we have witnessed the growing scope of ERP systems which essentially started out as back-office systems but have taken on more front-end roles. We have also witnessed such systems operating in support of more senior managers with business intelligence systems complementing decision-making. Advances in database and communication and collaboration (Internet) technologies and the evolution of open standards have all facilitated the evolution of information systems in the global organization. Today, it is often more appropriate to classify such systems as enterprise-wide systems (ES).

21. An ES is an organization-wide information system that integrates key business processes so information can flow freely between different parts of the organization. ES, considered by many to be the most important development in the corporate use of IT in the 1990s, presented a new model of corporate computing. In the form of ERP systems they allowed companies to replace their existing information systems, which were often incompatible with one another, with a single, integrated system. An ES streamlines a company's data flow and provides management with direct access to a wealth of real-time operating information. Unlike business information systems of the past, which were typically developed in-house and with a company's specific requirements in mind, ES (in the form of ERP systems) tend to be off-the-shelf solutions. They impose their own logic on a company's strategy, culture and organization, often forcing companies to change the way they do business. The popularity of ERP/ES is attributed to its potential to improve the profitability potential of an organization by reducing the time and costs of completing business activities.

38.3 MANUFACTURING PERSPECTIVE

22.   Having discussed information systems, in this section we consider the manufacturing perspective on the application of technology. Whereas the managerial perspective emphasizes the strategic, tactical and holistic application of information systems technology to help managers and administrators in particular, this section focuses more on operational demands on technology.

AUTOMATION OF MANUFACTURING PROCESSES

23.   Key to manufacturing is automation and control, replacing or enabling manual labour. **Automation**, using computer-based and mechanical technology to speed up the performance of existing tasks, has been implemented in manufacturing processes, material handling, inspection, assembly and packaging at increasing rates (Kalpakjian, Schmid and Kok, 2010). Beginning with the numerical control of machines (a method of controlling the movements of machine components through coded instructions), automation seeks to reduce costs, increase flexibility and facilitate making different parts with less operator skill. Operations may be continuously monitored and material handling improved particularly through the use of industrial **robots** and automated guided vehicles. Levels of automation typically depend on the processes used, the products to be made and production volumes.

CAD, CAM AND CIM

24.   Computer technology is pervasive and exists at many levels. **Computer-aided design (CAD)** refers to the use of a computer-based system for translating engineering concepts into engineering designs by means of programs incorporating data on (i) design principles and (ii) key variables (e.g. product size, shape, etc.). CAD programs are capable of providing three-dimensional representations on a screen. These representations can be rotated through a number of different perspectives. This form of computer modelling is extremely useful in the design process, as it enables detailed changes to be made, and their effects measured, with speed and accuracy. Computer-aided manufacture (CAM) is a general term which refers to any production system in which manufacturing plant and test equipment are controlled by computer. A CAM system can be expected to be faster, more consistent (and higher quality) and has the ability to achieve high production levels even when skilled craftsmen are in short supply.

25.   **Computer integrated manufacturing (CIM)** integrates the software and hardware needed for computer graphics, computer-aided modelling and computer-aided design and manufacturing activities, from initial product concept through its production and distribution in the marketplace (Kalpakjian, Schmid and Kok, 2010). CIM involves the total operation of an organization. Such systems comprise various subsystems which are integrated into a whole. Typical subsystems include business planning and support, product design, manufacturing process planning, process automation and control and production monitoring systems. Typically the output of one subsystem service is the input for another. Such systems may be clustered according to whether they fulfil the planning or business execution role. Thus CIM is seen as a more holistic concept that may include CAD, CAM and various automation technologies.

26.   Such technologies enable the organization to be more responsive, reduce inventory (and therefore cost) and gain better control of production. There are various elements to CIM such as industrial robots; automated materials handling, i.e. moving a part from one machine to another, and then to points of inspection, to inventory and finally to shipment; automated assembly systems; computer aided process planning; cellular manufacturing and flexible management systems. **Flexible manufacturing systems (FMS)** integrate all of the major elements of production into a highly automated system. Kalpakjian, Schmid and Kok (2010: p. 1132) argue that CIM systems have become the most important means of improving productivity, responding to changing market demands and enhancing the control of manufacturing and management functions. The relationship between a number of these technologies is summarized in Figure 38.2.

FIGURE 38.2 **Hierarchy of manufacturing systems**

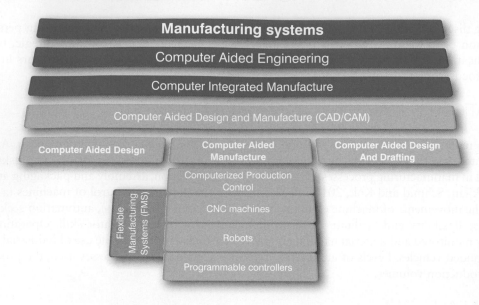

CONCLUSION

27. In this chapter we evaluated the role of technology in manufacturing, from the general and specific manufacturing standpoints. Initially focusing on information flows, we discussed the use of ERP systems in manufacturing. ERP systems and broader ES integrate the parts of the organization, its value and supply chain, to make the organization more responsive and efficient. In the second part we considered CIM. CIM systems have become the most important means of improving productivity, responding to changing market demands, and enhancing the control of manufacturing and management functions. Both sets of technologies represent efforts to integrate operations and processes in order to make manufacturers more effective and efficient.

QUESTIONS

1   Review the use of ERP and ES generally in manufacturing. In your answer you should contrast ES with functional systems, commenting on the advantages and disadvantages of ES such as ERP systems.

2   Evaluate the role of automation in manufacturing. In your answer you should comment on the application of technology at various stages of manufacturing and discuss benefits. You should also make reference to companies with which you are familiar to provide examples of automation in manufacturing.

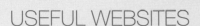

USEFUL WEBSITES

British Automation and Robot Association: **www.bara.org.uk**

REFERENCES

Greasley, A. (2009) *Operations Management*, 2nd edn, Wiley.

Kalpakjian, S., Schmid, S.R. and Kok, C. (2010) *Manufacturing, Engineering and Technology*, 6th edn, Prentice Hall.

Magal, S. and Word, J. (2009) *Essentials of Business Processes and Information Systems*, Wiley.

Møller, C. (2005) 'ERP II: a conceptual framework for next-generation enterprise systems?', *Journal of Enterprise Information Management*, 18(4): 483–497.

Porter, M.E. and Millar, V.E. (1985) 'How information gives you a competitive advantage', *Harvard Business Review*, 63(July/August): 149–174.

SKILL SHEET 11   **Operations Management**

This skills sheet provides a set of supply chain/operations tools to help the reader engage in the practice of operations (procurement, logistics and production). It should be noted that a simple overview is provided here and that operations specialists are more likely to utilize more sophisticated techniques. This skills sheet therefore provides an introduction to what can be a more complex skills set. The primary purpose here is to encourage the reader to appreciate key logistical and operational decisions.

Inventory Management Decisions and Models

Inventory management is a financial trade-off between inventory costs and stockout costs. The more stock, the more working capital is needed and the more stock depreciation observed. On the other hand if you do not have adequate stock, inventory stockouts occur, missing potential sales and possibility interrupting the whole production process. For many intermediaries inventory is generally the largest asset, as well as the largest expense item. Assessing inventory costs is therefore essential and has consequences for the finances of the business as well as its management. It helps businesses determine how much profit can be made from the inventory, how costs can be reduced (where changes can be made), which suppliers to choose, how capital must be allocated, etc.

In this skills sheet we first consider the decision about how much stock to order (or make). We explore the application of the EOQ algorithm in providing answers to this question. The second topic explores how to calculate key inventory costs. Some of the key inventory costs are inputs to the EOQ algorithm (e.g. cost per order and holding cost). In the third part we consider the decision of when to order and the reorder point. The reorder point (ROP) is the Inventory level of an item which signals the need for a replenishment order (PO). It is used when automating the PO process. Finally we consider Location Planning Analysis with the Centre of Gravity Method; a technique to assist in making location decisions (for the warehouse for example).

Whilst mathematics are used throughout this sheet the reader should not feel daunted by this as all formulae, algorithms and maths can be accomplished using spreadsheet functions and worked examples are provided.

1. Ordering Decisions – The Quantity to Order (Q): Economic Order Quantity (EOQ)

The EOQ is the optimum *quantity* of goods (optimum lot size/quantity for replenishment that minimizes total inventory costs) to be purchased at one time in order to minimize the annual total costs of ordering and carrying or holding items in inventory. EOQ applies only when demand for a product is constant over the year. There is a fixed cost for each order placed, regardless of the number of units ordered. There is also a cost for each unit held in storage, commonly known as *holding cost*. The most well-known EOQ formula is the Wilson Formula developed in 1913.

We want to determine the optimal number of units to order so that we minimize the total cost associated with the purchase, delivery and storage of the product. The required factors are the:

1. total demand for the year (D)
2. purchase price for each item (c)
3. fixed cost to place the order (K), and
4. storage (carrying cost) cost for each item per year (h).

$$Q = \frac{\sqrt{2DK}}{h}$$

Example:
At ScaterBoys (see case sheet 11) the annual demand for product 002-00051 (Jesus Fish Wheels) is 3545 (see Figure 4) i.e. D = 3545. The Cost per unit (c) = £8.50; this is how much ScaterBoys must pay the supplier for each product ordered. We assume the Cost per order (K) = £10 (see Section 2 for methods to determine this value) and the Annual carrying cost per unit (h) = £0.20 (see Section 2).

Calculation: THE QUANTITY TO ORDER (Q)

$$Q = \frac{\sqrt{2DK}}{h}$$

$$=$$

$$Q = \frac{\sqrt{2 + 3545 + 10}}{0.2}$$

$$= 595 \text{ units}$$

Thus, ScaterBoys should order 595 units each time they restock with this product and will therefore need to place six orders per year. Number of orders per year (based on EOQ) = D/Q

i.e. 3545/ 595 = 6

We can check whether this (595) is the best quantity to order using the formula:

Total cost = c × D + K (D/EOQ) + h (EOQ/2)
= 8.5 × 3545 + 10(3545/595) + 0.2 (595/2) = £30 251.58

If we check the total cost for any order quantity other than 595 (=EOQ), we should see that the cost is higher. For instance, supposing 300 units per order, then

= 8.5 × 3545 + 10(3545/300) + 0.2 (300/2) = £30 280.66

Now consider the current Q value used by ScaterBoys (see case sheet Figure 1): ScaterBoys typically orders 30 products in a single order (target level 40 – reorder level 10)

TC = 8.5 × 3545 + 10(3545/30) + 0.2 (30/2) = £31 317.16

Thus a shift from an order quantity of 30 to 595 would reduce total cost from £31 317.16 to £30 251.58, i.e. saving of £1065.58. This represents a significant reduction in inventory management cost.

There are several key assumptions to the model: The ordering cost is constant; the rate of demand is known, and spread evenly throughout the year; the lead time is fixed; the purchase price of the item is constant, i.e. no discount is available; the replenishment is made instantaneously; the whole batch is delivered at once and only one product is involved. Even if all the assumptions do not hold exactly, the EOQ gives us a good indication of whether or not current order quantities are reasonable. Variations on the formulae, to cope with discounts etc., exist. The EOQ formula can be modified to determine **production levels**. In this case the production quantity (Q) =

$$Q = \frac{\sqrt{2SD}}{PI}$$

Where S = Set-up costs; D = Demand rate; P = Production cost; and I = Interest rate (considered an opportunity cost, so the risk-free rate can be used).

2. Inventory Costs: Ordering, Carrying and Stockout Costs

Inventory costs are the costs related to storing and maintaining inventory over a certain period of time. Inventory costs fall into three main categories:

a. Ordering costs (also called Set-up costs)
b. Carrying costs (also called Holding costs)
c. Stockout costs (also called Shortage costs).

We made use of the ordering (K) and carrying (h) costs to compute the EOQ previously. We will now explain how they may be calculated/derived and also consider the costs associated with stockouts. As such costs are company specific they will be computed and provided by the company accounting or finance function.

a. Ordering Costs – Cost of Replenishing Inventory

In this section we wish to calculate the costs incurred every time we place an order (Calculating the cost of a PO). Ordering costs = the cost of the **ordering process** itself (clerical and system costs, independent of the number of units ordered) + the variable **inbound logistics** (transportation/shipping and reception – unloading and inspecting) costs. It is not easy to estimate the ordering cost, since it includes components that are business specific and even item specific: suppliers can be local or overseas, they can adopt rules to deliver only per palette instead of per unit, or only when a certain number of items are ordered; suppliers can provide volume discounts etc. The cost of raising a PO will be more or less the same whether it is for an order worth thousands of pounds or one worth only £5. In the case of ScaterBoys a PO may be raised by sales when taking an order or by procurement during inventory management. As the system generates the PO automatically only a small labour cost is incurred – approx. £2. The PO is emailed at little cost. Each PO will cause the receipt of an invoice from the supplier which must be received, approved, logged and paid. The cost is estimated at a further £3. Finally, the variable inbound logistics costs must be added.

b. Carrying Costs

Carrying costs may comprise the following: **Capital costs** (or financing charges – the interests on working capital and the opportunity cost of the money invested in the inventory), **Storage space costs** (the cost of building and facility maintenance – lighting, air conditioning, heating, etc., the cost of purchase, depreciation, or the lease, and the property taxes), **Inventory services costs** and **Inventory risk costs** (the risk that the items might fall in value over the period they are stored, shrinkage and obsolescence).

A classical way to determine the capital costs is to use a WACC (weighted average cost of capital). Capital costs are typically 5–15%. Inventory services costs include insurance, IT hardware and applications (Barcode/RFID equipment), also physical handling with the corresponding human resources, management, etc.

One standard rule of thumb suggests typical carrying costs are 25% of inventory value on hand. Another quick method of calculating the cost of carrying inventory is to add 20% to the current interest rate for borrowing money. For instance, if the rate is 3%, the carrying costs would be 3+20=23%, i.e. over 1 year, in the (23%) case, an intermediary would spend £230 for every £1000 carried in inventory.

Example:

ScaterBoys average inventory value = £300 000. **Storage space costs: 43 000; Inventory service costs: 10 000; Inventory risk costs: 10 000** (Shrinkage: 5 000, Obsolescence: 5 000).This represents a total of 63 000. To obtain a percentage, we divide this total by the average inventory value: 63 000/300 000 = 21%. We finally add the capital costs. Let us assume they are at 5% in this case, that is to say 15 000. In the ScaterBoys example, the total inventory carrying costs reaches 78 000 for an average inventory value of 300 000. The inventory carrying rate equals 21%+5%= 26%.

c.   Stockout Costs

To get a thorough revelation of the inventory costs, we should also add the stockout costs (or shortage costs), the costs incurred when stockouts take place. This can include the costs of emergency shipments, change of suppliers with faster deliveries, substitution to less profitable items, etc. However there will also be costs in terms of customer loss of the immediate or future sales (loyalty) or the general reputation of the company which will be harder to quantify. Calculating the cost of stockouts is in itself an immense topic that goes beyond the scope of this text. For simplicity we will assume a stock-out cost to be 25% of the customer sales order value at ScaterBoys.

3. When to Reorder

This section is intended for managers who want to implement a replenishment feature for (automated) inventory management. The ROP is the Inventory level of an item which signals the need for a replenishment order i.e. the ROP is the amount of stock that should trigger an order.

$$ROP = \text{Lead (time) demand} + \text{Safety stock}$$

Where the **lead demand** (also called lead time demand) is the total demand (expected customer orders) between now and the anticipated delivery time; this value is typically forecasted using time series analysis.

Example: How to compute safety stock and the ROP.

1. Paste the first row of (sales) data for ScaterBoys product 001-00019 into an Excel spreadsheet i.e.

Product	Total Quantity	Jan	Feb	Mar	Apr	May	Jun	Jul	Aug	Sep	Oct	Nov	Dec
001-00019	3122	161	285	210	321	30	685	246	380	120	275	246	76

2. Determine the **Lead time (months)** i.e. the time taken for supply (from when ScaterBoys raises a PO to the inbound goods arriving at the ScaterBoys warehouse). Assume this to be approximately 1 week i.e. 0.25 months.

3. Determine the percentage of time to avoid stockouts (some companies refer to this as a **service level**/factor) – the probability for the supplier of not having a shortage when a reorder is made. Assume this to be 75% i.e. 0.75.

4. Forecast sales for the next month(s). In this example we will assume the current month is September and the data in the above table for Oct-Dec is a forecast.

5. Determine the *lead time demand* (**Lead time (months)** × Forecast e.g. 0.25 ×120 = 30) – the amount ScaterBoys would expect to sell before the supplier order arrives.

6. Calculate the Deviation in the past sales (use STDEV in Excel for Jan – Sep) i.e. 222

7. Calculate the **Service factor** using the Inverse of the normal distribution as NORMSINV(Service level) i.e. NORMSINV(0.75) = 0.675

8. Calculate the **Lead time factor**: Square root of **lead time** to forecast ratio i.e. $\sqrt{0.25} = 0.5$

9. Calculate the **safety stock** by combining the standard deviation of past sales, Lead time factor and service factor i.e. $222 \times 0.5 \times 0.675 = 75$

10. Calculate the ROP as safety stock (75) + lead time demand (30) = 105

Thus ScaterBoys previously had a reorder level of 5 for product 001-00019 Mini First Aider (see Figure 1 for case sheet 11). We would recommend this be increased to 105 if stockouts are to be avoided. Replenishment is typically triggered when the inventory level equals the ROP (also called reorder trigger level), a setting from the system. When the ROP is reached, an order matching the EOQ is normally produced; this will typically be automated.

4. The Weighted Centre of Gravity (Facility Location Decisions)

Minimizing transportation costs is quite important in site selection projects for a new warehouse. One technique to assist in making location decisions is the 'centre of gravity' method which focuses on the transportation costs. With this method, the coordinates for the optimal location are proposed as an average of the coordinates of the various customers which are weighted according to the number of orders expected from each customer. This method is also called the Minisum method. The centre-of-gravity coordinates of the lowest cost location for a warehouse, $\overline{X}$ and $\overline{Y}$ is given by the formulae:

$$\overline{X} = \frac{\sum x_i V_i}{\sum V_i} \text{ and } \overline{Y} = \frac{\sum y_i V_i}{\sum V_i}$$

Where x_i = the x coordinate of a customer (or supplier) and y_i = the y coordinate of a customer (or supplier). V_i = the amount to be shipped (e.g. sales order frequency) to the customer (e.g. over the course of a year).

The coordinates will be on the Earth's surface in latitude and longitude. The latitude and longitude for each customer location must first be converted into Cartesian (x,y,z) coordinates. The x, y and z coordinates are then multiplied by the weighting factor (order frequency w) and added together. A line can be drawn from the centre of the Earth out to this new x, y, z coordinate, and the point where the line intersects the surface of the Earth is the geographic midpoint. This surface point is converted into the latitude and longitude for the midpoint. The midpoint is the optimum location for the warehouse. In practice the optimum location will also be influenced by other factors, such as transportation network, HR availability, the geography of the land, etc.

DETAILED STEPS:

Given the values for the first location (Kickflip Co) in the list:

Lat1, Lon1, Order Freq (e.g. see case sheet 11, Figure 13 and Figure 14:) 53.408371, -2.991573, 144)
Convert Lat1 and Lon1 from degrees **to radians**.
lat1 = lat1 × PI/180 i.e. 0.93215192207
lon1 = lon1 × PI/180 i.e. -0.0522127986637643
Convert lat/lon **to Cartesian coordinates** for first location.
X1 = cos(lat1) × cos(lon1) i.e. 0.60
Y1 = cos(lat1) × sin(lon1) i.e. -0.03
Z1 = sin(lat1) i.e. 0.80
Compute **weight** (by total orders) for first location (144).
Repeat steps for remaining locations in the list.
Compute combined total weight for all locations.
Total weight = w1 + w2 + ... + wn (e.g. 4631)
Compute weighted average x, y and z coordinates.
x = ((x1 × w1) + (x2 × w2) + ... + (xn × wn))/total weight i.e. 0.615083581
y = ((y1 × w1) + (y2 × w2) + ... + (yn × wn))/total weight i.e. 0.0881412041886892
z = ((z1 × w1) + (z2 × w2) + ... + (zn × wn))/total weight i.e. 0.7664733144
Convert average x, y, z coordinates **to latitude and longitude**. Note that in Excel and possibly some other applications, the parameters need to be reversed in the atan2 function, for example, use atan2(X,Y) instead of atan2(Y,X).
Lon = atan2(y, x) e.g. 0.142330593 in the example
Hyp = sqrt(x × x + y × y) e.g. 0.621366787
Lat = atan2(z, hyp) e.g. 0.889575299
Convert lat and lon to degrees.
lat = lat × 180/PI e.g. 50.9689102
lon = lon × 180/PI e.g. 8.154942264

Finally, type the coordinates into mapping software to view the optimum location of the warehouse (e.g. see **www.geomidpoint.com**).

Example in Excel:

		Customers	Kickflip Co	Yakwax	Neutral Density	Exist Clothing		Snot boards	Total
		W	144	114	224	166		16	
		Lat	53.408371						
		Lon	-2.991573						
	Radians	Lat	0.932151922						
pi/180	0.017453293	Lon	-0.052212799						
	Cartesian	X	0.595295213						
		Y	-0.031110305						
		Z	0.802904576						
	weighted XY	X	85.72251069						X 0.615083581
		Y	-4.479883916						Y 8.81E-02
		Z	115.6182589						Z 0.766473314
								Convert to Lat/ lon	
								Lon	0.142330593
								Hyp	0.621366787
								Lat	0.889575299
								Optimum location	
180/pi	57.29577951							Convert to degrees	
								Lon	8.154942264
								Lat	50.9689102

Example showing formulae (some of the columns hidden to fit)

		Customers	Kickflip Co	Sugar Sports	Snot boards		Total	
		W	144	212	16		=SUM(D2:AD2)	totweight
		Lat	53.408371	53.381129	43.696036			
		Lon	-2.991573	-1.470085	7.265592			
Radians		**Lat**	=D3*$B$7	=AC3*$B$7	=AD3*$B$7			
pi/180	=3.14159265359/180	**Lon**	=D4*$B$7	=AC4*$B$7	=AD4*$B$7			
Cartesian		**X**	=COS(D6) * COS(D7)	=COS(AC6) * COS(AC7)	=COS(AD6) * COS(AD7)			
		Y	=COS(D6) * COS(D7)	=COS(AC6) * SIN(AC7)	=COS(AD6) * SIN(AD7)			
		Z	=SIN(D6)	=SIN(AC6)	=SIN(AD6)			
weighted XY		**X**	=D9*D2	=AC9*AC2	=AD9*AD2	X	=SUM(D13:AD13)/$AF$2	Sum row/totweight
		Y	=D10*D2	=AC10*AC2	=AD10*AD2	Y	=SUM(D14:AD14)/$AF$2	
		Z	=D11*D2	=AC11*AC2	=AD11*AD2	Z	=SUM(D15:AD15)/$AF$2	
				Convert to Lat/ lon				
					Lon		=ATAN2(AF13,AF14)	
					Hyp		=SQRT((AF13 *AF13) + (AF14 * AF14))	
					Lat		=ATAN2(AF19,AF15)	
					Optimum location			
				Convert to degrees				
180/pi	=180/3.14159265359				Lon		**=AF18*B22**	
					Lat		**=AF20*B22**	

Section Thirteen
HR

CHAPTER 39
HUMAN RESOURCE MANAGEMENT

Key Concepts

- Employment relationship
- Generation X, Generation Y and the Baby Boomers
- Human capital (HC)
- Human resource management (HRM)
- Talent management
- Workplace and workforce

Learning Outcomes Having read this chapter, you should be able to:

- explain what is meant by the term HRM and how it relates to the management process
- explain the development of HRM
- discuss how changing demographics and the contemporary workplace are creating challenges for HR and their organizations
- explain what is meant by the war-for-talent and its relevance to today's organization
- explain the role of the HRM function
- list the key areas of HR policy and practice.

1.   An essential managerial role is to ensure the right person is recruited for any particular job. Similarly, every manager wants people who will do their best, without experiencing high turnover, or tribunal appearances for discriminatory or other illegal behaviours. This part of the book is concerned with managing people, both individually and collectively, in the workplace. It is relevant to all managers who share such concerns. Not only will this chapter help with an understanding of general aspects of managing people but it will also assist with understanding the specialist role of the dedicated HR function.

2.   **Human capital (HC)** is an economic and management construct referring to the knowledge, skills and other attributes of labour (people involved in productive work) that contribute to the development of a business or economy. Sometimes called *intellectual capital*, it is the collective value of the capabilities, knowledge, skills and commitment of an organizational workforce. HC theory is the view that people are worth investing in as a form of capital: that people's performance and the results achieved can

be considered as a return on investment and assessed in terms of cost and benefits (Bratton and Gold, 2012).

3.   Some scholars describe human capital management in terms of activities aimed at developing the intellectual assets of an organization. However, others consider the HC view as restricted – where people or employees are viewed as economic assets, as distinguished from other forms of (physical) capital, such as technology and buildings. Nevertheless, it is an important construct that allows us to conceptualize aspects of the workforce and their importance to the organization in accomplishing goals.

THE EMPLOYMENT RELATIONSHIP

4.   Each and every worker or employee in the organization, the HC or HR, has a relationship with their employer. The nature of the relationship between employees and their employer is an issue of central importance to HRM, (Bratton and Gold, 2012: p. 9). At the most basic, this relationship embraces an economic connection (pay). It also involves a legal relationship (rights and obligations affecting both parties) and a social relationship (employees observe social norms) which influences behaviour in the workplace.

5.   Bratton and Gold (2012: p. 12) further note that 'the **employment relationship** embodies an uneven balance of power'. More recently, this relationship has also been described in terms of a **psychological contract**, a two-way exchange of perceived promises and obligations between employees and their employer. There are unwritten expectations and understandings about mutual obligations. Thus, the employer–employee relationship should not be looked at simply in economic terms (a more traditional view). It is a significant human relationship of mutual dependency that has great impact on the people involved and from this relationship arise moral obligations involving both the employer and the employee.

6.   The concept of an individual employment relationship expands the (narrower) scope limited to a 'contract of employment', based on the criterion of subordination of the employee to the employer. The employment relationship must recognize that work has taken new forms, which may not fall within the classical common law definition of contracts of employment. Under this concept, employers and employees are assumed to have shared interests. The challenges facing the employment relationship are discussed by Sparrow and Cooper (2003). The employment relationship is important because of its effect on how employees and employers behave from day-to-day. It is the psychological contract that effectively tells employees what they are required to do in order to meet their side of the bargain and what they can expect from their job. The types of commitment employers and employees might make to one another are:

Employees	Employers
attend, punctually and work hard	provide interesting work, feedback and pay/benefits commensurate with performance
remain loyal and committed	maintain a pleasant and safe working environment, act fairly and provide opportunities for promotion
be flexible	offer reasonable job security
uphold company reputation, be honest and courteous	provide respectful treatment
contribute with new ideas, maintain skills, knowledge and competence	recognition for innovation or new ideas and opportunities for training and development

7.   Organizations wishing to succeed must obtain the most out of their human resource. In order to achieve this employers have to know what employees expect from their work. Employers must balance interests such as decreasing wage constraints with a maximization of labour productivity in order to achieve a profitable and productive employment relationship. Where the psychological contract is positive, increased employee commitment and satisfaction will have a positive impact upon business performance.

8.   The employment relationship also has implications for management style. In many organizations managers can no longer control the business 'top down' – they have to adopt a more 'bottom up' style. Vital information, needed by management, is known by employees from their interactions with customers

and suppliers. Other implications of the employment relationship may include a need for two-way dialogue between employer and employees and broader participation in decision-making. People want to know that their interests will be taken into account when important decisions are made; they would like to be treated with respect and are more likely to be satisfied and engaged with their job if they are consulted about change. We discuss this relationship further in Chapter 42.

9.   We have already discussed the meaning of management throughout the first part of this book. Managers are traditionally distinguished according to their function (for example, the production or marketing manager) and according to their level in the organizational hierarchy (for example senior, middle or first line manager). Employees in large organizations do not identify with any single person as the 'employer'. The line manager is important in making day-to-day decisions but employees are also affected by decisions taken by senior management and the HR function.

10.   The effective management of HR is a major determinant of success or failure in business. The goal of **human resource management** is to help an organization meet strategic goals by attracting and retaining employees and then managing them effectively. HRM is therefore concerned with the strategic management of HR to achieve a (sustainable) competitive advantage. Managing people however is not restricted to the HR department. It is part of the role of every manager or team leader responsible for the work of others.

11.   Managers often identify a need for new employees, leading to recruitment. In doing so they specify the work each employee will be required to do. Once employed they must lead, guide, develop and motivate them (refer back to Chapters 4–7). In order to maximize the return on investment from the organization's human capital (HC), larger firms establish a specialist HR function. HR specialists are typically used to support line managers, inculcate best HR practice, and ensure a fair, legal and consistent company-wide approach.

12.   This chapter focuses on the general role of the HR function. Subsequent chapters will review specific HR policies and practices in more detail. We will first explore the context for HR by discussing the contemporary workplace and working population. We will then return to the HR function and discuss this role in more detail – from both a strategic and operational (traditional) perspective.

39.1 HR CHALLENGES AND CONTEXT: THE CONTEMPORARY WORKPLACE, DEMOGRAPHICS AND THE WAR FOR 'TALENT'

13.   The **workplace** refers to the work setting in general and is typically a place, such as an office, store or factory, where people are employed and work. It is the location at which an employer provides work for an employee. Located within is the **workforce**, all the people engaged in or available for work, who are recruited from the wider society (sometimes referred to as the *labour market*), be it domestic or global. When discussing the workforce or available workers in a society, practitioners and academics often refer to **human capital**. This was discussed earlier. Given the important contribution the workforce can make as a source of new and existing employees for the organization, it is important to understand it. In the following paragraphs we will first consider key attributes of the society from which labour is drawn, considering factors such as the size of the labour pool, available skills, capabilities and knowledge. We will then consider the mix of values within the workforce and discuss how this presents challenges for those concerned with the management of people.

14.   In Chapter 12 we analyzed the business environment using the PESTEL framework. All of the PESTEL factors can influence HR in the workplace. Focusing on the social environment, Kelly and Ashwin (2013) discuss **demographic** trends and the implications for business. The three drivers of population change considered by them are fertility, life expectancy and migration. As we will see later, population change alters the challenges faced by the HR professional and every manager. According to the European Commission (EC) (2011) the EU population has now exceeded 500 million; this is approximately 7 per cent of the world's population (7 billion). The EC, in their Demography Report 2010, note 'The EU's demographic picture has become clearer: (population) growth is fuelled mainly by immigration, the population is becoming older (greater life expectancy) and more diverse' (increased migration and globalization).

15.   The impact of demographic ageing within the EU is expected to be of significance in the coming decades. Consistently low birth rates and higher life expectancy will change the shape of the EU's age pyramid; perhaps the most important change will be the marked shift towards a much older population. Consequently, the proportion of people of working age is shrinking whilst the relative number of those retired is expanding. The share of older persons in the total population will increase in the coming decades, as a greater proportion of the post-war baby boom generation (defined later) reaches retirement. This will lead to an increased burden on those of working age to meet the costs (reflected in government spending) of caring for the ageing population.

16.   In 2010 EU persons considered to be of working age (15 to 64 years old) accounted for 67 per cent of the population. However, the effect of the ageing population and migration may mean that the EU's population will be slightly higher in 2060, whilst the age structure of the population will be much older than it is now. The population of working age is expected to decline steadily (to 56 per cent), whilst elderly people will likely account for an increasing share of the population – those aged 65 years or over will account for almost 30 per cent of the EU's population by 2060 (17.4 per cent in 2010). One way to combat the shrinking workforce and economic dependency of the aging population will be to increase *retirement age*. Governments are also revising the *pension age*. The age issue poses challenges in the form of age discrimination law. In the EU, equality legislation makes it unlawful to discriminate against employees, job seekers and trainees because of their age.

17.   Migration is the main driver of population growth in most of the EU Member States and plays a significant role in the population dynamics of European societies; in recent years, the increase in the population of the EU has mainly been due to high net migration rates. Migratory movements are making the EU's population more *diverse* and creating new challenges and opportunities for European societies and their organizations. Migration, especially from non-EU countries, could provide a (temporary) relief from population ageing; since most people migrate primarily as young adults (aged 25–34). As young cohorts of foreigners feed progressively into the older national cohorts, the total population is rejuvenated and diversity increases. Migration flows impact upon the size and structure of the population. Unprecedented levels of immigration both from third countries (the term 'third country' means a country that is not a member of the Union) and within the EU (intra-EU mobility) over the past decade have substantially increased the proportion of EU inhabitants who do not live in their own native country or culture. There are an increasing number of European citizens who seek opportunities across national borders for study, work, and life experience, resulting in different forms of international connectedness across national borders.

18.   One country and organization level outcome of migration is **multiculturalism**. In the organizational studies context, it is another term for cultural differentiation or the existence of subcultures within an organization. Thus, the multicultural organization is an organization that contains many different cultural groups and values diversity. As organizations internationalize their operations, it is likely that the frequency with which employees will interact with people from different countries will increase. Further, through migration, domestic populations are becoming more diverse, suggesting that domestic organizations will also need to learn how to manage more heterogeneous and multicultural workgroups than they have managed previously. Immigration, changing demographics, globalization, increased international business and technology impact upon today's workforce which is older, more racially diverse, and more female, more varied. The twenty-first century workplace typically has a diverse (heterogeneous) workforce. Consequently there are rarely simple standard ways of managing such a workforce.

19.   Kelly and Ashwin (2013: p. 96) discuss how demographic and cultural changes impact upon the need for organizations to alter their policies, strategies, products, services and practices. All of these changes create a dynamic social environment from which customers, investors, employees and stakeholders of the organization will emerge. To be successful in dealing with people from other cultures, managers need knowledge about cultural differences and similarities amongst countries. They also need to understand the implications of the differences and the skills required to act and decide appropriately and in a culturally sensitive way.

20.   As society becomes more multicultural, so too does the workforce, both domestically and internationally. A competitive edge can be gained by optimizing the people resource of the organization. A critical challenge for senior management today is to turn cultural diversity into a differentiating advantage in an increasingly competitive global marketplace. Business reasons for managing diversity include: cost

savings – higher turnover costs (dissatisfied employees leaving the company), higher absenteeism rates and possible lawsuits on sexual, race and age discrimination. Winning the competition for talent, companies must attract, retain and promote excellent employees from different demographic groups. Companies cited as the best places to work for women and minorities have reported an increased inflow of applications (better recruitment opportunities). Companies who appreciate their workforce should reflect their consumer base, and benefit financially from improved marketplace understanding. A diverse workforce, with established customer relationships, is an example of a difficult-to-imitate resource that can confer a sustainable competitive advantage for the firm.

21.   There are, however, a number of counterarguments that may be presented, suggesting that diversity may actually be counterproductive for the firm. Diverse groups require more effort to integrate, coordinate and control. Minority members of groups may feel alienated and pushed out. Diversity integration requires a long-term commitment and the payback is often not as tangible or predictable as, for instance, investing in new product development.

22.   An organization's workforce composition may be diverse, composed of international or domestic values. Hewlett, Sherbin and Sumberg (2009), from the Centre for Work–Life Policy, conducted studies that reveal workplace values. They explored the composition of the workforce (different generations) whilst discussing changing HR practices. There are three key groups employed within today's workforce (see Figure 39.1): **Generation Y, Generation X** and before that the **Baby Boom generation**. Many HR professionals would argue that Gen Ys and Boomers share similar values and are eager to contribute to positive social change, and seek out workplaces where they can do that. They expect flexibility and the option to work remotely, but they also want to connect deeply with colleagues.

23.   Hewlett, Sherbin and Sumberg (2009) discuss shifting value propositions and life circumstances and suggest that both Boomers and Gen Ys are drawn to opportunities that allow time out (e.g. sabbatical leave)

FIGURE 39.1 Key groups employed within today's workforce

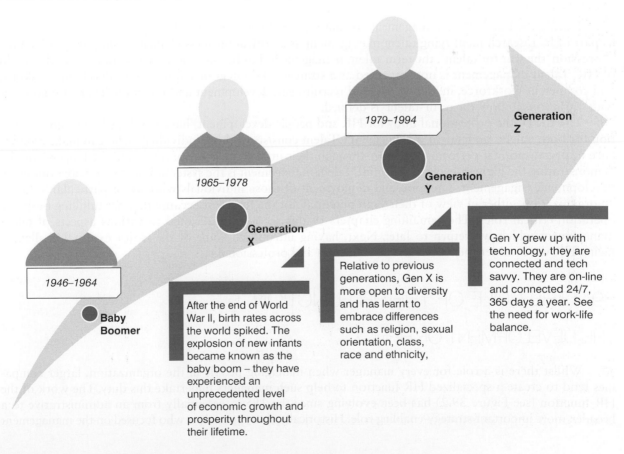

to explore passions and hobbies. Both groups see such breaks as opportunities for personal fulfilment. The study also found they share a heightened sense of obligation to make a positive contribution to society and to the health of the planet. Overwhelming majorities of Gen Ys and Boomers say that having flexible work options is important. Similar percentages say that **work–life balance** matters to them, so it is not surprising that many from both groups also wish for opportunities to work remotely. Having the freedom to choose when and where to work is of importance. However, such groups also enjoy teamwork and community. Most who want a remote option would prefer working from home just 1 day a week. Finally, Gen Ys and Boomers share a sense that financial gain is not the right reason to join or stay with an employer. Both generations rate four other forms of pay as at least as important as money: a great team, challenging assignments, a range of new experiences, and explicit performance evaluation and recognition. Such factors will influence the nature of the employment relationship discussed earlier.

24.   Companies whose employment offers align best with the shared values of Boomers and Gen Ys, will enjoy a major talent advantage argue Hewlett, Sherbin and Sumberg (2009). Offering discrete areas of work such as through specific projects may attract Boomers who can then reduce their work hours whilst utilizing and passing on their experience and knowledge. Employees want employers to be flexible and present opportunities to give back. Many companies support their employees' favourite causes, whether with release time for volunteering or with matching funds for contributions. Employers should recognize the sense of satisfaction employees may get from using vocational strengths to make a difference to a worthy cause. As people become more concerned about global climate change, many companies have discovered that a progressive work environment is deeply appreciated. Managers with open minds and newly energized growth plans will find ways to satisfy the workplace demands of the talent they seek. It will become increasingly important to monitor the changing attitudes of workers. The transformation of the workforce is ongoing. The organizations that thrive will be those which recognize their people's shifting values and preferences – and then find ways to make the work meaningful on those terms.

TALENT

25.   During the late 1990s, management consulting firm McKinsey coined the phrase the 'war for talent' as part of its research identifying talent management as a critical business challenge. Since they coined the expression 'the war for talent', the term 'talent management' has become increasingly common in the world of HR. **Talent management** is now regarded as a strategic and integrated approach to developing a skilled and competent workforce, involving targeted recruitment, development and retention. There are however wide variations in how the term 'talent' is defined.

26.   The CIPD (the professional body for HR and people development) have developed a working definition for both 'talent' and 'talent management': **Talent** consists of those individuals who can make a difference to organizational performance either through their immediate contribution or, in the longer-term, by demonstrating the highest levels of potential. Talent management is the systematic attraction, identification, development, engagement, retention and deployment of those individuals who are of particular value to an organization, either in view of their 'high potential' for the future or because they are fulfilling business/operation-critical roles. The remaining chapters of this section are devoted to various aspects of talent management which we return to later. Next, having introduced some of the major external challenges facing HR we consider the role of the HR function and professional.

39.2 THE ROLE OF THE HR FUNCTION

THE DEVELOPMENT OF HRM

27.   Whilst there is a role for every manager when managing people in the organization, larger companies tend to create a specialized HR function to help such managers undertake this duty. The work of the HR function (see Figure 39.2) has been evolving since the 1950s, essentially from an administrative to a broader, more important strategy-enabling role. Historically, those specialists who focused on the management

FIGURE 39.2 HRM functions, roles and activities

of employees tended to work for a business function labelled 'personnel management'; however, more recently this term has been replaced by many organizations with HR and HRM. The latter part of the twentieth century witnessed a radical change regarding how people were managed within organizations. There was a movement away from the idea of personnel management as an administrative and more operational function (the traditional view) to one that sought to ensure the organization had highly skilled, loyal and engaged employees who were a source of sustainable competitive advantage (the contemporary view). Aligned with this have been changes to the nature of the employment relationship as discussed earlier.

28.   Certain managers and professionals use the terms human resources and personnel interchangeably whilst others have argued a difference in the terms. For many scholars and practitioners the main difference centres on the role of the specialists. Whereas personnel management may be argued to be more administrative, HRM is integrated within strategic planning (Bratton and Gold, 2012). The contemporary HRM function may undertake a variety of activities, such as determining staffing needs and whether to use temporary staff or hire employees to fill these needs; recruiting and training the best employees; ensuring they are high performers; dealing with performance issues and ensuring HR practices conform to various regulations. Activities also include managing employee benefits and compensation, employee records and personnel policies.

29.   The CIPD believe that 'CEOs as well as HR directors are now likely to number talent management among their key priorities'[1]. In order for organizations to gain competitive advantage, they need to develop a strategic approach to talent management that suits their business and gets the best from their people. The CIPD also believe that HR specialists have an important role to play in providing support and guidance in the design and development of approaches to talent management that will fit the needs of the organization. 'They need to have a proper understanding of the key challenges facing the organization in attracting, recruiting, developing and retaining highly talented people to meet immediate and future strategic objectives and business needs'.

30.   The key HR activity in the evolving role of HR suggested by Bartlett and Ghoshal (2002: p. 37) is building human capital as a core source of competitive advantage. This presents a central role for HR in strategy. Bartlett and Ghoshal outline three major strategic tasks which align the HR function with the strategic challenge of developing the company's HC for sustainable competitive advantage:

- Building (HR systems, processes and culture)

- Linking (developing social networks – vital to knowledge management)

- Bonding (creating a sense of identity and belonging).

[1] www.cipd.co.uk/hr-resources/factsheets/talent-management-overview.aspx

LINE AND STAFF ASPECTS OF HRM

31.   The HR manager is an individual who typically acts in an advisory or staff capacity, working with other managers to help them deal with HR matters. More recently, HR managers have come to be viewed also as strategic partners who must work with senior management. Whilst all managers will have some involvement in activities such as recruitment, interviewing, selection and training, most organizations have a dedicated HR department. Whilst there is no common answer to the question of whether an organization needs a dedicated and full-time HR professional and recognizing that a company may choose to outsource this function, many argue the need to recruit such a manager when the organization size exceeds between 100 and 150; likewise you might expect to find around one full-time equivalent HR professional for each 100–150 employees. This is not a 'rule' but can guide expectations. The ratio of one HR person for every 100 employees has been in existence for some years and the most common HR-to-employee ratios are one to 100–200.

SCOPE AND FUNCTIONS OF HRM

32.   HRM seeks to organize work and manage **employment relations** and **engagement**. It covers areas from the level of the individual employee to that of the corporate strategy. At the operational and employee level it typically includes the sub-functions of HR planning, job design, recruitment and selection, performance management, training and development and rewards (Bratton and Gold, 2012). In this area HR management can play a significant role in organizational productivity. HR may also be linked with customer service and quality. At the strategic level it seeks to link the HR function with the strategic objectives of the organization in order to improve performance.

33.   Indeed Lepak and Gowan (2010) discuss managing employees for competitive advantage. They identify the primary HR activities as (1) work design and workforce planning, (2) managing employee competencies and (3) managing employee attitudes and behaviours. This influences the employee contribution which ultimately can drive competitive advantage. Mondy (2009) identifies five functional areas associated with 'effective' HRM: staffing, HR development, compensation, health and safety and employee relations. Additionally, HRM may have an international dimension where it focuses on the management of people operating in other countries (see Kelly, 2009).

34.   HR must also cope with a variety of environmental challenges such as changes in technology; labour force trends and demographics (diversity and the changing composition of the workforce); globalization (internationalization, joint ventures and partnerships, diversity and culture, etc.) and corporate social responsibility. Finally, from the political and legal environment (see PESTEL), legislation impacts upon HR practices such as recruitment and selection, compensation and reward and the rights of individuals to equal opportunities.

HR MANAGERIAL DUTIES

35.   In small organizations, line managers may carry out some or all of the typical duties associated with managing people. However, as the organization grows, and the need for specialized knowledge deepens, assistance may be provided from a dedicated HRM function. Aside from the line function (managing people in their own department) the HR manager has an advisory relationship and staff authority for other people in the organization. HR managers typically ensure that line managers are implementing the organization's HR policies and practices (functional authority) and will assist in hiring, training, evaluating, rewarding, counselling, promoting and dismissing employees. Additionally they may administer payroll and various benefit programmes and help line managers comply with equal opportunity and other relevant legislation. More recently, they are also likely to adopt both a strategic and international role.

39.3 STRATEGIC USE OF HR

36.   HR faces a number of challenges (Lepak and Gowan, 2010). These are presented in the form of organizational demands which manifest themselves in the strategy, culture and company characteristics (size and

stage of development for example). The strategy influences the types of jobs that must be performed to meet objectives. Culture influences how employees do their work, how managers and employees interact, and acceptable HR practices. Company size is likely to influence degrees of discretion (empowerment and autonomy) that managers may expect employees to display in their jobs. As companies increase in size we might expect to see higher degrees of job specialization. Similarly, we might expect higher degrees of formalization as companies seek to cope with increased complexity, communication and coordination challenges.

37.   Having agreed upon strategic goals, the organization, typically through the HR function, will then design and implement HR policies, programmes and practices in response. Such policies and practices are contingent upon the organization's internal and external environment (discussed earlier).

38.   According to Bartlett and Ghoshal (2002) skilled and motivated people are central to the operations of any company that wishes to flourish in the new age – 'In short, people are the key strategic resource, and strategy must be built on a HR foundation.' It is widely accepted that in order to compete in a rapidly changing environment, companies must improve their performance continually by reducing costs, innovating products and processes, and improving quality, productivity and speed to market. HR systems represent an opportunity to improve company performance. However, the HR contribution is not limited to making the organization more efficient but also more effective (Torrington *et al.*, 2009).

39.   Whilst it can be argued that it is the workforce itself (when highly skilled and motivated) that constitutes a source of sustainable competitive advantage, HR practices, when viewed collectively as an HR system, can be unique and difficult to replicate and may therefore be a source of sustainable competitive advantage. HR activities are thought to lead to the development of a skilled workforce and one that engages in functional behaviour for the organization; this results in higher operating performance, which translates into increased profitability.

40.   HRM thinking should consider the integration of HRM with business strategy, the development of distinctive corporate culture and the creation of a skilled, flexible and committed workforce which is adaptive to changing circumstances. The HR strategy is created to ensure the corporate goals are achievable. Contemporary organizations tend to adopt a dialogue whereby HR, as a functional strategy, may both be informed by and inform the corporate strategy. In this sense, HR may enable the creation of corporate strategy, making the organization more effective.

39.4 OPERATIONAL USE OF HR – POLICIES AND PRACTICES

41.   HR also has a role to make the organization more efficient. Ultimately the role of HR will be determined by the attitudes of the senior management of the organization. HR policies and practices typically include the following:

Recruitment

Training and development

Appraisal and performance

Employment services

Pay

Employee engagement and relations, and

Safety, health and welfare services.

As in other policy areas, HR policies are guidelines for behaviour, stating what the organization will do, or positively will not do, in relation to its employees and employee affairs. From policies derive more specific HRM practices. These are the HRM activities that have a direct impact on employees, e.g. types of compensation, staffing or resourcing methods, appraisal methods and forms of training and development. There are many choices amongst the array of possible practices and because they influence the behaviours of individuals, they need to be selected systematically to be aligned with the other HRM activities. HR practices are discussed in the remaining chapters of this section.

CONCLUSION

42. This chapter focused on human capital and its management in the organization – we considered HR as strategically important due to attributes which are difficult to imitate, thus ensuring any derived competitive advantage is sustainable. In particular we focused on the role of the specialist HR function in acquiring, developing and motivating HC in order to improve (productive) performance and develop a sustainable competitive advantage. The HR function develops and implements HR systems comprising the HR policies and practices. The HR role can be both strategic and operational. It is strategic in that the continued availability of HC must be assured in order for the strategy to be met. However, it must also be operational via the administration of certain HR practices such as resourcing, training and development and performance management.

QUESTIONS

1   Contrast the role of the HR function in the contemporary organization with that dominating much of the latter part of the twentieth century.

2   Discuss why organizations must now pay more attention to the nature of the external environment.

3   Evaluate how the HR function can contribute to corporate strategy.

USEFUL WEBSITES

Chartered Institute of Personnel Management **www.cipd.co.uk** International Labour Organization **www.ilo.org**

Institute for employment studies **www.employment-studies. co.uk/consult/index.php?id=hre&tab=work** Getting the most from your HR, L&D and OD functions

REFERENCES

Bartlett, C. and Ghoshal, S. (2002) 'Building competitive advantage through people', *MIT Sloan Management Review*, 43(2): 34–41.

Bratton, J. and Gold, J. (2012) *Human Resource Management Theory and Practice*, 5th edn, Palgrave Macmillan.

European Commission (2011) *Demography Report 2010 – Older, More Numerous and Diverse Europeans*, Luxembourg: Publications Office of the European Union.

Hewlett, S.A., Sherbin, L. and Sumberg, K. (2009) 'How Gen Y & Boomers will reshape your agenda', *Harvard Business Review*, 87(7/8): 71–76.

Kelly, P.P. (2009) *International Business and Management*, Cengage Learning EMEA.

Kelly, P. and Ashwin, A. (2013) *The Business Environment*, Cengage.

Lepak, D. and Gowan, M. (2010) *Human Resource Management International Edition*, Upper Saddle River: Pearson Education.

Mondy, R. (2009) *Human Resource Management: International Edition*, 11th edn, Pearson Education.

Sparrow, P.R. and Cooper, C. (2003) *The Employment Relationship – Key Challenges for HR*, Elsevier/ Butterworth-Heinemann.

Torrington, D., Hall, L., Taylor, S. and Atkinson, C. (2009) *Fundamentals of Human Resource Management: Managing People at Work*, Financial Times Press.

CHAPTER 40
RESOURCING: RECRUITMENT, SELECTION AND APPOINTMENT

Key Concepts

- Employee resourcing
- HR planning
- Job analysis
- Job description
- Recruitment
- Selection
- Social recruitment

Learning Outcomes Having read this chapter, you should be able to:

- evaluate the importance of recruitment and selection within organizations
- distinguish the typical stages of the recruitment and selection process
- list the typical content of a job description
- describe the common selection methods (application forms, interviewing, psychological testing and assessment centres)
- discuss the application of technology to the recruitment and selection process
- discuss the need for and methods to assure fairness in selection.

Vignette
RESOURCING AND TALENT PLANNING SURVEY 2013

The CIPD's annual Resourcing and Talent Planning survey examines organizations' resourcing and talent planning strategies and practices and the key challenges and issues they face. The 2013 survey report is based on 462 respondent organizations from the UK. 'Year on year we observe a fiercer war for talent, seeing the number of organizations reporting competition for well-qualified employees triple since 2009.' says Ksenia Zheltoukhova, Research Associate, CIPD. Nigel Heap of Hays recruiting added, 'Finding the right person for a job can transform a business as well as that person's life and having the right person in place has never been more important for organizations…Having an effective strategy in place to attract and retain employees is critical to an organization's success.'

Amongst the survey findings are the following points: more than two-thirds of organizations (surveyed) conduct recruitment activity in-house, whilst just over a quarter combine in-house and outsourcing approaches; the most effective methods for attracting candidates were through corporate websites and recruitment agencies; organizations were more likely to have increased recruitment spend on social and professional networking sites, commercial job boards and apprenticeships and more likely to have decreased spend on national newspaper advertisements and specialist journals/trade press; over half of organizations make use of social media in resourcing; interviews remain the most common selection method; the median recruitment cost of filling a vacancy was £5000 for senior managers/directors and £2000 for other employees; nearly three-fifths of organizations have a diversity strategy, rising to four-fifths of public sector organizations; and retaining employees has become an increasing challenge over the last few years.

1. The CIPD[1] believes that effective recruitment is central and crucial to the successful day-to-day functioning of any organization. Successful recruitment depends upon finding people with the right skills, expertise and qualifications to deliver organizational objectives and the ability to make a positive contribution to the values and aims of the organization. Recruitment is not only carried out to fulfil current needs. Recruiters should always be aware of and refer to future plans that have implications for organizational resourcing.

2. Effective HR planning can predict HR gaps and promote a focus on recruiting the right people to deliver business objectives, Pilbeam and Corbridge (2010: p. 155). **HR planning** is 'a rational approach to the effective **recruitment**, retention and deployment of people within an organization, including, when necessary, arrangements for dismissing staff'. HR planning identifies staffing needs and is therefore an input to the resourcing process. In other chapters we have noted the strategic importance of recruitment in securing talent for competitive advantage (see previous chapter) and as a means to develop organizational culture. The previous chapter also discussed the HR (people management) system. This chapter outlines the typical stages of the recruitment and selection process within organizations, and considers certain aspects of the process in greater detail. Some practitioners and scholars use the concept of **resourcing** to describe three main areas of HR activity: recruitment, selection and appointment (Martin, 2010). Others use this concept more broadly to include the process by which people are identified and allocated to perform necessary work.

3. Pilbeam and Corbridge (2010) extend the concept yet further, suggesting that 'people resourcing is that part of HRM which focuses on the recruitment and release of individuals from organizations, as well as the management of their performance'. They also suggest that it is now common to refer to this area of HRM as 'talent planning and resourcing'. They ask how organizations can resource talent into the organization. Indeed some practitioners and scholars now use the term talent acquisition interchangeably with recruitment and selection.

---

[1] http://www.cipd.co.uk/hr-resources/factsheets/recruitment-overview.aspx accessed 16 April 2014.

4. It will be helpful to distinguish 'recruitment' from 'selection'. The aim of recruitment is to ensure that the organization's demand for employees is met by attracting potential employees (candidates) in a cost-effective and timely manner; recruitment focuses on the identification of a vacancy (**job analysis**), identifying where likely candidates may be found, advertising, documenting and initial sifting. This is followed by **selection**. The aim of selection is to identify, from those coming forward, the individuals most likely to fulfil the requirements of the organization. Selection methods include **application forms** and CVs, interviews, **psychometric** testing, assessment centres and references. In simple terms, recruitment is concerned with attracting applicants, and selection is concerned with screening those applicants and choosing the preferred ones. The final stage of the selection process should be identification of the chosen applicants for the jobs. Typically, a job offer is made to the preferred applicant. If the job offer is accepted then the applicant is appointed. An outline of the resourcing process is shown in Figure 40.1.

FIGURE 40.1 **Resourcing process**

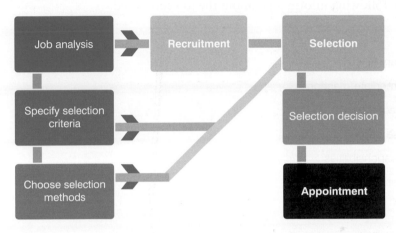

5. The recruitment and selection process is essentially a decision-making process (refer back to Figure 16.1). The first stages deal with defining a problem (the vacancy to be filled), recruitment activities are then used to collect data about alternative solutions (the candidates), selection is about choosing the solution, i.e. the preferred candidate and finally the decision must be implemented, i.e. appointment and induction. Given this and previous examples (e.g. strategy formulation, new product launch, the operations and marketing decisions) it is no wonder that Mintzberg felt that decision-making was possibly the most important of all managerial activities (see Chapter 16, para. 4).

   Activities may be performed by the manager owning the vacancy or HR or may be outsourced. Furthermore, they may be enabled by Internet and database technologies. We discuss each stage of the process in this chapter.

40.1 RECRUITMENT – ATTRACTING THE RIGHT PEOPLE

6. In this stage of the resourcing process a pool of applicants is generated. Recruitment activities may be carried out by operational/line managers, HR or a combination of the two. Typically HR will take the lead, providing a service to the line manager in need of new staff. It is important that such activities are conducted in a non-discriminatory and legal manner that sustains or enhances the good reputation of the organization. The key activities undertaken may include identification of a vacancy and the job analysis, identification of where likely candidates may be found, advertising, documentation (role and **person specification**, advert, application forms, standard letters, etc.) and initial sifting (shortlisting). Each are described in more detail before we consider the selection process.

JOB AND COMPETENCY ANALYSIS

7.   Resourcing starts with the identification of a vacancy and an analysis of the job. Pilbeam and Corbridge (2010: p. 159) refer to this as 'pre-recruitment'. Vacancies can arise through resignation, dismissal, increased workload or reorganization. Yet before proceeding, the case for recruitment should be presented. It will be prudent to ask the following questions: can elements of the job be distributed, eliminated or achieved through alternative means; does the predicted workload justify recruitment and does the filling of the vacancy fit with the HR plan? Such questions need to be considered in the context of the financial aspects of recruitment: the cost to recruit and select, payroll and benefits into the future. Should the case for recruitment be established then job analysis may follow.

8.   Job analysis helps us understand what people do at work. Information about the job role and its associated tasks are used to derive a specification of the knowledge, skills and abilities and other characteristics that are essential or desirable for a person performing the job role. This information helps determine the attributes that are to be assessed in order to make a decision about the suitability of a particular job candidate/applicant. Thus the product (output) of job analysis is a **job description**. The job description usually contains at least the following information about the job concerned:

- Job title

- Job grade/salary level

- Job title of immediate manager

- Number of direct reports

- Overall purpose of the job

- Principal job responsibilities

- Limits of authority

- Job location.

9.   In addition to a job description there is a description of the ideal person to fill the job. The 'candidate', or 'person(nel)' specification, as it is frequently called, is a summary of the knowledge, skills and personal characteristics required of the job holder to carry out the job to an acceptable standard of performance. This is an extremely important feature of the recruitment process, because it sets down a standard by which candidates for interview may be tested. The personal specification typically identifies the physical characteristics of the person, their attainments, qualifications and experience, general intelligence, specific aptitudes and abilities, interests, disposition and motivation. Whereas a job analysis focuses on the work, competency analysis may be described as worker-oriented analysis.

10.   The **competency-based approach** involves the development of a list of abilities and competencies (competency specification) necessary to perform a given job successfully and against which the applicant's performance can be assessed. This approach may be used in conjunction with job analysis or as an alternative to it.

11.   Having analyzed the job, the recruiter must now develop a strategy to promote it. The job description may be used, along with other company documentation to create the job advert. This advert must then be communicated with potential employees. The main approaches used to attract applicants include: advertising, websites, employee referrals, recruitment agencies and professional or educational associations; increasingly, companies are turning to social media to facilitate the process – a matter discussed later in this chapter. The choice of media will depend upon cost, time, equal opportunity and diversity legislation and regulations and the mobility of labour. Typically, adverts contain a specification of requirements, including basic educational requirements and previous relevant experience. The advert should contain information to attract potential applicants but also enable them to make a self-selection decision. The basic principles of an effective job advertisement (i.e. one that attracts sufficient numbers of the right kind of candidates) can be summarized as follows:

- Provide brief, but succinct, details about the position to be filled.

- Provide similar details about the employing organization.

- Provide details of all essential personal requirements.

- Make reference to any desirable personal requirements.

- State the main conditions of employment, especially the salary indicator for the position.

- State to whom the application or enquiry should be directed.

- Present the above information in an attractive form.

12. If an external advertisement has hit the target segment correctly, then only relatively small numbers of applications will be forthcoming, and most of these will be strong candidates for interview, and the difficulty will be to decide who not to invite. If the advertisement has been drawn up rather loosely, or has deliberately sought to attract a large segment of the labour market, then large numbers of applications can be expected, many of whom will be quite unsuitable. Shortlisting arrangements are necessary to select from the total number of applicants those who appear, from their application form, to be worthy of an interview. Pilbeam and Corbridge (2010: p. 157) discuss 'reduction' and the activity of eliminating unsuitable candidates. In drawing up a shortlist, it is common practice to divide the applications into three groups as follows:

1) Very suitable – must be interviewed.

2) Quite suitable – call for interview if insufficient numbers in category (1), or send holding letter.

3) Not suitable – send polite refusal letter, thanking them for their interest in applying.

13. Shortlisting may be a subjective exercise where the line manager or resourcing specialists simply trawl through the pack of received applications and choose the best few, or may be accomplished objectively by scoring applicant information and its relevance to the job. The applicants with the highest scores are deemed suitable for interview. This latter approach lends itself to the application of technology, a matter we revisit later in the chapter. In parallel with the advertising and initial sifting activities, the organization will prepare for the next stage (selection) by specifying selection criteria and choosing selection methods. Such methods will be described next.

40.2 SELECTION

14. The main outputs of recruitment include the outputs from job analysis: the *job description* and *competency specification* and the attributes which act as criteria for decision-making during selection. Selection is very much a two-way process – the candidate is assessing the organization, just as much as the organization is assessing the candidate. The main objective of selection, therefore, is to be able to make an acceptable offer to the candidate who appears, from the evidence obtained, to be the most suitable for the job in question. Selection is primarily about taking steps to assess whether or not the applicant will fit in with the organization, the department and team and the job itself.

15. Selection or assessment methods are used to determine the suitability of applicants for particular jobs. Methods vary in the amount of subjectivity utilized by selectors and in some cases methods may be subject to bias. For example, the bias introduced when attributing all of the characteristics of a person to a single differentiator, i.e. drawing a general impression or making a judgement about an individual on the basis of a single characteristic (such as the school they went to) is termed the **halo or horns effect**. When this is positive it is a 'halo' effect, when negative a 'horns' effect. The perception of a person is formulated on the basis of a single favourable or unfavourable trait or characteristic and tends to shut out other relevant characteristics of that person. Additionally, judging someone on the basis of one's perception of the group to which that person belongs is known as **stereotyping**. Selectors may be trained to overcome such bias. In addition, psychologists work to minimize bias from a range of selection methods that will be discussed next.

SELECTION METHODS

16. The first contact a job applicant has with an organization is usually via a curriculum vitae (CV) or an application form. These documents provide a summary of relevant biographical information such as

education and previous job experience. Application forms are similar to CVs but are organization-led. An application form or a letter of application tells an organization whether or not an applicant is worthy of an interview or a test of some kind. Application forms vary considerably in the way they are set out. Some require prospective candidates to answer routine questions in a form that gives them no opportunity to discuss their motives for applying or to talk about themselves in a general way. Others are very open-ended in their format, and require applicants to expand at some length on themselves and on how they see the job. In-between the two forms are several compromise versions, which aim to establish some kind of balance between closed and open questions. The answers to the closed questions supply the organization with routine information in a standardized form; the answers to the open questions provide a clue to the motives, personality and communication skills of the applicants.

17.   The selection interview, be it face-to-face, telephone, Skype, conference or other, is far and away the most common technique used for selection purposes. Unlike most other management techniques, it is employed as much by amateurs as by professionals. Few managers and supervisors carry out selection interviews regularly; many of them have received no formal training in the technique either, so it is not surprising to learn that research has shown that such interviews are frequently neither reliable nor valid. The measure of the reliability of an interview is the extent to which conclusions about candidates are shared by different interviewers; the measure of the validity of an interview is the extent to which it does measure what it is supposed to measure, i.e. the suitability of a particular candidate for a particular job. The main reasons why so many poor interviews are carried out are often associated with time, cost and limited information but include: (1) lack of training in interviewing technique, (2) lack of adequate preparation for an interview, (3) lack of time allocated to the interview itself and (4) the use of a sole interviewer rather than two or more. Such 'practical' constraints are likely to limit the quality of any resultant decision.

18.   Much has been written about selection interviewing, but most of the points made can be condensed into the following guide to good practice (Figure 40.2). This highlights the sort of issues which busy managers need to know about if they are to make optimum use of their own, and the candidates', time in the short period available for the interview. There are a few points arising from the guide which ought to be stressed. The first is the question of preparation. As with so many tasks, the better the preparation, the better the final result. It is very important to be properly prepared before an interview. It enables the interviewer to feel confident in themselves about their key role in the process, and enables them to exploit to the full the information provided by the candidate. It also helps to minimize embarrassment caused by constant interruptions, inadequate accommodation and other practical difficulties.

19.   Questioning plays a vital role in a selection interview, as it is the primary means by which information is obtained from the candidate at the time. Questions have been categorized in a number of different ways. There may be closed and open questions. The major differences between them are as follows: (1) closed questions are questions which require a specific answer or a yes/no response. For example: 'how many people were you responsible for in your previous job?' (specific) and (2) open questions require a person to reflect or elaborate on a particular point in their own way. An example of an open question is, 'what is it that attracts you about this job?' Open questions invariably begin with what? how? or why? Closed questions check information the candidate has already partly supplied on the application form, and to redirect the interview if the candidate is talking too much and/or veering off the point. Open questions tend to be employed once the interview is underway, with the object of allowing the candidate to demonstrate their knowledge and skills to the interviewer.

20.   Interview questions may also be categorized as behavioural, competency or situational. Behavioural interviews ask questions based upon key job requirements and invite interviewees to describe past experiences of performing such tasks; for example: describe a recent project that involved you working as part of a team. Competency-based interviews or questions are similar to behavioural but focus on a specific competency such as teamworking, problem-solving or leadership, etc. Both behavioural and competency-based interviews and questions focus on past behaviour. Situational interviews or questions are used to evaluate how a candidate might respond to a future challenge. The candidate may be given a scenario and asked what they would do in that situation.

21.   Interviews may be conducted on a one-to-one basis, but a two-to-one situation is also widely favoured, and there is still a lot of support for panel interviews, especially in the public services. In a two-to-one situation, the two interviewers usually agree amongst themselves as to how they will share the questioning and

FIGURE 40.2 Selection interviewing – guide to good practice

Be Prepared	Obtain available information, e.g. job details, candidate specification and application form. Arrange interview room. Ensure no interruptions. Plan the interview.
Welcome the Candidate	After initial courtesies, thank candidate for coming. Explain briefly what procedure you propose to adopt for the interview. Commence by asking relatively easy and non-threatening question.
Encourage Candidate to Talk	Ask open-ended questions. Prompt where necessary. Indicate that you are listening. Briefly develop points of interest raised by candidate.
Control the Interview	Direct your questions along the lines that will achieve your objectives. Tactfully, but firmly, clamp down on the over-talkative candidate. Do not get too involved in particular issues just because of your own interests. Keep an eye on the time.
Supply Necessary Information	Briefly add to information already made available to candidate. Answer candidate's questions. Inform candidate of the next steps in the selection procedure.
Close Interview	Thank candidate for his/her responses to your questions. Exchange final courtesies.
Final Steps	Write up your notes about the candidate. Grade, or rank, him/her for suitability. Operate administrative procedures regarding notifications etc.

information supplying during the interview. Frequently, in medium and large organizations, one of the two organizational representatives is an HR specialist, and the other is the (operational) 'client', seeking to fill the vacancy in question. The advantages of this type of interview are that whilst one interviewer is asking a question, or pursuing a point, the other can observe the candidate's reactions and make an independent evaluation of this response; and that each interviewer can specialize in his own areas of interest in the selection process, the 'client' concentrating on technical capability and the ability to fit into his team and the personnel member concentrating on the wider aspects of having such a person as an employee of the organization. The panel interview is an altogether different prospect for a candidate. In this case the individual candidate is faced by several interviewers. In the case of a panel interview, it is of greatest importance to decide who is going to ask which questions, and how the panel is to be chaired.

22.   In the final stage of the interview the candidate may be provided with any routine information about conditions of service and invited to ask questions. Taken as a whole, interviews are most useful for assessing the personal qualities of an individual. They help to answer questions such as 'is this candidate likely to be able

to fit into our team or our environment?' and 'has this particular candidate any special personal characteristics which give them an advantage over rivals?' Interviews are not so useful for assessing technical ability or the value of past experience. This is one of the reasons why organizations may consider using psychological tests to supplement information gained during interviews.

PSYCHOLOGICAL TESTS

23.   Psychological tests, or selection tests as they are often called, are standardized tests designed to provide a relatively objective measure of certain human characteristics by sampling human behaviour. Such tests tend to fall into four categories as follows:

- intelligence

- aptitude

- attainment, and

- personality tests.

24.   Checks for validity are designed to ensure that any given test measures what it sets out to measure, e.g. an intelligence test should be able to measure intelligence, and a manual dexterity test should be able to measure manual dexterity. Checks for reliability are designed to ensure that tests produce consistent results in terms of what they set out to measure. Thus, if a test which is carried out on an individual at a particular point in time is repeated, the results should be similar. The different categories of tests are as follows:

- **Intelligence tests**

  These tests are designed to measure thinking abilities. It is enough for our purposes to understand that general intelligence can be manifested by verbal, spatial or numerical ability, or a combination of these. Popular tests in use for personnel selection are often composed of several different sections, each of which aims to test candidates on the key ability areas to which we have just referred.

- **Aptitude tests**

  These are basically tests of innate skills. They are widely used to obtain information about such skills as mechanical ability, clerical and numerical ability and manual dexterity.

- **Attainment tests**

  These tests measure the depth of knowledge or grasp of skills which have been learned in the past – usually at school or college. Typical attainment tests are those which measure typing abilities, spelling ability and mental arithmetic, for example.

- **Personality tests**

  Where they are employed in work situations, they usually take the form of personality inventories – lists of multiple-choice questions in response to theoretical situations posed by the test designers – or of projection tests – where the candidate is required to describe a series of vague pictures or a series of inkblots. The aim of personality tests is to identify an individual's principal personality traits or dimensions, e.g. introverted or extroverted, sociable or isolated, etc.

25.   Psychological tests can provide useful additional or confirming information about a candidate for a position. They can supplement the information obtained from application forms and from interviews, and are particularly useful where objective information would be illuminating. Thus far we have described several assessment methods used in selection. Some organizations make use of assessment centres to provide information on candidates for jobs. They consist of multiple evaluations including job-related simulations, interviews and psychological tests. The strength of assessment centres is in the richness of the information they produce on candidates.

SOCIAL RECRUITMENT AND THE USE OF TECHNOLOGY IN ASSESSMENT

26. In this section we give brief consideration to the changing ways of searching for talent. With the emergence of the Internet and social media more specifically, new approaches have entered the sphere of recruitment. In the opening vignette, the CIPD's Resourcing and Talent Planning survey produced in partnership with Hays, we noted that organizations were more likely to have increased recruitment spend on social and professional networking sites. Social network sites (SNS) utilize Internet-based methods by which individuals and organizations can communicate with each other. Organizations are increasingly recognizing that social media has the potential to facilitate many aspects of engagement and communication with employees, potential recruits, customers and a range of stakeholders. Social media is based on informal interactions. In broad terms, social media is online technology for social interaction. This is in contrast with traditional media in which content is broadcast en masse, typically by a single organization.

27. Social media potentially offers speed, efficiency and the ability to target and attract specific, particularly suitable candidates in the recruitment process – the practice known as '**social recruitment**'. Examples of SNS and tools include blogs, Facebook, LinkedIn, podcast, Twitter, MySpace, etc. Thus social media is a broad category, encompassing practices such as podcasting, blogging, text messaging, Internet videos, and HR email marketing, which are some of the more widespread applications used in recruitment.

28. Early moves into online recruitment were initially the virtual equivalent of a traditional 'jobs board' that might publicize vacancies in employment offices or newspapers. However, this approach is quickly being superseded; following the idea of 'Web 2.0', the new emphasis for on-line recruitment has been on fostering interactive platforms, particularly via SNS. Companies are increasingly making use of social media at different stages of the recruitment process (see Figure 40.3), for example as a means to attract potential employees to their corporate recruitment website or more generally to foster a positive company image among the wider public. However, at present, social media tools and techniques are not a direct replacement for traditional hiring processes, but rather a supplement to them.

FIGURE 40.3 Social recruitment

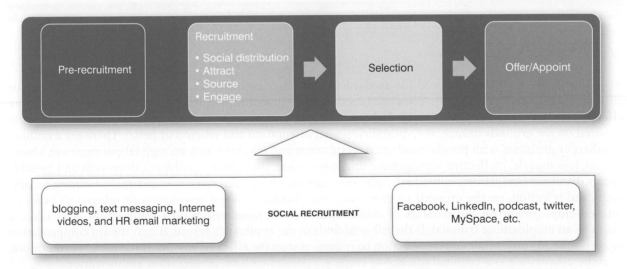

29. There are a wide range of benefits associated with using social media in recruitment, based largely on cost savings, increasing the pool of applicants reached, and being able to target recruitment at specific groups of potential candidates. There are also issues surrounding the accuracy of the information gained by the use of social media tools – there is no guarantee the information that individuals, or others, post on their SNS is accurate. Given the range of issues, one might reasonably expect organizations which are currently using social media as part of their recruitment strategies to have introduced some form of policy

in this area. There are also issues around the depth of the applicant pool that social media tools can access, giving rise to potential problems around diversity and discrimination, particularly in terms of reaching older candidates and those who are not as comfortable with using computers. This means that there are a number of legal aspects that employers should consider when thinking about using social media tools for recruitment. Furthermore, because social media tools tend to encourage fast and direct communication between individuals one might reasonably question whether their use signals a step-change for the recruitment practices within organizations.

30.   There are also a range of technologies to enable the 'testing' process. Databases and the Internet have provided an opportunity for organizations to process applications and conduct selection tests remotely. Multinationals, in particular, can benefit from 'e-testing' of new recruits, or promotion prospects, without having to incur all the costs involved in bringing individual candidates into a recruitment centre or HR office. Using the Internet it is possible to create interactive application forms, provide richer information about the job to applicants and request applicant information in a standard format. Today it is quite common for larger organizations to receive application forms and a CV (and other biodata) electronically. Information provided by the applicant can then be manipulated by software and a score of fit with the job calculated automatically. Scores may then be used to shortlist candidates. The advantages and disadvantages of e-testing can be summarized as follows:

Advantages	Disadvantages
– Reduction in costs of organizing tests.	– Lack of control over the test environment.
– Flexibility of timing of tests.	– Difficulty in ensuring consistency of treatment for all candidates.
– Faster scoring of test results.	
– Convenience and privacy for test.	– Possibility of candidates getting unauthorized help in responding to questions.
	– No immediate advice or support available to candidates who may be having difficulties understanding what they are being asked to do.
	– Possible lack of security of personal data.

FAIRNESS IN SELECTION

31.   Earlier we discussed the need for assessment and selection to be reliable and valid. It should also be ethical and conform to legal requirements. Good practice in recruitment and selection can result in a more effective, better motivated workforce. Labour turnover and absence can be reduced and discrimination avoided on the grounds of race, sex, disability, sexual orientation and religion or belief. There are a number of inherent problems with poorly-conducted recruitment and selection such as: high labour turnover, absenteeism, low morale, ineffective management and supervision, disciplinary problems, dismissals and possible unfair dismissal complaints. Individuals, who consider they have been discriminated against during recruitment and selection, on the grounds of their race, sex, disability, sexual orientation or religion or belief or refused employment on the grounds of membership or non-membership of a trade union, may make a claim to an employment tribunal. If the tribunal finds in the applicant's favour, it may award compensation or recommend some other course of action to reduce or stop the effect of any discrimination. Furthermore, in some countries it is a criminal offence to employ a person with no immigration authorization.

32.   Bratton and Gold (2012) discuss the legal context for the resourcing process, noting the importance of UK legislation and directives from the European Union. In particular they discuss the Data Protection Act (ensuring accuracy and protection of stored personal data, etc.), the Human Rights Act, Sex Discrimination Act, the Equality Act, the Race Relations Act, the Disability Discrimination Act, the Equal Pay Act and various other regulations. Collectively, this has made employment law something of a minefield. In general, it is the role of the HR Department to bring organizational resourcing practices in line with the provisions of the law.

33.   The Equality Act (2010) ensures consistency in what is needed to make the workplace a fair environment and to comply with the law. The Act covers the same groups that were protected by existing equality legislation – age, disability, gender reassignment, race, religion or belief, sex, sexual orientation, marriage and civil partnership and pregnancy and maternity – but extends some protections to groups not previously covered, and also strengthens particular aspects of equality law.

34.   Whilst it is advisable to seek legal guidance, the following checklist should help assure that recruitment and selection activities are performed in a legal and non-discriminatory manner:

- Create and adopt a resourcing (recruitment and selection) policy.

- Ensure interviewers are aware of the recruitment policy and are appropriately trained.

- Create and adopt an effective equal opportunities policy and approach.

- Use the person specification to avoid inadvertent discrimination.

- Consider whether an existing employee could be trained to do the job.

- Consider whether the work could be done by part-timers, job-sharers or home-based workers.

- The application form should only ask for information relevant to the job.

- Consider using a variety of methods to select the best candidate.

- When carrying out interviews, ensure that 'open-ended' questions are asked but do not ask questions which may be considered discriminatory.

- Keep all notes, including any rough jottings made during the interview – be prepared to give reasons for rejection to unsuccessful candidates who make a request.

35.   Approaches to recruitment vary worldwide. Variance may be determined by culture, law, government policy and other factors. Mistakes may be avoided when working to a checklist of recruitment activities, designed to minimize errors and thus avoid damaging the organization's image externally and HR/Personnel's reputation internally. A checklist helps to ensure a rational and logical approach to the recruitment of employees throughout the organization. Questions to be considered:

- Has the vacancy been agreed by the responsible manager?

- Is there an up-to-date job description for the vacant position?

- What are the conditions of employment (salary, hours, holidays, etc.) for the vacant position?

- Has a candidate specification been prepared?

- Has a notice of the vacancy been circulated internally?

- Has a job advertisement been agreed?

- Have details of the vacancy been forwarded to relevant agencies?

- Do all potential candidates (internal or external) know where to apply and in what form?

- What arrangements have been made for drawing up a shortlist of candidates?

- Have the interviewing arrangements been agreed, and have shortlisted candidates been informed?

- Have unsuitable candidates or candidates held in reserve, been informed of their position?

- Have offer letters been agreed and despatched to successful candidates?

- Have references been taken up, where necessary?

- Have suitable rejection letters been sent to unsuccessful shortlisted candidates, thanking them for their attendance?

– Have all replies to offer letters been accounted for?

– Have the necessary procedures for placement, induction and follow-up of successful candidates been implemented?

40.3 APPOINTMENT

36.   The final stage of the resourcing process should be the identification of the chosen applicants. Earlier we identified references as one form of selection method. Some organizations take up references prior to interview. However this can be time-consuming and costly, particularly as the majority will never be utilized. For this reason, many organizations take up references once the applicant has been chosen. References are normally obtained from the current or previous employer and the job offer may be made subject to satisfactory references.

JOB OFFER AND CONTRACT OF EMPLOYMENT

37.   Normally, the applicant is contacted with a formal offer of employment; a starting date is negotiated should this be accepted. The contract of employment is usually a written document that seeks to establish the basis of the working arrangements between employer and employee. A contract is only formed when an offer is made and accepted and a consideration has exchanged (Martin, 2010). It is important to note that a contract of employment does not have to be written to exist. It is also important to recognize the totality of a contract of employment will include things that are 'custom and practice' within the organization; elements from the law; and agreements with trade unions. In addition to the formal contract of employment, managers should also be mindful of the psychological contract – the unspoken and unwritten expectation that both parties have in relation to the role and responsibilities of each other (refer back to previous chapter).

CONTINGENCY PLANS

38.   In some cases, the preferred applicant may reject the job offer. In such cases, the organization may choose to offer the job to an applicant who narrowly missed out, may decide to repeat the recruitment process or withdraw the vacancy. When offering the job to the next preferred applicant, the organization should take steps to avoid that applicant perceiving they were 'second best'. Of course there are many HR related activities that follow the resourcing process. There is a need to induct the new employee and embark upon various strategies to retain them. Such activities will be explored in the following chapters.

CONCLUSION

39.   In this chapter we described the resourcing process in terms of recruitment, selection and appointment. Key recruitment activities include identification of a vacancy and the job analysis, identification of where likely candidates may be found, advertising, documentation and initial sifting. Many of the outputs from the recruitment sub-process form inputs to the selection process which aims to identify, from those coming forward, the individual(s) most likely to fulfil the requirements of the organization. The cornerstone of effective selection is the job analysis which defines the assessment criteria. Selection processes are designed on the assumption that there are job relevant individual differences between people, which can be assessed. A range of selection methods were described and the need for fairness argued. The output of the selection process is the identification of the chosen applicants. A job offer is made and an employment contract issued and signed. At this point, other aspects of the HR system associated with induction and employee retention are employed.

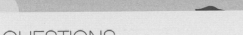

QUESTIONS

1   Highlight the difference between recruitment and selection – what is the selection process really about?

2   Discuss the role of personality measurement in the recruitment process: should a candidate's personality trait/scores be used to select/deselect them? Do you believe that personality can be measured? How helpful is personality assessment in enabling a manager to make predictions about a potential employee's future job performance? How valuable is personality assessment in enabling a career guidance counsellor to advise clients effectively on suitable and unsuitable career options?

3   Identify and describe the two main HR management processes used to attract qualified employees.

4   Identify and discuss, in sequence, the key activities involved in recruiting.

5   Discuss the purpose of the key activities involved in selecting workers and the devices used in selection.

6   The interview is a common method used to fill vacancies within the organization. With reference to the formal and informal, identify what is meant by the selection interview. You should also comment on the function of the interview.

7   Evaluate the role of technology in recruitment and selection.

8   Discuss the importance of fairness in selection and list typical activities which may be performed to ensure that recruitment and selection is conducted in a legal and non-discriminatory manner.

USEFUL WEBSITES

ACAS website **www.acas.org.uk** – templates and checklists – see Hiring new staff
The Equalities and Human Rights Commission **www.equalityhumanrights.com**

DTI Factsheets **www.dti.org.uk/publications**
Assessment Centres **www.assessmentcenters.org** – resources for the use of assessment centres

REFERENCES

Bratton, J. and Gold, J. (2012) *Human Resource Management Theory and Practice*, 5th edn, Palgrave Macmillan.
Pilbeam, S. and Corbridge, M. (2010) *People Resourcing and Talent Planning: HRM in Practice*, 4th edn, Financial Times Press.

Martin, J. (2010) *Key Concepts in Human Resource Management*, Sage.

CHAPTER 41
PERFORMANCE MANAGEMENT AND HUMAN RESOURCE DEVELOPMENT

Key Concepts

- Human resource development (HRD)
- Leadership and management development (LMD)
- Performance appraisal
- Performance management (PM)
- Performance management system (PMS)

Learning Outcomes Having read this chapter, you should be able to:

- clarify the nature and purpose of performance management and performance appraisal
- identify key elements of the appraisal form and explain the appraisal process
- understand the link between HRD, learning, training and development, and strategy
- review the role of learning, training and development activities within the organization
- discuss how learning and training needs are identified
- discuss how organizations may develop the capabilities of current or future managers (management development methods).

1. **Performance management** (PM) includes activities which ensure that goals are consistently being met in an effective and efficient manner. We can discuss the construct in terms of Rudyard Kipling's six honest serving men '(they taught me all I knew); their names are What and Why and When and How and Where and Who'. The Five Ws and one H are questions whose answers are considered basic in information-gathering. Returning to PM, the focus may be on the organization, a department, employee ('who') or even a particular process. However, in this chapter we focus on the individual employee. PM is a process, see Figure 41.1, used

FIGURE 41.1 The performance management process

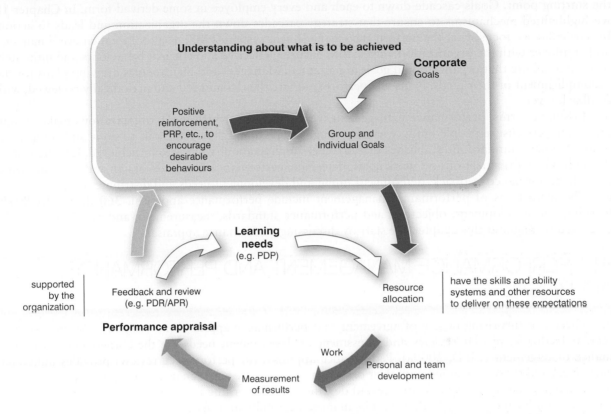

by organizations to align their resources, systems and people to strategic objectives (the 'why'). To that end it is concerned with making strategy happen throughout the organization. It involves managing both behaviour (the 'how') and results (the 'what') as a continuous process; thus the 'when' should be ongoing.

2. Managing employee performance and aligning their objectives facilitates the effective delivery of strategic and operational goals, a matter at the heart of HRM and its 'new' strategic orientation (refer back to Chapter 39); it is one of the major approaches to achieve high levels of organizational performance. According to the CIPD, performance management is a holistic process, bringing together many of the elements that make up the successful practice of people management including, in particular, learning and development (discussed later). It establishes shared understanding about what is to be achieved and is an approach to leading and developing people which will ensure that it is achieved.

3. Increasing emphasis on talent management has led many organizations to redefine PM, aligning it to the need to identify, nurture and retain employees who have a disproportionate impact on organizational performance. PM[1] comprises measurement, feedback and **positive reinforcement** and is also conceived as a tool to ensure that managers manage effectively – as part of which they ensure that the people or teams they manage:

- know and understand what is expected of them
- have the skills and ability to deliver on these expectations
- are supported by the organization in developing the capacity to meet these expectations
- are given feedback on their performance
- have the opportunity to discuss and contribute to individual and team aims and objectives.

[1] CIPD (2014), 'Performance management: an overview' Factsheet, Revised May 2013, available at **http://www.cipd.co.uk/ hr-resources/factsheets/performance-management-overview.aspx** accessed 19 April 2014.

4.   As a continuous process (Figure 41.1) organizations formulate corporate strategic goals which provide the starting point. Goals cascade down to each and every employee in some derived form. In Chapter 18 we highlighted mechanisms to ensure that strategy cascades down the organization and leads to action. In particular we focused on the performance management system (PMS) as a tool to align every manager and employee with the organization's goals, thus ensuring effective and efficient behaviours and ultimately helping to assure that organizational goals are attained. Managers and their reports draw up plans for the accomplishment of their goals. Plans and performance are then monitored and periodically reviewed, with feedback given.

5.   In simple terms, performance management is the means by which many organizations make certain that managers ensure people know what they ought to be doing, have the skills to do it and complete it to an adequate standard. It establishes shared understanding about what is to be achieved. It is the system through which organizations set work goals, determine performance standards, assign and evaluate work, provide performance feedback, determine training and development needs and distribute rewards.

6.   The main tools of performance management include performance appraisal, 360 degree feedback, learning and development, objectives and performance standards, measurement, and pay. These will be discussed throughout this chapter. We start by discussing performance appraisal.

41.1 PERFORMANCE MANAGEMENT AND PERFORMANCE APPRAISAL

7.   There is a surprising degree of agreement that **performance appraisal** (assessment), objective-setting, regular feedback, regular reviews and assessment of development needs are the cornerstones of performance management (CIPD, 2009a). Performance appraisal (or performance review) provides individual employees and those concerned with their performance, typically line managers, the opportunity to engage in a discussion about their performance and development. According to HRM philosophy, employees are an important business resource that must be managed carefully in order to maximize return on investment and achieve business objectives. In recent years, performance management and appraisal have become key features of an organization's drive towards achieving high performance and thus competitive advantage.

8.   Performance management has existed in the language of HR and people management since the 1980s. The underlying assumption of PM is that individual performance can be raised through a focus on setting and monitoring goals and aligning development and reward to individual aspirations and potential to grow and develop new skills. PM assumes that by raising individual levels of performance, organizational performance will also improve. Thus HRM aligns people strategies with business strategies by designing **performance assessment** systems which identify, develop and reward talent to achieve business objectives. The CIPD (2009b) tracked the evolution of PM since the early 1990s from a heavily bureaucratized procedure focused on objective-setting or merit rating, to a more wide-reaching and inclusive process, integrated with other related practices such as career management, talent management and development.

9.   Traditionally performance appraisal systems have provided a formalized process to review employee performance (Torrington et al., 2009). They tend to be centrally designed, usually by the HR function, requiring each line manager to appraise the performance of each of their employees, usually once a year. What is being appraised varies and may cover personality, behaviour or job performance, with measures being either quantitative or qualitative. Criteria such as the achievement of objectives, customer care, creativity, quality, flexibility, competence, productivity, teamwork may all feature in the process. Furthermore performance information may come from a variety of sources (different stakeholders and systems). Consequently every **performance management system** is different, with some being more effective than others.

10.   Traditional appraisals rate individuals on a list of qualities, primarily work-related attitudes and personality traits. They are used to ensure an individual's performance is contributing to business goals. Performance management is an ongoing or continuous process whilst performance appraisal is done at discrete time intervals. Performance appraisal is the systematic description of an employee's job-relevant strengths and weaknesses. Appraisal provides an analysis of a person's overall capabilities and potential, allowing informed decisions to be made in the process of engaging and managing (controlling) employees.

There are several reasons why appraisals are carried out in organizations. These may be summarized as follows, to:

- identify an individual's current level of job performance

- identify employee strengths and weaknesses

- enable employees to improve their performance

- provide a basis for rewarding employees in relation to their contribution to organizational goals

- motivate individuals

- identify training and development needs

- identify potential performance, and

- provide information for succession planning.

DEFINING AND MEASURING WORK PERFORMANCE

11.   For performance to be managed effectively, individuals must know the basis on which their performance will be measured – measures should be transparent. Performance assessment and appraisal necessitates a definition for performance and a means to measure it. In order to make comparisons between employees and to make the assessment process more valid and reliable, a number of practitioners seek to measure underlying components (job performance factors/competencies) of work performance that are common to all work roles. For example, Bartram (2005) listed eight 'great' factors of job performance:

Leading and deciding – takes control and exercises leadership. Initiates action, gives direction and takes responsibility.

Supporting and cooperating – supports others and shows respect and positive regard for them in social situations; puts people first, working effectively with individuals and teams, clients and staff; and behaves consistently with clear personal values that complement those of the organization.

Interacting and presenting – communicates and networks effectively; persuades and influences others successfully; and relates to others in a confident, relaxed manner.

Analyzing and interpreting – shows evidence of clear analytical thinking; gets to the heart of complex problems and issues; and applies own expertise effectively. Communicates well in writing.

Creating and conceptualizing – works well in situations requiring openness to new ideas and experiences; handles situations and problems with innovation and creativity; and thinks broadly and strategically.

Organizing and executing – plans ahead and works in a systematic and organized way; follows directions and procedures; and focuses on customer satisfaction and delivers a quality service or product to the agreed standards.

Adapting and coping – adapts and responds well to change; manages pressure effectively and copes well with setbacks.

Enterprising and performing – focuses on results and achieving personal work objectives; shows an understanding of business, commerce and finance; and seeks opportunities for self-development and career advancement.

12.   Other researchers and practitioners have generated similar lists, considering factors such as core task proficiency, demonstrated effort, teamwork and others. Our ability to define work performance is important because it impacts upon how it is measured and assessed. Performance data may derive from the judgements of the managers and other stakeholders who have contact with the employee or from objective data such as production data, e.g. the total number of sales made or revenue generated, etc. The most common form of performance data is still derived from managers' direct or indirect observation of employees in the workplace. Aside from direct observation, recently there has been an upsurge in the use of electronic methods, common in call centre environments.

13.   Both objective and subjective assessment data have their strengths and weaknesses. Objective/production data may be seen as fair in that it is difficult to dispute it but such data often measure not only the performance of the employee concerned but also other factors outside of their control. It does not measure behaviour but rather the outcomes of behaviour. Consequently, subjective data are often used. Despite this, many problems are typically reported when evaluating judgement as a performance assessment technique. Judgements which are subject to bias are often referred to as halos and horns. A considerable amount of work has been done on judgemental biases in rating and the tendency for managers to be lenient or severe in their assessments. Many assessors avoid using the high and low extremes of rating scales (central tendency) treating everybody as average. This fails to discriminate, making the process meaningless.

APPRAISAL PROCESS

14.   Performance appraisal involves two distinct processes: (1) observation and (2) judgement (Cascio and Aguinis, 2010). Observation processes include the perception and recall of specific behavioural events whilst judgement processes include the categorization, integration and evaluation of information. When observing and judging their employees, managers must be aware of the work and personal requirements of a particular job (refer back to job analysis), the required performance standard and must then describe the job-relevant strengths and weaknesses of each employee.

15.   At its simplest, the appraisal process can be depicted as in Figure 41.2. Any systematic approach to performance appraisal will include the completion of an appropriate appraisal form. This preparatory stage will be followed by an interview/review, in which the manager discusses progress with the employee. The result of the review is some form of agreed action. The action generally materializes in the shape of a personal development or job improvement plan, promotion to another job or to a salary increase, for example.

FIGURE 41.2 The appraisal process

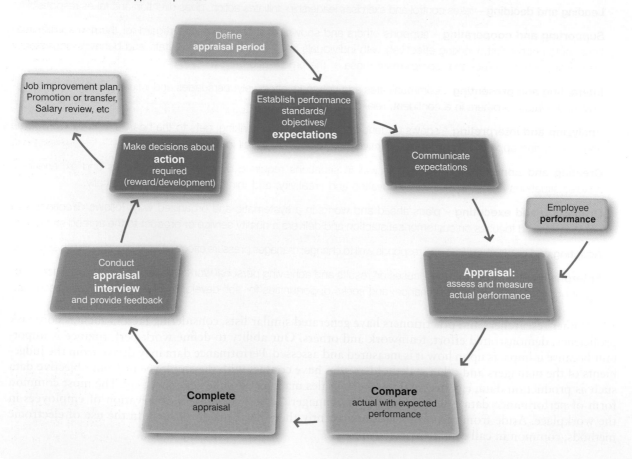

16.   Most appraisals are conducted by line managers on the employees who report to them, and so an element of formal authority is invariably present in the appraisal interview. However, in recent years, so-called 360° appraisals have been introduced by organizations keen to improve the appraisal process. A variety of stakeholders are consulted, so that appraisal becomes all-round rather than just top-down.

APPRAISAL FORMS

17.   An important component of the performance assessment stage is the use of appraisal forms – instruments used to document and evaluate performance. Appraisal forms usually include a combination of the following components: (1) employee information, job title, department, key dates, etc., (2) objectives, weighted in terms of importance (if a result approach has been adopted) and the extent to which they have been achieved, (3) competencies and indicators (if a behavioural approach has been adopted), (4) major achievements and contributions, (5) developmental achievements, i.e. the extent to which the employee has met developmental goals during the review period, (6) developmental needs, (7) stakeholder input, (8) employee comments and (9) signatures. There is no such thing as a universally correct appraisal form. However, generally desirable features include simplicity, relevancy, descriptiveness (include evidence and enable understanding by parties not present in the interview), adaptable, comprehensive, clearly defined competencies (where applicable) and has both a past and a future orientation.

18.   Appraisal criteria are generally either personality (behaviour) or results-oriented. Within each of these orientations appraisers are still required to 'measure' individual performance. They do so by using one or more scales for rating performance. Performance ratings may be intentionally or unintentionally distorted or inaccurate. It is important to understand how and why assessors may distort ratings. Assessors may provide inflated or deflated ratings. They may inflate ratings in order to maximize an employee's reward, encourage and motivate them or they may inflate ratings in order to avoid confrontation, make themselves look good or to get the employee promoted out of the manager's team. In some cases, the assessor may deflate ratings in order to send a message to or shock the employee.

19.   Thus the rating process may be influenced by emotions, hidden agendas and politics. Distorted ratings are clearly damaging for the organization's PMS and the HR professional will take steps to prevent conscious distortion of ratings. They will seek to train and make managers accountable for their ratings. It is important that assessors understand the company's reasons for implementing the PMS, how to collect performance information, how to minimize rating errors, use the appraisal form and manage the process.

20.   After the form has been completed, there is usually a need to compute an overall performance score. This enables subsequent decisions based on performance. There are two main methods used to compute the overall performance score: judgemental and mechanical (objective/ calculated). In the case of the former, the assessor will formulate an overall summary and in the case of the latter, category scores are simply added up; in many cases, category scores will be weighted to reflect the relative importance of each performance by dimension measured. Clearly the objective approach is more defensible and is less likely to be affected by assessor bias.

21.   Organizations must determine the period of time that should be included in the appraisal form – in many companies this will be a yearly activity; other companies may appraise employees more frequently, for example 6-monthly or quarterly. Organizations will also specify the best time to complete the reviews and this will normally be linked to the company's financial reporting year or the calendar year. Having considered the appraisal documentation and the validity and reliability of the performance information it contains (see Figure 41.2 'The appraisal process'), we can now turn to the next stage in the process, the appraisal interview/review conducted by the jobholder's manager.

PERFORMANCE APPRAISAL INTERVIEWS, REVIEWS AND EVALUATIONS

22.   A performance review is a fundamental process of the HR practices of an organization. It is a formal discussion as well as a documented process about an employee's development and performance, involving managers and HR. Meetings/interviews are required in order to discuss the performance system and set expectations, discuss self-appraisal, undertake the performance review itself, award and discuss rewards, discuss employee development needs and to set objectives for the following review period. Clearly some

of these tasks may take place together under one meeting; however, a number of organizations prefer to separate out certain tasks and include them in a separate meeting.

23.   The appraisal interview or performance review is the formal face-to-face meeting between the jobholder and their manager at which the information on the appraisal form is discussed and after which certain key decisions are made concerning salary, promotion and development, for example. The manner in which managers approach an appraisal meeting will be strongly influenced by their understanding of the purpose. Appraisal meetings can serve several purposes, to:

- evaluate the employees' recent performance
- formulate development plans
- identify problems and/or examine possible opportunities related to the job
- improve communication
- provide feedback on job performance to the employee
- provide a rationale for salary or performance-related pay reviews
- identify potential performance/possibilities for promotion or transfer, and
- identify training and development needs.

24.   Amongst other things, performance appraisals serve as an employee development tool. Feedback is used to bring about improvements in present performance. However, feedback must be delivered in the appropriate manner if it is to be motivating and encourage desirable behaviours. In addition, effective PM can result in increased employee engagement (Bratton and Gold. 2012: p. 253). In order to make appraisal interviews more effective, managers are encouraged to provide frequent performance feedback to employees and maintain comprehensive records of an employee's performance in their assigned roles. The manager should be trained in performance appraisal techniques and should understand the organization's PMS. They should encourage employees to prepare for appraisal interviews. This will typically mean explaining the appraisal system, categories, process and encouraging the employee to engage in self-appraisal prior to the meeting. During the appraisal interview, the manager should be specific, constructive and an active listener whilst encouraging employee participation. When setting goals for the next assessment period, the manager should be mindful of goal-setting theory (refer back to Chapter 5) and the need for employees to participate in goal-setting.

25.   Performance management is often linked to performance-related pay (PRP) – pay based on merit as assessed by a performance management process. PRP is believed to motivate people in their work, rewarding in a fair and transparent process. Aside from rewarding results and desirable behaviours, one of the key roles of performance appraisal and management is to bring about the modification of employee behaviours. It is important therefore to specify desirable behaviours and to devise intervention strategies that target undesirable behaviours or seek to strengthen desirable behaviours. Various intervention strategies exist and include the use of rewards, training (learning) and development and feedback. We consider learning and development in more detail next.

41.2 TRAINING, LEARNING AND DEVELOPMENT

26.   Employee development is a main route to improved organizational performance. The HR subsystems of learning, training and development help to ensure employees know what to do, why and also *how* to do it. New employees must be provided with the information required to function. They are typically inducted into the organization (see also orientation and on boarding) and may well be provided with initial training. The induction programme aims to make the employee feel welcome, provide them with the basic information they need to function effectively, enable the employee to understand the organization in a broad sense and therefore how their role contributes to organization's success, and socialize the employee into the organizational culture and way of doing things.

27.   Traditionally organizations made greater use of the term training, yet Torrington *et al.* (2009), as is fairly typical, prefer the term learning and development. They suggest there has been a considerable move

in the way that individual development is understood and characterized. They argue that we have moved from identifying training needs to identifying learning needs, 'the implication being that development is owned by the learner with the need rather than by the trainer seeking to satisfy that need'. This has implications for who identifies the needs and the way that those needs are met. Contemporary organizations pursue a partnership approach between the individual and organization. The partnership approach encourages employees to also take responsibility and ownership for their development.

28.   Cureton and Stewart (2014), discuss designing, delivering and evaluating learning and development, having 'reflected on how learning and development has changed in as little as a generation'. Like Torrington *et al.* they note that 'the most obvious change has seen the word training being replaced by learning'. They also suggest that more learning is now delivered at and through work, learning is done on-the-job and near-job as the distinctions between work and learning soften. Finally, they inform us that whilst the practitioner world has retained the title of learning and development, academics have preferred to use the term **human resource development (HRD)**.

29.   Gold *et al.* (2013) ask what HRD is about. Noting it to be a recent and abstract construct with no accepted meaning, they contrast two definitions: (1) organized learning experiences provided by employers, within a specified period of time, to bring about the possibility of performance improvement and/or personal growth and (2) planned interventions in organizational and individual learning processes. The former focuses on employers whilst the latter allows for a broader context. Despite this, they note that 'in professional contexts, the words training and development, are more common and are sometimes combined with learning, especially in job titles'. A key issue associated with HRD is the prospect of improving performance. This point is also emphasized by Price (2007), who defines HRD as a strategic approach to investing in human capital. It draws on other HR processes, including resourcing and performance assessment to identify actual and potential talent. HRD provides a framework for self-development, training programmes and career progression to meet an organization's future skill requirements. Likewise Bratton and Gold (2012: p. 283) see HRD as organized learning experiences to bring about performance improvement.

30.   Thus far we have identified learning and development as a means to enhance performance. Organizations must identify specific learning needs if they are to improve the contributions of individual employees. You may recall from the previous chapter that job analysis defines the tasks (work) and competencies employees need to perform effectively. Organizations use this information, along with performance measurements and review information, to determine learning and training needs. At a basic level, **learning and development** are needed to ensure that (recruited) employees are able to do their jobs well. Learning and development, therefore, are critical activities for ensuring the success of the company (Lepak and Gowan, 2009). However, it is not just new employees who require development. The changing environment results in change to products, equipment, facilities, procedures and the way work is done. Consequently, there is an ongoing need to ensure all employees are able to do their work well and accomplish goals.

31.   Learning, training and development may be considered at many levels within the organization. Strategically, the organization may focus on cultural issues, organizational learning and the **learning organization**; they may seek to align the development with corporate strategy. Of vital importance is the organizational and individual ability to learn – creating a learning climate. Contemporary organizations typically pursue entrepreneurial and innovative cultures in which learning is part of everyday work. Learning, training and development may also be considered at the group, team or individual level. There are a range of stakeholders to consider when addressing developmental needs.

32.   **Performance development reviews (PDR)** may be used to encourage individuals to think about how and in which ways they want to develop. This can lead to the drawing up of a **personal development plan (PDP)** setting out the actions they propose to take to meet their development needs. A 'traditional' term frequently used to describe well-organized training (and development) is **'systematic training'**. Whilst the systematic approach has its merits, rationality and efficiency, Torrington *et al.* (2009: p. 418) suggest it has been less prominent of late. Apart from not having a focus on learning it is somewhat mechanical and sluggish in the face of continual change. Despite this, the model or a modified version, has applicability in today's environment and has not been abandoned by many organizations. The model can be adapted to enable individuals to identify their learning needs and to do so in partnership with the organization.

33.   Learning, training and development needs may arise when a new employee commences work or when a current employee is underperforming (see earlier paragraphs of this chapter). Approaches for analyzing needs are often reactive and problem-centred focusing on employee performance shortfalls. In other cases

there are approaches which consider the needs of the job. In the previous chapter we discussed job analysis and the outputs of this activity, the job descriptions and job specifications that define specific duties and skills can be used to determine training required. When seeking to identify training needs it is typical then to focus on four main information sources:

- organizational-level data (mission, goals, products/services offered)

- job-level data (job descriptions and person specifications)

- individual data (**performance appraisal** data), and

- competence standards.

34.   Once development needs have been identified, learning opportunities can be identified. Figure 41.3 illustrates some of the different methods of on-the-job and off-the-job training, and indicates some of the advantages and disadvantages of each approach.

FIGURE 41.3 Summary of training methods

On-the-job training methods	Advantages	Disadvantages
On-the-job instruction	Relevant; develops trainee-supervisor links	Noise, bustle and pressure of workplace
Coaching	Job-related; develops boss-subordinate relationship	Subject to work pressures; may be done piecemeal
Counselling	Employee needs help and manager provides it	Counselling skills have to be developed
Delegation by boss	Increases scope of job; provides greater motivation	Employees may make mistakes or may fail to achieve task
Secondment	Increases experience of employees; creates new interest	Employee may not succeed in new position
Guided projects/action learning	Increases knowledge and skills in work situation, but under guidance	Finding suitable guides and mentors
Off-the-job training methods	**Advantages**	**Disadvantages**
(A) In-company		
Lectures/talks	Useful for factual information	One-way emphasis; little participation
Group discussions	Useful for generating ideas and solutions	Requires adequate leadership
Role-playing exercises	Useful for developing social skills	Requires careful organizing; giving tactical feedback is not easy
Skills development exercises e.g.: manual operations, communication skills, etc	A safe way to practice key skills	Careful organization required
(B) External		
College courses (long)	Leads to qualification; comprehensive coverage of theory; wide range of teaching methods	Length of training time; not enough practical work
College courses (short)	Supplement in-company training; independent of internal politics	May not meet client needs precisely enough
Consultants/other training organizations	Clients needs given high priority; fills gaps in company provision; good range of teaching methods	Can be expensive; may rely heavily on packages

35.   It is important to note that learning need not be planned. Employees may also learn from their experiences (emergent learning). Learning from experiences or activity was emphasized by Kolb (see the learning cycle) and by Honey and Mumford who described four learning styles: activists, reflectors, theorists and pragmatists.

36.   Internet technologies are used to enable e-learning which may be more cost-efficient, more timely, more flexible and therefore better value for money. e-Learning enables distant learning and learning at a time more convenient for the learner. Learning and training now involves a much wider range of activities which are typically blended to suit the needs of the learner. For many companies the resources placed in learning and development represent a considerable investment in time, money and human resources. This investment needs to be evaluated from time to time to ensure, so far as possible, that it is being deployed wisely.

41.3 LEADERSHIP AND MANAGEMENT DEVELOPMENT (LMD)

37.   Variations in the contexts and situations faced by leaders and managers have made defining **leadership and management development (LMD)** problematic. Where it is believed possible to specify a 'correct' way to lead or manage, LMD may be defined as a planned and deliberate process to help leaders and managers become more effective (Bratton and Gold, 2012: p. 331–3). In other cases it may be considered as a process

FIGURE 41.4 Management development system

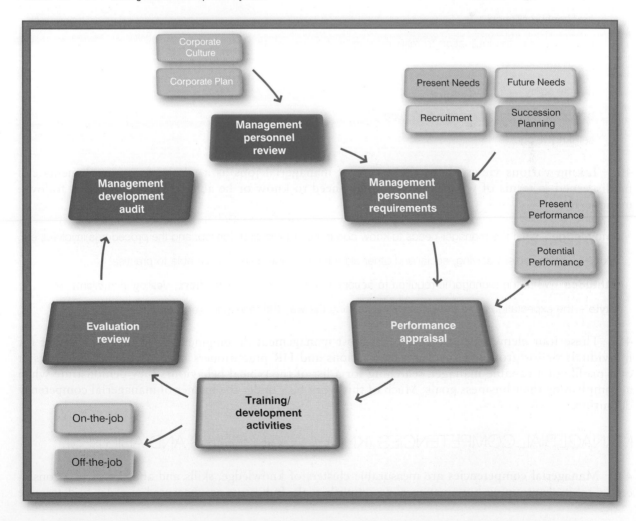

of learning for leaders and managers through recognized opportunities. Much of the following discussion focuses on LMD from the former perspective.

38. **Management development** is a systematic process for ensuring that an organization meets its current and future needs for effective managers; typical features include resourcing reviews (see HR planning), **succession planning**, performance appraisal and development (see figure 41.4). As was highlighted in the previous paragraph, prior to developing a manager we must have some idea about what constitutes a manager, what the managerial function should be and the knowledge skills and abilities (competencies) that are required for an effective managerial performance. We recap on what constitutes a manager before exploring the behaviours attributed to effective and efficient managers. Management development approaches vary according to whether we are dealing with the general or the specific, i.e. generic competencies employed in a range of situations and managerial roles or more technical skills associated with a specific job. The main emphasis here will be on generic competencies.

39. Pedler, Burgoyne and Boydell (2013) list the attributes of 'successful' managers. Their list comprises the following features of an effective manager:

– command of basic facts

– relevant professional knowledge

– continuing sensitivity to events

– analytical, problem-solving, decision-making and judgement-making skills

– social skills and abilities

– emotional resilience

– proactivity, i.e. the inclination to respond purposefully to events

– creativity

– mental agility

– balanced learning habits and skills, and

– self-knowledge.

40. Taking various views about the nature of managerial jobs as a whole, four key elements can be discerned in terms of what managers might need to know or be able to do. These are as follows: managerial,

knowledge – what the manager needs to know about the organization, the job, and the procedures involved, etc.

skills – what problem-solving, social and other skills the manager needs to be able to practise

attitudes – what the manager is required to accept in terms of coping with stress, dealing with clients, etc.

style – the expectations that people have concerning the way the manager exercises leadership.

41. These four elements can be found in most management development programmes, whether for individuals or for groups. However, organizations and HR practitioners have continued their pursuit of a profile of a capable manager, searching for a list of the typical behaviours they demonstrate when accomplishing their business goals. Much of this work falls under the banner of managerial competency definition.

MANAGERIAL COMPETENCIES (KNOWLEDGE, SKILLS AND ABILITIES)

42. **Managerial competencies** are measurable clusters of knowledge, skills and abilities (KSAs) considered vital in determining how managers accomplish goals. Indicators are measured in order to determine

the extent to which the manager possesses a competency. Each indicator is an observable behaviour that provides information about the relevant competency. In other words, the competency is not measured directly, we measure indicators that tell us whether the competency is present or not. An indicator is a behaviour that, if exhibited, suggests that the competency is present. Thus when describing a managerial competency, it is common to first define it and then describe the specific behavioural indicators that can be observed when a manager demonstrates the competency. It is also common to describe specific behaviours that are likely to occur when somebody does not demonstrate a competency.

43.   The Management Standards Centre (MSC) is the standards-setting body for National Occupational Standards (NOS) in management. The NOS for management and leadership are statements of best practice which outline the performance criteria, related skills, knowledge and understanding required to carry out various management and leadership functions effectively. The standards describe the activities/functions of management and leadership at various levels of responsibility and complexity. Therefore, they are relevant to anyone for whom management and leadership is, to a greater or lesser extent, part of their work. This applies to managers and leaders in all sizes and types of organization, and in all industries and sectors. The MSC argue the key purpose of management and leadership is to provide direction, gain commitment, facilitate change and achieve results through the efficient, creative and responsible deployment of people and other resources.

44.   Managers can use the standards to identify and describe the skills they need, and evaluate the skills they already have; employers can use the standards to evaluate the skills already in the workforce, identify skills gaps and plan training and recruitment. They can also be used as an aid to recruitment, selection and employee development. An example of a competency and indicators is shown in Figure 41.5.

FIGURE 41.5 Management standards: elements of performance

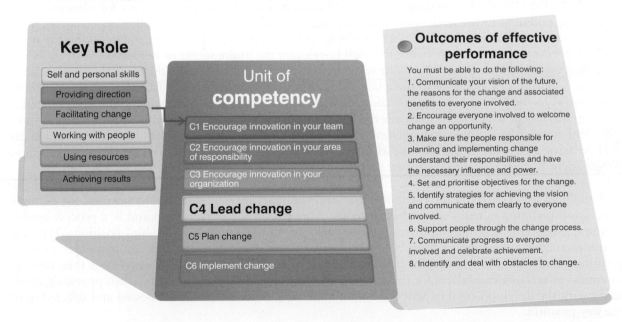

45.   Competencies are also used in the framework for National Vocational Qualifications (NVQs) and Scottish Vocational Qualifications (SVQs). Such frameworks provide qualifications based on required outcomes expected from the performance of a task in any work role, expressed as performance standards with criteria. These describe what competent people in a particular occupation are expected to be able to do. Having spent the past few paragraphs outlining managerial competencies and what managers should be able to do we must now turn our attention to the methods used to develop managers and make them competent in their current and future roles.

MANAGEMENT DEVELOPMENT METHODS

46.   Management development methods include coaching, counselling, project work, mentors, action learning, secondments, development centres, formal training courses, etc. The various methods employed in management development can be placed into four main categories, as follows:

- **Management education**: qualification-bearing courses run by universities or public-sector colleges, the emphasis is on acquiring knowledge and theory

- **Management training**: internal and external courses, off-the-job and focusing on acquiring specific knowledge and relevant job skills

- **Experiential learning**: 'learning by doing'; on-the-job experience usually with guidance from a more senior manager or colleague, and

- **Continuing professional development** (CPD): activities designed to update knowledge and learn new skills flexibly, using one or more of the previous three methods.

The most widely used experiential methods are as follows: coaching/guided experience, delegation, projects, secondments/job rotation. The emphasis in these experiential approaches is on learning whilst doing the job.

SUCCESSION PLANNING AND TALENT MANAGEMENT

47.   All organizations need to be able to find people with the right skills to fill key, leadership and senior management jobs. Management training and development activities alone cannot provide the hands-on experience that is crucial in making future leaders. Succession planning is a process for identifying and developing potential future leaders or senior managers, as well as individuals to fill other business-critical roles. Succession planning programmes typically include the provision of training and development activities and personalized work experience that will be relevant for future senior or key roles.

48.   Succession planning can also assist with the retention of talented individuals, as they are aware of internal opportunities available to them in seeking to progress their careers. Succession planning is therefore central to the internal element of talent management programmes. Succession planning is related to talent management which seeks to ensure the organization has a flow of people capable of meeting the need for talent at every level. Talent management seeks to maximize the contribution from all employees but can also be associated with the attraction, selection, retention, development and career management of those people identified as critical to the future success of the business (Martin, 2010).

49.   A succession plan is basically a plan for identifying who is currently in post and who is available and qualified to take over in the event of retirement, voluntary leaving, dismissal or sickness, for example. Succession planning is really about hiring people from within the organization and is a process used to identify, assess and develop employees systematically to fill higher level (leadership) positions. Typically, senior managers, with support from HR, will identify future senior managerial needs, particularly for key positions, and will specify the competencies required to function in the role. Management then turns its attention to creating candidates for these jobs. This means identifying potential and then providing candidates with the developmental experiences required. Finally, candidates will be assessed and selected to fill the key position.

CONCLUSION

50.   The adoption of a PMS can be seen as an attempt to integrate HRM processes with strategy. An organization's goals (business strategy) are translated ultimately into employee goals, with measurable performance indicators of their achievement. Appraisals are used to ensure an individual's performance is contributing to business goals. Learning and development needs derive from organizational goals, job descriptions and employee performance appraisals.

51. We defined what constituted management and then discussed what a competent manager should be able to do. Managerial competencies are measurable clusters of KSAs that are considered vital in determining how managers accomplish goals. Development techniques and methods such as coaching, counselling, project work, mentors, action learning, secondments, development centres, formal training courses, etc. were identified to develop the manager into a competent manager.

52. PM plays a key role in enhancing organizational performance, by ensuring that all individuals understand what is expected of them and are equipped with the skills and support to achieve this. The process drives *engagement*, a matter we discuss in the next chapter, by ensuring effective communication throughout the organization.

QUESTIONS

1 What advice would you give to an organization eager to implement a new performance appraisal process that is rigorous, fair and objective? In your answer you should explain the appraisal process, identify the typical components of an appraisal form and outline the main purposes of the appraisal interview.

2 Discuss the function and purpose of HRD and expand on your definition of the concept, highlighting key principles.

3 Discuss the four main categories of management development methods.

USEFUL WEBSITES

Learning and Skills Council: **www.lsc.gov.uk**
UK Lifelong Learning: **www.lifelonglearning.co.uk**
UK Department for Business, Innovation and Skills, BIS: **www.bis.gov.uk**
Performance Management & Appraisal Help Centre: **www.performance-appraisals.org**

DirectGov: **www.direct.gov.uk**
CIPD Performance management: **www.cipd.co.uk/subjects/ perfmangmt/general**
The Management Standards Centre: **www.management-standards.org** Standard setting for Management

REFERENCES

Bartram, D. (2005) 'The great eight competencies: a criterion-centric approach to validation', *Journal of Applied Psychology*, 90(6): 1185–1203.

Bratton, J. and Gold, J. (2012) *Human Resource Management Theory and Practice*, 5th edn, Palgrave Macmillan.

Cascio, W. and Aguinis, H. (2010) *Applied Psychology in Human Resource Management International Edition*, 7th edn, Pearson.

CIPD (2009a) 'Performance management in action: current trends and practice', CIPD – Survey report November 2009 – **www.cipd.co.uk.**

CIPD (2009b) *Performance Management: History and Foundations*, CIPD.

Cureton, P. and Stewart, J. (2014) 'Designing, Delivering and Evaluating Learning and Development', in Stewart, J. and Cureton, P. (2014) *Designing, Delivering and Evaluating Learning and Development: Essentials for Practice* (pp. 1–8), London: CIPD.

Gold, J., Holden, R., Iles, P. and Stewart, J. (2013) *Human Resource Development Theory and Practice*, 2nd edn, Palgrave Macmillan.

Lepak, D. and Gowan, M. (2009) *Human Resource Management International Edition*, Upper Saddle River: Pearson Education.

Martin, J. (2010) *Key Concepts in Human Resource Management*, Sage.

Pedler, M., Burgoyne, T. and Boydell, T. (2013) *A Manager's Guide to Self Development*, 6th edn, McGraw Hill.

Price, A. (2007) *Human Resource Management in a Business Context*, 3rd edn, Cengage Learning EMEA.

Torrington, D., Hall, L., Taylor, S. and Atkinson, C. (2009) *Fundamentals of Human Resource Management: Managing People at Work*, Financial Times Press.

CHAPTER 42
THE EMPLOYMENT RELATIONSHIP

Key Concepts

- Conflict and conflict resolution
- Dismissal
- Employee relations
- Employee voice
- Grievance
- Industrial relations
- Mediation
- Pay structure and pay progression
- Reward management

Learning Outcomes
Having read this chapter, you should be able to:

- discuss what is meant by the employment relationship and its importance to organizations
- explain how union–management (industrial) relations may address the collective aspects of the employment relationship
- explain employee voice and identify the mechanisms used to enable it
- discuss the need to protect employees and the role of HR in doing so
- comment on the argument that reward management is central to the effective management of the employment relationship
- evaluate conflict resolution approaches available to organizations and employees
- identify what deems a dismissal fair.

1. We introduced the *employment relationship* in Chapter 39, declaring the nature of the relationship between employees and their employer to be an issue of central importance to HRM. We also noted the employment relationship is important due to its effect on how employees and employers behave from day to day. The employment relationship describes the dynamic, interlocking economic, legal, social and psychological relations that exist between individuals and their work organizations (Bratton and Gold, 2012). It has also been described as a formal and informal relationship between the employing organization and an employee. The informal element

is sometimes referred to as the psychological contract – an undocumented understanding about the nature of employment within the organization. Regarded by neo-classical economists as an exchange of labour for pay, the employment relationship is also a power relationship in which the employer has the formal authority to direct effort towards specific goals, whereas the employee can – informally – frustrate the achievements of those objectives (Price, 2007).

2.   Building successful employment relationships is important and makes good business sense as organizations with good employment relationships tend to be more successful. There are many aspects of the employment relationship which may include:

Employee relations Industrial relations and employment rights Compensation, pay, reward and the minimum wage Managing conflict, disputes and grievance	Employee engagement Flexible working Employee communication Employee voice Discipline Ending the employment relationship	Working hours Holidays and leave Health, security, safety and welfare Absence/attendance management

   In this chapter we explore, at a high level, the topic and aspects listed above, commenting on links to PM (Chapter 41) and the role of HR (Chapter 39). The chapter builds upon and attempts to integrate a number of previous chapters, theories and concepts and is primarily focused on making the reader aware of this wide range of interrelated topics.

42.1 EMPLOYEE RELATIONS: AN OVERVIEW

3.   The term 'employee relations' was conceived as a replacement for the term 'industrial relations' – discussed later. However, according to Bratton and Gold (2012: p. 431), exactly what constitutes employee relations is not explicable. The expression 'employee relations' generally describes all those activities which contribute both formally and informally to the organization of the relationships between employers and their employees. In some instances these relationships are predominantly formalized as a result of collective bargaining between employers and trade unions as to the role, status and working conditions of employees. This aspect of employee relations is often called 'industrial relations'. However, employee relations can refer just as easily to arrangements worked out less formally between local management and their work teams, whether unionized or not. Because of its importance to national economies, employee relations has tended to be the focus of legislation. Thus, procedures such as balloting for possible strike action or the election of union representatives, or for the announcement of redundancies, are contained within legal parameters. Given the many facets to the concept, many scholars describe employee relations as an underlying philosophy, the body of work concerned with maintaining employer–employee relationships.

42.2 INDUSTRIAL RELATIONS

4.   Managing work and people in the workplace includes a collective dimension. Industrial relations concern the processes of regulation and control over the collective aspects of the employment relationship. A recent CIPD report, 'Managing employee relations in difficult times', concluded that dealing with the trade union relationship remains an issue in many workplaces but is not widely seen as problematic. Trade union influence is still an everyday reality for some, but continues to decline across the wider economy. Over the last 30 years in Britain there has been a marked shift in employee relations away from the more combative stance of union-led collective bargaining towards a more unified approach to management–employee relationships. This change has been accompanied by a strengthening of individual rights in the workplace, both in respect of the individual's relationships with management, and in respect of union members' rights vis-a-vis their union. The legal system now acts to support individuals in the workplace as well as collective groups represented by a union. The emphasis now is less on producing joint procedures and rules of behaviour, and more on gaining mutual commitment to organizational success within the framework of the law.

5.   Trade union membership in Britain has fallen quite substantially in recent years; levels reached their peak in 1979 and declined sharply through the 1980s and early 1990s. In 2012, the rate of union membership (union density) for employees in the UK fell to 26 per cent (1 in 4 employees). Nevertheless, trade unions still have an important watchdog role to perform, supported by law, to prevent management from acting in a purely arbitrary fashion. Nowadays it is more likely that groups of employees themselves – as empowered work teams – will contribute to the control of work and its key processes.

6.   Here we consider the relationship of management with employees, through the unions that represent them. Union–management relations address the collective aspects of the employment relationship and focus on the relations between organized employees (represented by a union) and management (Bratton and Gold, 2012). We will discuss the key features of union–management relations. In a non-unionized workplace, managers will typically have greater (unilateral) control and flexibility to impose their thinking upon the workforce. However, where a union is recognized there may be a greater need to negotiate before seeking change. Unions may seek control over employee rewards (such as pay), appraisals, learning and development, etc. Where management accept the legitimacy of trade unions they may move towards management by agreement. In the case of union acceptance, the organization will typically engage in **collective bargaining** as a process to regulate the employment relationship, to support their strategy.

7.   There are four notable types of trade union: (1) general unions (represent workers from all industries and companies, rather than just one organization or a particular sector), (2) craft unions (seeks to unify workers in a particular industry along the lines of the particular craft or trade in which they work), (3) industrial unions (workers in the same industry are organized into the same union – regardless of skill or trade) and (4) white-collar unions (a non-manual workers' union covering those in clerical and administrative jobs). Unions may also be affiliated to a larger organization that negotiates with the government, for example the Trades Union Congress (TUC) in the UK. Most trade unions (approximately 50–60 unions, representing over 6 million people) are affiliated to the TUC, which is the central confederation of unions in Britain. With the decline in both national collective bargaining and direct government intervention in industrial relations, this body has lost much of its former power, and this is reflected in its corresponding employer bodies, at least so far as their industrial relations influence is concerned.

8.   Essentially, a **trade union** is an organization of workers, which aims to protect and promote their interests in the workplace, mainly by means of collective bargaining and consultation with employers. Whilst some collective issues are handled by national bodies, such as unions and employers' associations, the majority of collective matters are dealt with in the workplace. In organizations where one or more trade unions are recognized for the purposes of bargaining and/or consulting on behalf of the employees, it is usual for workplace representatives to be appointed by the union members. These may be called 'shop steward', 'staff representative' (rep) or some other agreed term. Such representatives are employees of the organization who fulfil unpaid work on behalf of their trade union colleagues within a framework of rules agreed between the two parties – employer and union members. The work of a representative usually includes the following responsibilities: negotiating local conditions; dealing with members' problems in respect of pay, hours and other relevant conditions of employment; representing members in the course of disciplinary or grievance hearings; acting as a communication channel between members and the employer on relevant matters and acting as a link between the trade union and its members.

9.   Whereas historically the average workplace representative had a considerable amount of power to influence both employment conditions and working methods, the situation today is very different. The combined effects of increased competition, legal restrictions on arbitrary trade union sanctions and more flexible working methods have weakened the power once held by shop stewards and staff representatives.

10.   Collective bargaining is a system of negotiation involving both management and the union, i.e. union representatives and management jointly determine rules belonging to the employment contract. The outcome of union–management negotiations is a collective agreement. Collective agreements (or rules made) between employers and employees are usually divided into two categories: procedural agreements and substantive agreements. Substantive agreements deal with the substance of employee relations, i.e. actual terms and conditions of employment (pay, hours of work, holiday entitlements, etc.). Procedural agreements regulate the way in which substantive rules are made and understood and indicate how workplace conflicts are to be resolved. Matters covered by procedural agreements include negotiating rights for unions; scope of subjects for collective bargaining (i.e. what is negotiable); procedure to be followed in the case of a dispute between

the parties; and grievance and disciplinary procedures. Substantive agreements are usually renegotiated every 1 or 2 years, but procedural agreements are negotiated only as and when the parties feel the need to change or clarify the rules. Most procedural agreements require either side to give several months' notice of variation or termination of the agreement, whereas most substantive agreements run out automatically at the end of the period concerned.

11. The main body of rules in employee relations is drawn from the following:

- company/organization rules – these are usually generated by, and enforced by, managers

- collective agreements – jointly agreed rules or practices made by management representatives and employee representatives

- custom and practice – these are the informal rules which arise from the behaviour of managers and employees over a period of time; unlike the other rules just mentioned, these rules are not usually written down

- legal sources – these are the rules arising from statute, judicial precedent, and the common law, so far as they relate to employee relations

- codes of practice – these may be the codes of professional bodies, or those of bodies such as ACAS (the Advisory, Conciliation and Arbitration Service).

12. Rules affecting employees may be made therefore by management, by management with input from employees or by external bodies. In some cases employees will act collectively through trade unions and in other cases they may act alone. The previously discussed CIPD report, 'Managing employee relations in difficult times' also found that the main focus of employee relations is not on collective machinery but on individual relationships, a matter we consider in the following paragraphs.

42.3 EMPLOYEE ENGAGEMENT

13. The employee relationship may also be described in terms of degrees of *engagement*. We discussed 'organizing for engagement' in Chapter 23 (see Section 23.7 in particular). The achievement of business goals, discussed as a PM issue in the previous chapter, is increasingly dependent on delivery by front-line employees. Employers want engaged employees because they deliver improved business performance. Research has repeatedly confirmed a relationship between how people are managed and business performance. Thus, the importance of employee engagement as a key part of the employment relationship has increased. Indeed, employee engagement is a concept that has become increasingly mainstreamed into management thinking over the past decade. In Chapter 23 we discussed engaged employees, noting them to be committed to the organization, passionate about work, and dependable, showing high degrees of participation. It is generally seen as an internal state of being – physical, mental and emotional – that encompasses earlier concepts of work effort, organizational commitment and job satisfaction. Characteristic phrases used to describe employee engagement include discretionary effort, going the extra mile, feeling valued and passion for work.

14. In order to build an engaged workforce, organizations must rely on good people management and learning and development practices as discussed in the previous chapter. The 2009 MacLeod Review summarized four 'enablers' (drivers) that should be fundamentals of any engagement approach:

- Leadership that aligns the goals of employees (their jobs) with those of the organization.

- Managers who ensure that work is organized efficiently, motivate, empower, value, appreciate and support their employees.

- Employees feeling they are able to *voice* their ideas and be listened to, both about how they do their job and in decision-making in their own department, with joint sharing of problems and challenges and a commitment to arrive at joint solutions.

- 'Organizational integrity': stated values are embedded into organizational culture.

15.   The last of these, integrity, closely relates to the sense of fairness and trust in the organization and the psychological contract, which depend on employers delivering on their commitments. We discussed the psychological contract in Chapter 39. As well as these drivers, employee well-being (including work–life balance etc.) is often considered a vital 'hygiene factor' for employee engagement. Later in this chapter we consider working hours and flexible working (readers should also refer back to Chapter 21 where we discussed organizing work).

16.   Leaders and managers in all functions and at all levels should pay close attention to building employee engagement. HR is the most natural function to lead on this, using its 'employee advocacy' role to benefit organizational performance (CIPD 2013a) – **employee advocacy** concerns the responsibility of HR for clearly defining how management should be treating employees, making sure that employees have mechanisms to contest unfair practices, and representing the interests of employees within the framework of HR's primary obligation to senior management. – Successfully fostering employee engagement requires working with all areas of the business. Employers should especially pay attention to: giving employees meaningful voice, effective communications (discussed next), having managers demonstrate commitment to the organization and upholding the values of employee engagement in how they act, and fair and just management processes for dealing with problems and supporting employee well-being.

42.4 EMPLOYEE COMMUNICATION AND EMPLOYEE VOICE

17.   Communication – a fundamental process in the management of people – is an important aspect of employee engagement and the employee relationship. Communication was discussed in Chapter 25 where we argued a need for an engaged workforce and explored how organizations can strengthen relationships through internal communication. Communication is an integral part of organizational culture as discussed in Chapter 14. Senior managers (leaders) are responsible for setting out the organizational purpose. Clear and ongoing communication from all levels of management is needed to translate the purpose into the working lives of employees. Effective two-way communication, openness and transparency with information strengthens trust between employers and employees and can help to build the psychological contract, in which employees feel valued by their employer, and the employer values their employees' contributions.

18.   Responsibility for employee communication does not solely lie with a communications function (such as 'employee communications'). Every manager can play a central role and effective communication skills are an important element of good leadership. In larger organizations, responsibility for (internal) communications on strategic issues may lie with functions associated with HR and Learning and Development.

19.   Communication, however, must be two-way, a dialogue, up and down and across if it is to support engagement and build the employment relationship on mutual grounds. Earlier, when discussing industrial relations, we noted how collective bargaining provides employees with a say in decision-making (in unionized organizations). As union membership has declined so has collective bargaining, although it remains influential, particularly in the public sector. In the 1980s and 1990s, organizations became aware that those who became involved and engaged with their employees were likely to benefit from increased motivation and commitment. The MacLeod review of employee engagement, discussed earlier, identified 'voice' as one of the four key drivers of an engaged workforce. **Employee voice** is the two-way communication between employer and employee. It is the process of the employer communicating to the employee as well as receiving and listening to communication from the employee (CIPD, 2013b). The concept of employee voice focuses more on opportunities for employees to be involved in decisions collectively, whether through trade unions or by other means.

20.   There are a range of different and often complementary mechanisms for employee voice. In some cases employers (managers) wish to unleash employee ideas and opinions ('upward problem-solving'). In order to achieve this, organizations may use techniques such as suggestion schemes, attitude surveys and project teams. Employers may also seek employee participation through approaches such as employee forums, joint consultation and partnership schemes. Whilst the above listed communication approaches are formal, informal mechanisms (typically more important in smaller organizations) can be an effective form of voice. Organizations are increasingly making use of social media to provide employees with opportunities of conducting informal conversations with each other and contributing their opinions.

21.   In 'high performance workplaces', knowledge and skills are developed and better utilized, leading to high-value enterprises (CIPD, 2013b). With a greater voice the organization benefits from employees' skills and knowledge which can be better used, leading to higher productivity; feeling more valued, they are more likely to stay with the organization and to contribute more. The organization gains a positive reputation, making it easier to recruit good employees, conflict is reduced and cooperation between employer and employee is based on interdependence. Employees also benefit from having more influence over their work, leading to higher job satisfaction. Effective two-way dialogue, and particularly employee ability to feed views upwards, is clearly crucial to a productive employee relations climate.

42.5 WORKING HOURS, FLEXIBLE WORKING, HEALTH, SECURITY, SAFETY AND WELFARE

22.   The employment relationship includes the commitment of employees to be available for work and the employer to provide a safe and secure work environment. HR may again play a key role in both addressing and representing the needs of employees and ensuring that the organization fulfils its legal and moral obligations. The average full-time UK worker's hours are almost 40 per week, therefore by EU standards the UK has a high proportion of 'long hours' workers. A major review of the literature on the relationship between long hours working and health for the Health and Safety Executive (HSE) concluded that 'there is some evidence that working long hours can lead to stress or mental ill-health' (White and Beswick, 2003). There is a clear need then for employers to protect their employees from overwork since long hours are likely to have a negative impact on employment performance. The main regulations governing working time are the Working Time Regulations 1998 (WTR) which implement the provisions of the Working Time Directive (93/104/EC). They lay down minimum conditions relating to weekly working time, rest entitlements and annual leave, and make special provision for night workers. 'Working time' means any period during which the individual is working, is at the employer's disposal and is carrying out their activities or duties. The WTR currently provide employees with the following basic rights and protections:

- a limit of an average of 48 hours a week over a 17-week period which a worker can be required to work

- a limit of an average of 8 hours work in 24 hours which night workers can work

- a right to 11 hours rest a day

- a right to a day off each week

- a right to an in-work rest break if the working day is longer than 6 hours

- a right to 28 days paid leave for full-time workers per year.

23.   Flexible working was discussed in Chapter 21. The term 'flexible working' describes a type of working arrangement which gives some degree of flexibility on how long, where and when employees work. The flexibility can be in terms of working time, working location or the pattern of working. Examples of flexible working practices include: part-time or term-time working, flexitime, job-sharing, working from home, teleworking, zero hours contracts, etc. Arrangements can be formal or informal. Flexible working arrangements can play a vital role in organizational performance (a strategic tool). Such arrangements may be driven by the increased demand for an effective work–life balance, needs associated with employee (talent) acquisition, engagement and retention, advances in technology or even legislative changes (refer back to Chapter 39 and the discussion on the values and attitudes of Baby Boomers, Gen X/Y workers). HR's role should be to identify how various flexible working options can benefit both the organization and individuals, and then consider ways of implementing flexible working options.

24.   HR can also play a key role in (attendance) absence management, a significant cost and PM issue for businesses. Effective absence management involves finding a balance between providing support to help employees with health problems stay in and return to work, and taking consistent and firm action against employees who try to take advantage of organizational occupational sick pay schemes. A key element

in managing absence effectively is accurate measurement and monitoring. Measures can indicate when absence needs to be investigated. Monitoring absence allows the employer to identify trends and to explore underlying causes. The organization will normally implement absence policies that explain when and whom employees should notify if they are not able to attend work; and provide details of contractual sick pay terms and its relationship with statutory sick pay etc. Warning procedures for unacceptable absence may be used to make it clear to employees that unjustified absence will not be tolerated and that absence policies will be enforced. The ACAS Code of Practice Disciplinary and Grievance Procedures together with the employer's own procedures provide the main tools for addressing unacceptable absence. Effective absence management is also about supporting employees with health problems to stay in or return to work, such as through developing effective return-to-work programmes as part of an absence management strategy. A focus on employee well-being and health promotion can help avoid absence problems developing.

25.   Employee health, safety and wellness are important aspects of managing the employment relationship. Such matters are also influenced by relevant legislation. Contemporary health issues include workplace stress, alcoholism, smoking, bullying, workplace violence, etc. As suggested by Torrington, Taylor and Hall (2008: p. 527) there is always a conflict between the needs of the employer to push for increased output and the needs of the employee to be protected from the hazards of the workplace. They believe that the development of health, safety and welfare provision is interrelated with the development of HRM; the HR department has taken on the role of advising managers on the organization's legal obligations. After all, illness and injury lead to avoidable absence and a poor reputation for safety and welfare makes recruitment and retention difficult. Mathis and Jackson (2011: p. 468) discuss safety and security. Safety is a condition in which the physical well-being of people is protected and safety programmes seek to prevent work-related injuries and accidents. Similarly, security seeks to protect employees but from different threats, e.g. workplace violence.

42.6 COMPENSATION, PAY AND REWARD

26.   Bratton and Gold (2012) argue that reward management is central to the effective management of the employment relationship. Traditionally the aim of reward systems was to attract, retain and motivate staff. Contemporary organizations recognize that individuals are attracted, retained and motivated by a wide range of financial and non-financial rewards. This has resulted in the total reward approach to pay. HR will normally set policy and practice on reward management – management of pay, benefits and other forms of compensation. Bratton and Gold (2012: p. 363) discuss monetary rewards (wages, salaries and benefits) noting the reward function does not operate in isolation but has major knock-on effects for other HR policies and practices. To understand the crucial role that reward plays in managing the employment relationship, it is necessary to conceptualize it in its broadest sense. They suggest that an organization can provide two broad types of reward: extrinsic and intrinsic. Financial payments and working conditions are typically associated with extrinsic rewards. Intrinsic rewards, however, are referred to as psychological benefits. Refer back to motivation theory in Part 1 of this book. Consequently, Bratton and Gold (2012: p. 364) define reward as a package of monetary, non-monetary and psychological payments that an organization provides for its employees in exchange for a bundle of valued work-related behaviours. Reward is primarily but not exclusively the exchange of pay. The authors go on to define a reward strategy as an organization's plan and actions pertaining to the mix and total amount of direct pay (for example, salary) and indirect monetary payments (benefits) paid to various categories of employee.

27.   Whilst some smaller organizations manage without any form of pay structure at all (informal), larger organizations tend to implement pay structures with a specified number of pay grades, levels or bands. A pay structure then is a collection of pay grades, levels or bands, linking related jobs within a hierarchy that provides a framework for the implementation of reward strategies and policies within an organization. Pay spines are a similar approach, based on a series of incremental points that usually allow for service-related pay progression. Such arrangements are traditionally found in local government, universities or voluntary organizations. Pay structures are designed to ensure fairness and lawfulness, bring order and clarity and align reward strategy with the business strategy of the organization, such as encouraging high performance levels (refer back to discussion on performance related pay in the previous chapter). Pay progression refers

to the process by which an individual employee attains higher levels of pay within a range associated with a pay grade or band. This is separate from inflation-linked increases and/or the attainment of formal promotion to a higher grade or band.

28.   There are various methods for advancing individual employees along the pay ranges associated with their band or grade. With service-related increments an individual progresses through a number of incremental pay points with each year of service in the organization (usually up to a maximum point). This approach rewards the accumulation of expertise in the job and may also help with employee retention. The approach that links individual pay rises with an employee's performance is termed performance-related pay. A variation on this approach is team performance pay. At its highest levels, organizational performance can be used as a criterion for pay progression. Pay increases can also be pitched to keep pace with rates for similar jobs or regional pay levels in the external labour market.

29.   A key issue with regard to pay and work motivation is whether money can change work behaviours. This is an issue for the pay-performance relationship. Caruth and Handlogten (2001) cited in Bratton and Gold (2012) argued that a compensation system that rewards employees fairly according to efforts expended and results produced creates a motivating work environment.

30.   HR primarily deals with employee relations, whilst Payroll, a distinct function, administers the compensation of employees. Each department has its distinct functions, but they meet at times. HR responsibilities include hiring, promotions, salary determination, classifying and grading positions, company policy development, employee benefits, personnel data maintenance and employee compensation. HR must assure legal obligations are met in terms of discrimination and equality laws etc. Payroll, on the other hand, involves *calculating* wages, commissions, bonuses, severance pay, overtime, etc. Payroll also makes deductions from employees' wages for taxes etc. Payroll works with the Accounting department to ensure that wage deductions and other payroll expenses are paid and properly reported. For both departments to run smoothly, HR and Payroll must work together. In some organizations both departments ultimately report to HR whilst in others the Payroll function may report into Finance/Accounting. Additionally, it can be outsourced.

42.7 MANAGING CONFLICT, DISPUTES, DISCIPLINE AND GRIEVANCE

31.   Throughout this chapter we have discussed the employer–employee relationship. As with any relationship, the prospect of a breakdown exists. A **conflict** is a disagreement through which the parties involved perceive a threat to their needs, interests or concerns; it is a disagreement that may result in withdrawal of cooperation or, in an employee relations context, may result in some form of industrial action. **Conflict resolution** is the process which attempts to end the conflict between the disagreeing parties. In some cases the conflict may need to be resolved externally and this may involve hearing cases at an Employment Tribunal.

32.   The Employment Tribunals in England, Scotland and Wales, are independent judicial bodies which determine disputes between employers and employees over employment rights. A typical claim brought by an individual against his/her employer claiming breach of employment rights is called a 'single' claim. Other claims to employment tribunals come from individuals involved in collective workplace disputes – two or more workers bringing claims against (usually) a single employer. Claims that are linked as part of these collective disputes are referred to as multiple claims. In Employment Tribunals, the number of claims received in July to September 2013 was around 40 000 (in line with historical quarterly trends). A claim (either single or multiple) can be brought under one or more of different jurisdictions, for example under Age Discrimination and Equal Pay. The most common disputes are concerned with unfair dismissal (see Section 42.8), redundancy payments and employment discrimination. Over the past decade there has been a significant increase in employment rights legislation, providing additional avenues for employees to seek recourse through formal channels. People are also now more aware of their rights at work. This expanded legal framework means that, if employers do not manage conflict effectively, the consequences can be serious.

33.   Conflict (over performance, sickness absence and attendance, and relationships between colleagues for example) is an inherent part of the employment relationship. The ability to manage conflict remains a key issue for many organizations. Stages of conflict are shown in Figure 42.1. In some cases the dispute may be settled without a need to pursue a formal grievance procedure. Once formal procedures have been

FIGURE 42.1 The stages of conflict

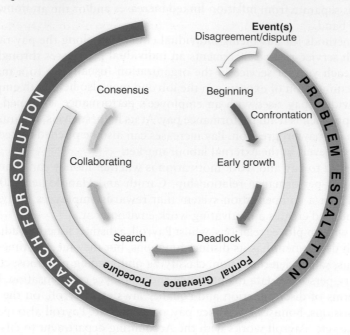

triggered, the tendency is for differences to become more adversarial. Mediation as a method or technique of resolving workplace issues represents an important shift from the traditional industrial relations framework, with its emphasis on formal discipline and grievance procedures, towards more of a 'win–win' approach consistent with the philosophy of HR management. Mediation is increasingly being used to resolve disputes in many areas of life. It is one of the processes within the alternative dispute resolution (ADR) spectrum and involves a neutral third party bringing two sides together with the aim of reaching a mutual agreement.

34.   Mediation is based on the principle of collaborative problem-solving, with a focus on the future and rebuilding relationships, rather than apportioning blame. Mediation is where an impartial third party, the mediator, helps two or more people in dispute to attempt to reach an agreement. Any agreement comes from those in dispute, not from the mediator. Mediation distinguishes itself from other approaches to conflict resolution, such as grievance procedures and the Employment Tribunal process, in a number of ways. Mediation is less formal, voluntary, morally binding but normally has no legal status and is owned by the parties. Mediation seeks to provide an informal and speedy solution to workplace conflict, and it can be used at any point in the conflict cycle. Mediation has many benefits including the improvement of relationships and retention of valuable employees; it also helps organizations avoid the costs involved in defending Employment Tribunal claims.

35.   Mediation needs to be promoted to employees as a flexible, confidential and less formal alternative to settling workplace disputes, and its potential advantages emphasized. The support of trade unions and employee representatives can be particularly useful in lending the use of mediation credibility and promoting trust in the process. There are different options for introducing mediation into an organization: one is to develop an in-house mediation scheme, with trained internal mediators. Another possible approach is to call on the services of external mediators when necessary.

DISCIPLINARY AND GRIEVANCE PROCEDURES

36.   When managers fail to create the desirable employee behaviours or encounter problematic undesirable behaviours they may have to resort to disciplinary action. Organizations establish rules to regulate the behaviour of workers. Disciplinary practices are then used to implement rules and make employee

behaviour more predictable. The discipline system should aim to provide a fair and consistent method for dealing with alleged inappropriate or unacceptable work behaviour. Fairness and transparency are promoted by developing and using rules and procedures for handling disciplinary and grievance situations. These should be set down in writing, be specific and clear (ACAS, 2009).

37. Discipline is about complying with the rules in order to produce a controlled and effective performance. The purpose of discipline is to encourage and improve behaviour and deter unacceptable behaviour. Disciplinary rules and procedures are necessary in order to manage employee relations in a fair and consistent manner. Rules set standards of conduct and performance in the workplace and the supporting procedures help to ensure employees adhere to these standards. Good practice in disciplinary matters is set out in an ACAS Code of Practice on disciplinary procedures.

38. A model disciplinary procedure should aim to correct unsatisfactory behaviour, rather than to punish it. It should specify, as fully as possible, what constitutes 'misconduct' and what constitutes 'gross misconduct'. It should then state what the most likely penalty is for each of these categories. In cases of proven 'gross misconduct', this is most likely to be immediate (or summary) dismissal, or suspension, followed by dismissal. In cases of less serious misconduct, the most likely consequence is that a formal warning will be given. For repeated acts of misconduct, it is likely that the employee concerned will be dismissed. So far as appeals are concerned, a model procedure should aim to ensure that appeals are dealt with quickly, so that the employee involved can be informed of the final decision without undue delay. Because of the serious implications of disciplinary action, only senior managers are normally permitted to carry out suspensions, demotions or dismissals. Other managers are normally restricted to issuing warnings.

39. A **grievance**, unlike a disciplinary matter, is first raised by the employee. The onus is on the employee to state the nature of the grievance and what, if anything, he or she wants done about it. In a work team where the manager or supervisor is in close touch with the members, issues that might lead to a grievance tend to be dealt with in the course of day-to-day problem-solving. Where, however, an issue is still not resolved satisfactorily from the employee's point of view, then a formal application may be made to raise the issue under the appropriate procedure. There is an ACAS Code of Practice on disciplinary and grievance procedures (the Code). It sets out principles employees and employers should follow to achieve a reasonable standard of behaviour in handling grievances.

40. Typical stages of a grievance process include:

The employee informs the employer about the nature of the grievance.

Employers arrange for a formal meeting to be held without unreasonable delay after a grievance is received.

The employee should be allowed to be accompanied at the meeting. Following the meeting a decision is made on what action, if any, to take. Decisions should be communicated to the employee, in writing, without unreasonable delay and, where appropriate, should set out what action the employer intends to take to resolve the grievance.

The employee is allowed to take the grievance further (appeal) if not resolved.

The appeal should be dealt with impartially.

The outcome of the appeal should be communicated to the employee in writing without unreasonable delay.

42.8 ENDING THE EMPLOYMENT RELATIONSHIP

41. Perhaps the final aspect of our focus on the employment relationship is its termination. **Dismissal** of an employee occurs when the employer terminates the contract, a fixed-term contract ends and is not renewed, or the employee leaves. Among the commonest reasons for dismissal are misconduct, inability to do the job and redundancy. A dismissal will normally be 'fair' provided the employer has one of the five specified reasons (see below) for the dismissal and has acted 'reasonably' in carrying it out. When somebody is dismissed, they often say they will claim 'unfair' or 'wrongful' dismissal. **Wrongful dismissal** occurs when the employer terminates the contract of employment, and in doing so breaches the contract (for example terminating a contract without giving the contractual notice period). The basis of **unfair dismissal** law is that employees have the right to be treated fairly. In such cases the employee must be able to demonstrate

that they were dismissed, and that this dismissal was not fair for a specific reason. To be fair, a dismissal must be due to redundancy, conduct or some other substantial reason, illegality or about capability (poor performance) or qualifications. Retirement is no longer a fair reason for dismissal.

42.   In addition, an employer must also have acted fairly and reasonably in the way they set about dismissing the employee. This involves following a fair procedure. See for example the ACAS Code of Practice on dealing with disciplinary and dismissal and grievance matters. Typically, the procedure will ensure that the employee is informed, in writing, of the alleged offence; there is a meeting with the employee and employer to discuss the alleged offence and the employee is allowed to be represented at this meeting by a trade union representative or colleague. Finally, the employee should have the opportunity to appeal against any sanction.

43.   **Constructive dismissal** occurs when the employee resigns as a result of the actions of the employer. The employer's actions must amount to a fundamental breach of the employment contract. Dismissing employees is sometimes necessary. However, it can be costly and can also damage the business. It should be considered only when other options have failed. Settlement agreements are a tool that can be used to deal with workplace problems. Most commonly they are used to help end an employment relationship in a mutually acceptable way. Settlement agreements (known as **compromise agreements** in Great Britain until 29 July 2013) are legally binding contracts which are used to end employment on terms agreed with the employee. Settlement agreements are normally used to bring an employment relationship to an end in a mutually agreed way. They are often used in situations where an employer and employee feel that their employment relationship is no longer working and a 'clean break' is the best way forward. They can also be used to reach an agreed and final conclusion to a workplace dispute or issue which does not result in an end to the employment relationship. Settlement agreements can be offered at any stage of an employment relationship.

CONCLUSION

44.   This chapter has explored many of the topics which may be considered under the general heading of the employment relationship philosophy and the role of HR, particularly from the viewpoint of employee advocacy. There are many arguments for organizations to allocate resources to the management and maintenance of the employment relationship (legal, moral, cost, etc.); HR, as part of the strategic role encompassed in HRM, has particular concerns with the impact on talent acquisition, retention and performance management in assuring that human capital is able to accomplish the organization's goals. Building successful employment relationships is important and makes good business sense as organizations with good employment relationships tend to be more successful.

QUESTIONS

1   Discuss why there has been a marked shift in employee relations away from the more combative stance of union-led collective bargaining towards a more unified approach to management–employee relationships.

2   Explain why employee communication and employee voice are important to the employment relationship.

3   Discuss the role of HR in assuring employees are available for work and how they enable the employer to provide a safe and secure work environment.

4   Evaluate whether reward management is central to the effective management of the employment relationship.

5   Evaluate the role of mediation as a collaborative problem-solving approach that can maintain a healthy employment relationship.

USEFUL WEBSITES

Office for National Statistics **www.statistics.gov.uk/cci/ nugget.asp?id=4** see Labour Market – Union Membership.

The Confederation of British Industry **www.cbi.org.uk** Department for Business, Innovation and Skills

Central Arbitration Committee **www.cac.gov.uk**

DirectGov Employment Trade unions **www.direct.gov.uk/en/ Employment/TradeUnions/DG_447**

ACAS **www.acas.org.uk**

IPA **www.ipa-involve.com/** The IPA is a British organization delivering partnership, consultation and employee engagement

Trades Union Congress **www.tuc.org.uk.**

REFERENCES

ACAS (2009) 'Disciplinary and grievance procedures', TSO (The Stationery Office) and available from: Online **www.tsoshop. co.uk** © Crown Copyright 2009.

Bratton, J. and Gold, J. (2012) *Human Resource Management Theory and Practice*, 5th edn, Palgrave Macmillan.

CIPD (2013a) 'Employee engagement Factsheet – Revised August 2013', available from **http://www.cipd.co.uk/ hr-resources/factsheets/employee-engagement.aspx.**

CIPD (2013b), 'Employee voice – Revised September 2013', available from **http://www.cipd.co.uk/hr-resources/ factsheets/employee-voice.aspx.**

MacLeod, D. and Clarke, N. (2009) *Engaging for Success: Enhancing Performance Through Employee Engagement*, London: Department for Business, Innovation and Skills. Available at: **http://www.bis.gov.uk/files/file52215.pdf** accessed 21 April 2014.

Mathis, R.L. and Jackson, J.H. (2011) *Human Resource Management*, 13th edn, South Western.

Price, A. (2007) *Human Resource Management in a Business Context*, 3rd edn, Cengage Learning EMEA.

Torrington, D., Taylor, S. and Hall, L. (2008) *Human Resource Management*, 7th edn, Financial Times Press.

White, J. and Beswick, J. (2003) *Working Long Hours*. Sheffield: Health and Safety Laboratory. (HSL/2003/02). Available at: **http://www.hse.gov.uk/research/hsl_pdf/2003/ hsl03-02.pdf.**

CHAPTER 43
INTERNATIONAL
HUMAN RESOURCE
MANAGEMENT

Key Concepts

- Cultural distance, cultural competence and culture shock
- Ethnocentric
- Internationalization
- International HRM
- Multinational company (MNC), global and multidomestic
- National culture
- Polycentric

Learning Outcomes Having read this chapter, you should be able to:

- identify HRM issues and problems arising from the internationalization of organizations
- explain the role of the IHRM function
- discuss factors which may impact upon HR policy and practice design and adoption in different countries of operation
- discuss how the HR function can help develop culturally competent employees
- explain how the HR function may support employees working in other countries.

1. Organizations now source, manufacture, market and conduct value-adding activities on an international scale. This poses new management challenges, particularly for HR, and necessitates the rise of the international manager or manager within an international organization who can acquire the requisite business knowledge and skills to enable the organization to perform in our ever-increasing globalized business environment. Not only is there a need to understand international business theory and practice, because international business activities are increasing, but there is also a need to understand domestic business since international organizations and their subsidiaries also have local challenges.

2. Globalization (see Part 4) and internationalization (discussed later) affect each and every business function. In this chapter we will focus on HR specifically. Since the early 1990s there has been a growing

interest in **international HRM (IHRM)**, reflecting the growing recognition that the effective management of HR internationally is a major determinant of success or failure in international business. In this chapter we establish the scope of IHRM, define key terms in international human resource management (IHRM) and outline the differences between domestic and IHRM. We also consider the context for IHRM, recognizing that the HR function and systems do not operate in a vacuum, and that HR activities are determined by, and influence internal organizational and external factors.

43.1 EXPLORING THE INTERNATIONAL CONTEXT

3.   In Chapter 12 we explored the domestic business environment. A company may offer its goods and services solely in its domestic market or wider in a global market. Clearly there is more opportunity associated with the latter but not all organizations become multinational. The domestic organization, headquartered at home, must decide whether or not to become a multinational organization and if not, will decide whether or not to export its goods and services (from production facilities at home). In the following paragraphs, using the PESTLE framework (refer back to Chapter 12, para. 3 and skill sheet 6), we outline key aspects of the environment from an international perspective. We will develop ideas further in the final part of the book.

POLITICAL ENVIRONMENT

4.   Acts of government create winners and losers in the marketplace. **Political systems** (the structures, processes and activities by which any nation governs itself) may be a source of opportunity or threat. The political system may be described in a number of ways, typically on a continuum between democracy and totalitarianism (such as communism, theocratic or secular totalitarianism). Systems exist on a continuum where power is centralized (with the government) at one extreme and decentralized at the other. A totalitarian regime is characterized by the centralization of power, an imposed authority (typically supported through a powerful military). The political system and factors are important for HR particularly because of their influence on employment law, the economy, equality and local content rules.

5.   **Political risk** arises from a variety of sources such as an unstable political system, policy change, conflict, poor political leadership or poor relations with other countries. Managers must be aware of how political risk can affect their organization and trade. In some cases, certain political risks will affect all organizations operating in or trading with a particular country whilst in other cases a particular industry or small group may be threatened. There are many types of political and associated risk such as security risks, corruption, civil protest and economic sanctions. There are a variety of consequences (business impacts) arising from such risk. Conflict, terrorism and kidnapping may disrupt business operations and revenue generation; local content requirements impact upon labour cost and quality of outputs and profits may be affected in the event of asset seizure (confiscation, expropriation or nationalization). In the last chapter we commented on the role of HR in relation to the safety, security and well-being of people; this role is clearly impacted by political risk.

ECONOMIC ENVIRONMENT

6.   In many ways, the economic systems of countries are becoming similar. Through the establishment of transnational rules, treaties, policies, agreements and law, countries are now more economically intertwined (economic integration) with one another, engaging in more international trade than ever before. International organizations, multinational companies (MNCs) in particular, adapt their strategies to benefit from integration, locating operations or forming strategic alliances and acquisitions that enable access to such markets. Economic and financial conditions affect HR in many ways. Such conditions (including wealth, inflation, interest and exchange rates) influence spending by governments, employers (budgets) and consumers. Key factors are likely to include unemployment levels, reward management (availability of financial resources for payments, inflation rate, wage rates, minimum wage, working hours, etc.), the nature of the workforce, competitive pressures, outsourcing and offshoring and travel expenditure.

SOCIO-CULTURAL ENVIRONMENT

7.   The social or socio-cultural factors in the macro-environment typically include social values, attitudes and beliefs, demographic trends, lifestyle preferences and skills (talent) availability. When organizations operate internationally they need to understand how people in other countries may differ. The construct used to describe such differences is termed (**national**) **culture** and cultural differences can create challenges within the business environment.

8.   Differences in culture (fit) may necessitate changes to business practices (e.g. the way the organization recruits and selects employees), management styles (e.g. democratic or autocratic), products and services. These are discussed later in the chapter. Differences in societies arise through education, religion, language and social systems inculcating values and meanings that become shared by the country's people. Differences may also arise as a result of the country's location, physical environment, geography and climate. The degree of difference between two countries impacts upon the extent of *adaptation* (alteration) required by an international organization. Where there is little alteration needed the organization may gain from knowledge transfer and economies of scale.

9.   A variety of frameworks exist that seek to measure *national culture*. Such frameworks (see for example, Hofstede) typically decompose the complex construct of culture into several dimensions. Typically, dimensions at the national and pan-national level are value-based, (dimensions at the organizational or sub-group level may include attitudes but are more likely to focus on behaviour and practice rather than on constructs directly related to the way we think). The starting point in comparing different cultures concerns how to define culture and the cultural dimensions to study. There is no standard definition of culture and no universal set of cultural dimensions. There are potentially many ways in which cultures can differ.

10.   In 1965, Geert Hofstede, working in the Personnel Research Department of IBM, performed a large survey regarding national value differences across the worldwide subsidiaries of this MNC; he compared the answers of over 100 000 IBM employees on the same attitude survey in different countries. Initially considering the 40 largest countries, he then extended it to 50 countries and three regions. He made use of factor analysis and other statistical techniques in order to identify his cultural dimensions.

11.   The cultural dimensions proposed by Hofstede can be used, in conjunction with other information, to evaluate cultural differences and therefore predict any needy adaptation by the international organization. Based on the empirical study, Hofstede proposed four dimensions of national culture (scores can be seen in Figure 12.3, the 'Culture dimension scores by country') that are widely cited in business textbooks and used by consultants and practitioners:

–   **Power distance** (PD) describes the extent to which the less powerful members of institutions and organizations within a country expect and accept that power is distributed unequally. Societies that are high on PD tend to expect obedience towards superiors and clearly distinguish between those with status and power and those without it. In such countries, superiors are supposed to initiate contact and subordinates will follow command without question (a rule orientation). Organizations in such countries tend to be bureaucratic, have tall hierarchies with consequences of slower decision-making.

–   **Uncertainty avoidance** (UA) is concerned with the extent to which the members of a culture feel threatened by uncertain or unknown situations. Societies that are high on uncertainty avoidance have a stronger tendency towards orderliness and consistency, structured lifestyles, clear specification of social expectations, and rules and laws to cover situations, fear of failure, less risk-taking, a belief in expertise (specialists and gurus), a preference for clear requirements and instructions, and orientation to rules, and lower readiness to compromise. In contrast, the people of countries where there is strong tolerance of ambiguity and uncertainty are used to less structure in their lives and are not as concerned about following rules and procedures.

–   **Individualism** (Ind) pertains to societies in which the ties between individuals are loose: everyone is expected to look after themselves. Collectivism as its opposite, pertains to societies in which people from birth onwards are integrated into strong cohesive in-groups. On the individualist side we find societies (like the USA and to some extent the UK) in which the ties between individuals are loose: everyone is expected to look after themselves and their immediate family. On the collectivist side, people from birth onwards are integrated into strong, cohesive in-groups, often extended families which continue protecting them in exchange for unquestioning loyalty. Members of collectivist cultures are more likely to favour group decision-making, value harmony and will engage in face-saving behaviours; members of individualist cultures emphasize autonomy, self-respect and independence. Individual achievement is highly valued in individualistic cultures.

 – **Masculinity** pertains to societies in which social gender roles are clearly distinct as opposed to overlapping. Countries with the least gender-differentiated practices tend to accord women a higher status and a stronger role in decision-making. They have a higher percentage of women participating in the labour force and more women in positions of authority. Men and women in these cultures tend to have similar levels of education.

TECHNOLOGICAL ENVIRONMENT

12.   We have already discussed the impact of technology on business. However, with regard to the MNC it is important to note that technology may be transferred from outside the organization or from within. For example, international organizations, the multinational in particular, may transfer the benefits of technologies developed in-house to their subsidiaries (intra-organizational transfer). Technology may also be transferred externally through franchises, licences and joint ventures. Different technologies impact upon work in different ways, changing the nature of work and therefore may impact upon the organization and structuring of work. The relationship between technology and work is captured in a theory known as **technological determinism**.

LEGAL SYSTEMS

13.   A legal system is the set of laws made and enforced to control the actions of people and organizations. Country's legal and political systems are interwoven. Laws may limit or open up opportunity, govern the conduct of business operations and manifest in the way business is performed. Organizations are required to obey the law otherwise they are likely to incur costs. Legal systems may be categorized in a number of ways and vary from country to country. Common law is used to describe a legal system based on precedent; civil law is based on written rules and theocratic law is based upon religious teachings. Legal-system-forces may influence or manifest in taxation, wage rates, minimum wage, health and safety requirements, employment age, employment contract, etc.

43.2 THE INTERNATIONALIZATION OF THE FIRM

14.   Having explored the international context we may now consider how domestic organizations become international. International strategy is concerned with choices about where the organization offers its products and services and where it locates value-adding activities. **Internationalization** is the process by which a company enters a foreign market. By internationalizing, the organization is able to broaden the size of its market and exploit opportunity for growth. International strategy considers not only where to locate facilities and activities but also how to enter different markets, i.e. the appropriate *entry mode*. Alternative market entry methods include:

(1)   Products are supplied from the organization's domestic operations:

  (a)   indirect exporting (the simplest and lowest cost method of market entry, products are sold overseas by other organizations), or

  (b)   direct exporting (the organization becomes directly involved in the presence of exporting), and

(2)   Products are supplied from the organization's overseas operations:

  (c)   foreign manufacturing strategies without direct investments (contract manufacturer, franchising and licensing)

  (d)   cooperative strategies (joint ventures and strategic alliances), and

  (e)   foreign manufacturing strategies with direct investment (wholly-owned subsidiary, company acquisitions and mergers).

15. Market-entry modes can be classified according to whether they require indirect or direct involvement by the organization and whether they involve both marketing and production or simply marketing. Thus, four different modes of entering an international market (see Figure 43.1) can be distinguished, where the successive stages represent higher degrees of international involvement:

FIGURE 43.1 Four different modes of entering an international market

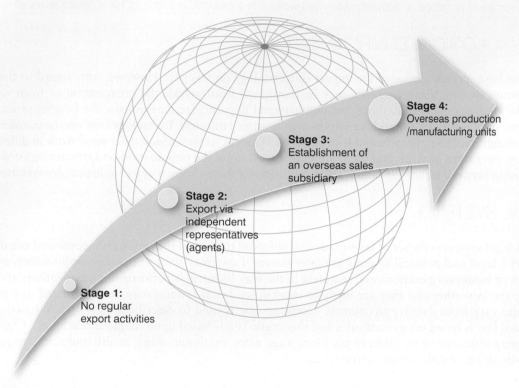

Stage 4:
Overseas production
/manufacturing units

Stage 3:
Establishment of
an overseas sales
subsidiary

Stage 2:
Export via
independent
representatives
(agents)

Stage 1:
No regular
export activities

43.3 INTERNATIONAL STRATEGY AND STRUCTURE IN MNCs

16. Eventually, international activities become too much for the domestic design to manage and the organization starts to place employees in overseas offices, subsidiaries and production facilities. With this follows added complexity, new coordination and control demands, new resource and task allocation problems and consequently a requirement for a new design and way of organizing (refer back to Chapters 20–24). Not only must the organizational design fit the demand of the environment, it must also accommodate the organization's evolving internationalization process, i.e. it must fit with the strategy. Typically, organizations start with a domestic structure (see Chapter 20) and may add an export department. From here, with continued growth in exports, a foreign subsidiary may be added, followed by an international division (organized along functional, product or area lines) before moving to a global structure. Once groups are formed and given an international scope they must compete for resources with the rest of the organization.

17. Common forms of organization design are listed below. Each of the three main designs emphasize a particular type of knowledge, i.e. knowledge of the area, product or function and this knowledge will vary in importance to different organizations. There are a number of advantages and disadvantages associated with integrated global structures:

- **Global functional** – more appropriate for companies offering similar products, using similar technology, with few products or customers. Managers can maintain highly centralized control over functional operations.

- **Global product** – each product is represented by a separate division and has its own functional departments, i.e. finance, production, sales and marketing specialists.

- **Global area** – probably the most common form of structure in larger international organizations. Area knowledge/needs are more important than product expertise or functional specialist knowledge. Local differences drive a focus on marketing and product adaptation.

18.   The globalization of business is making it more important than ever to understand how multinational enterprises (MNEs) can operate more effectively and efficiently. Global companies must be more than just a gathering of overseas subsidiaries with executive decisions made at the corporate centre. Companies must capture global-scale efficiency simultaneously, respond to national markets, and cultivate a worldwide learning capability for driving continuous innovation across borders. So far we have discussed the idea of internationalization, noting that not all organizations become multinational. However, we should not treat 'multinational' as a simple term. Multinationals are not always the same. The most popular classification of multinationals in the international business literature is probably Bartlett and Ghoshal's technology of strategic postures: global, multidomestic and transnational. Multinationals may be:

- **Global companies** which promote a convergence of consumer's preferences and strive to maximize standardization of production, which makes centralization and integration profitable. They benefit from home country specific advantages and export these abroad by creating replicas of the parent company. The global organization is an organization which trades internationally as if the world were a single and boundaryless entity.

- **Multidomestic organizations** (Local) by contrast, develop strategies for national responsiveness. Due to significant competitive differences between countries, the multidomestic strategy is determined by cultural, political and social national characteristics. The primary objective is the adapting of marketing and production strategies to specific local customer needs and government requirements. Products and policies conform to different local demands. The multidomestic organization is an organization that trades internationally as if the world were a collection of many different (country) entities.

- **Transnational enterprises (TNE)** operate a balanced combination of the multidomestic and global strategies. Although activities and resources may differ from country to country (decentralization), particular activities are coordinated and executed globally (centralization). The TNE is an international organization that standardizes certain aspects of its activities and output whilst adapting other aspects to local differences. In some cases such organizations may be categorized as 'glocal'.

43.4 UNDERSTANDING AND WORKING WITH OTHER CULTURES

19.   Many international business failures have been ascribed to a lack of cross-cultural competence (CC). Globalization opens many opportunities for business, but it also creates major challenges. An important challenge is the understanding and appreciating of cultural values, practices and subtleties in different parts of the world. To be successful in dealing with people from other cultures, managers need knowledge about cultural differences and similarities amongst countries. They also need to understand the implications of the differences and the skills required to act and decide appropriately and in a culturally sensitive way. Look back at Figure 12.3, the 'Culture dimension scores by country'. This is from the Hofstede data and can be used as one tool to explore how countries may be similar or different. However, similar to using information to assess a job candidate in the selection process, a variety of tools, data and insights must be employed in order to reveal aspects of a nation's culture.

20.   When considering the transfer of business practices from one subsidiary/office to that in another country it is useful to explore the cultural distance between them. Cultural distance aims to capture the overall difference in national culture between the home country and affiliates overseas. As the cultural distance increases, the difficulties facing business processes overseas also increase. A large cultural distance not only reflects a difference in cultural values, but also in many cases reflects a significant difference in other environmental variables.

21.   Given differences and their consequences it is not surprising to find companies seeking initiatives to develop their employee's cultural awareness. The fundamental intention of cross-cultural training is

to equip the learner(s) with the appropriate skills to attain cross-cultural understanding. People typically develop 'cross-cultural knowledge and awareness', becoming familiar with cultural characteristics such as values, beliefs and behaviours. This may lead to an ability to read into situations, contexts and behaviours that are culturally rooted and an ability to react to them appropriately (sensitivity). However, a mere understanding does not necessarily mean that an employee will be able to behave appropriately within any target country. 'Cross-cultural competence' is and should be the aim of all those dealing with multicultural clients, customers or colleagues.

22.   Cultural competence has been defined as a set of skills and attitudes that allow individuals to communicate effectively and appropriately with people who are different from themselves. Cultural knowledge has a positive effect on other (cross-cultural competence) attributes and maximizes intercultural competency. There are two different types of cultural knowledge: culture general (awareness and knowledge of cultural differences, components of culture, how cultural values are learned, and frameworks for understanding and comparing/contrasting different cultures); and culture specific (specific knowledge about another culture such as information about geography, economics, politics, law, history, customs, what to do and what not to do, etc.). Culture specific knowledge is both explicit and tacit. Consequently, culture specific knowledge is sometimes imparted through training in the classroom and in other cases through a process of socialization (such as through visits overseas) whereby awareness of behaviour is developed. Cross-cultural training enables the individual to learn both content and skills that will facilitate effective cross-cultural interaction by reducing misunderstandings and inappropriate behaviours.

43.5 INTERNATIONAL ASSIGNMENTS

23.   An international assignment is a temporary overseas task/work duty that may be short or long term. Long-term assignments tend to last between 2 and 5 years and involve moving the worker and family to the host country. The worker is expected to return 'home' after the assignment is completed. Short-term assignments can last from a few months to 1 year and involve moving only the worker abroad, not the family. Duties requiring a stay of less than 31 days duration per single visit are typically referred to as business trips.

24.   Preparing managers for work overseas remains a critical feature of international HRM. Typically the literature discusses expatriates as overseas workers though consideration is also given to the 'international manager' as a manager who is sent on an international assignment which may vary in length, and the transpatriates – individuals who operate globally rather than in specific local cultures. Expatriates need an understanding of the host culture and require skills that will enable them to choose the 'right' combination of verbal and non-verbal behaviours to achieve a smooth and harmonious relationship with their hosts in the foreign culture. Typically they require skills, such as adaptation, cross-cultural communication and partnership, work transition, stress-management, relationship building and negotiation techniques.

25.   The management of international assignments is a vast and complex subject, covering many different topics. It is therefore impossible within the scope of this section to do more than outline the important points to be considered. The main elements of international assignments include: resourcing, preparation, terms and conditions, remuneration, dual career problems and repatriation. International assignments incur substantial direct costs for the employer related to the relocation of the employee (and family), the provision of remuneration packages whilst abroad, repatriation costs and the recruitment and relocation of a replacement, if required. The costs of failure are also high and include damage done to relations with subsidiary staff, customers, suppliers and the local community. Some of the important implications of inadequate adjustment to international assignments are costly for both the organizations and individuals in terms of absenteeism, early return to the home country and lower performance. However, many companies still do not train managers for an international assignment. Lack of preparation generally has been associated with a higher expatriate failure rate.

26.   Hofstede (1997: p. 207) discusses intercultural encounters, suggesting that the simplest form of intercultural encounter is between one foreign individual and a new cultural environment – 'The foreigner

usually experiences some form of culture shock' (just as many higher education students do!). People on temporary assignment to a foreign cultural environment often report acculturation. Acculturation refers to the changes that occur as a result of first-hand contact between individuals of differing cultural origins. It is a process (see Figure 43.2) whereby an individual is socialized into an unfamiliar or new culture. The greater the acculturation, the more the language, customs, identity, attitudes and behaviours of the predominant culture are adopted. However, many expatriates experience difficulty in fully acculturating, only adopting the values and behaviours they find appropriate and acceptable to their existing cultures. It is a question of willingness and readiness.

FIGURE 43.2 Acculturation curve

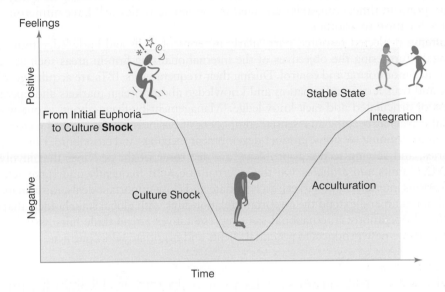

27.   There are several key areas to explore when selecting and preparing expatriates for assignment: adaptiveness, listening skills, empathy, respect for others, self-management, self-awareness, time management and political awareness. Self-awareness is key. An expatriate must be able to incorporate values, such as open-mindedness, high self-concept, non-judgmental attitudes, and social relaxation in order to understand the value of different cultures and become sensitive to the verbal and non-verbal cues of people from the foreign culture.

28.   Once the assignment is complete the employee returns home. The process of returning home at the end of an overseas assignment is termed repatriation. It is important to manage the repatriation process well if the experience is to benefit the employee and employer. Various studies found that employees who have completed an overseas assignment leave their company (often to join a competitor) soon after their return. This high rate of turnover impacts negatively on corporate effectiveness and efficiency by costing organizations in terms of losing a manager with valuable overseas experiences. This problem is exacerbated when both senior and high performing employees are specially selected for such assignments.

29.   Causes of employee turnover upon return from international assignments include: financial shock, psychological shock, lack of repatriation training, lack of career development, lack of positive corporate values related to the importance of an overseas assignment in the organization, and perceived impact of corporate turbulence on being able to place repatriates. Employees on international assignment often have greater autonomy and authority than similar domestic positions; they enjoy greater rewards and enjoy a high quality of life in the international assignment. Various surveys have revealed that many employees felt the return to the home office was not handled well and the repatriation process could have been handled much better. Repatriation training can help the person to set expectations about social and cultural readjustment challenges and thus reduce the re-entry culture shock. Organizations should consider progression and career planning with the repatriated employee, finding ways to utilize their knowledge and expertise upon

return. Not only does this make sense for the employer but will motivate the employee, raising esteem through recognition for the assignment.

30.   **International business travellers (IBTs):** IBTs are persons for whom a part – generally a major part – of their role involves international visits to foreign markets, facilities and projects. In the IHRM literature, staff movements tend to refer to those employees assigned to foreign operations for an extended period of time. Recently, there has been an observed trend towards increased use of non-standard (short term) international assignments. Changes are partly due to cost containment initiatives, as expatriates can be prohibitively expensive to support. In addition, multinational firms confront an increase in staff immobility, due to the rise in the number of dual-career couples, and other constraints, such as aged parents and single-parent families, along with changing work arrangements and shifting priorities that impact upon career choices. This compels companies to consider alternatives, with many using 'business trips' as a way of dealing with this issue. At any point in time, companies engaged in foreign activities will have numerous staff travelling from one country location to another.

31.   IBTs are often a neglected resource, particularly in terms of skills and knowledge transfer yet they play an important role in furthering the objectives of the internationalizing firm in areas such as sales, knowledge transfer, performance monitoring and control. During their frequent visits, IBTs are acquiring, collecting, assimilating, recording and transferring information and knowledge about foreign markets and operations. They are agents or carriers of articulated and tacit knowledge. 'Management-by-flying-about' is one-way of describing how international travel has become an essential component of business life. Group and regional meetings, staff briefing sessions, joint training sessions, product development meetings and cross-border project work, opening or closing factories, and solving technical problems are just some of the activities that involve international travel between MNC units and affiliates. On the external side, staff frequently undertake activities related to stakeholders in various international markets: to negotiate and close important deals, raise finance, sell products and services, and maintain and extend the important relationships with global stakeholders that are essential to smooth international operations. International sales representatives attend trade fairs, visit foreign agents and distributors, demonstrate new products to potential clients and negotiate sales contracts.

43.6 IHRM AND THE TRANSFER OF HR PRACTICES IN MNCs

32.   Thus far we have discussed work overseas and occasionally alluded to the role of IHRM in support. We will now take a closer look at the function. IHRM is about the worldwide management of human resources (Kelly, 2009). It concerns the processes and activities of people management which involve more than one national context. IHRM exists to assist organizations make the most effective use of their HR in the international context. The purpose of IHRM is to enable the MNE to be a global success. This entails being: (a) competitive through the world, (b) efficient, (c) locally responsive, (d) flexible and adaptable within the shortest of time periods, and (e) capable of transferring knowledge and learning across their globally dispersed units. Some scholars consider it to be the process of selecting, training, developing and compensating personnel in overseas positions. Others see it to be about global talent management. In the following paragraphs we take a closer look at more specific roles and functions often associated with IHRM.

33.   In some cases the HR function may develop practices for subsidiary use. In other cases subsidiaries will be autonomous, developing their own practices but in line with the overarching philosophy/policy framework. Policies and procedures constitute elements of the formal HR system and are used to influence HR related decisions throughout the organization. Statements of HR philosophy, whilst general, have the ability to prescribe limits on the actual treatment of individuals regardless of location.

34.   The glocal theme will affect the choice of appropriate HR practices, whether to inherit them from the parent company, adapt or create them locally. Transferring practices (diffusion) enables the beneficial transfer of knowledge and expertise across parts of the multinational company. Practices originate and become established in a given legal, institutional, political and cultural context. To some extent, they are dependent on this context and cannot operate in a different environment. The extent of this dependence varies from one area of HRM to another; in other words the diffusion ability of some practices is higher than that of others. Managers at the headquarters of the multinational may seek to operate a practice in a number of

countries that might be prevented from doing so by the legal, institutional and cultural constraints of the country to which the practice is directed. The country of origin, the way the multinational is structured, the way in which it established its foreign subsidiaries and the nature of production, integration or either, may constrain or facilitate the transfer of practices across borders.

35.   Beyond fitting in with the local environment and with the MNE, the local HR unit needs to fit in with its competitive strategy. That is, the local unit needs to develop HR practices that are not only consistent with the policies of the MNE, but also fit the competitive strategy of the unit (e.g. overseas subsidiary). The major objective of IHRM regarding internal operations is: being responsive to and effective in the local environment, yet willing and ready to act in a coordinated fashion with the rest of the MNE units. To facilitate local adaptation and fit, the subsidiary or local unit may staff the HR function with host-country nationals. In fact, this is one of the positions that MNEs seem to insist upon filling with a host-country national.

36.   The attitudes, values (see orientations) and overseas experiences of senior management at headquarters are likely to be significant influences on strategic IHRM. Three orientations can be described. The ethnocentric approach (using one's own set of standards and customs to judge all people, often unconsciously – a belief that home nationals are superior) may manifest as little autonomy in subsidiaries, strategic decisions are made at headquarters and key jobs at both domestic and foreign operations are held by headquarters' management personnel. In the case of a polycentric approach (a belief that host country cultures are different and as such local people are better placed to make business decisions), the MNE treats each subsidiary as a distinct national entity with more decision-making autonomy. Subsidiaries are usually managed by local nationals who are seldom promoted to positions at headquarters. This leads to considerable autonomy with regard to HR decisions and activities in local operations. Finally a geocentric approach (a belief that superiority is not equated with nationality) is characterized by a focus on ability.

RESOURCING: PLANNING, RECRUITMENT AND SELECTION

37.   In companies that function in a global environment, there is a need to distinguish between different types of employees. Traditionally, they are classified as one of three types:

Parent country national (PCN): The employee's nationality is the same as the organizations

Host country national (HCN): The employee's nationality is the same as the location of the subsidiary

Third country national (TCN): The employee's nationality is neither that of the organization nor that of the location of the subsidiary

Linking with parent company management orientations, ethnocentric staffing refers to the use of individuals from the home country to manage operations abroad; polycentric staffing involves the use of individuals from the host country to manage operations and geocentric staffing describes a situation where the best-qualified individuals, regardless of nationality, manage operations. In many organizations an employee's classification is tied to remuneration as well as benefits and opportunities for promotion.

38.   Resourcing (staffing) is a major international human resource (IHRM) practice that MNEs have used to help coordinate and control their far-flung global operations. Traditionally MNEs have sent PCNs or expatriates abroad to ensure that the policies and procedures of the home office were being carried out to the letter in foreign operations. As costs became prohibitive and career issues made these assignments less attractive, MNEs turned to TCNs and HCNs to satisfy international staffing needs. Whilst this approach solved the staffing need, it raised the concern about its ability to help with the needs for coordination and control (refer back to Section 10).

INTERNATIONAL PERFORMANCE MANAGEMENT

39.   As with other aspects of HR practice the key question is the extent to which an approach can be standardized. Scholars such as Armstrong and Taylor (2014: p. 482) suggest a standardized approach may be warranted for the sake of global integration, fairness and the mobility of global employees in particular. They cite research which suggests a trend towards standardization, finding little or no difference across the

world. Organizations may use global competencies, common evaluation processes and common approaches to rewards. This research commented, 'it was difficult therefore, to find many distinctive local practices'. However, there does seem to be some contradiction amongst researchers in this field. For example, Lucas, Lupton and Mathieson (2007: p. 173) argue there is evidence of limited convergence within the performance management systems of many countries. They cite various authors who suggest that it is cultural differences which make it difficult to standardize aspects of performance management practice.

40.   There are, however, several international performance management issues to consider. There may be a difference in perception, between the parent and host country, about what performance means. This may manifest as unclear or contradictory performance objectives of foreign operations. The parent company may lack understanding of the foreign environment and culture and it will be difficult for the international organization to maintain control over how line managers implement performance management. Cultural differences, particularly when contrasting the face-saving Asian cultures with an individualistic West, are likely to manifest in the way that performance feedback is provided. Furthermore, the implementation of a universal rating system may prove problematic.

REWARD

41.   In the following paragraphs we consider how the practice of reward management varies in different countries; how organizations reward those employees required to work outside their home country; and how organizations that employ local people in more than one country can manage their reward strategy. Organizations use their reward and benefits policies as a means of reinforcing organization culture throughout the world (Lucas, Lupton and Mathieson, 2007: p. 202). Unfortunately, this can create conflict with the host country national culture. In many countries there is now a minimum wage yet there is still considerable difference in wages paid in different countries. There is also considerable difference within any given country. Pay inequality, the difference between the top and bottom earners, is much greater in countries like the USA as compared with some Scandinavian countries for example. Within a country a number of factors can contribute towards this: density of union membership, centralization of collective bargaining, taxation policies, etc.

42.   National culture dimensions can explain country variations in basic, variable or performance related pay. For example, seniority-based pay systems and skill-based pay systems are more likely to be found in cultures with high uncertainty avoidance. Performance related pay is often associated with individualistic cultures. High levels of power distance over benefit packages related to status and high individualism is often associated with increasing use of flexible benefits.

43.   Earlier we discussed the complexity management requirements of IHRM. This is also apparent when seeking to manage reward on a global basis. As noted by Lucas, Lupton and Mathieson (2007: p. 215) an organization may have home employees based in several countries, employees from several countries in one location, and home and third country nationals in multiple locations. Furthermore, the organization may be using all of the types of assignment outlined earlier in this chapter. Consequently, some IHR professionals call for a global reward strategy whilst others recognize the difficulties associated with diversity in national practices. Those seeking to develop a global reward strategy need to recognize national differences in culture, taxation and local economic context. Any global reward strategy will need to be flexible if it is to be used around the world in different national contexts and might seek equity in pay for similar jobs around the globe. Such systems will need to be as simple as possible to administer whilst reflecting national differences. Similarly they will need to facilitate different forms of international working whilst attracting and retaining talent. Thus, the HR professional seeking to develop a global reward strategy will have a number of tensions and challenges to balance.

43.7 INTERNATIONAL LEADERSHIP AND DEVELOPING GLOBALLY MINDED MANAGERS

44.   Having considered the diffusion of practice we now consider the appropriateness of leadership and management styles around the world. Organizational leadership (Chapter 6) is the ability of an

individual to influence, motivate and enable others to contribute towards the effectiveness and success of the organizations of which they are members. We might now ask how to motivate and influence others in different cultures. We must ask whether the leadership theories are relevant or appropriate in different parts of the world and whether the local culture and environmental forces define situations that warrant specific leadership approaches, styles and behaviours.

45. To what extent is leadership culturally contingent? As with the domestic leader, the international leader must inspire and influence people anywhere in the world. Leadership is required within every organization around the world, however culture must be considered when contemplating the different theories of leadership. Situational determinants of leadership suggest that no single leadership style works well in all situations. Being a participative leader is more important in some countries as opposed to others. Once again, Hofstede's cultural dimensions provide a useful framework or model to study leader-subordinate relationships. Subordinates from high power distance countries are more likely to favour autocratic leadership whilst employees of lower power distance countries are more likely to prefer a consultative or participatory leadership style. An inappropriate style can be counter-productive in certain cultures.

46. If an organization is to accomplish its objectives, leaders and managers must encourage people to perform their jobs efficiently and effectively through a variety of motivational techniques. If we are to ensure people from any country or culture do what we want them to do, in the best interest of the organization, we must understand their needs and goals in order to motivate them. This necessitates an understanding of their values, attitude and beliefs and in particular those in relation to work. Work attitudes vary from country to country. Employees in certain countries expect to work longer hours, take shorter holidays and earn less money. In certain countries, particular motivational factors are relatively more important than others. Generally we cannot assume the universal applicability of motivational theories. International managers must make use of their cultural knowledge to infer the best means of motivating in that context.

47. Towards the end of the twentieth century, Bartlett and Ghoshal (1992) saw the development of a cadre of managers with a global mind set to be the only way in which organizations working across borders can create a common culture and deal effectively with the complexity inherent in international business. Companies must identify managers with global potential and provide them with various learning and development opportunities. For example, having one or more international assignments, working on cross-national teams and projects, and learning other languages and cultures contribute to making a manager more globally minded. Likewise, Paul Sparrow, Hugh Scullion and Elaine Farndale (cited in Scullion and Collings 2010: p. 39) discuss global talent management (GTM) and the new rules for the corporate HR function. When talking about GTM they define talent in terms of the key positions within an organization. This view of GTM means focusing on developing a global pool of people to fill these positions. In discussing responsibilities of the corporate HR role they argue a need for such professionals to champion processes (practices), and act as guardians of culture in particular.

CONCLUSION

48. IHRM involves the worldwide management of people. IHRM differs from HRM in a number of ways. IHRM is more complex, operating across national boundaries and it is therefore necessary to manage a wide mix of people. The HR professional must be culturally competent or at least have an awareness of national culture issues which may be utilized in the management of expatriates, overseas workers and the selection or adaptation of appropriate HR practices to use in other parts of the world. Furthermore, aside from choices about the extent to which parent company practices are utilized abroad, decisions will need to be made about the extent of decentralizing HR. There is a need to determine who will make resourcing decisions etc. Such decisions will be influenced by the fundamental strategy of the multinational – where it lies on the continuum between a global and multidomestic approach. Decisions will also be influenced by the orientation of key senior managers, the extent to which they are ethno or polycentric.

QUESTIONS

1   Explain the role of the IHRM function.

2   Discuss factors which may impact upon HR policy and practice design and adoption in different countries of operation.

3   Discuss how the HR function can help develop culturally competent employees.

4   Explain how the HR function may support employees working in other countries.

REFERENCES

Armstrong, M. and Taylor, S. (2014) *Armstrong's Handbook of Human Resource Management Practice*, 13th edn, Kogan Page.

Bartlett, C. and Ghoshal, S. (1992) 'What is a global manager?', *Harvard Business Review* (September/October): 124–132.

Hofstede, G. (1997) *Cultures and Organizations*, McGraw-Hill.

Kelly, P.P. (2009) *International Business and Management*, Cengage Learning EMEA.

Lucas, R., Lupton, B. and Mathieson, H. (2007) *Human Resource Management in an International Context*, CIPD.

Scullion, H. and Collings, D. (2010) *Global Talent Management*, Routledge.

SKILL SHEET 12   **HRM**

This skills sheet provides practical advice on writing HR policies and procedures, developing performance appraisal forms and determining staffing needs (workforce planning).

1. Writing the HR Policies

Introducing HR policies and procedures gives organizations the opportunity to offer a fair and consistent approach to managing their staff.

HR policies are a written source of guidance on how a wide range of issues should be handled within an employing organization. Certain HR policies and procedures are needed to comply with legal requirements. A written health and safety policy is required for any organization with five or more employees, whilst there are also important legislative provisions surrounding the setting out of formal disciplinary and grievance procedures.

An organization might have a distinct policy setting out its criteria for selection, together with other relevant policies for new joiners (such as induction). A reward policy might address areas such as how jobs are graded and performance rewarded; health, safety and well-being policies might cover topics such as attendance/absence etc.; employee relations policies might cover disciplinary and grievance matters, harassment and bullying.

Refer back to skills sheet 7 for advice on writing policy.

The first step is to **establish the need for a policy**. Then develop policy content and **draft policy**. Review and approve before implementing and communicating.

When introducing and reviewing HR policies, the following guidelines from the CIPD may be helpful:

- assess/audit what is already in existence, both formally and informally
- research and benchmark against other organizations' practice, particularly in the same sector or location
- analyze external factors (employment legislation etc.)
- consult with staff representatives and/or unions; establish steering groups/working parties to help with implementation

- set realistic timescales
- pilot draft policies
- offer specific guidance to managers
- include the policies as part of the induction process
- implement a continuous review process and ensure policies are complementary, flexible, practical and enforceable.

All policies should be written in plain English, avoiding jargon so that they are user-friendly and easily understood by all employees. It may be helpful to include a date of publication and/or most recent review. Policies should also indicate who should be contacted with queries about the content and who is responsible for updating and reviewing them.

A policy should include the following sections (Template):

POLICY NAME/TITLE
Purpose
The purpose sets out what the policy intends to accomplish, or the goal of the policy. For example, a health and safety policy may have a purpose of ensuring a safe and healthy workplace for all workers in compliance with the relevant health and safety legislation.

Scope
The scope outlines to whom the policy applies. It may apply to all staff and workers, or differentiate based on level, location, employment status or department.

Statement
The statement is the actual rule or standard the policy needs to communicate.

Responsibilities
Outline the responsibilities of the board, management and staff in regards to the policy as well as who is responsible for developing, maintaining, monitoring and implementing the policy.
If there are consequences for not complying with the policy (e.g., disciplinary), be sure to mention this. For example, 'Failure to comply with this policy could result in disciplinary measure up to and including just cause for termination of your employment.'

Definitions

Clearly define any terms used within the policy. If the terms are included in legislation that underpin the policy, ensure usage of the definitions from the legislation (e.g., disability, prohibited grounds, discrimination, harassment, workplace violence).

Questions

Identify the person or position employees can approach if they have questions.

References

Reference any other policies, documents or legislation that support the interpretation of this policy.

Effective Date

Indicate the date the policy came into effect and the date of any revisions.

Review Date

Indicate the date the policy is due to be reviewed.

Approval

Indicate who approved the policy and the date of approval (e.g., the Board, the Human Resources Policy Committee, the Executive Director)

EXAMPLE[1]

Title: Overtime

Scope: All employees

Overtime is only paid to staff members whose salary falls within Salary Range 1–6, for working in excess of 37 hours per week, provided that overtime worked is nondiscretionary (non-elective). Overtime is nondiscretionary when a supervisor/manager asks the employee to work and this usually involves a specific project outside normal work plans. Supervisors will give reasonable notice whenever overtime is needed so that the employee involved has sufficient time to make the necessary arrangements. Overtime compensation, either monetary or lieu time will not be provided to staff members graded 7 or above.

Questions about this policy may be directed to:

Effective Date:

Review Date:

Approved by:

---

[1] Sample policies are provided for reference only. Always consult current legislation to create policies and procedures for your organization.

Remember: a policy is a formal statement of a principle or rule that members of an organization must follow. A procedure tells members of the organization how to carry out or implement a policy. Policy is the 'what' and the procedure is the 'how to'.

An employee handbook describes the organization's policies and procedures. The handbook may also contain general information about the organization such as its priorities, the organization chart, the job classifications, whether positions are covered by a collective agreement and bargaining status for all groups of employees.

2. Writing HR Procedures

A procedure states what it is that will be done to implement the policy. Companies write procedures in order to make sure things are done without mistakes and omissions. Whilst policies guide the way people make decisions, procedures show the 'how to's' for completing a task or process. Procedures are action oriented, often instructional; they outline steps to take, and the order in which they need to be taken.

How to Write a Procedure:

1. **Gather Information** – detailed information on the process you are making into a procedure
2. **Draft the procedure** – don't worry about exact words and format at this stage. The main purpose is to include the information you need.
   Use the standard procedure format
   Write actions out in the order in which they happen – specify what it is that will be done, by whom and how
   Avoid too many words
   Use lists and bullets
   Use the active voice
3. **Presentation** – Consider using flow charts for example and use the following structure:

NAME OF ORGANIZATION
Unit name if specific to a unit
Page XXX of XXX pages
Issue Date:
Issue Number:

PROCEDURE
Title:

Purpose and scope: specify purpose of procedure, the area covered, exclusions

Responsibility: for implementing procedure: specify who will implement the procedure

Procedure: listing (or depicting) sequentially exactly what must be done and noting exceptions

Documentation: list documents to be used with the procedure and attach examples of completed documentation, if appropriate

Records: list any records created as a result of using the procedure, where they are stored and for how long

Authorization and date: signed and dated by the person authorizing the procedure

4. **Review and Pilot** – identify any gaps in the procedure by trialling the procedure with a user who was not involved in its development
5. **Redraft the procedure** on the basis of the review/trial
6. **Authorization** – refine and forward it to the relevant person for authorization and distribution
7. **Implementation**

Useful guidance can be found using the following resources:

– Discipline and grievances at work **http:// www.cipd.co.uk/hr-resources/factsheets/ discipline-grievances-at-work.aspx**
– ACAS (2009) Disciplinary and grievance procedures. Code of Practice 1. London: ACAS. Available at: **http://www.acas.org.uk**
– Absence measurement and management **http://www.cipd.co.uk/hr-resources/factsheets/ absence-measurement-management.aspx**

3. Performance Appraisal Forms

Performance appraisal (or performance review) is an opportunity for individual employees and those concerned with their performance, typically line managers, to engage in a dialogue about their performance and development, as well as the support required from the manager. The five key elements of the performance appraisal are:

Measurement – assessing performance against agreed targets and objectives, and behaviour/attitudes against espoused values.

Feedback – providing information to individuals on their performance and progress and on what is required to continue to perform well in the future, particularly in view of any change programme and evolution of job roles.

Positive reinforcement – emphasizing what has been done well and making only constructive criticism about what might be improved, and drawing out the importance of how things are done, as well as what is done, and ensuring effort is directed at value-adding activities.

Exchange of views – a frank exchange of views about what has happened, how appraisee's can improve their performance, the support they need from their managers to achieve this and their aspirations for their future career.

Agreement – jointly reaching an understanding by all parties about what needs to be done to improve and sustain performance generally and overcome any issues raised in the course of the discussion.

Form Structure:

The appraisal form provides a structure for the process. The first part of the form will typically contain essential **identifying data**: organization, division and department, year or period covered, name, position, location/site/based at/contact details (e.g., email), time in present position, length of service, etc. In order to avoid age discrimination it may be better to omit such data.

Part 2 of the form will often be **completed by the appraisee** before the interview/review: this part may start with a text box for the appraisee to indicate their understanding of their duties and responsibilities; the appraisee will typically list the objectives (and standards/targets) they set out to achieve in the past X months and utilize a rating scale to score their performance against each objective; there may be a section to then self-score certain skills and behaviours, capabilities or knowledge (for example they may rate their time management, communication, delegation, team working or IT skills, etc. Finally, there may be a section for the employee to look forward – objectives, activities, development opportunities, etc.

Part 3 (to be **completed before/during the appraisal by the appraiser –** where appropriate and then discussed and confirmed or amended in discussion with the appraisee during the appraisal): start with identifying data for the appraiser – name of appraiser, position and time managing appraisee; this will be followed by a section to describe the purpose of the appraisee's job. List the objectives the appraisee set out to achieve in the past X months with the measures or standards agreed – against each; comment on achievement or otherwise, with reasons where appropriate. Score the performance against each objective using an appropriate rating scale. Then score certain skills and behaviours, capabilities, competencies or knowledge (for example it may be appropriate to rate their time management, communication, delegation, team-working or IT skills, etc.). This may be role specific.

In some cases there will then be an **overall Annual Performance Rating** for the position, e.g. Performance during appraisal period

5 **Exceptional**: was consistently superior and significantly exceeded expectations.

4 **Highly effective**: frequently exceeded expectations.

3 **Proficient**: met expectations.

2 **Inconsistent**: met some, but not all expectations for the position. Performance improvement process should be initiated.

1 **Unsatisfactory**: consistently failed to meet minimum expectations for the position. Individual lacks or did not apply knowledge, skills or behaviour expected for the position. Performance improvement process should be initiated.

N/A New: Individual has not been in position long enough to fully demonstrate the competencies required for the position. This appraisal is provided for feedback purposes. Individual will, therefore, be formally reviewed and rated at a later agreed upon date.

Include free space for general comments by supervisor, supervisor's manager and employee.

Finally, the form will have space to be signed and dated by appraiser and appraisee.

Consideration may also be given to including space for
Action plans
Assessment of potential

Organizations typically write procedures for appraising performance which are usually based on an appraisal meeting.

Ratings examples:

A 1-4 scoring system gives less opportunity for middling, non-committal answers. 1 = little or no competence, 2 = some competence, but below level required for role, 3 = competence at required level for role, 4 = competence exceeds level required for role; Or: 1 = never meets standard, 2 = sometimes meets standard, 3 = often meets standard, 4 = always meets standard.

Performance criteria examples: Volume of work, Job knowledge, Safety awareness, Dependability, Teamwork, Attendance and punctuality, Work planning.

Useful resources: Managing staff – free documents to help you manage staff http://www.acas.org.uk/index.aspx?articleid=1438

4. Workforce Planning: Forecasting HR Needs

Organizations need to know how many people they need and with what capabilities to meet present and future business requirements.

According to the CIPD, *Workforce planning* is a core process of HRM that is shaped by organizational strategy and ensures the right number of people with the appropriate skills are in the right place at the right time to deliver short- and long-term organizational objectives. The term 'workforce planning' tends to embrace a diverse and extensive range of activities. Whilst the original concept of workforce planning fell out of favour around the early 1980s, as some commentators deemed it to be an inflexible process, more recent interpretations, based on less rigid forecasting, with more flexible target ranges and a greater role for contextual understanding, mean that the technique is an increasingly useful tool amongst the HR profession.

Workforce planning is about generating information, analyzing it to inform future demand for labour and then translating that into a set of actions that will develop and build on the existing workforce to meet that demand. The workforce planning process, see Figure 1, can take various forms but is really about operationalizing the business strategy (plans, forecasts and budgets) into a set of actions to ensure a workforce capable of delivering the organization's strategic goals and objectives.

FIGURE 1

Business Plans (Forecasts and Budgets)

↓

Demand Forecasts (numbers required)

↓

Supply Forecasts (numbers available)

↓

Compare demand and supply

↓

Action: no action, surplus or shortage

↓

Implement, Monitor and Evaluate

As indicated in Figure 1, workforce planning is an integral part of business planning. Plans (typically manifest as strategies and budgets) indicate the scale of business activity expected in the near future. Workforce planning interprets these plans in terms of people requirements. Planning may be approached quantitatively (hard) or qualitatively and subjectively (soft). It is not a precise science and is sometimes considered more an art. Despite this, many approach the process in a systematic manner.

Once the plans have been formulated there is a need for analysis. The analysis consists of two activities. The first activity is to estimate *demand* (number of people required) and the second activity is to estimate *supply* (number of people likely to be available). Demand may be forecast using a number of methods such as:

(1) **Quantitative forecast** – forecast data, typically used in the budgetary processes, this translated into activity levels for each functional department. For example, the sales budget could be translated into a manufacturing plan. It could be used to estimate the number of sales representatives or accounts staff to process expecting orders. Forecast can be used to determine the number of hours to be worked by product or process activity and to determine the skills and capabilities required to undertake the work.

(2) **Managerial judgement** – using this method, managers will consider the future workload of their departments and then forecast requirements.

(3) **Ratio – trend analysis** is carried out by analyzing existing ratios between an activity level and the number of employees working on that activity. The ratio may then be applied to forecasted activity levels to determine an adjusted number of people required. For example, presently an organization may have five people in the accounts department who process 1000 orders per day. Assuming they are not under or over-resourced this would mean that it requires one person for every 200 orders per day (1:200). Should the organization forecast a need to process 1400 orders per day they could determine the staffing level by dividing the forecast (1400) by 200, i.e. 7. Of course there will be a need to take account of possible improvements in productivity that may impact upon the ratio for the coming year.

(4) **Work – study techniques** are typically used to calculate how long operations should take and the number of people required. Such techniques may be used in combination with ratio-trend analysis.

In order to forecast future requirements, the organization must subtract demand from supply to determine whether there is a deficit or surplus rolling into the next year. Data may be set out as follows (see Figure 2):

FIGURE 2

Current staff level	
Annual staff turnover	e.g. 10%
Expected staff loss during the year	Current × turnover
Balance at end of year	Current − loss
Number required at end of year	<from demand forecast>
Number of new staff required	Required − Balance

Action is then undertaken to bring the required staff number in line with the actual staff number. This may involve recruitment and selection, improving productivity or downsizing and reducing hours.

Section Fourteen
Financial Aspects of Management

CHAPTER 44
FINANCIAL AND MANAGEMENT ACCOUNTING – AN INTRODUCTION

Key Concepts

- Accounting
- Balance sheet
- Cost accounting
- Financial accounting
- Management accounting
- Profit and loss account

Learning Outcomes   Having read this chapter, you should be able to:

- distinguish between financial accounting and management accounting
- outline what is meant by cost accounting
- explain the accounting process
- describe the principal (financial) statements of accounts
- explain how society assures financial statements are reported fairly.

1.   This chapter provides an introduction to accounting, the accounting process, financial statements and different types of cost. The next chapter will focus more on management accounting, budgeting and the use of financial information in internal decision-making.

2.   As yet, we have not discussed the management of financial resources within the organization. The system for recording and summarizing business transactions and activities designed to accumulate, measure and communicate financial information about economic entities for decision-making purposes is termed accounting. **Accounting** refers to the overall process of identifying, measuring, recording, interpreting and

communicating the results of economic activity; tracking business income and expenses and using these measurements to answer specific questions about the financial and tax status of the business, i.e. it is a system that provides quantitative information about finances. A simpler definition is provided by Black and Al-Kilani (2013); they suggest that accounting can be defined simply as the recording, summarizing and interpretation of financial information. In order to understand accounting, an appreciation of the decision-making process is required. We therefore advise a re-read of Chapter 16 before continuing.

3. Accounting is a language that communicates economic information to people and entities (stakeholders) that have an interest in an organization (Drury, 2012). They may come from within (e.g. managers and employees) or outside (e.g. shareholders, creditors and investors) of the organization. Each has its own requirement for information, the way it may be produced and communicated. Such information may concern the past, present or future. Thus accounting information may be used for investment decision-making, credit decisions, pricing decisions and investment decisions. It may also be used for inventory and logistics management (refer back to Chapter 40); operations management (Chapter 38); performance management (Chapter 41) and by the HR and marketing functions.

4. Drury (2012) distinguishes between financial, management and cost accounting. Whereas financial accounting is the use of accounting information for reporting to parties outside the organization, management accounting is concerned with the provisions and use of accounting information to managers within organizations, to provide them with the basis for making informed business decisions, thus allowing them to be better equipped in their management and control functions. The main differences between these two branches of accounting are based on legal requirements (more relevant to financial accounting), the time orientation (financial accounting more oriented to the past) and their focus; whereas financial accounting tends to focus on the whole business, management accounting may focus on parts of the organization. In the next chapter we consider the role of management accounting in providing information to managers for decision-making, planning, control and performance management.

5. In this chapter we outline the accounting system and process, how financial transactions are recorded and information generated for a range of stakeholders. We start by exploring the differences between management (internal) and financial (external) accounting in a little more detail, the financial accounting process and then consider financial statements as the information outputs. The three main financial statements (income, balance sheet and cash flow) are described as typical components of the company annual report. Later we link in with Chapter 13 and discuss the importance of assuring financial statements are reported accurately and fairly. Aspects of this chapter act as a foundation and introduction to the following chapter which will consider the role of accounting information in decision-making.

44.1 ACCOUNTING

6. It is not easy to provide a concise definition of accounting since the word has a broad application within businesses. A simple definition is the recording of financial or money transactions. Accounting is the systematic recording, reporting and analysis of the monetary financial transactions of a business; it is a system that provides quantitative information about finances. Accounting and accountancy also refers to the occupation of maintaining and auditing records and preparing financial reports for a business. Accounting refers to processes involved in providing information about a company's financial situation. This includes recording financial information and compiling it into financial statements for public use in assessing the financial health of a company.

7. Accounting is typically split into two key branches: financial accounting and management accounting. In simple terms, management accounting can be defined as the provision of information required by management for planning, organizing and control. Management accounting is concerned with information for management purposes and focuses on the internal running of the organization. Management accountants therefore help with strategy formulation, planning and decision-making and the safeguarding of assets. Throughout this book we have discussed competitive advantage in terms of cost (efficiency gains), differentiation (adding value), quality and speed of delivery. Management accounting has a role to play in contributing to sources of competitive advantage. Keeping costs low and being cost-efficient provides an organization with advantage.

8.   Financial accounts on the other hand are concerned with classifying, measuring and recording the transactions of a business. At the end of a period (typically a year), financial statements are prepared to show the performance and position of the business. The purpose of financial accounting statements is mainly to show the financial position of a business at a particular point in time and to show how that business has performed over a specific period. Financial accounts are geared towards external users of accounting information. To answer their needs, financial accountants draw up the profit and loss account, balance sheet and cash flow statement for the company as a whole. Certain companies are required to publish their annual report and accounts; others must file various documents and reports with Companies House.

44.2 COST ACCOUNTING

9.   Accounting systems measure costs and cost accounting is concerned with cost accumulation for inventory valuation to meet the requirements of external reporting and internal profit measurement (Drury, 2013: p. 20). Cost in the simple sense simply means an amount that has to be paid or spent to buy or obtain something. Despite this relatively simple definition there are many different types of cost to consider in management and accounting – for example, fixed or variable costs, opportunity and sunk costs. We have listed some of the important cost definitions in the table below:

COST OBJECT	Any activity for which a separate measurement of costs is desired
DIRECT MATERIAL COSTS	Material costs that can be specifically and exclusively identified with a particular cost object
DIRECT LABOUR COSTS	Labour costs that can be specifically and exclusively identified with a particular cost object
INDIRECT COSTS	Costs that cannot be identified specifically and exclusively with a given cost object, also known as overheads
PRIME COST	The sum of all direct manufacturing costs
COST ALLOCATION	The process of assigning costs to cost objects where a direct measure of the resources consumed by these cost objects does not exist.
PERIOD COSTS	Costs that are not included in the inventory valuation of goods and which are treated as expenses for the period in which they are incurred
PRODUCT COSTS	Costs that are identified with goods purchased or produced for resale and which are attached to products and included in the inventory valuation of goods
FIXED COSTS	Costs that remain constant for a specified time period and which are not affected by the volume of activity
VARIABLE COSTS	Costs that vary in direct proportion to the volume of activity
AVOIDABLE COSTS	Costs that may be saved by not adopting a given alternative
SUNK COST	Costs that have been incurred by a decision made in the past and that cannot be changed by any decision that will be made in the future
OPPORTUNITY COST	Benefit, profit or value of something that must be given up to acquire or achieve something else. Since every resource (land, money, time, etc.) can be put to alternative uses, every action, choice or decision has an associated opportunity cost
INCREMENTAL COSTS	The difference between the costs of each alternative action under consideration, also known as differential costs
MARGINAL COST	The addition to total cost resulting from the production of one additional unit of output

10.   Managers often want to know the cost of something, this is the cost object which could be a product, the cost to provide a service or run a department. If we were considering the cost of a product, as a manufacturing or merchandising organization, we would also be interested in the range of costs associated with the product. This might include raw materials, labour, plant and machinery. Costs that are

assigned to cost objects may be categorized as direct (such as parts or labour costs that can be specifically associated with a particular cost object) or indirect (for example the wages of all employees whose time cannot be identified with a specific product). Direct costs then can be traced easily and accurately to a cost object whilst the indirect costs cannot. In the case of indirect costs we normally make an estimate of resources consumed by cost objects using cost allocations.

11. Aside from understanding how to allocate costs it is also important for the manager to understand cost behaviour, the way in which a cost reacts or responds to changes in the level of business activity. Activity (volume) may be measured in terms of units of production or sales, hours worked, customers serviced, etc. Fixed and variable costs are often identified. Examples of fixed costs include salaries, leasing charges, insurance, property, equipment, etc. In the case of manufacturing, variable costs may include materials, energy and sales commissions.

12. As has been demonstrated above, the term cost has multiple meanings which must be understood in order to gain knowledge of accounting. Cost accounting provides the detailed cost information that management needs to control current operations and plan for the future. Since managers are making decisions only for their own organization, there is no need for the information to be comparable to similar information from other organizations. However, this is not the case with financial accounting which we discuss next.

44.3 FINANCIAL ACCOUNTING PROCESS

13. As was highlighted earlier, financial accounting is the part of accountancy concerned with the preparation of financial statements for shareholders, investors and other external stakeholders in the main. Financial accountancy is used to prepare accounting information for people outside the organization; it is the process of summarizing financial data taken from an organization's accounting records and publishing it in the form of annual reports. Financial accountants produce financial statements based on the accounting standards in a given jurisdiction. Thus, financial accounting aims at finding out results of an accounting year in the form of Profit and Loss Account and Balance Sheet. Cost accounting on the other hand aims at computing cost of production/service in a scientific manner and facilitates cost control and cost reduction. In financial accounting, cost classification is based on type of transactions, e.g. salaries, repairs, insurance, stores, etc. In cost accounting, classification is basically on the basis of functions, activities, products, process and on internal planning and control and information needs of the organization.

14. Wood and Horner (2010: p. 4) list three terms which they believe underpin much of the system of financial accounting: *assets*, *liabilities* and *capital* (or equity). The business uses assets (resources) as part of its activities. Liabilities represent the debts of the business and capital, typically in the form of money, refers to the resources supplied to the business by the owners.

15. The accounting process includes a sequence of activities involving recording the income and expenditure of an organization. Companies have an accounts or finance department to manage their accounting details. In smaller companies activities associated with book-keeping and accounts preparation may be outsourced. The function will record all the business transactions, and keep a track of the incomes and expenses of the business. The accounting department also helps to determine the correct financial position and standing of the business. For a systematic and accurate recording of transactions, accounting is important. The process is shown in Figure 44.1 and an outline of each activity is provided in the following paragraphs.

16. The first activity in the accounting process involves identifying a *transaction* or event, and finding the source documents for it. Business transactions may include buying supplies from vendors, selling goods to customers, payment of labour cost, salary of employees, etc. The source document of the transaction may be the invoice, purchase order, receipts, payment slips, etc. These source documents are also stored as a record of the transaction history. Book-keeping, in business, is the recording of financial transactions.

17. A record is made in the relevant entries of a journal. A *journal* is also called the 'Day book' or 'Book of original entry' because the transactions are recorded in a chronological order. Typical day books utilized in organizations include the sales, purchases, return inwards, return outwards and cash day books. Also, transactions are recorded in the journal using a double-entry system. An entry occurs in at least two

FIGURE 44.1 **Accounting process**

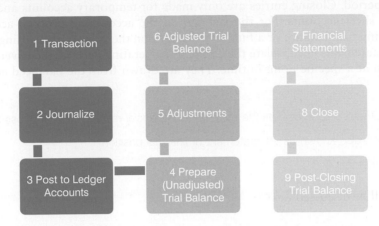

accounts one of which is debited and the other is credited. In the normal course of business, a document is produced each time a transaction occurs; for example sales and purchases usually have invoices or receipts. Book-keeping involves, first of all, recording the details of all of these source documents into journals. After a certain period, typically a month, the columns in each journal are each totalled to give a summary for the period. For an overview of processing financial data, ledgers, cash books, day books and journals see Black and Al-Kilani (2013: Chapter 2).

18.   The next activity to undertake is transferring the journal entries into the appropriate *ledger* accounts – a book or other collection of financial accounts. Whereas the journals/day books will contain more information, the ledger will only provide a small amount of information about transactions. This information is based on past transactions of these accounts and their current balances. Each transaction impacts upon the subsidiary ledgers and a collective sum is seen in the general ledger. A general ledger is a complete record of financial transactions over the life of a company. The ledger holds account information needed to prepare financial statements, and includes accounts for assets, liabilities, owners' equity, revenues and expenses. It is common practice to have three distinct ledges: a sales ledger (details of the debtors), a purchase ledger (details of creditors) and a general (or nominal) ledger.

19.   The next activity involves preparing a *trial balance*. This summarises the general ledger account balances, showing debit and credit columns. It is created to ensure that the debit amount is equal to the credit amount. The general purpose of producing a trial balance is to ensure the entries in a company's book-keeping system are mathematically correct. If any discrepancy is found in the amounts, it suggests an error in the posting of original transactions. Errors must be corrected immediately. A member of the accounts team will have to identify and rectify the errors by making the correct entries.

20.   The accounts function will have to make *adjusting entries* in order to record the accrued and deferred amounts. These are additional adjusting entries which may not be generated directly through the source documents. This may include expenses or incomes which had taken place but were not recorded in the books. For example, depreciation expenses will have to be recorded periodically for items like equipment, business vehicles, etc. Such adjusting entries are also posted in the journal and the general ledger.

21.   The accounts function then prepares the *adjusted trial balance* on the basis of the addition and subtraction of the entries. The adjusted trial balance is an internal document and is not a financial statement. The purpose of the adjusted trial balance is to be certain that the total amount of debit balances in the general ledger equals the total amount of credit balances.

22.   Once all accounts are updated, the trial balance is adjusted, and the debit and credit columns tally, it is possible to prepare the *financial statements*. The financial statements will include an Income Statement (Statement of Financial Performance), Balance Sheet (Statement of Financial Position), Cash Flow Statement, Statement of Retained Earnings and Notes to Financial Statements.

23.   Temporary accounts like expenses, revenues, dividend, gains, losses, owner's drawing accounts, etc. may then be closed. For this the journal entries must be closed. These balances are then transferred to the retained earnings account or the income summary account. It is reflected in the appropriate capital account

on the balance sheet. Thus, it leaves the accounts empty with a zero balance to enter the transactions for the new accounting period. Closing entries are only made for temporary accounts and not for permanent accounts or balance sheet accounts. For the last step in the accounting process, accounts will have to prepare the post-closing trial balance or a final trial balance on the basis of the closing journal entries.

24.   Thus financial statements encapsulate the company's operating performance over a particular period, and financial position at a specific point in time. They are drawn from the balanced accounts, which may include:

- the income statement, also known as the statement of financial results, profit and loss account, or P&L

- the balance sheet, also known as the statement of financial position

- the cash flow statement.

Each statement will be discussed next.

THE INCOME STATEMENT/THE PROFIT AND LOSS ACCOUNT

25.   The profit and loss account is a statement setting the total revenues (sales) for a period against the expenses matched with those revenues to derive a profit or loss for the period, i.e. it describes the trading performance of the business over the accounting period. The profit and loss account also provides a perspective on a longer time-period. The profit and loss account measures 'profit' – the amount by which sales revenue (also known as 'turnover' or 'income') exceeds 'expenses' (or 'costs') for the period being measured.

26.   The profit and loss statement presented in the annual accounts is a historical review of the revenue and expenditure activities of the company for the previous financial year. These statements may also be called Income and Expenditure or Revenue Accounts. They may be produced at other intervals during the year (e.g. monthly or quarterly) but in these circumstances the purpose is not to account to shareholders but to provide useful information to management. The conventional way of producing the profit and loss statement is to show gross sales' income (or turnover) less the cost of sales (materials, wages and other direct costs) to produce a gross profit figure, which is further reduced by the deduction of overheads (all the indirect costs of the business – rents, administration, salaries, etc.) to produce a net profit or surplus before tax. It is also usual to include items such as interest received and payable during the year, and exceptional items (which need to be explained in the notes to the accounts). Non-manufacturing companies omit the cost of sales step in the presentation of their accounts.

THE BALANCE SHEET

27.   Unlike the profit and loss account, the balance sheet does not serve to review activity over a year (or some other period), but presents a snapshot view of the company at a particular point in time. A balance sheet attempts to state what a company is worth at that time, rather than showing how much money it is attracting over a period of time, which is the role of the profit and loss account.

28.   The balance sheet summarizes the assets, liabilities and shareholders' equity of the organization. Assets describe the property owned by the business. Tangible assets include money, land, buildings, investments, inventory, vehicles or other valuables. Intangibles such as goodwill are also considered to be assets. It is normal practice to categorize assets as current or fixed (non-current). A fixed asset (capital asset) is a long-term, tangible asset, held for business use and not expected to be converted to cash in the current or upcoming fiscal year, such as manufacturing equipment, buildings and furniture. Fixed assets are sometimes collectively referred to as 'plant'. Assets expected to be converted into cash within 1 year are termed current assets. These include assets a company has at its disposal which can be converted easily into cash such as accounts receivable, work in process and inventory.

29.   Liabilities are obligations that legally bind an organization to settle a debt; a liability is a financial obligation, debt, claim or potential loss. Liabilities are reported on a balance sheet and are usually divided

into two categories: 'current liabilities' the term given to a balance sheet item which equals the sum of all money owed by a company and due within 1 year (also called payables or current debt) and long-term liabilities (non-current liabilities) – these liabilities are not expected to be liquidated within a year. They usually include issued long-term bonds, notes payables, long-term leases, pension obligations and long-term product warranties.

30. The accounting equation is the mathematical structure of the balance sheet. The accounting equation relates assets, liabilities and owner's equity:

$$\text{Assets} = \text{Liabilities} + \text{Owner's equity}$$

CASH FLOW STATEMENTS

31. The income statement, discussed previously, differs from a cash flow statement because the income statement does not show when revenue is collected or when expenses are paid. In financial accounting, a cash flow statement is a financial statement that shows a company's incoming and outgoing money (sources and uses of cash) during a specified time period (often monthly or quarterly). The statement shows how changes in balance sheet and income accounts affected cash and cash equivalents, and breaks the analysis down according to operating, investing and financing activities. As an analytical tool, the statement of cash flows is useful in determining the short-term viability of a company, particularly its ability to pay bills.

32. The balance sheet is a snapshot of a firm's financial resources and obligations at a single point in time, and the income statement summarizes a firm's financial transactions over an interval of time. These two financial statements reflect the accrual basis accounting used by firms to match revenues with the expenses associated with generating those revenues. The cash flow statement includes only inflows and outflows of cash and cash equivalents; it excludes transactions that do not affect cash receipts and payments directly. The cash flow statement is intended to provide information on a firm's liquidity and solvency.

44.4 GOVERNANCE

33. Management has a responsibility to ensure that financial information is fairly prepared, in accordance with relevant reporting requirements (see **Accounting standards** and **International Financial Reporting Standards (IFRS)**). To meet this responsibility companies introduce internal controls – procedures or systems designed to promote efficiency or assure the implementation of a policy or safeguard assets, avoiding fraud and error, etc.

34. Organizations employ **auditors** to assure control systems are working and typically outsource the auditing of financial statements to third-party (independent) auditors to ensure that financial statements are a fair representation of the financial position of the organization. However, the responsibility for adopting sound accounting policies, maintaining adequate internal control and making fair representations within financial statements rests with management. The auditors must obtain, through audits, reasonable assurance that the financial statements are free of error. When company account, financial statements are prepared, management make assertions about them. For example, they assert whether assets included in the balance sheet actually exist and whether all transactions and accounts that should be represented in the financial statements are included (completeness). Similar assertions are made about the value of assets and other issues concerning how the statements were prepared. Auditors make use of the financial statements and management assertions when conducting audits.

35. We discussed corporate governance in Chapter 13 (see Paras. 34–39). Corporate governance is an area that has developed very rapidly in the last decade; much of the recent emphasis has arisen from high-profile corporate scandals, globalization and increased investor activism. Corporate governance deals with the ways in which suppliers of finance, to commercial organizations, assure themselves of getting a return on their investment. Previously we discussed the importance of assuring financial statements are reported fairly. Corporate governance consists of the set of processes, customs, policies, laws and institutions affecting the way people direct, administer or control an organization. According to the Institute of Chartered Accountants, in England and Wales corporate governance is commonly referred to as a system by which

organizations are directed and controlled. It is the process by which company objectives are established, achieved and monitored.

36. Corporate governance is concerned with the relationships and responsibilities between the board, management, shareholders and other relevant stakeholders within a legal and regulatory framework. Corporate governance aims to protect shareholder rights, enhance disclosure and transparency, facilitate effective functioning of the board and provide an efficient legal and regulatory enforcement framework.

CONCLUSION

37. The system for recording and summarizing business transactions and activities designed to accumulate, measure and communicate financial information about economic entities for decision-making purposes, is termed accounting. Accounting refers to the overall process of identifying, measuring, recording, interpreting and communicating the results of economic activity; tracking business income and expenses and using these measurements to answer specific questions about the financial and tax status of the business, i.e. it is a system providing quantitative information about finances. Whereas financial accounting is the use of accounting information for reporting to parties outside the organization, management accounting is concerned with the provision and use of accounting information to managers within organizations, to provide them with the basis for making informed business decisions that will allow them to be better equipped in their management and control functions.

38. We need accounting and its products such as an organization's annual report as a platform upon which to build many decisions and activities. Organizations must follow specific rules and formats of presentation for their annual reports and financial statements. The key accounting event for any organization is the publication of the annual report which records the organization's (financial) performance over a book year. Whilst the balance sheet tends to remain somewhat of a mystery to those who are not accountants, the profit and loss account and the cash flow statement can be useful for many people in management as an indication of how well a business is progressing over the course of a year. Most managers, however, are more accustomed to dealing with finance at an operational level, i.e. at the level of department and section budgets, and it is to these aspects of finance that we turn to in the next chapter.

QUESTIONS

1 Distinguish between financial accounting and management accounting.

2 What is a profit and loss account and how might this help a range of stakeholders in either the management of or investment in a business?

3 Compare and contrast the profit and loss account with the balance sheet. What is the accounting equation? Compare and contrast the profit and loss account (income statement) with the cash flow statement.

4 What mechanisms exist to ensure that financial information is fairly prepared and reported?

USEFUL WEBSITES

Companies House **www.companieshouse.gov.uk** – The main functions of Companies House are to: incorporate and dissolve limited companies; examine and store company information delivered under the Companies Act and related legislation; and make this information available to the public.

CIMA **www.cimaglobal.com** – The Chartered Institute of Management Accountants

Institute of Chartered Accountants/England and Wales **www.icaew.co.uk**

REFERENCES

Black, G. and Al-Kilani, M. (2013) *Accounting and Finance for Business*, Pearson.

Drury, C. (2012) *Management and Cost Accounting*, 8th edn, Cengage Learning.

Drury, C. (2013) *Management Accounting for Business*, 5th edn, Cengage Learning.

Wood, F. and Horner, D. (2010) *Business Accounting Basics*, Financial Times Press.

CHAPTER 45
BUDGETING PROCESS, PRICING AND CAPITAL INVESTMENT DECISIONS

Key Concepts

- Budget
- Capital budgeting and capital rationing
- Capital investment decision
- Cost-volume-profit (CVP) analysis
- Financial management
- Master budget
- Net present value (NPV)
- Relevant costs

Learning Outcomes Having read this chapter, you should be able to:

- evaluate the purpose of budgeting in organizations
- discuss the process for developing budgets
- explain the purpose of investment appraisal
- apply investment appraisal techniques such as NPV and internal rate of return (IRR)
- discuss the utilization of financial information in decision-making

1.   **Financial management** means the effective and efficient management of funds (money) in such a way as to accomplish the objectives of the organization. It is a specialized function directly associated with senior management. In this chapter we explore financial management, essentially through the budgetary process, and key decisions based upon financial information such as pricing and internal investments (capital investment decisions); McLaney (2011: p. 75) states that investment decisions are at the heart of the management of all businesses ... errors in these decisions, can and do, prove fatal for many businesses. Today practically every type of organization practises some form of budgetary control. Budgets are used to implement strategy (see Chapter 17) by managing tactical issues and the allocation of resources to attain goals. The process of budgeting was briefly referred to in Chapter 18 (Strategy in Practice – see 18.6 Detailed Planning and Control Processes: Budgeting). We noted in that chapter that a budgetary control system is laid on the foundations of strategy (goals), forecasts, sales and production budgets, capital expenditure and cash budgets, and departmental/unit budgets. All these subsidiary budgets are integrated to form a **master budget** for the organization, which becomes in effect a projected profit and loss statement and balance sheet.

2.   Budgets are statements of desired performance expressed in financial terms. They represent the tactical or operational end of business activities, and can be applied to different organizational contexts in which individual managers are given responsibility for a particular unit of operation, which typically may be a

   revenue centre,

   cost centre, or

   profit centre.

Not only are budgets about short-term planning, decision-making and the implementation of strategy, they are also about coordination and control, i.e. they have multiple functions.

45.1 BUDGETS

3.   In Chapter 18 we noted budgeting is the implementation of the long-term plan (strategy) for the year ahead through the development of detailed financial plans, and a budget is a financial plan for implementing management decisions. We then outlined the important stages of the process. Budgets, quite simply, are plans expressed in numerical terms, usually in financial terms. They indicate how much should be spent, by which departments, when, and for what purpose (Thompson and Martin, 2005). All budgets should be prepared against the backcloth of wider organizational plans. They are, after all, a means to an end, which is the achievement of the organization's business or service objectives. Indeed, they are themselves specific and often quantified goals. Budgets are used to anticipate future costs and revenues, prioritize and control spending, and ensure that expenses do not exceed available funds and revenues.

4.   A number of budget types may exist within an organization such as capital budgets used to allocate resources for investment in buildings, plant and equipment; sales budgets (forecast) reflecting the flow of funds into the organization, and revenue or expenses budgets which concern the operating costs to be incurred when creating products and delivering services. Organizations devise budgetary processes to help with planning and control. In overall terms the process of developing budgets can be summarized as shown in Figure 45.1.

5.   Most *budgetary planning* embraces a period of 1 year or less, and some budgets are of a 'rolling' nature, i.e. they are amended each month or quarter in the light of what has transpired during the previous monthly or quarterly period. This ability to amend and adapt budgets, as well as to take other corrective action, is the essence of budgetary control.

6.   When management discuss results and, spending and performance against budget, they usually work from management reports prepared by their accountants (or management accountant in a large organization) using accounting information systems. Such reports show budgeted revenues and costs for the period or year to date (YTD), actual revenue and costs to date and the variances between them. This provides management with the opportunity to judge whether the variances are significant, and if so, what to do about them. The more detailed budgetary process, first presented in Chapter 18, is shown in Figure 45.2.

FIGURE 45.1 Budget development process (outline)

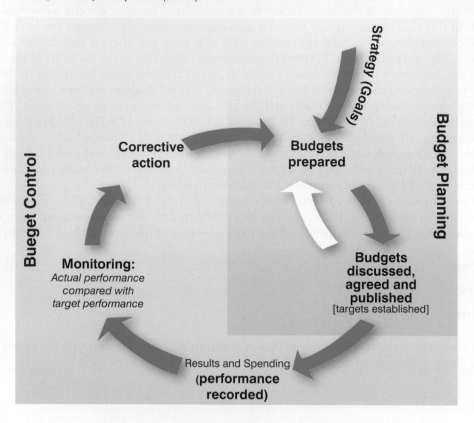

FIGURE 45.2 Budget development process (detailed)

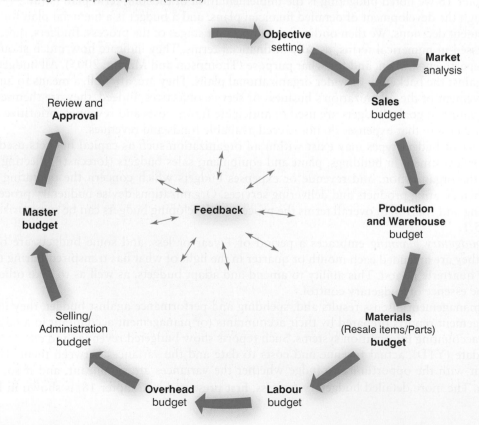

The budget process (see diagram) involves forecasting, setting goals (objectives) and conducting analysis, prior to investment decision-making. The company needs to estimate income and costs. An organization's leaders will need to know how much revenue the company is expected to generate in the forthcoming year. Either the marketing or sales (or both departments) contribute to such forecasts. There is a need to estimate price changes and the number of sales. This can either be done at a high level (marketing) or on a detailed product by product basis (sales forecast). A similar approach is taken for other business functions.

7. In the broadest sense, a budget is an allocation of money for some purpose. Budgeting has always been part of the activities of any business organization of any size. The budget not only limits expenditures; it also predicts income, profits, and returns on investment a year ahead. Budgeting is a collective (intra-organizational) negotiation process in which operating units (functions) prepare their plans in conformity with corporate goals. Each unit plan is intended to contribute to the achievement of those goals. Unit managers prepare forecasts of sales, operating costs overhead costs, and capital requirements. They calculate operating profits and returns on the investment they intend to use. The (master) budget itself is the projection of these values for the next year. As part of this process, in many organizations each unit presents its plans and budget to the management team (budget committee) and may, thereafter, make whatever changes result from instructions from or negotiations with the budget committee. Approved budgets then become the road-map for operations within the coming year.

Running in parallel with the master budget process is the capital investment process. This is discussed next.

45.3 INVESTMENT APPRAISAL AND CAPITAL BUDGETING

8. Recall from the strategy process that future company plans typically include goals and objectives for the future. Organizations, departments and their managers will develop competencies, talent, acquire resources, equipment, systems and facilities to develop advantages and enable the accomplishment of those goals and objectives. In many cases this will require the organization to spend money. Those decisions that involve current outlays (investment) in return for a stream of benefits in future years are termed capital investment decisions. In such decisions there is a significant period of time between the outlay and the recoupment of the investment. They are often important decisions.

9. Financial management involves making decisions about investment, sources of finance and how to manage the financial resources of organizations most efficiently. Capital budgeting is the process of analyzing and selecting various proposals for capital expenditures. The organization must establish mechanisms for developing, screening and selecting projects in which to invest. Investment decisions generally concern outlays of cash, the acquisition and development or use of assets and speculation. i.e. risk and reward. Capital budgeting techniques enable managers to compare different investment alternatives so that they can make informed choices about where the organization should invest its scarce resources.

10. A detailed version of the capital investment process is shown in Figure 45.3. Organizations first get 'FAT' – they Forecast costs and revenues, Analyze the environment and set Targets for the coming months (typically year). This can be used to define where the organization wants to go in the near future. Having accomplished this, the organization and its managers must determine the best way to get there (tactics), working to realize the targets (goals and objectives).

11. It is up to the managers to propose how they intend to accomplish this and identify the resources they will need. This is done by writing and presenting business cases and proposals for investment and resource allocation. A key input at this stage is the available financial (capital) resources of the organization. These will have been determined during the creation of the master budget and will have been calculated on the basis of retained profits and forecast revenues. The amount available for investment will act as a constraint on decision-making. The company will only be able to fund so much investment.

12. Investment decisions are important for all organizations. Organizations must raise finance (money) from various sources (internally and externally, from revenues, banks and other investors) which is then invested in assets such as plant, machinery and systems. Cash flows out of the organization when investments are made; however, the purpose of investment is to increase value and ultimately cause cash to flow into the organization. There is normally a time lag between flows and the organization must choose the most appropriate opportunities in which to invest, i.e. those that will increase shareholder wealth.

FIGURE 45.3 Capital investment process (detailed)

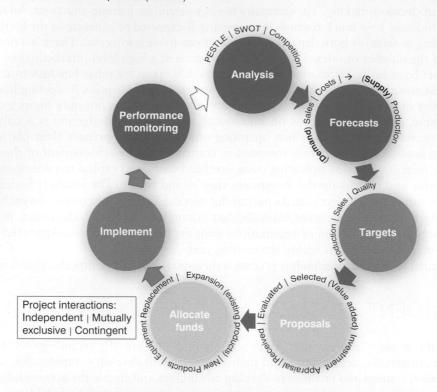

13.   The overall process of investment appraisal is based upon the rational economic decision-making process (refer back to Chapter 19). Once business objectives/goals have been set in the strategy-making process, investment opportunities and needs can be identified. Data are then assembled about costs and benefits associated with the investment opportunities (**cost benefit analysis,** CBA). It is rarely possible to fund all investment opportunities, or in some cases some opportunities may seek to tackle the same problem. It is therefore necessary to choose the projects in which to invest. These are then implemented and monitored.

14.   Investments are made to help the organization achieve its goals. Since there may be many ways to achieve goals there are often many initiatives and assets (such as new IT systems, new products, new factories, etc.) in which to invest to attain such goals. Investment opportunities arise in many ways either intentionally or by chance. Once an idea emerges, since it must compete for funding, it must be evaluated. To do this, the organization must describe the problem to be overcome by the investment, quantify the benefits of the investment and explain why investment is necessary to attain goals. Numerous quantitative approaches for evaluating investments are available such as net present value (NPV), internal rate of return (IRR), payback period and pay-off tables – some of which are discussed below. The main goal of such techniques and investment appraisal is to assess the profit (increase in wealth) for a given period.

APPRAISING INVESTMENTS: THE NET PRESENT VALUE METHOD

15.   Capital investments are likely to require the company to spend money over a number of years. Similarly, the benefits are likely to accrue over several years. The **net present value (NPV)** (also called discounted cash flow) measures the worth of a stream of cash flows (or savings), taking into account the time value of money. For example, imagine an organization wants to invest in a new production system that will either reduce costs or improve sales – each year for the next 5 years. The concept is based on the idea that money today is worth more than money in the future. The NPV is a logical, quantitative, practical evaluation procedure that evaluates opportunities which seek to maximize shareholder wealth.

The NPV of an investment is calculated by using a discount rate (typically the rate at which money is borrowed at e.g. 10% – the **cost of capital**) and a series of future payments (negative values) and income (positive values).

16. The calculation of NPV involves three simple yet non-trivial steps:

   (a) The first step is to identify the size and timing of the expected future cash flows generated by the project or investment and costs incurred (investment costs).

   (b) The second step is to determine the discount rate or the estimated rate of return for the project.

   (c) The third step is to calculate (typically using a spreadsheet) the NPV using the equations shown below: The NPV is calculated using the following formulae:

$$NPV = \sum_{i=1}^{n} \frac{Values}{(1+rate)^i}$$

17. £1000 is worth more now than it is one or more years into the future, i.e. we would not lend some person or entity that amount now and expect the same amount back 1 year later because of risk, inflation and interest foregone. The fact that money has a 'time value' makes investment appraisal more complicated. We need to be able to make comparisons between money now and money that may be paid out or flow into the company at some point in the future. In order to work out the value of a future cash sum we need to discount the sum by the amount of interest we could have earned over the period concerned and calculate the present value of the sum. For example, imagine a software company will be paid £1 000 000 in 1 year – what is the present value of the receivable? The present value of a future amount of income is:

Present Value (PV) = (Future Value)/(Rate)

18. If we assume the interest (discount) rate to be 10 per cent (0.1) then the present value of £1 000 000 = 1 000 000/1.1 = £909 091. That is to say, if we had £909 091 today and invested it with a bank offering 10 per cent interest we would turn our £909 091 investment into £1 000 000 over 1 year. The discount rate changes for each year in the future. For the first year it would be 1.1, for the second year 1.1^2 (1.21) and for the third year 1.1^3 (1.331) in this case as the cost of capital is 10 per cent.

19. Organizations do not have infinite sources of capital and in most cases will need to ration it. **Capital rationing** occurs whenever there is a budget ceiling, i.e. a constraint on spending. Rationing may be self-imposed ('soft') or there may be a limit to available external funds ('hard'). When selecting investment opportunities (projects) from a list it is advisable to order the list and then authorize projects in order until the available funds have all been allocated. However, it is better to order by the **profitability index** rather than simply the NPV, argues Drury (2012: p. 331). The profitability index = PV/investment required for any given opportunity/project. Furthermore, Drury (2012) recommends that only projects with a profitability index above 1.0 are acceptable.

APPRAISING INVESTMENTS: THE IRR METHOD

20. There are other techniques to evaluate investment opportunities. Many decisions involve a choice of whether to accept or reject a single investment opportunity. The IRR may be used to help with such decisions (it can be calculated using Microsoft Excel). IRR is sometimes referred to as 'economic rate of return (ERR)'. The **internal rate of return (IRR)** for an investment is the discount rate which makes the present value of the income stream total zero; the interest rate received for an investment, consisting of payments (negative values) and income (positive values) that occur at regular periods. In general, if the IRR is greater than the project's cost of capital, or hurdle rate, the project will add value for the company. To find the internal rate of return, IRR is defined by the equation:

NPV(C, t, IRR) = 0

21. In other words, the IRR is the discount rate which sets the NPV of the given cash flows made at the given times to zero. As a decision tool, the calculated IRR should not be used to rate **mutually exclusive**

projects, but only to decide whether a single project is worthy of investment. IRR is closely related to NPV, the net present value function. The major difference is that whilst NPV is expressed in monetary units, the IRR is the true interest yield expected from an investment expressed as a percentage.

22.   In many cases, an organization will consider numerous investment options. In some cases the options may seek to solve the same problem and compete with each other to the extent that only one of the options should be selected (mutually exclusive). In other cases, options may compete with each other for internal capital, i.e. the company may have a limited amount of money (the budget) to spend. When there are a number of non-mutually exclusive alternatives considered, various ranking criteria, such as return on investment (ROI) or more general cost benefit ratios provide a basis for evaluation.

23.   The rate of return (ROR) or ROI, or sometimes just return, is the ratio of money gained or lost on an investment relative to the amount of money invested. ROI is usually expressed as a percent rather than a decimal value. To calculate ROI, the benefit (return) of an investment is divided by the cost of the investment; ROI = (Gain from investment) – (Cost of investment)/Cost of investment Or ROI = (Annual revenue) – (Annual costs) / Initial investment Or % ROI = (Benefits / Costs) × 100 Or ROI = (Gain from investment – Cost of investment) / Cost of investment.

24.   Another way of looking at ROI is to calculate how many months it will take before benefits match costs and the investment pays for itself. This is called the **payback period**: payback period = costs / monthly benefits. The payback technique simply asks how long will it take for the investment to pay for itself out of the expected cash inflows. Proposals are typically ranked in order of highest ROI first and **are** selected until total initial investment exceeds a budget. Benefits can be quantified as revenues or cost savings. In either case, they should be converted to present values in order to take account of the time value of money. Ratios greater than '1' gener**ally indicate t**hat a proposal should be adopted if sufficient resources exist to support it.

25.   Many decisions involve a choice amongst several mutually exclusive alternatives. When only one alternative can be selected from many, the best choice can usually be identified by evaluating each alternative according to some criteria. The NPV or IRR may be used to choose between *competing* projects/choices. For decisions involving multiple criteria, simple scoring models are often used. The scoring model is a qualitative assessment of a decision alternative value, based on a set of attributes. For each decision alternative, a score is assigned to each attribute (which might be weighted), and the overall score used as a basis for selection.

26.   Financial decision-making is easy when only a single choice can be made (take it or leave it), i.e. if there is only one alternative (Hobson's choice). However, rather than only one alternative, most of the time a set of choices exist. It is also relatively easy to make decisions when the precise outcome of the decision is known. However this is rarely the case with contemporary management business decisions. Such decisions normally involve highly uncertain outcomes. Many decisions involve a selection from a small set of mutually exclusive alternatives with uncertain consequences; i.e. we are unsure what the benefits will be. In this scenario we must also define the outcomes, or events that may (savings and revenues) occur once a decision is made and over which the decision-maker does not have control. These outcomes provide a basis for evaluating risk associated with decisions. A useful tool for making decisions under uncertain conditions is the pay-off table; a pay-off table is a tool for organizing what is known about each alternative.

45.3 PRICING-PROFIT ANALYSIS

27.   When determining sales forecasts (as a part of the master budget process) the organization must decide whether to model existing or revised prices for its products and services. This will have a significant impact upon forecast sales volumes and revenues and therefore budgets. We considered pricing in Chapter 31 as a part of the marketing mix. Through Figure 31.4 we noted an area of price discretion between the price floor and ceiling. Accounting information is often an important input to pricing decisions. Also, the pricing decision will often be influenced by the cost of the product. Cost information then is of considerable importance, more so when the organization has control over pricing. Pricing decisions may be informed with reference to economic theory which explains how the optimal selling price is determined. For an introduction to economic theory relating to supply and demand and the market mechanism refer to Kelly and Ashwin (2013: Chapter 11).

28.   Drury (2012: p. 228) discusses the role of cost information in pricing decisions. He notes that in some firms prices are set by overall market supply and demand forces and the firm has little or no influence over

the selling prices of its products or services. This situation is likely to occur where there are many firms in an industry and there is little to distinguish their products from each other. Such firms are typically referred to as price takers. In contrast, firms selling products or services that are highly customized or differentiated have more discretion in setting prices. Such firms are typically referred to as price setters. Where firms are price setters, cost information is often an important input into the pricing decision.

29.   However, cost information is only one of many variables that should be considered in the pricing decision. The final price agreed upon will depend upon the pricing policy of the company. Price skimming (see also market skimming pricing) is a pricing strategy whereby a company charges the highest possible price that buyers who most desire the product will pay. It is an approach to pricing that attempts to exploit sections of the market that are relatively insensitive to price changes. The marketer sets a relatively high price for a product or service at first, and then lowers the price over time. Penetration pricing (see also Market penetration pricing) is an approach to pricing that involves charging low prices initially with the intention of gaining rapid acceptance of the product; it aims for rapid acquisition of market share. This is about setting a price below the prices of competing brands in order to penetrate a market and produce a larger unit sales volume.

45.4 COST-VOLUME-PROFIT ANALYSIS

30.   Planning often involves evaluating alternative courses of action. Managers will then compare the likely effects of each option before making choices. When setting targets and considering forecasts it is of interest to know information such as how many units must be sold to break even. Similarly it is useful to understand the relationship between volume and price and the impact of price increases or decreases on volume. Questions like this are answered through cost-volume-profit (CVP) analysis. This analysis examines the relationship between changes in activity (output) and changes in total sales revenue, costs and net profit (Drury, 2012: p. 168). Thus it allows us to predict what will happen to the financial results if a specified level of activity or volume fluctuates.

31.   Drury (2012: p. 172) discusses a numerical approach to CVP analysis. Using this approach it is possible to calculate break-even points, the number of units to be sold to obtain a specific profit target, the profit that would be derived from the sale of a specified number of units, the price to charge in order to sell a specified number of units that the specified profit and the sales volume required to meet specified additional costs.

Break-even point = fixed costs/contribution per unit

Units to be sold to obtain target profit = fixed costs + target profit/contribution per unit

45.5 MEASURING RELEVANT COSTS AND REVENUES FOR DECISION-MAKING

32.   In addition to the decisions already discussed, managers may need to decide, at some stage, whether to discontinue a product or a channel of distribution, make or buy, launch a new product or service or replace equipment. As noted by Drury (2012: p. 194) when decisions of this kind are being considered, special studies are often undertaken. In making such decisions, the manager should only consider those costs and revenues relevant to the alternatives under consideration. If the relevant costs and revenue data are included, the wrong decision may be made. Relevant costs and revenues are future costs and revenues that will be changed by a particular decision, whereas irrelevant costs and revenues will not be affected by that decision.

33.   In summary, so far we have discussed the strategic goals and objectives defining what the company wants to achieve, where it wants to get to in the future. We have discussed how the company calculates available financial resources based upon pricing and sales volume, then creates budgets. We have also discussed available resources as presented in the various budgets. Finally we have discussed how the company allocates those resources so that managers have what they need to accomplish goals. All of these activities are about planning for the short term. The next logical stage is implementation, where the organization works toward accomplishing its long and short-term plans. Management accounting and financial management also have a key role to play in monitoring and control (refer back to Figure 45.1). Control was discussed in Section 10 so we end this chapter with a brief explanation of the monitoring function, particularly in terms of the overall cash flow of the organization.

45.6 CASH FLOW FORECASTS

34.   Whereas a company may 'know' that the 'books' will balance over the course of the year this does not mean that spending can occur uncontrolled even if it is within the budget. Trading businesses, whether selling goods or services, need to know that they have enough cash available to fund their *immediate* operating expenses such as wages/salaries, rent, telephone charges, etc. If sufficient funds are not available from internal sources, then borrowings must be made – usually in the form of a bank overdraft (i.e. credit on the firm's current account). The usual way of keeping track of the cash position is to prepare a **net cash flow forecast**. This is essentially a budget which sets out the estimated receipts and payments of the business on a month-by-month basis over a period of 1 financial year. The net cash flow figure and balance for each column is expressed as a positive or negative sum. Thus it is easy to see at what stages of the year it may be necessary to borrow (or control costs) in order to finance the operating costs of the business. An outline example of a cash flow budget is shown at Figure 45.4.

35.   The cash flow budget in Figure 45.4 is a working document, unlike the cash flow statement referred to in the previous chapter, which is an end-of-year summary of the total cash position in the company concerned. As a working document, the cash flow budget is intended to provide a detailed (e.g. month-

FIGURE 45.4 Cash flow budget

Outline of a Cash Flow Budget					
Month	**Jan**		**Feb**		**Mar**	
	Budget	**Actual**	**Budget**	**Actual**	**Budget**	**Actual**
	£	£	£	£	£	£
Cash sales						
Cash from debtors						
Sale of assets						
Loans received						
Total Receipts (a)						
Payments:						
Cash purchases						
Payments to creditors						
Wages/Salaries						
Rent/Rates						
Repairs etc.						
Insurance						
Telephone						
Postage						
Stationery						
Transport						
Loan repayment						
Interest						
Bank charges						
Professional fees						
Other						
VAT payable (or refunded)						
Total Payments (b)						
Net Cash Flow (a–b)						
Opening Bank Balance						
Closing Bank Balance						

by-month) picture of the movement of funds in and out of the organization. A sufficiency of cash is vital for every business – it is literally the lifeblood of the system. Even if a business is actually and potentially profitable, it cannot survive without sufficient cash (liquidity), and there have been numerous businesses which have collapsed because, even though profitable and with a good product, they have experienced a 'cash crisis' and have been unable to meet their debts.

CONCLUSION

36.   In this chapter we explored financial planning and control mechanisms and techniques for allocating financial resources. We considered the provision of financial information to help managers make better decisions. Budgets are statements of desired performance, expressed in financial terms. They indicate how much should be spent, by which departments, when and for what purpose. All budgets should be prepared against the backcloth of wider organizational plans. Budgets are used to anticipate future costs and revenues, prioritize and control spending, and ensure that expenses do not exceed available funds and revenues. A generic budget development process was presented. Next we noted that businesses need to know they have enough cash available to fund their immediate operating expenses such as wages/salaries, rent, telephone charges, etc. The usual way of keeping track of the cash position is to prepare a cash flow forecast. This is a budget which sets out the estimated receipts and payments of the business on a month-by-month basis over a period of 1 financial year.

37.   Investment decisions are important for all organizations; the purpose of investment is to increase value and ultimately cause cash to flow into the organization. Once business objectives/goals have been set in the strategy-making process, investment opportunities and needs can be identified. Data are then assembled about costs and benefits associated with the investment opportunities (CBA). It is rarely possible to fund all investment opportunities, or in some cases some opportunities may seek to tackle the same problem. It is therefore necessary to choose the projects within which to invest. Numerous quantitative approaches for evaluating investments are available such as NPV, IRR, payback period and pay-off tables. The main goal of such techniques and investment appraisal is to assess the profit (increase in wealth) for a given period.

QUESTIONS

1   Evaluate the purpose of budgeting in organizations. In your answer you should comment on a number of budget types that may exist within an organization. You should also describe a generic budget development process.

2   Explain the role of investment appraisal within organizations and discuss how the NPV technique can help improve the quality of investment decisions.

USEFUL WEBSITES

Institute of Financial Services **www.ifsis.org.uk**

REFERENCES

Drury, C. (2012) *Management and Cost Accounting*, 8th edn, Cengage Learning.

Kelly, P.P. and Ashwin, A. (2013) *The Business Environment*, Cengage.

McLaney, E. (2011) *Business Finance: Theory and Practice, 9/E*, Financial Times/Prentice Hall.

Thompson, J.L. and Martin, F. (2005) *Strategic Management*, 5th edn, Cengage Learning EMEA.

SKILL SHEET 13   **Financial Management**

This skills sheet provides practical advice on the application of common investment appraisal methods (NPV, IRR and ROI). The aim is to help you understand what a Finance Manager may be talking about when discussing investment appraisal rather than turn you into a Finance Manager yourself! Applying the formulae in different contexts requires a specialist approach born out of experience.

The following problem will be solved using NPV, IRR and ROI:

ABC Company is a local business that sells physical goods to customers typically located within 50 miles of the factory/warehouse. They presently use one of three local couriers to deliver their product to customers. The annual courier bill has increased each year and is now £75 000 PA, a cost met by ABC. The Warehouse Manager proposes that ABC **purchase its own van** (£20 000) and recruit a driver (£2000/month) to enable them to fulfil their own deliveries. Additional costs include van maintenance-free for the first 3 years, after which it will cost an estimated £1500 PA. The only further cost is fuel which is estimated to cost £1500/month). The Warehouse Manager also investigates a second option where ABC **lease a van** for £5000 PA (inclusive of maintenance costs but excluding fuel).The MD asks the Finance Director which option should be pursued, if any. The Finance Director uses 10% as the cost of capital.

In answering this problem we consider the time value of money and therefore discount future cash flows.

Step 1: Lay out the costs by year:

Option 1 (Buy van)

Yr	0	1	2	3	4	5
Van	−£20 000					
Driver	−£24 000	−£24 000	−£24 000	−£24 000	−£24 000	−£24 000
Fuel	−£18 000	−£18 000	−£18 000	−£18 000	−£18 000	−£18 000
Maintenance	£0			−£1 500	−£1 500	−£1 500

Option 2 (Lease van)

Yr	0	1	2	3	4	5
Van	−£5 000	−£5 000	−£5 000	−£5 000	−£5 000	−£5 000
Driver	−£24 000	−£24 000	−£24 000	−£24 000	−£24 000	−£24 000
Fuel	−£18 000	−£18 000	−£18 000	−£18 000	−£18 000	−£18 000
Maintenance	£0	£0	£0	£0	£0	£0

Then summarize the Costs and Benefits

Option 1:

Yr	0	1	2	3	4	5
Out	−£62 000	−£42 000	−£42 000	−£43 500	−£43 500	−£43 500
In		£75 000	£75 000	£75 000	£75 000	£75 000

Option 2:

Yr	0	1	2	3	4	5
Out	−£47 000	−£47 000	−£47 000	−£47 000	−£47 000	−£47 000
In		£75 000	£75 000	£75 000	£75 000	£75 000

1. Calculating NPV – Worked Example

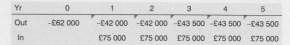

$$NPV = \sum_{i=1}^{n} \frac{Values}{(1 + rate)^i}$$

In Chapter 45 we discussed NPV. We suggested the first step is to identify the size and timing of the expected future cash flows generated by the project or investment and costs incurred (investment costs). This was done as step 1 above.

The second step is to determine the discount rate/estimated rate of return for the project. This step can be broken down into (a) determine the discount rate $(1+rate)^i$ and then (b) convert the combined costs and benefits for each future year into a present day value (PV).

a)   The discount rate is calculated as 1 + rate and in this case the rate is 10% (0.1) so this = 1.1; we must then raise this to the power (^) of 2 in the second year, 3 in the third year, etc. So the year 1 discount rate is simply 1.1; the year 2 rate is (1.1 × 1.1) = 1.21 and year 3 is (1.1 × 1.1 × 1.1) = 1.331.

b)   Present Value (PV) = (Future Value)/(Discount Rate).
If we take option 1 as an example, the PV for year 0 is simply the costs (£62 000) because the values are already in the present day. In the following year (1) we have to discount by the rate 1.1 so we sum the year 1 cost and benefit (−£42 000 and £75 000) = £33 000 and divide by the rate 1.1 i.e. PV (year 1) = £33/1.1 = £30 000.

The PV will always be a smaller figure because we are reflecting the time value of money. What we are saying, indirectly, is that if we had £30 000 today and invested it with a bank that paid 10% interest, in 12 months we would have £33 000; so £33 000 in 1 year is worth the same as £30 000 today.

We then repeat the exercise for the year 2 (PV) using the rate of 1.21 etc.

The complete set of PVs for option 1 are shown below:

FIGURE 1

Year	0	1	2	3	4	5
Out	−£62 000	−£42 000	−£42 000	−£43 500	−£43 500	−£43 500
In		£75 000	£75 000	£75 000	£75 000	£75 000
Net	−£62 000	£33 000	£33 000	£31 500	£31 500	£31 500
		1.1	1.21	1.331	1.4641	1.61051
PV	−£62 000	£30 000	£27 273	£23 666	£21 515	£19 559

The third step is to calculate the NPV. It is the 'Net' PV so we simply add up (sum) all of the PVs. Thus the NPV for option 1 is £60 013; as this is >0 it means that the investment decision is worth considering. Over the 5 years the company will be £60 013 better off. The key issue however is whether or not we could put our investment (capital) to better use. Remember we had to spend £62 000 up front.

We need to perform the same calculation with the data from the second option. This generates a slightly different NPV:

FIGURE 2

Year	0	1	2	3	4	5
Out	−£47 000	−£47 000	−£47 000	−£47 000	−£47 000	−£47 000
In		£75 000	£75 000	£75 000	£75 000	£75 000
Net	−£47 000	£28 000	£28 000	£28 000	£28 000	£28 000
		1.1	1.21	1.331	1.4641	1.61051
PV	−£47 000	£25 455	£23 140	£21 037	£19 124	£17 386
NPV	£59 142.03					

Overall, the second option adds slightly less value to the company in the long run but is a little less risky and does not tie up as much capital in the first year.

Using Spreadsheets

Whilst we showed the calculations longhand above, normally a spreadsheet would be used to compute the NPV. MS Excel has the NPV formulae built in. To use Excel, first type the data into a spreadsheet as shown above in step 1 (summary). Create the row for net values (a new row where you add the cost and benefit for each year). Then click in a cell below the data and click the formulas tab of the Excel ribbon. Click 'insert function' and type/select NPV. Either type 0.1 (for 10%) in the area for the 'rate' or type 0.1 in a cell in the spreadsheet and navigate to that cell from the NPV dialog. Next, where it says value1, click the button with the picture of a spreadsheet on and select the row of 'net' data in your spreadsheet but do not select the data in year 0. Then click OK. Next click in the NPV cell and at the end of the formula enter '+' and navigate to the net cell value for year '0'. Then click 'enter'. This should be the NPV value.

The NPV formula cell will look something like

=NPV(A57,E60:I60)+D58+D59

The cell references may be different because the data may be entered in different cells than here. On our spreadsheet, cell A57 contains the value of the cost of capital i.e. '0.1'; cells E60:I60 are the net values (sum of cost and benefit) for years 1–5 and cells D58 and D59 are the cost and benefit values for year 0. If confusing then use the Excel NPV help notes!

Remember when choosing how to allocate rationed capital (a budget) you want to select the best projects (that add the most value) therefore calculate the profitability index for each. To do this you must calculate overall PV/investment required. In this case calculate the PV as the sum of all discounted benefits and divide by the investment cost (refer to Chapter 45).

2. Calculating IRR – Worked Example

The IRR is the interest rate that makes the NPV zero. The IRR is a good way of judging different investments. First of all, the IRR should be higher than the cost of funds. If it costs 10% to borrow money, then an IRR of only 8% is not good enough.

Using Spreadsheets

IRR returns the IRR for a series of cash flows represented by the numbers in values.

Syntax: IRR (values, guess)

The 'Values' is an array or a reference to cells that contain numbers for which you want to calculate the IRR; the values must contain at least one positive value and one negative value to calculate the IRR. IRR uses the order of values to interpret the order of cash flows. So, be sure to enter payment and income values in the sequence required. The 'Guess' refers to a number that you estimate is close to the result of IRR. This is an optional input and can be left blank. If guess is omitted, it is assumed to be 0.1 (10 per cent). If IRR gives the #NUM! error value, or if the result is not close to what is expected, try again with a different guess value.

Using the 'net' row of Figure 1 as the 'values' the IRR computes to be 44%. However, using the 'net' row of Figure 2 as the 'values' the IRR computes to be 52%. There is a better rate of return from the second option because less money is invested up front. So, on NPV we might choose option 1 but on IRR may choose option 2.

3. Calculating ROI – Worked Example

The ROR or ROI, or sometimes just *return*, is the ratio of money gained or lost on an investment relative to the amount of money invested. ROI is usually expressed as a percentage rather than a decimal value.

To calculate ROI, divide the return (net profit) by the resources that were committed (investment):

$$\text{ROI (\%)} = (\text{Net profit} / \text{Investment}) \times 100$$

Thus the ROI for option 1 is:
Sum all net figures for years 1–5 = £160 500
then divide by the year 0 investment/costs of £62 000
then multiply by 100
= 259%

The ROI for option 2 is: 298%

Based on ROI we might select the leased van option (2).

Often there are criteria, other than financial, impacting upon investment appraisal decisions. There are qualitative considerations, politics and decision-maker predispositions to consider. With regard to the latter we might consider the risk attitudes of the decision-makers for example.

The risk neutral person exhibits a reaction to risk in line with its statistical probability. A risk averse person prefers the certain prospect to any risky prospect. Risk seekers choose among the risks that have negative consequences. A more risk averse person may prefer option 2 as they do not have to commit the same amount of up front capital and can pull out earlier if they prefer to revert back to using couriers.

Section Fifteen
Information Resource Management

CHAPTER 46
THE ROLE OF INFORMATION TECHNOLOGY AND BUSINESS INFORMATION SYSTEM: ENABLING STRATEGY AND WORK

Key Concepts

- Big data
- Business intelligence
- Business information system (BIS)
- Data
- Digital organization
- e-Commerce and e-business
- Explicit knowledge
- Information
- Tacit knowledge

Learning Outcomes Having read this chapter, you should be able to:

- differentiate between the concepts of data, information and knowledge
- explain what is meant by the term BIS
- discuss how information resources can be used to deliver value and help the organization compete
- explain the importance of knowledge management
- identify ways the use of the Internet and Internet (Net) technologies can help the organization compete, create wealth and add value
- explain what is meant by e-commerce and e-business.

1. In Chapter 8 we highlighted the important work of the Tavistock group and commented on how the best organizational performance is achieved by jointly optimizing both social and technical systems used in production. *Sociotechnical* systems refer to an approach which suggests that the social and technical subsystems within the organization should be designed in parallel to achieve an overall optimum system. We then (Chapter 9) discussed the contingency approach and the need to choose the best combination of the technological human and structural factors. Whilst we have discussed human and structural factors in detail we have yet to explore technological (and information system) factors which we explored briefly in Chapter 38. Technology, and more specifically, information systems, when used as a part of the sociotechnical system, can enable strategy and operations, a matter we explore in this chapter.

2. Laudon and Laudon (2014) comment on the growing interdependence between the ability to use information technology (IT) and the ability to implement corporate strategies and achieve goals; business firms invest heavily in information systems to achieve six strategic business objectives: operational excellence, new products, services and business models, customer and supplier intimacy, improved decision-making, competitive advantage and survival. In order to achieve its business objectives, a firm will need a significant investment in IT; similarly the IT platform can lead to changes in business objectives and strategies, i.e. it is a two-way relationship. Businesses shape their information systems and information systems shape businesses. The relationship between strategy and systems, the sociotechnical approach and aspects of contingency theory are reflected in Figure 46.1. People use systems, technology and other resources in an organized way to complete work (integrated business processes) and attain goals.

FIGURE 46.1 Contingency and congruence perspective

3.   Many scholars and practitioners have commented on the importance of IS and associated technologies to the contemporary organization. For example, Laudon and Laudon (2014) suggest that in 2012, more than 540 billion dollars was invested in IT. They also note that firms have increased IT investment faster than machinery and buildings; firms would much rather invest in IT because the returns on the investment are greater. Technology and associated systems allow business to be conducted at any time (time shifting) and any place (space shifting); digital firms are ideally suited for global operations which take place in remote locations and very different time zones. In the emerging, fully digital firm, significant business relationships are digitally enabled and mediated; core business processes are accomplished through digital networks and key corporate assets are managed digitally. Digital firms offer greater flexibility in organization and management.

4.   IS and IT represent important tools in achieving greater efficiency and productivity; they are a major enabling tool for new products, services and business models. Consider as examples Apple's iPad, Google's Android OS, and Netflix. They enable customer and supplier intimacy (refer back to CRM) and improve decision-making. Without accurate information managers must use best guesses and luck which may result in overproduction, underproduction, the misallocation of resources and poor response times. This can raise costs and lose customers.

5.   Alternatively, possessing and utilizing IT/IS appropriately is likely to lead to competitive advantage, delivering better performance, charging less for superior products, and responding to customers and suppliers in real time. IS help in the creating of value and investments in IT will result in superior returns, argue Laudon and Laudon (2014). In short, they help increase productivity and revenue.

6.   Evans, Martin and Poatsy (2014) comment on the kinds of software that small and large businesses use. Businesses use software to help them with the following tasks: finances and accounting (refer back to Chapters 44 and 45), desktop publishing, web page authoring, project management, CRM (see Chapter 34), ERP (see Chapter 38) and e-commerce. Productivity software programs include word processing, spreadsheets, presentations, databases, note taking and personal information management.

7.   In this chapter we focus on IS resources (hardware, software, communication technologies, people, data, information and knowledge). Systems theory (see Chapter 9) is used to unite such resources. Such resources enable the free flow of information throughout the organization in support of commerce, planning, decision-making, control and coordination. Later in the chapter we consider the role of Internet technologies as the 'glue' and 'conduit' for bundling resources together, making them available for work and value-adding activities. We will argue that IS resources are strategically important resources, enabling and informing strategy, creating capabilities and competencies when bundled with other resources.

46.1 INFORMATION RESOURCES: DATA, INFORMATION AND KNOWLEDGE

8.   The general management functions of planning, organizing, motivating and leading, coordinating and controlling, decision-making, performance managing, and all the major specialized business functions (especially marketing, operations and finance) and associated processes, benefit from information systems (IS) and information technology (IT). IS and associated technologies are omnipresent and enable strategy, tactics and operations. They are extremely important, enabling organizations to be more effective and efficient, to differentiate products and services whilst reducing costs. IS and associated technologies help companies to compete and offer value for money whilst enhancing customer satisfaction. Through the use of IS/IT, companies can reach and break into markets worldwide, operate 24/7, enable and empower employees, share knowledge, integrate work activities, improve the quality of working life, enable time compression and time-based advantages, improve communication and enable teamwork – especially over time and space.

9.   Data can be regarded as raw facts representing events occurring in organizations (such as business transactions) or the physical environment – objective measurements of the attributes (characteristics) of entities, such as people, places, things and events. The price of a product or service, the date of a customer order, contact details or an employee's date of birth, are all examples of data. Data may be generated during business or may be collected from external sources.

10. We can classify data in a number of ways, for example, data may be structured or unstructured. People use both types of data every day. Examples of 'unstructured data' may include audio, video and unstructured text such as the body of an email or word processor document. Data that resides in fixed fields within a record or file (relational databases and spreadsheets) is an example of structured data. Structured data are managed by technology that allows for querying and reporting against predetermined data types and understood relationships. Data structure is a way of storing data in a computer so that it can be used efficiently.

11. Data may be stored in paper-based (manual) or computer-based systems. A spreadsheet may be considered a simple database but its use is limited when considering many business problems. In many ways, the spreadsheet, for all its mathematical processing functionality, is little more than an electronic list. A database is a system or program in which structured data are stored. Databases may exist within or be external to the organization. There are many types of database such as the marketing databases (including CRM); databases support the major business operations of the organization. Transaction processing systems (TPS) are computerized systems that perform and record the daily routine transactions necessary to conduct the business (basic business transactions include purchasing, orders for goods and services, billing and payroll – banks, for example, handle millions of deposits and withdrawals each day); these systems serve the operational level of the organization. The records of such systems are typically stored within relational databases.

12. Data may be collected through manual or electronic means. For example, data can be captured using a keyboard, mouse, scanner, optical character or voice recognition, and as mentioned previously, through barcodes and RFID. Once stored (see Figure 46.2 Information system), queries and other programs may be used to access or edit the data. Data that has been *processed* (sorted, summarized, manipulated or filtered) so that it is meaningful to people is normally considered to be information.

FIGURE 46.2 Information system

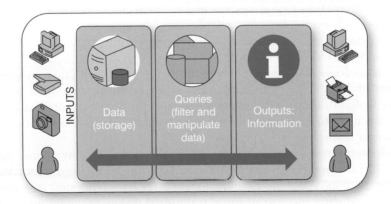

INFORMATION RESOURCES

13. Total sales of a product in a particular location during a particular time period or a strategic summary of strengths and weaknesses represent examples of information. The words information and data are used interchangeably in many contexts. This may lead to confusion, however, since they are not synonyms. Information is the summarization of data. Information may be communicated by formal (structured) or informal (e.g. casual conversation) means.

14. Information can add value to products and services and information flows can improve the quality of decision-making, collaboration, planning, coordination and control and internal operations. The importance of information has been brought into sharp focus by advances in information and communication technology (ICT), especially the explosion in the use of the Internet, to be discussed later in the chapter, which has opened new windows of opportunity for accessing and disseminating information.

15. Information reports (IS outputs) are typically generated through queries, gathering and manipulating the data required to create the report. Reports may then be communicated and disseminated in many ways. Information (the output) is created (the process) from data (the input) when it is required. In

many cases, therefore, there is no need to store information. Whereas data are typically the focus of the transaction processing system (TPS), information is at the heart of the management information system (MIS). The TPS serves the needs of operations (primary activities in the value chain) and stakeholders in the supply chain whereas the MIS serves the needs of managers, typically involved in tactical decision-making. However, this distinction becomes blurred within organizations granting employees and teams increased autonomy.

16.   MISs are systems designed to provide past, present and future routine information appropriate for planning, organizing and controlling the operation's functional areas in an organization. These systems provide feedback on organizational activities and help to support managerial decision-making. Information is of more value when available to the right people, in the right form and at the time they need it. In some cases the MIS may be a 'separate' system whilst in other cases it may describe the functionality added to an operational system as a module or application.

17.   Thus far, we have not only revealed the relationship between data and information but also identified information as an output of the information system. This output must be disseminated if managers and workers are to improve decision-making, planning, control and coordination. 'Dissemination' means the transmission of information, whether orally, in writing or by electronic means. The purpose of a dissemination activity is to ensure that information/knowledge is useful in reaching decisions, making changes or taking specific action and is available to those who can most benefit from it.

18.   IT also affects the traditional (physical) ways of delivering and communicating information, i.e. there is a separation between information and its carrier. Traditionally there was a trade-off between the richness of information (amount, quality and interactivity) and the reach (number of people involved in the information exchange): typically, the richer the information the smaller the reach. New technologies mean that information exchange is open and virtually cost-free.

19.   Dissemination may be achieved through traditional or electronic means. In the case of the latter, verbal channels such as presentations, meetings, the management chain, in-house newsletters, notice boards, seminars, employee reports, team briefings and telephone calls may be used. Communications technologies support the electronic dissemination of information; communications technology is used to transfer data/information from one physical location to another.

20.   Collaboration technologies help us to share information with each other (communication), coordinate our work efforts and resources with each other (coordination), and work together cooperatively on joint assignments (collaboration). Groupware tools and the Internet, intranets, extranets and other computer networks are used to support and enhance communication, coordination, collaboration and resource sharing amongst teams and work groups.

21.   Technology (telecommunications and software applications) can overcome geographic barriers, enabling the capture of information about business transactions from remote locations; time barriers – providing information to remote locations immediately after it is requested (see virtual organization); overcome cost barriers, reducing the cost of more traditional means of communication and can support linkages for competitive advantage (overcome structural barriers).

KNOWLEDGE RESOURCES

22.   Knowledge and information are closely related and, as was the case with data and information concepts, on occasions the two terms are used interchangeably (see Figure 46.3). Many see knowledge as the understanding, awareness or familiarity acquired through education or experience. Others see knowledge as applying experience to problem-solving. The source of knowledge as education or experience has led many to divide the concept in two classes: it may be about 'Knowing-that' (explicit) or 'Know-how' (tacit). Explicit knowledge is 'knowledge and understanding which is codified, expressed and available to anyone' – like the contents of this book; the knowledge that deals with objective, rational and technical knowledge (data, policies, procedures, software, documents, etc.). Tacit knowledge (also termed 'sticky' knowledge), on the other hand, is mainly intangible knowledge that is typically intuitive and not recorded since it is part of the human mind; the knowledge that is usually in the domain of subjective, cognitive and experiential learning. It is highly personal and hard to formalize. Thus, explicit knowledge is more easily confused with information; tacit knowledge with skills, abilities and competencies.

FIGURE 46.3 Knowledge information data (KID) resources

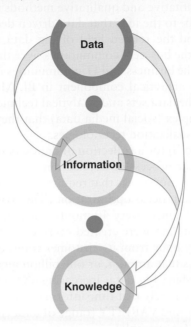

23. A system that facilitates knowledge management (KM) by ensuring knowledge flow from those who know to those who need to know throughout the organization is termed a knowledge management system (KMS). Once knowledge can be captured, the issue of where and how to store it arises. There are two knowledge management models (one for tacit and one for explicit knowledge) – the knowledge network and knowledge repository model (hybrid models also exist). In some cases databases may be used to simplify the task of identifying where knowledge exists (more likely when the knowledge is tacit), and in other cases the databases may be used to actually store knowledge (more likely when the knowledge is explicit). Technology is crucial to the success of the KMS.

24. KMSs are developed using three sets of technologies: communication, collaboration and storage. Communication technologies allow users to access the knowledge they need and to communicate with each other – especially with experts (email, the Internet, corporate intranets and other web-based tools provide communication capabilities). Collaboration technologies provide the means to perform group work. Groups can work together on common documents at the same time (synchronous) or at different times (asynchronous); in the same place, or in differing locations. Aside from recognizing the importance of technology-enabled networks it is important to also recognize the importance of people networks in KM initiatives. After all it is ultimately people that create, use and share knowledge. Thus there is a role for both the IT and HR functions in KM initiatives.

DATA MANAGEMENT AND BIG DATA

Vignette

The total amount of information storage technology grew from less than one 730Mb CD per person in 1993, to 61 CDs per person in 2007. This would create a stack of CDs that would reach beyond the moon!

25. The growth in the quantity and diversity of data has led to data sets larger than is manageable by the conventional, hands-on management tools. To manage these new and invaluable data sets, new methods

of data science and new applications in the form of predictive analytics, have been developed. Generally, data science is the application of quantitative and qualitative methods to solve business problems. Many of today's business practitioners subscribe to the idea that data-driven decisions are better decisions. Business intelligence and analytics (BI&A) and the related field of big data analytics have become increasingly important in both the academic and the business communities over the past two decades. Business intelligence (BI) became a popular term in the business and IT communities in the 1990s; later, **business analytics** was introduced to represent the key analytical component in BI. More recently, big data and big data analytics have been used to describe the data sets and analytical techniques in applications that are so large (from terabytes to exabytes) and complex (social media data) that they require advanced and unique data storage, management, analysis and visualization technologies.

26.   **Big data** is the term (and buzzword) for a collection of data sets so large and complex that it becomes difficult to process using traditional data processing applications. Gartner suggests 'Big data is high volume, high velocity and/or high variety information assets that require new forms of processing to enable enhanced decision-making, insight discovery and process optimization'. The world's technological per-capita capacity to store information has roughly doubled every 40 months since the 1980s (Hilbert and López, 2011); as of 2012, 2.5 exabytes (2.5×10^{18}) of data were created every day. It is estimated that Wal-mart collects more than 2.5 petabytes of data every hour from its customer transactions. A petabyte is one quadrillion bytes of text. An exabyte is 1000 times that amount, or one billion gigabytes. Many academics and practitioners use the '3Vs' model for describing big data: increasing VOLUME (amount of data), VELOCITY (speed of data in and out – real-time or nearly real-time information makes it possible for a company to be much more agile than its competitors), and VARIETY (range of data types and sources – the huge amounts of information from social networks, for example).

27.   **Business intelligence** is a topic of growing importance for business (Lycett, 2013). It encompasses the data infrastructure, applications, tools and best practices required for the effective capture, representation and delivery of data to inform decision-making and action; a BI system discovers not-yet-known patterns, trends and other useful information gleaned from large amounts of data that can help improve the organization's performance. Data are thus the underlying resource for BI. Arguably, it is the increasing availability of data (so-called 'big data' ultimately) that provides the impetus for BI. Volume proposes that there is key benefit in being able to process large amounts of data; and Variety proposes that data are cluttered in reality, coming from many sources in many different forms. More recently, value has emerged as an additional and, perhaps, integrating 'V' – doing something valuable with the data is important! A recent report found that top-performing organizations made decisions based on rigorous analysis. Increasingly, however, analytic insight is used within top-performing organizations to guide both future strategies and day-to-day operations.

28.   Duncan Shaw has a research interest in and blogs about big data and big data analytics. He notes that firms are gathering more and more data about their customers and how their supply chains operate. Customers are expecting services to be evermore personalized to their individual wants and needs. The possibilities for using these data for improving services, creating new products and services and meeting customers' needs are huge, but doing it properly is incredibly challenging. He believes the real promise of 'big data' is about extending our capabilities of perception, understanding and manipulation to macro levels that are much bigger than those we normally think about and operate on – and micro levels that are much smaller than we have analyzed and worked with before. We are starting to use new analytical tools and techniques to push back both the micro and the macro frontiers of space, time and organizational complexity.

29.   Big data (and analytics) enables managers to decide on the basis of evidence rather than intuition; thus managers rely less on subjective decision-making and educated guesses and more on objective or 'fact' based decision-making. For that reason it has the potential to revolutionize management. The big data movement seeks to glean intelligence from data and translate that into business advantage. We explore how data and other information resources may provide advantage and an ability to compete next.

46.2 COMPETING WITH INFORMATION RESOURCES

30.   The idea of competing with information resources is an old one. Porter and Millar (1985) in their landmark article, 'How Information Gives You Competitive Advantage', discuss the impact of information

and technology on the business we do and the way in which we do it. They review the impact upon internal operations and relationships with other organizations (suppliers, customers, rivals, etc.). Porter and Millar also examine how such resources alter industry structures, support cost or differentiation strategies and spawn entirely new businesses (competition). Whilst technologies, the volume, velocity and variety of data sources have changed, the underlying purpose has changed less and we explore this next.

31. Internal operations are conceptualized as the value chain – discussed in Chapter 10. According to Porter and Millar (1985: p. 151), 'to gain competitive advantage over its rivals, a company must either perform these activities at a lower cost or perform them in a way that leads to differentiation and a premium price (more value)'. Information resources and technology may therefore enable the organization strategy by reducing cost or enabling it to add value and do things differently.

32. Information resources and technology may determine industry structure (see five forces, Chapter 12), competitive advantage (lower costs/enhanced differentiation) and new business. IT can increase buyer-power (making product information more readily available, enabling comparisons to be made between suppliers); raise or lower barriers-to-entry (dependent on the needs and cost technology investments); make it easier to create substitute products and increase rivalry.

33. As the acquisition of IS shifted more to off-the-shelf products the ability of organizations to compete through the IS alone diminished since rivals could purchase the same or similar systems. Knowledge resources therefore became the more 'superior' of the information resources in the late 1990s and are most often associated with *sustainable* competitive advantage; superior and sustainable because of the difficulties faced by rivals when seeking to copy such resources. The 'knowledge-based view' (KBV) focuses upon knowledge as the most strategically important of resources; it is an outgrowth of the RBV. Under the 'knowledge-based-view of the firm', knowledge is seen as the resource upon which organizations base their competitive strategies. However, big data analytics may be reversing the table to some degree.

34. Organizations may need to develop their infrastructure before seeking to implement specific knowledge management initiatives. Three key infrastructures, technical, structural and cultural, enable the creation, sharing and use of knowledge. In order to leverage infrastructure, KM processes must also be present in order to store, transform and transport knowledge throughout the organization. These processes enable the organization to capture, bring together and transfer knowledge in an efficient manner.

35. Many scholars have identified processes associated with KM. Three common knowledge processes are: knowledge generation, knowledge codification and knowledge transfer/realization. Knowledge generation includes all processes involved in the acquisition and development of knowledge. Knowledge codification involves the conversion of knowledge into accessible and applicable formats. Knowledge transfer includes the movement of knowledge from its point of generation or codified form to the point of use.

46.3 TYPES OF BIS

36. Thus far we have discussed many different types of IS and technology utilized in the organization. At this point we might ask, 'What is a business information system?' An IS is a system designed to produce information that can be used to support the activities of managers and other workers; or interrelated components working together to collect, process, store and disseminate information to support decision-making, coordination and control in an organization. Similarly, it is (1) A set of people, procedures and resources that collects, transforms and disseminates information in an organization. (2) A system that accepts data resources as input and processes them into information products as output.

37. At the highest level we might distinguish two types of IS: formal and informal. Formal systems rest on accepted and fixed definitions of data and procedures, operating with predefined rules whilst informal systems are unstructured, i.e. 'office gossip networks' that use unstated rules of behaviour. With informal systems there is no agreement on what constitutes information or on how it will be stored and processed. In many ways, the use of the terms 'formal' and 'informal' is consistent with the way such terms have been used previously within this book. It is common to subdivide the formal system into (1) manual (i.e. paper and pencil) and (2) computer-based systems. Computer-based information systems (CBIS) rely on computer hardware and software technology (the technical foundation) to process and disseminate information.

38.   We may describe system parts in terms of a particular resource type (hardware, software, data) or as a collection of resources bound through some sub-goal; for example, we might discuss the part of a system responsible for interfacing with other systems or the part responsible for processing bookings rather than payments. Parts are related in as much as they may share data inputs or the outputs of one part become the inputs of another. Parts may also come together in order to fulfil some higher order goal (see holism). As an example, consider a hotel management system. One part of the system will manage the reservation process and allocate rooms; another may take and process payments and yet another may allocate goods and services to guests enabling them to charge a restaurant meal to their room. However, the charging of services to a room is dependent upon the guest being registered in the system and a room having been allocated. Similarly, invoice generation is dependent upon customer details having been entered.

39.   Classifying computer-based information systems is not unlike classifying cars. Cars have a series of common components no matter what the make or model: wheels, engine, fuel, steering and seats. In some cases a car may be placed in more than one category and in some cases it is difficult to categorize. IS also have common components: inputs, processes and outputs and sometimes storage. They tend to be categorized according to their use, the user and purpose.

40.   A functional business system is a system designed to support a specific activity of the organization. Business applications have traditionally served the functional areas of an organization, such as: production; inventory; purchasing; accounting; HR; inbound and outbound logistics and marketing and sales.

A selection of functional systems are described below:

- Accounting information systems

- Sales and marketing systems

- Inventory systems

- Production and manufacturing systems include production control, computer aided manufacturing and workflow management systems

- Packaging and distribution systems include logistical planning and customer database-labelling systems

- HR systems include payroll database, skills, training and development, employee record and payroll systems

- Purchasing systems.

Functional systems serve the specific and local needs of parts of the organization and are developed using specific programming languages. Typically they have their own database(s), data structures, operating systems and other idiosyncrasies. However, as was noted in Chapter 38, the idea of the functional system has broadly given way to the integrated concept of the enterprise system as typified by the ERP and CRM systems.

46.4 NET TECHNOLOGIES

41.   Thus far we have discussed different types of BIS. However, aside from significant advances in database technologies and business applications, the 1990s also witnessed significant advances in networking and communication technologies. Indeed the Internet, associated technologies and mobile technologies have revolutionized business and life generally. The key to understanding the Internet is the concept of connectivity. The Internet is simply a global network of interlinked computers, operating on a standard protocol which allows data to be transferred between otherwise incompatible machines. The word itself simply means a 'network of networks'.

42.   The digital organization is an 'organization where nearly all significant business processes and relationships with customers, suppliers and employees are digitally enabled, and key corporate assets are managed through digital means'. The Internet is the primary technology for the digital firm and organizations use the Internet for communication, coordination and the management of the organization (e-business). The Internet and other networks have made it possible for businesses to replace manual and

paper-based processes with the electronic flow of information. Net technologies manifest in the form of the inter, intra and extra-nets.

43.   An intranet is a network inside an organization that uses Internet technologies to provide an Internet-like environment within the organization for information sharing, communications, collaboration and the support of business processes. Intranets can significantly improve communications and collaboration within an organization. Intranet software browsers, servers and search engines can help companies and individuals navigate and locate the business information required.

46.5 COMPETING WITH NET TECHNOLOGY: E-COMMERCE AND E-BUSINESS

44.   Many see e-commerce as simply buying and selling using the Internet; for some, e-commerce is more than electronic financial transactions, extending it to all electronically mediated transactions between organizations, and any third party with which it deals. Others have defined e-commerce with a broad scope, as the exchange of information across electronic networks, at any stage in the supply chain, whether within an organization, between businesses, between businesses and consumers, or between the public and private sector, whether paid or unpaid.

45.   e-Business, on the other hand, is the transformation of key business processes through the use of Internet technologies; the buy-side, e-commerce transactions with suppliers and the sell-side e-commerce transactions with customers can also be considered key business processes. Thus, e-business is seen as a larger concept, embracing e-commerce plus the internal (process) aspects of the digital organization.

46.   Whilst the Internet presents new opportunities it also intensifies competition and shifts power to buyers. Porter (2001) considers the consequences of the Internet, presenting arguments for the changing nature of competition and the resultant challenges for strategy formulation. The Internet has created new industries; however, its greatest impact has been to enable the reconfiguration of existing indus-tries previously constrained by high costs for communicating, gathering information or accomplishing transactions. Internet technology provides buyers with easier access to information about products and suppliers, thus strengthening buyer bargaining power. The Internet mitigates the need for such things as an established sales force or access to existing channels, reducing barriers to entry (see disintermediation). Market places automate corporate procurement by linking many buyers and suppliers electronically. The benefits to buyers include low transaction costs, easier access to price and product information, convenient purchase of associated services and, sometimes, the ability to pool volume. The benefits to suppliers include lower selling costs, lower transaction costs, access to wider markets and the avoidance of powerful channels.

47.   By enabling new approaches to meeting needs and performing functions, it creates new substitutes and channels. As an open system, companies have more difficulty maintaining proprietary offerings, thus the rivalry amongst competitors is intensified. On the Internet, buyers can often switch suppliers with just a few mouse clicks, and new web technologies are systematically reducing switching costs even further. The use of the Internet also expands the geographic market, bringing many more companies into competition with one another. A number of businesses are able to increase revenue through network effects which can create demand-side economies of scale and raise barriers to entry. However, the openness of the Internet makes it difficult for a single company to capture the benefits of a network effect.

48.   Internet technologies tend to create greater pressure for companies to engage in destructive price competition. In general, Internet technologies erode profitability by shifting power to customers. The great paradox of the Internet is that the very benefits – making information widely available; reducing the diffi-culty of purchasing, marketing and distribution; allowing buyers and sellers to find and transact business with one another more easily – also make it more difficult for companies to capture those benefits as profits. Much of the value, however, is absorbed by customers and may not result in expected wealth creation for the business. The Internet is an enabling technology – a powerful set of tools which rarely offers a direct competitive advantage. Internet technology itself is not a source of advantage because it is readily available to all. Competitive advantages arise from traditional strengths fortified through Internet technology, by tying a company's activities together in a more distinctive system (Porter, 2001).

CONCLUSION

49. Information resources include data, information and knowledge. Such resources, with associated technologies, are an important source of competitive advantage that enables value creation, managerial and operational work, strategy, effectiveness and efficiency in organizations around the world. Internet and mobile technologies present opportunities but also intensify competition. Internet technology itself is not a source of advantage because it is readily available to all. Competitive advantages arise from traditional strengths fortified through Internet technology – by tying a company's activities together in a more distinctive system. Recently there have been significant developments in big data, business intelligence and analytics. Companies face the ongoing challenge of embracing and applying such technologies to meet organizational goals and at the same time provide a source of advantage over rivals. In the next chapter we consider how organizations acquire and implement information systems and technologies and the role of the IT function in support.

QUESTIONS

1   Summarize the main purposes of IS within organizations.

2   The words data and information are used frequently in business. Define and distinguish the two concepts and explain what constitutes an IS.

3   Explain how organizations compete with information resources, systems and technology. Which of the

information resources do you believe is most important to strategy and competitive advantage? Explain your answer.

4   Explain what is meant by e-commerce, e-business and the digital organization.

REFERENCES

Cetindamar, D., Phaal, R. and Probert, D. (2010) *Technology Management – Activities and Tools*, Palgrave.

Chaffey, D. (2011) *E-Business and E-Commerce Management*, 5th edn, FT/Prentice Hall.

Evans, A., Martin, K. and Poatsy, M.A. (2014) 'Technology in Action, Complete: *Pearson New International Edition*, 10th edn, Pearson.

Hilbert, M. and López, P. (2011) 'The world's technological capacity to store, communicate, and compute information'. *Science*, 332(6025): 60–65.

Laudon, J.P. and Laudon, K.C. (2006) *Management Information Systems – Managing the Digital Firm*, 9th edn, Pearson Prentice Hall.

Laudon, K.C. and Laudon, J.P. (2014) *Management Information Systems, Global Edition*, 13th edn, Pearson.

Lycett, M. (2013) 'Datafication': making sense of (big) data in a complex world', *European Journal of Information Systems*, 22: 381–386.

Porter, M.E. and Millar, V.E. (1985) 'How information gives you a competitive advantage', *Harvard Business Review*, 63: 149–174.

Porter, M.E. (2001) 'Strategy and the Internet', *Harvard Business Review*, (March): 62–78.

CHAPTER 47
MANAGING INFORMATION RESOURCES

Key Concepts

- Acquisition process
- Information resource management (IRM)
- Information systems infrastructure
- Project management
- Systems analysis
- Systems development life cycle (SDLC)

Learning Outcomes   Having read this chapter, you should be able to:

- describe the essential components of an organization's IS infrastructure
- discuss managerial issues associated with managing an organization's IS infrastructure
- understand the role of the IS department and its relationship with end users
- describe, with reference to the acquisition process, how organizations acquire IS and IT
- describe, with reference to the SDLC, how organizations develop software applications
- discuss the role of project management in the development of software applications and implementation of IT.

Vignette

Projects to implement IS often fail and if that were not bad enough, implemented systems can also fail – both resulting in high business costs.

WHY YOUR IT PROJECT MAY BE RISKIER THAN YOU THINK

Flyvbjerg and Budzier (2011) reached a worrying conclusion after conducting a large global study of IT change initiatives. They examined 1471 projects, comparing their budgets and estimated performance benefits with the actual costs and results. They found that over one in four projects overran on cost. However, one in six of the projects studied had a cost overrun of 200 per cent and a schedule overrun of almost 70 per cent. They suggested that planners consistently underestimated the costs and overestimated the benefits of IT projects.

THE DEVASTATING EFFECT ON BUSINESS WHEN CORE SYSTEMS FAIL

Globalscape's survey (reported in 2014) found that 60 per cent of enterprise employees who estimated the financial cost of downtime on their organization said that a single hour without critical systems costs their company between $250 000 and $500 000 – and one in six reported that 1 hour of downtime can cost $1 000 000 or more.

1.   As the opening vignette highlights, companies are critically dependent on IS and technologies but frequently fail to implement them as intended. In the last chapter we considered how IS are used to increase productivity, attain organizational goals and provide competitive advantage. Businesses rely on an **information systems infrastructure** (consisting of hardware and competing platforms, system software (application and operating systems), storage, networking and telecommunications services including Internet platforms, data management services and data centres) to support their decision-making business processes and competitive strategy (Valacich and Schneider, 2014: p. 128).

2.   Enterprise-wide infrastructure includes services such as email, the corporate website, company intranets and an array of enterprise-wide software applications. This infrastructure, along with other information resources, must be managed if the organization is to use such resources effectively and efficiently. Creating and managing a coherent infrastructure creates challenges in terms of investment decisions, coordination, dealing with scalability (the ability to adapt applications as business needs grow), change and governance. The creation and maintenance of the infrastructure requires significant capital investment decisions (refer back to Chapter 45).

3.   **Information resource management (IRM)** encompasses all activities related to the controlling, organizing, maintaining, planning, acquiring and securing of (information) systems and IT resources. The key activities can be remembered through the compass acronym in 'en*compass*es'! We will explore the activities throughout this chapter. In particular we will discuss the organization and role of the IS department, how the organization acquires and develops IS and technologies, the use of project management to deliver information resources and solutions to business problems, and the need to secure and protect information resources. We will discuss what IS specialists do (their roles, tasks and responsibilities) and the role of the IS function. Linked to this we will consider the organization and location of IS in terms of reporting lines and degrees of centralization.

47.1 ORGANIZING AND PLANNING (STRATEGY): IS STRATEGY, THE IT/IS FUNCTION, ROLES AND RESPONSIBILITIES

4.   The organization must determine *who* will control and manage the information systems and technology infrastructure. Some organizations allocate this responsibility to each division or department whilst others create a specialized business function to manage related issues. In some organizations people discuss the IT department whilst in others it may be referred to as the IS department or something similar. Information system (IS) is the study of complementary networks of hardware and software (see IT) that people and organizations use to collect, manipulate, process, create and distribute data and information. On the other

hand, information technology (IT) is the application of computers and telecommunications equipment to store, retrieve, transmit and manipulate data, often in the business situation. Whilst the terms may be used interchangeably, information technology is seen as a subset of the IS. The information system refers to a set of interrelated components of which IT forms a part. When discussing roles and responsibilities confusion may also arise from related concepts such as e-commerce, e-business and knowledge management – all of which may be found in the IS/ IT or some other department(s).

5.   In many ways the IS function is similar to the HR function. Traditionally, both were seen in supporting (administrative and operational) roles. However, in recent years their roles have become increasingly strategic. They are seen as enablers of strategy and the key resources needed to attain competitive advantage and accomplish organizational goals. Given their changing roles, we also observed changes to the views on how they should be organized. With regard to the IS function, organizations have pursued service, partnership, vendor and strategic advantage models. Traditional approaches featured in the 1960s and were followed by database-driven approaches the following decade. In the 1980s there was an emphasis on business functions and functional information systems. In the 1990s, with the advent of the Internet and enterprise systems, there was a new focus on integrating systems and an external focus; what Laudon and Laudon (2014: p. 200) referred to as the 'enterprise computing era'. More recently, approaches are being influenced by mobile technologies, cloud computing, the pursuit of business analytics and the use of IS to enable strategy (enterprise and KMS) – the so-called 'cloud and mobile computing era'. Once again, parallels may be drawn with HR. Both functions are specialists that share the responsibility for management of their resources with the rest of the business. The management of information resources is shared between the end-user (the person who actually uses a particular system) and the IS department.

6.   Those responsible for organization design must decide to whom the IS (services) department, if created, will report. Like HR, the IS department traditionally had a more operational role and may not therefore have reported directly to the CEO. However, this has become increasingly strategic as information resources enable the attainment of corporate goals and the creation of competitive advantage. Traditionally (when typically referred to as the data-processing department) they may have reported to the accounting or finance organization, an administrative group or operating division. As noted by Pearlson and Saunders (2013), many organizations recognized that certain strategic areas of the IS organization required more focused guidance. This recognition led to the creation of new positions, such as the chief information officer (CIO), chief knowledge officer, chief technology officer, chief telecommunications officer, chief network officer and even the chief information security officer.

7.   Contemporary organizations are more likely to have a board level chief information officer reporting directly to the CEO. The CIO is the highest-ranking corporate officer (senior manager) in charge of IS and IT; oversees the planning, development and implementation of IS and serves as leader to all IS professionals in the organization.

8.   In recognition of the need to incorporate the views of the whole company, many organizations establish a *steering committee* in order to set direction, allocate resources and oversee the actions of the IS department/division. The department like HR needs to achieve two-way strategic alignment; the IT strategy should both inform and be informed by the corporate strategy. There is also a need to develop effective relationships with line management and foster good relationships (partnerships) with end-users; there is also a need to manage good relationships with vendors; they should quickly develop and implement new systems, build and manage infrastructure; and finally the department must ensure it has the right talent, organized to meet its goals and mission.

9.   As has already been noted there are many ways in which the IS/IT function can be organized. The IS department consists of specialists, such as programmers, systems analysts and IS managers, Laudon and Laudon (2014). Programmers write the software instructions for computers; systems analysts liaise with the rest of the organization and translate business problems and requirements into information requirements and systems; and IS managers are leaders of teams of programmers and analysts, project managers, etc. There is no magic formula for determining the ratio of IS professionals to end-users and this will depend upon the degree of centralization and extent of roles and responsibilities and outsourcing; ratios of between 1:50 and 1:100 are common.

10.   Amongst the *roles* of the IS function is the provision and management of IS infrastructure, long-term research and the facilitation of end-user computing. In this latter role there is a need to enable users

to conceptualize IS problems (typically a role for the **systems analyst** – an IT professional who analyzes business problems and recommends technological solutions); to select or design the appropriate technology and system and then to implement it. In this capacity, the IS specialist would typically adopt an internal consultancy role. In many organizations they may have to compete with external consultants and IS and IT vendors.

11.   The distribution and division of roles and responsibilities between the specialist IS function and the line business unit (location of the end-user) will continue to present a tension to manage within any organization. Generally, we might expect to find the strategic planning (setting strategic direction), communications network management (establishing infrastructure systems), management of shared databases and information resources to be the responsibility of the IS function. They are also likely to scan for emerging technologies and facilitate the transferring of technology throughout the organization. Other traditional IT activities include managing the data centre (a facility used to house computer systems and associated components typically used by organizations for the remote storage, processing or distribution of large amounts of data) and network, application design, development and maintenance and the procurement, installation and maintenance of desktop hardware. More recent IT activities include standards and technology planning, supplier/vendor management, security and business continuity planning. The technical planning for applications and aspects of business analysis may be the responsibility of the line. There will always be some end-user computing development but the development and acquisition of more sophisticated systems is likely to be a shared responsibility.

12.   From a structural and organizational design standpoint, IS and IT specialists (professionals) may be grouped in a number of ways and may exist as a centralized or decentralized organization. There is much debate about the extent of centralization and decentralization and companies exist in various places along this continuum. A centralized approach makes the application of standards an easier job and presents the organization with economies of scale advantages (one voice when dealing with vendors). This approach also enables knowledge sharing within the profession and makes the recruitment of IS/IT talent easier. However, the centralized approach is less responsive to local needs, making support slower. Furthermore, investment in IS resources may be outside the control of local business units. The decentralized approach is more flexible and enables close partnership between this specialized function and the line business unit. The middle ground is often described as federalism – an approach that seeks to distribute power, hardware, software, data and personnel between a central IS group and local units (Pearlson and Saunders, 2013).

13.   Finally, we have discussed *outsourcing* on a number of occasions in this textbook and the concept is often applied to various aspects of the IS function. Organizations will question whether they should have an IS function and which aspects of their responsibilities may be outsourced. In the remaining sections of this chapter we will take a closer look at the processes used by organizations to acquire and develop systems and finally outline the need and methods used to protect information resources. We have selected these areas as they are responsibilities involving any line managers as part of their job, i.e. they are processes that are shared with the IS professional.

47.2 ACQUIRING SYSTEMS AND TECHNOLOGY

14.   Thus far we have identified BIS types but have not yet explained how they find their way into the organization. We address this challenge in this section, discussing the acquisition process and the five Ss first (Figure 47.1) and then the development process (Figure 47.2) later. First we ask, Why do organizations initiate IS projects? This is the 'start' stage in the acquisition process. In some cases projects are 'failure driven', i.e. faults in existing system(s) and in other cases may be 'aspiration driven' i.e. new opportunities are presented. The BIS may be obtained from within or outside the organization and may exist already (off-the-shelf) or be specially developed (bespoke) for the organizational problem at hand. Acquiring a BIS is not unlike purchasing a new suit of clothes. In some cases the suit fits perfectly (bespoke) but costs more, takes time to create and may have particular flaws. In other cases a purchase can be readymade, off-the-peg. This suit is common, cheaper but may not fit so well!

15.   Thus, acquisition refers to the approach for sourcing the BIS. Alternative acquisition methods include: (1) procurement off-the-shelf – purchased from a software vendor, (2) bespoke development – 'built from

FIGURE 47.1 Acquisition process

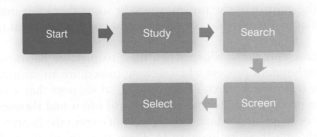

scratch' and (3) end-user-developed – either (a) built by the IT department (internal developers) or by (b) the end-user themselves. Hence acquisition is how a company obtains the technologies valuable for its business, based on the buy–collaborate–make decision. Technologies might be developed internally, by some form of collaboration, or acquired from external developers. The management of acquisition differs on the basis of the choice made (Cetindamar, Phaal and Probert, 2010).

16. The acquisition methods cited may be compared and evaluated using criteria such as delivery time, cost, quality (bugs) and how closely they meet needs, i.e. are fit-for-purpose. Bespoke solutions score better with this latter criterion but are poor when judged against the others. The standard off-the-shelf solution tends to be the opposite. i.e. good on all criteria except the fit with business needs. Acquisition method is therefore linked with generic strategy – a tailor-made system supporting a differentiation and an off-the-shelf supporting a cost advantage.

17. The second stage of the acquisition process involves a feasibility STUDY. The key stages of the acquisition process can be remembered using the five Ss. The feasibility study is the activity that occurs at the start of the project to ensure that the project is a viable business proposition. The feasibility report (output) analyzes the need for and impact of the system and considers different alternatives for acquiring software; seeks an overview of a problem and a rough assessment of whether feasible solutions exist, prior to committing resources. The study outputs include the feasibility report and recommendation to proceed and will include high level requirements and a cost–benefit analysis. The cost–benefit analysis will involve investment appraisal (refer back to Chapter 45) and may document a TELOS analysis.

18. The TELOS analysis includes: Technical feasibility which determines whether a proposed solution can be implemented with the available hardware, software and technical resources; the Economic feasibility is an assessment of the costs and benefits of different solutions to select that which gives the best value (i.e. will the new system cost more than the expected benefits?); Legal feasibility assesses whether it is lawful to use the information system in the way intended – the organization may end up breaking data privacy laws etc.; Organizational feasibility reviews how well the solution meets the needs of the business and anticipates problems such as resistance to the system if insufficient training occurs (considers the effect of change given a company's culture and politics); alternatively, some describe Operational feasibility – an assessment of how the new system will affect the daily working practices within the organization (is the system workable on a day-to-day basis?); and finally the Schedule feasibility considers whether or not the preferred system can be implemented in the desired timescales.

19. As part of the study or afterwards, the organization must SEARCH for alternative solutions to the identified business problem. In cases other than end-user development or development by the IT department, the organization will either search for and select an off-the-shelf solution or find a developer to build one for them. Interactions with external suppliers often take the form of the request for information (RFI); request for proposals (RFP) or request for quote (RFQ). The purpose of the RFI and RFP is to identify possible solutions to the IS problem; they typically constitute a detailed list of questions submitted to vendors of packaged software or other computer services to determine if the vendor's product can meet the organization's specific requirements. The RFQ is a request for pricing quote(s) specifications related to a required product, by a prospective purchaser. Such requests mark the beginning of the SCREENING and SELECTION sub-process. From here, as with the generic problem-solving process, companies will select

their preferred solution through a competitive tendering process and mechanisms to identify the solution that most meets their requirements. A variety of stakeholders may become involved in the acquisition process, depending upon the culture of the organization. In some cases this may be a centralized and in other cases a decentralized activity. External consultants and consultants from the solution provider may also support the process.

20.   The acquisition process may stand alone when used to procure hardware but may be integrated with a broader systems development process when seeking to acquire an information system (application software etc.). We consider this process next. Prior to doing so we note that a variety of stakeholders are likely to be involved in the process and the line manager will often find themselves an active participant and even manager of the process/project. Managers should not expect the IS professional to take automatic ownership of the process though they are likely to facilitate and consult on it. At the end of the day it is a process to deliver a solution to a business problem and it is likely that the line or business manager will know more about the problem than the IS professional. The latter will know how to manage the process and is likely to have the desired systems analyst skills to model the problem and write system requirements in a manner useful by the developer/programmer.

47.3 DEVELOPING SYSTEMS

21.   When a system does not already exist it must be developed. Systems development concerns the activities that go into producing an IS solution to an organizational problem or opportunity. Regardless of the type of IS to be implemented, common activities are undertaken at the start, middle and end of each project. Whilst there are many development models, mostly based on generic problem-solving approaches (refer back to decision-making, Chapter 16), we focus on the best known here, the systems development life cycle (SDLC), also known as the waterfall or stepwise model. Developed in the 1950s and 1960s, this is the traditional methodology used to develop, maintain and replace IS; it is the sequence in which a system is created from initiation, analysis, design, implementation, build and maintenance.

22.   The model may be applied in different ways. For example, more detail and rigour may be evident for the development of a more expensive system or one that is to be built from scratch as opposed to one that may have already been developed. End-user development tends to neglect the feasibility, analysis, design and testing phases and the design and build phases are relatively insignificant for off-the-shelf acquisition. The traditional IS development cycle (see Figure 47.2) is based upon the following stages:

Systems Investigation (Initiation): this stage seeks to answer the question, what system do we need and why? Typically, this stage includes a cost–benefit analysis as part of a feasibility study. In many cases the aforementioned acquisition process may be viewed as the sub-process of the SDLC and utilized here. The main output at this stage is the decision as to whether to proceed with the project and if so, a project plan will be created and resources allocated.

Systems Analysis: this stage seeks to answer the question, what exactly should the system do? This stage includes a detailed analysis of the information needs of end-users, the organizational environment, and any system currently used to develop the functional requirements of a new system. These first two stages are non-technical and require little knowledge of IT or programming. They require knowledge of the business. The outputs of this stage include a report documenting the business requirements of the new system.

Systems Design: this stage develops specifications from the requirements for the hardware, software, people, network and data resources of the system. The information products the system is expected to produce are also designated. Various conceptual, logical and development models will be created for the programmers to follow.

Systems Implementation: here the organization develops or acquires the hardware and software needed to implement the system design. Programmers may write code and 'build' the system software. Testing of the system and training of people to operate and use the system are also part of this stage. Finally, the organization converts to the new system. Four options are generally considered when changing over from the old system (paper or computer-based) to the new system: (1) Parallel conversion – the old and new systems are used concurrently

FIGURE 47.2 Systems development life cycle (SDLC)

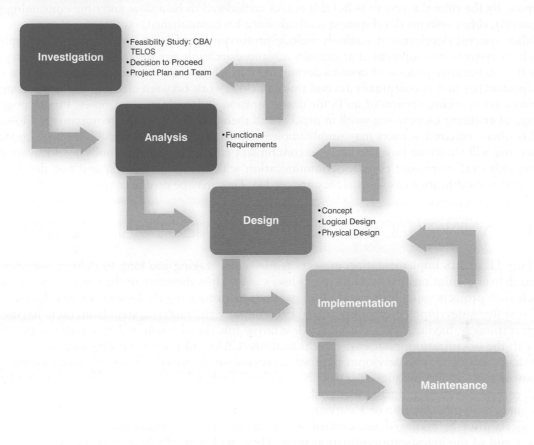

until the new system is demonstrably stable and reliable, (2) Pilot conversion – the system is trialled in a limited area before it is deployed more extensively across the business, (3) Phased conversion – this changeover method involves introducing different modules of the new system sequentially and (4) Direct cutover strategy – where the new system completely replaces the old one on an appointed day. Conversion methods vary in the amount of associated risk, cost and complexity. Legacy data may then be migrated onto the new system, user profiles created and then the system will be handed over to the user.

Systems Maintenance: in this (final) stage, management uses a post-implementation review process to monitor, evaluate and modify the system as needed and on an ongoing basis.

23. Traditionally the model stages were conducted sequentially; however, developers learned this created problems as new requirements, highlighted after the analysis stage, were not incorporated into the design. Consequently, the implemented system was not a quality system in that it did not fully fit and meet the user's requirements. The model was therefore improved and, during the project, previous stages may be revisited as indicated by the reverse arrows in Figure 47.2.

24. It is important to note the different roles and responsibilities throughout the project. The first two stages may be undertaken by non-technical people: the investigation stage makes use of employees from the target department, i.e. where the users are located, and the analysis stage by systems analysts. The design stage is undertaken by IT specialists whilst implementation tasks may be shared between the users and the IT function. Implementation involves change management and the reader should refer back to Chapter for more detail.

25. The SDLC and variants allow a structured and disciplined approach to be taken in the design, development and implementation of IS. Whilst it seeks to ensure a close fit with business needs (through thorough requirement capture and modelling) it has been criticized for being implemented as a linear sequen

steps, such that requirements may have changed before the system is built and will therefore no longer be fit for purpose by the time the system is built. It is also considered to be a slow and time-consuming process. Consequently, other systems development methods have been established.

26. Other systems development methods include prototyping and agile development. **Prototyping** is an approach to systems development that exploits advanced technologies for using trial-and-error problem-solving. It is an iterative process of systems development in which requirements are converted to a working system (prototype) that is continually revised through close work between analysts and users. A **prototype** is a preliminary working version of an IS for demonstration and evaluation purposes. Prototyping has the advantage of enabling users to see work in process and therefore develop their requirements. However, the method is often criticized as users may simply implement the prototype which will have been created using shortcuts and will therefore be more likely to contain software bugs. **Agile methods** are software development methods that emphasize constant communication with clients (end-users) and fast development of code, as well as modifications as soon as they are needed. They may be used in conjunction with prototyping.

47.4 PLANNING (TACTICAL LEVEL): PROJECT MANAGEMENT

27. Many IT or BIS implementation projects fail by either taking too long to deliver, overspending or failing to deliver a solution that actually meets user's needs. It is therefore in the organization's interest to approach such projects using frameworks and methods incorporating the lessons (knowledge) of the past. Pitfalls in systems development projects, mistakes commonly encountered, stem from users having unrealistic expectations or having little involvement; low cross- functional involvement; requirements with a lack of 'fit' with the organization; poor cost–benefit analysis (CBA) and poor resourcing of projects.

28. Systems acquisition and development processes previously discussed are typically managed using project management tools and techniques. A **project** is a one-time undertaking (a set of activities) with a beginning and end, carried out to meet a particular goal (such as the development of a new product, construction of a new building, or implementation of a software system) within cost, schedule and quality objectives.

29. Projects must be managed and controlled. Under the SDLC a project team will normally be identified at the end of the investigation/initiation stage. There will normally be a project manager and budget, the amount and distribution of resources allocated. Project control is responsible for the monitoring of the project objectives of cost, time and quality as the project progresses. In many cases there may be a project board, a structure to oversee the project and link to wider organizational initiatives. In the case of enterprise system implementations there are likely to be several interrelated projects considering not just the software but also changes to structure, processes and culture.

30. **Project management** refers to the combination of systems, techniques and people used to control and monitor activities undertaken within the project; it coordinates the resources necessary to complete the project successfully. It involves all activities associated with planning, scheduling and controlling projects. Managers use a **project management framework** which is a structured approach, such as PRINCE or PMBOK, to ensure that all steps are covered and stakeholders considered in completing a project. Competent project managers are vital for project success. They will create and implement the **project plan**. This shows the main activities within the project, providing an overall schedule and identifying resources needed for project implementation. The plan (a Gantt or Pert chart and work breakdown structure) can be used coordinate the activities of the **project team** – a collection of employees from different work areas in an anization brought together to accomplish a specific task within a finite time.

Chaffey and White (2011: p. 329) discuss methodologies to support the project management process, that in the UK, PRINCE2 is an established methodology used on many public service projects. is methodology the project is divided into manageable stages and roles and responsibilities clearly he project is driven by the business case which describes the organization's justification and t for the deliverable. The methodology encourages involvement of management and stakehold-riate, during the project.

ct plan **work breakdown structure** (the definition of, and the relationship between, the packages in project management, each work package can be allocated its own objectives that fit in with the overall work breakdown structure; it is a statement of all the work (tasks) that must be completed in a project) will often be modelled on the key activities of the SDLC. However, in some cases the project does not go according to plan. A runaway project is a systems development project that requires much more spending or time to complete than budgeted or scheduled. Many statistics suggest that more than half of all IS projects fail to deliver either in terms of budgeted cost, solving the defined problem or on-time delivery. Assuming that the IS is implemented successfully, and handed over to the user, the need to protect it arises. Whilst security will have been designed into the system we outline further measures to protect information resources in the next and final section of this chapter.

47.4 PROTECTING INFORMATION RESOURCES

33.   It is the responsibility of end-users and IS professionals to protect information resources from threats (hacking, fraud, sabotage, etc.). Resources may be vulnerable in any number of ways and it will be important to ensure that data remain confidential and have integrity and that information resources remain available to users in order to avoid business disruption (refer back to the opening vignette). **Confidentiality** is about ensuring information is accessible only to those authorized to have access. **Integrity** concerns safeguarding the accuracy and completeness of information and processing methods. Finally, **availability** describes the property of being accessible and usable upon demand by an authorized entity. The three attributes of information security can be remembered by the CIA acronym.

34.   There are many ways to protect information resources (Kelly, 2005). The IS department will often write and manage relevant IS security policies and ensure compliance throughout the organization. They will also procure and implement more sophisticated controls such as cryptographic controls. These are used to authenticate system users and protect data and messages over networks. The reader is likely to be familiar with logical access control, a concept used to assure confidentiality that consists essentially of three components: Identification, Authentication of the user and/or the equipment; and Authorization, i.e. restrictions on what the user is able to do. Identification and authentication are the first two steps. A user will then be allowed to access the system as permitted by their authorizations. The identification and authentication of a user may make use of three classes of basic techniques. These classes may be used either on their own or in combination. They are: something known exclusively to the user (userID and passwords, etc.), something possessed (such as tokens, keys, swipe card, etc.) or a unique physical attribute (biometric techniques). The userID and password is the common form of access control implemented in the business system. Users should be given advice on passwords and rules may be included in policy statements. Similarly, rules may be applied automatically through software that may enforce password changes and their format.

35.   In the event that data are corrupted, systems become unavailable or there is a significant breach of confidentiality (privacy) the organization will normally initiate its business continuity plan, see Chapter 29 (Paras. 31–36).

CONCLUSION

36.   In this chapter we have considered how the organization acquires, develops and implements IS and IT. We introduced two key processes: acquisition and development and discussed the use of project management tools and techniques and methods to coordinate activities in a manner likely to ensure solutions are delivered on time whilst meeting cost and end-user functionality requirements.

37.   We recognized that a range of stakeholders are involved in the acquisition, development and use of BIS and that roles and responsibilities may be allocated to end-users or IS professionals. We also discussed the important aspects of the IS and IT infrastructure, noting a need to allocate responsibility for business information resources to a dedicated and specialist IS function. Finally we discussed the need to ensure that BIS and associated resources remain available and that the content is kept confidential with integrity.

QUESTIONS

1 Identify and describe typical business information resources and discuss who should have responsibility for their management.

2 Evaluate the acquisition and systems development processes.

3 Discuss why it is important for organizations to protect their information resources. In your answer, you should comment on a selection of methods used to secure such resources.

USEFUL WEBSITES

The Official PRINCE2 (PRojects IN Controlled Environments)
Website **www.prince-officialsite.com**

REFERENCES

Cetindamar, D., Phaal, R. and Probert, D. (2010) *Technology Management – Activities and Tools*, Palgrave Macmillan.

Chaffey, D. and White, G. (2011) *Business Information Management*, 2nd edn, Financial Times Press.

Kelly, P. (2005) *Information Systems Risk*, Witherbys.

Laudon, K.C. and Laudon, J.P. (2014) *Management Information Systems, Global Edition*, 13th edn, Pearson.

Pearlson, K.E. and Saunders, C.S. (2013) *Strategic Management of Information Systems, International Student Version*, 5th edn, Wiley.

Valacich, J. and Schneider, C. (2014) *Information Systems Today, International Edition*, 6th edn, Pearson.

SKILL SHEET 14 | Information Resource Management

This skills sheet provides practical advice on the implementation of IS and management of information resources. In particular we explain how to create a feasibility study.

A feasibility study for a new IS may be written by the novice (non-IT manager) or the systems analyst. Whether reading, writing or presenting the feasibility study, as a manager, you will need to have some understanding of the structure and purpose of this document. There are many ways to write such a document and we highlight the more common content below. More detail may be required, in certain sections, if a bespoke system is to be acquired rather than one from off-the-shelf. The detail and writing style may also be influenced by the intended audience who may be internal managers (users) and decision-makers or external consultants and software developers.

1. Writing the Feasibility Study

A feasibility study is a preliminary study undertaken to determine and document a project's viability. It is a formalized, written approach to evaluating an idea and can help identify: (1) if the idea is viable or not, (2) useful facts and figures to aid decision-making and (3) alternative approaches and solutions to an identified business problem. Below we suggest one alternative structure for the study (see Figure 1). Each section is then described.

FIGURE 1

Title page
Executive Summary
Revision/Document History sheet
Contents page
Acronyms and Abbreviations
Introduction
A.   Company background
B.   Problem definition/Needs analysis
C.   High-level (Outline design of) system requirements
D.   Business models, information and data flows, etc.
E.   Proposed system
F.   Alternative systems
G.   TELOS
Conclusion/Recommendation(s)
Appendices

Executive Summary

The executive summary is the most important part of a business document. It is the first (and sometimes the only) part people will read. It is normally written last as it is simply a brief summary of the (whole) document, not an introduction. Its purpose is to inform managers, with little time to read the whole document, providing an overview that will indicate how much to read and what actions will probably be needed. Paragraphs should be short and concise. Executive summaries should make sense, even when the original report has not been read. Make sure the problem is defined in clear, understandable terms. The solution must be presented so that it tackles the problem effectively. In some cases it may be helpful to add a Summary sheet of the important findings and recommendations. This may include the purpose, description of the project; technical features; schedules of net benefits and capital requirements; benefit-cost ratios and NPV/IRR; project benefits and costs; proposed financial plan and projected cash flows and recommendations for implementation.

Revision/Document History Sheet

It is likely the document will be amended on more than one occasion as feedback is received from different readers. Document history and version control is used to record detail of minor and major amendments (reviews) to documentation. It allows anyone accessing the document to know if it is the most current version; when it was last amended; what was changed from the previous version; and who approved the document including any amendments made to it. A formal change process should be used to identify, control, track and show changes: e.g.

Version/Date	Title	Brief Description/ Comments	Circulation	Authorization (Date Approved/ Approved by)
Draft 0.1				
Version 1				

The Introduction

State the purpose, aims and rationale of the study. Include a scope statement. The scope statement helps to manage stakeholder expectations. The scope of the project outlines the objectives of the project and the goals that need to be met to achieve a satisfactory result. Clarify the limitations or parameters of the project and identify clearly any aspects that are not to be included. In specifying what will and will not be included, the project scope must make clear to the stakeholders, senior management and team members involved, what will be delivered. After introducing the problem and developing background material, you should explain your approach.

A. Company Background

A brief description of the business to assess more possible factors which could affect the study; it may be necessary to include the mission statement and company goals if the proposed system is to influence their attainment. In some cases the organization structure, processes and SWOT analysis may also provide relevant context for the reader.

B. Problem Definition/Needs Analysis

A problem is a perceived gap between the existing state (the system now) and a desired state.
It is important to be clear about the problems to be solved through the implementation of a new system. A succinct statement of the core problem should be provided, followed by an outline of the business problems to be solved. Consider using cause and effect analysis, Pareto analysis and other problem-solving frameworks. Consider using the PIECES Framework – a checklist for identifying problems with an existing IS:

Performance

INFORMATION (AND DATA): Lack of necessary information; Information overload; accuracy; Information that is not timely to its subsequent use; Data not captured/in time to be useful; Data are not accurately captured – contain errors; Data are captured redundantly – same data are captured more than once; Data are stored redundantly in multiple files and/or databases; Stored data are not accurate; Data are not secure; Data are not well organized; Data are not accessible etc.

ECONOMICS: Costs; Costs are too high; Profits.
CONTROL (AND SECURITY): Too little security or control; Redundantly stored data are inconsistent in different files or databases; Data privacy regulations or guidelines are being (or can be) violated; Processing errors are occurring (either by people, hardware or software); Decision-making errors are occurring; Controls inconvenience customers or employees; Excessive controls cause processing delays.
EFFICIENCY: Wasted time; Data are redundantly input, copied or processed; Information is redundantly generated; Effort required for tasks is excessive.
SERVICE: The system produces inaccurate/inconsistent /unreliable results; Not easy to learn, use; Inflexible; Incompatible with other systems.
Summarize the analysis: Is there a need to improve: (1) the performance of the system, (2) information (and data), (3) economics, (4) control, (5) efficiency of people and processes or (6) service to customers, suppliers, colleagues, partners, etc.

C. High-Level (Outline Design Of) System Requirements

In this section outline what the (hypothetical) system is required to do; it is a 'wish' list. In most cases the services of a systems analyst from the IS department may be enlisted to help write the system (software) requirements specification. This part of the study will normally address, at a high (user) level,[1] the following: functionality – what the software is supposed to do; external interfaces – how does the software interact with people and other systems; performance – what is the speed, availability, response time, etc. of various system functions; attributes – what are the security considerations etc. Finally, are there any design constraints to be imposed?

Requirements are elicited from the business through consultation. This involves interviewing managers and key staff, observations and the study of existing systems and their documentation. In some cases it may be deemed appropriate to use questionnaires which can be sent to system users. Consideration may also be given to the use of workshops and brainstorming sessions or prototyping. Requirements analysis is the process of studying user needs to arrive at a definition of system or software requirements. *Functional requirements* (FRs) describe the functionality desired

---

[1] A high-level description is one that is more abstracted, describes overall goals and systemic features, and is more concerned with the system as a whole. In many ways it may be viewed as a preliminary design, an overview.

of a problem solution; they describe fully what the software will do. A non-functional requirement is a requirement that specifies criteria that can be used to judge the operation of a system. Broadly, functional requirements define what a system is supposed to do and non-functional requirements (NFRs) define how a system is supposed to be. Functional requirements are usually in the form of 'system shall do <requirement>'. In contrast, non-functional requirements are in the form of 'system shall be <requirement>', an overall property of the system as a whole or of a particular aspect and not a specific function. Non-functional requirements are often called qualities of a system. A requirement is often assumed to be a property that is expected to be true of the system: The system shall …. It is traditional to use the verb shall for property requirements. Requirements will often be structured in a hierarchical relationship. Requirements are often communicated in table form – an example is presented below:

Requirement Reference	Title	Requirement & (Source of Requirement)	Rank (E – Essential/ D – Desirable)	Comment
FRs				
1.1				
NFRs				
2.1				

The PIECES framework can be applied to defining requirements. For example, non-functional requirements can be classified by focusing on the same categories: Performance, Information, Economics, Security, Efficiency and Service. The PIECES framework can also be used as a checklist for ensuring that functional requirements are covered. Typically non-functional requirements fall into areas such as: Accessibility, Capacity, Compliance, Documentation, Disaster recovery, Efficiency, Effectiveness, Fault tolerance, Interoperability, Maintainability, Privacy, Portability, Quality, Reliability, Resilience, Response time, Robustness, Scalability, Security, Stability, Supportability and Testability.

D. Business Models, Information and Data Flows, Etc.

Include any diagrams/models used to analyze the organization.

E. Proposed System

In this section provide a description of any Proposed System, functions, etc. Include a general statement of the system; give a brief description of what the proposed system will do, highlighting where it meets the specified business requirements of the organization.

F. Alternative Systems

In this section provide a description of each Alternative System. In many cases, like considering job applicants, you will score and rank each alternative. A Feasibility Analysis Matrix is often used to compare alternatives when there are multiple selection criteria and none of the alternatives is superior across the board. An example is provided below:

Criteria e.g. FR/NFRs	Weighted importance	Alternative system 1	Alternative system 2	Alternative system 3
1.1 Shall support automated reordering using EOQ	1	100% / 1	50% / 0.5	75% / 0.75
Etc.				
Total Score				

A detailed scoring and comparison of alternative systems is likely to use functional and non-functional requirements as criteria. Each alternative system will then be scored as to the extent to which it fulfils the criteria. Alternatively, a high-level matrix may be utilized and the TELOS factors (see next) used as criteria.

G. TELOS

The proposed (and often the alternative) system(s) are evaluated using the TELOS framework. This is used to consider whether solutions (systems) are technically, economically, legally and organizationally/operationally feasible and whether they can be delivered in the required timescales (scheduling feasibility). Each is discussed in more detail below.

Technical Feasibility: Assessing technical feasibility is to evaluate whether the new system will perform adequately and whether an organization has ability to construct a proposed system or not. The technical assessment helps answer the questions such as whether the technology needed for the system exists, how difficult it will be to build, and whether the firm has enough experience using that technology. If there is insufficient expertise in-house it may be necessary to look outside the organization.

Economic Feasibility (Cost/Benefit Analysis (CBA)):
To assess economic feasibility, management has to analyze costs and benefits associated with the proposed project. In most cases precise costs and benefits may not be known but will need to be estimated. First think of the tangible costs that are easy to determine and estimate, such as hardware and software cost, or labour cost. However, in addition to these tangible costs, there are also some intangible costs, such as improved service or decision-making, or operational inefficiency. One methodology for determining the costs of implementing and maintaining IT is Total Cost of Ownership (TCO). On the other hand, IT/IS projects can provide many benefits, both tangible and intangible, to an organization. The tangible benefit, such as cost saving or increased revenue, would be easier to estimate whilst intangible benefits are harder to quantify. There are several economic evaluation methods available to assess an investment. The most widely used method is the NPV – refer back to previous skills sheet. Ensure the total estimated cost of the project, projected cash flow and profitability are made clear. It is often desirable to present key information in a structured table of costs and benefits.

Legal and Contractual Feasibility:
Legal feasibility determines whether the proposed system conflicts with the legal requirement or not. Identify relevant laws and discuss conformance.

Operational Feasibility:
It is important to understand how the new systems will fit into the current day-to-day operations of the organization. It may be appropriate to discuss strategic, cultural, structural and style 'fit'.

Schedule Feasibility:
To assess the duration of the project – whether it will take too long to complete before it is useful. System analysts have to estimate how long the system will take to develop, and whether all potential time frames and the completion date schedules can be met. Also, one needs to determine whether the deadlines are mandatory or desirable.

At the end of a feasibility study a **conclusion** is taken whether to carry on with the project or not. The conclusion will often include recommendations such as whether to proceed, which system/approach to proceed with or appropriate next steps.

2. Creating System Models

The systems analyst often uses models in order to represent aspects of the system, just as the architect might draw plans of buildings. Models may be used in any of sections A-F of Figure 1. Models are simplified abstractions often expressed with a precise graphical or textual notation; with a specific language of symbols. In this skills sheet we will focus on simple models such as the context diagram, information flow diagram (IFD), decision flow diagram and entity relationship diagram (ERD). However, the reader may uncover more sophisticated models and modelling languages. For example, the Unified Modelling Language (UML) is a language used to specify, visualize and document the artefacts of an object-oriented system.

Context Diagram (or a System Context Diagram (SCD)):
The context diagram is a simplified diagram, which is useful for specifying the boundaries and scope of the system. This diagram is a high level view of a system. The context diagram depicts an entire system as a single process with its major inputs and outputs. In particular, the context diagram can: provide overview of existing system; allow documentation and actions to be modelled; facilitate production of information flow diagrams and allow physical processes to be modelled quickly and easily. The context diagram can provide a useful system overview and facilitates the identification of stakeholders and their influence. It is used to show: (1) the system for which requirements are gathered, (2) the parts that need to interact with the system and (3) a brief note about the interaction between each part and the system. This can be seen in Figure 2. Create a context diagram by drawing a circle in the centre of the page. Label the circle with the name of your system. If it has no name then simply label the circle as 'System'. Then list each of the external entities around your system and draw a line between the entity and the system. Note what information is passed and who it is passing it (the system or the entity).

FIGURE 2 Example context diagram

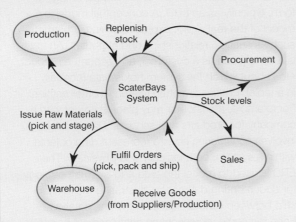

shown as rectangles and the flow of information with connecting lines and directional indicators (arrow heads). In some cases the connecting line may be annotated with detail of the data/information and media type that flows between the business functions. The IFD reveals stakeholders and the inputs/outputs they rely on or provide for operations and function. We can investigate how functions receive or share information within the BIS and the purpose to which it is put. The Information Flow Diagram (IFD) is one of the simplest tools used to document findings from the requirements determination process. After determining the requirements of a system, then use the IFD to document the results. The aim is to diagnose or map out which information is flowing where, between whom, when and how. To draw a diagram we need to discover who needs or uses what information and then draw links. An IFD usually uses 'blobs' or boxes to decompose the system and subsystems into elemental parts. Lines drawn between the blobs then indicate how the information travels from one system to another. The Blobs or Boxes represent sources and destinations of information. Arrows represent the flow of information.

Information Flow Diagrams (IFD): The IFD is a simple diagram showing how information is routed between different parts of an organization (and other stakeholders). It has an information focus rather than a process focus. IFDs enable the identification of entities that both send and receive data/information within a BIS. Functions such as HR and Finance are

FIGURE 3 IFD example

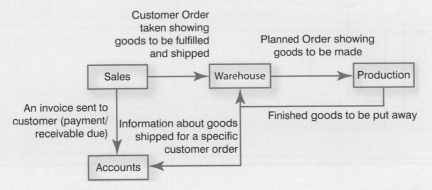

Decision Flow Diagram: Decision Flow Diagrams, also known as logic flow charts, are used to illustrate the flow of actions and decisions within a process. The diamond symbol (which shows a decision) has one point of entry – but may have two points of exit (yes or no). A process is depicted with a rectangle and arrows show the flow of information. All flow diagrams have a start/stop point normally represented by a thin rectangle with curved ends. Decisions and activities should link the start and end of the process/subprocess though several routes through the diagram will be possible.

FIGURE 4   Example decision flow diagram

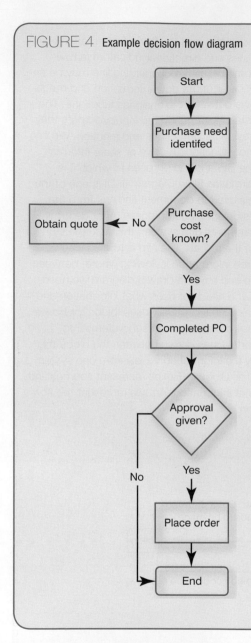

Entity Relationship Diagram (ERD): Data structures are normally represented in a conceptual or logical form, typically as an ERD. A conceptual model is a model of the real world, expressed using constructs such as entities, relationships and attributes. An entity is a thing (such as a customer, an account, a product, etc.) about which the system holds data (normally in a table). Entities are often related to other entities. For example, a customer may place an order with a company for products and services. Data modelling involves considering how to represent data objects within a system, both logically and physically. The ERD is used to model the data and is a methodology for documenting databases, illustrating the relationship between various entities within the database. Each rectangle represents an entity and will normally become a table in the database.

FIGURE 5 Example ERD

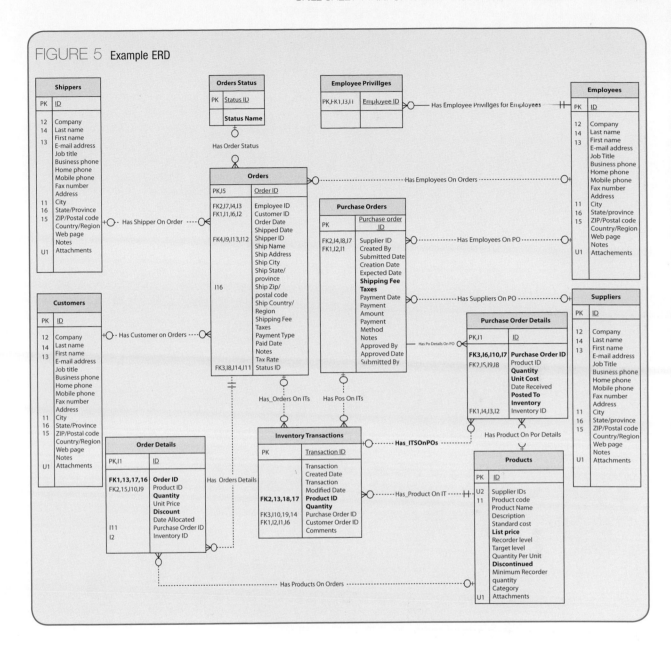

PART IV
GLOBAL MANAGEMENT

This final part of the book comprises two chapters. We consider the impact of globalization on leadership, management and operations and ask how managers can make themselves and their organizations more effective and efficient. In Part 3 we focused on functional management and will now contemplate aspects of leading the organization and managing such functions on a global level, i.e. global marketing, global operations, global research and development, global HRM (and cross-cultural management) and global financial management. Chapter 48 will consider aspects of leading globally. In Chapter 49 we start by revisiting aspects of cultural intelligence and managing diversity and then consider the various global managerial issues in business functions.

Section Sixteen
Global Management

CHAPTER 48
LEADING GLOBALLY

Key Concepts

- Global-local dilemma
- Global economy
- Globalization of markets
- Globalization of production
- Glocal
- Transnational corporations

Learning Outcomes Having read this chapter, you should be able to:

- discuss how global forces shape business environments
- identify universal attributes of the global business leader
- discuss cultural determinants of global leadership styles
- explain the global-local dilemma
- distinguish between global and multi-domestic strategies.

1. In the final part of this book we consider the impact of globalization on leadership, management and operations and ask how managers can make themselves and their organizations more effective and efficient. In Part 3 we focused on functional management and will now contemplate aspects of leading the organization and managing such functions on a global level, i.e. global marketing, global operations, global research and development, global HRM (and cross-cultural management) and global financial management. This chapter will consider aspects of leading globally and is organized into three sections. First we build on Chapter 12, taking a closer look at the global business environment. We will then build on Chapter 6 and consider leading in the global context and finally we build on Chapter 17, discussing strategies associated with global challenges and the internationalization process.

48.1 GLOBAL BUSINESS ENVIRONMENT (GBE)

2. In Chapter 12 (refer back to 12.3) we introduced the global business environment (GBE). We defined globalization (para. 28) and explored national culture in brief. Globalization, a process that gained momentum throughout the latter part of the twentieth century, now seems to touch and impact upon every person worldwide and every type of business activity in all sizes of organization (Kelly and Ashwin, 2013: p. 348). Its forces

may manifest as threats and opportunities. Threats in terms of increased competition, challenges in terms of constraints posed through legislation, codes and standards, and opportunities for growth and efficiency gains.

3.   Globalization is about the interconnectedness and interdependence between people, organizations and governments. It has been facilitated by technology, political and economic integration, international trade and the motivation of consumers, investors, politicians, workers, tourists and a range of people throughout the world. The forces behind globalization are many and varied; Globalization is a supranational concept whose forces influence the political, economic, social, technical, legal and ecological and environmental factors discussed already within this book. Goldin and Reinert (2012) define globalization as an increase in the impact of forces, which span national boundaries, on human activities (economic, social, cultural, political and technological – all of which can interact).

4.   Globalization is a multifaceted construct. The term global economy is used to describe an integrated world economy with unrestricted and free movement of goods, services and labour transnationally. The economies of most of the world's nations have become increasingly interconnected. International economic activity includes the worldwide integration of markets for goods, services, labour and capital. Thus the global economy can be considered as economic activity spanning many nations of the world, with little regard for national borders. Some consider the development of an increasingly integrated global economy, marked especially by free trade, free flow of capital and the utilization of cheaper foreign labour markets, as the definition of globalization, see for example the Merriam-Webster Dictionary.

5.   Companies may now not only import and export more easily but can also establish their operations overseas. Consequently, there has been a rapid growth in transnational corporations (TNCs – operate in more than one country at a time but differ from traditional MNCs in that they do not identify themselves with one national home) and MNCs. Many organizations now source, manufacture, market and conduct value-adding activities on an international scale. This poses new management challenges and necessitates the rise of the international manager or manager within an international organization who can acquire the requisite business knowledge and skills to enable the organization to perform in our ever-increasing GBE.

6.   A key issue for many organizations now concerns how they view the world: do they see it as a single and growing market or a collection of markets? This worldview will shape different strategies (to be discussed later in this chapter). Three decades ago, Theodore Levitt published 'The Globalization of Markets' in the *Harvard Business Review* (1983). Levitt proposed a new commercial reality as the emergence of global markets for standardized consumer products on a previously unimagined scale of magnitude. 'A powerful force drives the world toward a converging commonality, and that force is technology', Levitt (1983). Well-managed companies have moved from emphasis on customizing items to offering globally standardized products that are advanced, functional, reliable and low priced. They benefit from enormous economies of scale in production, distribution, marketing and management. He argued companies must learn to operate as if the world were one large market. However, as noted at the start of this paragraph, this is not the only worldview driving global strategies.

7.   The multinational and the global corporation are not the same thing. The multinational corporation operates in a number of countries (multi-domestic), and adjusts its products and practices in each – at high relative costs. The global corporation operates with resolute constancy – at low relative cost – as if the entire world (or major regions of it) were a single entity; it sells the same things in the same way everywhere. Levitt was discussing two different strategies, a matter we explore later in this chapter. Whilst there are many global companies, in support of Levitt's predictions, the notion that the 'multinational corporation' was drawing to a close has not proven to be true. The global corporation caters less well for local differences in taste.

8.   So what is meant by the term the globalization of markets? For many the globalization of markets means the expansion and access of businesses to reach the needs of customers worldwide. It may be described as the moving away from an economic system in which national markets are distinct entities, isolated by trade barriers and barriers of distance, time and culture, and towards a system in which national markets are merging into one global market (Kelly and Ashwin, 2013: p. 353).

GLOBALIZATION FORCES: SHAPING NATIONAL ENVIRONMENTS

9.   The multi-domestic organization must analyze each country and determine its 'local' differentiated approach as to how it will compete and operate; it will analyze the PESTLE factors in each country it operates in as it sees the world as a collection of markets. Similarly, managers of domestic firms must

understand how their local environment is changing as a result of such forces. Kelly and Ashwin (2013: p. 357) summarized the relationship between global forces and the national environment (see Figure 48.1). Whilst, in some cases, such changes may be viewed as challenges or even threats, globalization may bring opportunities and benefits to those firms seeking growth through overseas sales or efficiency gains through value chain fragmentation or gains through other aspects of the way they manage their supply chains. Kelly and Ashwin (2013) emphasize an interconnected/interdependent world. The extent to which the behaviour of one country depends upon others is a matter of interdependence and the state of being interconnected – connected reciprocally – is a worldview which sees a oneness in all things.

FIGURE 48.1 Globalization and the national (PESTLE) environment

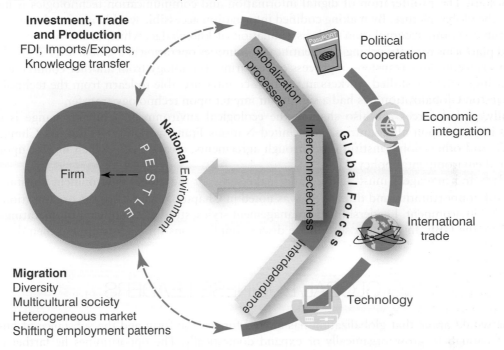

10. As depicted in Figure 48.1, global forces shape each of the nation's PESTLE factors. Global forces shape the political and legal environment. When nations join with others in a trade or political bloc, they give up some national sovereignty. The EU has built considerable political integration over a period of several decades. But it is far from a unified state and substantial sovereignty still remains with the EU's member governments. In a globalizing world, nations feel pressure to join trade and political pacts. Often, these international groupings erode national democracy.

11. Global forces are also shaping the economic environment. The combined effects on the level of economic activity of individual countries will in turn affect the global economy. More and more it has become important for government economists to consider international business cycles. The periodic and irregular expansions and contractions in world output can be measured by changes in real world GDP. Globalization is often associated with increased international trade and financial linkages and consequently the synchronization of international business cycles. International trade linkages generate both demand and supply-side overflows across countries, which can increase the degree of business cycle synchronization.

12. Global forces are shaping the social environment. Liberalization leads to increased migration and this can lead to changes in the social environment, impacting upon national culture, increasing diversity and introducing the concept of multiculturalism. Immigration impacts upon culture, making the society more heterogeneous and multicultural; immigrants bring their values, traditions and cultural practices which may then alter the cultural characteristics of the host country. Migration is the main driver of population growth in most of the EU Member States and plays a significant role in the population dynamics of European societies; in recent years, the increase in the population of the EU Member States has mainly been due to high net migration rates. Globalization, amongst other factors, is changing the nature of the

workplace and as a result, managers must ask constantly how they can make best (and fairest) use of HR to meet organizational goals. Today's workforce is older, more racially diverse, more female and more varied. Within such environments the management aim remains to maximize benefits and minimize costs and to enable all workers to achieve their full potential.

13.   Global forces shape the technological environment. Ultimately, much of research, science and technology manifests as goods, supplied through business to solve everyday living problems, and provide entertainment. **Technological diffusion** refers to the spreading of new technologies within and between economies. Communication technologies and behaviours impact upon diffusion. For example, the UNESCO science report (2010) comments upon the number of Internet users – a variable used to gauge whether easier access to information and knowledge has provided opportunities for a more rapid diffusion of science and technology. The proliferation of digital information and communication technologies is increasingly modifying the global picture. By making codified information accessible worldwide, it is having a dramatic effect on the creation, accumulation and dissemination of knowledge, whilst at the same time providing specialized platforms for networking by scientific communities operating at a global level. A similar concept to diffusion is technology transfer – a process of acquiring technology from another country, especially in manufacturing; whereby skilled workers in the host country are able to learn from the technology of the foreign investor. Globalization has had a significant impact upon technology transfer.

14.   Finally, global forces are also shaping the ecological environment. Climate change is caused by many and impacts upon all countries. The United Nations Framework Convention on Climate Change (UNFCCC) and other global institutions, through agreements, create forces which impact upon regional and national environmental policy.

15.   Leaders and managers must analyze and make sense of the global environment constantly if they are to identify opportunities and threats. As was noted in Chapter 9, aspects of the organization are determined by the environment. Leadership and management styles, strategies and ways of operating will all be influenced by the GBE. In the next section we discuss implications for leadership and then discuss global strategy further.

48.2 DEVELOPING GLOBAL BUSINESS LEADERS

16.   Some would argue that globalization has altered forever the form and the substance of business. No longer is it enough to grow organically or expand domestically. The opportunities lie farther afield, and competitiveness on an international scale requires new skills and a more finely tuned worldview. From discussions so far we might conclude that geographic and cultural boundaries have become blurred and that our notion of leadership needs to be reconsidered in the context of globalization. Pankaj Ghemawat, Professor of Strategic Management, has focused for nearly two decades on studying globalization and thinking through its implications for business; he believes that companies must cultivate leaders for global markets.

17.   In the era of globalization, companies must develop leaders who can operate throughout the world, lead global teams, and create strategies that are effective both globally and locally. There are a number of views as to what knowledge and skills such a leader should acquire and how they should acquire them (experience or training and education). Some argue the new leader must have functional knowledge and analytical skills, yet be adept at leading teams. They must have a global mindset (refer back to Chapter 43.7) that combines an openness to and awareness of diversity with an ability to see common patterns across countries and markets.

18.   Adler and Bartholomew (1992) argued that global leaders need to develop cross-cultural competencies: they must understand business environments worldwide; and sociocultural differences; beyond understanding they must be able to work and communicate simultaneously with people from many cultures and not only should they behave they must also think in a culturally sensitive way – they should not be ethnocentric but learn to relate to people from other cultures from a position of equality rather than cultural superiority. Other scholars have added to this list suggesting that global leaders need skill in creating and articulating transcultural visions.

19.   Globalization opens many opportunities for business, but it also creates major challenges. An important challenge is the understanding and appreciating of cultural values, practices and subtleties in different parts of the world. We might ask to what extent is leadership culturally contingent? Do leaders need to act differently when leading in different parts of the world? The Global Leadership and Organizational

Behaviour Effectiveness research program (GLOBE), has demonstrated that what is expected of leaders, what leaders may and may not do, and the status and influence bestowed on leaders, vary considerably as a result of the cultural forces in the countries or regions in which the leaders function.

20.   The meta-goal of the GLOBE research programme is to develop an empirically based theory to describe, understand and predict the impact of cultural variables on leadership and organizational processes and the effectiveness of these processes. A central question in this part of the research concerns the extent to which specific leadership *attributes* and *behaviours* are universally endorsed as contributing to effective leadership and the extent to which the endorsement of leader attributes and behaviours is culturally contingent (House *et al.*, 1999).

21.   House and his colleagues identified over 20 specific leader attributes and behaviours that are universally viewed as contributing to leadership effectiveness. For them, organizational leadership is the ability of an individual to influence, motivate and enable others to contribute towards the effectiveness and success of the organizations of which they are members.

22.   In Chapter 6 (see para. 5) we introduced perspectives on leadership and management from Gary Yukl. He rightly identifies a major issue concerning the extent to which leadership theories developed and tested in one culture can be generalized to different cultures (Yukl, 2010: p. 454). He notes that globalization and changing demographic patterns are making it more important for leaders to understand how to influence people with different values, beliefs and expectations. Leaders are increasingly confronted with the need to influence people from other cultures and successful influence requires a good understanding of these cultures. He also believes that some aspects of a leadership theory may be relevant to all cultures but other aspects may only be applied to a particular type of culture.

23.   Commenting on the GLOBE project and cultural value dimensions (drawn from the work of Hofstede) and leadership, Yukl (2010: p. 460) suggests that in high power distance countries an autocratic style may be favoured; in low power distance cultures (refer back to Chapter 12, para. 35) such as Western Europe, a participative leadership style is viewed as a more favourable approach, and in developing countries with a high power-distance-culture, people may prefer a paternalistic style that combines autocratic decisions with supportive behaviour. He also notes that when there is high uncertainty avoidance, valued qualities include being reliable, orderly and cautious, rather than flexible, innovative and risk-taking. In the case of individualistic cultures the emphasis on individual rights and autonomy makes it more difficult to create a strong culture of shared values. Because people are more motivated to satisfy their self-interests and personal goals in an individualistic culture, it is more difficult for leaders to inspire strong commitment to team or organizational objectives.

24.   In a similar way, Northouse (2010: p. 349) uses the GLOBE findings to summarize relevant profiles for leading in different parts of the world. In Eastern European countries, an ideal example of a leader would be an independent self-centred and autocratic or autonomous person, able to inspire teams whilst being attentive to human needs. This contrasts with the Nordic Europe leadership profile where an ideal leader is highly visionary and participative, diplomatic and inspiring. The leadership profile of the Confucian Asian countries describes a leader who is self-protective, team and humane oriented (supportive, considerate, compassionate and generous); this type of leader does not invite others to be involved in goal-setting or decision-making. Of course these are broad generalizations that may be used with other contextual information to help managers lead when working in such cultures.

25.   In summary we have suggested that globalization presents challenges for how we lead and whilst there may be universal leader attributes (common to many cultures) there are also culture specific ways to lead in certain countries. Wherever the location practised, managers as leaders require foresight and must be trustworthy, just, dynamic, motivational, decisive, communicative, honest, encouraging, and dependable whilst being good team builders, negotiators and win–win problem-solvers. They must be culturally sensitive and not ethnocentric. A leader shapes organizational purpose, direction and goals. It is then important to determine how purpose, direction and goals are attained. This leads us to consider global strategies.

48.3 DEVELOPING GLOBAL STRATEGIES

26.   Johnson, Whittington and Scholes (2011: p. 265) note that operating in different geographical markets is a challenge for all kinds of organizations nowadays. When discussing international strategy they focus

on drivers for internationalization (market demand, cost advantages-scale economies, the need to respond to competitor moves); geographical advantages (location); market selection (global customers, similar customer needs, etc.) and mode of entry. They then recognize the organization must face difficult questions about what kinds of strategies to pursue in the markets. Here the key problem is the so-called global-local dilemma. This relates to the extent to which products and services may be standardized across national boundaries or need to be adapted to meet the requirements of specific national markets (2011: p. 274).

27.   According to Kelly (2009) there are a number of fundamental questions every international company must answer such as: What do we do? Why are we here? What kind of company are we? What kind of company do we want to be? What is our current strategy? What is happening in the GBE? What are our goals? In which markets and in which geographic areas will we compete? What products and services will we offer and to whom? What technologies will we employ? What capabilities and capacities will we require? What will we make by ourselves and what will we buy (outsource) from others? Finally, how will we compete? The answers to such questions may be provided through strategic problem-solving activities. Strategy is concerned with how the international organization will achieve its aims and goals. International strategy is concerned with choices about where the organization offers its products and services and where it locates value-adding activities (2009: p. 89).

28.   Strategies are driven by opportunities and threats. Earlier we outlined how business environments (the PESTLE factors) were shaped by global forces. Globalization can bring increased competition and costly constraints through legislation, codes or standards. On the other hand, firms can benefit by penetrating the global marketplace to grow sales and reduce costs. Business benefits are clustered around production and the supply chain, investment, sales growth and the pursuit of advantage.

29.   Globalization of production refers to the sourcing of goods and services from locations around the globe to take advantage of national differences in the cost and quality of factors of production like land, labour and capital. Globalization through increased competition forces companies to locate particular operations (activities and resources) in those places where they can be performed most efficiently. Organizations do this by relocating production facilities to other countries or by outsourcing certain activities to companies in other countries. However, globalization (and the Internet) do not merely benefit the larger organization, they have created unprecedented opportunities for small- and medium-sized businesses.

30.   Whereas globalization is a process impacting upon the firm, internationalization (introduced in Chapter 43) refers to the firm's process of entering foreign markets and exploiting the benefits liberalization brings. Geographical scope describes the multinationality of the organization. Global strategies change the locations from where organizations may purchase inputs, sell outputs to, locate activities performed in the value chain and find intellectual capital.

31.   Internationalization is a significant force shaping the competitive environment of business. Internationalization occurs through trade and direct investment and has implications for strategy formulation or formation either in terms of opportunity to expand markets or through the threats posed by overseas competitors. International strategy is concerned with choices about where the organization offers its products and services and where it locates value adding activities. Organizations pursue international strategies for a number of reasons: homogenization of customer demand (globalization) leading to economies of scale, access to different markets for economies of scope and growth and to serve the needs of global customers. By internationalizing, the organization is able to broaden the size of its market.

32.   International strategy considers not only where to locate facilities and activities but also how to enter different markets, i.e. the appropriate entry mode (see Chapter 43). There are a number of benefits associated with such strategies. Such a strategy should enable efficiency advantages. First there is opportunity to produce more, which may enable economies of scale through both experience and the ability to spread fixed costs over a greater number of units. Second there will be scale benefits in the ability to replicate knowledge and technology within the organization. Once created, knowledge can be reused at close-to-zero cost if it can be transferred. As has already been mentioned, efficiencies may also be gained from locating different activities in different places. Furthermore, organizations may make use of positive cash flows in one region to cross-subsidize and invest in another region.

33.   However, as discussed earlier in the chapter, organizations have fundamentally different views of world markets and these are reflected in strategy. Two broad generic international strategies can be distinguished: (1) the global strategy – assumes a single market and offers a standard product(s) to meet customer

needs wherever customers are located. This is essentially a cost leadership strategy, exploiting economies of scale and other cost efficiencies and (2) the multi-domestic strategy – assumes variance in customer needs according to their location and therefore pursues a differentiation strategy, adapting products and services to meet unique local requirements. The extent to which services may be standardized across national boundaries or need to be adapted to meet specific local requirements is often referred to as the global-local dilemma.

34. In practice, organizations rarely pursue a pure and a single generic strategy and seek out a position between the two. Most large multinational and transnational organizations face the need to tailor their product or service to some extent. Whilst there are many benefits to an international strategy such as economies of scale and scope, access to new markets for growth and the exploitation of location advantages, the organization becomes much more complex, requiring more money and time to be spent on coordination, collaboration, communication, formalization and control. Consequently not all organizations benefit from internationalization in the same way and some may not benefit at all.

35. As was noted, a global strategy is one that views the world as a single market. This means that customers are assumed to be similar across country boundaries and that there is therefore little or no need for differentiation at the country level; consequently, more decisions are likely to be made at headquarters. However, laws and government regulations, variance in disposable income, national culture and country infrastructure may impact upon products and services and the means by which they are delivered to customers.

36. Global strategies are very much about integration whilst other international business strategies may focus on differentiation. In the case of some products and services there are national differences in customer preferences and as a consequence the organization must consider customer needs in different locations. Products and services must then be designed or adapted to meet those needs. However, in some cases common basic designs and common components can reduce the cost of national differentiation. Flexible manufacturing systems, computer-aided design and manufacture with lean production processes help create customized products at a lower cost.

37. Reconciling conflicting forces for global efficiency and national differentiation represents one of the greatest strategic challenges facing the international or multinational corporation. Many organizations opt for a hybrid approach – one of global localization, i.e. 'glocal'. In such cases the organization will seek to standardize aspects of the product or service and primary activities where scale economies are substantial and will differentiate where national preferences are strongest. Whether or not the international organization pursues a global or a local strategy will impact upon the organizational structure and management systems (the internal environment of the firm). Business units such as IT, Research and Development and Procurement can be more centralized or at least organized at a global level since it is likely that scale economies can be attained through sharing such resources across the whole organization. The downstream and primary activities of Marketing and Customer Service and the secondary activities associated with Human Resource Management are more likely to reflect local differences. Whilst manufacturing lies somewhere inbetween, it has strong globalization potential, being located near raw materials, low-cost or highly skilled labour.

38. Internationalization, globalization and increasing competition has amplified the importance of supply chain management (SCM) to managers working within international organizations. Major SCM activities include: running overseas plants or coordinating international activities, selection of transformation processes; forecasting; capacity planning; inventory management; planning and control, purchasing and logistics. From a practical standpoint, one of the attractions of developing international operations is the low labour cost available in many of the less developed nations. However, the low labour cost is not enough to offset the low labour productivity in some of these nations. Extremely low wages do not offset the differences in labour productivity in some of the reforming economies. This would suggest that to be an effective international operations manager, a sophisticated understanding of international differences is essential. The objectives of SCM include (1) maximize efficiency and effectiveness of the total supply chain for all players and (2) maximize the opportunity for customer purchase by ensuring adequate stock levels at all stages of the process. Internet and associated technologies are vital to SCM since managing relationships with customers, suppliers and intermediaries is based on the flow of information and the transactions between these parties. Organizations seek to enhance the supply chain in order to provide a

superior value proposition (quality, service, price and fulfilment times), which they do by emphasizing cost reduction, increased efficiency and consequently increased profitability. Not only can we conceive of the supply chain as an opportunity to increase profits, it may also be viewed as a sequence of events intended to satisfy customers. Typically, it will involve procurement, manufacture and distribution, together with associated transport, storage and IT.

39.   Whatever the strategy pursued by the organization it will need to pay attention to sources of competitive advantage. These have been discussed throughout the book and throughout this chapter we have recognized how various cost advantages may benefit the global organization. Whether pursuing a global or multi-domestic strategy, international organizations must remain responsive. This is accomplished through integration, coordination and control. In Chapter 49 we focus on managing and operating globally and discuss various methods that can be used to make the organization more responsive.

CONCLUSION

40.   With the rapid pace of globalization and economic integration, cross-cultural leadership has become an important topic for research and focus for management attention. Whereas culture may determine certain specific aspects of leadership, some leadership attributes are deemed to be universal and important for effective leadership wherever a manager is working. For example, being a visionary, decisive, dynamic, dependable, honest and trustworthy and a team integrator seem to be ideal leader attributes around the globe. Leaders are visionaries that drive organizational purpose and goals. These are attained through strategies which have been influenced by globalization. Companies may be global, local or glocal depending on how they see the world and their products and services.

QUESTIONS

1   Explain how forces of globalization impact upon domestic markets.

2   Select three admired business leaders with whom you are familiar and evaluate the attributes which make them good global business leaders.

3   Select two multinational companies with which you are familiar and suggest, with reasons, whether they are likely to pursue a global, glocal or multi-domestic strategy.

REFERENCES

Adler, N.J. and Bartholomew, S. (1992) 'Managing globally competent people', *Academy of Management Executive*, 6(3): 52–65.

Goldin, I. and Reinert, K. (2012) *Globalization for Development – Meeting New Challenges*, Oxford University Press.

House, R., Hanges, P., Ruiz-Quintanilla, S.A. and Dorfman, P. (1999) 'Cultural influences on leadership and organizations: Project GLOBE', *Advances in Global Leadership*, 1: 171–233.

Johnson, G., Whittington, R. and Scholes, K. (2011) *Exploring Strategy: Text and Cases*, 9th edn, Prentice Hall.

Kelly, P. and Ashwin, A. (2013) *The Business Environment*, Cengage.

Kelly, P. (2009) *International Business and Management*, Cengage Learning EMEA.

Levitt, T. (1983) 'The globalization of markets', *Harvard Business Review*, 61(3): 92–102.

Northouse, P.G. (2010) *Leadership, Theory and Practice*, 5th edn, Sage Publications.

UNESCO (2010) *UNESCO Science Report 2010*, Paris: United Nations Educational, Scientific and Cultural Organization.

Yukl, G. (2010) *Leadership in Organizations: Global Edition*, 7th edn, Pearson Higher Education.

CHAPTER 49
MANAGING GLOBALLY

Key Concepts

- Country attractiveness
- Emotional intelligence
- Ethno relative
- Foreign exchange risk
- Political intelligence
- Social intelligence

Learning Outcomes   Having read this chapter, you should be able to:

- describe, using the 'SPICE' acronym, the types of managerial intelligence required to operate globally
- describe, using the 'SPACE' acronym, the dimensions of social intelligence (SI)
- discuss the specific challenges faced by the global marketing manager
- explain why transnational corporations (TNCs) may globalize innovation practice
- discuss the global financial management issues of foreign exchange risk and transaction exposure
- discuss how a firm's international strategy may impact upon its global IT needs.

1.   We discussed the global mindset and globally minded managers in Chapter 43. In this chapter we start by revisiting aspects of cultural intelligence and managing diversity and then consider the various global managerial issues in business functions. As we dedicated Chapter 43 to IHRM we will not discuss global HRM further in this chapter. Managing globally is about leading, planning, organizing, motivating and controlling in a more complex setting (Figure 49.1). There are more factors to consider when managing in the international company. This requires not only a good understanding of business theory and challenges associated with operating globally, but also requires cultural, social, political and emotional intelligence if managers are to make things happen wherever in the world they are working.

FIGURE 49.1 **Managing globally**

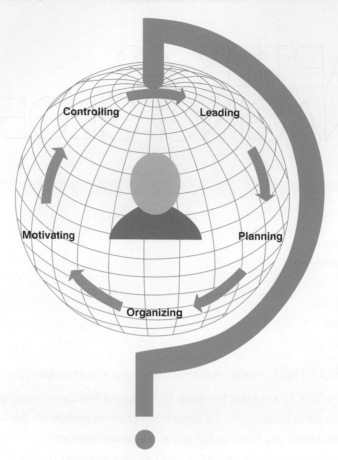

49.1 CULTURAL INTELLIGENCE REVISITED

2.   In Chapter 15 we discussed diversity and in para. 6 noted how globalization was altering the nature of the workplace. Aside from the need to avoid ethnocentric thinking, there is a need to recognize and avoid prejudice. Successful managers tend to be **ethno relative**, they are comfortable with many standards and customs and have an ability to adapt behaviour and judgements to a variety of interpersonal settings; they learn to cope with different regional, national, corporate and professional cultures.

3.   **Prejudice** is an attitude, typically associated with negative feelings, that involves a pre-judgement about the members of a group. Throughout life we become conditioned to thinking in ways that generalize and stereotype others. Such thinking may result in behaviours categorized as prejudiced, privileged or oppressive. Such thoughts and the behavioural consequences have significant implications for managing globally and managing a diverse workforce. Although usually rooted in some truth, stereotypes often do more harm than good. Stereotypes arise when we act as if all members of a culture or group share the same characteristics. There are many indicators of group membership such as race, age, gender that may be used by the manager. In some cases the assumed characteristics are respected (positive stereotype) and in other cases may be disrespected (negative stereotype).

4.   During our working lives repeatedly we encounter and form perceptions about other people. We typically make judgements about the kind of person they are and often arrive at such judgements using limited information. Judgements are made to guide our behaviour in relation to the people concerned. It has been shown that first impressions of another person are important. We often rely on a single striking characteristic such as their nationality, or gender, etc. to make judgements about them (the halo effect – as

was discussed in Chapter 40 (selection)). If this judgement is favourable we allocate a halo, if not, horns. The halo effect is a perceptual error and may cause us to filter out later information which is not consistent with our earlier judgement. We tend to give more favourable judgement to people who have characteristics in common with us. This can create problems when operating globally as not everyone will be like us. The halo effect can be used to describe problems in many business situations.

5. Bias in person perception may also take place during perceptual organization when we group together people who seem to us to share similar characteristics – stereotyping. Stereotypes are over-generalizations which enable us to shortcut the evaluation process and make predictions about an individual's behaviour. Stereotypes are formed when we ascribe generalizations to people based on their group identities and the tendencies of the whole group rather than seeing a person as an individual. In this case the grouping may be national, professional, gender or other.

6. Stereotyping can help explain why some people may be treated differently (discriminatory behaviour) from others. In some cases certain groups may be discriminated against. Prejudice and other discriminatory behaviours have consequences in the organization. If people feel that they are not being treated fairly their motivation and performance is likely to be affected; people may leave the organization or be absent from work. This will impact upon cost, productivity and performance. Ultimately it will impact upon a variety of talent management dimensions.

7. When managing globally, to be successful in dealing with people from other cultures, aside from being fair and treating people equally, global managers or managers of the diverse workforce need knowledge about cultural differences and similarities amongst countries. They also need to understand the implications of the differences and the skills required to act and decide appropriately and in a culturally sensitive way. Cultural intelligence is the ability to make sense of unfamiliar contexts and then blend in. While it shares many of the properties of emotional intelligence (the ability to perceive, to integrate, to understand and manage one's own and other people's feelings reflectively), a high cultural intelligence quotient (CQ) goes one step further by equipping a person to distinguish behaviours produced by the culture in question from behaviours that are peculiar to particular individuals and those found in all human beings. A *quotient* simply reflects the degree to which a specific quality or characteristic (cultural intelligence in this case) exists.

8. One critical element that cultural intelligence and emotional intelligence share is a propensity to suspend judgement – *to think before acting*. Cultural intelligence resides in the body (managers will not win over their foreign hosts or colleagues simply by showing they understand their culture; their actions and demeanour must prove that they have already to some extent entered their world) in the heart (self-belief and confidence), as well as the head. Earley and Mosakowski (2004) identify six cultural intelligence profiles:

The 'provincial' is effective when working with people of similar background but runs into trouble when venturing farther afield.

The 'analyst' deciphers methodically a foreign culture's rules and expectations by resorting to a variety of elaborate learning strategies.

The 'natural' relies entirely on intuition rather than on a systematic learning style.

The 'ambassador', like many political appointees, may not know much about the culture just entered, but will communicate convincingly at belonging there.

The 'mimic' has a high degree of control over actions and behaviour, if not a great deal of insight into the significance of the cultural cues picked up.

The 'chameleon' possesses high levels of all three CQ components and is a very uncommon managerial type.

9. Cultural intelligence is just one of many types of intelligence required by the global manager. Palmer *et al.* (2001) explore the relationship between emotional intelligence (EI) and effective leadership and management (L&M). They note that interpersonal skills have become more integral to effective L&M. L&M roles should motivate and inspire others, foster positive attitudes at work and create a sense of contribution and importance with and amongst employees. In their study they found that leaders, who considered themselves

to motivate and inspire subordinates to work towards common goals, reported that they monitored and managed emotions both within themselves and others.

10.　Sensing when a subordinate needs a more or less challenging task depends on the ability to monitor emotions, i.e. monitoring when a subordinate is bored or frustrated with a given task. Similarly, sensing when a subordinate requires feedback may first involve monitoring and detecting the existence of emotions that suggest this need, but in this case, also managing their emotions or feelings: for example, monitoring and detecting feelings from subordinates such as not being appreciated for one's work, and managing their emotions, perhaps by providing positive feedback to elevate feelings of not being appreciated. Thus EI or EQ is of significant importance to the practising manager operating at home or globally.

11.　Aside from having EQ, CQ and cognitive intelligence (IQ), effective managers also possess PQ (political quotient), a relatively new business acronym. PQ involves acknowledgement of power at the workplace. PQ is the capacity to interact strategically in a world where government, business and wider society share power to shape the future in a global economy (Reffo and Wark, 2014) and is the art of *making things happen* through people you do not control. When managing globally this can be about knowing where the power lies in subsidiaries and offices located around the world. Embracing the aforementioned types of 'management' intelligence, Owen (2006) presents a formula for management as MQ = IQ + EQ + PQ.

12.　Various scholars have discussed the idea of multiple intelligences (see for example, Albrecht, 2013). He believes the concept of multiple intelligences (MI) – the idea that we are equipped with a range of mental competencies, not just IQ – is now widely accepted. He and others embrace a further intelligence type of significance to the manager. We all know that getting along with people is important to business success but we are just beginning to understand that this ability represents a particular kind of intelligence, one that can be nurtured and developed (Albrecht, 2004). The social quotient (SQ), is a term that has been used to define the result of a measure that describes one's overall level of social intelligence (SI). It is the capacity to negotiate complex social relationships and environments effectively; the ability to get along well with others, and to win their cooperation with you. Sometimes referred to simplistically as 'people skills' (interpersonal or social skills), SI includes an awareness of situations and the social dynamics that govern them, and a knowledge of interaction styles and strategies to help a person achieve their objectives in dealing with others. Managers with a low SQ/SI tend to make people feel devalued, cross, frustrated, guilty or otherwise inadequate; such managers have an inability to connect with people and influence them effectively. Those with a high SQ make people feel valued, respected, acknowledged, encouraged or competent and tend to be much more effective in dealing with others.

13.　Albrecht (2013) presents a model for describing, assessing and developing SI. He suggests five key dimensions of SI which are easily remembered using the 'SPACE' acronym. The 'SPACE' framework is described here: at work, around the world, managers find themselves in many different situations. Situational awareness (or social awareness) describes an ability to observe and understand the context of a situation managers may find themselves in, and to understand the ways in which the situation dictates or shapes the behaviour of the people in it. In addition to *Situational* awareness, *Presence* describes the impression, or 'message' a manager may send to others through behaviour. Work colleagues, peers, subordinates and others will tend to make inferences about a manager's character and capability based on the behaviours they observe. *Authenticity* is the extent to which others perceive a manager as acting from honest, ethical motives, and the extent to which they sense that their behaviour is congruent with their personal values. *Clarity* is the ability to express ideas clearly, effectively and with impact. It involves a range of 'communicating' skills such as listening, feedback, paraphrasing and skilful use of language, skill in using metaphors and figures of speech and the ability to explain things clearly and concisely. Finally, *empathy* is the skill of building connections with people – the capacity to get people to meet you on a personal level of respect and willingness to cooperate; creating a mutual feeling between yourself and another person.

14.　In summary, we might develop a management formula for operating globally that suggests effective and efficient management is about having SPICE! (Social, Political, Intelligence, Cultural and Emotional quotient):

$$M = \Sigma \: S \: P \: I \: C \: E$$

suggesting that managers require a cluster of 'intelligences'.

MANAGING GLOBAL (CROSS-CULTURAL) TEAMS

15.   Wherever managers work at a global level they are likely to encounter groups of people. Having discussed the multiple intelligences required by managers and prior to discussing specific functions we consider briefly the management of multicultural teams and the special considerations that may be required. You may recall that we discussed groups and teams in Chapter 7. In para. 40 we discussed the development of multicultural teams as a result of globalization. Furthermore, in Chapter 15 we commented on potential benefits and challenges associated with diversity and therefore multicultural teams. Global firms make use of teamwork through committees, taskforces, project and cross-functional teams. Multicultural teams may perform either significantly worse or better than monocultural (homogeneous) teams. Whilst they enable a multiplicity of perspectives, experiences and viewpoints this must be harnessed through effective group working, communication and on occasions conflict management. The absence of this may lead to miscommunication and misunderstanding which may manifest itself as a need to take longer over certain group tasks. We discussed stages of group development in Chapter 7, para. 8. A number of studies have suggested that it can take diverse cultural groups longer to develop and reach the norming stage. However, once performing they are endowed with capabilities, including critical problem-solving and creativity. Furthermore they have deeper insights into marketplace problems.

16.   In a similar manner, Kelly (2009) notes that globalization changes the composition of the adult classroom, increasing diversity and bringing new associated teaching and learning problems; problems with group work. He notes that group diversity may have either a positive or negative effect on performance. Based upon an empirical study he produces a model suggesting how groups are formed and how cohesive they are has a significant impact upon group performance outcomes and group motivated effort. People like to have some say regarding who is in their group or team but realize that they may not have full control over the group formation and allocation process. When members choose their own group they tend to use subjective, emotionally charged thinking processes. This may not create the ideal group structure and is unlikely to result in the creation of a diverse group as people select members that are most like themselves in terms of nationality, gender and experience. The manager, on the other hand, may use objective criteria to select group members for a project. Managers are often more concerned with performance outcomes than social interaction. Yet Kelly's findings suggest that often a hybrid approach can yield better group results. Allowing members some choice regarding team selection will increase social cohesion thus enhancing motivation and ownership of group performance issues.

49.2 GLOBAL MARKETING

17.   Having explored the multiple intelligences of any manager operating globally we now outline a selection of key issues related to specialist functions, starting with global marketing. The organization uses research to determine if there is demand for its products elsewhere in the world and if there is, seeks to estimate potential market share so that the opportunity can be quantified. Determining opportunity is a complex challenge and requires analysis of end customers' needs and buying behaviour, intermediaries, competitors and the industry as well as the wider environment. Given the large number of countries worldwide there is a need to focus attention – a company does not have the resources to operate in every country from day one. Researchers typically scan markets to identify which countries have the potential for growth, which are the best prospects for the firm. Identified countries are then qualified through assessment of accessibility, profitability and market size (**country attractiveness**).

18.   The scanning stage identifies countries where marketing opportunities exist. Opportunities may exist in countries already serviced by existing suppliers (existing markets); in countries where no company has yet offered a product of potential (latent market) and where a future opportunity may exist (incipient market). At the scanning stage, the manager researching international markets is identifying and then analyzing opportunities in order to evaluate which markets to prioritize for further investigation. When country attractiveness is high and the company's products, services and capabilities are highly compatible, a significant opportunity exists. Opportunity is also hunted by competitors. Competitor analysis starts with an assessment of the competitive environment. Relevant competitors are identified and primary competitors

determined. A common measure of their relative competitive strength is their respective market share, i.e. the proportion of total sales volume they have captured. Next, information is gathered about the strengths and weaknesses and capabilities of the most important competitors.

19.   Once a country is selected the marketer must make key decisions as typified by those discussed in the marketing mix chapters earlier in the book. Such decisions will be influenced by the organization's world-view. In the previous chapter we discussed the globalization of markets and the predictions of Theodore Levitt. His arguments were based on the convergence of consumer needs and behaviours that would erase national differences and lead to the standardization of marketing policies (Lasserre, 2012: p. 228). In Section 11 of this book (marketing management) we identified understanding customer needs as a prime task of the marketing manager. If customer needs are indeed converging (of which there is more evidence in some product categories than others) then products could be standardized.

20.   Product standardization, customer segmentation and branding can be considered at the global level. Some customers may indeed be classified as global customers (large global corporations for example) and a brand is global when the product or service it represents is marketed across the world under its name. There are now many 'global' brands. There are several criteria for inclusion in Interbrand's (a brand consultancy) annual Best Global Brands report. The brand must be truly global and needs to have transcended geographic and cultural boundaries successfully. It must have expanded across the established economic centres of the world and be establishing a presence in the major markets of the future. Leading global brands include Apple, Google, Coca-Cola, IBM, Microsoft, GE, McDonalds, Samsung, Intel and Toyota. Global brands reinforce corporate identity and bring savings in communication costs but ignore national differences.

21.   A further key challenge for the marketer working globally concerns pricing (discussed in Chapter 31), i.e. should the organization set a consistent pricing policy across borders? Lasserre (2012: p. 235) notes that global pricing has the advantage of protecting brand integrity and makes it easier to service the needs of global customers. Differential country pricing can lead to arbitrage (the purchase and sale of an asset in order to profit from a difference in the price) and the creation of grey markets (goods sold at a lower price than that intended by the maker; the goods are often bought cheaply in one national market, exported and sold at a higher price in another; the unauthorized sale of new, branded products diverted from authorized distribution channels or imported into a country for sale without the consent or knowledge of the manufacturer).

22.   Sales and distribution are probably the marketing mix elements that are the most difficult to standardize globally Lasserre (2012: p. 241). This is due to language differences, differences in social codes and negotiation practice as applied to commercial processes, the distance between prospects and customers, local laws and distribution structures. Frequent sales to a dispersed customer base tend to require a distributed salesforce; infrequent sales to a small customer base may obviate the need for a local salesforce.

23.   In summary, see Figure 49.2, there are several major decisions to be made in global marketing. The first problems concern the identification of target markets and whether or not to internationalize. Having assessed global market opportunities the organization must then decide which markets to enter, how to enter and compete. The ability of the product to meet customer needs, the price, promotional communications and distribution network (the marketing mix) will all impact upon sales. The international organization must make decisions about what to standardize and what to adapt to the local market – should they change the product, the price, the message or the distribution network in each of the countries within which they operate? All of the decisions require information derived from analysis and analytical tools. Decisions will also have implications for supply chain management and other business functions.

49.3 GLOBAL INNOVATION (R&D)

24.   Firms rely on innovation to create and adapt products and processes to meet customer needs. The internationalization of innovation continues to lag behind the internationalization of finance, distribution and manufacturing, but it is now experiencing a rapid proliferation. For decades, the dominant position of many scholars has been that innovation, in contrast to most other stages of the value chain, is highly immobile. Firms had a strong incentive to concentrate innovation in their home countries. However, recent

FIGURE 49.2 Major decisions in global marketing

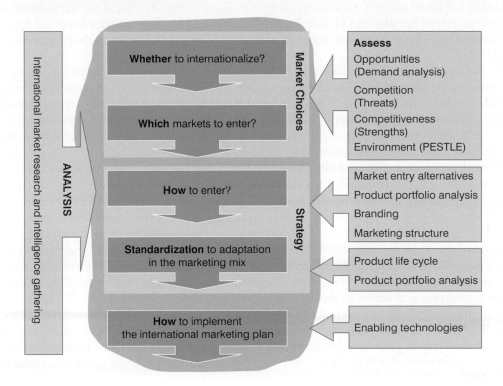

empirical research on globalization has established the centre of gravity has shifted beyond the national economy.

25.   Innovation is often, though not exclusively, associated with R&D. UNCTAD (2005) – the principal organ of the United Nations General Assembly dealing with trade, investment and development issues – define R&D as consisting of four types of activities: basic and applied research, and product and process development. *Basic research* is original experimental work without a specific commercial aim, frequently undertaken by universities. *Applied research* is original experimental work with a specific aim. *Product development* is the improvement and extension of existing products. *Process development* is the creation of new or improved processes. UNCTAD discuss emerging patterns and drivers of the globalization of R&D. They suggest the traditional view (the 1950s and 1960s) was that R&D activities by TNCs were undertaken mainly at home. However, in the current global environment characterized by rapidly changing technologies and shorter product life cycles, TNCs are offshoring (defined as the location or transfer of activities abroad) more and more R&D in different parts of the world through both foreign direct investment (FDI) and technology alliances. Reflecting the increased internationalization of R&D, foreign affiliates are assuming more important roles in many host countries' R&D activities (UNCTAD, 2005: p. 6).

26.   The rise of corporate R&D abroad and the growing importance of some developing economies as locations for R&D-related FDI reflect the combined impact of the global economic environment (global competition) and technological progress in particular. Not all aspects of R&D activity have been globalized to the same extent though. UNCTAD distinguish several different types of R&D units: (1) Technology transfer units are closely linked to manufacturing units and are established to adapt a parent's products and processes to local conditions in host countries, (2) Indigenous technology units are set up to develop new and/or improved products for local markets, (3) Regional technology units are established to develop new and/or improved products for regional markets and (4) Global technology units are set up when a single product is envisaged for the global market. Thus different aspects of R&D are globalized dependent upon the firm's strategy, i.e. global, local or glocal.

27.   Cited in UNCTAD (2005), Robert Pearce discusses, 'The globalization of R&D'. He suggests that a difference in demand conditions between countries (i.e. market heterogeneity) is an important determinant

of global R&D activity. Globalization, in many industries and product groups, has not led to demand standardization but often instead, to an increased willingness to manifest localized taste differences. Thus, the in-depth research of Bartlett and Ghoshal showed that many successful TNCs benefited from a willingness to respond to local taste differentiation, rather than seeking to override it (perhaps in pursuit of economies of scale).

28. Pearce discusses two types of classificatory system: First, typologies have been derived to distinguish different emphases in overall global R&D programmes of TNCs; second, typologies have been generated to distinguish the different roles played by individual R&D laboratories in TNC networks. As efficiency-seeking TNCs reconfigure global-supply networks and reallocate production responsibility for particular goods to new affiliates in potentially lower-cost locations, support laboratories facilitate this transfer process by helping these affiliates to assimilate, apply and, where relevant, adapt these technologies.

29. A key attribute of managing globally should be the ability to create and diffuse quickly new products and processes. We discussed 'organizing for innovation' in Chapter 22. In para. 21 we noted that organizations may create dedicated departments tasked to innovate (e.g. R&D, product development, market development and new process technology). When managing globally the organization must decide where to locate various innovation departments. This will be heavily influenced by the strategy, i.e. global or local. A global strategy will tend to centralize R&D type departments as the products and processes are standardized for the world. A local strategy will emphasize differentiation so that products and services may be customized to meet the needs of local markets. They will set up innovation centres in the local country for proximity to the market and access to skilled and knowledgeable people (local talent). The decentralized or local approach has the benefit of proximity to market and access to other research institutions such as local universities. Thus there may be multiple innovation sites in the multidomestic firm and a smaller number in the global firm. Despite an increasing internationalization of R&D activities by multinational firms, a major portion of corporate R&D still tends to be concentrated in firms' home countries, (Belderbos, Leten and Suzuki, 2013).

49.4 GLOBAL FINANCIAL MANAGEMENT

30. Thus far we have discussed global marketing and innovation, the functions that create and channel offerings to the global marketplace. However, this requires investment in different parts of the world which will then generate cash flows from different regions and countries. Lasserre (2012: p. 363) identifies four central global financial management issues: hedging against currency fluctuation, investing, capital structure and trading (cross-border transactions). We will focus on hedging as the other issues were dealt with in Chapter 45. When trading internationally, the organization must determine which currency to accept in the exchange process. Consequential issues then emerge and a necessity to manage exchange rate risk may become necessary.

31. Managing money in the global organization necessitates a consideration of risk. Such organizations not only face traditional investment and credit risks but must also consider political, economic and exchange rate risks. Political risk refers to the likelihood of political forces causing dire changes in a country's business environment that will adversely affect the profit and other goals of a particular organization. Economic risk concerns the probability that events, including economic mismanagement, will cause drastic changes in a country's business environment which again adversely affect the profit and other goals of a particular organization. Foreign exchange risk is the risk that changes in exchange rates will harm the profitability of a commercial transaction.

32. An important consideration when managing globally is to consider that currencies fluctuate in value against each other. Companies operating globally are exposed to these currency fluctuations. Cash flow can be positively or negatively affected (transaction exposure). Furthermore, the valuation of assets and liabilities can also be affected by currency variations. Transaction exposure describes the extent to which income from individual transactions is affected by fluctuations in foreign exchange values; and may result in unexpected losses (or gains). Transaction exposure may occur when a company borrows in a given currency to finance an investment that generates revenues in another currency. It may also occur when a company makes a sale in a different country. In both cases, with the passage of time, the exchange rate may have altered at the time money is exchanged, resulting in transaction gains or losses.

33.   For example, a consultancy firm operating globally may be headquartered in country A but contracted to deliver services to a firm in country B. The agreement may specify that invoices and payment be in the currency of country B. If at the time of the sale and signing contracts the exchange rate meant that one unit of currency A equalled one unit of currency B then any subsequent change to that rate will affect the value of the contract. If the value of currency B decreases then any future payments would have less value in country A and vice versa. This could have a significant impact upon the profitability of the sale and work, more so for the small to medium enterprise. For this reason, companies may employ a variety of hedging techniques to reduce this risk (technique of reducing risk by settling risky transactions at predetermined fixed terms, used very often to manage risks resulting from currency variations). They may seek to fix the exchange rate or invoice in the home country currency. Other techniques include the use of currency swaps and options or future/forward contracts. In Chapter 44 we discussed financial statements and the global firm may make use of a variety of techniques to adjust for currency fluctuations.

49.5 GLOBAL IT

34.   If marketing or operations decisions result in the establishment of overseas subsidiaries and offices then new IT challenges are created for the IT/IS department(s). Employees will need access to information systems and technologies wherever they are working. Integrating worldwide information systems is a significant challenge for the company operating globally as it is likely to have complex heterogeneous IT systems. When companies acquire subsidiaries they often acquire their legacy systems. The global IT problems are related to the firm's international strategy, i.e. whether they standardize (global) or differentiate (local).

35.   The multidomestic or 'local' strategy gives priority to local responsiveness (differentiation) in each worldwide location. National units tend to have considerable autonomy (decentralized) and typically have local, independently-run IT operations and enterprise systems. Typically, each national unit manages its own IT/IS operations; they are autonomous. However, installations tend to be linked to parent systems for financial reporting purposes. Parent (HQ) integration occurs primarily through financial reporting structures. These organizations prefer a high degree of customization of ERP or other enterprise system functionality to meet local market needs; they opt for distributed information architectures with stand-alone local databases. Organizations operating globally and adopting this strategy face unique challenges. The near absence of centralized control and standardization often results in multiple and varied ERP/enterprise system (ES) configurations across national units. Application functionality can also vary across multiple platforms, making it difficult to obtain an integrated/holistic view of crucial business data. They are, however, engineered to operate in the most efficient and effective manner dictated by local conditions.

36.   Organizations following a global strategy place high priority on operational efficiency and standardization. They require high levels of control and low levels of coordination. These organizations are structured around centralized 'hubs', with strategic decision-making concentrated at HQ. HQ drives IT activities with an eye towards maximizing operational efficiency. The national units have limited freedom to adopt the strategies, products and systems passed down to them by the parent company. At the enterprise level, organizations implementing a global strategy tend to use a 'single-financial/single-operation' logical structure. HQ manages and distributes ERP operations to national units through interfaces. Cost savings are achieved using vendor-recommended default configurations for user profiles, parameters and business processes. Global standardization affords further savings by requiring only limited customization of ERP functionality. Organizations using a global strategy follow centralized information architectures with HQ appropriately linked to national units. The installation of a centralized database also affords stronger HQ control.

37.   Finally, organizations adopting a transnational (or glocal) strategy are structured as integrated networks with specialized but interdependent strategic and operational decision-making functions; they embrace the dual need for efficiency (integration) and being local (differentiation). These organizations create competitive advantages which are location specific and efficiency driven. They gain location advantages by dispersing their value-creating activities wherever this can be best done and at the cheapest cost. They gain economic efficiencies by leveraging their worldwide knowledge base and by acquiring economies

of scale. These organizations tend to adopt an integrated global IT approach that emphasizes common systems and core applications for shared worldwide functionality. They also encourage adaptation to meet local requirements.

38.   Organizations adopting a transnational strategy have found it difficult to meet worldwide needs for coordination and integration effectively. Since resources and capabilities can be centralized or decentralized, organizations must tailor the ERP package to meet the dual needs of national responsiveness and global operational efficiency. At the enterprise level, these organizations use a 'single-financial/multi-operations' logical structure when implementing their ERP systems. Such a structure has allowed organizations to accommodate different business processes for multiple product lines. Functional modules are dispersed to national locations. However, all installations and databases must be integrated. Each national unit is configured to leverage its unique value-adding capabilities, therefore the design of user profiles, the selection of appropriate parameters, and the adoption of business processes is detailed and time-consuming. Organizations that use a transnational strategy opt for a high degree of customization of ERP functionality to suit the unique needs of their local markets. Those organizations with a transnational strategy tend to use hybrid architectures. These are distributed information architectures with integrated databases. Such a configuration requires the ERP vendor to provide software that is open and easily migratable.

CONCLUSION

39.   Managing in the global business environment requires multiple intelligences; there is a need to 'SPICE' up management when managing globally! In order to be effective and efficient the global manager should not only be culturally intelligent but also cognitively, emotionally, politically and socially intelligent. Functional managers face new and complex challenges when seeking to manage globally. The Marketing Manager must think about standardization in terms of the product, brand and price in particular. The Innovation Manager must consider where to locate research and development activities in support of the international strategy. Investing and trading worldwide exposes the organization to various financial risks which must be considered by the Financial Manager. Once the value chain has been fragmented and operations or subsidiaries established in other countries, the global IT Manager needs to ensure systems are accessible and available. However, the parent company will want certain data and information to be available in order to support timely decision-making and the production of financial statements. Thus there will be a call to integrate certain aspects of the IS worldwide.

QUESTIONS

1   Evaluate the importance of the multiple intelligences required of the global manager.

2   Discuss the specific challenges faced by the marketing, innovation, finance and IT functions when operating globally.

REFERENCES

Albrecht, K. (2004) 'Social intelligence: beyond IQ', *Training*, 41(12): 26–31.

Albrecht, K. (2013) 'Triune intelligence', *Personal Excellence*, 18(8): 6.

Belderbos, R., Leten, B. and Suzuki, S. (2013) 'How global is R&D? Firm-level determinants of home-country bias in R&D', *Journal of International Business Studies*, 44(8): 765–786.

Earley, P. and Mosakowski, E. (2004) 'Cultural intelligence', *Harvard Business Review*, 82(10): 139–146.

Kelly, P. (2009) 'Group work and multicultural management education programmes', *Journal of Teaching in International Business*, 20(1): 80–102.

Lasserre, P. (2012) *Global Strategic Management*, 3rd edn, Palgrave Macmillan.

Owen, J. (2006) *How to Manage*, Pearson.

Palmer, B., Walls, M., Burgess, Z. and Stough, C. (2001) 'Emotional intelligence and effective leadership', *Leadership and Organization Development Journal*, 22(1): 5–10.

Reffo, G. and Wark, V. (2014) *Leadership PQ – How Political Intelligence Sets Successful Leaders Apart*, Kogan Page.

United Nations Conference On Trade And Development (UNCTAD) (2005) 'Globalization Of R&D and Developing Countries – Proceedings of the Expert Meeting', Geneva, 24–26 January 2005, United Nations Publication, printed in Switzerland – available from http://unctad.org/en/docs/iteiia20056_en.pdf.

Glossary

360 degree feedback The assessment and feedback of someone's performance by a number of people who may include his or her manager, subordinates, colleagues and customers (also known as multi-source feedback).

7S model A model for organizational analysis and dynamics including components: strategy, structure, systems, style, staff, shared values and skills.

A

ABC analysis Also called Pareto analysis or the rule of 80/20, is a way of categorizing inventory items into different types depending on value and use.

Absence management The development and application of policies and procedures designed to reduce levels of absenteeism.

Accountability This is the ultimate responsibility which managers cannot delegate. While managers may delegate authority, they remain accountable for the decisions and actions of their subordinates.

Accounting Is the recording of financial or money transactions. Accounting is the systematic recording, reporting and analysis of financial transactions of a business.

Accounting standards Rules for preparing financial statements.

Acculturation Refers to the changes that occur as a result of first-hand contact between individuals of differing cultural origins. It is a process whereby an individual is socialized into an unfamiliar or new culture.

Acquisition (systems) How a company obtains the technologies valuable for its business.

Actor–observer effect When we judge others we tend to assume that failure is due to their lack of ability rather than caused by the situation.

Adaptability culture Encourages entrepreneurial values, norms, beliefs.

Adaptive system In general, an adaptive system has the ability to monitor and regulate its own performance. In many cases, an adaptive system will be able to respond fully to changes in its environment by modifying its behaviour.

Added value The value added to a product or service by an organization through the work (transformational process) which they perform.

Adhocracy A type of organization design which is temporary, adaptive and creative, in contrast with bureaucracy which tends to be permanent, rule-driven and inflexible.

Adjourning When a group disperses after goals have been met.

Administrative controls Formalized standards, rules, procedures and disciplines to ensure that the organization's controls are properly executed and enforced.

Advertising A paid-for form of non-personal communication that is transmitted through mass media (television, radio, newspapers, magazines, direct mail, outdoor displays and the Internet).

Agency problem Parties in an agency relationship differ in their decision-making objectives.

Agile methods Software development methods that emphasize constant communication with clients (end-users) and fast development of code, as well as modifications as soon as they are needed.

Agile supply chain Ability of firms in a supply chain to respond quickly to frequent changes in consumer preferences and levels of demand.

Annual report Document detailing the business activity of a company over the previous year, and containing the three main financial statements: Income Statement, Cash Flow Statement, Balance Sheet.

Application forms (blanks) Usually sent out to jobseekers who respond to some kind of job advertising. The form or blank is a template for the presentation of personal information that should be relevant to the job applied for. This ensures that all candidates provide the desired range of information in the same order of presentation to facilitate comparison and preparation of a shortlist for further selection procedures.

Appraisal A process that provides analysis of a person's overall capabilities and potential, allowing informed decisions to be made for particular purposes.

Arbitrage The purchase and sale of an asset in order to profit from a difference in the price.

Area structure The organization is structured according to geographical areas.

Assertiveness The quality of being self-assured and confident without being aggressive.

Assessment centres Centres used to provide information on candidates for jobs. They typically consist of multiple evaluations including job-related simulations, interviews and psychological tests.

Assumptions Deeply held beliefs that guide behaviour and tell members of an organization how to perceive and think about things.

Asynchronous communication The sending and receiving of messages in which there is a time delay between the sending and receiving; as opposed to synchronous communication.

Attribution theory The way in which individuals make sense of other people's behaviour through attributing characteristics to them by judging their behaviour and intentions on past knowledge and in comparison with other people they know.

Audit An evaluation (official inspection or examination) of a person, organization, system, process, enterprise, project or product.

Auditor Professional accountant appointed by a company to prepare its annual accounts in accordance with applicable regulatory rules, and from an independent perspective.

Authority The right to make particular decisions and to exercise control over resources.

Automation Using the computer to speed up the performance of existing tasks.

Autonomous work groups A work team with delegated responsibility for a defined part of an organization's activities with the freedom to organize its own resources, pace of work and allocate responsibilities within the group.

Availability (systems) The property of being accessible and usable upon demand by an authorized entity.

B

Baby boomer A person born in the years following the Second World War, when there was a temporary marked increase in the birth rate.

Balance sheet A statement that lists the assets of a business or other organization, at some specified point in time, together with the claims against those assets.

Barcode A series of thick and thin lines that identifies the product.

Basic assumptions A term used by Schein to refer to the origins of values and cultural artefacts in organizations. Basic assumptions are shared and deeply embedded presuppositions about issues such as whether human beings do or should live for the moment (immediate gratification) or see their activities as a means to a future end or goal (deferred gratification).

Basic force-field model A change model which proposes that any situation is held in place as the result of the balance of change and restraining forces acting upon it.

Batch production A type of manufacturing process where items are moved through the different manufacturing steps in groups or batches.

Behavioural control A form of control based on direct personal supervision which is responsive to the particular needs of the tasks, the abilities of the manager and the norms of the organization.

Behaviouralism An approach to job design that aims to improve motivation hence performance by increasing job satisfaction.

Belief system (formal) The explicit set of organizational definitions that senior managers communicate formally and reinforce systematically to provide basic values, purpose and direction for the organization.

Big data The term (and buzzword) for a collection of data sets so large and complex that it becomes difficult to process using traditional data processing applications.

Bill-of-materials (BOM) A document/form stating the required quantity of materials for each operation to complete the product, inventory data and the production plan to determine when material needs to be produced or acquired (ordered).

Biodata Scoreable information about a job applicant.

Book-keeping The recording of financial transactions.

Boston Matrix (Also called the BCG Matrix, the Growth-Share Matrix and Portfolio Analysis).

Brand A name, term, design, symbol or any other feature that identifies one seller's goods or service as distinct from those of other sellers.

Brand equity The marketing and financial value associated with a brand's strength in a market.

Branding The process of creating and developing successful brands.

Break-even analysis The technique of comparing revenues and costs at increasing levels of output in order to establish the point at which revenue exceeds cost, that is the point at which it 'breaks even'.

Budget A financial plan to manage the spending and saving of money.

Budgeting The implementation of the long-term plan for the year ahead through the development of detailed financial plans.

Bureaucracy Describes a form of business administration based on formal rational rules and procedures designed to govern work practices and organization activities through a hierarchical system of authority (see Standardization, Centralization, Formalization, Specialization).

Bureaucratic culture Prevalent in stable and predictable environments where employee behaviour is governed by formal rules, standard operating procedures and hierarchical control.

Business analytics The skills, technologies, applications and practices for continuous iterative exploration and investigation of past business performance to gain insight and drive business planning.

Business continuity The activity performed by an organization to ensure that critical business functions will be available to customers, suppliers and other entities that must have access to those functions.

Business continuity management (BCM) A holistic management process that identifies potential threats to an organization and the impacts to business operations those threats, if realized, might cause, and which provides a framework for building organizational resilience with the capability of an effective response that safeguards the interests of its key stakeholders, reputation, brand and value-creating activities.

Business continuity planning (BCP) Coordinated efforts aimed at avoiding discontinuities in operations and taking action to deal with their consequences, including reactivating operations as soon as possible.

Business ethics The accepted principles (beliefs and values) of right or wrong governing the conduct of business people.

Business information system (BIS) Specific information system used to support business.

Business intelligence (BI) Information gleaned from large amounts of data, usually a data warehouse or on-line databases; a BI system discovers not-yet-known patterns, trends and other useful information that can help improve the organization's performance.

Business model The organization's essential logic for consistently achieving its principle objectives – explains how it consistently makes money, highlights the distinctive activities and approaches that enable the firm to succeed – to attract customers and deliver products and services profitably.

Business plan A document that summarizes how an entrepreneur will organize a firm to exploit an opportunity, along with the economic implications of exploiting that opportunity.

Business process A specific ordering of work activities across time and place, with a beginning, an end and clearly identified input and output.

Business process management (BPM) Systematic, structured approach to analyze, improve, control and manage processes with the aim of improving the quality of products and services.

Business process orientation A process orientation means that the company focuses on business processes as opposed to a functional business orientation where a company organizes along functional lines, such as sales and production.

Business process re-engineering (BPR) The redesign of business processes in an effort to reduce costs, increase efficiency and effectiveness, and improve quality. BPR is characterized as radical rather than incremental in its approach to change and broad rather than narrow in its organization impact.

Business strategy Describes how the organization competes within an industry or market.

Buying behaviour The decision processes and actions of people involved in buying and using products.

C

Capacity The maximum production possible – The amount of work a production unit, whether individual or group, can accomplish in a given amount of time.

Capital budgeting The process of analyzing and selecting various proposals for capital expenditures.

Capital investment decisions Those decisions that involve current outlays (investment) in return for a stream of benefits in future years.

Capital rationing Occurs whenever there is a budget ceiling, i.e. a constraint on spending.

Centralization The degree to which the authority makes certain decisions is located at the top of the management hierarchy.

Change agents Any person seeking to promote, further support, sponsor, initiate, implement or help to deliver change within the organization.

Change model An abstract representation describing the content or process of changes.

Channel cannibalization The decrease in sales through an existing channel due to the introduction of a new channel.

Channels A medium through which a company directs its messages to customers.

Charismatic leadership The ability to exercise leadership through the power of the leader's personality.

Chief executive officer (CEO) The highest-ranking executive or administrator in charge of management; the singular organizational position that is primarily responsible for carrying out the strategic plans and policies of an organization.

Churn rate The proportion of contractual customers or subscribers who leave a supplier during a given time period.

Classical approach to management The organization is thought of in terms of its purpose and formal structure and this approach aims to identify how methods of working can improve productivity. Emphasis is placed on the planning of work, the technical requirements of the organization, principles of management and the assumption of rational and logical behaviour.

Classical decision theory A theory which assumes that decision-makers are objective, have complete information and consider all possible alternatives and their consequences before selecting the optimal solution.

Coalition building The forming of partnerships to increase pressures for or against change.

Code of ethics A set of ethical-behaviour rules developed by organizations or by professional societies.

Collective agreements The results of collective bargaining are expressed in agreements; these are principally procedure agreements and substantive agreements; they are not legally enforceable in the UK. (See also Procedure Agreements and Substantive Agreements.)

Collective bargaining The process of negotiating wages and other working conditions collectively between employers and trade unions, it enables the conditions of employees to be agreed as a whole group instead of individually.

Commitment Construct that represents the consumers desire to continue a relationship.

Communication The activity of conveying information.

Communication climate in an organization The prevailing atmosphere, open or closed, in which ideas and information are exchanged.

Communication process The transmission of information between entities.

Communication strategy The macro-level communication choices we make based on organizational goals and judgements about others' reactions, which serve as a basis for action.

Communications Essentially the process by which views and information are exchanged between individuals or groups; usually refers to the system of communication in use, but can also mean personal skills of communication.

Communications technology Technology that is relevant to communications, the Internet, satellite communications, mobile telephony, digital television.

Company's memorandum and articles of association The documents needed to form a company – In the UK, a company must draw up a Memorandum of Association to document and record details of the firm. The memorandum provides basic information on a business or association in the UK and with the Articles of Association, forms the company's charter or constitution. The memorandum may be viewed by the public at the office in which it is filed.

Competence Work-related knowledge, skill or ability held by an individual.

Competency-based approach The development of a list of abilities and competencies necessary to perform successfully a given job, and against which the applicant's performance can be assessed.

Competitive advantage Used interchangeably with distinctive competence to mean relative superiority in skills and resources.

Competitive dynamics How one firm responds to the strategic actions of competing firms.

Competitive strategy Competitive strategy is concerned with the basis on which a business unit might achieve competitive advantage in its market.

Computer integrated manufacturing (CIM) Involves the total operation of an organization – integrates the software and hardware needed for computer graphics, computer-aided modelling and computer-aided design and manufacturing activities, from initial product concept through its production and distribution in the marketplace.

Computer-aided design (CAD) software Software that allows designers to design and build production prototypes, test them as a computer object under given parameters, compile parts and quantity lists, outline production and assembly procedures, and then transmit the final design directly to milling and rolling machines.

Computer-aided manufacturing (CAM) software Software that uses a digital design such as that from a CAD system to directly control production machinery.

Concurrent feedback Information which arrives during our behaviour and which can be used to control behaviour as it unfolds.

Confidentiality Ensuring that information is accessible only to those authorized to have access.

Configuration The shape of the organization's role structure – the structures, processes and relationships through which the organization operates.

Conflict A disagreement through which the parties involved perceive a threat to their needs, interests or concerns.

Conflict resolution The process which attempts to end the conflict between the disagreeing parties.

Constructive dismissal Dismissal where the employee is 'forced' to leave their job against their will because of the employer's conduct (breach of contract).

Content theories of motivation These theories attempt to explain those specific things which actually motivate the individual at work and are concerned with identifying people's needs, the strength of those needs and the goals they pursue in order to satisfy those needs.

Contingency approach An extension of the systems approach that implies organizational variables (e.g. strategy, structure and systems) and its success or performance is dependent upon environmental influences (forces). There is, therefore, no one best way to structure or manage organizations; rather it must be dependent upon the contingencies of the situation.

Contingency approach to organization structure A perspective which argues that an organization, to be effective, must adjust its structure in a manner consistent with the main type of technology it uses, the environment within which it operates, its size and other contextual factors.

Contingency theory of leadership A view which argues that leaders must alter their style in a manner consistent with aspects of the context.

Continuous change Organizational changes that tend to be ongoing, evolving and cumulative.

Control Ensuring plans are properly executed; assuring the organization functions as planned.

Control mechanism The individual, molecular units of organizational control (e.g. standards, policies, norms) that are applied in control processes.

Control system Configurations of multiple formal and informal control mechanisms.

Control target Specific elements of organizational transformation processes (i.e. impotence, behaviours or outputs) to which control mechanisms are intended to be applied.

Controlled performance Setting standards, measuring performance, comparing actual with standard and taking corrective action if necessary.

Controllee Target of control.

Controller Person who selects (chooses) control mechanisms and systems to achieve their goals; a person or thing that directs or regulates something.

Coordination The process of linking and integrating functions and activities of different groups (assuring resources work well together towards the common goal).

Core competence Those capabilities fundamental to the organization's strategy and performance.

Core values Core values are the principles that guide an organization's actions.

Corporate communication A set of activities involved in managing and orchestrating all internal and external communications aimed at creating a favourable point of view among stakeholders on which the company depends.

Corporate culture Defined by Bower (1966) as 'the way we do things around here'. Trice and Beyer (1984) elaborated this as: 'the system of ... publicly and collectively accepted meanings operating for a given group at a given time'. Hofstede (1994) describes corporate culture as 'the psychological assets of an organization, which can be used to predict what will happen to its financial assets in 5-years time'. See also 'Culture'.

Corporate governance The system used to control and direct a company's operations.

Corporate social responsibility (CSR) The responsibility of an organization for the economic, social, ethical and environmental impacts of its activities.

Cost accounting Accounting concerned with cost accumulation for inventory valuation to meet the requirements of external reporting and internal profit measurement.

Cost behaviour The way in which a cost reacts or responds to changes in the level of business activity.

Cost benefit analysis (CBA) The assessment of resources used in an activity and their comparison with the value of the benefit to be derived from the activity. Choice and evaluation of competing solutions should take account of NPV and changing price levels.

Cost centres A unit which serves other parts of the organization (e.g. HR, IT, Accounts, etc) and which is allocated a budget based on the costs of operating the service at an agreed level; Cost centres account for related expenses – they add to the cost of an organization, but only indirectly add to its profit.

Cost of capital Price of money.

Cost-volume-profit (CVP) analysis Examines the relationship between changes in activity (output) and changes in total sales revenue, costs and net profit.

Country attractiveness Measure that reflects that countries have a potential for growth, and may offer prospects for the firm. Identified countries are qualified through assessment of accessibility, profitability and market size.

Courier A company that transports commercial packages.

Creativity The ability to produce novel and useful ideas and can lead to new products and services, novel applications and cost savings.

Crisis An abnormal situation, or even perception, which is beyond the scope of everyday business and which threatens the operation, safety and reputation of an organization.

Crisis management The process by which a business or other organization deals with a sudden emergency situation.

Critical success factor Product features that are particularly valued by customers, hence, where the organization must outrival competition.

Cross-docking Technique used extensively in the retail industry where a product arrives at a warehouse or distribution centre and is quickly processed and shipped to a retail store.

Cross-functional processes Cross-functional business processes are processes that span across several different departments of one business.

Cultural A branch of study concerned with observing and explaining cultural differences in human behaviour.

Cultural artefacts Phenomena accessible to the senses, including architecture, myths, rituals, logos, type of personnel employed and so on, which signify the values in an organization's culture.

Cultural competence Set of skills and attitudes that allow individuals to communicate effectively and appropriately with people who are different from themselves.

Cultural distance Cultural distance aims to capture the overall difference in national culture between the homecountry and affiliates overseas. As the cultural distance increases, the difficulties facing business processes overseas also increase.

Cultural intelligence Cultural intelligence reflects a person's capability to adapt as they interact with others from different cultural regions. An individual with a high level of cultural intelligence has: the cognitive skills that allow them to function effectively in a new culture; the motivational impetus to adapt to a different cultural environment and the ability to engage in adaptive behaviours.

Culture Shared ways of thinking and behaving (uniformity).

Culture shock Psychological process affecting people living and working abroad that may affect their work performance.

Customer acquisition All marketing activities and strategies used by organizations to attract new customers.

Customer loyalty The feeling of attachment to or affection for a company's people, products or services. These feelings manifest themselves in many forms of customer behaviour.

Customer relationship management (CRM) Uses technology-enhanced customer interaction to shape appropriate marketing offers designed to nurture ongoing relationships with individual customers within an organization's target markets.

Customer satisfaction When an exchange meets the needs and expectations of the buyer.

Customer switching The action through which a customer changes supplier.

Cybernetic system A system with reference to the components and operation of feedback control (see self-regulation).

Cycle time The time it takes a product to go from beginning to end of a production process; i.e. the time it is work-in-process.

D

Dashboard A graphic presentation of organizational performance. Dashboards display in an easy-to-grasp visual manner metrics, trends and other helpful information that are the result of processing of business intelligence applications.

Data Raw facts.

Database A system or programme in which structured data are stored.

Decision Commitment of resources.

Decision-making The process of making choices from among several options.

Decision support system (DSS) A computer-based information system that combines models and data in an attempt to solve semi-structured problems with extensive user involvement.

Decision tree A diagram showing the sequence of events, decisions and consequent actions that occur in a decision-making process.

Decision-making approach An approach to management that focuses on managerial decision-making and how organizations process and use information in making decisions.

Defection The loss of any portion of that customer's business.

Delayed feedback Information which is received after a task is completed, and which can be used to influence future performance.

Delegation A distinct type of power sharing process that occurs when a manager gives subordinates the responsibility and authority for making certain decisions previously made by the manager.

Demographic Key variables concerning age, sex, occupation, level of education, religion and social class.

Design (structure) purpose The primary purposes of design are to divide and allocate work and then coordinate and control that work so that goals are met.

Development Anything that helps a person to grow, in ability, skills, confidence, inter-personal skills, understanding, self-control and more.

Diagnostic control system Formal IS used to monitor organizational outcomes and correct deviations from preset standards of performance.

Diamond of competitive advantage Configuration of four sets of attributes (factor conditions, demand conditions, supporting industries and inter-firm rivalry) which, in Porter's theory, determine a nation's competitive advantage.

Differentiation The degree to which the tasks and the work of individuals, groups and units are divided up within an organization.

Digital organization An organization where nearly all significant business processes and relationships with customers, suppliers and employees are digitally enabled and key corporate assets are managed through digital means.

Direct channel structure Where the product goes directly from the producer to the final customer.

Direct distribution channels Distribution channels in which products are sold directly from producers to users.

Direct marketing The use of non-personal media, the Internet or telesales to introduce products to customers, who then purchase the products by mail, telephone or the Internet.

Discrimination Usually refers to unfair treatment of an individual or group on grounds of their sex or race.

Disintermediation The process of doing away with 'middlemen' from business transactions.

Dismissal The termination of an employee's contract of employment either by the employer, or by the employee himself in circumstances where the employer's conduct justifies such a step (constructive dismissal); dismissal may be with or without notice.

Dissemination The transmission of information, whether orally, in writing or by electronic means.

Disseminator role Managers scan their environments, monitor their own units and disseminate the information they collect.

Distribution channel Interlinked stages and organizations involved in the process of bringing a product or service to the consumer or industrial user.

Diversity All the ways in which we differ.

Division of labour An approach to job design that involves dividing a task down into relatively small parts, each of which is accomplished by a single person.

Divisional structure A design whereby an organization is split into a number of self-contained business units, each of which operates as a profit centre.

Domestic A business's home market.

Downstream The other operations in a supply chain between the operation being considered and the end customer.

E

e-business Using Internet technologies as the platform for internal business operations, electronic commerce and enterprise collaboration.

e-commerce All electronically mediated information exchanges between an organization and its external stakeholders (see sell-side and buy side e-commerce).

Economic order quantity (EOQ) The order size minimizes the total cost of ordering and carry inventory.

Economies of scope The value of a firm's products or services increases as a function of the number of different businesses in which that firm operates.

Education Formal learning outside (and often before entering) the workplace.

Effectiveness Doing right things.

Efficiency Doing things right.

Efficient supply chain Designed for efficiency and low cost by minimizing inventory and maximizing efficiencies in process flow.

Electronic data interchange (EDI) The use of IT to integrate order processing with production, inventory, accounting and transportation.

Emotional intelligence The ability to perceive, to integrate, to understand and manage one's own and other people's feelings reflectively.

Employee advocacy The responsibility of HR for clearly defining how management should be treating employees, making sure that employees have mechanisms to contest unfair practices, and representing the interests of employees within the framework of HR's primary obligation to senior management.

Employee engagement Refers to the individual's involvement and satisfaction with, as well as enthusiasm for, work.

Employee involvement A participative, employer-led, process that uses the input of employees and is intended to increase employee commitment to an organization's success.

Employee relations Employee relations is an alternative label for 'industrial relations'. It is not confined to unionized collective bargaining but encompasses all employment relationships. It goes beyond the negotiation of pay and benefits to include the conduct of the power relationship between employee and employer.

Employee resourcing That element of HRM concerned with obtaining and retaining a workforce with the necessary skills, competencies, values, attitudes and other attributes.

Employee voice The two-way communication between employer and employee. It is the process of the employer communicating to the employee as well as receiving and listening to communication from the employee.

Employment relations Concerned with the relationships between the policies and practices of the organization and its staff and the behaviour of work groups.

Employment relationship A psychological contract, a two-way exchange of perceived promises and obligations between employees and their employer. There are often expectations and understandings about obligations.

[Empowerment] A climate whereby employees are allowed [freedom], autonomy and self-control over their [area of] responsibility for decision-making.

[End user] A person who actually uses a particular [product].

[Engagement] Refers to the individual's involvement and [satisfaction with, a]s well as enthusiasm for, work.

Engagement culture Where the majority of employees feel valued and are committed to the organization and its goals.

Enterprise resource planning (ERP) systems Large, integrated, computer-based business transaction processing and reporting systems. ERP systems pull together all of the classic business functions such as accounting, finance, sales and operations into a single, tightly integrated package that uses a common database.

Enterprise risk management (ERM) A process, effected by an entity's board of directors, management and other personnel, applied in strategy setting and across the enterprise, designed to identify potential events that may affect the entity, and manage risk to be within its risk appetite, to provide reasonable assurance regarding the achievement of entity objectives.

Enterprise system An IS that integrates information from all functional areas of an organization with the goal of providing a more whole or complete information resource for the organization.

Entrepreneurship Identification and exploitation of previously unexploited opportunities.

Environmental determinism A perspective which claims that internal organizational responses are wholly or mainly shaped, influenced or determined by external environmental factors.

Episodic change Organizational changes that tend to be infrequent, discontinuous and intentional.

e-procurement The electronic integration and management of all procurement activities including purchase request, authorization, ordering, delivery and payment between a purchaser and a supplier.

Equity theory A theory of motivation which focuses on people's feelings of how fairly they have been treated in comparison with the treatment received by others.

Ethnorelative Being comfortable with many standards and customs and having an ability to adapt behaviour and judgements to a variety of interpersonal settings.

Ethnocentric A belief that home nationals are superior.

European quality award (EQA) A quality award organized by the European Foundation for Quality Management (EFQM), it is based on the EFQM excellence model.

Expatriate A citizen of one country working in another country.

Expectancy theory A process theory which argues that individual motivation depends on the valence of outcomes, the expectancy that effort will lead to good performance, and the instrumentality of performance in producing valued outcomes.

Experiential learning Learning from doing.

Explicit knowledge Knowledge and understanding which is codified, expressed and available to anyone.

Export Selling products in a country other than the one in which they were made.

Extrinsic Valued outcomes or benefits provided by others, such as promotion, pay increases, a bigger office desk, praise and recognition.

Extrinsic motivation A form of motivation that stresses valued outcomes or benefits provided by others, such as promotion, pay increases, a bigger office desk, praise and recognition.

F

Factors of production Resources, such as land, labour and capital used to produce goods and services.

Feedback (in the context of interpersonal communication) the processes through which the transmitter of a message detects whether and how that message has been received and decoded.

Figurehead role The manager performs ceremonial and symbolic duties as head of the organization/team or department.

Filtering A sender's manipulation of information so that it will be seen more favourably by the receiver.

Finance A branch of economics concerned with resource allocation as well as resource management, acquisition and investment; deals with matters related to money and markets.

Financial accounting Reporting of the financial position and performance of a firm through financial statements issued to external users on a periodic basis.

Financial control In financial control the role of the centre is confined to setting financial targets, allocating resources, appraising performance and intervening to avert or correct poor performance.

Financial management The effective and efficient management of funds (money) in such a way as to accomplish the objectives of the organization.

Finished goods Product ready for sale – items that are ready to be moved to a customer.

First-mover advantage Exists where an organization is better off than its competitors as a result of being first to market with a new product, process or service.

Five forces framework Identifies the five most common threats faced by firms in their local competitive environments and the conditions under which these threats are more or less likely to be present; these forces are the threat of entry, of rivalry, of substitutes, of buyers and of suppliers.

Flexible manufacturing systems (FMS) Integrate all of the major elements of production into a highly automated system.

Flexible working An arrangement whereby the start and finish times of a worker may be varied whilst not exceeding the daily/weekly hours of a normal working day/ week over a predetermined period.

Flexitime Flexible working hours: A system enabling employees to vary their working hours in a particular period, provided they do attend during certain 'core hours', e.g. 10:00 hours – 16:00 hours.

Flow chart A pictorial summary that shows, with symbols and words, the steps, sequence and relationship of the various activities involved in the performance of a process.

Flow production A type of manufacturing process that closely resembles a production line process. Typically adopted in order to produce highly standardized goods or services, usually around the clock in very high volumes.

Flow shop processes Organized around a fixed sequence of activities and process steps, such as an assembly line to produce a limited variety of similar goods or services.

Force-field analysis A process of identifying and analyzing the driving and restraining forces associated with a change.

Foreign exchange risk The chance of a loss due to an adverse movement in exchange rates.

Formal communication Formal communication involves presenting information in a structured and consistent manner. Such information is normally created for a specific purpose, making it likely to be more comprehensive, accurate and relevant than information transmitted using information communication. An example of formal communication is an accounting statement. See Informal communication.

Formal management controls A firm's budgeting and reporting activities that keep people higher up in a firm's organizational chart informed about the actions taken by people lower down in the organizational chart.

Formal organization The collection of work groups that has been consciously designed by management to maximize efficiency and achieve organizational goals.

Formalization The degree to which instructions, procedures, etc. are written down.

Forming The initial formation of a group and the first stage in group development.

Forward vertical integration A firm incorporates more stages of the value chain within its boundaries and those stages bring it closer to interacting directly with final customers.

Freight forwarder An agent who serves as an intermediary between the organization shipping the product and the actual carrier, typically on international shipments.

Functional business (information) systems Systems to support different primary and secondary activities such as the manufacturing, order processing, accounting or HR systems. Functional systems serve the specific and local needs of parts of the organization and are developed using specific programming languages. Typically they have their own databases, data structures, operating systems and other idiosyncrasies.

Functional business system A system designed to support a specific primary activity of the organization.

Functional layout A type of layout where resources are physically grouped by function.

Functional structure The organization is structured according to functional areas such as finance, marketing and HR.

G

Gantt chart A graphical tool used to show expected start and end times for project activities, and to track actual progress against these time targets.

Gender discrimination Many countries, including all members of the EU, have sex discrimination and equal pay legislation. However, informal psychological and organizational barriers continue to bar the progress of women. The processes of occupational segregation and sex-typing of jobs continue so that women tend to be concentrated at the base of most organizational hierarchies in jobs which are less prestigious and lower paid than those favoured by men.

Generation X The generation born after that of the baby boomers (roughly from the early 1960s to mid-1970s), typically perceived to be disaffected and directionless.

Generation Y The generation born in the 1980s and 1990s, comprising primarily the children of the baby boomers and typically perceived as increasingly familiar with digital and electronic technology.

Generic business strategies Another name for business-level strategies, which are cost leadership and product differentiation.

Generic routes to competitive advantage Cost leadership, differentiation and focus; not mutually exclusive.

Geocentric approach A belief that superiority is not equated with nationality (sees the world as a single market – global).

Geographical scope Describes the multinationality of the organization.

Glass ceiling Expression used to denote a subtle barrier to women's promotion to senior posts in an organization, and usually implying that it is kept in place by men's innate prejudice against women in senior management positions.

Global A form of international organizational design where foreign subsidiaries are modelled on the parent companies' domestic approach (replication) – standardization and centralization are emphasized in order to achieve integration.

Global company Promotes a convergence of consumer's preferences and strives to maximize standardization of production, which makes centralization and integration profitable.

Global economy An integrated world economy with unrestricted and free movement of goods, services and labour transnationally.

Global sourcing Global sourcing: purchasing services and components from the most appropriate suppliers around the world regardless of their location.

Global strategy Assumes a single market and offers a standard product(s) to meet customer needs wherever they are located.

Globalization Growth and integration to a global or worldwide scale.

Globalization of markets The expansion and access of businesses to reach the needs of customers worldwide.

Globalization of production Trend by individual firms to disperse parts of their productive processes to different locations around the globe to take advantage of differences in cost and quality of factors of production.

Global-local dilemma (glocal) The extent to which products and services may be standardized across national boundaries or need to be adapted to meet the requirements of specific national markets.

Goal theory A theory of motivation that is based on the premise that people's goals or intentions play an important part in determining behaviour. Goals guide people's responses and actions and direct work behaviour and performance, leading to certain consequences or feedback.

Governance Exercise of authority and control.

Grey market Goods sold at a lower price than that intended by the maker; the goods are often bought cheaply in one national market, exported and sold at a higher price in another.

Grievance Concerns, problems or complaints that employees raise with their employers.

Group An association of two or more individuals who have a shared sense of identity and who interact with each other in structured ways on the basis of a common set of expectations about each other's behaviour.

Group cohesiveness The extent to which members of a group interact, cooperate, are united and work together effectively. Generally, the greater the cohesiveness within a group, the more rewarding the experience is for the members and the higher the chances are of success.

Group dynamics The behavioural interactions and patterns of behaviour that occur when groups of people meet.

H

Halo or horns effect The perception of a person is formulated on the basis of a single favourable or unfavourable trait or characteristic and tends to shut out other relevant characteristics of that person; when this is positive it is a 'halo' effect, when negative a 'horns' effect.

Hawthorne studies A series of studies exploring aspects of group working within the Western Electric Company in the USA during the late 1920s and early 1930s.

Hedging A technique of reducing risk by settling risky transactions at predetermined fixed terms. Used very often to manage risks resulting from currency variations.

Hierarchy of needs A theory of motivation developed by Maslow which states that people's behaviour is determined by their desire to satisfy a progression of physiological, social and psychological needs.

Holism The total of a system is greater than the sum of its parts.

Homophily bias (i.e. love of the same) is the tendency of individuals to associate and bond with similar others. This is often expressed in the adage 'birds of a feather flock together'.

Homosocial reproduction The tendency of people to identify with particular groups (e.g. same gender) and then define these groups as the in-group and all other groups as out-groups. The in-group is then positively discriminated towards.

HR planning A rational approach to the effective recruitment, retention and deployment of people within an organization, including, when necessary, arrangements for dismissing staff.

HR system A set of distinct activities, functions, policies and processes that are directed at attracting, developing and maintaining the human resources of an organization.

Human capital (HC) An economic and management construct referring to the knowledge, skills and other attributes of labour (people involved in productive work) that contribute to the development of a business or economy. Sometimes called intellectual capital, it is the collective value of the capabilities, knowledge, skills and commitment of an organizational workforce.

Human resource development (HRD) A strategic approach to investing in HC. It draws on other HR processes, including resourcing and performance assessment to identify actual and potential talent. HRD provides a framework for self-development, training programmes and career progression to meet an organization's future skill requirements.

Human resource management (HRM) A philosophy of people management based on the belief that HR are uniquely important to sustained business success. An organization gains competitive advantage by using its people effectively, drawing on their expertise and ingenuity to meet clearly defined objectives. HRM is aimed at recruiting capable, flexible and committed people, managing and rewarding their performance and developing key competencies.

Human resource planning (HRP) A process which anticipates and maps out the consequences of business strategy on an organization's HR requirements. This is reflected in planning of skill and competence needs as well as total headcounts.

Human resource strategy Overall plan for staffing, developing and rewarding employees and outsourced human resources tied to business objectives.

Hygiene factors Aspects of work which remove dissatisfaction but do not contribute to motivation and performance, including pay, company policy, supervision, status, security and working conditions are known as hygiene or context factors.

I

Identity The company's defining attributes such as its vision and values, its people, products and services.

Image The company as seen through the eyes of its stakeholder groups.

Import The purchase of goods or services from a buyer in another country.

Inbound logistics The management of material resources entering an organization from its suppliers and other partners.

Inclusive climate A work environment where employees do not feel or perceive themselves to be excluded from activities to which they would normally expect to participate if they wanted to; broad participation is encouraged.

Industrial relations The processes of regulation and control over the collective aspects of the employment relationship.

Informal communication. This describes information that is transmitted by informal means, such as casual conversations between members of staff. The information transmitted in this way is often less structured and less detailed than information transmitted by formal communication. In addition, the information may be inconsistent or may contain inaccuracies. Furthermore, the information may also include a subjective element, such as personal opinions. See Formal communication.

Informal management controls Include a firm's culture and the willingness of employees to monitor each others' behaviour.

Informal organization The network of relationships between members of an organization that form of their own accord, on the basis of common interests and companionship.

Information Data that have been processed (sorted, summarized, manipulated, filtered) so that they are meaningful to people.

Information resource management (IRM) All activities related to the controlling, organizing, maintaining, planning, acquiring and securing of (information) systems and IT resources.

Information system (IS) A set of people, procedures and resources that collects, transforms and disseminates information in an organization – accepts data resources as input and processes them into information products as output.

Information systems infrastructure (consisting of hardware and competing platforms, system software (application and operating systems), storage, networking and telecommunications services including Internet platforms, data management services and data centres) to support their decision-making, business processes and competitive strategy.

Information technology (IT) The hardware and software that are used to store, retrieve and manipulate information.

Innovating organization Organizations designed to do something for the first time – those that recognize and formalize the roles, processes, rewards and people practices which naturally lead to innovations.

Innovation The first, practical, concrete implementation of an idea done in a way that brings broad-based, extrinsic recognition to an individual or organization.

Inputs The resources introduced into a system for transformation into outputs.

Insourcing The use of resources within the firm to provide products or services.

Institutions Rules, norms and beliefs that describe reality for the organization, explaining what is and what is not, what can be acted upon and what cannot.

Integration The required level to which units in an organization are linked together, and their respective degree of independence (integrative mechanisms include rules and procedures and direct managerial control).

Integrity (systems) Safeguarding the accuracy and completeness of information and processing methods.

Interdependence The extent to which the behaviour of the components of a system depend upon one another.

Intermediary Brings together buyers and sellers.

Internal analysis Identification of a firm's organizational strengths and weaknesses and of the resources and capabilities that are likely to be sources of competitive advantage.

Internal rate of return (IRR) The internal rate of return (IRR) is the discount rate which delivers a NPV of zero for a series of future cash flows. It is a discounted cash flow (DCF) approach to valuation and investing.

International business travellers (IBTs) Persons for whom a part – generally a major part – of their role involves international visits to foreign markets, facilities and projects.

International Financial Reporting Standards (IFRS) International accounting standards, designed to harmonize reporting standards in different countries, which are gradually supplanting national accounting standards.

International HRM (IHRM) Processes and activities of people management which involve more than one national context.

Internationalization The gradual process of taking organizational activities into other countries.

Internet An international network of computers, cables and satellite links that enables individuals to communicate worldwide through their personal computer or workplace server.

Intranet Internal, in-company Internet networks for routine communications, fostering group communications, providing uniform computer applications, distributing the latest software or informing colleagues of marketing developments and new product launches.

Intrapreneur A person within a large corporation who takes direct responsibility for turning an idea into a profitable finished product through assertive risk-taking and innovation.

Intuitive decision-makers Cognitive style that describes people who approach a problem with multiple methods in an unstructured manner, using trial and error to find a solution.

Inventory A list of the items held in stock.

Inventory management Planning, coordinating and controlling the acquisition, storage, handling, movement, distribution and possible sale of raw materials, component parts and subassemblies, supplies and tools, replacement parts and other assets needed to meet customer wants and needs.

Item A single article that is kept in stock, it is one entry in the inventory.

J

Job The set of tasks an individual performs.

Job analysis The process of job analysis is that of gathering and analyzing job-related information. This includes details about tasks to be performed as part of a job and the personal qualities required to do so. Job analysis can provide information for a variety of purposes including: determining training needs, development criteria, appropriate pay and productivity improvements. For resourcing purposes, job analysis can generate job and personnel specifications.

Job characteristics model A model of job enrichment based on the need to incorporate a number of core job dimensions (skill variety, task identity, task significance, autonomy and feedback) into the design of a job.

Job description A statement of the overall purpose and scope of a job, together with details of its tasks and duties; the description is a product of job analysis.

Job design Involves determining the specific job tasks and responsibilities, the work environment and the methods by which the tasks will be carried out to meet the goals of operations.

Job enlargement The horizontal increasing of job responsibility, i.e. by the addition of tasks of a similar nature to be distinguished from job enrichment.

Job enrichment The process of vertically increasing the responsibilities of a job, by the addition of motivators, e.g. more discretion, improved job interest, etc.

Job rotation The moving of a person from one job or task to another in an attempt to add variety and help remove boredom. It may also give the individual a holistic view of the organization's activities and be used as a form of training.

Job satisfaction An attitude or internal state which is associated with the working environment and working experiences. In recent years it has been closely associated with improved job design and work organization and the quality of working life.

Job sharing An arrangement that allows two or more individuals to split a traditional 40-hour-a-week job.

Job simplification An approach to job design based on a minimization of the range of tasks into the smallest convenient size to make the job efficient and cost-effective.

Jobbing processes Processes that deal with high variety and low volumes, although there may be some repetition of flow and activities.

Jobbing production The process for making a one-off, or low volume, product to a customer specification.

Just-in-time (JIT) Methods of managing inventory (stock) whereby items are delivered when needed in the production process instead of being stored by the manufacturer.

K

Kaizen Japanese term for continuous improvement.

Knowledge What people understand as a result of what they have been taught or have experienced. Knowledge may then be applied to solve problems.

L

Lateral communication Communication within an organization which exists between individuals in different departments or sections, especially between individuals on the same level.

Leadership The process of influencing others to understand and agree about what needs to be done and how to do it, and the process of facilitating individual and collective efforts to accomplish shared objectives.

Leadership and management development (LMD) A planned and deliberate process to help leaders and managers become more effective.

Lean production A term commonly used to refer to JIT production.

Learning and development The process of ensuring that the organization has the knowledgeable, skilled and engaged workforce it needs.

Learning organization An organization skilled at creating, acquiring and transferring knowledge, and at modifying its behaviour to reflect new knowledge and insights.

Lifetime customer value (LCV) The net profit attributed to the entire future relationship with a customer.

Limited company A corporation with shareholders whose liability is limited by shares.

Line relationship The links, as shown on an organizational chart, that exist between managers and staff whom they oversee directly.

Loading The amount of work that is allocated to a work centre.

Locus of control An individual's generalized belief about internal (self-) control versus external control (control by the situation or by others).

Logistics The management of both inbound and outbound materials, parts, supplies and finished goods.

Logistics management The coordination of activities of the entire distribution channel to deliver maximum value to customers: from suppliers of raw materials to the manufacturer of the product, to the wholesalers who deliver the product, to the final customers who purchase it.

Loyalty programmes Structured marketing efforts that reward, and therefore encourage, loyal buying behaviour – behaviour which is potentially beneficial to the firm.

M

Machine bureaucracy A type of organization which possesses all the bureaucratic characteristics. The important decisions are made at the top, while at the bottom, standardized procedures are used to exercise control.

Macro-environment The wider environment of social, legal, economic, political and technological influences in which the organization is situated.

Maintenance The activity of caring for physical facilities so as to avoid or minimize the chance of those facilities failing.

Make-to-order (MTO) Operations that produce products only when they are demanded by specific customers.

Make-to-stock (MTS) Operations that produce products prior to their being demanded by specific customers.

Management Coordinated activities (forecasting, planning, deciding, organizing, commanding) to direct and control an organization.

Management accounting The process of identifying, measuring, analyzing, interpreting and communicating information for the pursuit of an organization's goals.

Management by objectives (MBO) A technique to establish individual performance objectives which are tangible, measurable and verifiable. Individual objectives are derived or cascaded from organizational goals. Top managers agree their own specific objectives compatible with the organization's goals but restricted to their own areas of responsibility. Subordinates do the same at each lower level, forming an interlocked and coherent hierarchy of performance targets.

Management development A systematic process for ensuring that an organization meets its current and future needs for effective managers; typical features include manpower reviews, succession planning, performance appraisal and training.

Management information systems (MIS) A computer-based information system used for planning, control, decision-making or problem-solving.

Management style The approach managers use to deal with people in their teams, also called leadership style.

Managerial authority A person's right to exercise power based on the belief that his or her actions are legitimate and in alignment with accepted standards appropriate to conduct.

Managing diversity The management of diversity goes beyond equal opportunity and embodies the belief that people should be valued for their differences and variety. Diversity is perceived to enrich an organization's human capital. Whereas equal opportunity focuses on various disadvantaged groups, the management of diversity is about individuals.

Market segment A market segment is a group of customers who have similar needs that are different from customer needs in other parts of the market.

Market segmentation The division of customer markets into groups of customers with distinctly similar needs.

Market skimming pricing New product pricing in which a high price is set to skim maximum revenues from the market, layer by layer.

Market surveys Structured questionnaires submitted to potential customers, often to gauge potential demand.

Market test An experiment in which a product is made available to buyers in one or more test areas, after which purchases and consumer responses to its distribution, promotion and price are measured.

Market-based view of strategy An outside-in approach to competitive strategy; firms identify the opportunities and threats in their external environment (see also the complementary resource-based view approach to strategy which is defined as an inside-out approach to strategy).

Marketing The processes associated with the transfer of goods from, and the relationships between, producer and consumer – it is also concerned with anticipating the customers' future needs and wants – marketing involves researching, promoting, selling and distributing products or services.

Marketing audit A systematic examination of the marketing function's objectives, strategies, programmes, organization and performance.

Marketing communication The diffusion of persuasive information about a product aimed at key stakeholders and consumers within the target market segment.

Marketing concept The philosophy that an organization should try to provide products that satisfy customers' needs through a coordinated set of activities that also allows the organization to achieve its goals.

Marketing mix The tactical 'toolkit' of the marketing programme; product, place/distribution, promotion, price and people variables that an organization can control in order to appeal to the target market and facilitate satisfying exchange.

Marketing plan The written arrangements for specifying, implementing and controlling an organization's marketing activities and marketing mixes.

Marketing planning A systematic process of assessing marketing opportunities and resources, determining marketing objectives and developing a thorough plan for implementation and control.

Marketing research The process of gathering, interpreting and disseminating information to help solve specific marketing problems or take advantage of marketing opportunities.

Marketing strategy A plan indicating the opportunities to pursue specific target markets to address the types of competitive advantages that are to be developed and exploited, and maintenance of an appropriate marketing mix that will satisfy those people in the target market(s).

Mass production Processes that produce goods in high volume and relatively low variety.

Master budget A document that brings together and summarizes all lower level budgets and which consists of a budgeted profit and loss account, a balance sheet and cash flow statement.

Material handling The function that physically moves materials around a warehouse or between operations.

Material requirements planning (MRP) A planning process (usually computerized) that integrates production, purchasing and inventory management of interrelated products.

Matrix management A system of management operating in a horizontal as well as vertical organization structure, where, typically, a manager reports to two superiors – one a departmental/line manager and the other a functional/project manager.

McGregor's Theory X and Theory Y Theory X managers consider workers as lazy and having to be driven to achieve performance. Theory Y managers consider workers enjoy the experience of work and have a desire to achieve high performance. McGregor believed that managers managed their staff on the basis of these beliefs, irrespective of actual employee approach to work.

Mechanistic system A rigid system of management practice and structure which is characterized by a clear hierarchical structure, specialization of task, defined duties and responsibilities and knowledge centred at the top of the hierarchy.

Mediation A form of third-party intervention in negotiations in which a neutral person recommends a non-binding agreement.

Metric Measurements that facilitate the quantification of some particular characteristic (like an objective or goal); they quantify results.

Micro-environment The immediate environment including customers, competitors, suppliers and distributors in which the organization is situated.

Micro-management Involvement in the detailed control of the activities in one's area of responsibility.

Mission statement A mission statement is a statement of the overriding direction and purpose of an organization.

Motion study The study of the individual human motions that are used in a job task with the purpose of trying to ensure that the job does not include any unnecessary motion or movement by the worker.

Motivation A driving force that encourages an individual to behave in particular ways as they seek to achieve a goal.

Multicultural Relating to or containing several cultural or ethnic groups.

Multicultural organization An organization that contains many different cultural groups and values diversity.

Multiculturalism A phenomenon, trend or the characteristics of a society which has or is moving towards many different ethnic or national cultures mingling and coexisting freely. Taken literally, it refers to the existence of several different cultures (rather than one national culture) significantly represented within a country. Also considered to be an ideology that favours and deliberately fosters the presence of many cultures in society, each with equal rights – a doctrine asserting the value of different cultures coexisting within single society.

Multidomestic organization An organization that trades internationally as if the world were a collection of many different (country) entities.

Mutually exclusive Options may be seeking to solve the same problem and competing with each other.

N

National culture Culture, including a sense of identity and belonging, which distinguishes and unites people, linking them to a territorial homeland, usually a nation state.

Need for achievement (nAch) A general concern with meeting standards of excellence, the desire to be successful in competition and the motivation to excel.

Need for power (nPow) The desire to make an impact on others, change people or events and make a difference in life.

Net cash flow The net (summed) flow of cash into or out of a business over some time period.

Net present value (NPV) An investment appraisal technique that determines the amount of money an investment is worth, taking into account its cost, earnings and the time value of money.

Niche strategy A firm reduces its scope of operations and focuses on narrow segments of a declining industry.

Non-verbal communication Gestures and facial expressions which convey meaning within a particular linguistic context.

Norming The third stage of group development during which members of the group establish guidelines and standards and develop their own norms of acceptable behaviour.

O

Offshoring Moving production and service provision to countries with low wages but similar or even higher skills (the location or transfer of activities abroad).

Open system Considers the organization's structures, systems, processes and external environment to be inter-related and able to affect one another.

Operational risk The risk of loss resulting from inade-quate or failed internal processes, people and systems or from external events.

Operations (production) function That part of the organ-ization with responsibility for operations management.

Operations and supply chain strategy A functional strategy that indicates how structural and infrastructural elements within the operations and supply chain areas will be acquired and developed to support the overall business strategy.

Operations management The planning, scheduling and control of the activities that transform inputs into finished goods and services.

Operations planning A business process that helps organizations plan and coordinate operations and supply chain decisions over a tactical time horizon.

Operations strategy The overall direction and contri-bution of the operation's function with the business; the way in which market requirements and operations resource capabilities are reconciled within the operation.

Opinion formers People who exert personal influence because of their profession, authority, education or status associated with the object of the communication process. They are not part of the same peer group as the people they influence.

Opinion leader Person who is especially admired or possesses special skills and therefore exerts more influ-ence over certain purchases made by others.

Opportunity Favourable or advantageous circumstance that may shape or facilitate goals.

Order picking The process of pulling items from inven-tory to fill a customer order.

Organic system A fluid and flexible system of manage-ment practice and structure which is characterized by the adjustment and continual redefinition of tasks, a network structure of control, authority and communica-tion and where superior knowledge does not necessarily coincide with positional authority.

Organization A group of people with a common purpose who work together to achieve shared goals (see formal organization and informal organization).

Organizational climate The prevailing atmosphere surrounding the organization – the level of morale and strength of feelings or belonging, care and goodwill among members – organizational climate is based on the perceptions of members towards the organization.

Organizational change The alteration of organiza-tional components (such as the mission, strategy, goals, structure, processes, systems, technology and people) to improve the effectiveness or efficiency of the organization.

Organizational design The design of an organization patterns its formal structure and culture. It allocates purpose and power to departments and individuals. It lays down guidelines for authoritarian or participative management by its rigidity or flexibility, its hierarchical or non-hierarchical structure.

Organizational structure The way in which the interre-lated groups of an organization are constructed.

Orientation and onboarding Introducing a new employee to his or her job and the organization.

Outbound logistics The management of resources supplied from an organization to its customers and intermediaries such as retailers and distributors.

Outputs The completed products or services of a system.

Outsourcing The practice of having goods or services provided by an outside organization.

P

Package tracking The process of localizing deliveries at different points of time during sorting, warehousing and package delivery to verify their origin and to predict and aid delivery.

Packaging The development of a product's container and label, complete with graphic design.

Paradigm A paradigm is the set of assumptions held relatively in common and taken for granted in an organization.

Pareto analysis A general law found to operate in many situations that indicates that 20 per cent of something causes 80 per cent of something else, e.g. 20 per cent of effort in one area gains 80 per cent of the results.

Partnership When you go into business with someone else (more commonly associated with professional services such as accountants, solicitors and doctors).

Pay progression The process by which an individual employee attains higher levels of pay within a range associated with a pay grade or band.

Pay structure A collection of pay grades, levels or bands, linking related jobs within a hierarchy that provides a framework for the implementation of reward strategies and policies within an organization.

Payback period An investment appraisal technique that assesses how long it takes for initial cash investment to be repaid from cash receipts generated by the investment.

Peer control A type of (horizontal) control that occurs when people who are of the same organizational level or in the same field exert control over their peers; a process whereby peers encourage others to act in ways desirable to achieving the objectives of the people who initiate the control.

Penetration pricing New product pricing that aims for rapid acquisition of market share.

Perception A mental process used to manage sensory data.

Perception theory The process of selecting, organizing and interpreting information inputs to produce meaning.

Perfect order A term used to refer to the timely, error-free provision of a product or service in good condition.

Perfectly competitive industry When there are large numbers of competing firms, the products being sold are homogeneous with respect to cost and product attributes, and entry and exit are very low cost.

Performance appraisal The process of assessing the performance of an employee in his job; appraisal can be used for salary reviews, training needs analysis and job improvement plans, for example.

Performance assessment One of the many people management techniques which 'classify and order individuals hierarchically' (Townley, 1994, p.33). Modern assessment is often focused on competencies. See also 'Appraisals'.

Performance development reviews (PDR) A formal assessment of the job performance of an employee with the intention of instituting change if necessary – often used to encourage individuals to think about how and in which ways they want to develop.

Performance management (PM) Activities which ensure that goals are consistently being met in an effective and efficient manner.

Performance management system (PMS) A systematic attempt to link organizational strategy to employees through the integration of activities that assess, appraise, develop and reward employees.

Performing The fourth stage of group development during which the group concentrates on the performance of the common task.

Person specification A list of the knowledge, experience and skills necessary for a person to be able to perform a particular job.

Personal development plan (PDP) A programme for improving one's performance and capability.

PESTEL The PESTEL framework categorizes environmental influences into six main types: political, economic, social, technological, environmental and legal.

Picketing Trade union activity where groups of workers in dispute with their employers attend at their own place of work for the purpose of peacefully persuading other workers not to leave or enter the premises for work; the persons in attendance are the pickets, and the area they are picketing is called the picket line.

Place or distribution Is essentially about how you can place the optimum amount of goods and/or services before the maximum number of members of your target market, at times and locations which optimize the marketing outcome, i.e. sales.

Planning The formalization of what is intended to happen at some time in the future; concerns actions taken prior to an event, typically formulating goals and objectives and then arranging for resources to be provided in order to achieve a desired outcome.

Policy A guiding principle designed to influence decisions, actions, etc.

Political quotient (PQ) The art of making things happen through people you do not control.

Political risk The likelihood that political forces will cause dire changes in a country's business environment that will adversely affect the profit and other goals of a particular organization.

Political systems Structures and processes by which a nation state is governed.

Polycentric A belief that host country cultures are different and as such local people are better placed to make business decisions.

Positive reinforcement The attempt to encourage desirable behaviours by introducing positive consequences when the desired behaviour occurs.

Postmodernism A more recent view of organizations and management that rejects a rational, systems approach and accepted explanations of society and behaviour. Postmodernism places greater emphasis on the use of language and attempts to portray a particular set of assumptions or versions of the 'truth'.

Power The ability of individuals or groups to persuade, induce or coerce others into following certain courses of action.

Power culture A form of culture that depends on a central power source that exerts influence throughout the organization.

Practice An accepted method or standardized activity.

Prejudice Prejudice is an attitude, usually with negative feelings, that involves a prejudgement about the members of a group.

Price bundling When a product or service is offered together with another complementary product or service which is not available separately in order to make the original product or service seem more attractive.

Price setters Firms that have some discretion over setting the selling price of their products or services.

Price skimming A pricing strategy whereby a company charges the highest possible price that buyers who most desire the product will pay.

Price takers Firms that have little or no influence over setting the selling price of their products or services.

Price variable The aspect of the marketing mix that relates to activities associated with establishing pricing policies and determining product prices.

Principle-centred leader A leadership type based upon morals and ethical principles.

Principles of management Fourteen elements of what being a manager involved, developed by Fayol.

Procedure agreement A collective agreement setting out the procedures to be followed in the conduct of management–union relations with particular reference to negotiating rights, union representatives, disputes and grievance procedures. (See also Substantive Agreement.)

Process A structured set of activities designed to produce a specified output for a particular customer or market.

Process theories of motivation These theories look at motivation as the outcome of a dynamic interaction between the person and their experiences of an organization and its management. Such processes depend critically on the sense individuals make of their experiences at work.

Procurement The act of getting possession of something from a supplier.

Product Anything that is capable of satisfying customer needs.

Product cannibalization Where one product within a company's range reduces sales of other products in its range.

Product development A strategy of increasing sales by improving present products or developing new products for current markets.

Product development process The overall process of strategy, organization, concept generation, product and marketing plan creation and evaluation, and commercialization of a new product.

Product differentiation Refers to one way in which firms can maintain their competitive advantage; they differentiate their product, in ways that appeals to the customer, from all others on the market.

Product layout (assembly line) arranges activities in a line according to the sequence of operations that are needed to assemble a particular product. Each product will have its own line.

Product life cycle The four major stages through which products move: introduction, growth, maturity and decline.

Product mix The set of all product lines and items that an organization offers for sale to buyers.

Product portfolio The variety of products manufactured or supplied by an organization.

Product portfolio analysis A strategic planning tool that takes a product's market growth rate and its relative market share into consideration in determining a marketing strategy.

Production order An order to produce a specific quantity of material within a predefined time frame. It contains all of the relevant information required for completion of the process, including how much should be manufactured, and when, as well as information about the work-site and all high level steps involved.

Production process The way that businesses create products and services.

Production run Completion of all tasks is associated with a production order.

Production schedule Statement of how many finished items are to be produced and when they are to be produced.

Productivity Economic measure of efficiency that summarizes the value of outputs relative to the value of inputs used to create them.

Profit and loss account A statement that sets the total revenues (sales) for a period against the expenses matched with those revenues to derive a profit or loss for the period.

Profit centre A part of an organization that directly adds to its profit/run as a business with profit objectives; it is a subset of the business for which senior managers want to track income and expenses.

Profitability index Used to compare the profitability of alternative investments; it is calculated by dividing the present value of the total cash inflow from an investment by the initial cost of the investment.

Project An undertaking with a beginning and end, carried out to meet established goals within cost, schedule and quality objectives.

Project management The combination of systems, techniques and people used to control and monitor activities undertaken within the project; it coordinates the resources necessary to complete the project successfully.

Project management framework A structured approach, such as PRINCE2 or PMBOK, to ensure that all steps are covered and stakeholders considered in completing a project.

Project plan This shows the main activities within the project, providing an overall schedule and identifying resources needed for project implementation.

Project team A collection of employees from different work areas in an organization brought together to accomplish a specific task within a finite time.

Promotion Communication with individuals, groups or organizations in order to facilitate exchanges by informing and persuading audiences to accept a company's products.

Promotional mix The combination of five key communication tools: advertising, sales promotions, public relations, direct marketing and personal selling.

Prototype Preliminary working version of an IS for demonstration and evaluation purposes.

Prototyping An approach to systems development that exploits advanced technologies for using trial-and-error problem-solving.

Psychological contract An unwritten agreement that sets out what management expects from an employee and vice versa.

Psychometric tests Written tests that assess a person's aptitude and personality in a measured and structured way. Such tests are often used by employers as part of their recruitment and selection processes.

Public relations A planned and sustained effort to establish and maintain goodwill and mutual understanding between an organization and its target publics.

Publicity Non-personal communication in news-story form about an organization and/or its products that is transmitted through a mass medium at no charge.

Purchase order (PO) A document that authorizes a supplier to deliver a product or service and that often includes key terms and conditions, such as price, delivery and quality requirements.

Purchasing The organizational function, often part of the operations function, that forms contracts with suppliers to buy in materials and services.

Pure risk Situation in which there are only the possibilities of loss or no loss.

Push strategy Information is just 'pushed' by the seller towards the buyer.

Q

Quality Degree to which a set of inherent characteristics fulfils requirements.

Quality circles These are meetings of group of workers committed to continuous improvement in the quality and productivity of a given line of production.

Quality management Refers to systematic policies, methods and procedures used to ensure that goods and services are produced with appropriate levels of quality to meet the needs of customers.

Quality management system (QMS) A systematic approach to proactively managing quality based on documented standards and operating procedures. The best known QMSs are those based on the ISO 9000 series of quality standards.

Quality of working life An individual's overall assessment of satisfaction with their job, working conditions, pay, colleagues, management style, organization culture, work-life balance, training, development and career opportunities.

Quality standard A framework for achieving a recognized level of quality within an organization. Achievement of a quality standard demonstrates that an organization has met the requirements laid out by a certifying body.

Queuing theory A mathematical approach that models random arrival and processing activities in order to predict the behaviour of queuing systems (also called waiting line theory).

R

Radio frequency identification (RFID) Technology that enables identification of an object (such as product, vehicle or living creature) by receiving a radio signal from a tag attached to the object.

Rational model of organization A perspective which holds that behaviour within an organization is not random, but that goals are clear and choices are made on the basis of reason in a logical way. In making decisions, the objective is defined, alternatives are identified and the option with the greatest chance of achieving the objective is selected.

Rational–economic A method which assumes that decision-making is and should be a rational process consisting of a sequence of steps that enhance the probability of attaining a desired outcome.

Rational–economic concept of motivation Motivational theory suggesting employees are motivated by their economic needs.

Rational–legal authority Authority derives from a person's office/position as bounded by the rules and procedures of the organization (see also legitimate authority).

Readiness for change A predisposition to welcome and embrace change.

Recruitment Locating, identifying and attracting capable applicants.

Reinforcement The encouragement of particular behaviours through the application of positive and/or negative rewards.

Relationship marketing Places emphasis on the interaction between buyers and sellers, and is concerned with winning and keeping customers by maintaining links between marketing, quality and customer service.

Relevant costs Future costs and revenues that will be changed by a particular decision, whereas irrelevant costs and revenues will not be affected by that decision.

Repatriation The process of returning home at the end of an overseas assignment.

Request for information (RFI) A request to vendors for general, somewhat informal, information about their products.

Request for proposal (RFP) A document specifying all the requirements and soliciting a proposal from vendors who might want to bid on a project or service.

Request for quotation (RFQ) A formal request for suppliers to prepare bids based on the terms and conditions set by the buyer.

Resistance to change The desire not to pursue change.

Resourcing That element of HRM concerned with obtaining and retaining a workforce with the necessary skills, competencies, values, attitudes and other attributes.

Responsibility An obligation placed on a person who occupies a certain position in the organization structure to perform a task, function or assignment.

Revenue centre (income centre) is a unit such as a sales section within an organization where income is accumulated and identified with a specific project or organizational entity; the manager is held accountable for the revenue generated by the subunit.

Reverse channel Channel that allows for returning goods, parts or packaging.

Reverse logistics (returns) The return of products by customers. The items flow in a reverse direction, from the buyer back to the seller.

Reward A package of monetary, non-monetary and psychological payments that an organization provides for its employees in exchange for a bundle of valued work-related behaviours.

Reward management Management of pay, benefits and other forms of compensation.

Reward strategy Sets out what the organization intends to do in the longer term to develop and implement reward policies, practices and processes that will further the achievement of its business goals.

Risk culture An organization's propensity to take risks as perceived by the managers in the organization.

Risk management The process whereby methodically, organizations address the risks associated with their goals and activities.

Risk management audit Systematic, independent and documented process for obtaining evidence and evaluating it objectively in order to determine the extent to which the risk management framework, or any selected part of it, is adequate and effective.

Risk management process Systematic application of management policies, procedures and practices to the activities of communicating, consulting, establishing the context, and identifying, analyzing, evaluating, treating, monitoring and reviewing risk.

Risk taking The practice of taking action or making decisions which might lead to either desirable or undesirable consequences.

Robot A machine capable of carrying out a complex series of actions automatically.

Role culture A form of culture that is based on logic and rationality and relies on the strength of the functions of specialists in, for example, finance or production. The interactions between the specialists is controlled by procedures and rules.

Role set The collection of persons most immediately affected by the focal person's role performance, who depend upon the focal person for their own role performance and who therefore have a stake in it.

S

Safety stock Inventory needed to prevent stockouts.

Sales and operations planning A process to develop tactical plans by integrating marketing plans for new and existing products with the management of the supply chain.

Scheduling A term used in planning and control to indicate the detailed timetable of what work should be done, when it should be done and where it should be done.

Scientific management A school of classical management theory, dating from the early twentieth century, based on the application of work study techniques to the design and organization of work in order to maximize output – increased productivity (to find the 'one best way' of performing each task); it is a form of job design theory and practice which stresses short, repetitive work cycles; detailed, prescribed task sequences; a separation of task conception from task execution; and motivation based on economic rewards (see also Taylorism, after Frederick Taylor who was influential in founding its principles).

SCM See Supply chain management.

Scorecard A framework for setting and monitoring business performance and strategy – metrics are structured according to customer issues, internal efficiency measures, financial measures and innovation.

Segmentation The process of grouping customers in heterogeneous markets into smaller, more similar or homogeneous segments – customers are aggregated into groups with similar needs and buying characteristics.

Segmentation variables or bases The dimensions or characteristics of individuals, groups or businesses that are used for dividing a total market into segments.

Selection Screening job applicants to ensure the most appropriate candidates are hired.

Self-serving bias A situation whereby individuals attribute success to their abilities and failure to the situation.

Semi-structured decisions Decisions where only part of the problem has a clear-cut answer provided by an accepted procedure.

Sequencing rules Rules used to determine the order in which jobs should be processed when resources are limited and multiple jobs are waiting to be done.

Service The application of human and mechanical efforts to people or objects in order to provide intangible benefits to customers; an intangible product involving a deed, a performance or an effort that cannot physically be possessed.

Settlement agreement (known as compromise agreements in Great Britain until 29 July 2013) are legally binding contracts which are used to end employment on terms agreed with the employee.

Sex discrimination Discriminatory or disparate treatment of an individual because of his or her sex.

Sexism The belief or attitude that one gender or sex is inferior to or less valuable than the other.

Shipper A company that transports or receives goods.

Shop floor Location in factories where industrial or manufacturing workers are employed.

Situational approach A viewpoint that emphasizes the importance of the environmental situation in determining (organization) behaviour.

Situational awareness (or social awareness) describes an ability to observe and understand the context of a situation managers may find themselves in, and to understand the ways in which the situation dictates or shapes the behaviour of the people in it.

Six Sigma An approach to improvement and quality management that originated in the Motorola Company but which was widely popularized by its adoption in the GE Company in America. Although based on traditional statistical process control, it is now a far broader 'philosophy of improvement' that recommends a particular approach to measuring, improving and managing quality and operations performance generally.

Social capital Refers to features of social organization, such as networks, norms and trust that facilitate coordination and cooperation for mutual benefit.

Social communication model An interactive, conversational approach to communication in which formerly passive audience members are empowered to participate fully.

Social identity theory Part of the self-concept which comes from our membership of groups.

Social quotient (SQ) The capacity to negotiate complex social relationships and environments effectively; the ability to get along well with others, and to win their cooperation with you.

Social recruitment The process of sourcing or recruiting candidates through the use of social platforms.

Socio-technical system A subdivision of the systems approach which is concerned with the interactions between the psychological and social factors and the needs, demands of the human part of organization and its structural and technological requirements.

Span of control A measure of the number of employees who report to one supervisor or manager.

Specialization The degree to which an organization's activities are divided into specialist roles.

Speculative risk A condition in which there is a possibility of loss or gain.

Sponsorship The financial or material support of an event, activity, person, organization or product by an unrelated organization or donor.

Staff relationship A link between workers in advisory positions and line employees – staff employees use their specialized expertise to support the efforts of line employees who may choose to act on the advice given.

Staging A location used to prepare items for use.

Standardization The degree to which an organization lays down standard rules and procedures.

Stereotypes Stereotypes are formed when we ascribe generalizations to people based on their group identities and the tendencies of the whole group rather than seeing a person as an individual.

Stereotyping Judging someone on the basis of one's perception of the group to which that person belongs.

Stock All items stored by organizations for future use.

Storming The second stage of group development which involves members of the group getting to know each other and putting forward their views.

Strategic choice The process whereby power-holders within organizations decide upon courses of strategic action.

Strategic communication Communication aligned with the company's overall strategy.

Strategic control Strategic control is concerned with shaping the behaviour in business units and with shaping the context within which managers are operating.

Strategic decision-making Determining the long-term objectives, resources and policies of an organization.

Strategy Strategy is the direction and scope of an organization over the long term, which achieves advantage in a changing environment through its configuration of resources and competencies with the aim of fulfilling stakeholder expectations.

Strong culture A culture in which the core values are intensely held and widely shared (homogeneous).

Structure The structure of an organization is the way in which employees are formally divided into groups for coordination and control.

Structured decisions Decisions that are repetitive, routine and have a definite procedure for handling them.

Styles of leadership Suggests that successful leadership is about the style of behaviour adopted by the leader, usually described as falling within an autocratic – democratic scale.

Substantive agreement A collective agreement dealing with terms and conditions of employment, e.g. wages, hours of work, holidays, etc. (See also Procedure agreement.)

Subsystem One part of numerous interdependent elements that comprise the wider system.

Succession plan A plan for identifying who is currently in post and who is available and qualified to take over in the event of retirement, voluntary leaving, dismissal or sickness.

Succession planning A process through which senior-level openings are planned for and ultimately filled.

Supply The action of providing what is needed or wanted.

Supply chain A network of manufacturers and service providers that work together to convert and move goods from the raw materials stage through to the end-user. These manufacturers and service providers are linked together through physical flows, information flows and monetary flows.

Supply chain management The management of all activities that facilitate the fulfilment of a customer order for a manufactured good to achieve satisfied customers at reasonable cost.

Supply management The methods and processes of corporate buying.

Sustained competitive advantage A competitive advantage that lasts for a long period of time; an advantage that is not competed away through strategic imitation.

Symbols Symbols are objects, events, acts or people which express more than their intrinsic content.

Systematic training Training that is specifically designed, planned, implemented and evaluated to meet defined needs.

Systems analyst An IT professional who analyzes business problems and recommends technological solutions.

Systems approach A management approach which is focused on the total work of the organization and the interrelationships of structure and behaviour and the range of variables within the organization. The organization is viewed within its total environment and emphasizes the importance of multiple channels in interaction.

Systems development life cycle (SDLC) A model for developing a system based on a traditional problem-solving process with sequential steps and options for revisiting steps when problems appear.

Systems thinking A holistic approach to analysis that focuses on the way a system's constituent parts interrelate and how systems work over time and within the context of larger systems.

T

Tacit knowledge Mainly intangible knowledge that is typically intuitive and not recorded since it is part of the human mind; the knowledge that is usually in the domain of subjective, cognitive and experiential learning. It is highly personal and hard to formalize.

Talent What people have when they possess the skills, abilities and aptitudes that enable them to perform effectively in their roles.

Talent management A strategic and integrated approach to developing a skilled and competent workforce, involving targeted recruitment, development and retention.

Tall hierarchical structure An organization that has narrow spans of control and a relatively large number of levels of authority.

Task culture A form of culture which is task or job oriented and seeks to bring together the right resources and people and utilizes the unifying power of the group.

Taylorism An approach to management based on the theories of F.W. Taylor. See also 'Scientific management'.

Team Implies a small, cohesive group that works effectively as a single unit through being focused on a common task.

Team role A pattern of behaviour, characteristic of the way in which one team member interacts with another, where performance facilitates the progress of the team as a whole.

Technological determinism The argument that technology can be used to explain internal aspects of the organization.

Technological diffusion The spreading of new technologies within and between economies.

Technology The creation, usage, and knowledge of tools, machines, crafts, techniques, systems or methods of organization in order to solve a problem or perform a specific job, in this case operations, manufacturing or service provision.

Telecommunications The exchange of information in any form (e.g., voice, data, text and images) over networks.

Tendering An administrative mechanism to determine effective competition procedures – suppliers make a formal written offer to carry out work, supply goods for a stated price.

Theory of constraints (TOC) An approach to visualizing and managing capacity that recognizes that nearly all products and services are created through a series of linked processes, and in every case, there is at least one process step that limits throughput for the entire chain.

Theory Z The management style (characteristic of many Japanese companies) that combines various aspects of scientific management and behaviouralism; the characteristics include long-term employment, development of company-specific skills, participative and collective decision-making and a broad concern for the welfare of workers.

Third-party logistics providers (3PLs) Suppliers that handle some or all parts of the logistics requirements for other companies.

Threat Circumstances with the potential to cause loss or harm and may hinder goal achievement.

Throughput (the rate of production) The output rate of a production process.

Tight control Severe limitations applied to an individual's freedom.

Time and motion studies Measurement and recording techniques which attempt to make operations more efficient.

Time management Refers to a range of skills, tools and techniques used to manage time when accomplishing specific tasks, projects and goals.

Total quality management (TQM) A quality approach that emphasizes a continuous process of improvement, through the involvement of people.

Touchpoint (point of contact) Describes the interface of a product or brand with customers before, during and after a transaction.

Trade union An organization of employees whose principal purpose is to negotiate with employers about terms and conditions of employment and other matters affecting the members' interests at work. (See also Certified trade union.)

Traditional authority Authority based on the belief that the ruler had a natural right to rule. This right is either God-given or by descent and tradition. The authority enjoyed by kings and queens would be of this type.

Training Any intervention aimed at increasing an individual's knowledge or skills.

Traits approach to leadership Assumes leaders are born and not made. Leadership consists of certain inherited characteristics, or personality traits, which distinguish leaders from followers. Attention is focused on the person in the job and not the job itself.

Transaction exposure The extent to which income from individual transactions is affected by fluctuations in foreign exchange values.

Transaction processing systems (TPS) Computerized systems that perform and record the daily routine transactions necessary to conduct business.

Transactional approach The (traditional) transactional approach to marketing is a business strategy that focuses on solitary, point of sale transactions; it is focused on a single objective, and that is making the sale and a sale is a one-time/one-off event.

Transactional change Changes to components of the organization such as the structure, systems and processes.

Transformational change A fundamental change impacting upon the whole organization (the leader, mission, strategy and culture).

Transnational corporations (TNCs) Operate in more than one country at a time but differ from traditional MNCs in that they do not identify themselves with one national home.

Transnational enterprises (TNE) An international organization that standardizes certain aspects of its activities and output whilst adapting other aspects to local differences.

Transpatriates Individuals who operate globally rather than in specific local cultures.

Transport modes Methods of moving goods; these include railways, motor vehicles, inland waterways, airways and pipelines.

Transportation The process of moving a product from where it is made to where it is purchased and used.

Trigger of change Any disorganizing pressure indicating that current systems, procedures, rules, organization structures and processes are no longer effective.

Trust Involves judgements about reliability and integrity and is concerned with the degree of confidence that exists between buyers and sellers, that each will fulfil their obligations and responsibilities.

U

Uncertainty Situations where the probability of the outcome of events is unknown as opposed to risk situations where each outcome has a known probability.

Unfair dismissal Dismissal whereby an employer does not have a good reason for dismissing an employee or does not follow the company's formal disciplinary or dismissal process/procedure.

Unit The standard size or quantity of a stock item.

Unstructured decisions Unstructured decisions tend to involve complex situations, where the rules governing the decision are complicated or unknown. Such decisions tend to be made infrequently and rely heavily on the experience, judgement and knowledge of the decision-maker.

Upside risk The opposite to downside risk, typically emphasizing benefits and rewards (generally beyond expectations).

Upstream The processes which occur before manufacturing or conversion into a deliverable product or service, usually dedicated to obtaining raw materials from suppliers.

V

Value-added activities Activities that customers perceive as adding usefulness to the product or service they purchase.

Value analysis A term used to describe an analytical approach to the function and costs of every part of a product with a view to reducing costs whilst retaining the functional ability; sometimes known as value engineering.

Value chain A model for analysis of how work activities can add value to products and services delivered to the customer and thus add a margin of value to the organization.

Value proposition What the customer gets for their money.

Value system The supply chain within which an organization's value chain is located, i.e. includes producers, suppliers, distributors and buyers.

Vendor managed inventory Is a partnering initiative for improving multi-firm supply chain efficiency, where the buyer shares inventory information with its vendors (or suppliers), so that the vendors can manage the inventory for the buyer.

Vertical communication Communication flows up and down the management hierarchy.

Vertical integration Extension of the organization's activities into adjacent stages of productions, i.e. those providing the organization's inputs or outputs.

Virtual organization Uses information and communications technology to operate without clearly defined physical boundaries between different functions.

VRIO framework Four questions that must be asked about a resource or capability to determine its competitive potential: the questions of value, rarity, imitability and organization.

W

Warehouse Any location where stocks are held.

Warehousing The design and operation of facilities for storing and moving goods.

Weak culture A culture in which the core values are not intensely held or widely shared (heterogeneous).

Weighted centre of gravity method A logistics decision modelling technique that attempts to identify the best location for a single warehouse, store or plant, given multiple demand points which differ in location and importance.

Work breakdown structure A statement of all the work that has to be completed in a project.

Work centre A collection of resources (people, machines, etc.) assembled together to undertake specific work tasks.

Work design The procedure of designing in advance all the features of a task or job, specifying the way in which the operator will work in relation to the workplace, the physical and social environment and all other relevant aspects.

Work–life balance The balance between work, family, personal and leisure activities.

Workforce All the people engaged in or available for work, who are recruited from the wider society (sometimes referred to as the labour market), be it domestic or global.

Working time Any period during which the individual is working, is at the employer's disposal and is carrying out their activities or duties.

Workplace Refers to the work setting in general and is typically a place, such as an office, store or factory, where people are employed and work.

Wrongful dismissal When the employer terminates the contract of employment, and in doing so breaches the contract.

Z

Zero-hours contracts An arrangement by an employer to provide work but without actually guaranteeing any.

Credits

The following Figures, Tables, Vignettes have all been reproduced with permission of the copyright holders and the credit lines are listed below:

Case Study page 3 Source: Reproduced with permission © Dr Phil Kelly 2013 (adapted from Magal, S. and Word, J. (2009), 'Essentials of Business Processes and Information Systems', Wiley).

Urwick's 10 Principles page 31 Source: L.F. Urwick, 1952, Notes on the Theory of Organization, AMA. Reproduced with permission.

Figure 5.1 page 58 Source: Adapted from Vroom, V.H (1964) *Work and Motivation*. copyright © Victor Vroom. Reproduced with permission.

Figure 6.4 page 76 Source: Adair, J. (1973) *Action-Centred Leadership*. Copyright © John Adair. Reproduced with permission.

Figure 12.2 page 152 Source: Adapted from Hofstede, G. (1980) *Cultures Consequences: International Differences in Work-related Values*. p. 336. Copyright © Geert Hofstede BV. Reproduced with permission.

Figure 17.2 page 205 Source: Corporate Strategy (1965) H. Igor Ansoff. Reproduced by permission of the Ansoff Family Trust.

Figure 17.3 page 205 Source: The BCG Portfolio Matrix from the Product Portfolio Matrix © 1970, The Boston Consulting Group. Reproduced with permission.

Figure 28.2 page 342 Source: Data from http://www.iso.org/iso/home/standards/certification/iso-survey.htm, reproduced with the permission of ISO.

Figure 29.4 page 351 Source: Adapted from A *Risk Management Standard* (2002) Published by the Institute of Risk Management (www.theirm.org). Reproduced with permission.

Figure 31.1 page 377 Source: The Boston Consulting Group (1970) Product Portfolio Matrix. Copyright © The Boston Consulting Group. Reproduced with permission.

Chapter 40 Vignette page 476 Source: Produced with the kind permission of the Chartered Institute of Personnel and Development (CIPD) www.cipd.co.uk/hr-resources/survey-reports/resourcing-talent-planning-2013.aspx.

Additional referencing citations for the following Figures, Tables, Vignettes are listed below:

Chapter 4

Vignette Source: Adapted from http://www.thedailystar.net/beta2/news/it-takes-two-to-tango/ The Daily Star © 2013 Published: Friday, June 21, 2013.

Figure 4.2 Source: Abraham H. Maslow, Robert D. Frager and James Fadiman, 1987, *Motivation and Personality 3*rd edition.

Chapter 6

Figure 6.2 Source: Adapted from 'How to Choose a Leadership Pattern' in *Harvard Business Review* (Mar/Apr 1958) by R. Tannenbaum and W. Schmidt (1957).

Figure 6.3 Source: Adapted from Likert, R.K. (1961) New Patterns of Management.

Chapter 7

Vignette Source: Europa press release Reference: IP/10/1643 Date: 02/12/2010 http://europa.eu/rapid/press-release_IP-10-1643_en.htm#PR_metaPressRelease_bottom.

Chapter 8

Vignette Source: Adapted from an article written by Miyoung Kim (2013), 'Samsung misses forecast as smartphone worries deepen', Published Friday, Jul. 05 2013, http://www.theglobeandmail.com/report-on-business/samsung-misses-forecast-as-smartphone-worries-deepen/article13015606/.

Chapter 9

Vignette Source: Adapted from Greenfield, D. (2013), 'How Well Do You Handle Change?', accessed from http://www.automationworld.com/how-well-do-you-handle-change on 8th July 2013.

Figure 9.2 Source: 'Organizational Frame Bending: Principles of Managing Reorganization' in *The Academy of Management Executive* by D.A. Nadler and M. Tushman. Copyright © 1989 by Academy of Management (NY). Reproduced with permission of The Academy of Management (NY) via Copyright Clearance Center.

Chapter 14

Vignette Source: Adapted from Chitkara, P. and Davidson, V. (2013), 'Shifting to a digital culture - Government agencies need to create a culture that not just tolerates digitization but embraces it', CIO magazine, Copyright 2013 IDG Communications. www.cio.com.au/article/523036/shifting_digital_culture/ accessed August 2013.

Chapter 15

Table 15.1 Source: www.ukcae.co.uk Accessed 20 August 2013.

Chapter 17

Vignette Source: Adapted from Ira Kalb, Business Insider (2013), available at www.businessinsider.com/apple-changes-its-marketing-strategy-for-the-better-with-the-5s-and-5c-introduction-2013-9, published Sep. 10, 2013, accessed 12 September 2013.

Chapter 19

Vignette Source: Adapted from Cokins, G. (2013) www.cgma.org/magazine/features/pages/20138186.aspx CGMA Magazine online accessed 27 September 2013 Copyright © 2011-2013 Chartered Institute of Management Accountants.

Chapter 20

Figure 20.1 Source: Adapted from Mintzberg, H. (1983) 'Structural configurations' Structure in Fives: Designing Effective Organisations. pp. 11, 280–281.

Chapter 21

Vignette Source: Adapted from Channel 4 © 2013 http://blogs.channel4.com/siobhan-kennedy/grim-reality-life-hours-contracts/466.

Chapter 23

Vignette Source: Adapted from Improving employee engagement in the NHS – discussion roundup; A summary of the key points from an online discussion on improving employee engagement within the NHS, Guardian Professional, Wednesday 23 October 2013 available online from www.theguardian.com/health-care-network/2013/oct/23/improve-employee-engagment-nhs-roundup accessed 24 October 2013.

Chapter 24

Figure 24.2 Source: Kelly, P.P. (2009), International Business and Management, Cengage Learning EMEA.

Chapter 26

Figure 26.1 Source: Adapted from Mintzberg (1994).

Chapter 29

Vignette Source: Adapted from www.bangkokpost.com/business/news/381697/winning-with-risk-in-an-uncertain-world.

Chapter 34

Figure 34.4 Source: Adapted from Keaveney (1995).

Chapter 46

Vignette Source: Hilbert and López (2011: p. 62).

Chapter 47

Vignette Source: Flyvbjerg, B. and Budzier, A. (2011), 'Why Your IT Project May Be Riskier Than You Think', Harvard Business Review, Sep2011, Vol. 89 Issue 9, pp. 23–25; Press release www.globalscape.com/news/2014/4/30/new.globalscape.study.details.the.devastating.effect.on.business.when.core.systems.fail.

Chapter 48

Figure 48.2 Source: Kelly and Ashwin (2013), The Business Environment, Cengage Learning: Andover.

Chapter 49

Figure 49.2 Source: Adapted from Kelly (2009).

Index